CANADIAN PERSONNEL MANAGEMENT AND HUMAN RESOURCES

SECOND EDITION

William B. Werther, Jr.
Professor
Arizona State University

Keith Davis
Professor
Arizona State University

Hermann F. Schwind
Associate Professor
Saint Mary's University

Hari Das
Associate Professor
Saint Mary's University

Frederick C. Miner, Jr.
Associate Professor
Saint Mary's University

McGraw-Hill Ryerson Limited
Toronto Montreal New York Auckland Bogotá
Cairo Guatemala Hamburg Johannesburg Lisbon
London Madrid Mexico New Delhi Panama Paris
San Juan São Paulo Singapore Sydney Tokyo

CANADIAN PERSONNEL MANAGEMENT AND HUMAN
RESOURCES, Second Edition. Copyright © McGraw-Hill
Ryerson Limited, 1985, 1982. PERSONNEL MANAGEMENT
AND HUMAN RESOURCES, Second Edition. Copyright ©
McGraw-Hill Inc., 1985, 1981. All rights reserved. No part of
this publication may be reproduced, stored in a retrieval
system, or transmitted, in any form or by any means,
electronic, mechanical, photocopying, recording, or
otherwise, without prior written permission of McGraw-Hill
Ryerson Limited.

ISBN 0-07-548913-9

2 3 4 5 6 7 8 9 0   THB   4 3 2 1 0 9 8 7 6 5

Printed and bound in Canada

Care has been taken to trace ownership of copyright
material contained in this text. The publishers will gladly
take any information that will enable them to rectify any
reference or credit in subsequent editions.

Canadian Cataloguing in Publication Data

Main entry under title:

Canadian personnel management and human resources

Includes index.
ISBN 0-07-548913-9.

1. Personnel management. 2. Personnel management –
Canada. I. Werther, William B.

HF5549.C36 1985   658.3   C85-098500-5

About the Authors

WILLIAM B. WERTHER, JR. received his Ph.D. (Phi Beta Kappa) from the University of Florida, where he taught for two years before joining the faculty at Arizona State University.

He has written three books and over forty articles on a variety of employee relations topics. His writings have appeared in *The Personnel Administrator, Personnel Journal, Compensation Review, Labor Law Journal, California Management Review*, and other major business publications.

Dr. Werther has served as a consultant to a number of leading firms in the aerospace, aluminum, communications, electronics, hospitality, and steel industries and has worked in the U.S. with local, state, and federal government agencies. His consulting work has involved both diagnostic assistance and over 200 executive development seminars. He is also a labour arbitrator, listed with the National Panel of Arbitrators for the American Arbitration Association and the Federal Mediation and Conciliation Service, and is a member of the American Society of Personnel Administration, the Academy of Management, and the Industrial Relations Research Association.

KEITH DAVIS has been Professor of Management at Arizona State University, College of Business Administration, since 1958. He is the author of prominent books on management and the consulting editor for approximately eighty books in the McGraw-Hill Book Company's Series in Management. He is a Fellow in both the Academy of Management and the International Academy of Management.

Davis received his Ph.D. from Ohio State University and has taught at the University of Texas and Indiana University. His fields of work are management, organizational behaviour, the grapevine, and social issues that affect management. He has been visiting professor at a number of universities, most recently at the University of Western Australia (1974) and the University of Central Florida (1978). He has also taught in a variety of management development programs in business, universities, and government.

Two of Davis's most popular books are *Human Behavior at Work: Organizational Behavior* (7th ed., 1985) and (with William C. Frederick and Robert L. Blomstrom) *Business and Society: Concepts and Policy Issues* (4th ed., 1980), both published by McGraw-Hill Book Company. He has also contributed chapters to over 90 other books, and he is the author of over 150 management articles in journals such as *Harvard Business Review, Academy of Management Journal, Management International*, and *California Management Review*. Three of his books have been translated into other languages.

HERMANN F. SCHWIND, who has been associated with Saint Mary's University in Halifax since 1976, brings fifteen years' experience in industry to his academic work. After studying mechanical and industrial engineering in Germany, he joined Zeppelin-Metallwerke, the German Caterpillar dealer, as a service manager and later training director. He next came to North America to earn a B.B.A. and an M.B.A. at the University of Washington, and a Ph.D. at the University of British Columbia.

Besides having worked and studied in Germany, the U.S., and Canada, Dr. Schwind has served as a visiting professor at Sophia University in Tokyo and the Institute for International Studies and Training near Mt. Fuji, and has undertaken comparative studies of the German, Canadian, and Japanese industrial relations systems. His major area of interest, however, is the personnel field, wherein he has served as a consultant to the Canadian travel and banking industries. His scholarly contributions include over forty papers and articles on such topics as performance appraisal, job analysis, cross-cultural management training, industrial relations systems, unionization of middle managers, and training evaluation. In addition, he has contributed chapters to four books on personnel management and performance measurement.

Dr. Schwind is a member of the Administrative Science Association of Canada, the Academy of Management, and the Canadian Psychological Association. He is presently vice president of the Halifax & District Personnel Association.

HARI DAS received his Ph.D. from the University of British Columbia, where he taught for two years before joining the Department of Management at Saint Mary's University, Halifax. He is currently an associate professor at the university and has served as the director of the MBA program.

Dr. Das has written several articles in the areas of performance appraisal, human resource accounting, organizational crisis management, corporate strategic planning, and training evaluation. His writings have appeared in *Canadian Journal of Behavioural Sciences, The Canadian Personnel & Industrial Relations Journal, Human Resource Planning, Journal of Social Research, Indian Journal of Industrial Relations, Group and Organization Studies,* and *Journal of Management Studies and Exchange.*

Dr. Das has served as a consultant to a number of organizations in the iron, dairy, electronics, furniture, and rubber industries in addition to his work with local and state government agencies in India. The projects he has handled include implementation of management-by-objectives techniques, assessment of training and development needs of managers, and organization and methods analysis. He is a member of several professional associations in and outside Canada, including the American Psychological Association, the Academy of Management, and the Administrative Sciences Association of Canada. He has also served as an academic reviewer for professional meetings and journals and as a leader of several management development seminars in and outside Canada.

FEDERICK C. MINER, JR. has taught at Saint Mary's University, Halifax, since graduating from the Ph.D. program at the University of Minnesota in

1976. He is currently an associate professor at the university and has served as chairman of the Department of Business Administration and director of the MBA program.

Recently he was academic reviewer and editor of the 1981 proceedings of the Administrative Sciences Association of Canada, Organizational Behavior Division, and was elected program chairman for that division's 1982 National Conference. He has published and presented over twenty academic articles in such areas as leadership, attitude change, organizational development, and conflict resolution. He is also active in the consulting area, where he has been involved in organizational development, quality of work life, long-range planning, and strategy determination activities.

Contents

PART 2   PREPARATION AND SELECTION

PART 3   DEVELOPMENT AND EVALUATION

PART 4 PERFORMANCE, COMPENSATION, AND PROTECTION

PART 5   LABOUR-MANAGEMENT RELATIONS

PART 6   PERSONNEL MANAGEMENT IN PERSPECTIVE

APPENDIX

INDEXES

Preface

We believe that personnel departments will play a key role in determining the success of our organizations, and of our society, during the remaining years of the twentieth century.

The Authors

PURPOSE

This book is about the personnel department's role in dealing with human resources. Its purpose is to introduce the foundations and challenges of modern personnel management in Canada. It presents the key concepts, issues, and practices of this exciting field without being encyclopedic. The focus is practical, emphasizing the applications of this knowledge, so that readers will gain a useful understanding of the subject, whether they seek careers in personnel management or in other disciplines.

It was extremely gratifying to see the broad acceptance of the first edition of this book by Canadian universities and colleges. It has been adopted at over thirty institutions and is the bestselling personnel text in Canada. Students and instructors have found that it is both readable and teachable because of its balanced coverage and varied features. Those who are in management development programs and personnel careers will find it to be a useful addition to their personal libraries. But regardless of their orientation, readers will sense our belief that people are the ultimate resource for any employer. How well an organization obtains, maintains, and retains its human resources determines its success or failure. And the success or failure of our organizations shapes the well-being of every person on spaceship Earth.

BALANCED COVERAGE

Throughout the book, we have aimed for a balanced coverage of both traditional materials and emerging concerns. First, we explore the well established concepts and practices that form the core of modern personnel management; then we go beyond these to discuss the challenges and innovations that confront today's personnel professionals.

The book is organized into six parts, each with a brief overview explaining the importance of its contents. Part 1, "Foundations and Challenges," makes clear the dynamic nature of personnel management and human resources; it discusses the internal and external challenges, including those related to the issues of job discrimination and quality of work life, that are now shaping the field. Part 2, "Preparation and Selection," covers the selection process and the preparation it requires, discussing job analysis information, human resource planning, and recruitment. Part 3, "Development and Evaluation," discusses the importance of preparing people for new challenges through training, development, career planning, and change and organizational development; performance appraisals are explored as a method of giving feedback to people and the personnel department.

Part 4, "Performance, Compensation, and Protection," reviews the many ways a personnel department can contribute to a more effective organization; here motivation, compensation, benefits, safety, communications, stress, counselling, and discipline are discussed. Part 5, "Labour-Management Relations," examines the union-management framework, union organizing and bargaining, and collective agreement administration. Part 6, "Personnel Management in Perspective," reveals how personnel departments evaluate their own effectiveness and discusses the future challenges to personnel management and human resources.

Within this format, emerging concerns that exhibit significant potential are included. In some cases, an entire chapter is devoted to these concerns; for example, see Chapter 4 (The Quality of Work Life), Chapter 6 (Human Resource Planning), Chapter 10 (Career Planning), and Chapter 11 (Change and Organizational Development). In other cases, innovative ideas are incorporated into the appropriate chapters; for example, see the issue of accreditation in Chapter 2 (Environmental Challenges), behaviour-anchored rating scales in Chapter 12 (Performance Appraisal), flexible work schedules and employee assistance programs in Chapter 15 (Employee Benefits and Services), and stress in Chapter 18 (Stress, Counselling, and Discipline).

KEY FEATURES

Although balanced and thorough coverage is the most important feature of this book, we believe that readers and instructors want more than that. Comments from colleagues and students convince us that an introductory personnel management text must also be readable and teachable. It should:

- Capture the interest of the readers
- Reflect the flavour and challenges of this exciting field
- Provide instructors with a flexible teaching tool

To enhance the book's appeal to both students and instructors, we have incorporated a variety of features that add relevance and interest to the material:

1. *Real-life examples.* The book contains over 200 anecdotes and examples drawn from the case histories of business and government organizations. These are integrated into the text material to illustrate and reinforce key concepts.

2. *Two-colour figures.* There are over 125 two-colour figures that illustrate concepts and their relationships while adding visual variety to the book.

3. *Chapter objectives.* Each chapter begins with a list of five learning objectives that prepare the reader for the major ideas ahead. (Students will also find these objectives to be useful review tools.)

4. *Chapter opening quotation.* Each chapter is headed by a brief quotation from a leading authority in the field, to stimulate interest and provide a perspective on the chapter.

5. *Opening issue.* The text of each chapter starts with an issue that focuses attention on the different perspectives discussed in the following pages.

6. *Chapter summary.* Each chapter concludes with a brief summary of its main thoughts.

7. *Terms for review.* Following the summary is a list of the key terms introduced in the chapter. (These terms are italicized in the chapter text.)

8. *Review and discussion questions.* Each end-of-chapter section includes several review and discussion questions. Some of these request a summarization of the ideas found in the chapter; others, an application of the chapter's concepts to specific problems.

9. *Chapter incidents.* Each chapter presents real or invented case histories, called "incidents," that are suitable for classroom discussion or independent study. These classroom-tested exercises emphasize the application of the material in the chapter to realistic situations that readers may encounter.

10. *References.* Each chapter provides a mix of classic and current references that enable the reader to pursue topics in greater depth.

11. *Appendix: How to Find a Job.* This section will be useful as part of the reader's studies and during future job searches.

12. *Glossary.* Since this book is intended as an introduction to personnel management and human resources, a thorough glossary is included in the Appendix. This material is useful as a reference and review tool.

SUPPLEMENTARY MATERIALS

To augment the balanced coverage and interest-building features of the book, a comprehensive, one-volume combined instructor's manual and test bank is available to adopters.

Instructor's Manual. The manual portions of the volume comprise: Section I, with a sample course syllabus, alternative course designs, suggested term projects, a film and videotape bibliography, and other instructional resources; Section II, with chapter-by-chapter materials such as lecture notes keyed to chapter outlines, experiential in-class exercises, answers to review and discussion questions, and comments on chapter incidents; and Section IV, with a complete set of transparency masters selected from the figures in the text.

Test Bank. The test bank, Section III of the volume, presents approximately 1,000 questions drawn from the text material. Questions include true-false, multiple choice, essay, and other formats.

ACKNOWLEDGEMENTS

The writing of a book usually requires the cooperation and support of many people. We are indebted to Dan A. Ondrack of the University of Toronto for his thorough review of the manuscript. We also appreciate the advice and support received from Philippe J. Bussy, Labour Canada, Flemming Holm of the Canadian Human Rights Commission, D. Scott MacCrimmon and Eve Giannini of Thorne Stevenson & Kellogg, N. S. Allen of the Pay Research Bureau, and G. Edward Sutherland of William M. Mercer Ltd. Not forgotten should be the encouragement and assistance provided by Jim Saunders, Sponsoring Editor, and Kathy Roulston, Production Editor, at McGraw-Hill Ryerson Limited. We are also grateful for the moral support received from and the working climate created by our deans and colleagues.

William B. Werther, Jr.
Keith Davis
Hermann F. Schwind
Hari Das
Frederick C. Miner, Jr.

Part *1*

Foundations and Challenges

A personnel department helps people and organizations reach their goals. But it faces many challenges along the way. These challenges arise from the demands of people, organizations, and the work environment. Other challenges result from the need to create meaningful jobs and avoid discrimination.

The first four chapters of this book explore these challenges. Your success as a personnel specialist or manager depends on how you meet these challenges. You are affected because organizations touch your life every day. How well organizations succeed also determines your well-being and the well-being of society.

Chapter *1*

The Challenges of Personnel Management

Most observers ... expect the 1980s to be a period of readjustment for western economies ... this could mean increasing tension between workers and employers as they clash over the issue of job security and the size of their respective shares of national income.

Gerald A. Regan[1]

CHAPTER OBJECTIVES

After studying this chapter, you should be able to:
1. **Explain** the purpose and objectives of personnel management.
2. **Discuss** the major activities associated with personnel management.
3. **Describe** the responsibilities for personnel management held by all managers.
4. **Identify** the key jobs in a personnel department.
5. **Diagram** the relationship among basic personnel management functions.

For what accomplishment will the twentieth century be remembered? Unlocking the fury of the atom? Landing on the moon? Developing and refining computers? While less than two decades remain in this century, the most noteworthy accomplishment is hard to pinpoint. It may not even have happened yet. But a quick review of major events reveals a common element: organizations.

A large part of today's Canada (originally known as Rupert's Land) was opened up to settlers by the Hudson's Bay Company. Canada is the world's largest producer of newsprint, nickel, and asbestos, thanks to the efforts of several companies and small organizations in those industries. The Canadian Broadcasting Corporation, which owns and operates several radio and television stations and networks, brings you the news, music, and entertainment. In each case, it is organizations that have marshalled the resources needed to achieve these results.

Even on a more day-to-day basis, organizations play a central role in our lives. The water we drink, the food we eat, the clothes we wear, and the vehicles we drive are products of organizations. When future historians view our era, they may see twentieth-century organizations as our greatest accomplishment. Certainly, they will agree with this assessment:

> Organizations are the most inventive social arrangements of our age and of civilization. It is a marvel to know that tens of thousands of people with highly individualized backgrounds, skills, and interests are coordinated in various enterprises to pursue common institutionalized goals.[2]

People are the common element in all organizations. *They* create the objectives, the innovations, and the accomplishments for which organizations are praised. When looked at from the perspective of the organization, people are resources. They are not inanimate resources, such as land and capital; instead, they are *human resources*. Without them, organizations would not exist. The following incident shows how decisively important human resources can be.

TransCanada Minerals was a small company that owned several nickel and zinc leases. In exchange for several million dollars, it sold all its mineral claims. Total balance sheet assets consisted of some office furniture, miscellaneous prospecting equipment of little value, and nearly $8 million on deposit with the Royal Bank of Canada. While the president of the company looked for investments in the brewing industry, one of the firm's few remaining geologists discovered a large deposit of zinc. Within a short period the company's stock doubled.

It can be seen that although TransCanada Minerals' balance sheet did not list the human "assets," these resources were at work. Before the zinc discovery, a casual observer would have considered the $8-million deposit as the company's most important asset; afterward, he would have considered the mineral claim the major asset. However, a keen observer would have noted that neither the bank account nor the mineral claim could be of great value without capable people to manage them.

More and more top managers are beginning to recognize that organizational success depends upon careful attention to human resources. The case of Delta Air Lines provides a long-standing example of effective personnel management:

C. E. Woolman was a major force in the creation of Delta Air Lines. As its long-time president, he stamped his image on the company through his employee relations philosophy. He treated employees like they were part of a large family. Personnel policies and management actions were designed to take care of Delta's human resources. The company went beyond merely promoting from within and offering superior wages and benefits.

For example, when other airlines furloughed employees during fuel crises and the air traffic controllers' strike, Delta put surplus pilots and flight attendants to work selling tickets, loading bags, and even washing airplanes. Through these turbulent times, not one full-time Delta employee was laid off. As Delta's senior vice president for administration and personnel observed, "The whole company saw what we did for the pilots and flight attendants . . . to keep paychecks coming and benefits intact. . . . And I think the company is better off for what we did. Everyone knows we went the extra mile for them, and so today our folks seem to be willing to go the extra mile for us."3

A year after these comments were made, Delta gave its employees an 8% raise while many other employers were actually cutting wages. The majority of Delta's employees responded by chipping in to buy their employer a 30-million dollar Boeing 767 jet.

As the above two examples illustrate, people and organizations depend upon each other. Individual employees rely on organizations for jobs, and society needs organizations to provide goods and services. As well, it is obvious that organizations need human resources to exist. As a slogan at one Union Carbide plant puts it, "Assets make things possible, people make things happen."

THE CENTRAL CHALLENGE

During the rest of this century, the interdependence of individuals, organizations, and society is almost sure to grow. As the challenges shown in Figure 1-1 become more complex, society will face increasing demands to feed the hungry, find new forms of energy, cure diseases, curb inflation, lower unemployment, and meet other challenges we cannot imagine. Individuals and society as a whole will respond to these opportunities through our most creative invention: organizations. The better organizations work, the more easily society can meet the challenges and opportunities of this century and the next. *Therefore, the central challenge of our age has become continued improvement of our organizations, both private and public.*

How can organizations be improved? Organizations improve through the more effective and efficient use of their resources. *Effective* means producing the right goods or services in a way that society deems appropriate. In Delta's case, effective means providing safe and reliable air transportation of people and freight. But Delta must do more than just the right things: it also must perform its activities in the right ways. Since Delta competes with other carriers, it must be efficient to survive. *Efficient* means that an organization must use the minimum amount of resources needed to produce its goods and services. If Delta, for example, can do a better job of scheduling its planes with the same amount of other resources, it can serve more customers with fewer planes, pilots, and fuel. Other airlines must then serve more customers with fewer planes to remain competitive. The result for society is an improvement in the industry's productivity.

Productivity refers to the ratio of an organization's outputs (goods and services) to its inputs (people, capital, materials, and energy). (See Figure 1-2.) Productivity increases as an organization finds new ways to use fewer resources to produce its output. In a business environment, productivity improvement is essential for long-run success. Through gains in productivity, managers can reduce costs, save scarce resources, and enhance profits.

Figure 1-1
THE CENTRAL CHALLENGE OF ORGANIZATIONS

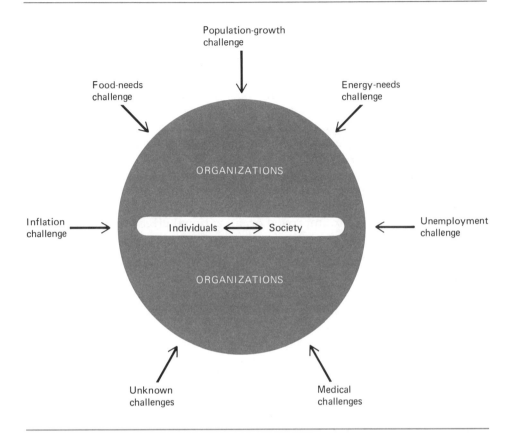

In turn, improved profits allow an organization to provide better pay, benefits, and working conditions, which is the strategy that Delta used before deregulation. The result can be a higher quality of work life for employees, who are more likely to be motivated toward further improvements in productivity. Personnel departments contribute to improved productivity *directly* by finding better, more efficient ways to meet their objectives and *indirectly* by improving the quality of work life for employees.[4]

To meet society's needs and challenges, organizations establish objectives. Objectives are then achieved through the use of resources. If organizations are to be improved, resources must be used more effectively. This chapter begins the explanation of how organizations properly use one resource: people. It shows the purpose, objectives, and activities of personnel management and human resources. The chapter ends with an overall framework in the form of a model. Subsequent chapters expand the framework and provide details.

Figure 1-2
PRODUCTIVITY DEFINED AS A RATIO

$$\text{PRODUCTIVITY} = \frac{\text{OUTPUTS (GOODS AND SERVICES)}}{\text{INPUTS (PEOPLE, CAPITAL, MATERIALS, ENERGY)}}$$

THE RESPONSE OF PERSONNEL MANAGEMENT

As society's challenges have become more complex, organizations have responded with increased sophistication. One area of advancement has been the management of human resources, also called *personnel management. It exists to improve the effectiveness of human resources in organizations.* This purpose guides the study and practice of personnel management. Academically, the study of personnel management requires a description of what human resources managers do *and* a prescription as to what they should do. In practice, this purpose demands that human resources contribute—directly or indirectly—to improved organizational effectiveness.

PERSONNEL MANAGEMENT: PURPOSE AND OBJECTIVES

The purpose of personnel management is to provide organizations with an effective work force. To achieve this purpose, the study of personnel management reveals how employers obtain, develop, utilize, evaluate, maintain, and retain the right numbers and types of workers. The importance of these activities is illustrated by this example:

The Atlantic Brewery always sought the best workers it could find. "Best" meant, among other things, brightest and most reliable. Usually, the company recruited students from surrounding schools and universities. With one job, however, this strategy created problems. The job required the worker to stand in the bottling plant eight hours a day inspecting beer bottles for damage. The work floor was damp, noisy, and full of fumes coming from the beer tanks. Employees usually quit within four months.

Bright, ambitious persons found this simple, repetitive job boring. Probably, a solution for this would be to give the job to individuals with lower ambitions and career expectations. Personnel management can succeed only when it provides a work force appropriate to the jobs to be done.

In practice, personnel management achieves its purpose by meeting objectives. *Objectives* are benchmarks against which personnel management actions are evaluated. Sometimes these objectives are carefully thought out and put in writing; more often, they are never formally stated. Either way, objectives guide the personnel management function in practice. To do this, personnel objectives must recognize challenges from society, the organization, the personnel function, and the people who are affected. These challenges lead to four objectives common to personnel management.

• *Societal objective.* To be responsive to the needs and challenges of society while minimizing the negative impact of such demands upon the organization. The failure of organizations to use their resources for society's benefit may result in restrictions on the organizations.[5] For example, society may pass laws that limit personnel decisions.

• *Organizational objective.* To recognize that personnel management exists to contribute to organizational effectiveness. Personnel management is not an end in itself; it is only a means of helping the organization achieve its primary objectives. Simply stated, personnel's role is to serve the rest of the organization.

• *Functional objective.* To keep the personnel management contribution on a level appropriate to the organization's needs. Resources are wasted when the personnel department is more or less sophisticated than the organization demands. The department must be appropriate for the organization it serves.

• *Personal objective.* To assist employees in achieving their personal goals, at least insofar as these goals enhance the individual's contribution to the organization. If the personal objectives of employees are ignored, employee performance may decline, or employees may even leave the organization.

These four objectives are beacons that guide the day-to-day activities of personnel management. By keeping these objectives in mind, one can see the reasons behind the many activities these departments perform.

PERSONNEL MANAGEMENT ACTIVITIES

To fulfill these objectives, personnel specialists engage in activities that lead to an effective work force for the organization. These activities exist to obtain, develop, utilize, evaluate, maintain, and retain employees. Figure 1-3 shows how these activities contribute to the purpose of personnel management if all four objectives are met. When other nonhuman resources also contribute properly, the organization achieves its overall objectives, which are to meet societal needs and challenges. As the figure points out, personnel activities are essential to organizational objectives and the needs of society.

Figure 1-3
THE RESPONSE OF PERSONNEL MANAGEMENT TO SOCIETAL NEEDS AND CHALLENGES

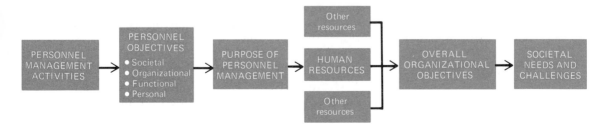

KEY PERSONNEL ACTIVITIES

Personnel activities are those actions taken to provide the organization with an effective work force. Some of the more important ones are described in the following paragraphs.

Once an organization grows beyond a few employees, attempts are made to estimate the organization's future human resource needs through an activity called *human resource planning*. With an idea of future needs, *recruitment* seeks to secure qualified job applicants to fill those needs. What results is a pool of applicants who are screened through a *selection process*. This process chooses those people who meet the needs uncovered through human resource planning.

Since new workers seldom fit the organization's needs exactly, they must be *trained* to perform effectively. Subsequent human resource plans reveal new demands upon the organization. These demands are met by recruitment of additional workers and by *development* of present employees. Development teaches employees new skills to ensure their continued usefulness to the organization and to meet their personal desires for advancement. Then as demands change, *placement* activities transfer, promote, demote, lay off, or even terminate workers.

To check on these various personnel activities, individual performance is subject to *appraisal*. This activity not only evaluates how well people perform, but also indicates how well personnel activities have been carried out. Poor performance might mean that selection, training, or developmental activities should be reconsidered. Or there may be a problem with employee motivation and satisfaction.

When employees perform acceptably, they must receive *compensation*. This form of reward includes wages, salaries, and a wide variety of fringe benefits such as insurance and vacations. Some rewards are *required services* dictated by *legal compliance*, such as the Canada Pension Plan, safe working conditions, and the like. *Communications* and *counselling* efforts are other techniques used to maintain employee performance and satisfaction.

If personnel management activities do not meet employee needs successfully, workers may band together to take collective action. Then personnel management is confronted with a new situation, *union-management relations*. To respond to collective demands by employees, personnel specialists may have to negotiate a *collective agreement* and administer it.

Even when personnel activities appear to be going smoothly, modern personnel departments apply *controls* to evaluate their effectiveness. Besides traditional budgetary limitations, the personnel department may elect to conduct an evaluation of each activity's effectiveness in meeting the personnel management objectives.

Figure 1-4 matches these different activities against the four personnel management objectives previously discussed. The figure shows that each activity contributes to one or more personnel objectives. For example, appraisal contributes to organizational, functional, and personal objectives.

Figure 1-4
THE RELATION OF PERSONNEL MANAGEMENT ACTIVITIES TO PERSONNEL MANAGEMENT OBJECTIVES

Personnel Management Objectives	Supporting Activities
1. Societal objective	**a.** Legal compliance **b.** Required services **c.** Union-management relations
2. Organizational objective	**a.** Human resource planning **b.** Recruitment **c.** Selection **d.** Training and development **e.** Appraisal **f.** Placement **g.** Control activities
3. Functional objective	**a.** Appraisal **b.** Placement **c.** Control activities
4. Personal objective	**a.** Training and development **b.** Appraisal **c.** Placement **d.** Compensation **e.** Control activities

RESPONSIBILITY FOR PERSONNEL MANAGEMENT ACTIVITIES

The responsibility for personnel management activities rests with *each manager*. If a manager does not accept this responsibility, then personnel activities may be done only partially or not at all.

When a manager finds that personnel work seriously disrupts other responsibilities, this work may be reassigned. The assignment might be to a worker or a specialized department that handles personnel matters. This process of getting others to share the work is called *delegation*. But delegation requires the manager to assign duties, grant authority, and create a sense of responsibility; if these three elements are not explained clearly to the delegate, delegation often fails. And even though others may have been asked to handle personnel activities, the manager still remains responsible. Delegation does not reduce a manager's responsibility; it only shares that responsibility with others. For example, many managers ask a senior worker to train new employees. However, if the senior worker errs and the new employee makes a costly mistake, the manager will properly be held responsible by superiors.

THE ORGANIZATION OF PERSONNEL MANAGEMENT

A separate personnel department is created only when personnel activities would otherwise become a burden to other departments in the organization, i.e., when the expected benefits of a personnel department usually exceed its costs. Until then, managers handle personnel activities themselves or delegate them to subordinates.

When a personnel department emerges, it is typically small and reports to some middle-level manager. Figure 1-5 illustrates a common placement of a personnel department at the time it is first formed. The activities of such departments are usually limited to maintaining employee records and helping managers find new recruits. Whether the department performs other activities depends upon the needs of other managers in the firm.

As demands on the personnel department grow, it increases in importance and complexity.[6] Figure 1-6 demonstrates the increased importance by showing the head of personnel reporting directly to the chief operating officer, who is the company president in this figure. The greater importance of the head of personnel may be signified by a change in title to vice president. In practice, increased complexity also results as the organization grows and new demands are placed on the personnel department; jobs in the department become more specialized. As the department expands and specializes, it may become organized into highly specialized subdepartments.

Figure 1-5
THE PERSONNEL DEPARTMENT IN A SMALL ORGANIZATION

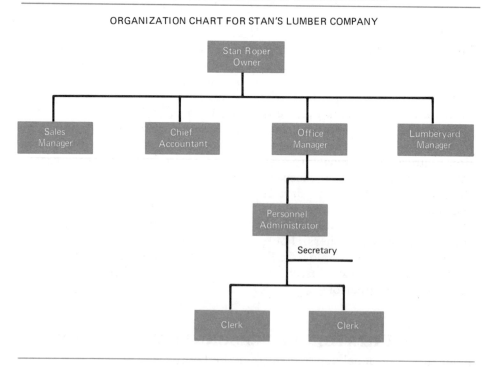

ORGANIZATION CHART FOR STAN'S LUMBER COMPANY

Figure 1-6
THE HIERARCHY OF JOBS WITHIN A LARGE PERSONNEL MANAGEMENT DEPARTMENT

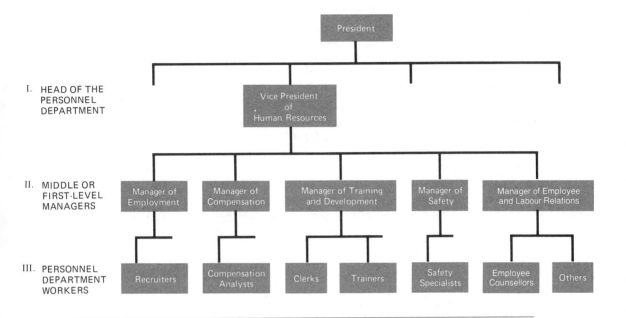

DEPARTMENTAL COMPONENTS

The subdepartments of a large personnel department approximately correspond with the personnel activities already mentioned. For each major activity, a subdepartment may be established to provide the specialized service, as shown in Figure 1-6. The employment department, for example, handles recruitment and selection. Other divisions perform the activities implied by their names in the figure. This specialization allows members of the personnel department to become extremely knowledgeable in a limited number of personnel activities.

Activities not shown in Figure 1-6 are shared among the different sections. For example, employment, training, and development managers may share in human resource planning and placement. Performance appraisals are used to determine pay, and so the compensation division may assist managers in appraising performance. Required services fall to the benefits and safety sections. Control activities, communications, and counselling are divided among all subdepartments, with employee and labour relations doing much of it. Employee and labour relations sections also provide the official union-management coordination.

KEY ROLES IN PERSONNEL

The personnel department contains a hierarchy of jobs, as also shown in Figure 1-6. The top job varies in importance and title in different organizations.[7] When the department is first formed, the head of it is often called a personnel manager, director, or administrator. The title of vice president of personnel or vice president of human resources is more likely when the department's contribution, sophistication, and responsibility have grown. If unions make a major demand on the personnel function, the title typically becomes director or even vice president of industrial relations.

Personnel departments in large organizations have a variety of positions whose holders report to the top person. The manager of employment assists other managers with recruiting and selection. The compensation manager establishes fair pay systems. The training and development manager provides guidance and programs for those managers who want to improve their human resources. Other activity managers contribute their expertise and usually report directly to the head of personnel.[8]

Activity managers may be supported by an assortment of specialists, secretaries, and clerks who carry out the department's activities. It is the specialists in large organizations who actually do the recruiting, training, and other necessary tasks. And it is these specialist positions which are sought by college graduates starting careers in personnel.

THE SERVICE ROLE OF PERSONNEL

Personnel departments are service departments. They exist to assist employees, managers, and the organization. Personnel managers do not have the authority to order other managers in other departments to accept their ideas. Instead, the personnel department has only *staff authority*, which is the authority to advise, not direct, managers in other departments.

Line authority, possessed by managers of operating departments, allows these managers to make decisions about production, performance, and people. It is the operating managers who normally are responsible for promotions, job assignments, and other people-related decisions. Personnel specialists merely advise line managers, who alone are ultimately responsible for employee performance.

In highly technical or extremely routine situations, the personnel department may be given *functional authority*. Functional authority gives the personnel department the right to make decisions usually made by line managers or top management. For example, decisions about fringe benefits are technically complex, so the top manager may give the personnel department the functional authority to decide the type of benefits offered employees. If each department manager made separate decisions about benefits, there might be excessive costs and inequities. To provide control, uniformity, and the use of expertise, functional authority allows personnel specialists to make crucial decisions effectively.

The size of the personnel department affects the type of service provided to employees, managers, and the organization. In small departments, the personnel manager handles many of the day-to-day activities related to the organization's human resource needs. Other managers bring their problems directly to the head of personnel, and these meetings constantly remind the personnel manager of the contribution expected.

When the personnel function grows larger, more problems are handled by subordinates. Not only do personnel managers have less contact with lower-level managers, but others in the personnel department grow increasingly specialized. At this point, personnel managers and their subordinates may lose sight of the overall contributions expected of them or the limits on their authority. Experts sometimes become more interested in perfecting their specialty than in asking how they may serve others. While improving their expertise, they may fail to uncover new ways of serving the organization and its employees. Or specialists may try to exercise authority they do not have. For example, consider what happened at a fast-growing maker of minicomputers.

For the past five years, Harris Minicomputers Limited had grown at an average rate of 25% a year. To keep up with this growth, the personnel department manager, Earl Bates, used budget increases to hire new recruiters. His strategy meant that the personnel department was well prepared to find new employees. But recruiting specialists paid little attention to other human resource problems. In one month, three of the company's best computer design engineers quit to go to work for a competitor. Before they left, they were interviewed. They complained that they saw desirable job openings being filled by people recruited from outside the organization. No design engineer had been promoted to supervisor in three years. So each of these engineers found jobs where the promotion possibilities looked better.

When Earl reminded these engineers that they lacked experience or training as supervisors, one of them commented that the company should have provided such training. With the next personnel department budget increase, Earl hired a specialist in employee training and development.

The personnel manager and the recruiting specialists at Harris Minicomputers overlooked the variety of activities that the personnel department is supposed to perform. And they failed to identify the services that the organization needs from the personnel department. They also did not recognize the connection between different personnel management activities.

THE PERSONNEL MANAGEMENT MODEL

Personnel management is a system of many interdependent activities. These activities do not occur in isolation. Virtually every one affects some other personnel activity.

In preparing a bid for the construction contract, an estimator miscalculated the human resource requirements. Too many unskilled workers and too few skilled employees were hired. As the construction of the hockey arena fell behind schedule, supervisors tried to get the work done more quickly. This speedup led to complaints from the union. Finally, the project manager realized the problem. The manager fired one-third of the unskilled workers and replaced them with skilled cement masons and *carpenters. This decision led to legal problems over unemployment compensation claims, and the higher-paid skilled workers caused the original payroll estimates to be wrong. The personnel manager had to intervene. The arena seats were in place by the first home game. But the contractor lost $385,000 on the job.*

As this illustration shows, personnel management activities are connected. A poor decision about human resource requirements led to problems in employment, placement, legal compliance, union-management relations, and compensation. When personnel activities are viewed as a whole, they form an organization's personnel management system.

A SYSTEMS MODEL

When activities are related, a system exists. A *system* is two or more parts (or subsystems) working together as an organized whole with identifiable boundaries, inputs, and outputs.[9] Examples are everywhere. A car is a system composed of subsystems called the engine, the transmission, the radio, and so on. A human body is a system with respiratory, digestive, circulatory, and other subsystems. Moreover, cars, people, and personnel departments all have identifiable boundaries, inputs, and outputs.

Figure 1-7 shows how personnel management activities form an interconnected system with boundaries. It indicates that each activity (or subsystem) relates directly to every other activity. For example, the challenges faced by personnel departments affect their selection of employees. The selection subsystem influences the department's development and evaluation of human resources. In addition, each subsystem is affected by the personnel department's objectives and the external environment in which personnel management takes place.

Thinking in terms of systems is useful. It causes one to recognize the relationships between parts. If one adopts a systems view of personnel, the relationships between personnel activities are less likely to be overlooked. In the example of the hockey arena, the manager, when firing one-third of the unskilled workers, failed to take into account the interdependence of the subparts of the personnel system.

Systems thinking also requires the recognition of the system's boundaries, which mark the beginning of its external environment. The environment is an important consideration because most systems are open. An *open system* is one affected by the environment. Organizations and people are an open system because they are affected by their environments. Personnel management is also an open system, influenced by the external environment. The arena contractor's organization was an open system because laws, unions, and other elements in the environment affected the manager's decision to replace unskilled workers.

The following brief discussion of this model's parts explains the role of major personnel subsystems and serves as a preview to the six parts of this book and its major topics. (Each part is identified below and in the foregoing model by a roman numeral.)

Figure 1-7
A MODEL OF THE MAJOR PERSONNEL MANAGEMENT SUBSYSTEMS

I
FOUNDATIONS
AND
CHALLENGES

VI
PERSONNEL
MANAGEMENT
IN
PERSPECTIVE

II
PREPARATION
AND
SELECTION

OBJECTIVES
• Societal
• Organizational
• Functional
• Personal

V
LABOUR-MANAGEMENT
RELATIONS

III
DEVELOPMENT
AND
EVALUATION

IV
PERFORMANCE,
COMPENSATION,
AND
PROTECTION

I. *Foundations and challenges.* Personnel management faces many challenges in dealing with human resources. These challenges arise from the environment in which organizations operate; economics, markets, pressure groups, professional ethics, and government are just a few environmental factors. Perhaps the most pervasive environmental force is government requirements for equal employment opportunity. Challenges also spring from within the organization. For example, other departments compete with the personnel department for larger budgets. Or personnel departments are sometimes expected to improve the quality of work life within the organization. These challenges and others usually demand that the personnel department find ways to make jobs more meaningful and more productive.[10] To perform effectively, personnel specialists need to consider a broad spectrum of challenges before undertaking traditional personnel activities.

II. *Preparation and selection.* To meet their challenges, personnel departments commonly develop a human resource information base. Data are gathered about each job and the organization's future human resource needs.[11] With this data base, employment specialists are then able to recruit and select new workers.

III. *Development and evaluation.* Once hired, new employees are oriented to the company's policies and procedures. A sound human resource information system also indicates which employees need training and development. Training is often provided by personnel departments to enable workers to do their jobs better. On the other hand, development helps new and old employees prepare for future responsibilities. Truly effective developmental activities are preceded by career planning, wherein individuals attempt to identify their career objectives. Periodically, employees are evaluated through formal performance appraisals. Appraisals give workers feedback on their performance and can help the personnel department identify weaknesses.

IV. *Performance, compensation, and protection.* Personnel specialists help provide the organization with effective performers. To ensure good performance, personnel specialists may assist with improving employee motivation and satisfaction. One important element in maintaining employee satisfaction is compensation programs. These include wages, benefits, and other services the employer makes available. Satisfaction is also maintained through company communications, counselling, and disciplinary activities.

V. *Labour-management relations.* For a variety of reasons, employees may decide to join together and form self-help groups called unions. When this happens, the personnel department is usually responsible for handling the organization drive, negotiating a contract with the union, and administering the contract once signed.

VI. *Personnel management in perspective.* As with any social system, personnel departments need to uncover their successes and failures through self-evaluation. Increasingly, sophisticated personnel departments conduct audits of the various subsystems in order to implement solutions to emerging problems. At the same time, personnel specialists seek to remain aware of future challenges in order to anticipate their impact on the organization and its human resources.

AN APPLIED SYSTEMS VIEW

Since personnel subsystems affect each other, personnel specialists must remain aware of this interdependency. Perhaps the most effective way to

Figure 1-8
THE INPUT-OUTPUT SIMPLIFICATION OF THE PERSONNEL MANAGEMENT SYSTEM

INPUTS	TRANSFORMATION PROCESS	OUTPUTS
● Challenges	● Personnel management activities	● Human resource contributions
● Human resources	● Recruiting	● Capable workers
● Education	● Selection	● Motivated workers
● Skills	● Others	

recognize possible implications is through systems thinking. Figure 1-8 provides a simplified visual model for applying systems thinking.

An applied systems view describes personnel activities as taking *inputs* and *transforming* them into *outputs*. Then the personnel specialist checks on the results to see if they are correct. This checking process produces *feedback*, which is information that helps evaluate success or failure. Consider the situation faced by Carol Torres, the personnel manager at Municipal General Hospital:

A predicted shortage of medical technologists caused Carol to start an in-house development program to prepare six lab assistants to become licensed medical technologists. After fifteen months, they finished the program and passed the provincial certification test. Since the program was a success and the shortage had grown worse, eight more lab assistants were recruited for the second program.

The prospect of a shortage was one *input*. Another *input* was the lab assistants who signed up for training. The program itself was the *transformation process* that created the desired *output*, a new supply of technologists. When all six technologists passed the provincial certification test, those results gave Carol *feedback* that the program was a success.

In summary, the personnel management system transforms inputs into desired outputs. The inputs are challenges (usually in the form of information) and human resources. Through personnel activities, these inputs are transformed into the desired outputs, which become feedback to the personnel management system.

In practice, systems thinking helps personnel specialists identify the key variables with which they are dealing. After viewing new information as an input, specialists decide what the desired output is. With inputs and outputs known, decision makers draw on their knowledge of personnel activities to transform the inputs into outputs in the most effective way. To verify their success, they acquire feedback about the outcome. Negative feedback means that other inputs (information or people) are needed or that the transformation process (a specific personnel activity) is malfunctioning. Negative feedback demands corrective action.

PROACTIVE VERSUS REACTIVE PERSONNEL MANAGEMENT

Personnel departments cannot always wait for feedback and then respond, however. To wait may expose the organization to damage from the external environment. For example, reconsider Carol Torres's situation when she learned of the impending shortage of technologists:

Carol Torres: *My department budget must be increased by $12,000 so we can train more technologists.*

Anna Newman: *Hold on! The municipality has put a freeze on the hospital budget for six months and as director of administrative services my hands are tied. Why not wait until we can show the Municipal Council of Supervisors complaints from the doctors. Then the shortage will be real and we can get the board to react to it.*

Carol Torres: *But then we will probably have to spend $15,000 for training. We will probably have to pay another $30,000 for overtime to the technologists we now have while we train new ones. Besides, with all that overtime, error rates will jump and so will lawsuits for faulty lab work. All I need is $12,000, but I need it now.*

Anna was suggesting that Carol's department wait until an actual problem occurred and then react. Carol wanted to take action in anticipation of the problem without waiting for the feedback of doctor's complaints or lawsuits. Anna's approach to this personnel challenge was reactive, while Carol's was proactive.

Reactive personnel management occurs when decision makers respond to human resource problems. *Proactive* personnel management occurs when human resource problems are anticipated and corrective action begins before the problem exists.[12]

PERSONNEL MANAGEMENT APPROACHES

Throughout this chapter several approaches to personnel management stand out. They provide complementary themes that we will pursue throughout the book to keep personnel management and human resources in their proper perspective. They include:

• *Human resource approach.* Personnel management is the management of *human* resources. Thus human resource management should be done professionally—in fact, humanely![13] Proper human resource management can result in substantial benefits to the organization.

• *Management approach.* Personnel management is a responsibility of every manager, not only of Personnel. The personnel department only provides a service for other departments; in the final analysis, the performance and well-being of each worker depend upon that worker's immediate supervisor.

• *Systems approach.* Personnel management takes place within a larger system, the organization. Therefore, personnel management must be evaluated with respect to the contribution it makes to the whole. In practice, experts must recognize that the personnel management model is an open system of interrelated parts, each of which affects the others and is influenced by the external environment.

• *Proactive approach.* Personnel management can increase its contribution to employees, managers, and the organization by anticipating problems and challenges. Efforts that are merely reactive compound problems and miss opportunities.

As for the question of precisely how personnel management and human resources are affected by the environment, the next chapter reviews the major environmental challenges.

SUMMARY

The central challenge of our age is the effectiveness of organizations. Personnel management exists to improve the contribution made by human resources to organizations.

Personnel management fulfills its purpose by obtaining, developing, utilizing, evaluating, maintaining, and retaining an effective work force. To carry out its role, personnel management needs to satisfy several objectives generated by society and the organization. The objectives are achieved through a variety of activities. These activities are the responsibility of all managers, but many of them may be delegated to a personnel department. Personnel departments often begin as small offices that grow as the demands upon the organization increase.

The activities of a personnel department are best viewed as a system of actions, each of which affects others directly or indirectly. Personnel specialists take information and human resources as prime inputs and use different personnel activities to produce outputs that help the organization achieve its objectives. Ideally, personnel experts undertake this role proactively.

TERMS FOR REVIEW

Human resources	Staff authority
Productivity	System
Personnel management	Open system
Purpose of personnel management	Inputs and outputs
Effectiveness	Feedback
Delegation	Reactive
Labour-management relations	Proactive

REVIEW AND DISCUSSION QUESTIONS

1. What is productivity and why is it important to organizations?
2. Give the purpose, definition, and objectives of personnel management.
3. Explain the relationship between societal needs and the activities of a personnel department.
4. Diagram a large-scale personnel department and label the likely components of such a department.
5. Of what use is a systems model of personnel management?
6. Explain the difference between proactive and reactive approaches to personnel management.
7. Suppose your employer is planning a chain of high-quality restaurants to sell food products it already produces. Outline what areas of personnel management will be affected.
8. If a bank is going to open a new branch in a distant city, with what inputs will the personnel department be concerned? What activities will the personnel department need to undertake in the transition to a fully staffed and operating branch? What type of feedback do you think the personnel department should seek after the branch has been operating for six months?

INCIDENT 1-1
THE BIRTH OF A PERSONNEL DEPARTMENT

In 1970, Karen and Alice Bloodsworth decided to form a business to advise women executives on financial planning. Their decision coincided with a rapid increase in women executives. By the end of the 1970s, Alice was still handling all personnel records, employment, and compensation for sixty employees in three cities in eastern Canada.

Talking with Karen, Alice listed the following reasons why she thought a personnel department should be formed.

A. *"I don't like to do recruiting or interviewing."*

B. *"The personnel paperwork interferes with my time to line up new accounts."*

C. *"Certainly, someone else could do this personnel work better."*

D. *"I've never had any training in personnel work, and I fear I might be unknowingly breaking laws."*

E. *"Without a personnel department, there is no one to whom I can delegate these thankless personnel tasks."*

F. *"I've done this personnel work long enough."*

It was decided to hire a recent graduate of a reputable university for training as a personnel manager.

1. Of the reasons Alice gave, which should properly be considered in deciding whether to start a personnel department? Which should be ignored?
2. What is Alice's view of personnel management?
3. If you were hired to fill the new opening of personnel director, what personnel responsibilities do you think Alice would delegate to you?

INCIDENT 1-2

PERSONNEL DECISION MAKING AT CALGARY IMPORTERS LIMITED

Calgary Importers Limited is a very large importer of linens, china, and crystal. It has branch offices in six provinces and has long been plagued by problems in its personnel practices. These problems led to the following discussion between the vice president of personnel and the vice president of distribution:

Rob Whittier: *You may not agree with me, but if we are going to have consistency in our personnel policies, then key personnel decisions must be centralized in the personnel department. Otherwise, branch managers will continue to make their own decisions differently. Besides, the personnel department has the experts. If you needed financial advice, you would not ask your doctor; you would go to a banker or other financial expert. When it comes to deciding compensation packages or hiring new employees, those decisions should be left to experts in salary administration or selection. To ask a branch manager or supervisor to make those decisions deprives our firm of all of the expertise we have in the department.*

Henri DeLahn: *I have never questioned your department's expertise. Sure, the people in personnel are more knowledgeable than the line managers. But if we want those managers to be responsible for the performance of their branches, then we must not deprive those managers of their authority to make personnel decisions. Those operating managers must be able to decide whom to hire and whom to reward with raises. If they cannot make those decisions, then their effectiveness as managers will suffer.*

1. If you were the president of Calgary Importers Limited and were asked to resolve this dispute, whose argument would you agree with? Why?
2. Can you suggest a compromise that would allow line managers to make these decisions consistently?

INCIDENT 1-3

PEOPLE, PRODUCTIVITY, AND PROFITS AT DELTA AIR LINES

Delta Air Lines was used as an example early in the chapter because it represents an organization that is successful in a variety of ways. Its treatment of employees, its profitability, and its productivity help set the standards for its industry.

To continue its success, Delta's personnel policies try to ensure good treatment of its human resources. So pervasive is the commitment to its people that the organization evokes a strong commitment—even zeal—from its employees. Some of Delta's policies include:

* *Reassignment of employees to avoid layoffs, even at the expense of short-term profits and productivity.*
* *Payment of wages that are five to ten cents per hour above the rates paid to unionized workers in other airlines.*
* *Fringe benefits that are considered some of the most generous in the industry and that provide employees with sound economic security in the event of disability or retirement.*
* *Rewards for employees who do an exceptional job of helping passengers in need of assistance.*

• *Communications from top management with all employees in groups of twenty-five to thirty every year-and-a-half.*

Although good planning, modern planes, lean staff, and effective equipment scheduling contribute to Delta's favourable record, the core of its success is those people who do the planning and scheduling, and who serve the customers. By creating and maintaining an effective work force, Delta has been able to grow and prosper in times when other airlines have declared bankruptcy.

1. Since Delta must pay approximately the same for its planes, equipment, fuel, and facilities as other airlines, how can it pay higher wages and fringe benefits and still remain one of the industry's most profitable carriers?
2. From this incident, give examples of how Delta's management uses the human resource, management, systems, and proactive approaches discussed in the chapter.

REFERENCES

1. Gerald A. Regan, "Preparing for the Microelectronic Revolution," *The Canadian Personnel & Industrial Relations Journal*, January 1981, p. 32.
2. Robert Granford Wright, "Managing Management Resources through Corporate Constitutionalism," *Human Resource Management*, Summer 1973, p. 15.
3. "Delta: The World's Most Profitable Airline," *Business Week*, August 31, 1981, p. 71.
4. Harold C. White, "Personnel Administration and Organizational Productivity: An Employee View," *Personnel Administrator*, August 1981, pp. 37–42, 44, 46, 48.
5. Harold A. Gram, Gunther Brink, and John Smola, *Business Policy in Canada*, Toronto: John Wiley & Sons (Canada) Ltd., 1980, pp. 453–457.
6. David E. Dimick, "Who Makes Personnel Decisions?" *The Canadian Personnel & Industrial Relations Journal*, January 1978, pp. 23–29.
7. Roger Kenny, "The Future Top Personnel Executive," *The Personnel Administrator*, December 1978, pp. 17–19. See also John Sussman, "Profile of the Successful Personnel Executive," *The Personnel Administrator*, February 1980, pp. 77–82.
8. Herbert E. Meyer, "Personnel Directors Are the New Corporate Heroes," *Fortune*, February 1976, pp. 84–88, 140. See also Wendell French and Dale Henning, "The Authority-Influence Role of the Functional Specialist in Management," *Academy of Management Journal*, September 1966, pp. 187–203.
9. Rabindra N. Kanungo and Harish C. Jain, "Why Behavioral Science in Management?" in H. C. Jain and R. N. Kanungo (eds.), *Behavioral Issues in Management*, Toronto: McGraw-Hill Ryerson Ltd., 1977, pp. 4–5.
10. Rabindra N. Kanungo, Gerald J. Gorn, and Henry J. Dauderis, "Motivational Orientation of Canadian Anglophone and Francophone Managers," in Jain and Kanungo (eds.), op. cit., pp. 85–99. See also James G. Goodale, "Job and Personal Factors Affecting Worker Attitudes and Performance," in Jain and Kanungo (eds.), op. cit.
11. T. F. Hercus, "Management Inventory Systems," *The Canadian Personnel & Industrial Relations Journal*, January 1973, pp. 22–29.
12. Paul R. Westbrook, "A Practical Approach to Personnel," *Personnel Journal*, September 1977, p. 459. See also Alfred W. Hill, "How Organizational Philosophy Influences Management Development," *Personnel Journal*, February 1980, pp. 118–120, 148.
13. C. W. Memeth and J. I. A. Rowney, "Professionalize or Perish," *The Canadian Personnel & Industrial Relations Journal*, January 1981, pp. 27–31. See also Walter R. Nord and Douglas E. Durand, "What's Wrong with the Human Resource Approach to Management?" *Organizational Dynamics*, Winter 1978, pp. 13–25.

Chapter 2

Environmental Challenges

The manager of the 1980s will be operating in a much more turbulent, a much less predictable environment. . . . The manager of the 1980s will have to understand the impact of changing societal values . . . communicate with customers and environmentalists who don't speak the language of business and who are unimpressed with the compelling logic of the bottom line.

Max Clarkson[1]

CHAPTER OBJECTIVES

After studying this chapter, you should be able to:

1. **Discuss** the challenges that led to the study of personnel management.
2. **Identify** the forces that have shaped the role of personnel management as it is practised today.
3. **Isolate** the challenges to personnel management that come from within the organizations served.
4. **Describe** the challenge of professionalism facing the personnel field.
5. **Put** personnel management concepts into an understandable framework.

Personnel management occurs within an environment filled with challenges. These challenges make personnel management an appealing career choice for people who seek an opportunity to help others.

"Why would you want to go into personnel management as a career? There are so few challenging things to do," commented Tom Corlini, the resident assistant in Mike Ferguson's dorm.

"I like to work with people," Mike confidently responded.

"Come on, name two jobs where you don't work with people," chuckled Tom. "Why not major in something more challenging?"

"Like what? I think the personnel field will be challenging. Not only do you work with people, but you help them—help them get jobs, promotions, and other personal objectives. There are challenges of recruiting new workers, developing training programs, and coping with constantly changing demands. When changes take place in

society, people in organizations are usually affected. And when people in organizations are affected, personnel management is involved. You name two interesting jobs with more challenge," Mike argued.

Not every personnel specialist is as enthusiastic about personnel work as Mike. But few practitioners ever complain that their careers in personnel lack challenge.

Challenges to personnel practices may result from changes within the historical, external, organizational, or professional environments. Although some challenges are unique to a firm or an industry, many of them affect personnel professionals in all organizations. For example, most personnel practices have historical origins earlier in this century that have led most personnel departments to use similar methods and procedures. However, today's practitioners must adapt these practices or create new ones to meet the challenges that result from the external, organizational, and professional environments in which they work. Their proactive responses assume an awareness of their organization's environment and how it may affect their efforts. An example of how the policies and practices of human resources departments are affected by technological changes is illustrated in the *Ottawa-Carleton Transit* case:

Ottawa-Carleton Regional Transit Authority planned to introduce a computerized traffic scheduling system and informed the union about its plans shortly after the signing of a two-year collective agreement. The union foresaw a loss of several jobs and was very concerned about these proposals. It filed an application to the Canadian Labour Relations Board complaining that the employer had not given proper notice of the change and that the proposed changes went beyond simple changes in job descriptions.
Source: Ottawa-Carleton Regional Transit Commission and Amalgamated Transit Union Locals 1502 and 279, 1982, 1 Can. LRBR 172.

The changes in the external environment meant that the transit authority had to adapt its business and human resource strategies to the new realities. The sources of the major challenges facing the personnel management system are shown in Figure 2-1; the rest of this chapter explains these challenges. Throughout the book, we will return to these challenges to see how they affect the specific personnel activities.

HISTORICAL CHALLENGES

The field of personnel management did not suddenly appear. It evolved into its present form. A review of this evolution shows how the efforts of early pioneers led to today's more proactive methods. By tracing this evolution, we also can sense the newness and growing importance of personnel management.

EARLY CAUSES AND ORIGINS

The origins of personnel management are unknown. Probably the first cave dwellers struggled with problems of utilizing human resources. Even the

Figure 2-1
**A MODEL OF THE PERSONNEL MANAGEMENT SYSTEM AND ITS MAJOR
ENVIRONMENTAL CHALLENGES**

Bible records selection and training problems faced by Moses.[2]

During the thousands of years between Moses and the Industrial Revolution, there were few large organizations. Except for religious orders (the Roman Catholic Church, for example) or governments (particularly the military), small groups did most of the work. Whether on the farm, in small shops, or in the home, the primary work unit was the family. There was little need for a formal study of personnel management.

The Industrial Revolution changed the nature of work. Mechanical power and economies of scale required large numbers of people to work together. Big textile mills, foundries, and mines sprung up in England and then in North America. Collectively, people were still an important resource, but the Industrial Revolution meant greater mechanization and unpleasant working conditions for many workers.

By the late 1800s, a few employers reacted to the human problems caused by industrialization and created the post of *welfare secretary*. Welfare secretaries existed to meet worker needs and to prevent workers from forming unions. Social secretaries, as they were sometimes called, helped employees with personal problems such as education, housing, and medical needs. These early forerunners of personnel specialists also sought to improve working conditions for workers. The emergence of welfare secretaries prior to 1900 demonstrates that the personnel activities in large organizations had already become more than some top operating managers wanted to handle. Thus social secretaries marked the birth of specialized human resource management, as distinct from the day-to-day supervision of personnel by operating managers.

SCIENTIFIC MANAGEMENT AND HUMAN NEEDS

The next noteworthy development was scientific management. The scientific management showed the world that systematic, scientific study of work could lead to improved efficiency. Their arguments for specialization and improved training furthered the need for personnel departments.

Stimulated by the developments of scientific management and early unions, the first decades of this century saw primitive personnel departments replace welfare secretaries. These new departments contributed to organizational effectiveness by maintaining wages at proper levels, screening job applicants, and handling grievances. They also assumed the welfare secretary's role of improving working conditions, dealing with unions, and meeting other employee needs.

By World War I, personnel departments were becoming common among very large industrial employers. But these early departments were not important parts of the organizations they served. They were record depositories with advisory authority only. At that time, production, finance, and marketing problems overshadowed the role of personnel management. The importance of personnel departments grew slowly as their contribution and responsibilities increased.

From the end of World War I until the Great Depression in the 1930s, personnel departments assumed growing roles in handling compensation, testing, unions, and employee needs. More and more attention was paid to employee needs. The importance of individual needs became even more pronounced as a result of the research studies in the United States at Western Electric's Hawthorne plant during this period. These studies showed that the efficiency goals of scientific management had to be balanced by considerations of human needs. These observations eventually had a profound impact on personnel management. But the Depression and World War II diverted attention to more urgent matters of organizational and national survival.

MODERN INFLUENCES

The Depression of the 1930s led citizens to lose faith in the ability of business to meet society's needs. They turned to government. Government intervened to give workers minimum wages and the right to join labour unions. In 1940 Canada started an unemployment insurance program to help alleviate financial problems during the transition from one job to another. In general, the government's emphasis was on improving employee security and working conditions.

This outpouring of legislation during the 1930s helped to shape the present role of personnel departments by adding legal obligations. Organizations now had to consider societal objectives and the need for legal compliance, which elevated the importance of personnel departments. In practice, personnel departments were made responsible for discouraging unionization among employees. But with new-found legal protection, unions grew dramatically. These organizing successes startled many organizations into rethinking their use of *paternalism*, their "management knows best" approach to employee welfare. Personnel departments began replacing paternalism with more proactive approaches that considered employee desires. When workers did organize, responsibility for dealing with unions also fell to the personnel department, sometimes renamed the industrial relations department to reflect these new duties.

Personnel departments continued to increase in importance during the 1940s and 1950s. The recruiting and training demands of World War II added to the credibility of personnel departments that successfully met these challenges. After the war, personnel departments grew in importance as they contended with unions and an expanding need for professionals such as engineers and accountants. The increasing attention given to behavioural findings led to concern for improved human relations. These findings helped underscore the importance of sound personnel management practices.

In the 1960s and 1970s the central influence on personnel was again legislation. Several laws were passed which affected the working conditions, wage levels, safety, and health and other benefits of employees. These acts began to provide personnel department managers with a still larger voice— a voice that began to equal those of production, finance, and marketing executives in major corporations.

EXTERNAL CHALLENGES

Organizations are surrounded by an external environment filled with variables—variables over which the organization has little influence. This leaves personnel departments with two choices: to wait for the variables to change and then react, or to anticipate what changes will take place and plan accordingly.

The Depression of the 1930s caused the birthrate to decline. The Prairies were severely hit by the Depression and the population actually declined in Saskatchewan during the 1930s and 1940s. This meant fewer people in the 35-to-44 age range during the late 1960s and throughout the 1970s. This age group is the primary source of middle-level managers. Reactive personnel departments did little until the shortage became acute. Proactive personnel departments implemented training programs in the early 1960s to groom lower-level managers to fill the foreseeable shortages.

Personnel departments could do nothing about the lower birthrates, but proactive firms treated this change as an input and developed programs to transform their employees into capable workers before the shortage of human resources harmed operations.

The specific external challenges that face personnel management vary. The most common ones include technology, economics, changes in the labour force, cultural values, and government. The steps that personnel specialists follow to keep up with these diverse changes are outlined in Figure 2-2. As it explains, personnel experts must constantly watch the environment for changes and evaluate their implications for the organization. Once conceived, proactive plans are developed and implemented. Their success is determined through feedback about the changes. Although numerous challenges face personnel management, the major ones are discussed in the following sections.[3]

Figure 2-2
STEPS IN DEALING WITH ENVIRONMENTAL CHALLENGES

---

1. Monitor the environment. Personnel specialists must stay informed about likely changes in the environment by belonging to professional associations, attending seminars, furthering their formal education, and reading widely.

2. Evaluate the impact. As new information is acquired, personnel experts ask: "What impact will this information have on the organization today? Tomorrow?" Specialists must diagnose the future meaning of today's events.

3. Take proactive measures. Once changes and their impact are evaluated, personnel specialists implement approaches that help the organization reach its goal.

4. Obtain and analyze feedback. The results of proactive personnel activities are then evaluated to see if the desired outcomes were brought about.

TECHNOLOGICAL CHALLENGES

Technology influences personnel management in two general ways. One way is for technology to change entire industries.

The technology of cars and airplanes modified the transportation industry. Automobile and aviation companies grew. Growth created demand for more employees and training. For those already employed within this industry, growth provided promotional opportunities. Railways were also affected by the same technology, but the per-

sonnel management challenges differed. Revenue lost to cars, trucks, and airplanes limited growth. Advancement opportunities—even employment opportunities— shrank. Personnel departments in these companies had to reduce the work force and create early retirement systems.

Automation is the other main way technology affects personnel management.

The introduction of computers into banks changed employment needs. Before computers, personnel specialists recruited large numbers of unskilled and semiskilled clerks. Computers, however, required highly skilled programmers and systems analysts. Also needed were semiskilled employees to process information into computer-usable form. To outsiders, banks changed little. But their personnel departments had to change recruiting and training programs significantly.

One specific form of automation that is likely to have a significant impact on organizations is *robotics*. As robots become more common and sophisticated, they will affect organizational productivity and the quality of work life of employees. Their increased use seems assured since their cost relative to human resources is declining.[4] One recent survey of 206 Canadian chief executives by Andrew Templer found that the major reasons for introducing robots into the workplace were the increasing cost of labour, concern over product quality, concern over the loss of market share, declining productivity of employees, and the general trend towards robotization in Canadian industry.[5] The same study also found that lack of skilled manpower, employee unwillingness to perform certain types of jobs, and top management values also contributed to the prevailing trend. Only 16% of Templer's respondents had actually introduced robots in their workplace at the time of the survey; however, another 15% were preparing for their use in the near future and 38% were actively considering their use in the long term. Nonavailability of capital and poor employee and union attitudes were cited as the major barriers to the introduction of robots in the workplace. In the future it would seem that hazardous and boring jobs will be taken over by robots. Dangerous jobs—such as working with toxic chemicals and paints—will be changed by substituting robots for people. Likewise, highly repetitive assembly tasks increasingly will be taken over by robots during the late 1980s and early 1990s. General Motors, for example, plans to use more than 1,500 robot painters by 1990, when it will have more than 13,000 robots doing welding, assembly, and other work.[6] New jobs will appear from robotics engineers to robotics technicians and assemblers. The result will be more challenges for personnel departments to recruit and train these specialists. Those jobs that remain are likely to be upgraded in importance and pay because those who control and maintain the robots will require higher-level skills than the less-skilled workers who will be replaced.

The bad news is that personnel professionals may have to contend with increased worker alienation, since job opportunities may shrink along with opportunities for socialization on the job. To effectively utilize expensive robots, more and more factories may find it necessary to work two or three shifts a day. If these changes do occur on a wide scale, personnel departments will face even more challenges in recruiting and retaining qualified workers. And it is likely that these departments will become more involved with helping line managers introduce robots into the workplace in ways that minimize employee fears of displacement and unemployment.[7] It is also possible that automation will adversely affect the overall quality of work life.[8]

Yet another factor that has very great significance for the personnel manager is the increasing computerization of major organizational functions. The computer has already become (and will increasingly become) an essential part of most organizations. Some of the possible consequences of computerization on organizations are shown in Figure 2-3.

Figure 2-3
POSSIBLE CONSEQUENCES OF COMPUTERIZATION ON ORGANIZATIONS

- Increased delegation of decision making to lower levels (with clearly established constraints), with implications for the training function, performance evaluation, and reward systems.
- More unit-level data analysis with implications for performance evaluation procedures.
- Changes in work procedures, increasing the importance of frequent job analysis, greater focus on job design, more flexible procedures, etc.
- Increased separation between managers and computer specialists, necessitating new reporting procedures, leadership training, and performance evaluation measures.
- Task specialization and fragmentation, with implications for all personnel activities.
- Changed work hours and procedures affecting several of the personnel functions.

Source: A talk given by F. C. Miner on "Impact of Computers on Management Training," Saint Mary's University, Halifax, March 16, 1984.

The *exact* effects of computerization on decision making will vary from one organization to another (depending on size, management practices, technology, culture, etc.). Figure 2-3 is intended to show some broad patterns in this context. The significance of these trends for personnel selection, training, and evaluation practices cannot be overemphasized.

ECONOMIC CHALLENGES

The business cycle challenges the skills of personnel specialists. A recession creates a need to maintain a competent work force and reduce labour cost. Decisions to reduce hours, lay off workers, or accept lower profit levels intimately involve personnel departments. The more carefully personnel departments monitor the economy, the better they can anticipate the organization's changing needs. This means control strategies can be less drastic because they are begun sooner.

Gemini Contractors supplied roofing and siding materials to the construction industry. When in 1977 the personnel manager of the company, monitoring the monthly earning figures of that industry, noticed the earnings beginning to drop, he recommended an employment "freeze" and no new workers were hired. Sure enough, Gemini's sales to the construction industry in 1978 were about half those of a few years back; yet no one was put on layoff because normal employee departures had reduced labour costs sufficiently.

On the other hand, as the economy expands, the demand for new employees and training programs grows. Voluntary departures by employees also increase. These developments bring pressure for higher wages, better benefits, and improved working conditions. Personnel departments must act cautiously, however. Overstaffing, bloated benefit programs, and high wages aggravate the problems of a declining business cycle.

The more closely personnel departments monitor the economy the better they can anticipate the organization's changing needs. Sometimes personnel departments can even develop proactive policies that anticipate changes in the business cycle.

A large electronics firm uses contract labour to staff its human resource needs during periods of peak business activity (contract labour consists of persons who are hired— and often trained—by an independent agency that supplies other companies with needed human resources for a fee). When this electronics firm finds that it needs electronic component assemblers to finish a project, for example, it recruits, hires, and trains most of these people through its own personnel department. But some of the workers it uses will be contracted from a temporary help agency. Not only can the agency provide extra staff more quickly, but these agency workers do not become the firm's employees; instead, they work for their agency and are assigned by it to meet the temporary need for more workers. When the project is completed or when the business cycle declines, the electronics firm informs the agency that it needs fewer of these temporary contract workers. The result is that the personnel department is able to meet the staffing needs of its divisions while providing high levels of employment security to its own employees.

This policy of using contract labour is another example of how proactive personnel departments seek ways to meet the needs of an organization and its employees while remaining sensitive to the firm's economic environment. In the electronics example, the firm did not wait for the economy to go up or down and then react. Rather, it developed policies that allowed the organization to adjust smoothly to changes caused by technological, economic, and other challenges.

DEMOGRAPHIC CHALLENGES

The *demographics* of the labour force describe the composition of the work force: the education levels, the age levels, the percentage of the population participating in the work force, and other population characteristics.[9] Demographic changes occur slowly, are usually known in advance, and are well measured. Decisions to have smaller families in the 1930s, 1960s, or 1970s, for example, take decades to influence the work force. Increases in the educational levels of the population are another slow-moving trend.

Figure 2-4
POPULATION AND LABOUR FORCE GROWTH IN CANADA

Year	Population (15 years of age and over; in 000s)	Labour Force	% Labour Force Participation (15 years of age and over)		
			Male	Female	Both Sexes
1966*	13,083	7,493	79.8	35.4	57.3
1971*	14,872	8,639	77.3	39.4	58.1
1976	16,701	10,203	77.6	45.2	61.1
1980	18,053	11,573	78.4	50.4	64.1
1981	18,375	11,904	78.4	51.7	64.8
1982	18,664	11,958	77.0	51.7	64.1
1983	18,917	12,183	76.7	52.6	64.4

* All estimates are for fifteen years of age and over.
Source: Statistics Canada, *The Labour Force*, Bulletin No. 71-001, 1966–1981.

Projections of demographic developments are made available by Statistics Canada. Figure 2-4 shows the population and labour force growth in Canada. The figure indicates increasing labour participation by women. There is also a shift from employment in primary and extractive industries to service and professional jobs. Figure 2-5 indicates the shift in proportions of the labour force employed in different industries over the last two decades. Apparently, occupations employing white-collar workers (e.g., clerical, professional, sales) are increasing in number, while those employing blue-collar workers (e.g., skilled and semiskilled technicians) are decreasing. Figure 2-6 shows the educational attainment of Canadians over the years. As may be seen, this has increased dramatically in the past several years and is expected to maintain its upward trend. More and more Canadian adults seem to like the idea of going back to school, as the following quote points out:

> Across the country thousands of Canadian adults are now hitting the books. Twenty years ago an adult would have been painfully conspicuous in a classroom of undergraduates. But the notion that education ends abruptly after high school or university has been challenged by a new generation of lifelong learners. No fewer than two million Canadians over 25 are now refusing to bury learning along with their year books. . . .
> At the University of Guelph urban teachers mingle with airline pilots for evening classes on sheep farming—all hoping to become part-time farmers. Union members spend weekends at Simon Fraser University in British Columbia studying the art of negotiating. At the tiny Université Saint Anne in Church Point, N.S., a boat building program is graduating adults who hope to revive a local ship building yard. At Rankin Inlet, N.W.T., RCMP officers while away hours with degree-earning corresponding courses. . . .[10]

The impact of education on labour productivity and employee expectations is obvious and requires little further discussion.

Changes in demographics challenge personnel specialists to anticipate their impact on the organization. For example, the low birthrate of the 1960s and 1970s indicates a potential shortage of teenage workers for the service industry in the late 1980s and a shortage of middle-management talent near the end of the next decade. Demographic changes may also reflect shifts in cultural values.

Figure 2-5
DISTRIBUTION OF EMPLOYMENT BY MAJOR OCCUPATIONAL GROUPS

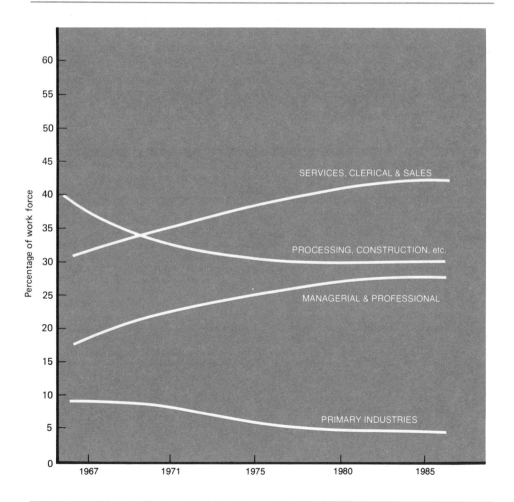

Source: Statistics Canada, *The Labour Force*, Bulletin No. 71-001, 1967–1981 and Bulletin No. 94-736, 1975–1981.

Figure 2-6
EDUCATIONAL ATTAINMENT OF CANADIAN WORKERS

Educational Level		Years		(Projected)	
Attained	1961	1971	1981	1985	2000
Elementary School	45.3	25.8	15.2	12.3	6.8
Secondary School	46.2	52.7	53.0	50.2	48.5
Post-Secondary Level	8.5	21.4	31.8	37.5	44.6

Source: W. D. Wood and P. Kumar (ed.), *The Current Industrial Relations Scene in Canada 1981*, The Industrial Relations Centre, Queen's University, Kingston, 1981; *The Labour Force*, Dec. 1981; Statistics Canada: *The Changing Educational Profile of Canadians*, Ottawa, 1980.

One of the impending issues for personnel managers is what *Maclean's* termed "our coming old age crisis."[11] In 1983, two million Canadians were over 65; this number will more than triple when the baby boom generation starts to retire (see Figure 2-7). As Edward Harvey predicts, an increasingly hectic scramble for future jobs may be one consequence as the fear of post-retirement poverty motivates employees to hold on to their current jobs.[12] This may create fresh concerns and problems for the personnel manager who is likely to be faced with unprecedented bottlenecks in professionalized and unionized industries.

Figure 2-7
GROWTH OF MIDDLE AGED AND ELDERLY IN THE WORK FORCE
(All Figures in 000s)

Year	Age Group						Total	
	45-54 Years		55-64 Years		65 Years & Up			
	Popu-lation	In Labour Force	Popu-lation	In Labour Force	Popu-lation	In Labour Force	Popu-lation	In Labour Force
1971	2,261	1,528	1,711	970	1,662	197	5,634	2,695
1975	2,420	1,672	1,854	1,005	1,808	199	6,082	2,876
1980	2,454	1,799	2,085	1,124	2,115	189	6,654	3,112
1981	2,461	1,828	2,132	1,139	2,180	190	6,773	3,157
1982	2,465	1,826	2,179	1,151	2,243	191	6,887	3,168
1983	2,471	1,857	2,229	1,163	2,301	190	7,001	3,210

Source: Statistics Canada, *The Labour Force*, Bulletin No. 71-001, 1971–1983.

Yet another crisis currently facing the Canadian economy is youth unemployment. (See Figure 2-8.)

Figure 2-8
YOUNG AND OUT OF WORK

In Coquitlam, B.C., 23-year-old engineering technologist Darren Bartel invests 20 hours a week watching television or lying on the beach because the reality of 13 months of unemployment has dashed his dreams of a promising future. In Halifax 19-year-old high school dropout Phillip Downey has discovered that no employer will hire him because he lacks skilled training and on-the-job experience. And in

Calgary, Vivian Hertz, the 17-year-old daughter of an unemployed gas station attendant, is so distraught because she cannot find work that she spends entire days in bed, staring at the ceiling and waiting in vain for a reply from any of the hundreds of companies to which she has applied. Bartel, Downey and Hertz are all victims of one the most potentially dangerous social problems that Canada has had to face since the Depression of the 1930s.

For the more than half a million unemployed young Canadians the summer of 1984 offers no rewards of youthful exuberance or sunny optimism. Instead, because of the economic slowdown and the fierce competition from the baby boom generation that preceded them to the job market, they are unable to find work at the very time that society expects them to begin laying the foundations of adulthood. The most pessimistic analysts talk of the danger of social unrest and the creation of a "lost generation"—a hardcore group of alienated youths for whom the temporary protection of unemployment insurance payments and welfare is gradually becoming a straitjacket of lifelong dependency.

Aftershock: The dimensions of the problem are staggering. Of the more than 1.3 million Canadians listed as officially unemployed in June, fully 531,000 were youths—whom Statistics Canada defines as people between 15 and 24 years old. And although the unemployment rate for young people has improved slightly over the past year as the economy struggled toward recovery, it is still 17 per cent, almost double the 8.7-per-cent jobless rate for those 25 and over. To meet the crisis the federal government is spending an average of $3.6 million a day this year on programs designed solely to lessen the number of unemployed young people. Officials estimate that an additional $3 billion will go toward unemployment benefits and welfare payments to unemployed youth.

Limbo: Among the thousands searching for work even higher education is not the guarantee of success that it once represented. After graduating from the British Columbia Institute of Technology two years ago as a mechanical engineering technologist, Bartel spent eight months looking for work. He finally won a position at the University of British Columbia, but that job ended after five months, and he has not had a steady job since, despite making roughly 130 calls to prospective employers in his field. Said his mother, Patricia Bartel: "I feel badly for him. It is very depressing for young people right now." Added Darren: "We were all quite surprised when we graduated. The grads before us all had their pick of three or four jobs. Then, in January, 1982, it was like somebody turned off the tap. It has been like that ever since." Now, Bartel said, he is willing to take a job in any related field as long as there is some opportunity for advancement. "It is like being in limbo," he said. "My plans were to be living on my own by now and in a career position, working my way up the ladder."

Crisis: And without adequate education many of today's youths will find it more difficult than ever to find a job. A May survey by StatsCan showed that the national unemployment rate for youths with a Grade 8 education or less was 28.6 per cent. For those with a high school diploma it fell to 19.3 per cent, while the rate for those with a university degree was only 15 per cent. "The kids with only a high school education have a tough road ahead," said Rev. Harold Parsons, who operates St. Michael's Mission in a church basement in the shadow of Montreal's opulent Place des Arts complex.

Source: From the article by Ross Laver. Reprinted with permission from *Maclean's*, July 16, 1984, pp. 34–37.

Some available research has shown a link between unemployment and poor physical and mental health. Leandre Desjardins, chairman of the Canadian Mental Health Association (CMHA) suggests that unemployment may lead to poor health because of poor diet, stress, and inactivity.[13] The unemployed also periodically go through emotional highs and lows (called a "roller-coaster effect" by CMHA). The longer a young person remains unemployed, the less the person will be able to adjust to the discipline required in steady jobs and to maintain good work habits. As Elizabeth Beale, chief economist with the Atlantic Provinces' Economic Council pointed out, "if someone is unemployed for the first five or six years of his adult life, then their ability to hold a job suffers drastically."[14] Alienation, a sense of hopelessness, and an increasing crime rate may be some of the many social costs associated with youth unemployment. Clearly, the challenges facing the human resource managers are complex indeed.

CULTURAL CHALLENGES

As cultural values change, personnel departments discover new challenges. The increased participation of women in the labour force is an example of a cultural change that has demographic implications.

Between 1970 and 1980 the labour force in Canada grew by roughly three million workers. The participation of women (as a percentage of the total labour force) grew from 37% to 44% during that decade.[15] The old cultural value judgment that "men work and women stay home" underwent radical modification during that period. This shift carries implications for personnel management. For example, child-care facilities provided by the employer will become a more common demand confronting personnel departments. Sick days—paid days off for illness—may become "personal leave days" so that working parents can care for the needs of children.

Changing attitudes toward work and leisure have confronted personnel departments with requests for longer vacations, more holidays, and varied workweeks.[16] Supervisors increasingly turn to personnel departments for help with employee motivation. Even attitudes toward honesty are reflected in the growing rates of employee theft with which many personnel departments must contend.

Over the last several decades, Canadian society has developed through advanced industrialization toward what has been called the post-industrial stage.[17] As mentioned earlier, this has led to a shift in labour force from primary, extractive occupations to secondary (manufacturing and processing) and service industries. In the past fifteen years, women's employment has increased by approximately 80%. More and more young persons have also been entering the work force. This increase in the number of women and young persons working has led to some changes in the expectations and demands of the labour force.

There has also been a change in Canadian values in recent years. The Canadian national character has been described succinctly in the past as a "conservative syndrome"[18] made up of a tendency to be guided by tradition, to accept the decision-making functions of elites, and to put a strong emphasis on the maintenance of order and predictability. Canadians are typically viewed as a hybrid product of several nationalities and ethnic groups "not quite as American as the Americans, not quite as British as the British . . . and not quite as French as the French."[19] However, in recent years Canada's national self-image has changed somewhat (witness the new Constitution, with its Charter of Rights and Freedoms). The coexistence of Anglophones and Francophones along with dozens of other national, racial, and ethnic groups, each with its unique cultural and social background, makes Canadian society a "vertical mosaic."[20] (See Figure 2-9.) This has led to a few unique issues and problems for the personnel administrator. Sociologists who have compared Canadian patterns with those of the U.S. have suggested that in Canada the "sorting" of people proceeds in terms of ascriptive criteria (e.g., sex, ethnic origin).[21] For example, in Canada gender is a clearer indicator of where men or women will be located in the labour force than it is in the U.S. Another study on occupational distribution by ethnic origin found that the cultural pluralism ideal in Canada (in contrast to the so-called "melting pot" ideal in the U.S.) results in unequal job placement of different ethnic groups.[22] Greater governmental intervention has at times been necessary to eliminate such imbalances; the Canadian Bill of Rights of 1960 is an example. More discussion of this issue will be found in the next chapter.

Figure 2-9
FROM OLD COUNTRY TO A NEW MOSAIC

When Irshad Khan, an engineer, arrived in Calgary 29 years ago, he was the first East Indian in the city. At least that is how it seemed to him. "There just weren't any others," he says. "It was a small Canadian city at the end of the world. I mingled with the Canadians, and they accepted me." Now he can enjoy such cultural amenities as being able to dine out at his favorite curry restaurant, the Taj Mahal. And last week, along with other East Indians, he attended a dinner dance for the Sri Lanka Canada Association. Khan admits that immigration has irrevocably changed the character of his adopted city. He is equally impressed by the effects of an influx of eastern Canadians. "There are so many people from other parts of the country here," he said, "that a native Calgarian is a novelty. I shake hands whenever I meet one."

When the 1981 census put a mirror to Canada's features, they appeared at first glance to be familiar. White faces predominated. Eighty-four per cent had been born in Canada, and 76 per cent had at least one British ancestor. Even the francophone former leader of the Quebec Liberal party, Claude Ryan, had obvious Irish antecedents, and a man by the name of Waldo McIntosh held the title of paramount chief of the Cree Nation. But in large areas of English Canada the country was no longer a primarily Anglo-Saxon nation. And the latest data confirmed that Canada's immigrant population was growing. While the actual number of arrivals in the 1970s dropped in comparison to the 1960s, more newcomers were staying in Canada. At the same time, the Canadian birthrate was falling. As a result, between 1971 and 1981 the foreign-born population rose by one per cent or almost 250,000 people.

Meanwhile, Canadians themselves were on the move. As they uprooted and transplanted themselves in the search for a better life, many Canadians found themselves strangers in their own homeland. According to the census, almost one in three Canadians had changed provinces. Easterners flocked to Alberta, British Columbia and Ontario, while the Ontarians and, in greater numbers, Quebecers, left their native provinces.

In addition to their cultures, the newcomers have brought their values, their ambitions and, in some cases, their money. In the past two years alone, 3,291 immigrants entered Canada under the "entrepreneurial and self-employed" category, bringing with them $1.1 billion worth of investment and employing more than 7,900 Canadians.

Still, there is no statistical proof that racism is increasing. And Prof. Anthony Richmond, who emigrated from Britain 23 years ago, points out that compared to his native country, which only last summer witnessed ugly clashes between blacks and whites in the poorer suburbs of London, Canada has adapted remarkably well to having one of the world's higher immigration rates. Flor Cadigal, host of a Winnipeg radio program, agrees. Said Cadigal, who arrived from the Philippines in 1976: "I'm going to spend the rest of my life in Canada because it's the best place in the world to raise kids. Life here is great."

Source: Val Ross, *Maclean's*, July 4, 1983, pp. 20–21.

It is, of course, impossible to identify every changing value in any society. However, organizations represent only a small sample of society, so as cultural values change, personnel departments can anticipate the impact of some of the changes and act accordingly. Failure to make the attempt can lead to lower effectiveness or government involvement.

GOVERNMENT CHALLENGES

Few challenges encountered by personnel departments are as overwhelming as those presented by government. Government—through the enforcement of laws—has a direct and immediate impact on the personnel function. The federal and provincial laws that regulate the employee-employer relationship challenge the methods personnel departments use. Some laws, such as the Canada Labour Safety Code of 1968, make major demands on personnel departments. The impact of these laws has helped elevate the importance of personnel decisions.

Government involvement in the employment relationship seeks to achieve societal objectives—usually the elimination of practices considered contrary to public policy. To personnel specialists, government involvement requires compliance and proactive efforts to minimize the organizational consequences. At appropriate points throughout this book, employee-related laws are explained, to illustrate the challenges modern personnel departments encounter and the actions they must take.

In 1983 the British Columbia government sought to rewrite the rules of bargaining, especially in the public sector. Bill 3, the Public Sector Restraint Act, attempted to remove job security from civil servants, while Bill 2, the Public Service Labour Relations Amendment Act, if passed, would have had the effect of stripping unions of the right to negotiate a variety of items, including work scheduling. The proposals would have also limited wage increases and reduced the importance of the Human Rights Commission within the province. The proposed legislation immediately sparked off a series of strike threats, including those from the 40,000 member British Columbia Government Employees Union (BCGEU). The Solidarity Coalition, a 950,000 member protest movement, threatened a general strike all over the province.

ORGANIZATIONAL CHALLENGES

Besides external demands, personnel departments find current challenges within the organizations they serve. Internal challenges arise because employers pursue many objectives. These objectives require trade-offs between financial, sales, service, production, employee, and other goals. Since personnel objectives are just one set among many in the eyes of top management, personnel managers must confront internal challenges with a balanced concern for other needs. The employer does not exist solely, or even largely, to meet personnel objectives. Rather, personnel departments exist to assist the organization in meeting its other objectives successfully. Personnel departments find several internal challenges in helping the organization achieve its objectives. Included are challenges from unions, informational needs, and organizational character.

UNIONS

Unions represent an *actual* challenge in unionized companies and a *potential* challenge in those that are not. In companies with unions, the employer and the union sign a labour agreement that specifies compensation (wages and benefits), hours, and working conditions. The agreement limits the personnel activities of supervisors and personnel departments. For both, the challenge is to achieve objectives without violating the agreement.

Karl McPheters wanted to promote Jill Wang to chief switchboard operator because Jill was an excellent employee. The labour contract called for promotions to go to the most experienced worker, which meant Pam Hale. To promote Jill, Karl found Pam a production job at more money. She took it. This now made Jill the senior switchboard operator and next in line for the promotion. The contract was honoured, and management achieved its objective of promoting the best person, Jill.

Employees *without* unions are affected too. To retain the flexibility of nonunion status, personnel departments implement compensation policies, hours of work, and working conditions similar to those found in unionized operations. Here the personnel challenge is usually determined by top management: try to operate so that unionization is discouraged. For example, in November 1980, Michelin Tires actively lobbied with the provincial government in Nova Scotia to discourage unionization within its plants and was successful in its attempt.[23]

The emerging challenges confronting western industrial countries, according to one author, would seem to be to identify new policies and programs that are consistent with the economic realities of the 1980s and 1990s.[24] Unions are increasingly drawing closer to Social Democratic and Labour parties; in other cases they are realizing how important it is to maintain their close ties with each other and to coordinate their efforts if they are to maintain their power in the wake of Conservative administrations in several countries. Employers caught between increasing labour costs and declining profit margins in several of the traditional industries may turn to personnel managers for their "expert" handling of the situation. What are the causes of industrial disputes? Are they identifiable or are they too diffuse? Are there other alternatives to work stoppages? Which of the available alternatives are consistent with present-day values and social aspirations? These are some of the questions to which personnel managers will be required to find adequate answers in the future.[25]

INFORMATION SYSTEMS

Personnel departments require large amounts of detailed information. Increasingly, the quality of the personnel department's contribution depends on the quality of its information. Such questions as the following hint at just a very few of these information requirements:

• What are the duties and responsibilities of *every* type of job in the organization?
• What are the skills possessed by *every* employee?
• What are the organization's future human resource needs?
• How are external constraints affecting the organization?
• What are the current trends in compensation of employees?

And this list could be continued for pages!

Clearly, the acquisition, storage, and retrieval of information present a significant challenge. To meet this challenge, personnel departments increasingly rely on computer-based information systems—systems that store detailed information about employees, jobs, laws, unions, economic trends, and other internal and external factors. But massive information systems challenge the personnel department's ability to safeguard the privacy of employee records. And failure to provide such safeguards may well lead to increased government intervention in the form of privacy legislation.[26]

ORGANIZATION CHARACTER

Every employer is unique. Similarities between organizations can be found among their parts, but each whole organization has a unique character.[27] *Organization character* is the product of all the organization's features: its employees, its objectives, its technology, its size, its age, its unions, its policies, its successes, and its failures. Organization character reflects the past and shapes the future.

The challenge for personnel specialists is to adjust proactively to the character of the organization. For example, it is sometimes overlooked that objectives can be achieved in several acceptable ways. This idea, called *equifinality*, means there are usually many paths to any given objective. The key to success is picking the path that best fits the organization's character.

Personnel manager Aaron Chu feared that a request that he be permitted to hire a training assistant would be turned down. So instead of asking for funds to hire someone, Aaron expressed concern that poor supervisory skills were contributing to employee complaints and some resignations. He observed at the weekly management meeting that unskilled replacements could lead to rising labour costs.

Knowing that top management were concerned that the company remain a low-cost producer, Aaron was not surprised when the plant manager suggested hiring "someone to do training around here." Aaron got a budget increase for training. By adjusting to the organization's character, he achieved his objective.

PROFESSIONAL CHALLENGES

The newest challenge for personnel experts is professionalism. Personnel management skills are too important to organizations and society to be ignored; external and internal challenges require practitioners who are at least minimally qualified. Since the actual capabilities of practising personnel experts vary widely, it became increasingly evident during the 1970s that professionalism of the personnel management field was needed. Kumar, in his study of personnel managers, personnel and industrial relations officers, and personnel clerks, concluded that:

> Against the background of growing professionalism and complexity in personnel and industrial relations, the P&IR staff in Canada appears to be under-educated and under-trained. A majority of managers and personnel officers have only a high school education with little vocational training. Only two-fifths have had any university education and only one in four has a university degree.[28]

Several formal programs are currently available for educational training in personnel and its related areas.[29] However, as pointed out by Memeth and Rowney, several of the available college and certificate programs in personnel management may only enhance the technical and job-related skills of the persons involved.[30] This has led many a top executive to lose faith in the personnel staff's ability to think in terms of the entire organization rather than in terms of a few departments or individuals involved.[31] In the words of Burack and Miller:

> To meet the changing needs and circumstances of organization, substantive changes in the orientation of personnel specialists, let alone curriculum, faculty preparation and pedagogical techniques will be demanded. For example, the descriptive and recipe approaches to personnel or human resources management should be replaced by a more comprehensive approach, which incorporates policy, environment and people and particularizes these to specific organizational or situational conditions.[32]

The personnel education programs should thus focus not merely on human resource management but on developing flexible and broad decision makers in an organizational context.[33] Further, to build the profession of personnel management, *accreditation/certification* would seem to be called for.

THE ISSUE OF ACCREDITATION/CERTIFICATION

The American Society for Personnel Administration (ASPA) established, in late 1975, standards and credentials for accreditation in the field of personnel management. The credentials are now earned through successful completion of various tests by a candidate. This ensures a minimum level of competence among those who receive a professional designation from ASPA.

ASPA created four professional designations to distinguish between different levels of specialists and generalists in the personnel field. Specialists have to pass a test in one area of personnel management. Generalists must pass tests in three areas for the designation of accredited personnel manager (APM) or four areas to receive the accredited executive in personnel (AEP) designation. Tests are given by ASPA in the following areas:

1. Employment, placement, and personnel planning
2. Training and development
3. Compensation and benefits
4. Health and safety
5. Employee and labour relations
6. Personnel research

Canada has been somewhat slow in the move towards certification of personnel managers. While it is generally agreed that the establishment of a uniform standard of education and minimum professional qualifications would further the interests of personnel practitioners and would also provide a better framework for the administration of upgrading courses, the efforts toward certification have been only recent.[34] In the past, the Council of Canadian Personnel Associations (CCPA) has been a national voice for personnel and industrial relations practitioners in Canada, and this organization has been suggested by some writers as the appropriate body to institutionalize and administer a certification program.[35] The council had moved in this direction by developing a certificate program in personnel and industrial relations areas. The more recent efforts at certification, however, have been made on a provincial level in Ontario, Manitoba, and Quebec.

In one recent survey, involving 154 personnel practitioners in Canada, a majority of the respondents recommended five or more years of work experience as a requirement for effective performance in personnel and industrial relations jobs. On formal education and training, approximately two-thirds of the respondents felt that a university degree was an essential requirement for such jobs. Also, those respondents who considered personnel and industrial relations as a professional vocation stated that in addition to a good general education, candidates should have received a prescribed course of academic training. [36]

Figure 2-10 shows a comparison of three lists of courses, one required for the CCPA certificate program, one required for the Personnel Association of Ontario (PAO) Certificate Program, and one generated by a survey conducted at Queen's University. [37] As may be seen from the figure, there is considerable similarity among the three lists. [38]

From the available findings, it would appear that considerable interest now exists in equipping personnel practitioners to adequately meet the challenges and complexities of the times. It should be noted, however, that certification alone does not make personnel management a profession. Some argue that the field will never become a profession because there is no common body of knowledge. Personnel management is not a clearly

Figure 2-10

SUBJECT AREAS IN CCPA, PAO, AND KUMAR'S SURVEY OF PERSONNEL MANAGERS

CCPA

1. Organizational Management
2. The Personnel Function
3. Management Principles and Organizational Behaviour
   or
   Labour Relations

Options (any 3)

1. Communications
2. Compensation
3. Program Design and Evaluation
4. Introductory Economics
5. Interviewing and Counselling
6. Training and Development
7. Quantitative Methods

PAO

Tier I (all)

1. Labour Economics
2. Organizational Behaviour
3. Finance/Accounting
4. Personnel Research
5. Personnel Administration

Tier II (any 3)

1. Industrial Relations
2. Manpower Planning
3. Training and Development
4. Compensation
5. Health and Safety

**Kumar Survey
(In order of importance)**

1. Human Resource Management
2. Sociology/Psychology
3. Management Skills
4. Industrial Relations
5. Economics/Labour Economics
6. Labour Law

7. Communication Skills
8. Labour Relations
9. Collective Bargaining
10. Statistics/Computers
11. Organizational Theory/Behaviour
12. Labour History

Source: D. A. Ondrack, "P/IR Professional Certification in Ontario: The PAO Model," paper presented at a symposium on professional education in P/IR, Canadian Industrial Relations Association (CIRA), Dalhousie University, Halifax, N.S., May 26, 1981.

separate discipline like law, medicine, or economics. It draws on a variety of disciplines.

Individual personnel practitioners have little control over their activities, and this limits their professionalism. Unlike self-employed physicians or attorneys, who are independent decision makers, or teachers, who have some traditionally guaranteed rights under tenure rules, personnel experts are dependent upon the direction of top management and have few rights. And unlike most professionals, personnel managers have no legal certification or licensing requirements. Even ASPA's accreditation program is voluntary. As a result, there are no standard codes of conduct or ethics that are widely recognized. So there is little reason for the public to recognize the personnel field as a profession.

While debate will continue over whether the field of personnel is or will become a profession, the field is *becoming* more professional through the leadership of agencies like the Council of Canadian Personnel Associations, the Personnel Association of Ontario, and similar organizations in other provinces, and through enlightened practitioners and more advanced university education in personnel management. The result is a challenge that goes beyond organizational boundaries: can the personnel management field become a profession?[39]

PERSONNEL MANAGEMENT IN PERSPECTIVE

Amid historical, external, internal, and professional challenges, it is important to keep personnel management in perspective. Its purpose is to assist in the attainment of organizational objectives with maximum effectiveness. Personnel management only aids other departments. It does not direct operations or decide organizational objectives.

The authority of personnel management is limited. Although research shows that personnel managers perceive themselves as having more authority than they really do, their authority is usually viewed as *advisory* (or staff) *authority.*[40] That is, personnel managers primarily advise and assist, not decide and direct. In recent years, however, the complexity of the employment environment has meant that personnel managers get more *decision-making* (or line) *authority.*

James Turner has been personnel manager for B.C. Lumber Yards for seven years. James usually recommended to department managers the best three applicants he could find for each opening. The department managers then made the final hiring decision. But because some of these managers made statements to applicants that could be interpreted as racially or sexually discriminatory, lawsuits resulted. Eventually, therefore, the owners of B.C. Lumber Yards decided to grant James the final hiring authority.

James and many of his peers in other companies now have more decision-making authority as the result of environmental changes. Authority to manage other departments still remains with the managers in those departments, however. In using their advisory and decision-making authority, personnel experts must recognize different groups within the organization. Research shows that executives and lower-level managers have different expectations about personnel activities.[41] Figure 2-11 illustrates the dozen most important personnel activities as viewed by executives. Note how these perceptions differ from the perceptions of lower-level managers. For example, executives give selection testing a ranking much different from that of managers. Likewise, health and safety concerns are more important to lower-level managers than to executives, according to this survey. To be effective, personnel specialists must determine the areas of concern to different levels of management. Otherwise their advisory authority will be less effective and more likely ignored.

Figure 2-11
THE IMPORTANCE OF DIFFERENT PERSONNEL FUNCTIONS AS PERCEIVED BY EXECUTIVES AND LOWER-LEVEL MANAGERS

	Rankings by Executives	Rankings by Managers
Fringe benefits	1	1
Selection testing	2	16
Orientation of new employees	3	3
Recruiting	4	11
Job descriptions	5	21
Training	6	8
Selection	7	13
Personnel surveys	8	12
Complaints and grievances	9	5
Health and safety	10	2
Employee communications	11	14
Civil rights	12	6

Source: Harold C. White and Robert E. Boyton, "The Role of Personnel Administration: A Management View," *Arizona Business*, October 1974, p. 19.

The vesting of personnel specialists with authority is important because often the resources of their departments are extremely limited. With no real authority and few resources, the personnel department will be hard put to deal with the burden of its several challenges (see Figure 2-12). These challenges, which result from the historical, external, organization, and professional environment, affect the personnel department's ability to achieve its purpose of contributing to the organization's effectiveness. Moreover, this burden is likely to grow in the future, unless personnel specialists can take proactive measures to meet these challenges.[42]

Perhaps the biggest challenge to the practice of personnel management comes from the need to avoid discrimination in staffing. With the increase of women in the Canadian work force there has been more pressure for affirmative-action programs such as those in the U.S.[43] As well, Murray has

Figure 2-12
PERSONNEL MANAGEMENT CHALLENGES IN PERSPECTIVE

pointed out the need for integrating disadvantaged persons into the work force.[44] Today the Canadian human rights program is moving in this direction. While the goals and results of these programs are still somewhat modest, the human rights commissions in various jurisdictions have set up training programs aimed at improving the positions of minorities. Details of these and other programs are given in the next chapter.

SUMMARY

The practice of personnel management is shaped by a variety of environmental challenges. These challenges arise from the historical, external, organizational, and professional demands confronting personnel specialists.

The historical challenges began with the pressures of the Industrial Revolution, which led to the scientific study of work and workers. As the tools available to managers became more sophisticated, the need for specialists in personnel management and human resources grew. Early in this century personnel departments emerged to deal with these demands. Today personnel departments are responsible for meeting the external, organizational, and professional issues that affect employees.

The external challenges to personnel management come from several different sources. The major external concerns are created by changing technologies, economic cycles, demographic developments, cultural changes, and government involvement. Each of these factors influences the ways in which personnel departments meet their objectives.

Organizational challenges include those elements within the organization that personnel departments cannot ignore if they are to be successful. Unions are one obvious example. They demand that management meet and satisfy their economic objectives within the constraints imposed by labour organizations. Even employers who do not have a union must be aware of actions that can cause workers to unionize. A professionally managed personnel department must develop and maintain a sophisticated data base in order to be effective. The urgency of the need for information and the best way of implementing personnel activities, however, are dependent on unique aspects of the organization involved.

The newest challenge to personnel management is professionalism. The important role that personnel departments and their members play in modern organizations requires a professional approach and professionally trained staff. Although personnel experts face obstacles in reaching the status of professionals, the growing importance of this function requires practitioners to strive for the high standards associated with this status.

If personnel departments can successfully meet the environmental challenges discussed in this chapter, they are more likely to contribute effectively to the goals of the organization and its people.

TERMS FOR REVIEW

Scientific management
Paternalism
Reactive and proactive approaches
Environmental challenges
Robotics
Computerization
Economic challenges

Demographics
Canadian values
Government challenges
Character of an organization
Professional challenges
Accreditation/Certification
Authority

REVIEW AND DISCUSSION QUESTIONS

1. Assuming you do *not* work in the personnel department, would you prefer to work for a company with a proactive or a reactive personnel department? Why?
2. Identify and briefly describe the major external challenges facing personnel managers. How have the external developments of the 1960s and 1970s influenced personnel management?
3. Would the professionalization of personnel management help personnel experts meet internal and external challenges? How?
4. Find two recent news items and explain how these developments might affect the demands made on the personnel department of some employer.
5. Suppose the birthrate during the 1980s was double the low rates of the 1970s. What implications would this growth have in the years 2000 and 2010 for (a) grocery stores, (b) fast-food restaurants, (c) the Canadian Armed Forces, (d) large metropolitan universities?
6. Why do you think people would want to work in a personnel department, besides "liking to work with people"? What challenges would most likely appeal to you?

7. Assuming you are entrusted with the responsibility of identifying criteria for accreditation, what qualifications and experience would you prescribe for "personnel and industrial relations" jobs? Why?
8. What items should go into a code of ethics for professional personnel and industrial relations managers?
9. Evaluate the impact of governmental policies on organizations by carefully recording the events in British Columbia since 1983.

INCIDENT 2-1
A POSSIBLE TECHNOLOGICAL SCENARIO

Sometime within the near future electronic technology will advance to the point where the average home will have:

   • *A computer console and access to several on-line computer systems via satellite communications.*
   • *A television set (with more than a hundred working channels fed by a cable system) that serves as a visual display for computer outputs and inputs.*
   • *A photocopy machine connected to the television that permits photocopies of screen information.*
   • *A two-way video phone.*

At that point, serious people will start asking, "Why do we still follow the primitive ritual of going to work? Why don't we do our jobs at home, since most workers are now white-collar information handlers?" And then the practice of going to work, which began with the Industrial Revolution, will end for some workers. Of course, people will still work; some will even have to continue to "go to work." But most people will stay at home, plugged into a worldwide information grid.

1. Assuming this scenario comes true during your career, what implications does it hold for our culture and our society? For personnel management?

INCIDENT 2-2
GOVERNMENT INTERVENTION

Since the 1930s, federal and provincial governments have increased their regulations of how employers treat employees. Laws have been passed that permit workers to join unions, require employers to pay minimum wages, ensure safe and healthy work environments, prohibit discrimination, and restrict the freedom of employers to make personnel decisions in other areas.

Some futurists believe the trend of increasing government intervention will continue. To support their argument, these thinkers point to Japan and Europe, where government involvement is far more extensive than in Canada. They believe that federal and provincial governments will require employers to provide even greater job security against layoffs, develop more extensive training programs for the disadvantaged and handicapped, and follow other regulations that will further limit personnel decisions.

Other experts think that the trend of growing government involvement is beginning to end. Tax complaints, deregulation of the industries, and the demographic trend toward an older population are the evidence these people cite in support of their position. They also argue that regulation cannot continue if Canadian firms are to remain competitive in international markets.

1. Which trend do you think will manifest itself and why?
2. If government regulation continues to increase, how will personnel departments be affected?

REFERENCES

1. Max S. E. Clarkson, Professor of Management, Faculty of Management Studies, University of Toronto, *The Financial Post*, March 19, 1977, p. 20.
2. Moses was confronted by one of the earliest recorded personnel challenges when Jethro, his father-in-law, advised:

    And thou shalt teach them ordinances and laws, and shalt shew them the way wherein they must walk, and the work they must do.

    Moreover, thou shalt provide out of all the people able men . . . to be rulers. . . .

    Exod. 18:20–21.
3. For another view of challenges likely to confront personnel management, see Lawrence A. Wrangler, "The Intensification of the Personnel Role," *Personnel Journal*, February 1979, pp. 111–119; Campbell R. McConnell, "Why Is U.S. Productivity Slowing Down?" *Harvard Business Review*, March–April 1979, pp. 36–38, 42, 44, 48, 50, 54, 56, 60; and "The Future," *Business Week*, September 3, 1979, p. 169ff.
4. George L. Whaley, "The Impact of Robotics Technology upon Human Resource Management," *Personnel Administrator*, September 1982, p. 70.
5. Andrew Templer, "The Behavioural Implications of Introducing Robots and Other Forms of New Technology into Canadian Industry," *ASAC Organizational Behaviour Division Proceedings*, vol. 5, Guelph, Ontario: University of Guelph, 1984, pp. 171–179.
6. "GM's Ambitious Plans to Employ Robots," *Business Week*, March 16, 1981, p. 31.
7. George L. Whaley, op. cit., pp. 61–63. See also John Dodd, "Robots: The New Steel Collar Workers," *Personnel Journal*, September 1981, pp. 688–695.
8. A. N. Azim, "A Discussion of Quality of Work Life," *ASAC Organizational Behaviour Division Proceedings*, vol. 5, Guelph, Ontario: University of Guelph, 1984, pp. 26–34.
9. Sylvia Ostry and Mahmood A. Zaidi, *Labour Economics in Canada*, 2nd. ed., Toronto: Macmillan of Canada, 1972.
10. *Maclean's*, August 9, 1982, p. 30.
11. "Our Coming Old Age Crisis," *Maclean's*, January 17, 1983, p. 24.
12. Edward Harvey, Professor of Sociology, University of Toronto, quoted in *Maclean's*, op. cit., p. 24.
13. Leandre Desjardins, quoted in *Maclean's*, July 16, 1984, p. 36.
14. Elizabeth Beale, quoted in *Maclean's*, July 16, 1984, p. 37.
15. Statistics Canada, *The Labour Force*, Bulletin Nos. 71-001 and 94-702, 1970–1981.
16. John D. Owne, "Workweeks and Leisure: An Analysis of Trends, 1948–75," *Monthly Labour Review*, August 1976, pp. 3–8.
17. Frank G. Vallee and Donald R. Whyte, "Canadian Society: Trends and Perspectives," in Harish C. Jain (ed.), *Contemporary Issues in Canadian Personnel Administration*, Scarborough: Prentice-Hall of Canada, 1974, pp. 29–42.
18. Vallee and Whyte, op. cit., p. 31.
19. Ibid.
20. John Porter, *The Vertical Mosaic: An Analysis of Social Class and Power in Canada*, Toronto: University of Toronto Press, 1965. See also V. V. Murray, "Canadian Cultural Values and Personnel Administration," in Harish C. Jain (ed.), *Contemporary Issues in Canadian Personnel Administration*, Scarborough: Prentice-Hall of Canada, 1974.
21. Vallee and Whyte, op. cit., p. 34.
22. Porter, op. cit., pp. 60–63.
23. Frank M. Covert, "Bill 98 'will protect employees in the long run,' " *The Mail-Star*, December 16, 1980, p. 4.
24. Solomon Barking, "Troubled Worker Militancy: Challenges Confronting Western Industrial Relations Systems," *Relations Industrielles*, 1983, vol. 38, no. 4, pp. 713–729.
25. A. W. R. Carrothers, "An Outlook on Labour Relations in Canada," *Relations Industrielles*, 1983, vol. 38, no. 3, pp. 648–657.
26. John Rahiya, "Privacy Protection and Personnel Administration: Are New Laws Needed?" *The Personnel Administrator*, April 1979, pp. 19–21, 28.
27. William B. Wolf, "Organizational Constructs: An Approach to Understanding Organizations," *Journal of the Academy of Management*, April 1968, pp. 7–15. See also Robert Granford Wright, *Mosaics of Organization Character*, New York: Dunellen Publishing Company; Inc.
28. P. Kumar, "Personnel Management in Canada—A Manpower Profile," *The Canadian Personnel & Industrial Relations Journal*, 23 (1976): 33.
29. J. I. A. Rowney and C. W. Memeth, "Educational Programs for Professionalism," *The Canadian Personnel & Industrial Relations Journal*, 26 (November 1979): 10–14.
30. C. W. Memeth and J. I. A. Rowney, "Professionalize or Perish," *The Canadian Personnel & Industrial Relations Journal*, January 1981, pp. 27–31.

31. Ibid.
32. E. H. Burack and E. L. Miller, "The Personnel Function in Transition," *California Management Review*, 18 (3) (Spring 1976): 36.
33. Memeth and Rowney, loc. cit.
34. J. P. Siegel, D. A. Ondrack, and R. F. Morrison, "Education and Development of Employee Relations Staff: A Survey of Current Practices," *The Canadian Personnel & Industrial Relations Journal*, 21 (March 1974): 25–34.
35. Memeth and Rowney, loc. cit.
36. Pradeep Kumar, "Professionalism in Canadian Personnel and Industrial Relations" *The Canadian Personnel & Industrial Relations Journal*, October 1980, pp. 34–41.
37. Pradeep Kumar, *Professionalism in the Canadian P/IR Function: Report of a Survey*, Queen's University, Industrial Relations Centre, 1980.
38. D. A. Ondrack, "P/IR Professional Certification in Ontario: The PAO Model," paper presented at a symposium on professional education in P/IR, Canadian Industrial Relations Association (CIRA), Dalhousie University, Halifax, N.S., May 26, 1981.
39. George Ritzer, "The Professionals: Will Personnel Occupations Ever Become Professions?" *The Personnel Administrator*, May–June 1971, pp. 34–36.
40. Wendell French and Dale Henning, "The Authority-Influence Role of the Functional Specialist in Management," *Academy of Management Journal*, September 1966, p. 203.
41. Harold C. White and Robert E. Boynton, "The Role of Personnel: A Management View," *Arizona Business*, October 1974, pp. 17–21; see also Harold C. White and Michael N. Wolfe, "The Role Desired for Personnel Administration," *The Personnel Administrator*, June 1980, pp. 87–97.
42. Robert A. Holmes, "What's Ahead for Personnel Professionals in the '80's?" *The Personnel Administrator*, June 1980, pp. 33–37, 82.
43. Jane Burton, "Studies on the Status of Canadian Women," *The Labour Gazette*, July 1976, pp. 377–380; *Women in the Labour Force: Facts and Figures*, Ottawa: Labour Canada Women's Bureau, 1973.
44. David Murray, "Integration of the Disadvantaged," *The Canadian Personnel & Industrial Relations Journal*, May 1976, pp. 30–31.

Chapter 3

The Challenge to Discrimination

I think we may have been only subconsciously aware of how easily we relegated people to second-rate status in the past. You may think that second-rate or second-class are terms that are too strong in this context, but I assure you that to the people who were thus categorized these terms are not exaggerated.

R. G. L. Fairweather[1]

CHAPTER OBJECTIVES

After studying this chapter, you should be able to:
1. **Identify** the jurisdictions of Canadian human rights legislation.
2. **List** the major provisions of the Canadian Human Rights Act.
3. **Cite** the remedies for violations.
4. **Explain** the effect of human rights legislation on the role of human resource specialists.
5. **Outline** an affirmative-action program.

A major challenge to personnel management is to provide equal employment opportunities without regard to people's race, religion, sex, national origin, or age. Common sense dictates such a policy, but there are also laws that prohibit certain forms of discrimination. No other laws—perhaps no other single development—rival the impact that these have on personnel management.

College intern: *What major changes has the personnel field undergone since you started with the company?*

Personnel manager: *Well, when I started in 1960, there was almost no government involved. You could hire, promote, and fire anyone you wanted.*

Intern: *Can't you still do that today?*

Manager: *Not really. Today, many companies have affirmative-action plans. These plans set goals for hiring, training, and promoting to ensure that every person has equal employment opportunities.*

Intern: *Well, since they are the company's plans, I don't see how government is involved.*

Manager: *The plans are developed to show the government our intention to eliminate discrimination. If we do not meet these goals, we could lose our federal government contracts, or worse.*

Intern: *What could be worse than losing contracts?*

Manager: *Litigation! Human rights commissions could sue us, and so could those people who thought we had discriminated against them. Suits are tremendously expensive and time consuming, even when we win.*

Intern: *I see. Have there been other changes in personnel management as significant as government involvement?*

Manager: *Not in my opinion. Sure, there have been many changes. Personnel management is a dynamic field. But government's influence on the employment relationship is the biggest change of all, especially with respect to equal employment opportunity.*

As this discussion indicates, many aspects of personnel management (shown in Figure 3-1) are affected by human rights legislation. In fact, few of the challenges discussed in this book affect human resource management as extensively as government. It shapes the role of personnel management through the use of laws aimed at the employment relationship. Government's attention to the employment relationship results from the present nature of society. No longer is Canada primarily a nation of farmers, fishermen, and small proprietors. It is a nation of wage earners. This means that the well-being of society increasingly depends upon the employment relationship.

To avoid flooding the courts with complaints and the prosecution of relatively minor infractions, federal and provincial governments often create special regulatory bodies, such as commissions and boards, to enforce compliance with the law and to aid in its interpretation. Examples are the various human rights commissions and labour relations boards, who evaluate complaints and develop legally binding rules, called *regulations*. Personnel specialists become involved because legislation and regulations affect the employment relationship. The involvement creates three important responsibilities. First, human resource experts must stay abreast of the laws, their interpretation by regulatory bodies, and court rulings. Otherwise, they will soon find their knowledge outdated and useless to the organization. Second, they must develop and administer programs that ensure company compliance. Failure to do so may lead to the loss of government contracts, poor public relations, and suits by regulatory bodies or affected individuals. Third, they must pursue their traditional roles of obtaining, maintaining, and retaining an optimal work force. No organization benefits from compliance with government constraints at the expense of a well-qualified work force.

SCOPE OF EMPLOYMENT LAWS

Usually, employment-related laws and regulations are limited in scope; their impact on the personnel management process is confined to a single personnel activity. For example, minimum-wage laws specify the lowest amount an employer can pay for each hour worked; in spite of their impor-

Figure 3-1
**A MODEL OF THE PERSONNEL MANAGEMENT SYSTEM AND ITS MAJOR
ENVIRONMENTAL CHALLENGES**

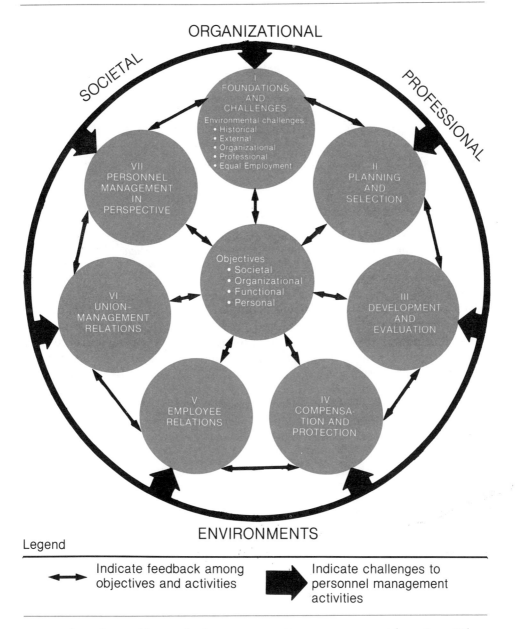

Legend

←→ Indicate feedback among objectives and activities	➡ Indicate challenges to personnel management activities

tance, these laws affect only the compensation management function. Other
personnel activities—selection, training, and labour relations—are largely
unaffected.

Human rights legislation, however, is an exception. Its role is not limited to a single personnel activity. Instead, human rights legislation affects nearly every personnel function: human resource planning, recruiting, selection, training, compensation, and labour relations. Since these laws are a major challenge to personnel management, this chapter deals exclusively with them.

HUMAN RIGHTS LEGISLATION: AN OVERVIEW

Human rights legislation is a family of federal and provincial acts that have as a common objective the provision of equal employment opportunity for members of *protected groups*. These acts outlaw discrimination based on race, colour, religion, national origin, sex, or age. Under special circumstances, they also outlaw discrimination against handicapped persons. Figure 3-2 summarizes these two layers of employment laws. Discrimination between workers on the basis of their effort, performance, or other work-related criteria remains both *permissible* and *advisable*.

Shelly Rossie complained to her provincial Human Rights Commission and charged her former employer with discrimination. When questioned, she insisted to the commission that the "real" reason for her discharge as a welder was that the company discriminated against women in "traditionally" male jobs. Shelly's case was dismissed when the company showed the commission records of her excessive absenteeism and poor productivity. (Undoubtedly, the company's case was strengthened when, later, a woman was hired to replace Shelly.)

Human rights legislation does permit employers to reward outstanding performers and penalize insufficient productivity. Its only requirement is that the basis for rewards and punishments be work-related—not a person's race, sex, age, or other prohibited criteria.

Figure 3-2
TYPES, SOURCES, OBJECTIVES, AND JURISDICTION OF CANADIAN HUMAN RIGHTS LEGISLATION

Type	Source	Objectives and Jurisdiction
Federal Law	Passed by Parliament and enforced by federal Human Rights Commission	To ensure equal employment opportunities with employers under federal jurisdiction
Provincial Law	Enacted by provincial governments and enforced by provincial human rights commissions	To ensure equal employment opportunities with employers under provincial jurisdiction

THE CANADIAN HUMAN RIGHTS ACT

The Canadian Human Rights Act was passed by Parliament on July 14, 1977, and took effect in March 1978. The act proclaims that

every individual should have an equal opportunity with other individuals to make for himself or herself the life that he or she is able and wishes to have, consistent with his or her duties and obligations as a member of society, without being hindered in or prevented from doing so by discriminatory practices based on race, national or ethnic origin, colour, religion, age, sex or marital status, or conviction for an offence for which a pardon has been granted or by discriminatory employment practices based on physical handicap.[2]

The act applies to all federal government departments and agencies, and Crown corporations, and to business and industry under federal jurisdiction—such as banks, airlines, and railway companies—in their dealings with the public and in their employment policies.

In areas not under federal jurisdiction, protection is given by provincial human rights laws. Each of the ten Canadian provinces has its own antidiscrimination laws, which are broadly similar to the federal law. Figure 3-3 compares federal and individual provincial human rights legislation as to different grounds of discrimination prohibited.

The Canadian Human Rights Act identifies nine different types of discrimination which are prohibited.

RACE AND COLOUR. It is sometimes difficult to see which of these two characteristics is the actual basis of discrimination; often both are involved. The discrimination can be intentional or unintentional, subtle or very open, as two examples will show:

A bank in a small town advertised a position specifying that the applicant should have a pleasing appearance, and requested that a recent photograph be submitted. The bank personnel were all Caucasian. A black community leader filed a discrimination complaint which was settled when the bank agreed to include human rights training in its courses on interviewing, personnel selection, and counselling.

The Western Guard Party of Toronto was operating a tape-recorded message which could be heard by telephone. The message proclaimed the supremacy of the white race and attacked Jews for being determined to destroy the white race by means of communism. The party refused to withdraw or change the messages. The Human Rights Commission therefore held a tribunal, which found the messages to be discriminatory and ordered the respondents to refrain from using this subject matter in any future messages.[3]

NATIONAL OR ETHNIC ORIGINS. It is also illegal for personnel decisions to be influenced by the national or ethnic origins of applicants or of their forebears. Hence the discrimination process can be either direct or indirect. The refusal to hire or promote people because of their national or ethnic origins is a direct and obvious violation:

A Canadian citizen originally from Haiti was refused entrance into the Armed Forces because he was not eligible for security clearance until he had lived in Canada for at least ten years. He had been in this country for six years and was unusually highly qualified in every other respect. During investigation of his complaint, the Armed Forces agreed to invoke a rule already in place which allowed for the 10-year residency requirement to be waived for exceptional candidates. He was cleared and offered enrolment as an officer cadet.[4]

Figure 3-3

PROHIBITED GROUNDS OF DISCRIMINATION IN EMPLOYMENT

Jurisdiction	Federal	British Columbia	Alberta	Saskat-chewan	Manitoba	Ontario	Quebec	New Brunswick	Prince Edward Is.	Nova Scotia	Newfound-land	Northwest Territories	Yukon
Race	●	●	●	●	●	●	●	●	●	●	●	●	●
National or ethnic origin[1]	●			●	●	●	●	●	●	●	●		●
Ancestry[2]		●	●	●		●		●				●	●
Nationality or citizenship				●	●	●					●		
Place of origin		●	●	●		●		●			●		
Colour	●	●	●	●	●	●	●	●	●	●	●	●	●
Religion	●	●	●	●	●		●	●	●	●	●		●
Creed[3]		●	●		●			●	●	●	●	●
Age	●	● (45-65)	● (45-65)	● (18-65)	●	● (18-65)	●	● (19+)	● (18-65)	● (40-65)	● 19-65	●	
Sex	●	●	●	●	●	●	●	●	●	●	●	●	●
Pregnancy or childbirth	●						●						
Marital status	●	●	●		●	●	●	●	●	●	●	●	●
Family status	●				●	●					●		
Pardoned offence	●						●				●		
Record of criminal conviction		●				●	●						
Physical handicap or disability	●		●	●	●	●	●	●	●	●	●	●	
Mental handicap or disability	●				●	●	●				●		
Dependence on alcohol or drug	●												
Place of residence												●	
Political belief		●			●		●		●		●		
Assignment, attachment or seizure of pay[4]										●			
Source of income					●					●			
Social condition[4]							●						

Figure 3-3 (cont.)

PROHIBITED GROUNDS OF DISCRIMINATION IN EMPLOYMENT

Jurisdiction	Federal	British Columbia	Alberta	Saskatchewan	Manitoba	Ontario	Quebec	New Brunswick	Prince Edward Is.	Nova Scotia	Newfoundland	Northwest Territories	Yukon
Language							●						
Social origin[4]											●		
Harassment[5]	●					●	●						
Sexual orientation							●						
Without reasonable cause		●											

1 New Brunswick includes only "national origin."
2 Saskatchewan, Alberta and the Northwest Territories include in the same ground "ancestry or place of origin."
3 Creed usually means religious beliefs.
4 In Quebec's charter, "social condition" includes assignment, attachment or seizure of pay and social origin.
5 While not technically a "ground," the federal and Quebec statutes ban harassment on all grounds. Ontario prohibits sexual harassment.

This chart is for quick reference only. For interpretation or further details, call the appropriate commission.
Source: Canadian Human Rights Commission, September 1983.

An example of an indirect violation is the following. In one case (which will be detailed later) the hiring requirements for a certain job specified that the candidate had to be 5′8″ (173 cm). But reflection reveals that such a standard disproportionately discriminates against Asian-Canadians, who tend to be shorter than descendants of immigrants from European countries. So, although the height rule may not *intend* to discriminate, the *result* is discriminatory.

RELIGION. A person's religious beliefs and practices should not affect employment decisions. An employer must accommodate an employee's religious practices, unless those practices present undue hardship to the employer.

A Moslem employee of a communications company lost his job over the question of having time off each week to attend prayers at his mosque. After conciliation, a settlement was reached, which did not impose undue hardships on the employer, by which the employee was allowed to take 1½ hours per week of leave without pay. He was reinstated with retroactive pay and benefits.[5]

If an employer does not make a reasonable attempt to accommodate workers' religious practices, he or she can be found guilty of violating the Human Rights Act.

AGE. The use of age as an employment criterion has lately been the object of considerable attention. Many employers consider that the laying-down of minimum or maximum ages for certain jobs is justified, although evidence is rarely available that age is an accurate indication of one's ability to perform a given type of work.

The General Pilotage Regulations require that a pilot be removed from the eligibility list after reaching the age of 50. A special human rights tribunal found that such a regulation was invalid and ordered that pilots affected by this rule be restored into their former positions. An appeal court set aside the tribunal's decision on the basis that the removal of the pilots from the eligibility list because of age was not a discriminatory practice. The Canadian Human Rights Commission appealed to the Supreme Court of Canada, but the appeal was denied.[6]

Age consideration also has important implications for collective bargaining, where seniority rights are often based on the age of an employee (as opposed to seniority based on length of service).

In the collective agreement between Wardair Canada and the Canadian Association of Passenger Agents, age was the determining factor for ranking of employees on the seniority list when hired on the same day. Following a complaint, the seniority list has been revised and in future, when two or more employees are hired on the same day, their seniority will be determined by company seniority, by starting following completion of training and—if two employees are still tied—by drawing of lots.[7]

The law makes an exception, however, when it comes to retirement age. It is not considered a discriminatory practice if a person's employment is terminated because that person has reached the *normal age of retirement for employees working in similar positions.*

SEX. The Canadian Human Rights Act also prevents discrimination on the basis of an individual's sex. Not only is it illegal to recruit, hire, and promote employees because of their sex; it is unlawful to have separate policies for men and women. For example, it is discriminatory to reserve some jobs for men only or women only. It is even illegal to apply similar standards to men and women when such standards arbitrarily discriminate more against one sex than against the other. When standards discriminate against one sex (or race, national or ethnic origin, religion, age, or marital status), the burden is on the employer to prove that the standards are necessary.

A woman complained that she had been refused an interview for a job as a bus driver because she was under the minimum height requirement of 5'8" (173 cm). She claimed that this height requirement discriminated against women. After conciliation, the case was settled with the company discontinuing the practice of requiring applicants to be 5'8" for drivers' jobs. Two women under 5'8" have since been hired. The Canadian Human Rights Commission informed the company that it would monitor driver application records for one year. The complainant has been paid $3,500 for lost wages and general damages.[8]

Although the standard did not discriminate against women per se, the arbitrary height requirement tended to exclude most female applicants. To keep the height rule, since it discriminates against women, the employer must show that it is necessary given the nature of the job. If this cannot be shown, the employer can be compelled to drop the requirement.

One issue that falls under the topic of sex discrimination has made headlines lately: that of *equal pay for work of equal value*. This is not to be confused with the concept of *equal pay for equal work*. The latter provision was part of the Canadian Labour Code from the beginning. It made it against the law to pay a woman less if she did the *same* work as a man; this "equal pay for equal work" concept was incorporated into the Canadian Human Rights Act later. But then the act went even further, making it illegal to discriminate against women on the basis of job *value* (or content).[9]

A nurse in a federal penitentiary complained that male health care officers, many of whom were less qualified than trained nurses, were being paid at a higher level than nurses performing work of equal value. In the settlement of the complaint, the nurses' salaries in that region will be raised to the level of the health care officers by means of an equalization adjustment.[10]

That the "equal pay for work of equal value" concept can be very costly was shown in the case of 390 federal library science employees—mostly women—who earned less than historical researchers—mostly men—though the library science work was claimed to be of equal value. The settlement, requiring individual salary increases of up to $2,500 a year, cost the federal government $2.4 million. The implication for personnel people is that they had better make very sure their wage and salary system does not subtly discriminate on the basis of sex.

MARITAL STATUS. The idea of what constitutes a family has undergone considerable changes in Canadian society in recent years. Non-traditional families, such as those resulting from so-called "common law" marriages, or single-parent families, are now far more numerous than in the past. But there is still a strong feeling that the traditional family is a unique institution deserving special consideration.

The Canadian Human Rights Act spells out quite clearly that any discrimination based on marital status is illegal.

A woman was denied a job with the CBC because her husband was already employed by the corporation at the same station. After a complaint and hearing, the CBC changed its employment practices, which formerly discriminated on the basis of marital status, and placed the woman in a position in the same station in which her husband was employed.

There is an interesting side-issue here which typically arises in Canada, and which should be brought to the attention of personnel practitioners. Under the Official Languages Act, the French and the English wording of a piece of legislation have equal force in law. In the French wording of the Canadian Human Rights Act, "situation de famille" is used, not "état civil," a term which relates more precisely to marriage only. "Situation de famille," however, includes close family relationships other than marriage.

Based on this broad definition the Canadian Human Rights Commission initiated action against Canadian Pacific Airlines. The complaint alleged that
CP Air's policy of hiring the children of its employees for summer jobs was
discrimination on the prohibited ground of "situation de famille." CP Air's
application for a writ of prohibition was dismissed by a federal court.[11]

PARDONED CONVICTS. The Canadian Human Rights Act prohibits discrimination against a convicted person if a pardon has been issued for the
offence. Pardon may be granted by a parole board after five years following
release, parole, or the completion of a sentence. So far only one case of discrimination of this nature has been brought to the attention of the Canadian
Human Rights Commission, but the case was resolved without any action
taken by the Commission.

*A person convicted and paroled on a drug offence applied for a job with a government
agency dealing with drug abuse. He was denied employment because of his conviction. Subsequently, the National Parole Board granted his request for a full pardon.
The government agency maintained, however, that, pardoned or not, he remained a
security risk and that being without a criminal record was a bona fide occupational
requirement of a correctional service's staff. He appealed to the Canadian Human
Rights Commission, and after the commission's investigation, the government agency
decided that a criminal record would not, in fact, inhibit the applicant's ability to
meet the requirements of the job, and, satisfied that he was suitable, offered him the
position.*[12]

The Canadian Human Rights Commission has also been approached by
several persons who claim to have been refused employment on the basis of
their *arrest* record, even when the arrest did not lead to a conviction. These
persons are without legal protection since the Canadian Human Rights Act
does not address this type of discrimination. For the personnel manager
this does not mean that all applicants can be asked for their arrest record. It
must still be shown that it is relevant to the job. For this reason the Commission has advised employees under federal jurisdiction that applicants
should not be asked "Have you ever been convicted of an offence?" It is
recommended—if such information is legitimately needed for employment
purposes—that the question be phrased: "Have you ever been convicted of
an offence for which you have not received a pardon?" (See Recruitment
and Interviewing Guide in the appendix to Chapter 3.)

PHYSICAL HANDICAP. No person should be denied employment solely for
the reason of his or her being disabled, e.g., blind, deaf, or confined to a
wheelchair. Of course, there are exceptions. A blind person cannot be a
truck driver, or a deaf person a telephone operator. However, the principle
of "reasonable accommodation" has been established. It means that an
employer can be expected to take reasonable measures to make available a
suitable job to a person with a physical handicap if it does not impose undue hardships on the organization.

A man was refused a technician's job because he failed a hearing test. However, he had been tested without his hearing aid; he asserted that he could perform the job using a hearing device. Medical advisors for the company claimed that the job required perfectly normal hearing. After conciliation the company agreed that with a hearing aid the man would be able to do the job. The complaint was settled with the complainant being hired as a technician and paid damages of $750.

Many organizations have established rigid physical standards for certain jobs without being able to show that these standards are truly relevant to the requirements of the job. Some complainants have been refused jobs when their disability might be a problem in a speculative situation, e.g., the firm might argue that a deaf person would be unable to hear a fire alarm. Other complainants have been disqualified for jobs not because they are physically handicapped now, but because they may become so in the future.

A machinist who had suffered an injury to his leg was refused a position on the hypothesis that at some time in the future he might develop complications which might affect his ability to work, which might in turn lead to a finding against the employer for compensation. After an investigation by the Canadian Human Rights Commission, the company had to agree that its assumptions were highly speculative. In the settlement, the complainant was paid the additional wages, approximately $2,000, that he would have earned if he had not been denied the position, as well as compensation in respect of his feelings and self-respect.[13]

EXCEPTIONS. An employer is permitted to discriminate against protected groups when a *bona fide occupational requirement* exists, i.e., when the employer has a justifiable reason for discriminating. For example, a designer of women's fashions, hiring models, would be allowed to discriminate against men. This type of discrimination is also legal in cases involving handicapped people: a trucking company can refuse to hire blind or deaf people as truck drivers. Obviously, discrimination in these situations ought to be permitted—a bona fide occupational requirement certainly exists.

EMPLOYER RETALIATION. As with most employment laws, it is a separate violation to retaliate *in any way* against those who exercise their rights according to the Human Rights Act. Those who file charges, testify, or otherwise participate in any human rights action, are protected by law. If a supervisor tries to "get even" with an employee who filed charges, he or she violates the act.

ENFORCEMENT. The responsibility for the enforcement of the Canadian Human Rights Act lies in the hands of a specially created Canadian Human Rights Commission. It consists of a Chief Commissioner, a Deputy Chief Commissioner, and from three to six other members—all appointed by the Governor in Council. The Chief Commissioner and his deputy are full-time members. Full-time members are appointed for a term of not more than seven years, and part-time members for a term of not more than three years.

The commission deals with complaints it receives concerning discriminatory practices covered by the act. The commission may also act on its own when it perceives a possible infraction. It also has the power to issue guidelines interpreting the act. It has wide powers, including the establishment of tribunals which may order cessation of the discriminatory practice and the adoption of measures to ensure that it will not recur, as well as compensation.

Figure 3-4 summarizes the CHRC enforcement procedures. Any individual or group may file a complaint with the commission, given that they have reasonable grounds to believe they have been discriminated against. The commission may refuse to accept the complaint if it is submitted by

Figure 3-4
CANADIAN HUMAN RIGHTS COMMISSION ENFORCEMENT PROCEDURE

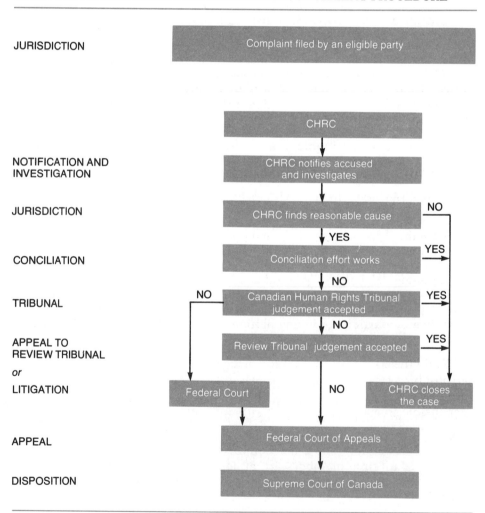

someone other than the person who allegedly has been discriminated against, unless the alleged victim permits investigation of the claim.

It is also possible for the commission itself to initiate a complaint, if it has reasonable grounds to assume that a party is engaging in a discriminatory practice.

The commission has to deal with any complaint filed with it if it involves a federal government department or agency or any business or industry under federal jurisdiction. The same is true for commissions and organizations at the provincial level. Commissions, however, may refuse to deal with complaints if other procedures seem more appropriate, if the complaint seems trivial or made in bad faith, or if too much time has elapsed since the alleged discrimination took place.

After a complaint has been accepted by the commission, an investigator is appointed to gather facts about the case. The investigator submits a report to the commission recommending a finding of either substantiation or non-substantiation of the allegation. If the allegation is substantiated, a settlement may be arranged in the course of the investigation, or the commission may, after adoption of the investigator's report, appoint a conciliator.

Should the parties involved be unable to reach a *conciliation agreement*, a Human Rights Tribunal consisting of up to three members—most consist of one—may be appointed to investigate the complaint. Figure 3-5 describes the discretion of the tribunal in settling a complaint.

Figure 3-5
DISCRETION OF A CANADIAN HUMAN RIGHTS TRIBUNAL

A Canadian Human Rights Tribunal can order a violator to:

- **Stop** the discriminatory practice.
- **Restore** the rights, opportunities, and privileges denied the victim.
- **Compensate** the victim for wages lost and any expenses incurred as a result of the discriminatory practice.
- **Compensate** the victim for any additional cost of obtaining alternative goods, services, facilities, or accommodation as a result of the discriminatory practice.
- **Develop** and implement affirmative-action programs to equalize opportunity for certain groups which have suffered from discriminatory practices in the past.

Should the tribunal find that the discriminatory practice was maintained purposely or recklessly, or that the victim's feelings of self-respect have suffered as a result of the practice, it may order the person or organization responsible to compensate the victim appropriately.

A person who obstructs an investigation or a tribunal, or fails to comply with the terms of a settlement, or reduces wages in order to eliminate a discriminatory practice, can be found guilty of an offence punishable by a fine and/or jail sentence. If the guilty party is an employer or any employee organization, the fine might be up to fifty thousand dollars. For individuals the penalty might be up to five thousand dollars.[14]

In the Western Guard Party case mentioned earlier (see under the section "Race and colour") the tribunal had ordered that the party cease preparing recorded telephone messages that expose persons to hatred or contempt because of their religion or race. When the respondents persisted with their messages, the Canadian Human Rights Commission successfully moved in the Court that the respondents be found guilty of contempt. The party's leader, John Ross Taylor, was sentenced to one year in jail and the Western Guard Party was sentenced to a $5,000 fine. The respondents appealed their conviction and sentence to the Federal Court of Appeals and the Supreme Court of Canada, but both let the conviction stand. [15]

AFFIRMATIVE ACTION

The Canadian Human Rights Act gives the Canadian Human Rights Commission great latitude in pursuing the enforcement of the act. One way for the commission to comply with the intent of the act to improve equal employment opportunities for special groups is for it to encourage what are often called *affirmative-action programs.*

Section 15(1) of the act specifies special programs as a legitimate mechanism for improving the opportunities of a group through the elimination, reduction, or prevention of discrimination.

It is not a discriminatory practice for a person to adopt or carry out a special program, plan, or arrangement designed to prevent disadvantages that are likely to be suffered by, or to eliminate or reduce disadvantages that are suffered by, any group of individuals when those disadvantages would be or are based on or related to the race, national or ethnic origin, colour, religion, age, sex, marital status, or physical handicap of members of that group, by improving opportunities respecting goods, services, facilities, accommodation, or employment in relation to that group.

Such programs are developed by employers to remedy past discrimination or to prevent discrimination in the future. It usually implies on the part of the organization a self-evaluation with regard to hiring, promotion, and compensation practices. If discrepancies are found, it would be good personnel practice to check the criteria used for different personnel decisions, adjust them if necessary, and make sure that they are consistently applied.

Affirmative-action programs exist for several reasons. From a practice standpoint, employers seldom benefit by excluding people who belong to some particular group. To exclude an entire class of workers, such as women or minorities, limits the labour pool available to the personnel department. Open discrimination can also lead to negative public relations, boycotts by consumers, and government intervention. [16] To ensure that such discrimination does not occur, employers often develop affirmative-action programs voluntarily.

Regardless of the reasons or goals of such programs, personnel departments should adhere to the guidelines discussed below and summarized in Figure 3-6.

EXHIBIT COMMITMENT. No matter how favourably the personnel department is viewed by others in the organization, the president of the company

Figure 3-6
MAJOR STEPS IN AFFIRMATIVE-ACTION PROGRAMS

1. **Exhibit** strong employer commitment.
2. **Appoint** a high-ranking director.
3. **Publicize** commitment internally and externally.
4. **Survey** the work force for underutilization and concentration.
5. **Develop** goals and timetables.
6. **Design** remedial and preventive programs.
7. **Establish** control systems and reporting procedures.

should support the affirmative-action program in writing. Anything less than total backing from top officials raises questions about the sincerity of the organization's commitment in the eyes of government agencies, courts, and employees. To exhibit this commitment forcefully, company officials may make raises, bonuses, and promotions dependent upon each manager's compliance.

APPOINT A DIRECTOR. Some member of the organization should be responsible for affirmative action. Commonly, the vice president of personnel is appointed director, although day-to-day implementation may be delegated to a compliance specialist in the personnel department.

Pearl Kays was made the affirmative-action officer for the Daily Times Newspaper. *Most department managers at the* Times *were supportive of Pearl's efforts. But a pressroom supervisor felt affirmative action was "hogwash." Whenever Pearl needed this supervisor's assistance, she would draft an interoffice memo to the supervisor and have the personnel manager sign it.*

PUBLICIZE COMMITMENT. Equal employment and affirmative action are meaningless unless publicized externally and internally. Outside the company, sources of potential recruits must be made aware of the new policy. School guidance counsellors, employment agencies, and officers of Canada Employment Centres are likely candidates for notification. The phrase "an equal-opportunity employer" is frequently used on company stationery and in classified ads to further publicize the policy.

Internally, managers at all levels need to be aware of the new commitment. This means more than simply informing them of the policy. Equal employment has to be viewed as their responsibility too. Personnel managers cannot be the only ones responsible for equal opportunity. They must enlist the active support of *all* managers.

SURVEY THE WORK FORCE. The personnel department needs to know how the composition of the employer's work force compares with the composition of the work force in the labour market. For example, if the employer's mix of male and female employees differs significantly from the labour market from which the employer attracts workers, then it is possible that discrimination has occurred. When a survey of the employer's work force indicates such differences, the employer may find examples of underutilization or concentration. *Underutilization* exists when a company or department has a smaller proportion of protected class members than is found in the labour market. For example, when a company has no female managers even though the labour market is 37% female, underutilization exists. *Concentration* is just the opposite. It occurs when protected class members are concentrated in a few departments out of proportion with their presence in the labour market.

At the Northern Telephone & Telegraph Company 100% of the telephone operators and 25% of the supervisors were female. The labour market was 33% female. Alan Taylor, the personnel manager, realized that the job of operator was an example of concentration and the supervisors' position an example of underutilization, so he developed a series of goals and timetables to eliminate these problems.

DEVELOP GOALS AND TIMETABLES. When, through surveys, underutilization and concentration are found (possibly consequences of past discrimination) personnel specialists should set up goals and timetables to eliminate them. In the case of Northern Telephone & Telegraph, Alan set a three-year goal of 25% male operators and 50% female supervisors. He hoped that in a subsequent five-year plan he could achieve the same male/female ratio in the company's labour force as existed in the local labour market.

DESIGN SPECIFIC PROGRAMS. To reach goals, personnel specialists must design both remedial and preventive programs. *Remedial programs* correct problems that already exist. Alan's remedial program at the phone company was to train and promote more women into supervisory positions. He also sought more male applicants for operator openings.

Preventive programs are more proactive. They involve an assessment of personnel policies and practices. Policies that discriminate (such as height rules) or practices that continue past discrimination (such as hiring exclusively from employee referrals) must be eliminated.

ESTABLISH CONTROLS. An affirmative-action program is likely to fail unless controls are established. Personnel specialists and line managers must perceive their rewards as depending upon the success of the affirmative-action plan. To evaluate that success, monthly, quarterly, and yearly benchmarks should be reported directly to the director of the program and to the president or another senior official.

HUMAN RIGHTS LEGISLATION IN PERSPECTIVE

Equal employment laws have a broad impact on the practice of personnel management in three major areas. One obvious effect is on personnel activities; another is on people who are not directly protected by these laws. The third effect, on line management, may be even more serious.

FUNCTIONAL IMPACT

Virtually every personnel function is affected by equal-employment opportunity and affirmative-action plans:

• *Human resource plans* must reflect the organization's affirmative-action goals.

• *Job descriptions* must not contain unneeded requirements that exclude members of protected classes.

• *Recruiting* must ensure that all types of applicants are sought without discriminating.

• *Selection* of applicants must use screening devices that are job-relevant and nondiscriminatory.

• *Training and developmental* opportunities must be made available to workers without discrimination.

• *Performance appraisal* must be free of biases that discriminate.

• *Compensation programs* must be based on skills, performance, and/or seniority and cannot discriminate against jobholders in other respects.

Even when personnel specialists know their *intent* is not to discriminate, they must carefully review the results of these personnel functions to ensure that the *results* are not discriminatory. Otherwise, lawsuits may arise and the current affirmative-action plan may need to be revised or scrapped.

REVERSE DISCRIMINATION

The use of affirmative-action plans can lead to charges of reverse discrimination against employers. These charges usually arise when an employer seeks to hire or promote a member of a protected group over an equally (or better) qualified candidate who is not a member of the protected group. For example, if an employer has an affirmative-action program that gives preference to women over men when promotions occur, a qualified male may sue the employer and claim that he was discriminated against because of his sex.

Charges of reverse discrimination may place personnel departments in a difficult position. On one hand, the personnel department is responsible for eliminating concentration and underutilization. On the other hand, to give preference to members of a protected class (such as women, for example) raises questions about whether the personnel department is being fair.[17]

For example, if the attitudes expressed in Figure 3-7 are representative of most male employees, it is easy to imagine how special treatment toward women would evoke strongly negative feelings. These negative feelings could easily lead to frustration, tensions, employee turnover, and lower employee satisfaction.[18]

Figure 3-7
**REACTIONS OF MALE EMPLOYEES TOWARD ORGANIZATIONAL
TREATMENT OF WOMEN**

Attitude Expressed	Percentage Agreeing
Favouritism toward Women	
Women can get complaints resolved more easily than men.	19
Women are given too many breaks.	13
Organizations are forced by law to favour women.	26
Promotion and Training	
Promotion opportunities are greater for women than for men.	50
Recently there has been more emphasis on training women than on training men.	23
Favouritism is shown when it comes to special opportunities for development.	10
Women and Power	
Management is afraid of women's liberation.	27
It would be disastrous if women got much control or power.	17
I resent women's attempts to get more power.	14
Women have too much say on policies and decisions.	5
Men's and Women's Place	
Some jobs should remain men's jobs and other jobs should remain women's jobs.	45
A woman's place is in the home.	26
Men should always be the backbone of the organization.	21

Source: Benson Rosen and Thomas H. Jerdee, "Coping with Affirmative Action Backlash," *Business Horizons*, August 1979, p. 17. Used by permission.

Although preferential treatment will always raise questions of fairness, the Canadian Human Rights Act declares affirmative-action programs non-discriminatory if they fulfill the spirit of the law as outlined in Section 15(1). So far, reverse discrimination has not been an issue in Canada.

LINE MANAGEMENT

The implementation of an affirmative-action program may cause line managers to feel a loss of authority.[19] Operating managers may lose the right to make final hiring and promotion decisions. To achieve the objectives of the plan, the personnel department may even have to overrule line managers. In time, supervisors may believe that members of protected classes are getting different treatment. If workers also sense an element of reverse discrimination, conflicts may arise which lessen the effectiveness of the work group.

To overcome potentially damaging side effects of affirmative-action plans, personnel specialists must educate line managers—particularly first-line supervisors. Training programs, seminars, and explanations of personnel decisions affecting protected groups must be given to managers. Otherwise, their support and understanding of affirmative action is likely to be low;[20] and, in turn, the perceived quality of the work environment may decline.

A LANDMARK DECISION ON AFFIRMATIVE ACTION

In August 1984, a federal human rights tribunal issued its first decision with regard to a *mandatory* affirmative-action program in Canadian history.[21] The tribunal ordered Canadian National Railways to hire women for one in four nontraditional or blue-collar jobs in its St. Lawrence region until they hold 13% of such jobs. CN was also required to implement a series of other measures, varying from abandoning certain mechanical aptitude tests to modifying the way it publicizes available jobs. The decision arose from a complaint laid against CN in 1979 by a Montreal lobby group, Action Travail des Femmes. The goal of 13% would roughly correspond to the proportion of women in blue-collar jobs in industry generally. Currently, women represent approximately 4% of CN employees.

SUMMARY

Government is a significant variable that strongly shapes the role of personnel management. It influences personnel through laws governing the employment relationship. Most of these laws are limited in scope; however, equal-employment laws influence nearly every personnel activity.

The two sources of equal-employment laws are the federal and provincial human rights statutes. The Canadian Human Rights Act of 1978 applies to federal government departments and agencies, Crown corporations, and businesses and industries under federal jurisdiction, such as banks, airlines, and railway companies. Areas not under federal jurisdiction are protected by provincial human rights laws. Each of the ten Canadian provinces has its own antidiscrimination laws which are broadly similar to the federal law.

To eliminate past discrimination and ensure future compliance, many organizations have developed affirmative-action programs. These programs are designed to identify areas of past and present discrimination, develop affirmative goals, and implement corrective programs.

The appendix to this chapter contains a "recruitment and interviewing guide" which describes acceptable and unacceptable questions to ask during job interviews and on application forms.

TERMS FOR REVIEW

Regulations
Canadian Human Rights Act
Provincial antidiscrimination laws
Canadian Human Rights
  Commission
Equal pay for work of equal value

Bona fide occupational
  requirements
Conciliation agreement
Affirmative-action programs
Underutilization
Concentration

REVIEW AND DISCUSSION QUESTIONS

1. Suppose during your first job interview after graduation you are asked, "Why should a company have an affirmative-action plan?" How would you respond?
2. If you are a supervisor in the production department of a textile mill and an employee demands to be allowed to miss work on Fridays for religious reasons, what would you do? Under what circumstances would you have to let the employee have time off? Under what circumstances could you prohibit it?
3. List the major prohibitions of the Canadian Human Rights Act.
4. Since a personnel department is not a legal department, what role does personnel play in the area of equal-employment law?
5. Suppose you are told that your first duty as a personnel specialist is to construct an affirmative-action plan. What would you do? What types of information would you seek?
6. What conditions would have to be met before you could bring suit against an employer who discriminated against you because of your sex?
7. During the rest of this decade, do you think more groups will receive special legislation to protect them from discrimination? Which groups might get additional protection?

INCIDENT 3-1

METROPOLITAN HOSPITAL'S AFFIRMATIVE-ACTION NEEDS

A large metropolitan hospital in Ontario recently developed an affirmative-action program. Under the program the hospital agreed to promote two women into supervisory ranks for each man promoted. This practice was to continue until 40 to 45% of all supervisory jobs in the hospital were held by women.

The need for the first supervisory promotion occurred in the medical records department. The manager of medical records was one of the few female managers in the hospital. Nevertheless, she argued that Roy Biggs should become a medical records supervisor since he was best qualified. Roy had two years of medical school and was a graduate of a medical-records program at the local community college. The assistant director of hospital operations agreed that Roy should get the promotion. The equal-employment compliance specialist in the personnel department argued that Kate VanDam should get the promotion because of the affirmative-action program and because she had more seniority and experience in the department than Roy. The records manager, the assistant administrator, and the compliance specialist decided that the personnel manager should make the final decision.

1. What weight would you give to (a) Kate's seniority and experience, (b) Roy's superior training, (c) the recommendation of the records manager, (d) the new affirmative-action program?
2. What are the implications for the affirmative-action program if Roy gets the job? What are the implications for the employees presently taking job-related courses if Kate gets the promotion?
3. What decision would you make if you were the personnel manager?

EXERCISE 3-1
CARVER JEWELLERY COMPANY

The Carver Jewellery Company Ltd. has the following work force composition:

Job Classes	Male	Female	White	Black	Asian	Native peoples
Executive	9	1	10	0	0	0
Management	71	9	79	0	1	0
Salaried/Commission	43	31	74	0	0	0
Hourly Paid	24	164	168	10	8	2

An analysis of the local labour force from which Carver draws its employees is as follows:

Male	Female	White	Black	Asian	Native peoples
53%	47%	84%	8%	3%	5%

On the basis of this information:
1. Identify which job classes at Carver exhibit underutilization.
2. Identify which job classes at Carver exhibit concentration.

REFERENCES

1. R. G. L. Fairweather, Chief Commissioner of the Canadian Human Rights Commission, in an address to the Federal Institute of Management, Halifax, N.S., November 3, 1980.
2. Canadian Human Rights Act, Paragraph 2, Subsection (a).
3. These cases have been taken from either "Summary of Decisions Taken by the Canadian Human Rights Commission," Ottawa: Government of Canada, 1979, or "Annual Report of the Canadian Human Rights Commission," Ottawa: Government of Canada, 1980. Used with permission.
4. Ibid.
5. Ibid.
6. Ibid.
7. Ibid.
8. Ibid.
9. Hermann F. Schwind, "Equal Pay for Work of Equal Value," *Commercial News*, a publication of the Halifax Board of Trade, July 1981, pp. 28–31.
10. Canadian Human Rights Commission, op. cit. in note 3.
11. "Annual Report of the Canadian Human Rights Commission," 1980, p. 33.
12. "Correctional Service Agrees To Hire Pardoned Ex-Convict," *Release*, a publication of the Canadian Human Rights Commission, Ottawa: Government of Canada, undated.
13. Canadian Human Rights Commission, op. cit. in note 3.

14. Canadian Human Rights Act, Paragraph 46, Section 2, (a), (b).
15. *Peterborough Examiner*, April 8, 1981.
16. Tove Helland Hanner, "Affirmative Action Programs: Have We Forgotten the First Line Supervisor?" *Personnel Journal*, June 1979, pp. 384–389.
17. Eleanor Holmes Norton, "Comment on the Bakke Decision," *The Personnel Administrator*, August 1978, pp. 26–28.
18. Benson Rosen and Thomas H. Jerdee, "Coping with Affirmative Action Backlash," *Business Horizons*, August 1979, pp. 18–19.
19. Hanner, loc. cit.
20. Ibid.
21. Margot Gibb-Clark, "CN ordered to recruit more women in landmark human-rights decision," *Globe and Mail*, August 23, 1984, pp. 1–2.

APPENDIX TO CHAPTER 3
RECRUITMENT AND INTERVIEWING GUIDE

Subject	Unacceptable Practices	Acceptable Practices	Comments
Name	• Asking for maiden name of applicant. • Asking for previous name when name was changed by court order or otherwise.	• Asking for name under which applicant has been educated or employed.	
Address	• Asking for foreign addresses (which may indicate national origin).	• Asking for place and duration of current and previous addresses in Canada.	
Age	• Asking for birth certificate, baptismal record, or any other documents or information regarding age of applicant.	• Asking whether applicant has attained minimum age, or has exceeded maximum age, applying to employment by law.	Verification of age may be obtained after hiring.
Sex	• Asking about sex of applicant on the application form. • Using different or coded application forms for males and females.		Correspondence to applicants may be addressed to their home with or without the prefixes Mr., Mrs., Miss, Ms.; e.g. "Dear Mary Smith."
Marital Status	• Asking whether applicant is single, married, remarried, engaged, divorced, separated, widowed, or living common law. • Asking about applicant's spouse, e.g. "Is spouse subject to transfer?" • Asking for number of children or other dependents.	• Asking if applicant is willing to travel or to be transferred to other areas of the province or country, if this requirement is job related.	Such information, if required for tax or insurance purposes, may be required after hiring.

RECRUITMENT AND INTERVIEWING GUIDE (cont.)

Subject	Unacceptable Practices	Acceptable Practices	Comments
	• Asking about child-care arrangements. • Asking whether applicant is pregnant, on birth control, or has future childbearing plans.		
National or Ethnic Origin	• Asking about birthplace. • Asking about nationality of parents, grandparents, relatives, or spouse. • Asking about ethnic or national origin, e.g. requiring birth certificate, asking for mother tongue. • Asking whether applicant is native-born or naturalized. • Asking for date citizenship received. • Asking for proof of citizenship.	• Asking if the applicant is legally entitled to work in Canada.	An employer may ask for documentary proof of eligibility to work in Canada after hiring.
Medical Information	A medical examination will necessarily reveal prohibited information about an applicant, such as his or her age, race, or sex. For this reason employers should conduct medical examinations after the hiring decision is made. Employers may indicate on application forms that the job offer is conditional on the applicant's passing a medical examination.		
Organizations	• Asking applicant to list all clubs or organizations he or she belongs to.	• Asking for such a list with the proviso that applicant may decline to list clubs or organizations which may indicate a prohibited ground of discrimination.	The request should only be made if membership in organizations is necessary to determine job qualifications.

RECRUITMENT AND INTERVIEWING GUIDE (cont.)

Subject	Unacceptable Practices	Acceptable Practices	Comments
Height and Weight			Height and weight requirements may be discriminatory if they screen out disproportionate numbers of minority-group individuals or women and if they cannot be shown to be essential for the performance of the job.
Relatives	• Asking for relationship to applicant of next of kin to be notified in case of emergency.	• Asking for name and address of person to be notified in case of emergency.	
References	• Asking any question of a person given as a reference that would not be allowable if asked directly of the applicant.		
Criminal Conviction	• Asking whether applicant has ever been convicted of an offence.	• Asking whether applicant has been convicted of an offence for which no pardon has been granted.	The CHRA permits discrimination based on a criminal conviction for which a pardon has not been granted. However, it discourages inquiries into unpardoned criminal convictions unless the particular conviction is relevant to job qualification; e.g., a theft and fraud conviction is relevant to a job requiring honesty, but a conviction for marijuana possession is not.

RECRUITMENT AND INTERVIEWING GUIDE (cont.)

Subject	Unacceptable Practices	Acceptable Practices	Comments
Optional Inquiries	• Making any of the above prohibited inquiries, even if marked "optional" on the application form.		
Military	• Asking about all military service.	• Asking about Canadian military service.	Asking about all military service is permissible if military experience directly relates to the job applied for.
Languages	• Asking about mother tongue or where language skills were obtained.	• Asking which languages applicant speaks, reads, or writes, if job-related.	Testing or scoring an applicant in English or French language proficiency is not approved unless English or French language skill is a requirement for the work to be performed.
Race or Colour	• Asking anything which would indicate race, colour, or complexion, including colour of eyes, hair, or skin.		
Photographs	• Asking for photograph, or taking of photograph.		Photos may be required after hiring for identification purposes.
Religion	• Asking about religious affiliation. • Asking about willingness or availability to work on a specific religious holiday.	• Asking about willingness to work a specified work schedule.	It is the duty of the employer to accommodate the religious observances of the applicant, if it is reasonably possible to do so.

RECRUITMENT AND INTERVIEWING GUIDE (cont.)

Subject	Unacceptable Practices	Acceptable Practices	Comments
	• Asking about church attended, religious holidays, customs observed, or religious dress. • Asking for reference or recommendation from pastor, priest, minister, rabbi, or other religious leader.		After hiring, inquiry about religion to determine when leave of absence might be required for religious observances, is permitted.
Physical Handicap	• Asking about all physical handicaps, limitations, or health problems which would tend to elicit handicaps or conditions not necessarily related to job performance.	• Asking whether applicant has any physical handicaps or health problems affecting the job applied for. • Inquiry as to any physical handicaps or limitations that the applicant wishes to be taken into consideration when determining job placement.	A physical handicap is relevant to the job if: (a) the handicap would be hazardous to the applicant, coworkers, clients, or the public; (b) the handicap would prevent the applicant from performing the duties of the job satisfactorily.

Chapter *4*

The Quality of Work Life

... why I think the quality of work life movement is so critical has to do with the fact that certain mutually reinforcing global trends—namely technology and bigness—threaten to smother the individual, unless we take measures to counteract them. I believe that workplace democracy and job redesign comprise one such measure.

Gerald A. Regan[1]

CHAPTER OBJECTIVES

After studying this chapter, you should be able to:
1. **Explain** why personnel specialists are interested in the quality of work life.
2. **Identify** the efficiency and behavioural considerations in job design.
3. **Discuss** the different techniques used to improve jobs and the quality of work life.
4. **Recognize** the nature of autonomous work groups in improving the quality of work life.
5. **Place** quality of work life in perspective with other personnel challenges.
6. **Explain** the concept of the quality circle.

Beyond the challenge of providing equal employment opportunities, personnel departments also seek to improve the quality of work life. Efforts to improve the *quality of work life (QWL)* make jobs more productive *and* satisfying. Although many different techniques are used to improve the quality of work life, most involve the participation of the workers who are affected.

Bob Walters: *My job is very boring. All I do all day long is install the motors on electric typewriters. Every day it is the same task. I realize that someone must do it, but surely the job could be more fun.*

Stan Browne: *Well, several supervisors have talked with us in personnel about some of these assembly-line jobs. But the plant manager's big concern is maintaining pro-*

ductivity. Any changes we make could not mean fewer units per day. What do you suggest?

Bob Walters: *I know high production is necessary to compete against foreign typewriters. But why can't several of us on the line be responsible for entire subassemblies instead of being responsible just for the parts we install?*

Stan Browne: *Well, what difference would that make?*

Bob Walters: *Probably not much difference. But when we got bored with one job we could swap jobs among us. Besides, when someone got behind, we could all pitch in.*

Stan Browne: *Maybe we should get together with the supervisor and the other workers and discuss this at lunch.*

The quality of work life is affected by many factors: supervision, working conditions, pay, benefits, and the design of the job. But it is the nature of the job that most intimately involves the worker. Even if management gave Bob Walters a pay raise, new benefits, improved working conditions, and excellent supervision, his job would still be boring. For most people a good work life means an interesting, challenging, and rewarding job. Admittedly, not all employee dissatisfactions can be solved by redesigning jobs. Technology, production economies, and even tradition may block change. In Bob Walters' case, however, changing the job may be the best way to improve the quality of his employment in the typewriter factory.

When jobs need to be redesigned, the changes are often handled by operating managers without direct involvement of the personnel department. But other managers seek the assistance of the personnel department because it can help match human needs with job needs. Either way, personnel specialists need to be knowledgeable about how to improve the quality of work life through job design.

Knowledge of job design is also important if personnel departments are to respond proactively to the organizational, environmental, and behavioural challenges listed in Figure 4-1. Changes in any of these factors may affect the design of jobs and the quality of work life. If the impact of these changes can be anticipated, personnel departments are better able to respond. Consider how a knowledge of job design allowed one personnel manager to be proactive:

The development of a semiautomated steam box meant that Industrial Supply Service needed fewer employees to iron the uniforms the company rented. Instead of hand-ironing cotton uniforms, Industrial Supply changed to permanent press ones that only needed a four-minute trip through the steam box to remove wrinkles. Since Helen Edgmon, the personnel manager, understood the work flow in the laundry room, she stopped hiring new workers when the steam box was ordered. She immediately began training the displaced ironers to fill other job openings.

Without an understanding of these jobs in the laundry room, Helen could not have undertaken such a proactive approach. She would have been forced to react by laying off workers. And layoffs do not contribute to societal, organizational, or employee objectives of stable employment.

Perhaps the most important need for understanding how job design affects quality of work life is the obvious point: *Jobs are the link between peo-*

Figure 4-1
ENVIRONMENTAL, ORGANIZATIONAL, AND BEHAVIOURAL FACTORS
THAT INFLUENCE JOB DESIGN AND QUALITY OF WORK LIFE

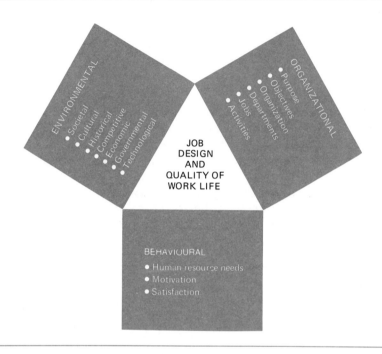

ple and the organization. Job openings are the reason organizations need human resources. If personnel departments are going to help the organization obtain and maintain a desired work force, people specialists must have a thorough understanding of job designs. The personnel management model from Chapter 1 is developed further in Figure 4-2 to indicate that quality of work life is an important challenge to personnel management. Every one of the major personnel activities in Figure 4-2 presupposes that personnel experts understand the organization's jobs. Without this knowledge, personnel cannot assist managers in redesigning jobs or performing other QWL activities.

THE PERSONNEL DEPARTMENT'S ROLE

The role of the personnel department in QWL efforts varies widely, although it is involved in almost every undertaking. In some organizations top management has appointed an executive to ensure that QWL and productivity efforts occur throughout the organization.[2] In most cases, these executives have a small staff and must rely on the personnel department for help with employee training, feedback from attitude surveys, and other support.[3] In other organizations, the personnel department is responsible for

Figure 4-2
A MODEL OF THE PERSONNEL MANAGEMENT SYSTEM

initiating and directing the firm's QWL and productivity efforts.

Perhaps the most crucial role that the personnel department plays is winning the support of key managers. Management support—particularly top management support—appears to be a near universal prerequisite to successful QWL programs.[4] When full support from all levels of management does not exist, proactive personnel departments seek ways to document the success of individual QWL efforts.[5] By substantiating employee satisfaction and financial benefits, which range from lower absenteeism and turnover to higher productivity and fewer accidents, the personnel department can help convince doubting managers.[6] One telephone company, for example, achieved better sales from its phone installers, a reduction in lost inventory, fewer strikes, better employee attitudes, and improved productivity as a result of its QWL effort. Without the documentation of these favourable results, top management perhaps would not have given its on-going and strong support.

The remainder of this chapter takes a closer look at the key elements in job design, the trade-offs personnel specialists face between different design choices, and the tools of job design. Following this, there is a review of some specific approaches to QWL before concluding with a discussion of barriers that personnel departments are likely to encounter.

ELEMENTS OF JOB DESIGN

To understand job design, Figure 4-3 provides a framework that identifies the goals of job design and the major demands it faces. The demands on job design are organizational, environmental, and behavioural. When they are carefully considered and correctly matched with a proper job design, the result is a productive and satisfying job. But when inputs or desired outputs are overlooked, problems result. For example, consider the following situation:

Cal and Doris Shaeffer own the Shaeffer Car Rental Agency. Greg, a high school drop-out, works weekends. Cal and Doris each give him parts of their job they dislike: fetch-

Figure 4-3
THE JOB DESIGN INPUT/OUTPUT FRAMEWORK

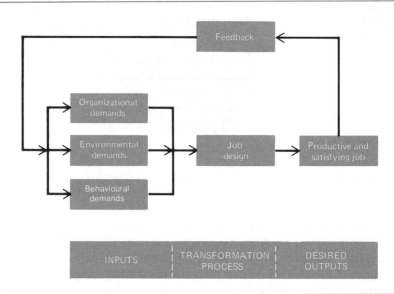

ing cars for customers, putting in gas, and posting the week's entries into the ledger. As a result, Greg's satisfaction and motivation are low.

Consider how Greg's job design compares with the model in Figure 4-3. The Shaeffers designed Greg's job to reflect their personal objectives, not organizational objectives. No apparent thought was given to Greg's needs. As a result, the job was not very satisfying to Greg. Nor did it make efficient use of his time; Greg faced long stretches with nothing to do followed by periods of hectic activity each time a plane landed. Obviously, the quality of his work life was quite low under these circumstances.

Even if the Shaeffers had weighed the organization's objectives and Greg's needs, the job design may still have been ineffective. To create an effective job design requires an understanding of the factors listed in Figure 4-4. These organizational, environmental, and behavioural elements of job design cannot be ignored if the demands placed on jobs are to be met. Had the Shaeffers considered the guidelines suggested by Figure 4-4, Greg's motivation and satisfaction might have been higher. Since these elements help ensure a high quality of work life, managers and personnel specialists should be familiar with them.

Figure 4-4
ELEMENTS OF JOB DESIGN

Organizational Elements	Environmental Elements	Behavioural Elements
• Mechanistic approach • Work flow • Work practices	• Employee abilities and availability • Social expectations	• Autonomy • Variety • Task identity • Feedback

ORGANIZATIONAL ELEMENTS OF JOB DESIGN

Organizational elements of job design are concerned with efficiency. Efficiently designed jobs allow a highly motivated and capable worker to achieve maximum output. This concern for efficiency was formalized by management scientists around the turn of the century. They devoted much of their research to finding the best ways to design efficient jobs. Their success with stopwatches and motion pictures even gave rise to a new discipline, industrial engineering. They also contributed to the formal study of management as a separate discipline. From their efforts, we have learned that specialization is a key element in the design of jobs. When workers are limited to a few repetitive tasks, output is usually higher. The findings of these early researchers are still applicable today. They can be summarized under the heading of the mechanistic approach.

MECHANISTIC APPROACH. The mechanistic approach seeks to identify *every* task in a job so that tasks can be arranged to minimize the time and effort of workers. Once task identification is complete, a limited number of tasks are grouped into a job. The result is *specialization*. Specialized jobs lead to short *job cycles*, the time to complete every task in the job. For example:

An automotive assembly-line worker might pick up a headlight, plug it in, twist the adjustment screws, and pick up the next headlight within thirty seconds. Completing these tasks in thirty seconds means this worker's job cycle takes one-half a minute. The job cycle begins when the next headlight is picked up.

Headlight installation is a specialized job. It is so specialized that training takes only a few minutes. And the short job cycle means that the assembler gains much experience in a short time. Said another way, short job cycles require small investments in training and allow the worker to learn the job quickly. Training costs remain low because the worker only needs to master one job.

This mechanistic approach stresses efficiency in effort, time, labour costs, training, and employee learning time. Today, this technique is still widely used in assembly operations. It is especially effective when dealing with poorly educated workers or workers who have little industrial experience. But the efficient design of jobs also considers such organizational elements as work flow and work practices.

WORK FLOW. The flow of work in an organization is strongly influenced by the nature of the product or service. The product or service usually suggests the sequence of and balance between jobs if the work is to be done efficiently. For example, the frame of a car must be built before the fenders and doors can be added. Once the sequence of jobs is determined, the balance between jobs is established.

Suppose it takes one person thirty seconds to install each headlight. Then in two minutes, an assembler can put on four headlights. If, however, it takes four minutes to install the necessary headlight receptacles, then the job designer must balance these two interrelated jobs by assigning two people to install the receptacles. Otherwise, a production bottleneck results. Since the work flow demands two receptacle installers for each headlight installer, one worker specializes in right-side receptacles and the other specializes in left-side receptacles.

WORK PRACTICES. Work practices are set ways of performing work. These may arise from tradition or the collective wishes of employees. Either way, the personnel department's flexibility to design jobs is limited, especially when such practices are part of a union-management relationship. Failure to consider work practices can have undesired outcomes.

In the United States, General Motors decided to increase productivity at its Lordstown, Ohio, plant by eliminating some jobs and adding new tasks to others. These design changes caused workers to stage a strike for several weeks because traditional practices at the plant had required a slower rate of production and less work by the employees. The additional demands on their jobs by management were seen as an attempt by the company to disregard past work practices.[7]

ENVIRONMENTAL ELEMENTS OF JOB DESIGN

A second aspect of job design concerns environmental elements. As with most personnel activities, job designers cannot ignore the influence of the external environment. In designing jobs, personnel specialists and managers should consider the ability and availability of potential employees. At the same time, social expectations also have to be weighed.

EMPLOYEE ABILITIES AND AVAILABILITY. Efficiency considerations must be balanced against the abilities and availability of the people who are to do the work. When Henry Ford made use of the assembly line in the United States, for example, he was aware that most potential workers lacked any automobile-making experience. So jobs were designed to be simple and require little training. Thought must be given to who will actually do the work. An extreme example underlines this point.

Governments of less developed countries often think they can "buy" progress. To be "up to date," they seek the most advanced equipment they can find. Leaders of one country ordered a computerized oil refinery. This decision dictated a level of technology that exceeded the abilities of the country's available work force. As a result, these government leaders have hired Europeans to operate the refinery.

In less developed nations, the major risk is that jobs may be too complex. But in industrial nations with highly educated workers, jobs that are too simple can produce equally disturbing problems. For example, even when unemployment rates are high, many simple and overly specialized jobs are sometimes hard to fill, as long-standing newspaper want ads for dishwashers and cleaners attest.

SOCIAL EXPECTATIONS. The acceptability of a job's design is also influenced by the expectations of society.[8] Many uneducated immigrants to this country during the early days of the railway industry readily accepted highly specialized jobs that demanded long hours and hard physical labour. Often they had fled countries where jobs were unavailable; this made a job —any job—acceptable. Today, industrial workers are much better educated and have higher expectations about the quality of work life. Although work flow or work practices may suggest a particular job design, the job must meet the expectations of workers. Failure to consider these social expectations can create dissatisfaction, low motivation, hard-to-fill job openings, and a low quality of work life.

BEHAVIOURAL ELEMENTS OF JOB DESIGN

Successful job designs consider behavioural elements if workers are to have a high quality of work life. Jobs cannot be designed by using only those elements that aid efficiency. To do so overlooks the human needs of the people who are to perform the work. Instead, job designers draw heavily on behavioural research to provide a work environment that helps satisfy individual needs. Higher-level needs are of particular importance. One pair of researchers provided a useful framework when they suggested:

> People with a strong desire to satisfy higher order needs perform their best when placed on jobs that were high on certain dimensions. These were:
>
> • Autonomy—responsibility for work
> • Variety—use of different skills and abilities
> • Task identity—doing the whole piece of work
> • Feedback—information on performance[9]

AUTONOMY. *Autonomy* is having responsibility for what one does. It is the freedom to control one's response to the environment. Jobs that give workers the authority to make decisions provide added responsibilities that tend to increase their sense of recognition and self-esteem. The absence of autonomy, on the other hand, can cause employee apathy or poor performance.[10]

A common problem in many production operations is that employees develop an "I don't care" attitude because they believe they have no control over their jobs. On the bottling line of a small brewery, teams of workers were allowed to speed up or slow down the rate of the bottling line as long as they met daily production goals. Although total output per shift did not change, there were fewer cases of capping machines jamming or breaking down for other reasons. When asked about this unexpected development, the supervisor concluded, "Employees pride themselves on meeting the shift quota. So they are more careful to check for defective bottle caps before they load the machine."

VARIETY. A lack of variety may cause boredom. Boredom in turn leads to fatigue, and fatigue causes errors. By injecting variety into jobs, personnel specialists can reduce fatigue-caused errors. Being able to control the speed of the bottling line in the brewery example added variety to the pace of work and probably reduced both boredom and fatigue.

One research study found that diversity of work was partially responsible for effective performance.[11] And another study found that autonomy and variety were major contributors to employee satisfaction.[12]

TASK IDENTITY. One problem with some jobs is that they lack any *task identity*. Workers cannot point to some complete piece of work when a job lacks task identity. They have little sense of responsibility and may lack pride in the results. After completing their job, they may have little sense of accomplishment. When tasks are grouped so that employees feel they are making an identifiable contribution, job satisfaction may be increased significantly.[13]

The Crosswell and Black chartered accounting firm had two bookkeepers assigned to billing the firm's clients. One bookkeeper prepared and mailed the monthly bills, and the other one received incoming payments and credited them to each client's account. When problems arose, a partner in the firm had to check with both bookkeepers to find the cause of the problem. Since neither of them was completely responsible for individual accounts, neither took great interest in preventing errors. Mr. Crosswell decided to split the accounts equally between the bookkeepers and let each one prepare, mail, and post bills for the clients assigned to them. Besides making fewer errors, both bookkeepers expressed satisfaction with the arrangement and greater interest in the special needs of "their" clients.

FEEDBACK. When jobs do not give the worker any feedback on how well the job is being done, there is little guidance or motivation to perform better. By letting employees know how they are doing relative to the daily production quota in the brewery example, workers received feedback that allowed them to adjust their efforts. In the accounting firm example, each bookkeeper received feedback on client errors and was able to implement changes in billing or posting procedures to avoid future problems. In both examples, feedback led to improved motivation.[14]

BEHAVIOURAL AND EFFICIENCY TRADE-OFFS

Behavioural elements of job design tell personnel specialists to add more autonomy, variety, task identity, or feedback. But efficiency elements point to greater specialization, less variety, minimal autonomy, and other contradictory elements. Thus to make jobs more efficient may cause them to be less satisfying. Conversely, satisfying jobs may prove to be inefficient. What should personnel specialists do?

There is no simple solution. Instead, personnel experts often make trade-offs between efficiency and behavioural elements. Figure 4-5 depicts the most significant trade-offs faced by job designers in the personnel department.

GRAPH A: PRODUCTIVITY VERSUS SPECIALIZATION

The assumption that additional specialization means increased output is true only up to some point. As jobs are made more specialized, productivity climbs until behavioural elements such as boredom offset the advantages of further specialization. In Figure 4-5A, additional specialization beyond point *b* causes productivity to drop. In fact, jobs that are between *b* and *c* can have their productivity *increased* by reducing the degree of specialization.

GRAPH B: SATISFACTION VERSUS SPECIALIZATION

Another interesting relationship exists between satisfaction and specialization. Here satisfaction first goes up with specialization and then additional specialization causes satisfaction to drop quickly. Jobs without any specialization take so long to learn that frustration and feedback are helped by some specialization. When specialization is carried past point *b* in Figure 4-5B, satisfaction drops because of a lack of autonomy, variety, and task identification. Notice that even while satisfaction is falling in graph B, productivity may still increase in graph A, from *a* to *b*. Productivity continues

Figure 4-5

EFFICIENCY VERSUS BEHAVIOURAL TRADE-OFFS IN JOB DESIGN

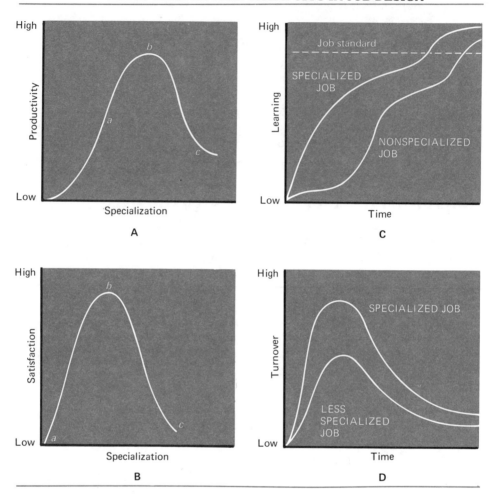

to go up only if the advantages of specialization outweigh the disadvantages of dissatisfaction.

GRAPH C: LEARNING VERSUS SPECIALIZATION

When a job is highly specialized, there is less to learn than in a nonspecialized job. Therefore, it takes less time to learn a specialized job. Graphically, this means that the rate of learning more quickly reaches an acceptable standard (shown as a dashed line). In the short run, the nonspecialized job takes longer to learn.

GRAPH D: TURNOVER VERSUS SPECIALIZATION

Although overspecialized jobs are quicker to learn, the lower levels of satisfaction generally associated with them can lead to higher turnover rates.

When turnover rates are high, redesigning the job with more attention to behavioural elements may reduce this "quit rate."

JOB REDESIGN TECHNIQUES

The central question often facing job designers is whether a particular job should have more or less specialization. As can be seen in graph A in Figure 4-5, the answer depends on whether the job is near point *a*, *b*, or *c*. Jobs near point *a* may need more specialization to increase their output. Those jobs near point *c* require less specialization to become more effective. Analysis and experimentation are the only sure ways to determine where a particular job is located on graph A.

UNDERSPECIALIZATION

When personnel specialists believe jobs are not specialized enough, they engage in *work simplification*. That is, the job is simplified. The tasks of one job may be split into two. Unneeded tasks are identified and eliminated. What is left are jobs that contain fewer tasks.

When the Allyndale Weekly Newspaper *operated with its old press, Guy Parsons could catch the newspapers as they came off the press, stack them, and wrap them. But when a new high-speed press was added, he could not keep up with the output. So the circulation manager simplified Guy's job by making him responsible for stacking the newspapers. Two part-time high school students took turns catching and wrapping the papers.*

The risk of work simplification is that jobs may be so specialized that boredom causes errors or resignations. This problem is more common in advanced industrial countries that have a highly educated work force. In less developed countries, highly specialized factory jobs may be acceptable and even appealing because they provide jobs for workers with limited skills.

OVERSPECIALIZATION

As the labour force in advanced industrial societies becomes more educated and affluent, routine jobs that are very specialized, such as assembly-line positions, hold less and less appeal for many people. These jobs seldom offer opportunities for accomplishment, recognition, psychological growth, or other sources of satisfaction.

To increase the quality of work life for those who hold such jobs, personnel departments can use a variety of methods to improve jobs through redesign. The most widely practiced techniques include job rotation, job enlargement, job enrichment, and work-group enrichment. Taken together, these techniques are usually referred to as quality of work life programs. When jobs are believed to be overly specialized, personnel specialists often recommend one of these approaches.

JOB ROTATION. *Job rotation* is rotation of employees from job to job. Rotation breaks the monotony of highly specialized work by calling on different skills and abilities. The organization benefits because workers become competent in several jobs rather than only one. Knowing a variety of jobs also helps the worker's self-image and personal growth, and makes him or her more valuable to the organization.

Personnel experts should caution those who want to use job rotation. It does not improve the jobs themselves; the relationships between tasks, activities, and objectives remain unchanged. It may even postpone the use of more effective techniques while adding to training costs. Implementation should occur only after other techniques have been considered.

JOB ENLARGEMENT. *Job enlargement* means the expansion of the number of related tasks in a job, i.e., adding similar duties to provide greater variety. Enlargement reduces monotony by expanding the job cycle and drawing on a wider range of employee skills. According to one summary of job design research:

IBM reported job enlargement led to higher wages and more inspection equipment, but improved quality and worker satisfaction offset these costs. The Maytag Company claimed that production quality was improved, labour costs declined, most workers preferred enlarged jobs, overall efficiency increased, and management had more flexibility in scheduling production. [15]

JOB ENRICHMENT. *Job enrichment* means the addition of new sources of needed satisfaction to jobs. This increases worker responsibility, autonomy, and control. Adding these elements to jobs is sometimes called *vertical loading. Horizontal loading* occurs when the job is expanded by simply adding related tasks, as with job enlargement. Job enrichment sees jobs as consisting of three elements: plan, do, control.[16] Job enlargement (or horizontal loading) adds more things to *do*. Enrichment (or vertical loading) attempts to add more responsibility for *planning* and *control*. These additions to the job, coupled with rethinking the job itself, often lead to increased motivation and other improvements.

In a pilot project with one unit of the Data Capture section of Statistics Canada, job enrichment and other changes resulted in increased employee satisfaction, lower absentee rates, increases in the quality and quantity of work done, and improved relationships between the union and management.

One employee recalled that prior to the changes, "we were watched every second. We weren't able to talk. We had no responsibility or variety in our work. We'd just go to the basket and take the job that was on top." The changes implemented included more variety and more worker responsibility, both for completing the work and for attendance, hiring, training, appraisals, and discipline. Aside from the success indicators already mentioned, when the rest of the section was asked whether they were interested in being involved in similar changes for their units, 171 of the remaining 177 employees were in favour. [17]

Job enrichment, however, is not a cure-all; if it were, this book could end here. Job enrichment techniques are merely tools, and they are not applied universally. When the diagnosis indicates jobs are unrewarding and unchallenging and limit the motivation and satisfaction of employees, personnel departments *may* find job enrichment to be the most appropriate strategy. Even then, however, job enrichment faces problems.

One author has listed twenty-two arguments against job enrichment.[18] The most compelling points are the existence of union resistance, the cost of design and implementation, and the scarcity of research on long-term effects. Another criticism of job enrichment is that it does not go far enough. To enrich the job and ignore other variables that contribute to the quality of work life may simply increase dissatisfaction with the unimproved aspects of the job environment. There is a need to go beyond job enrichment in some work situations.[19] Last but not least, the cultural values and social expectations surrounding the organization have to be carefully considered before any job redesign attempts are made.[20]

QUALITY CIRCLES

A *quality circle* is a small group of employees with a common leader that meets regularly to identify and solve work-related problems.[21] When quality circles started in Japan, they were called "quality control circles," because their primary focus was to improve the poor quality of products manufactured in Japan.

ORIGINS OF CIRCLES

Following World War II, the small island nation of Japan lacked virtually all types of resources except human ones. Japan found that to buy sufficient foodstuffs and raw materials it had to export. But in the 1950s and even the early 1960s, "Made in Japan" meant poor quality to many buyers. Government and business leaders realized that to import raw goods, add value, and export required the production of quality products which the world would buy. With the assistance of such United States experts as Drs. Demming and Juran, the concept of quality control circles was born in Japanese factories in the early 1960s. By the 1980s, most medium and large Japanese manufacturers had quality control circles in place among hourly employees. This effort began as a quality improvement program that has since become part of many Japanese managers' routine procedures and a key part of the QWL effort in many Japanese firms.

In the 1970s Lockheed Corporation and others adopted this approach to QWL and, with a few modifications, began using it in North America. The imported version is simply called "quality circles" or "employee participation groups," although many firms customize the name. For example, Tektronix, Inc. calls them "Tek Circles"; Control Data Corporation calls them "Involvement Teams"; and Union Carbide calls them "Pride Circles," which stands for *P*roductivity through *R*ecognition, *I*nvolvement, and *D*evelopment of *E*mployees.

UNIQUE CHARACTERISTICS

Whatever they are called, quality circles (QC) are unique among the many QWL efforts being tried by North American firms. First, membership in the circle is voluntary for both the leader (usually the supervisor) and the members (usually hourly paid workers).[22] Typically, supervisors are given a brief explanation of the QC concept and asked if they want to start a circle. If yes, the supervisor's employees are given a briefing and volunteers are sought. Shortly thereafter training begins.

Second, the creation of quality circles is usually preceded by in-house training. Supervisors typically get two or three days of training. Most of the time is devoted to discussions of small-group dynamics, leadership skills, and indoctrination in the QWL and QC philosophies. About a day of the training is spent on different approaches to problem solving, such as those explained in Figure 4-6. Once the supervisor is trained, his or her employees are usually given one day of intensive training, primarily in the problem-solving techniques of Figure 4-6. Part of this training also explains the supervisor's role as the group's discussion leader and the concept of the quality circle.

Third, as is pointed out in the training, the group is permitted to select the problems it wants to tackle. Management may suggest problems of concern to it, but the group decides which ones to select. Ideally, the selection process is made not by democratic vote but by consensus, in which everyone agrees on the problem to be solved first. (If management has pressing problems to be solved, they can be handled in the same way that problems were resolved before the introduction of quality circles.) The reason for relying on group consensus to select the problem is to allow employees to take on problems of concern and inconvenience to *them.*

At Solar Turbines International (a Caterpillar Tractor Company subsidiary), employees were frustrated by the lack of power hand tools. They studied the lost production time caused by waiting for tools and showed management how to save more than $30,000 dollars a year by making a $2,200 investment in additional hand tools.

The employees at Solar Turbines did not select this problem to save management money; they did it because of the inconvenience that insufficient tools caused them. The fact that it saved more than a dozen times what it cost to fix is a typical by-product of successful quality circle efforts.

When employees select the problems they want to work on, they are likely to be more motivated to find a solution—and they are more likely to be motivated to remain in the circle and solve problems in the future.

QC PROCESS

After the training is completed, employees and their supervisor agree on a time and begin meeting, usually once a week for an hour. At the first meeting the supervisor often reviews the ground rules. Circles are intended to tackle problems in that group's area of responsibility. Company pay policies, union contracts, problems in remote departments, and personality

Figure 4-6
QUALITY CIRCLE DECISION-MAKING TOOLS

1. Brainstorming. Brainstorming is a process by which members of the circle provide their ideas on a stated problem during a freewheeling group session. Some circles do request that members present their ideas in turn to ensure that each one participates.

2. Pareto Analysis. Pareto analysis is a means of collating data that is provided to employees by staff assistants or is collected by the workers themselves. Often this data describes types or causes of production problems. The data is then arranged in descending order of frequency, usually on a bar chart like the following. The bar chart helps workers to identify the most important causes of problems in order of priority.

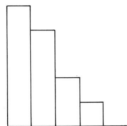

3. Cause & Effect. A cause-and-effect, or fishbone, diagram begins with a known effect, such as a defective part. From that effect, members of the circle use brainstorming and their knowledge of the production or service process to identify possible causes, in such standard areas as machines, people, methods, or materials.

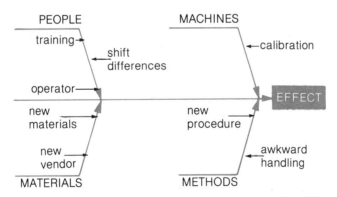

Each "bone," or branch, of the "fishbone" represents a possible cause of the effect under study. Once the group has identified all possible causes through brainstorming, members usually collect data on these causes to determine the source of the problem.

4. Statistical Tools. Workers also are taught a variety of statistical concepts to help them objectively determine causes of production problems. Common methods include random sampling, probability sampling, and the ability to compute arithmetical means and variances.

issues are usually excluded from consideration. Instead, employees are asked to focus on how they can make their job easier. As a quality circle leader at Control Data Corporation once stated, "If we find ways to make the job easier, we cannot help but improve the QWL and productivity."

Following the discussion of ground rules, the group uses brainstorming to create a list of problems to be solved. Then through discussion, one is selected for further study and research. Data are collected about the problem and analyzed to see if there is a pattern from which causes and effects may be identified. If no pattern exists, the effect under study may be put into a "fishbone" diagram (Figure 4-6) so that additional brainstorming on other possible causes may be uncovered. These possible causes are ranked as to their likelihood by the group and then the most significant ones are researched.

Once a cause has been found for the problem, the group develops a solution. In its training, the group is taught to be able to justify the cost of the solution. For example, at Solar Turbines the workers believed that a $2,200 dollar outlay by the company was justified because of the potential to save more than $30,000 in the first year.

At this point the group assembles its research, its proposed solution, and its justification for a presentation to management. This presentation explains to management the problem and the circle's recommended course of action. It also gives the circle members an opportunity for recognition by higher levels of management. Management, of course, reserves the right to accept or reject the recommendation, although more than 80% of a circle's ideas are typically accepted.[23]

Once an idea is presented, the burden falls to management to give the circle a timely authorization to implement the suggestion or an explanation as to why it is rejected. In the meantime, the circle begins the process over again and starts on another problem. This cycle repeats itself until the group solves all the problems it wishes to handle or until the members of the circle decide to disband. Circles usually disband when supervisors act autocratically rather than participatively or when upper levels of management repeatedly and arbitrarily reject circles' recommendations.

FACILITATORS AND CIRCLE COORDINATION

Most organizations with multiple circles find that a coordinator or *facilitator* is needed. This person may be a line manager or a personnel specialist. Facilitators need good interpersonal skills—particularly the ability to communicate and train. The first facilitator usually receives five days of specialized training through the International Association of Quality Circles or the American Productivity Center. These training programs concentrate on teaching the facilitator about quality circles and how to administer a QC effort. Training in teaching and consulting skills is typical too. Likewise, the facilitator also receives considerable training in group dynamics and the ability to coach supervisors. The facilitator reports to the *steering committee*, which includes the top manager and his or her staff.

Once circles are operating, the facilitator may serve as a consultant to those supervisors who need additional help with their circles. The facilitator also serves as a link among the circles and others in the company who may have specialized knowledge needed by the circle to solve its problems.

COSTS AND BENEFITS OF QUALITY CIRCLES

Quality circles have few costs to the organization. The primary expenditures are related to training. Included here are the costs of developing the training materials and the training of facilitators, supervisors, and employees. Perhaps the major cost of training is the wage and salaries paid to the trainees while they are being trained. Interestingly, the time spent in the circle meetings is not considered a significant cost because most facilitators and supervisors find that circle members get as much work done in thirty-nine hours as they did in forty hours, before quality circles.

Solar Turbines International kept detailed track of their start-up costs over the first eighteen months. They included the costs of training materials, facilitator salaries, and the wage costs for employees while they were in training and attending circle meetings. The total amount spent was $79,000. However, during the same time period, documented and fully audited first-year savings from circle suggestions amounted to $90,000. And most of the circle ideas continued to save the company money during the second and subsequent years. After the start-up period, the facilitator estimated in a conversation with one of the authors that the annual savings were $3.00 for each dollar Solar Turbines spent on its quality circle effort.[24]

The measurable dollar savings from quality circle efforts are probably not the major benefits, however. Companies like Solar, Tektronix, Westinghouse, and others report that circles mean enhanced QWL for employees. Communications between supervisors and employees improve because they develop a less autocratic relationship. Supervisors and employees also learn to think more like executives because they begin to solve problems systematically and to cost-justify their recommendations. Often higher-level managers can spot particularly articulate employees who show promise to be supervisors based on their efforts in the circle group. In fact, some plant managers view it as their primary employee and supervisory development program, aside from solving workplace problems. They see quality circles as an effective way to train supervisors and workers, because circles allow the application of newly learned skills. The result may be a growing cadre of managers and personnel specialists with exceptional "people skills."[25]

TEAM-BUILDING VARIATIONS

Quality circles are a very specialized form of *team building*. Some companies have undertaken other approaches to creating cohesive teams among their supervisors and employees. Some of these team approaches are a slight variation on the quality circle approach. The major difference is that the teams may consist of people from different departments, so they are more like a task force. Also, teams may exist only to solve one problem and then disband. Boeing uses a single-focus task force called "Tiger Teams." Generally these teams are assembled to solve some production-delaying problem that the supervisor and employees cannot overcome.

These various forms of team building share a common underlying philosophy: groups of people are usually better at solving problems than is an individual. And even though the "purpose" of these teams is to solve problems, a by-product is improved quality of work life.[26]

SOCIO-TECHNICAL SYSTEMS

Another approach to QWL efforts are socio-technical systems. *Socio-technical systems* are interventions into the work situation that restructure the work, work groups, and relationship between workers and the technologies they use to do their jobs. More than just enlarging or enriching a job, these approaches may result in more radical changes in the work environment, as an article in *Business Week* points out:

> At a Siemens plant in Karlsruhe, West Germany, workers assembling electronics products used to perform simple tasks over and over, spending less than one minute on each unit as it moved along a belt conveyor. Today many employees work in groups of three to seven at well designed 'work islands', where they can avoid boredom by rotating jobs, socializing, and working in cycles of up to 20 minutes rather than a few seconds.[27]

This rearrangement of the social and technical relationships on the job offers workers an opportunity for greater QWL. This "humanization" of the workplace seems to be most advanced in West Germany, where the government even funds 50% of selected work restructuring and retraining efforts of private industry.[28]

West Germany also has done considerable work in the area of ergonomics. *Ergonomics* is the study of the biotechnical relationships between the physical attributes of workers and the physical demands of the job, with the object of reducing physical and mental strain in order to increase productivity and QWL. Germans have made considerable strides in reducing the strain of lifting, bending, and reaching, through their ergonomic approach to structuring jobs, arranging equipment, and lighting.

Through ergonomics and socio-technical approaches to work, West Germany appears to lead the world in modifying assembly lines and increasing the worker's job cycle to minimize boredom and dissatisfaction. Individual work stations are being used that allow workers to assemble significant subassemblies which may take ten minutes or more. Through buffer stocks of partially completed products, employees are increasingly freed from the tedium of the assembly line.

CODETERMINATION

One of the first attempts at industrial democracy on a broad scale occurred in West Germany under the name codetermination. *Codetermination* allows workers' representatives to discuss and vote on key management decisions that affect the workers through formal sessions with company management. This form of industrial democracy has since spread through most of free Europe. As a result, decisions to close plants or lay off large numbers of workers meet with far more formal resistance in Europe than in North America. On the plus side, however, European firms are forced to plan more carefully their human resource needs and seek export markets to offset national economic cycles. Since major Canadian corporations operate in Europe under codetermination, personnel management in multinational corporations is affected. For international personnel experts, codetermination is a consideration in the design of overseas jobs. In North America, the first steps toward codetermination may have begun when Chrysler Corporation appointed the president of the United Automobile Workers to its board of directors in the early 1980s.

AUTONOMOUS WORK GROUPS

A more common, albeit still rare, approach to employee involvement is autonomous work groups. *Autonomous work groups* are teams of workers without a formal, company-appointed supervisor who decide among themselves most matters traditionally handled by a supervisor. These groups of workers typically decide daily work assignments, the use of job rotation, new-employee orientation, training, and production schedules. Some groups even handle recruitment, selection, and discipline. Perhaps the two best known experiments with these approaches are the Gaines Pet Food plant in the United States and Volvo's Kalmar plant in Sweden. These experiments are summarized in Figure 4-7.

Figure 4-7
A SUMMARY OF GAINES'S AND VOLVO'S EXPERIENCES WITH AUTONOMOUS WORK GROUPS

Gaines Pet Food

At the Gaines Pet Food plant, jobs were radically changed. No longer were workers assigned specific tasks in traditional jobs. Instead, teams of workers were held responsible for a group of tasks that previously constituted several separate jobs. For example, the work group was held responsible for packaging and storing the completed products, instead of each worker having a narrow job that included only a few tasks in the packaging and storing operations. Employees were assigned to a work group, not a job. They were free to participate in the group decision-making processes. Members developed work schedules, interviewed new employees, performed quality control checks, maintained machinery, and performed other diverse activities. The work-group enrichment led to reduced overhead, higher productivity, better product quality, and lower turnover and absenteeism.

Volvo's Kalmar Plant

Volvo, the Swedish automobile producer, sought to design a more humane car production environment. It built the Kalmar plant around the concept of work teams, rather than the traditional assembly line. Again, workers were assigned to teams, not jobs. Teams built subsystems of the car: doors, cooling systems, engines, and other key components. Buffer stocks of partially completed cars reduced the dependence of one group on another. The physical work environment was made as quiet as the latest technology permitted.

The results of this experiment with autonomous work groups are not clear. Volvo claims higher satisfaction levels among employees because of the design changes, but productivity has remained behind that of other plants for years.

Whether these experiments at Gaines and Volvo herald a radically new approach to the quality of work life is still uncertain. Such innovations do illustrate the need of some employers and employees for more innovative solutions to the trade-off between efficiency and behavioural considerations. More, not less, attention will have to be paid by personnel experts to changing the socio-technical relationship in order to meet changing expectations about jobs. Improving the quality of work life may mean completely redesigning factories and workplaces, as Volvo and Gaines have done, to satisfy environmental and behavioural needs while maintaining efficiency.

In the refund services branch of Air Canada's finance department in Winnipeg, where over 50,000 refunds were processed monthly, an innovative program involving workers, union, and management resulted in major work changes. Rather than specializing in one task, clerks learned a variety of skills and were formed into work teams with greater autonomy in handling refunds for their region. These changes are in part credited with an increase in job satisfaction and morale and with a 30% increase in job performance.[29]

Steinberg Limited, a grocery store chain that employs over 25,000 people, with branches in Quebec, Ontario, and New Brunswick, created autonomous and semi-autonomous production groups in their frozen-foods distribution centre in Dorval. By involving the employees in the creation and development of a new work environment, significant job improvements materialized. Prior to the change the absentee rate was 15% and the production of the employees involved was similar to that of other employees. However, the quality of working life (QWL) process employed resulted in significant increases in morale, a three-and-a-half-year absence of complaints from the stores receiving distribution-centre deliveries, an absentee rate of 5% (other centres had a 12% rate), and a productivity rate 35% higher than the old frozen-foods distribution centre.[30]

QWL is more likely to improve as workers demand jobs with more behavioural elements. These demands are likely to emerge from an increasingly educated work force that expects more challenge and autonomy in jobs and more participation in decisions traditionally reserved to management. In Europe codetermination is more than thirty years old and still growing in popularity. And in both Europe and North America, experiments by Gaines, Volvo, and other employers indicate that such new arrangements are economically feasible.[31]

If the population of industrial countries continues to grow at the slow rates of the last two decades, the scarcity of new workers entering the labour force will allow workers to be more selective, assuming the recessionary trends of the more recent years are reversed. Then employers may be forced by economic necessity to redesign jobs to achieve a higher quality of work life.[32] Or, as has happened in Europe, government may decree programs to improve the quality of work life.[33] In any event, increased on-the-job autonomy and participation in decision making seem likely during the coming decades.

Personnel departments will play an even more important role in organizations as social expectations increase the pressure for more autonomy. Rotation, enlargement, enrichment, and redesigning of jobs will be priorities. The training of present workers will receive greater attention from personnel departments. To attract scarce human resources, personnel departments may have to offer a wide variety of part-time and full-time work schedules from which employees can choose the hours and days they wish to work. Whether these changes mean that any one approach to employee involvement will become more common is uncertain. What seems virtually certain, however, is the growing trend of employees toward participation in decisions affecting them.

QWL ON THE NATIONAL SCENE

In 1976, in the speech from the throne, the federal government's support for QWL was announced. The responsibility for the QWL program was assigned to the Employment Relations and Conditions of Work branch of Labour Canada. The activities of this organization over the past few years have been quite diverse. Rather than getting directly involved in QWL activities, it has opted for a policy of supporting and promoting QWL concepts and activities. This has been pursued by its being represented at and sponsoring conferences and workshops, publishing QWL information (including *Quality of Working Life: The Canadian Scene*), and providing some financial and technical assistance for QWL training and research projects. This branch of Labour Canada has also endeavoured to develop a network of qualified QWL individuals across the country.

At the provincial level, most activities are less institutionalized. However, in 1978 Ontario established a QWL centre in its Department of Labour. The centre's activities include consultation, information services, research and field activities, and educational programs. It also publishes a journal entitled *QWL Focus*. McGill University has a QWL centre and there is presently a QWL forum in British Columbia. Yet these organizations represent only a small part of QWL activities in Canada. More and more public and private organizations are becoming involved in QWL.

BARRIERS TO QUALITY OF WORK LIFE

As with many personnel department programs, barriers to implementation can undermine the success of any quality of work life program. These barriers are commonly erected by employees, management, or unions. Each of these groups usually fears the effect of unknown change. Even when the process and probable results are explained, the incentives for change may be too few.

To overcome these barriers, the personnel department usually must explain the need for change and the hoped-for results, and give whatever assurances it can. Workers and unions are sometimes suspicious because they may feel that any program to management's advantage is not likely to benefit them. Management often resists the change because it doubts that the benefits of change justify the potential disruption of production or service.

Although there is no certain way to gain the support of every group, most successful attempts at implementing quality of work life require broad participation. Through the participation of key managers, union officials, and affected employees, personnel specialists are more likely to overcome the barriers to new programs.[34] For example, consider how British Columbia Forest Products Ltd., MacKenzie Sawmill Division, was able to implement a program.[35]

Faced with an annual turnover rate of 200%, the company and the unions involved at MacKenzie collaborated with a research team to investigate the labour turnover problems. After a three-month pilot study that was coordinated by a joint steering committee comprising management, union, and research representatives, it was decided to begin an extensive change program in one of the company's three sawmills, "C" mill.

The "C" mill manager hoped that increased worker participation would lead to improvements in safety, quality, cost control, and production, but he also expressed his conviction that "working in the sawmill should not be like a jail sentence that we endure in order to live ... [it] should be something that we enjoy doing and get some satisfaction or feeling of accomplishment from."

To implement the program, it was necessary to obtain the cooperation and support of the various organizational and individual units involved. After the management, union, and research people involved had reached agreement on the project, an unprecedented general meeting of all the plant's employees was called by the plant manager, and the sawmill was shut down. The mill manager described the project and explained that its intent was to involve the work force in the diagnosis and solution of work problems in the mill. However, some workers wondered whether they even wanted to be involved in such a program, and initially they all felt some degree of bewilderment and suspicion, because this approach to solving problems was quite alien to the company's previous practices.

During the next few weeks, numerous meetings were held with the various shifts of workers and foremen within the departments. It was agreed that the program should start in the most crucial part of the mill, the log infeed area, where the tree logs were transformed into rough lumber.

For each shift, decision-making groups were formed (comprised largely of workers), which identified problems, did research, and made decisions related to production and other work-related projects. It was decided that if these groups could not reach a consensus on how a problem should be solved, the decision would be postponed or delayed.

The types of decisions reached encompassed all areas of the production operation; they involved technological work procedures, organizational role, and structure changes. Six months after the initiated activities in the infeed area, the QWL project was extended to another part of the plant, the planer mill.

The results achieved by a more participative and involved form of decision-making were significant. Production rose from 350,000 units of lumber per day to over 410,000. There were no recorded safety accidents during this same period. The absentee rate in "C" mill fell by over 50% and turnover was reduced to less than 30%. In the planer mill production efficiency rose from 50 to 70%. Absenteeism dropped from two per shift to one person every two shifts. As is evident, these represent significant improvements in morale and job satisfaction.

QUALITY OF WORK LIFE IN PERSPECTIVE

The quality of work life represents another layer of challenges to personnel management. Proactive personnel departments must find better ways to achieve QWL. Otherwise, the purpose of personnel management remains only partially fulfilled at best. But as important as the challenge of improving the quality of work life is, it represents only one in a long line of challenges facing personnel departments.

These other challenges must be met if personnel management is to contribute to the organization's success. Although the quality of work life is important, personnel experts cannot disregard the challenges of fulfilling the purpose, objectives, and activities assigned to the personnel department. Nor can the environmental and equal-employment challenges be overlooked in designing jobs for maximum efficiency. All these challenges must be met simultaneously. The rest of this book explains how proactive personnel departments meet these challenges through a blend of traditional and innovative activities to achieve a high-quality work life through productive and satisfying jobs.

SUMMARY

Jobs are the link between organizations and their human resources. The combined accomplishment of all jobs allows the organization to meet its objectives. Similarly, jobs represent not only a source of income to workers but also a means of fulfilling their needs. However, for the organization and its employees to receive these mutual benefits, jobs must provide a high quality of work life.

To achieve a high quality of work life requires jobs that are well designed. Effective job design seeks a trade-off between efficiency and behavioural elements. Efficiency elements stress productivity; behavioural elements stress employee needs. The role of personnel specialists is to achieve a balance between these trade-offs. When jobs are too specialized, job designers may simplify the job by reducing the number of tasks. If jobs are over-specialized, they must be expanded or enriched.

Quality of work life efforts are systematic attempts by organizations to give workers a greater opportunity to take part in decisions that affect the way they do their job and the contribution they make to their organization's overall effectiveness. They are not a substitute for good, sound personnel practices and policies. However, effective QWL efforts can supplement other personnel actions and provide improved employee motivation, satisfaction, and productivity. QWL is most commonly improved through employee involvement. Whether that involvement is in solving workplace problems or participating in the design of jobs, employees want to know that their contribution makes a difference.

Many approaches to QWL exist. Aside from job design, one of the most popular is an import from Japan, quality circles. A quality circle is a small group of employees from the same work area who meet regularly with their supervisor to identify and solve workplace problems. Quality circles afford workers a chance to make a meaningful contribution by participating in decisions that affect them. Other forms of team building are similar to quality circles, although different groupings or objectives might be sought. Socio-technical systems seek to change the human and technical relationship that exists in the workplace. Typically, employees are involved in making these changes. Codetermination involves giving workers a formal voice in management decisions. Although common in Europe, it is almost nonexistent in Canada. Autonomous work groups also are uncommon, but have been more widely found in Canada than has codetermination. These groups consist of employees who collectively assume the supervisor's role of deciding work schedules, job assignments, and other duties typically reserved to first-level supervisors.

Management support and a long-term perspective are essential to any successful QWL effort. Unless the barrier of management support is overcome, even short-term success is unlikely.

TERMS FOR REVIEW

Quality of work life (QWL)	Brainstorming
Specialization	Pareto diagrams
Job cycle	Cause-and-effect diagrams
Autonomy	Facilitators
Task identity	Steering committee
Work simplification	Team building
Job rotation	Socio-technical systems
Job enlargement	Ergonomics
Job enrichment	Codetermination
Quality circles (QC)	Autonomous work groups

REVIEW AND DISCUSSION QUESTIONS

1. What role do personnel specialists play in ensuring a high quality of work life?

2. What are the major challenges of job design?

3. In their attempts to use autonomous work groups, Volvo and Gaines Pet Food had different outcomes with regard to productivity. Since Swedish workers are highly educated and enjoy a standard of living at least equal to that of workers in Canada and the United States, what other differences might account for these different outcomes?

4. What problems would you expect to arise in an organization that had carefully designed its jobs for maximum efficiency without careful consideration of each employee's individual priority of needs?

5. What were the contributions of scientific management to the design of jobs? What are the advantages of highly specialized jobs?

6. Suppose you have been assigned to design the job of ticket clerk for Air Canada.
   (a) Would you recommend highly specialized job designs to minimize training or very broad jobs with all clerks cross-trained to handle multiple tasks? Why?
   (b) Would you change your answer if you knew that employees tended to quit the job of ticket clerk within the first six months? Why or why not?

7. Assume that you were told to evaluate a group of jobs in a boat-building business. After studying each job for a considerable amount of time, you identified the following activities associated with each job. What job redesign techniques would you recommend for these jobs, if any?
   (a) *Sailmaker*. Cuts and sews material with very little variety in the type of work from day to day. Job is highly skilled and takes years to learn.
   (b) *Sander*. Sands rough wood and fibreglass edges almost continuously. Little skill is required in this job.
   (c) *Sales representative*. Talks with customers, answers phone inquiries, suggests customized additions to special-order boats.
   (d) *Boat preparer*. Cleans up completed boats, waxes fittings, and generally makes the boat ready for customer delivery. Few skills are required for this job.

8. Suppose you are a plant or division manager and you want to create a high QWL environment. Why could you not simply order it done and expect a high QWL environment almost immediately?

9. Explain where quality circles started and what makes them unique compared to other QWL efforts. What is management's responsibility after a quality circle group makes its presentation to management?

INCIDENT 4-1

JOB DESIGN AT MARKETING NEWSLETTERS, INC.

Marketing Newsletters, Inc. is a small Montreal company that produces several different types of newsletters. These are sold to companies and individual salespeople. Although each series of letters has a different market, they all provide readers with useful tips on how to be more effective at selling.

Pierre Martel, president of Marketing Newsletters, discovered he could sell these letters by carefully tailoring them to the concerns of different types of specialized salespeople. For example, one letter was directed at new-car salespeople. Another was directed at sellers of industrial supplies. Although the sales of each letter were modest, Pierre succeeded in developing a new newsletter market about every three months.

In Pierre's firm there were two developmental editors, two copy editors, and two marketing editors. The developmental editors sought out likely authors to write and develop newsletters. The copy editors were responsible for editing each newsletter before it was printed and mailed. The marketing editors were responsible for advertising and for building the circulation of each newsletter.

Whenever a newsletter did not meet its sales goal, the marketing editors blamed the copy editors for not producing a quality product. In turn, the copy editors would complain that they could only improve so much on the quality of the contributions, and they blamed the developmental editors for not finding better writers.

Suppose Pierre asked you to help him solve the problem of identifying responsibility for the success or failure of each newsletter.

1. What suggestions would you make to Pierre about the way the editors' jobs are designed?
2. If each editor were made responsible for developing, editing, and selling selected newsletters, what advantages would result for the firm? For the editors?
3. If each editor were completely responsible for several newsletters, what kinds of favourable trade-offs might be encountered in the newly designed jobs?

INCIDENT 4-2
COOPERATION, QWL, AND SPACE

Psychologists Joseph Brady and Henry Emurian at Johns Hopkins Hospital have been doing research to learn how to increase productivity and reduce friction on future space missions. Under research grants from NASA, they are "... studying the psychological and physiological effects of prolonged confinement on two- and three-person 'microsocieties.' Their goal is to develop behavioural guidelines for the most productive individual and group performance, with the least social friction, on future space and underwater missions."*

Their studies have revealed the not-too-surprising conclusion that rewards and incentives are better motivators than sanctions and controls, and that cooperation leads to greater individual performance and greater satisfaction within the group.

* For a more detailed explanation of this study, see Berkeley Rice, "Space-Lab Encounters," *Psychology Today*, June 1983, pp. 50–58.

1. Assume for the sake of this incident that these findings are applicable to larger societies called organizations. What implications do you see in these studies for improving the QWL in organizations?
2. If you were a supervisor with six employees working for you, how could these findings make your quality circle group become more effective? Suggest specific actions you would implement to improve the effectiveness of the quality circle based on this brief research summary.

EXERCISE 4-1
A GOOD WORK ENVIRONMENT

Think of some work-related situation that you have found enjoyable. Think of the job and identify the features which made it more enjoyable than other jobs you have held. The job need not have been a formal, full-time job. It may simply have been some temporary job or even some chore you have had to perform. Make a list of those characteristics of the job which made it so enjoyable.

1. In reviewing your answers with others, do you find any similarities between your list and the lists of others who did different jobs?
2. Do these characteristics indicate what job features provide a good work situation?

REFERENCES

1. Gerald A. Regan, quoted in "Minister of Labour on QWL," *Quality of Working Life: The Canadian Scene,* 3 (1980) (4): 25.
2. William B. Werther, Jr., and William A. Ruch, "Chief Productivity Officer," Working Paper, Bureau of Business Research, College of Business Administration, Arizona State University, 1982.
3. William A. Ruch and William B. Werther, Jr., "Productivity Strategies at TRW," *National Productivity Review,* Spring 1983, p. 116.
4. William B. Werther, Jr., "Out of the Productivity Box," *Business Horizons,* September/October 1982, p. 56.
5. Martha Glenn Cox and Jane Covey Brown, "Quality of Work Life: Another Fad or Real Benefit?" *Personnel Administrator,* May 1982, pp. 49–53.
6. Werther, "Out of the Productivity Box," op. cit., pp. 51–52.
7. Barbara Garson, "Luddites in Lordstown," *Harper's,* June 1972, pp. 68–73.
8. Bernard Blisher and Tom Atkinson, "Anglophone and Francophone Differences in the Perceptance of the Quality of Work Life in Canada," Paper presented at IXth World Congress of Sociology, Uppsala, Sweden, August 1978.
9. J. R. Hackman and E. E. Lawler III, "Employee Reactions to Job Characteristics," in W. E. Scott and L. L. Cummings (eds.), *Readings in Organizational Behavior and Human Performance,* Homewood, Ill.: Richard D. Irwin, Inc., 1973, p. 231. For a detailed summary of research on job design see C. L. Hulin and M. R. Blood, "Job Enlargement, Individual Differences, and Worker Responses," *Psychological Bulletin,* 1968, pp. 41–55. For a more recent summarization see Jon L. Pierce and Randall B. Dunham, "Task Design: A Literature Review," *The Academy of Management Review,* October 1976, pp. 83–97.
10. Frederick Herzberg, Bernard Mausner, and Barbara Snyderman, *The Motivation to Work,* New York: John Wiley & Sons Inc., 1959. See also E. F. Stone and L. W. Porter, "Job Characteristics and Job Attitudes: A Multivariate Study," *Journal of Applied Psychology,* 1975, pp. 57–64.
11. G. E. Farris, "Organizational Factors and Individual Performance: A Longitudinal Study," *Journal of Applied Psychology,* 1969, pp. 87–92.
12. Stone and Porter, op. cit.
13. Hackman and Lawler, op. cit.
14. Edward E. Lawler III, "Job Attitudes and Employee Motivation: Theory, Research, and Practice," *Personnel Psychology,* Summer 1970, p. 234.
15. Richard W. Woodward and John J. Sherwood, "A Comprehensive Look at Job Design," *Personnel Journal,* August 1977, p. 386.
16. M. Scott Myers, *Every Employee a Manager,* New York: McGraw-Hill Book Company, 1970.
17. Jennifer Trapnell, "Quality of Working Life at Statistics Canada," *Quality of Working Life: The Canadian Scene,* 2 (1979) (3): 11–14.
18. Robert H. Schappe, "Twenty-Two Arguments against Job Enrichment," *Personnel Journal,* February 1974, pp. 116–123.
19. William B. Werther, Jr., "Beyond Job Enrichment to Employment Enrichment," *Personnel Journal,* August 1975, pp. 438–442.
20. Natalie Lam, "Work Orientations: A Crosscultural Comparison and Relevance for Participative Management," Working Paper No. 84-21, Ottawa: University of Ottawa, 1984. Also see R. N. Kanungo, G. J. Graen, and H. J. Dauderis, "Motivational Orientation of Canadian Anglophone and Francophone Managers," *Canadian Journal of Behavioural Science,* 1976, 8, 107–121.
21. William B. Werther, Jr., "Quality Circles: Key Executive Issues," *Journal of Contemporary Business,* Vol. 11, No. 2, N.D., pp. 17–26.
22. Frank Shipper, "Quality Circles Using Small Group Formation," *Training and Development Journal,* May 1983, p. 82.

23. See, for example, "Tektronix Inc." *Case Study 17* (American Productivity Center), 1981, pp. 1–3.
24. "Quality Circles: Key Executive Issues," op. cit., p. 26.
25. "A Serendipitous Training Ground for Managers," *Business Week*, February 15, 1982, p. 52T.
26. Dutch Landen, "Beyond Quality Circles," *Productivity Brief 12* (American Productivity Center), April 1982, pp. 1–7.
27. "Moving Beyond Assembly Lines," *Business Week*, July 27, 1981, pp. 87, 90. By special permission, © 1981 by McGraw-Hill, Inc.
28. Ibid.
29. Paul Roddick, "Work Improvement Plan at Air Canada," *Quality of Working Life: The Canadian Scene*, 1 (1978) (Autumn): 2.
30. Pierre Pelletier, "Semi-Autonomous and Autonomous Production Groups," *Quality of Working Life: The Canadian Scene*, 3 (1980) (1): 22–25.
31. Daniel Zwerdling, *Democracy at Work*, Washington: Association for Self-Management, 1978.
32. Timothy J. Keaveny, Robert E. Allen, and John H. Jackson, "An Alternative to Legislating the Quality of Work Life," *The Personnel Administrator*, April 1979, pp. 60–64, 79. See also Keith Davis and William C. Frederick, *Business and Society*, 5th ed., New York: McGraw-Hill Book Company, 1980, pp. 353–356.
33. Ted Mills, "Europe's Industrial Democracy: An American Response," *Harvard Business Review*, November-December 1978, pp. 143–152. See also Kenneth A. Kouach, Ben F. Sands, Jr., and William W. Brooks, "Is Codetermination a Workable Idea for U.S. Labor-Management Relations?" *MSU Business Topics*, Winter 1980, pp. 49–55.
34. George W. Bohlander, "Implementing Quality-of-Work Programs: Recognizing the Barriers," *MSU Business Topics*, Spring 1979, pp. 37–39.
35. Bert Painter, "Experiences of Employee Participation in Decision-Making," *Quality of Working Life: The Canadian Scene*, 1 (1978) (Autumn): 5–19.

Part 2

Preparation and Selection

A company hires employees to meet its objectives. To staff effectively, it first studies its jobs and then plans its human resource needs. Then it recruits applicants. From these recruits, it selects those who best meet its needs.

The next four chapters discuss the procedures used in selecting employees. As either a personnel specialist or a manager, you are affected. The quality of workers you select helps to shape the company's success and yours. You are also affected each time you look for a job.

Chapter 5

Job Analysis

*True Human Resource Development (HRD) professionals are concerned
with the organizing (or reorganizing), and designing (or redesigning), and
structuring (or restructuring) of line functions and the people and
machines performing them. . . .*

Ross Hennigar[1]

*To be concerned about the design of work is to be concerned about
tapping the tremendous wellspring of productivity tied up in the
motivation of people to perform.*

Richard W. Woodman and John J. Sherwood[2]

CHAPTER OBJECTIVES

After studying this chapter, you should be able to:
1. **Explain** why personnel departments must have job analysis
   information.
2. **List** the major methods of collecting job analysis information.
3. **Identify** the type of information needed to develop job descriptions.
4. **Describe** several different methods of setting job performance
   standards.
5. **Explain** different techniques for grouping like jobs into families.

In the previous chapter, we discussed the *ideal* job characteristics that contribute to the quality of work life. This chapter explains how personnel
specialists discover the *actual* characteristics that presently exist in each
job. This knowledge forms the beginnings of a human resource information
system that helps personnel specialists perform effectively. The need for
this information is made clear by the following dialogue:

Service manager: *Before we had a personnel department, we took care of people matters pretty well. Now we have a personnel department, and there is too much paperwork on each job. I wonder if it is a help or a hindrance.*

Personnel manager: *I can sympathize with your views. Before the department was set
up, you probably had complete authority for people matters. Right?*

Service manager: *I sure did! And I did it without a lot of paperwork.*

Personnel manager: *Sure you did. You know every job in the service department, in
and out. You had all the information you needed stored in your experiences.*

Service manager: *That is my point. If I got along without all this paperwork, why can't your department?*

Personnel manager: *Why? Because you deal with those jobs every day. You've probably done most of them yourself. But my department is also responsible for jobs in sales, production, warehouse, supervision, and others. Without the paperwork describing these jobs, we would have no idea of their requirements.*

Jobs are at the core of every organization's productivity. If they are designed well and done right, the organization makes progress toward its objectives. Otherwise, productivity suffers, profits fall, and the organization is less able to meet the demands of society, customers, employees, and others with a stake in its success. The importance and implications of well-designed jobs are perhaps best illustrated by an example:

Rapid growth in a Calgary construction company led to an increase in the number of invoices and a decrease in the quality and timeliness of its departments' performance. Consultants who were hired to look into the problems faced by the company conducted workshops and taught organizational members to apply job diagnostic tools to their activities. The result of all these activities was a 12.3% increase in the number of invoices processed, a saving of $15,200 in salaries and overtime, and a better understanding among the workers of the importance of their work roles.

Not all attempts to restructure jobs succeed as well as this example. However, improvements in productivity, quality, and cost often begin with the jobs employees do. For a personnel department to be effective, its members must have a clear understanding of the jobs found throughout organizations. But with hundreds—or even thousands—of jobs, it is nearly impossible for the personnel professionals in large companies to know the details of every job. The solution is an effective human resource information system that contains detailed information about every job in the organization. With this written or electronically stored information, personnel specialists can quickly learn the details of any job. This knowledge is crucial to the success of a personnel department, especially in large corporations, because it enables personnel specialists to be more proactive in their efforts to assist the organization. Without this information base, personnel would be less able to redesign jobs, recruit new employees, train present employees, determine appropriate compensation, and perform many other human resource functions.

When there is no personnel department all personnel matters are handled by managers. Since operating managers are familiar with the jobs they supervise, they do not need recorded job information. They already know the characteristics, standards, and human abilities required of every job.

After a personnel department is created, however, knowledge about jobs and their requirements must be collected through job analysis. *Job analysis* systematically collects, evaluates, and organizes information. It is done by specialists called *job analysts*, who gather data about each position (though not necessarily about the individual jobs available).

One insurance company has 150 clerical employees who process incoming premium payments. Each job is the same. Therefore, job analysis only requires a random sam-

ple of these positions. Data collection on a few of these jobs generates an accurate information base for all 150 positions. Job analysts can then understand the premium clerk's job without studying each clerk's individual characteristics.

Recorded job information plays a crucial role in personnel departments. It supplies the minimum data to do many personnel activities. Figure 5-1 lists major personnel actions that are affected by job analysis information. Even before a personnel department exists, successful managers consider the informal job information they have acquired. Personnel departments merely formalize the collection, evaluation, and organization of this information.

Figure 5-1
MAJOR PERSONNEL MANAGEMENT ACTIONS THAT RELY ON JOB ANALYSIS INFORMATION

1. **Evaluate** how environmental challenges affect individual jobs.
2. **Eliminate** unneeded job requirements that can cause discrimination in employment.
3. **Discover** job elements that help or hinder the quality of work life.
4. **Plan** for future human resource requirements.
5. **Match** job applicants and job openings.
6. **Determine** training needs for new and experienced employees.
7. **Create** plans to develop employee potential.
8. **Set** realistic performance standards.
9. **Place** employees in jobs that use their skills effectively.
10. **Compensate** jobholders fairly.

This chapter describes the specific information sought by job analysis and the techniques used to collect it. The chapter also examines how the data are converted into useful tools that form the basis of a human resource information system.

COLLECTION OF JOB ANALYSIS INFORMATION

Job analysts gather information about jobs and jobholder characteristics. The function of job analysis is to provide information not only about the job itself, but also about what it calls for in employee behaviour.[3] Before studying jobs, analysts typically study the organization—its purpose, design, inputs (people, materials, and procedures), and outputs (products or services). They may also study industry and government reports about the jobs to be analyzed. In all cases, however, the major aim of job analysis is to provide the basic clues for identifying predictors and measures of job behaviour.[4] Armed with a general understanding of the organization and its work, job analysts:

- Identify the jobs to be analyzed.
- Develop a job analysis questionnaire.
- Collect job analysis information.

JOB IDENTIFICATION

Analysts identify every different job in the organization before they collect job information. This process is simple in small organizations because there are few jobs to uncover. In large companies analysts may have to construct lists of jobs from payroll records, organization charts, or discussions with workers and supervisors. If job analysis has been done before, previous records may be used. Moreover, existing job descriptions, process specifications, and various records and reports relating to organizational performance may also help in establishing the nature of the various jobs.[5]

QUESTIONNAIRE DEVELOPMENT

To study jobs, analysts develop checklists or questionnaires that are sometimes called job analysis schedules. These questionnaires seek to collect job information uniformly. They uncover the duties, responsibilities, human abilities, and performance standards of the jobs investigated.

It is important to use the same questionnaire on similar jobs. Analysts want differences in job information to reflect differences in the jobs, not differences in the questions asked. Uniformity is especially hard to maintain in large organizations: when analysts study similar jobs in different departments, only a uniform questionnaire is likely to result in usable data.

After two appliance producers merged, each initially retained its separate personnel departments and separate job analysis schedules. As a result, all the production supervisors evaluated by one form had their jobs and pay substantially upgraded. The supervisors in the other plant had identical jobs, but they received only modest pay raises.

As the example points out, similar jobs should be studied with identical checklists. Otherwise, job analysis adds confusion. This does *not* mean that the personnel department is limited to one questionnaire. Job analysts often find that technical, clerical, and managerial jobs require different checklists. Different checklists, however, should never be applied to similar jobs.

What are the questions asked in a job analysis questionnaire? Figure 5-2 shows an abbreviated sample form.

Figure 5-2
A JOB ANALYSIS QUESTIONNAIRE

BREVARD GENERAL HOSPITAL
Job Analysis Questionnaire
(Form 110-JAQ)

A. Job Analysis Status

1. Job analysis form revised on _____
2. Previous revisions on _____
3. Date of job analysis for specified job _____
4. Previous analysis on _____
5. Job analysis is conducted by _____
6. Verified by _____

ont.)

LYSIS QUESTIONNAIRE

ntification

title _____ **2.** Other titles _____

ision(s) _____ **4.** Department(s)_____

le of supervisor(s) _____

C. Job Summary

Briefly describe purpose of job, what is done, and how. _____

_____

D. Duties

1. The primary duties of this job are best classified as:

_____ Medical _____ Technical _____ Managerial

_____ Clerical _____ Professional

2. List **major** duties and the proportion of time each involves:

a. _____. _____ %

b. _____. _____ %

c. _____. _____ %

3. List other duties and the proportion of time each involves:

a. _____. _____ %

b. _____. _____ %

c. _____. _____ %

4. What constitutes successful performance of these duties? _____

_____

5. How much training is needed for normal performance of these duties?

_____

_____

_____

E. Responsibility

1. What are the responsibilities involved in this job and how great are these responsibilities?

Responsibility for:	Extent of Responsibility	
	Minor	Major
a. Equipment operation	_____	_____
b. Use of tools	_____	_____
c. Materials usage	_____	_____
d. Protection of equipment	_____	_____
e. Protection of tools	_____	_____
f. Protection of materials	_____	_____
g. Personal safety	_____	_____
h. Safety of others	_____	_____
i. Others' work performance	_____	_____
j. Other (Specify _____)	_____	_____

Figure 5-2 (cont.)
A JOB ANALYSIS QUESTIONNAIRE

F. Human Characteristics

1. What physical attributes are necessary to perform the job? _____

_____

2. Of the following characteristics, which ones are needed and how important are they?

Characteristic	Unneeded	Helpful	Essential
1. Vision	_____	_____	_____
2. Hearing	_____	_____	_____
3. Talking	_____	_____	_____
4. Sense of smell	_____	_____	_____
5. Sense of touch	_____	_____	_____
6. Sense of taste	_____	_____	_____
7. Eye-hand coordination	_____	_____	_____
8. Overall coordination	_____	_____	_____
9. Strength	_____	_____	_____
10. Height	_____	_____	_____
11. Health	_____	_____	_____
12. Initiative	_____	_____	_____
13. Ingenuity	_____	_____	_____
14. Judgment	_____	_____	_____
15. Attention	_____	_____	_____
16. Reading	_____	_____	_____
17. Arithmetic	_____	_____	_____
18. Writing	_____	_____	_____
19. Education (Level _____)	_____	_____	_____
20. Other (Specify _____)	_____	_____	_____

3. Experience for this job:
   _____ a. Unimportant
   _____ b. Includes _____ (months) as (job title)_____

4. Can training be substituted for experience?
   _____ Yes   How: _____
   _____ No   Why: _____

G. Working Conditions

1. Describe the physical conditions under which this job is performed. _____

_____

2. Are there unusual psychological demands connected with this job? _____

_____

3. Describe any unusual conditions under which the job is performed.

_____

_____

_____

Figure 5-2 (cont.)
A JOB ANALYSIS QUESTIONNAIRE

H. Health or Safety Features

    1. Describe fully any health or safety hazards associated with this job. _____

    2. Is any safety training or equipment required? _____

I. Performance Standards

    1. How is the performance of this job measured? _____

    2. What identifiable factors contribute most to the successful performance of this job?

J. Miscellaneous Comments

    Are there any aspects of this job that should be especially noted?_____

Job Analyst's Signature	Date Completed

STATUS AND IDENTIFICATION. The first two headings in the figure show how current the information is and identify the job being described. Without these entries, users of job analysis data may rely on out-of-date information or apply it to the wrong job. Since most jobs change over time, out-dated information may misdirect other personnel activities.

At Brevard General Hospital, new job analysis information had not been collected for two years on the job of billing clerk. The outdated information indicated that book-keeping experience was the major skill needed by billing clerks. But once the hospital's entire billing system had been computerized, bookkeeping skills became unimportant; instead, billing clerks needed typing skills to process billing information into the computer.

DUTIES AND RESPONSIBILITIES. Many job analysis schedules briefly explain the purpose of the job, what the job accomplishes, and how the job is performed. This summary provides a quick overview. The specific duties and responsibilities are also listed to give more detailed insight into the position. Questions on responsibility are expanded significantly when the checklist is applied to management jobs. Additional questions map areas of responsibility for decision making, controlling, organizing, planning, and other management functions.

HUMAN CHARACTERISTICS AND WORKING CONDITIONS. Besides information about the job, analysts need data about the people who do the work. This section of the checklist uncovers the particular skills, abilities, training, education, experience, and other characteristics that jobholders need. It is invaluable when filling job openings or advising workers about new job assignments.

Information about the job environment improves understanding of the job. Working conditions may explain the need for particular skills, training, knowledge, or even a particular job design. Likewise, jobs must be free from recognizable health and safety hazards. Knowledge of hazards allows the personnel department to redesign the job or protect workers through training and safety equipment. Unique working conditions also influence hiring, placement, and compensation decisions.

During World War II, one airplane manufacturer had problems installing fuel tanks inside the wings of the bombers it was building. The crawl space was extremely narrow and cramped. These tight conditions caused considerable production delays. When the personnel department learned about this situation, it recruited welders who were less than 5 feet tall and weighed under 100 pounds.

PERFORMANCE STANDARDS. The job analysis questionnaire also seeks information about job standards, which are used to evaluate performance. This information is collected on jobs with obvious and objective standards of performance. When standards are not readily apparent, job analysts may ask supervisors or industrial engineers to develop reasonable standards of performance.

DATA COLLECTION

There is no one best way to collect job analysis information. Analysts must evaluate the trade-offs between time, cost, and accuracy associated with each method.[6] Once they decide which trade-offs are most important, they use interviews, questionnaires, employee logbooks, observations, or some combination of these techniques.

INTERVIEWS. Face-to-face interviews are an effective way to collect job information. The analyst has the job checklist as a guide, but can add other questions where needed. Although the process is slow and expensive, it allows the interviewer to explain unclear questions and probe into uncertain answers. Both jobholders and supervisors typically are interviewed. The analyst usually talks with a limited number of workers first. Then interviews with supervisors verify the information. This pattern ensures a high level of accuracy.

MAIL QUESTIONNAIRES. A fast and less costly option is a mail questionnaire developed from the job analysis checklist. This approach allows many jobs to be studied at once and at little cost. However, there is less accuracy because of misunderstood questions, incomplete responses, and unre-turned questionnaires. Supervisors can also be given mail questionnaires to verify employee responses.

EMPLOYEE LOG. An employee log or diary is a third option. Workers periodically summarize their tasks and activities in the log. If entries are made over the entire job cycle, the diary can prove quite accurate. It may even be the only feasible way to collect job information.

New Brunswick Brokers' three dozen account executives each handled a bewildering array of activities for clients. Since interviews and questionnaires often overlooked major parts of the job, the personnel department suggested a logbook. Most account executives initially resisted, but eventually they agreed to a one-month trial. The personnel department obtained the information it wanted, and account executives learned how they actually *spent their days.*

Logs are not a popular technique. They are time-consuming for jobhold-ers and personnel specialists. This makes them costly. Managers and workers often see them as a nuisance and resist their introduction. More-over, after the novelty wears off, accuracy tends to decline as entries be-come less frequent.

OBSERVATION. Another approach is direct observation. It is slow, costly, and potentially less accurate than other methods. Accuracy may be low because the analysts may miss irregularly occurring activities. But observa-tion is the preferred method in some situations. When analysts question data from other techniques, observation may confirm or remove doubts. The existence of language barriers may also necessitate the observation ap-proach, especially in cases involving foreign-language workers.

COMBINATIONS. Since each method has its faults, analysts often use two or more techniques concurrently.

A lumber company had six facilities scattered throughout Canada and the United States. To interview a few workers and supervisors at each facility was considered prohibitively expensive; to rely only on questionnaire data was thought to be too in-accurate. So the personnel department both interviewed selected employees at the home office and sent questionnaires to other facilities.

Combinations can ensure high accuracy at minimum cost, as the example implies. Personnel departments may even use combined methods when all employees are at the same location. Regardless of the technique used, the job analysis information is of little value until analysts convert it into more usable forms.

USES OF JOB ANALYSIS INFORMATION

Through the preparation and collection phases of job analysis shown in Figure 5-3, personnel departments obtain information about jobs. Then this information is put into such usable forms as job descriptions, job specifica-tions, and job standards. Together, these applications of job analysis infor-

Figure 5-3
THE THREE PHASES OF JOB ANALYSIS INFORMATION

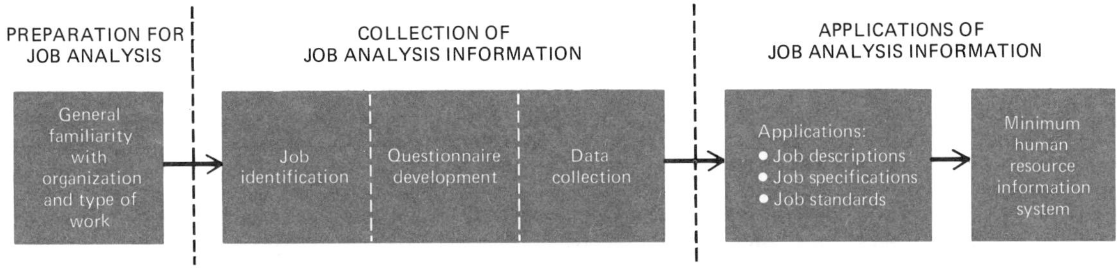

mation provide a minimum human resource information system. The remainder of this chapter discusses these applications.

JOB DESCRIPTIONS

A *job description* is a written statement that explains the duties, working conditions, and other aspects of a specified job. Within a firm, all the job descriptions follow the same style, although between companies, form and content may vary. One approach is to write a narrative description that covers the job in a few paragraphs. Another typical style breaks the description down into several subparts, as shown in Figure 5-4.[7] This figure shows a job description that parallels the job analysis checklist which originally generated the data.

In a job description, the section on job identity may include a *job code*. Job codes use numbers, letters, or both to provide a quick summary of the job. These codes are useful for comparing jobs. Figure 5-5 explains the code used in the *Canadian Classification and Dictionary of Occupations* (CCDO). It is an alphanumeric code that helps arrange jobs into occupational groups. This classification is based on, among other things, the kind of work performed, the materials or equipment used or produced, the standards to be met, the education or training required, the working conditions, and the relationship to coworkers of the jobholder.[8]

The job identity section contains other useful information.

• *Date.* The date is essential. It tells subsequent users how old the description is. The older the description, the less likely it is to reflect the job as now done.

• *Author.* The writer of the description is identified so that questions or errors can be brought to the attention of the author.

• *Location.* The department (or departments) where the job is located helps identify the job for future reference. Location references may include division, plant, or other organization breakdowns.

• *Job grade.* Job descriptions may have a blank for later addition of the

Figure 5-4
A JOB DESCRIPTION

BREVARD GENERAL HOSPITAL
Job Description

Job Title:	Job Analyst	**Job Code:**	166.088
Date:	January 3, 1985	**Author:**	John Doakes
Job Location:	Personnel Department	**Job Grade:**	
Supervisor:	Harold Grantinni	**Status:**	Exempt

Job Summary: Collects and develops job analysis information through interviews, questionnaires, observation, or other means. Provides other personnel specialists with needed information.

Job Duties: Designs job analysis schedules and questionnaires. Collects job information.
Interacts with workers, supervisors, and peers.
Writes job descriptions and job specifications.
Reports safety hazards to area manager and safety department.
Verifies all information through two sources.
Performs other duties as assigned by supervisors.

Working Conditions: Works most of the time in well-ventilated modern office. Data collection often requires on-site work under every working condition found in company. Works standard 8 a.m. to 5 p.m., except to collect second-shift data and when travelling (one to three days per month).

The above information is correct as approved by:

(Signed) _____   (Signed) _____
              Job Analyst   **Department Manager**

---

job grade or level. This information helps rank the job's importance for pay purposes.

• *Supervisor.* The supervisor's title may be listed to help identify the job and its relative importance.

• *Status.* Analysts may identify the job as exempt or not from overtime laws.

JOB SUMMARY AND DUTIES. After the job identification section, the next part of the description is the job summary. It is a written narrative that concisely summarizes the job in a few sentences. It tells what the job is, how it is done, and why. Most authorities recommend that job summaries specify the primary actions involved. Then in a simple, action-oriented style, the job description lists the job duties. Figure 5-4 provides an example of this style.

This section is important to personnel specialists. It explains what the job requires. The effectiveness of other personnel actions depends upon this understanding, because each major duty is described in terms of the actions expected. Tasks and activities are identified. Performance is emphasized. Even responsibilities are implied or stated within the job duties. If employees are in a union, the union may want to narrow the duties associated with specific jobs.

Before the union organized, the employee job descriptions contained the phrase "or other work as assigned." The union believed supervisors abused this clause by assigning idle workers to do unrelated jobs. With the threat of a strike, management removed the phrase, and supervisors lost much of their flexibility in assigning work.

WORKING CONDITIONS. A job description also explains working conditions. It may go beyond descriptions of the physical environment. Hours of work, safety and health hazards, travel requirements, and other features of the job expand the meaning of this section.

APPROVALS. Since job descriptions affect most personnel decisions, their accuracy should be reviewed by selected jobholders and their supervisors. Then supervisors are asked to approve the description. This approval serves as a further test of the job description and a further check on the collection of job analysis information. Neither personnel specialists nor managers should consider approval lightly. If the description is in error, the personnel department will become a source of problems, not assistance.

In explaining the job of foundry attendant to new employees, personnel specialists at one firm relied on an inaccurate job description. Many new employees quit the job during the first two weeks. When asked why, most said the duties were less challenging than they were led to believe. When analysts checked, it was found the job description had never been verified by the supervisors.

Figure 5-5
EXPLANATION OF JOB CODES IN THE CANADIAN CLASSIFICATION AND DICTIONARY OF OCCUPATIONS (CCDO)

Each occupational definition in the *Canadian Classification and Dictionary of Occupations* (CCDO) has a seven-digit code number, a title, and an industry designation; for example, 9173-110 TAXI DRIVER (motor trans.). The first four digits of the code number represent the major, minor, and unit groups which categorize occupations in successively finer detail; for example, 11 represents managerial, administrative, and related occupations (major group), 111 officials and administrations unique to government (minor group), and 1111 members of legislative bodies (unit group). The last three digits provide a code number within the classification structure for each occupation; for example 4133-110 TELLER (bank and finance) and 6191-110 JANITOR (any industry).

Occupational descriptions include five selected occupational characteristics and appear as coded digits or letters. These are: the general educational development needed for the job (GED), the specific vocational preparation needed (SVP), the environmental conditions within which the work is performed (EC), the physical activities involved in the work (PA), and the demands made on the worker and the worker's function in relation to data, people, and things (DPT). The codes GED and SVP reflect the training-time requirements of occupations independently of years of schooling (or other standards commonly used) of job incumbents; they also arrange occupations in each unit group in order of complexity. The EC code indicates the relevant physical surroundings of a worker; noise, mechanical hazards, fumes, and dust are examples of the kind of factors considered. The PA code expresses both the physical requirements of the occupation and the physical capacities (or traits) a worker must have to meet those requirements; for example, seeing, lifting, climbing, etc. The DPT code indicates the worker's functional relationships to data (for example, analyzing, synthesizing), people (negotiating, supervising), and things (handling, tending).

Aptitudes required for each job (APT), apart from the above, are also coded. The factors included are intelligence (G), verbal ability (V), numerical ability (N), spatial ability (S), form perception or the ability to perceive pertinent details in objects (P), clerical perception ability (Q), eye-hand motor coordination (K), finger dexterity (F), manual dexterity (M), eye-hand-foot coordination (E), and colour discrimination (C). Five levels, i.e. five codes, are used for every aptitude except intelligence, for which only four levels are used.

The interest factors (INT) required for the particular job are also shown in the CCDO coding. Five pairs of interest factors are provided such that a positive concern for one factor of a pair usually implies rejection of the other factor (for example, routine, concrete, organized work vs. abstract, creative work). Finally, the temperament or personality requirements (TEMP) are shown against each job. Twelve such factors are used in CCDO.

Given below is an example of CCDO job coding.

8739-170   Tree Trimmer (elec. power, telecom.)

Trims trees to clear right-of-way for communication and electric power lines to minimize storm and short-circuit hazards:

Climbs trees to reach branches interfering with wires and transmission towers, using climbing equipment. Prunes treetops and branches, using saws and pruning shears. Trims damaged trees and paints stumps to prevent bleeding of sap. Removes broken limbs from wires, using extension pole. Fells trees interfering with power service, using chain-saw.

Works from bucket of extended truck boom to reach branches as required.

GED: 2   SVP: 3   PA: M 2 4   EC: 0 4 6   DPT: 687

	APT	INT	TEMP
G V N S P Q K F M E C			
4 4 5 4 4 5 4 4 3 3 5	3 1		2 3 Y

Source: *Canadian Classification and Dictionary of Occupations*, Vols. 1–2, Canada Employment and Immigration, 1971.

Figure 5-6
A JOB SPECIFICATION SHEET

BREVARD GENERAL HOSPITAL
Job Specification

Job Title:	Job Analyst	**Job Code:**	166.088
Date:	January 3, 1985	**Author:**	John Doakes
Job Location:	Personnel Department	**Job Grade:**	
Supervisor:	Harold Grantinni	**Status:**	Exempt

Skill Factors

Education: College degree required.

Experience: At least one year as job analyst trainee, recruiter, or other professional assignment in personnel area.

Communication: Oral and written skills should evidence ability to capsulize job data succinctly.

Effort Factors

Physical demands: Limited to those normally associated with clerical jobs: sitting, standing, and walking.

Mental demands: Extended visual attention is needed to observe jobs. Initiative and ingenuity are mandatory since job receives only general supervision. Judgment must be exercised on job features to be emphasized, jobs to be studied, and methods used to collect job data.
Decision-making discretion is frequent.
Analyzes and synthesizes large amounts of abstract information into job descriptions, job specifications, and job standards.

Working Conditions

Travels to hospital clinics in municipality from one to three days per month.
Travels around each work site collecting job information.
Works mostly in an office setting.

JOB SPECIFICATIONS

The difference between a job description and a job specification is one of perspective. A job description defines what the job does; it is a profile of the job. A *job specification* describes what the job demands of employees who do it and the human factors that are required.[9] It is a profile of the human characteristics needed by the job. These requirements include experience, training, education, physical demands, and mental demands. Since the job description and specifications both focus on the job, they are often combined into one document. The combination is simply called a job description. Whether part of a job description or a separate document, job specifications include the information illustrated in Figure 5-6. The data to compile specifications also come from the job analysis checklist.

Job specifications contain a job identification section if they are a separate document. The subheadings and purpose are the same as those found in the job identification section of the job description.

A job specification should include *specific* tools, actions, experiences, education, and training, i.e. the *individual* requirements of the job. For example, it should describe "physical effort" in terms of the special actions demanded by the job. "Lifts 100-pound bags" is better than "Lifts heavy weights."[10] Clear behaviour statements give a better picture than vague generalities.[11] Specifications of mental effort help personnel experts determine the intellectual abilities that are needed. Figure 5-6 contains several examples of the kind of information about physical and mental efforts needed by job analysts for a hospital.

Do the working conditions make any unusual demands on jobholders? The working conditions found in job descriptions may be translated by job specifications into demands faced by workers. Figure 5-7 provides examples for the job of hospital orderly. It shows that a simple statement of working conditions found in the job description can hold significant implications for jobholders. For example, compare points 2 and 3 under the job description column with points 2 and 3 under job specifications.

Figure 5-7

TRANSLATION OF WORKING CONDITIONS FOR JOB DESCRIPTION TO JOB SPECIFICATION

Hospital Orderly	
Job Description Statement of Working Conditions	**Job Specifications Interpretation of Working Conditions**
1. Works in physically comfortable surroundings.	1. (Omitted. This item on the job description makes no demands on jobholders.)
2. Deals with physically ill and diseased patients.	2. Exposed to unpleasant situations and communicable diseases.
3. Deals with mentally ill patients.	3. May be exposed to verbal and physical abuse.

JOB PERFORMANCE STANDARDS

Job analysis has a third application, *job performance standards*. These standards serve two functions. First, they become objectives or targets for employee efforts. The challenge or pride of meeting objectives may serve to motivate employees. Once standards are met, workers may feel accomplish-

Figure 5-8
DIAGRAM OF A JOB CONTROL SYSTEM

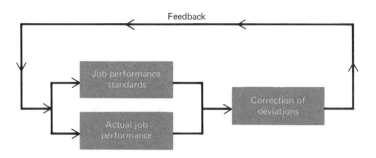

ment and achievement. This outcome contributes to employee satisfaction. Without standards, employee performance may suffer.

Second, standards are criteria against which job success is measured. They are indispensable to managers or personnel specialists who attempt to control work performance. Without standards, no control system can evaluate job performance.[12]

All control systems have four features: standards, measures, correction, and feedback. The relationship between these four factors is illustrated in Figure 5-8. Job performance standards are developed from job analysis information, and then actual employee performance is measured. When measured performance strays from the job standard, corrective action is taken. That is, personnel experts or line managers intervene. The corrective action serves as feedback to the standards and actual performance. This feedback leads to changes in either the standards (if they were inappropriate) or actual job performance.

In the Toronto Trust Company, current standards dictated that each loan supervisor review 250 mortgage-loan applications per month. Yet the actual output averaged 210. When more recent job information was collected, analysts discovered that since the standards had been first set, several new duties had been added for each supervisor. Corrective action resulted in new job designs, revised job descriptions, and more realistic standards.

Job standards are a key part of any control system. When the standards are wrong, as in the trust company example, they alert managers and personnel specialists to problems that need correction. The example also underscores the need for keeping job analysis information current.

Job standards are obtained either from job analysis information or from alternative sources. Job analysis information is usually sufficient for jobs that have the following features:

• Performance is quantified.
• Performance is easily measurable.

- Performance standards are understood by workers and supervisors.
- Performance requires little interpretation.

Jobs with short work cycles often exhibit these features. An example is an assembly-line job. For these jobs, questions on the job analysis checklist may generate specific, quantitative answers. When confirmed by supervisors, this information becomes the job performance standard. Figure 5-9 shows the job dimensions for professors teaching organizational behaviour courses in Canada. Figure 5-10 elaborates some "effective" and "ineffective" behaviours associated with one performance dimension, "teaching style." Clear behavioural descriptions of job performance such as these facilitate a more accurate appraisal of the performer.[13] More details of behaviourally oriented performance appraisals will be discussed in Chapter 12.

ALTERNATIVE SOURCES OF STANDARDS

Although job analysis information does not always provide a source of job standards, it is necessary even if analysts use other means to develop reasonable standards. The most common alternative sources of job standards are work measurement and participative goal setting.

Figure 5-9
EMPIRICALLY DERIVED PERFORMANCE DIMENSIONS OF PROFESSORS TEACHING BEHAVIOURAL SCIENCES IN CANADA

Performance Dimension	Key Aspects Covered
1. Course outlining and structuring	Definition of the course objectives; inclusion of student needs and expectations into the outline; provision of detailed schedule for lectures and assignments in class.
2. Coverage of material	Nature, relevance, scope, and depth of course content and readings; linkage to other disciplines.
3. Teaching style	Actual behaviour within the classroom, including leadership style used within classroom.
4. Teaching methods	Variety, relevance, and usefulness of various teaching methods and aids used.
5. Evaluation	Objective definition of evaluation criteria; extent of feedback given to students about their performance; flexibility displayed in evaluation methods.
6. Interaction outside class	Instructor being available for consultation outside class; friendliness, interest, and help given by him/her to students.
7. Flexibility and responsiveness	Flexibility and responsiveness displayed by instructor. Sensitivity to student needs.

Source: Hari Das, Peter J. Frost, and J. Thad Barnowe, "Behaviourally Anchored Scales for Assessing Behavioural Science Teaching," *Canadian Journal of Behavioural Science*, Vol. II, no. 1, January 1979, p. 82.

Figure 5-10
SCALE SCORES AND "EFFECTIVE" AND "INEFFECTIVE" BEHAVIOURAL ANCHORS FOR "TEACHING STYLE" PERFORMANCE DIMENSION OF UNIVERSITY PROFESSORS

Scale Score	Behavioural Anchor
6.73	Could be expected to provide real-life and personal examples to explain a concept.
5.81	Could be expected to speak with considerable energy and enthusiasm.
2.10	Could be expected to give dull lectures which are repetitive of the textbook.
1.70	Could be expected to use abstract and difficult language in his/her lectures.
5.39	Could be expected to lay emphasis on many students participating in class discussions rather than students only giving right answers.
3.71	Could be expected to spend considerable class time in stating his/her personal views on different matters.
6.44	Could be expected to encourage students to ask questions and answer their questions without "putting them down."
5.89	Could be expected to take considerable effort to learn names of students and engage in conversations.
5.46	Could be expected to treat his/her students as equals within class.
4.39	Could be expected to secure participation of individual students by asking them specific questions.

Source: Hari Das, Peter J. Frost, and J. Thad Barnowe, "Behaviourally Anchored Scales for Assessing Behavioural Science Teaching," *Canadian Journal of Behavioural Science*, Vol. II, no. 1, January 1979, p. 83.

WORK MEASUREMENT

Work measurement techniques estimate the normal performance of average workers; the results dictate the job performance standard. Such techniques are applied to nonmanagerial jobs and are created from historical data, time study, and work sampling. They may be used by the personnel department, line management, or industrial engineering. Regardless of who applies work measurement techniques, however, job analysis information is also needed.

HISTORICAL DATA. Historical data can be obtained from past records if job analysis does not supply performance standards. For example, the number of shirts produced per month by a clothing manufacturer indicates how many sleeves, collars, and buttons should be sewn on by each worker. One weakness of this approach is that it assumes past performance is average performance. Another weakness is that historical data are useless on new jobs. However, if production records are reviewed for long-standing jobs, historically based standards may be more accurate than standards drawn from a job analysis checklist.

TIME STUDY. *Time studies* produce standards when jobs can be observed and timed. Time studies identify each element within a job. Then each element is timed while being repeated by an average worker using the standard method of doing the job. The average times for each element of the job are summed up to yield the *rated job time*. Allowances for rest breaks, fatigue, or equipment delays are added to produce a *standard time*. The standard time allows personnel specialists to compute performance standards.

Assume a typist can type a page of straight copy in an average of eight minutes, based on several direct observations. To this rated job time of eight minutes, allowances for changing paper, replacing typewriter ribbons, taking rest breaks, etc., are added. The total is a standard time of twelve minutes. This means that the typist's standard of performance should be an average of one page of typing per twelve minutes, or five an hour.

WORK SAMPLING. How does the analyst know the number of minutes to add for allowances? Allowances are usually set through *work sampling.* By making 300 observations of typists at different times during the day over a two-week period, for example, analysts might discover that the typists were actually typing two-thirds of the time. If eight minutes of uninterrupted typing are required to type a page, then the standard time can be computed by dividing the rated time of eight minutes by the fraction of time spent working, or two-thirds in this example. The result is a standard time of twelve minutes. Mathematically, the computation is:

Rated time ÷ observed proportion of work time used = standard time

OR

8 minutes ÷ $2/3$ = 12 minutes

Standards for some jobs cannot be determined by either job analysis information or work measurement. In service or managerial jobs, output may reflect changing trade-offs. For example, the number of customers handled by a grocery checkout clerk depends on how busy the store is and on the size of each customer's purchases. But standards are still useful, even though they are difficult to set. In some cases, mutual agreement between the worker and the manager—participative goal setting—is more likely to be effective.

PARTICIPATIVE GOAL SETTING
When a job lacks obvious standards, managers may develop them participatively through discussions with subordinates. These conversations discuss the purpose of the job, its role in relation to other jobs, the organization's requirements, and the employee's needs. The employee gains insight into what is expected. Implicit or explicit promises of future rewards may also result. From these discussions, the manager and the employee reach some jointly shared objectives and standards.[14] The process may even lead to greater employee commitment, morale, satisfaction, and motivation. Since

objectives are usually for individual positions (instead of jobs), they are seldom included in job descriptions.

Performance standards sometimes are set participatively with union leaders. Labour leaders understand the important role of job analysis information, and they may insist on negotiating performance standards for jobs. These negotiated agreements are written into legally enforceable contracts.

In one paper products company, management decided to increase production rates by 5% to meet customer demand. After this was done, the union threatened legal action because the new standards conflicted with those in the labour contract. Management was forced to retain the old standard.

THE HUMAN RESOURCE INFORMATION SYSTEM

Job descriptions, job specifications, and job standards are the minimum data base needed by personnel departments. Together, these outputs of job analysis information explain each job. Supported with this information, personnel specialists can make intelligent decisions concerning jobs and human resources.[15] But there are three problems with the minimum human resource information system as it has been explained so far: organization, legal considerations, and the scope of the data base.

ORGANIZATION OF THE DATA BASE

Whether job information is on written forms or in computer memories, it is organized around individual jobs. Although this is useful, personnel departments also need job analysis information that is organized around job families. *Job families* are groups of jobs that are closely related by similar duties, responsibilities, skills, or job elements. The jobs of clerk, typist, clerk-typist, and secretary constitute a job family, for example. These groups allow personnel departments to facilitate job rotation programs, permanent job transfers, and other personnel decisions.

Job families can be constructed in several ways. One way is by careful study of existing job analysis information. Matching of the data in job descriptions can identify jobs with similar requirements. A second method is to use the codes in the *Canadian Classification and Dictionary of Occupations* (Figure 5-5). Similarities in the job codes indicate similarities in the jobs.

The third approach is the *position analysis questionnaire*. The position analysis questionnaire (also called the PAQ) is a standardized, preprinted form that collects specific information about job tasks and worker traits. Through statistical analysis of the PAQ responses, related jobs are grouped into job families.

LEGAL CONSIDERATIONS

For the most part, job analysis information is an internal matter that is affected little by external challenges. But when personnel specialists rely on job analysis information to pursue other external activities, such as hiring, legal considerations arise in the area of compliance with Human Rights Legislation. For example, charges of discrimination may result from the unequal impact of some needless job requirement:

In one instance, an employer required a high school diploma for nearly all jobs within the company except those in the labour pool. When the need for a diploma was challenged, the employer could not show that it was absolutely necessary to perform many of the jobs for which it was officially required and although this requirement was applied equally to all applicants, it had an unequal impact on minority-group applicants. As a result, many persons belonging to such groups were offered labour-pool jobs only.

Further, needless job requirements exclude potentially qualified individuals from consideration, which may reduce the effectiveness not only of hiring but of other personnel activities.

SCOPE OF THE DATA BASE

Job descriptions, job specifications, and job standards provide only a narrow data base. Arranging these data into job families helps, but more information is demanded for the purpose of some personnel management activities. Thus job analysis information is only the first part of a sophisticated human resource information system. Additions to this information system are made through other personnel activities discussed throughout the book.

SUMMARY

Job analysis information provides the foundations of an organization's human resource information system. Analysts seek to gain a general understanding of the organization and the work it performs. Then they design job analysis questionnaires to collect specific data about jobs, jobholder characteristics, and job performance standards. Job analysis information can be collected through interviews, juries of experts, mailed questionnaires, employee logs, direct observation, or some combination of these techniques. Once collected, the data are converted into such useful applications as job descriptions, job specifications, and job standards.

Job analysis information is important because it tells personnel specialists what duties and responsibilities are associated with each job. This information then is used when personnel specialists undertake other personnel management activities such as job design, recruiting, and selection. Jobs are the link between organizations and their human resources. The combined accomplishment of every job allows the organization to meet its objectives. Similarly, jobs represent not only a source of income to workers but also a means of fulfilling their needs. However, for the organization and its employees to receive these mutual benefits, jobs must provide a high quality of work life.

TERMS FOR REVIEW

Job analysis	Work measurement
Job description	Time studies
Job code	Work sampling
Job specification	Job families
Job performance standards	Position analysis questionnaire

Canadian Classification and Dictionary of Occupations (CCDO)

REVIEW AND DISCUSSION QUESTIONS

1. What types of raw data do the questions on a job analysis checklist seek to obtain? Are there other data you should seek for management jobs?
2. What are the different methods of collecting job analysis information, and what are the advantages and disadvantages of each technique?
3. What is the purpose of (a) job descriptions, (b) job specifications, (c) job performance standards?
4. How can performance standards be set for production jobs when job analysis information is insufficient? How would you set standards of performance for a research scientist if you were chief scientist?
5. Describe three ways jobs can be grouped into job families.
6. Suppose that you were assigned to write the job descriptions for a shirt factory in Toronto employing mostly Chinese immigrants who spoke little English.
   (a) What methods would you use to collect job analysis data?
   (b) If a manager in the shirt factory refused to complete a job analysis questionnaire, what reasons would you use to persuade that individual to complete it?
   (c) If, after your best efforts at persuasion failed, you still wanted job analysis information on the manager's job, how would you get it?

INCIDENT 5-1

HEDGES ELECTRONICS COMPUTERIZED JOB DATA

Hedges Electronics is a small manufacturer of remote access consoles, cathode-ray-tube display terminals, and other on-line computer equipment. The remote consoles and cathode displays are widely used within the company. Through the consoles, most managers can store and retrieve data from the company's main-frame computer. This information appears on cathode-ray displays, which are similar to small television screens.

One day, since most line and staff managers were familiar with on-line equipment, it was decided to store the human resource information system on the main computer. Then when managers or personnel specialists needed a job description, they could simply secure one from the computer.

After computerizing all human resource information, job analysts began to notice that job descriptions, job specifications, and job standards were constantly being changed by jobholders. It seemed that whenever a manager or worker reviewed a job description or job specification that seemed outdated, he or she would "write in" a correction on the computer's memory.

Thus although in the beginning personnel specialists were glad that workers were showing an interest by updating the computerized job analysis information, they eventually became worried because workers with the same job titles had different views of their jobs. Changes would come from almost anyone, and there was no consistency in style or content.

To eliminate this problem, a subroutine was programmed into the computer that prevented unauthorized changes. Job analysts then reviewed the job descriptions and job specifications to ensure uniformity of style. Line and staff managers could still obtain copies of job analysis information.

1. Assume that you are the personnel manager at Hedges. What procedures would you lay down that would ensure that the restudied job analysis information was correct?
2. Given the ability of most managers to "communicate" directly with the computer, does Hedges Electronics have a new way to collect job analysis information? Explain.

EXERCISE 5-1
PREPARATION OF A JOB DESCRIPTION

As discussed in the chapter, there are several ways to collect job analysis information. One way is through observation. Using the form in Figure 5-2, complete parts C through J for the job of professor. After you have completed those sections of the job analysis questionnaire, use the format in Figure 5-4 and write a job description for the job of professor. When you are finished, look up the definition of professor *provided in the* Canadian Classification and Dictionary of Occupations.

1. How does the description in the *Canadian Classification and Dictionary of Occupations* vary in format and content from the one you wrote?
2. What parts of a professor's job are most important, in your opinion?

REFERENCES

1. Ross Hennigar, "Today's Human Resource Manager," *The Canadian Personnel & Industrial Relations Journal,* 23(4) (September, 1976): 12.
2. Richard W. Woodman and John J. Sherwood, "A Comprehensive Look at Job Design," *Personnel Journal,* August 1977, pp. 384–385.
3. Harish C. Jain (ed.), *Contemporary Issues in Canadian Personnel Administration,* Scarborough: Prentice-Hall of Canada Limited, 1974, pp. 54–55.
4. Marvin D. Dunnette, "Studying Jobs and Job Behaviour," in Jain (ed.), op. cit.
5. Dunnette, op. cit., p. 60.
6. J. D. Dunn and Frank M. Rachel, *Wage and Salary Administration: Total Compensation Systems,* New York: McGraw-Hill Book Company, 1971, pp. 139–141.
7. Herbert G. Zollitsch and Adolph Langsner, *Wage and Salary Administration,* 2nd ed., Dallas: South-Western Publishing Co., 1970, pp. 290–301.
8. Canada Employment and Immigration, *Canadian Classification and Dictionary of Occupations 1971,* Vols. 1–2, Ottawa: Information Canada, 1971. See also Canada Employment and Immigration, *Updates on CCDO,* Ottawa: Information Canada (published for major groups annually).
9. Zollitsch and Langsner, op. cit., pp. 301–311. See also Allan N. Nash and Stephen J. Carroll Jr., *The Management of Compensation,* Monterey, Calif.: Brooks/Cole Publishing Company, 1975, pp. 116–117.
10. Paul Sheibar, "A Simple Selection System Called 'Job Match,'" *Personnel Journal,* January 1979, p. 26.
11. Dunnette, op. cit.
12. Tom Laufer, "A Practical Tool For Evaluating Clerical Jobs," *The Canadian Personnel & Industrial Relations Journal,* 25(2) (March 1978): 10–16.
13. Tom Janz, "Estimating the Standard Deviation of Job Performance: A Behavioural Approach," *Administrative Sciences Association of Canada (Organizational Behaviour Division) Meeting Proceedings,* Vol. 2, Part 5, 1981, pp. 70–78. See also Tom Janz, "Behaviour Relationship Scales: Behaviour Observation Scales for Small Samples," Simon Fraser Discussion Series 80.6.3, Department of Business Administra-

tion, Simon Fraser University, B.C., 1980; Hari Das, Peter J. Frost and J. Thad Barnowe, "Behaviourally Anchored Scales for Assessing Behavioural Science Teaching," *Canadian Journal of Behavioural Science*, Vol. 11, no. 1, January 1979, pp. 79–88.
14. William B. Werther, Jr. and Heinz Weihrich, "Refining MBO through Negotiations," *MSU Business Topics*, Summer 1975, pp. 53–59.
15. William P. Anthony, "Get to Know Your Employees—The Human Resource Information System," *Personnel Journal*, April 1977, pp. 179–183, 202–203.

Chapter 6

Human Resource Planning

Through human resource planning, management prepares to have the right people at the right places at the right times to fulfill both organizational and individual objectives.

James W. Walker[1]

CHAPTER OBJECTIVES

After studying this chapter, you should be able to:
1. **Explain** why small organizations seldom use human resource planning and why large organizations are using it more frequently.
2. **Identify** the factors that change an organization's demand for human resources.
3. **Discuss** the shortcomings of human resource forecasting techniques.
4. **Develop** a skills inventory as part of a human resource audit.
5. **Recommend** solutions to shortages or surpluses of human resources.

Human resource planning improves the personnel department's contributions to the organization's objectives. Perhaps more than any other human resource activity, planning allows the personnel department to be proactive rather than reactive.

Sy Wolfe: *All I ever seem to do is "put out fires." Every day different department heads tell me they need new employees. Well, we are a service department, so we rush around and try to find someone. And I thought being a city personnel manager would be a snap.*

Jean-Marie Gasse: *Why don't you do like we do in the police department and develop plans?*

Sy Wolfe: *Plans? How am I supposed to know who is going to quit?*

Jean-Marie Gasse: *You don't need to know exactly. Try estimating job vacancies. No one tells us when crimes or accidents are going to happen. We try to anticipate the need for traffic and crime squads for each shift based on past experience.*

Sy Wolfe: *Your idea would be fine in a police department, but there are too many different jobs in city government to create human resource plans.*

OVERVIEW OF HUMAN RESOURCE PLANNING

Human resource planning systematically forecasts an organization's future supply of, and demand for, employees.[2] By estimating the number and types of employees that will be needed, the personnel department can better plan its recruitment, selection, training, career planning, and other activities. Human resource planning—or employment planning, as it is also called—allows the department to staff the organization at the right time with the right people. Not only can it help companies meet their equal-employment goals, but human resource plans also help firms implement their short- and long-range strategic business plans.

If an organization is not properly staffed with the right numbers and types of people, short- and long-range corporate plans may fail. Of course, production, financial, and marketing plans are important cornerstones of a company's strategic plans. More and more executives realize, however, that well-conceived human resource plans are another cornerstone of company plans.[3] For example, the decision of high technology firms like Northern Telecom, IBM, and others to develop new products and enter new markets often depends on the availability of qualified technical and support staff. Without sufficient engineering talent, market opportunities can be lost to more appropriately staffed competitors.

Ideally, all organizations should identify their short-run and long-run employee needs through planning. Short-range plans point out job openings that must be filled during the coming year. Long-range plans estimate the human resource situation two, five, or occasionally ten years into the future. Examples of employment planning are more common in large organizations because it allows them to:

- **Improve** the utilization of human resources.
- **Match** personnel activities and future organization objectives efficiently.
- **Achieve** economies in hiring new workers.
- **Expand** the personnel management information base to assist other personnel activities and other organizational units.
- **Make** major demands on local labour markets successfully.
- **Coordinate** different personnel management programs such as affirmative-action plans and hiring needs.

A small organization can expect similar advantages, but the gains in effectiveness are often considerably less because its situation is less complex. In fact, the benefits of human resource planning for small firms may not justify the time and costs. Consider the different situations faced by a small- and large-city government.

Rural City employs twenty workers and is growing 10% a year. Metropolis has 8,000 employees, and Sy Wolfe estimates it is growing by 5%. That means 400 new employees plus replacements for those who leave. If it costs $400 to find and hire a typi-

cal employee, Rural City will spend $800 to hire two more workers. Metropolis will spend $160,000 just to add new employees. If employment planning saves 25%, Rural City's manager cannot justify detailed planning efforts for $200. But for $40,000, Metropolis can afford a specialist and still save thousands of dollars after planning expenses are deducted.

Nevertheless, knowledge of human resource planning is useful to personnel specialists in *both* small and large organizations. It shows small employers the human resource considerations they will face should they expand rapidly. (For example, if Rural City attracted several large factories to its area, expansion of city services would depend partly on the city's human resource planning.) Large organizations can benefit from knowledge of employment planning because it reveals ways to make the personnel function more effective.

This chapter examines the two dimensions of human resource planning. It begins with an explanation of how the personnel department estimates future job openings, and ends by showing the methods used by personnel experts to isolate potential sources of employees.

THE DEMAND FOR HUMAN RESOURCES

An organization's future demand for people is central to employment planning. Most firms try to predict their future employment needs (at least informally), but they may not estimate their sources of supply. For example, one study found that employers are two times more likely to estimate demand than supply.[4] The challenges that determine this demand and the methods of forecasting it merit brief review.

CAUSES OF DEMAND

Although countless challenges influence the demand for human resources, changes in the environment, the organization, and the work force are usually involved.[5] These factors are common to both short-range and long-range employment plans. The causes of these changes are summarized in Figure 6-1. Some of these causes are within the organization's control and others are not.

Figure 6-1
CAUSES OF DEMAND FOR HUMAN RESOURCES IN THE FUTURE

External	Organizational	Work Force
• Economics	• Strategic plans	• Retirements
• Social-political-legal	• Budgets	• Resignations
• Technology	• Sales and production forecasts	• Terminations
• Competitors	• New ventures	• Deaths
	• Organization and job designs	• Leaves of absence

EXTERNAL CHALLENGES. Developments in the organization's environment are difficult for personnel specialists to predict in the short run and sometimes impossible to estimate in the long run. Reconsider the example of the small-city government. City planners seldom know of major factory relocations until shortly before construction begins. Other *economic* developments have a noticeable effect but are difficult to estimate. Examples include inflation, unemployment, and interest rates. High interest rates, for example, often curtail construction and the need for construction workers.

Social-political-legal challenges are easier to predict, but their implications are seldom clear. The impact on human resource planning of the Canadian Human Rights Act, passed in 1977, is still somewhat unclear. Although most large firms have established affirmative-action programs, the results of a change from the notion of "equal pay for equal work" to that of "equal pay for work of equal value" (see Chapter 3), will have profound implications. Likewise, the effect of patriating the Constitution with a Charter of Rights will not really be known for many years.

Technological changes are difficult to predict and difficult to assess. Many thought the computer would mean mass unemployment, for example. Today it is a major growth industry employing hundreds of thousands directly or indirectly. Very often human resource planning is complicated by technology because it tends to reduce employment in one department while increasing it in another.

Competitors are another external challenge that affects an organization's demand for human resources. Employment in the automobile and steel industries barely grows partially because of foreign competition. But in the electronics industry, competition causes lower prices, larger markets, and additional employment.

ORGANIZATIONAL DECISIONS. Major organizational decisions affect the demand for human resources. The organization's *strategic plan* is the most influential decision.[6] It commits the firm to long-range objectives—such as growth rates and new products, markets, or services. These objectives determine the numbers and types of employees needed in the future. If long-term objectives are to be met, personnel specialists must develop long-range human resource plans that accommodate the strategic plan. In the short run, planners find that strategic plans become operational in the form of *budgets*. Budget increases or cuts are the most significant short-run influence on human resource needs.

Sales and production forecasts are less exact than budgets, but may provide even quicker notice of short-run changes in human resource demand.

The personnel manager for a nationwide chain of furniture outlets observed a sharp decline in sales, brought on by a recession. The personnel manager quickly discarded the short-run human resource plan and imposed an employment freeze on all outlets' hiring plans.

New ventures mean new human resource demands. When begun internally, the lead time may allow planners to develop short-run and long-run employment plans. But new ventures begun by acquisitions and mergers cause an immediate revision of human resource demands. For example, any of these decisions can lead to new organization and job designs. A reorganization, especially after a merger or an acquisition, can radically alter human resource needs. Likewise, the redesign of jobs changes the required skill levels of future workers.

WORK-FORCE FACTORS. The demand for human resources is modified by employee actions. Retirements, resignations, terminations, deaths, and leaves of absence all increase the need for human resources. When large numbers of employees are involved, past experience usually serves as a reasonably accurate guide. However, reliance on past experiences means that personnel specialists must be sensitive to changes that upset past trends.

Presently, Jim Santino keeps close track of employees nearing retirement so that his human resource plan remains accurate. Although the establishment of a mandatory retirement age in Canada is not considered discriminatory, as it is in the United States, the law could change. In such a case, Jim could no longer use his past experience as a guide to predicting when older workers would retire. Such a change would force Jim to seek other ways of forecasting his short-term human resource needs.

FORECASTING TECHNIQUES

Human resource forecasts are attempts to predict an organization's future demand for employees. As Figure 6-2 shows, forecasting techniques range from the informal to the sophisticated. Even the most sophisticated methods are not perfectly accurate; instead, they are best viewed as approximations. Most firms only make casual estimates about the immediate future. As they gain experience with forecasting human resource needs, they may use more sophisticated techniques (especially if they can afford the specialized staff). Each of the forecasting methods in Figure 6-2 is explained below.

Figure 6-2
FORECASTING TECHNIQUES FOR ESTIMATING FUTURE HUMAN RESOURCE NEEDS

Expert	Trend	Other
• Informal and instant decisions	• Extrapolation	• Budget and planning analysis
• Formal expert survey	• Indexation	• New-venture analysis
• Delphi technique	• Statistical analysis	• Computer models

EXPERT FORECASTS. *Expert forecasters* rely on those who are knowledgeable to estimate future human resource needs. At the first level of complexity, the manager may simply be convinced that the work load justifies another employee.

Manager: *Water and gas bills should be mailed by the tenth of each month. How come they haven't gone out?*

Worker: *I know they should, but we are shorthanded. We used twenty-five hours overtime every week this month. And each billing cycle still takes thirty-four days.*

Manager: *Well, we better get personnel to hire us another clerk. We could pay the salary through lower overtime costs.*

The example of the billing clerk illustrates an informal and instant forecast. But it is not part of a systematic planning effort. A better method is for planners to *survey* managers, who are the experts about their department's future employment needs. The centralization of this information permits formal plans that identify the organization's future demands.

Additional sophistication can be added to the survey approach with the Delphi technique. The *Delphi technique* is to solicit estimates from a group of experts, usually managers. Then personnel department planners act as an intermediary, summarizing the various responses and reporting the findings back to the experts. The experts are surveyed again after they get this feedback. Summaries and surveys are repeated until the experts' opinions begin to agree on future developments. (Usually four or five surveys are enough.) For example, the personnel department may survey all production supervisors and managers until an agreement is reached on the number of replacements needed during the next year.

TREND PROJECTION FORECASTS. Perhaps the quickest forecasting technique is to project past trends. The two simplest methods are extrapolation and indexation. *Extrapolation* involves extending past rates of change into the future. For example, if an average of twenty production workers were hired each month for the past two years, extrapolation indicates that 240 production workers will probably be added during the upcoming year.

Indexation is a method of estimating future employment needs by matching employment growth with some index. A common example is the ratio of production employees to sales. For example, planners may discover that for each million-dollar increase in sales, the production department requires ten new assemblers.

Extrapolation and indexation are crude, short-run approximations because they assume that the causes of demand—external, organizational, and work-force factors—remain constant, which is seldom the case. They are very inaccurate for long-range human resource projections. The more sophisticated *statistical analyses* make allowances for changes in the underlying causes of demand.[7]

OTHER FORECASTING METHODS. There are several other ways planners can estimate the future demand for human resources. One approach is through *budget and planning analysis*. Organizations that need human resource planning generally have detailed budgets and long-range plans. A study of department budgets reveals the financial authorizations for more

Figure 6-3

STAGES OF COMPLEXITY AND SOPHISTICATION IN HUMAN RESOURCE FORECASTING

Stage 1	Stage 2	Stage 3
Managers discuss goals, plans, and thus types and numbers of people needed in the short term.	Annual planning budgeting process includes human resource needs.	Using computer-generated analyses, examine causes of problems and future trends regarding the flow of talent.
Highly informal and subjective.	Specify quantity and quality of talent needs as far as possible.	Use computer to relieve managers of routine forecasting tasks (such as vacancies or turnover).
	Identify problems requiring action: individual or general.	

Source: James W. Walker, "Evaluating the Practical Effectiveness of Human Resource Planning Applications," *Human Resource Management*, Spring 1974, p. 21.

employees. These data plus extrapolations of work-force changes (resignation, terminations, and the like) can provide short-run estimates of human resource needs. Long-term estimates can be made from each department or division's long-range plans.

When new ventures complicate employment planning, planners can use new-venture analysis. *New-venture analysis* requires planners to estimate human resource needs by comparison with firms that already perform similar operations. For example, a petroleum company that plans to open a coal mine can estimate its future employment needs by determining them from employment levels of other coal mines.

The most sophisticated forecasting approaches involve computers. *Computer models* are a series of mathematical formulas that simultaneously use extrapolation, indexation, survey results, and estimates of work-force changes to compute future human resource needs. Over time, actual changes in human resource demand are used to refine the computer's formulas.

One expert suggests that there are four levels of complexity in human resource forecasting.[8] These stages of forecasting sophistication are summarized in Figure 6-3. As can be seen, they range from informal discussions to highly complex computerized forecasting systems. The more sophisticated techniques are found among large organizations that have had years of experience in human resource planning. Small firms or those just beginning to forecast human resource needs are more likely to start with Stage 1 and progress to other stages as planners seek greater accuracy.

Figure 6-3 (cont.)
STAGES OF COMPLEXITY AND SOPHISTICATION IN HUMAN RESOURCE FORECASTING

Stage 4

On-line modelling and computer simulation of talent needs, flows, and costs to aid in a continuing process of updating and projecting needs, staffing plans, career opportunities, and thus program plans.

Provide best possible current information for managerial decisions.

Exchange data with other companies and with government (such as economic, employment, and social data).

HUMAN RESOURCE REQUIREMENTS

Figure 6-4 depicts an overview of the key considerations involved in estimating demand for human resources. It shows that forecasts translate the causes of demand into short-range and long-range statements of needs. The resulting long-range plans are, of necessity, general statements of *probable* needs. Specific numbers are either omitted or estimated.

Figure 6-4
COMPONENTS OF THE FUTURE DEMAND FOR HUMAN RESOURCES

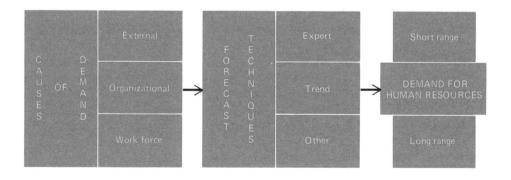

Figure 6-5

A PARTIAL STAFFING TABLE FOR A CITY GOVERNMENT

METROPOLIS
CITY GOVERNMENT
STAFFING TABLE

Date Compiled: _____

Budget Code Number	Job Title (As Found on Job Description)	Using Department(s)	Anticipated Openings by Months of the Year												
			Total	1	2	3	4	5	6	7	8	9	10	11	12
100–32	Police Recruit	Police	128	32			32			32			32		
100–33	Police Dispatcher	Police	3	2					1						
100–84	Meter Reader	Police	24	2	2	2	2	2	2	2	2	2	2	2	2
100–85	Traffic Supervisor	Police	5	2			1			1			1		
100–86	Team Supervisor —Police (Sergeant)	Police	5	2			1			1			1		
100–97	Duty Supervisor —Police (Staff Sergeant)	Police	2	1					1						
100–99	Shift Officer— Police (Inspector)	Police	1	1											
200–01	Car Washer	Motor Pool	4	1			1			1			1		
200–12	Mechanic's Assistant	Motor Pool	3				1			1			1		
200–13	Mechanic III	Motor Pool	2	1									1		
200–14	Mechanic II	Motor Pool	1						1						
200–15	Mechanic I (Working Supervisor)	Motor Pool	1	1											
300–01	Clerk IV	Administration	27	10			5			6			6		

Short-term plans are more specific and may be reported as a staffing table, as in Figure 6-5. A *staffing table* lists the future employment needs for each type of job. The listing may be a specific number or an approximate range of needs, depending on the accuracy of the underlying forecast. Staffing tables (also called manning tables) are neither complete nor wholly accurate. They are only approximations. But these estimates allow personnel specialists to match short-run demand and supply. They help operating departments run more smoothly and can enhance the image of the personnel department.

Sy Wolfe: *If you are selected as the city's human resource planner, how will your employment projections help the city?*

Jean-Marie Gasse: *Earlier you commented that the personnel department spent considerable time reacting to daily requests for new employees. Some requests are for replacements, and others are for new employees for expanding city services. Right?*

Sy Wolfe: *Yes, but . . .*

Jean-Marie Gasse: *My employment projections will allow your department to stop reacting to openings after the fact. Instead, people could be found and prepared in anticipation of job openings.*

Sy Wolfe: *If we could do that, it would really reduce the disruptions managers experience while waiting for replacements to be found, assigned, and taught their jobs.*
Jean-Marie Gasse: *Yes. And their usual gripes about how long it takes the personnel department to fill jobs would diminish greatly.*

With specific estimates of future human resource needs, personnel specialists can become more proactive and systematic. For example, a review of Figure 6-5 shows that the city's personnel department must hire thirty-two police academy recruits every three months. This knowledge allows recruiters in the personnel department to plan their recruiting campaign so that it peaks about six weeks before the beginning of the next police academy class. The advanced planning allows the department to screen applicants and notify them at least three weeks before the class begins. For those still in school or otherwise unable to be ready that quickly, recruiters can inform them when the following class begins. If the personnel department waited for the police department to notify them, notification might come too late to allow a systematic recruiting and screening process. Staffing tables enable recruiters to be proactive and better plan their activities.

THE SUPPLY OF HUMAN RESOURCES

Once the personnel department makes projections about future human resource demands, the next major concern is filling projected openings. There are two sources of supply: internal and external. The internal supply consists of present employees who can be promoted, transferred, or demoted to meet anticipated needs. For example, Jean-Marie Gasse (in the previous dialogue) works in the police department of Metropolis but is applying for a transfer into the personnel department. She is part of the internal supply of human resources to the city government. The external supply consists of people in the labour market who do not work for the city. These include employees of other organizations and those who are unemployed.

Figure 6-6 illustrates the major supply considerations that confront human resource planners. As can be seen, internal and external considerations are intertwined. For ease of explanation, they are discussed separately.

Figure 6-6
FACTORS THAT DETERMINE THE FUTURE SUPPLY OF HUMAN RESOURCES

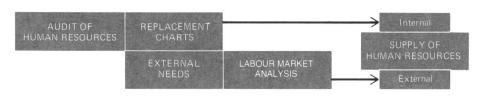

INTERNAL SUPPLY ESTIMATES

Estimates of the internal supply are more than merely counting the number of employees. As Figure 6-6 implies, planners audit the present work force to learn about the capabilities of present workers. This information allows planners to estimate tentatively which openings can be filled by present employees. These tentative assignments usually are recorded on a replacement chart. Considering present employees for future job openings is important if workers are to have life-long careers with their employer rather than just dead-end jobs.

Audits and replacement charts also are important additions to the personnel department's information base. With greater knowledge of employees, the department can more effectively plan recruiting, training, and career-planning activities. Personnel can also help meet its affirmative-action goals by identifying internal minority candidates for job openings. Since audits and replacement charts are important to proactive personnel work, they are explained more fully below.[9]

HUMAN RESOURCE AUDITS. *Human resource audits* summarize each employee's skills and abilities. When referring to nonmanagers, the audits result in *skills inventories*. Audits of managers are called *management inventories*. Whatever name is used, an inventory catalogues each employee's skills and abilities. This summary gives planners a comprehensive understanding of the capabilities found in the organization's work force.

An example of a skills inventory is found in Figure 6-7. It is divided into four parts. Part I can be completed by the personnel department from employee records. It identifies the employee's job title, experience, age, and previous jobs. Part II seeks information about skills, duties, responsibilities, and education of the worker. From these questions, planners learn about the mix of employee abilities. The personnel department may collect these data through phone or face-to-face interviews. Or the questions may be sent to the employee through the company mail.

The employee's future potential is briefly summarized by the immediate supervisor in Part III. Performance, readiness for promotion, and any deficiencies are noted here. The supervisor's signature helps ensure that the form's accuracy is reviewed by someone who knows the employee better than the personnel specialists. Part IV is added as a final check for completeness and for the addition of recent employee evaluations, which give more insight into past performance.

To be useful, inventories of human resources must be updated periodically. Updating every two years is sufficient for most organizations if employees are encouraged to report major changes to the personnel department when they occur. Major changes include new skills, degree completions, changed job duties, and the like. Failure to update skills inventories can lead to present employees being overlooked for job openings within the organization.

Figure 6-7

SKILLS INVENTORY FORM FOR METROPOLIS CITY GOVERNMENT

Part I (To be completed by personnel department)
1. **Name** _____   2. **Employee Number** _____
3. **Job Title** _____   4. **Experience** _____ Years
5. **Age** _____   6. **Years with City** _____
7. **Other Jobs Held:**

    With City: Title _____ From _____ to _____

                    Title _____ From _____ to _____

    Elsewhere: Title _____ From _____ to _____

                    Title _____ From _____ to _____

Part II (To be completed by employee)

8. **Special Skills.** List below any skills you possess, even if they are not used in your present job. Include types and names of machines or tools with which you are experienced.

      Skills: _____

                _____

  Machines: _____

      Tools: _____

9. **Duties.** Briefly describe your present duties.

_____

10. **Responsibilities.** Briefly describe your responsibilities for:

      City Equipment: _____

           City Funds: _____

    Employee Safety: _____

Employee Supervision: _____

11. **Education.** Briefly describe your education and training background:

	Years Completed	**Year of Graduation**	**Degree and Major**
High School:	_____	_____	_____
University:	_____	_____	_____
	_____	_____	_____
Job Training:	_____		
Special Courses:	_____		

Part III (To be completed by personnel department with supervisory inputs)

12. **Overall Evaluation of Performance** _____

_____

13. **Overall Readiness for Promotion** _____

    To What Job(s): _____

      Comments: _____

14. **Current Deficiencies** _____

_____

15. **Supervisor's Signature** _____ **Date:** _____

Part IV (To be completed by personnel department representative)

16. **Are the two most recent performance evaluations attached?** ____ Yes ____ No
17. **Prepared by** _____ **Date:** _____

Management inventories should be updated periodically, since they also are used for key personnel decisions. In fact, some employers use the same form for managers and nonmanagers. When the forms differ, the management inventory requests information about management activities. Common topics include:

- Number of employees supervised
- Total budget managed
- Duties of subordinates
- Types of employees supervised
- Management training received
- Previous management duties

REPLACEMENT CHARTS. *Replacement charts* are a visual representation of who will replace whom in the event of a job opening. The information for constructing the chart comes from the human resource audit. Figure 6-8 illustrates a typical replacement chart. It shows the replacement status of only a few jobs in the administration of a large city.

Figure 6-8
A PARTIAL REPLACEMENT CHART FOR A MUNICIPAL GOVERNMENT

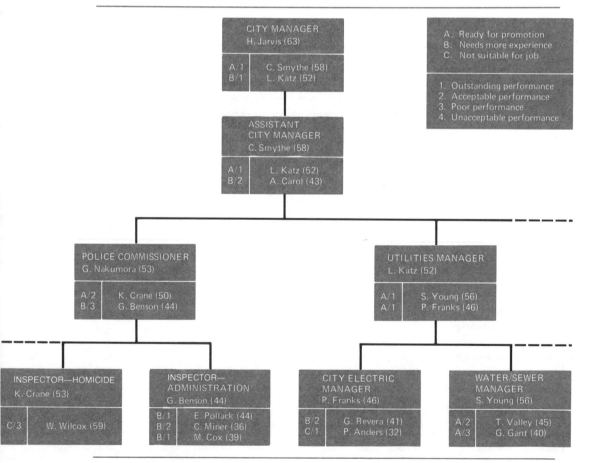

Although different firms may seek to summarize different information in their replacement charts, the figure indicates the minimum information usually included. The chart, which is much like an organization chart, depicts the various jobs in the organization and shows the status of likely candidates. Replacement status consists of two variables: present performance and promotability. Present performance is determined largely from supervisory evaluations. Opinions of other managers, peers, and subordinates may contribute to the appraisal of present performance. Future promotability is based primarily on present performance and the estimates by immediate superiors of future success in a new job. The personnel department may contribute to these estimates through the use of psychological tests, interviews, and other methods of assessment. Replacement charts often show the candidates' ages.

Personnel and management decision makers find these charts provide a quick reference. Their shortcoming is that they contain little information.[10] To supplement the chart—and, increasingly, to supplant it—personnel specialists develop replacement summaries. *Replacement summaries* list likely replacements and their relative strengths and weaknesses for each job. As Figure 6-9 shows, the summaries provide considerably more data than the replacement chart. This additional information allows decision makers to make more informed decisions.

Most companies that are sophisticated enough to engage in detailed human resource planning computerize their personnel records, including job analysis information and human resource inventories. Then through a simple computer program, planners can compile replacement summaries each time a job opening occurs. These summaries also show which positions lack human resource backups. In the long run, the personnel department can encourage employees to upgrade their capabilities and prepare for future vacancies. In the short run, an opening without a suitable replacement requires someone to be hired from the external labour market.

Whether replacement charts or summaries are used, this information is normally kept confidential. Confidentiality not only guards the privacy of employees, but prevents dissatisfaction among those who are not immediately promotable.

EXTERNAL SUPPLY ESTIMATES

Not every future opening can be met with present employees. Some jobs lack replacements to fill an opening when it occurs. Other jobs are entry-level positions; that is, they are beginning jobs which are filled by people who do not presently work for the organization. When there are no replacements or when the opening is for an entry-level job, there is a need for external supplies of human resources.

EXTERNAL NEEDS. Employer growth and the effectiveness of the personnel department largely determine the need for external supplies of human

Figure 6-9
A REPLACEMENT SUMMARY FOR THE POSITION OF CITY MANAGER

Replacement Summary for the Position of   City Manager

Present Office Holder   Harold Jarvis   **Age** 63

Probable Opening   In two years   **Reason** Retirement

Salary Grade   99 ($78,500 yearly)   **Experience** 8 years

Candidate 1   Clyde Smythe   **Age** 58

Current Position   Assistant City Manager   **Experience** 4 years

Current Performance   Outstanding   **Explanation**   Clyde's performance evaluations
by the City Manager are always the highest possible.

Promotability   Ready now for promotion.   **Explanation**   During an extended illness of the
City Manager, Clyde assumed all duties successfully, including major policy decisions
and negotiations with city unions.

Training Needs   None

Candidate 2   Larry Katz   **Age** 52

Current Position   Utilities Manager   **Experience** 5 years

Current Performance   Outstanding   **Explanation**   Larry's performance has kept costs
of utilities to citizens 10 to 15% below that of comparable city utilities through careful planning.

Promotability   Needs more experience.   **Explanation**   Larry's experience is limited to
utilities management. Although successful, he needs more broad administrative experience
in other areas. (He is ready for promotion to Assistant City Manager at this time.)

Training Needs   Training in budget preparation and public relations would be desirable
before promotion to City Manager.

---

resources. Growth is primarily responsible for the number of entry-level job openings. Obviously, a fast-growing firm has more beginning-level vacancies. The number of higher-level openings also depends on how well the personnel department assists employees to develop their capabilities. If workers are not encouraged to expand their capabilities, they may not be ready to fill future vacancies. The lack of promotable replacements creates job openings that need to be filled externally.

LABOUR MARKET ANALYSIS. The personnel department's success in finding new employees depends on the labour market. Even when unemployment rates are high, many needed skills are difficult to find.

In January 1984 the unemployment rate was 12.4%. However, personnel departments that sought managers and administrators had to compete in a labour market with only 4.7% of these people unemployed.[11]

In the short run, the national unemployment rate serves as an approximate measure of how difficult it is to acquire new employees. Personnel specialists realize that this rate varies for different groups as well as from province to province and city to city.

In 1984 there were some wide variations. The unemployment rate in Saskatchewan during January was 8.6%. But in Newfoundland the rate was 21.7%.[12]

Regardless of the unemployment rate, external needs may be met by attracting employees who work for others. In the long run, local developments and demographic trends have the most significant impact on labour markets.[13] Local developments include community growth rates and attitudes. For example, many farm towns find their population declining. When they attempt to attract new business, employers fear declining population may mean future shortages in the local labour market. So the new businesses often locate elsewhere. The lack of jobs results in still more people leaving the local labour market. Conversely, growing cities are attractive to employers because they promise even larger labour markets in the future.

COMMUNITY ATTITUDES. Community attitudes also affect the nature of the labour market. Antibusiness or no-growth attitudes may cause present employers to move elsewhere. The loss of jobs forces middle-class workers to relocate, and the shrinking work force discourages new businesses from becoming established.

DEMOGRAPHICS. Demographic trends are another long-term development that affects the availability of external supply. Fortunately for planners, these trends are known years in advance of their impact.

The low birthrates of the 1930s and early 1940s were followed by a baby boom during the late 1940s and 1950s. When the post–World War II babies started to go to university in the 1960s, the low birthrates of the 1930s led to a shortage of university teachers. These demographic trends were already in motion by 1950. Long-range human resource planning, which was sensitive to demographic developments, could have predicted the shortage soon enough for proactive universities to take corrective action.

Canada Employment and Immigration publishes both short- and long-term labour force projections. One document, *Ford Occupational Imbalance Listing* (FOIL), is a quarterly publication that estimates both labour market demands (by occupation) and supply characteristics. A longer-term projection, typically six years, is provided by the *Canada Occupational Forecasting Program* (COFOR). This document is available in both national and provincial versions, but it forecasts only demand requirements. Statistics Canada also publishes reports on labour-force conditions on a monthly, quarterly, annual, and occasional basis. Information is available on: total labour force projections by geographic, demographic, and occupational variables; labour income; census data; and population projections by sex and province over various years. For example, Figure 6-10 shows the

Figure 6-10
CHANGES IN THE TOTAL LABOUR FORCE

Age, Both Sexes	Projected Numbers (Thousands)		
	1985	1990	1995
16 years and over:	19,589	20,821	22,013
16 to 24	4,036	3,569	3,557
25 to 54	10,718	12,012	12,891
25 to 34	4,640	4,997	4,702
35 to 44	3,565	4,201	4,705
45 to 54	2,513	2,814	3,484
55 years and over:	4,834	5,239	5,565
55 to 64	2,284	2,308	2,340
65 and over	2,551	2,931	3,225

Source: Statistics Canada, *Population Projections for Canada and the Provinces 1976–2001*, Catalogue 91-520, Ottawa: Industry, Trade, and Commerce, 1979.

projected composition of the work force by age from 1985 to 1995. These data have implications for many businesses.

Fast-food restaurants depend on 16- to 24-year-olds for many jobs. But by 1995 this group will have declined by approximately 500 thousand. At the same time, population growth and the trend toward eating more meals away from home will cause an increased demand for fast-food employees.

IMPLEMENTATION OF HUMAN RESOURCE PLANS

Figure 6-11 summarizes the key concepts discussed throughout the chapter. The left side of the figure identifies the major causes of human resource demand, which are external, organizational, and work force factors. These causes of demand are forecast by experts, trend data, or other methods to determine the short- and long-range demand for human resources. This demand is fulfilled either internally by present employees or externally by newcomers. The internal supply is shown in replacement charts which are based on audits of the organization's human resources. Sources of external candidates are identified by analysis of the labour market. The results include short- and long-range human resource plans that are fulfilled by an internal and external staffing process.

Once the supply and demand of human resources are estimated, adjustments may be needed. When the internal supply of workers exceeds the firm's demand, a *human resource surplus* exists. Most employers respond to a surplus with a hiring freeze. This freeze stops the personnel department from filling openings with external applicants. Instead, present employees are reassigned. Voluntary departures, called *attrition*, slowly reduce the surplus.[14] If the surplus persists, leaves of absence are encouraged.

Layoffs, the temporary withdrawal of employment to workers, are also used in cases of a short-run surplus. If the surplus is expected to persist into the foreseeable future, employers often encourage early retirement on

Figure 6-11
SUPPLY AND DEMAND CONSIDERATION IN HUMAN RESOURCE PLANNING

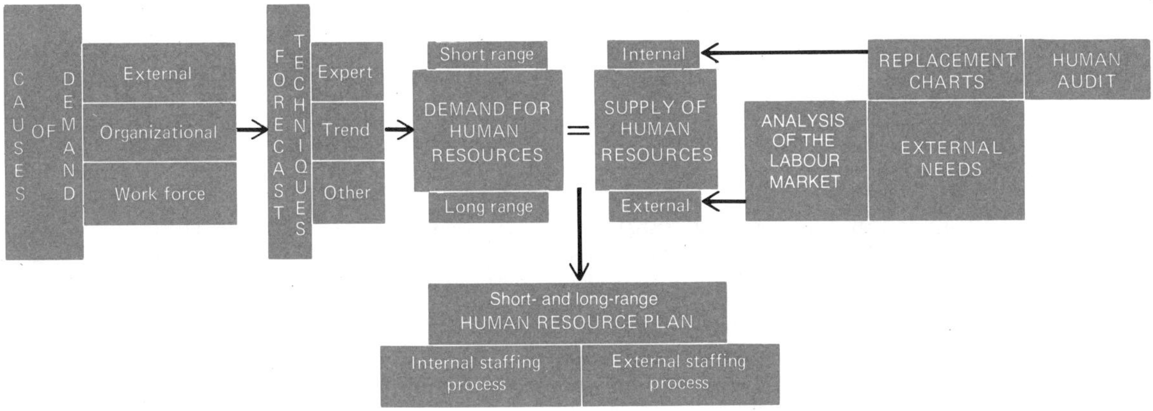

a *voluntary* basis. Should the surplus still persist, employees are discharged. The blow of discharge may be softened through formal *outplacement* procedures, which help present employees find new jobs with other firms. These efforts may include the provision of office space, secretarial services, photocopying machines, long-distance phone calls, counselling, instructions on how to look for work, and even invitations to competitors to meet with employees.[15]

If the internal supply cannot fulfill the organization's needs, a human resource *shortage* exists. Planners have little flexibility in the short run. They must rely on the external staffing process and find new employees. In the long run, responses can be more flexible. Planners can use the internal staffing process; that is, they can redouble efforts to have employees develop the necessary knowledge, skills, and attitudes.

Whether staffing needs are met internally or externally, planners must consider their employer's affirmative-action plan. That plan, as discussed in Chapter 3, contains the company's strategy for undoing past discrimination and guarding against future discrimination. As internal and external candidates are selected to fill job openings, these decisions must match the goals and timetables found in the affirmative-action plan. The human resource plan also indicates how likely it is that the employer's affirmative-action goals will be met. For example, even modest goals of increasing minority representation in a company are unlikely to happen if the human resource plan indicates that no new hiring is planned and the company intends to reduce overall employment through attrition.

The human resource plan does more than serve as a check on the likelihood of the affirmative-action plan's success. It is an important part of an organization's *human resource information system*. The information contained in the plan serves as a guide to recruiters, trainers, career planners, and other human resource specialists. With the knowledge of the firm's internal and external employment needs, personnel specialists, operating managers, and individual employees can direct their efforts toward the organization's future staffing needs. Managers can groom their employees through specific training and development efforts. Even individual employees can prepare themselves for future openings through education and other self-help efforts.

SUMMARY

Human resource planning requires considerable time, staff, and financial resources. The return on this investment may not justify the expenditure for small firms. Increasingly, however, large organizations use human resource planning as a means of achieving greater effectiveness. Human resource planning is an attempt by personnel departments to estimate their future needs and supplies of human resources. Through an understanding of the factors that influence the demand for workers, planners can forecast specific short-term and long-term needs.

Given some anticipated level of demand, planners try to estimate the availability of present workers to meet that demand. Such estimates begin with an audit of present employees. Then possible replacements are identified. Internal shortages are resolved by seeking new employees in the external labour markets. Surpluses are reduced by normal attrition, leaves of absence, layoffs, or terminations.

As can be seen in Figure 6-11, both the external and internal staffing processes are used to meet human resource plans. The figure also summarizes the key concepts discussed in this chapter. The next two chapters explain the external staffing process in detail. Then Part 3 of the book discusses the internal staffing process.

TERMS FOR REVIEW

Strategic plan	Skills inventories
Forecasts	Replacement charts
Delphi technique	Replacement summaries
Extrapolation	Labour market analysis
Indexation	Attrition
Staffing table	Outplacement

REVIEW AND DISCUSSION QUESTIONS

1. Why is human resource planning more common among large organizations than among small ones? What are the advantages of human resource planning for large organizations?
2. List and briefly describe the factors that cause an organization's demand for human resources to change.

3. What is a staffing table? Of what use is it to human resource planners?

4. What is the purpose of a human resource audit? Specifically, what information acquired from a human resource audit is needed to construct a replacement chart?

5. Suppose human resource planners estimated that several technological innovations suggest that your firm will need 25% fewer employees in three years. What actions would you take today?

6. Suppose you managed a restaurant in a winter resort area. During the summer it was profitable to keep the business open, but you need only one-half the cooks, tables servers, and bartenders. What actions would you take in April when the peak tourist season ended?

7. Review the demographic trends in Figure 6-10. What industries might have problems finding enough employees externally in 1995?

8. If your company locates its research and development offices in downtown Windsor, Ontario, the city is willing to forgo city property taxes on the building for ten years. The city is willing to make this concession to help reduce its high unemployment rate. Calgary, Alberta, your company's other choice, has a low unemployment rate and is not offering any tax breaks. Based on just these considerations, which city would you recommend and why?

INCIDENT 6-1
EASTERN UNIVERSITY'S HUMAN RESOURCE NEEDS

For years Eastern University had operated at a deficit. This loss was made up from the provincial budget, since Eastern was provincially supported. With the inflation of the 1970s and 80s, the drain on the province's budget had tripled to $71 million by 1982.

Several members of the provincial cabinet had heard that university enrolments were to continue to decline during the 1980s. A decline in enrolment would lead to overstaffing and even large deficits. The president of the university hired Bill Barker to develop a long-range human resource plan for the university. An excerpt from his report stated:

> *The declining birthrates of the 1960s and 1970s mean that there will be a decline in university-age students at least to the year 2000. If the university is to avoid soaring deficits, it must institute an employment freeze now. Furthermore, a committee should be formed to develop new curricula that appeal to those segments of the work force that are going to experience rapid growth between now and the year 2000.*

Zach Taylor, president of Eastern University, argued, "An employment freeze would cut the university off from hiring new faculty members who have the latest training in new areas. Besides, our enrolments have grown by 2 to 4% every year since 1970. I see no reason to doubt that trend will continue."

1. Assuming you are a member of the provincial cabinet, would you recommend that the university implement an employment freeze or not?

2. If Bill Barker had used national birthrate information, what other population information could the president use to support his argument that the university will probably keep growing?

3. Are there any strategies you would recommend that would allow the university to hire newly trained faculty and avoid serious budget deficits in the 1990s if enrolments do drop?

INCIDENT 6-2
HUMAN RESOURCE PLANNING IN THE BELL SYSTEM

For many years, the American Telephone and Telegraph Company has been the largest private employer in the United States. At a recent conference on human resource planning, Mr. W. S. Cashel, Jr., vice chairman and chief financial officer of AT&T, made the following observations about employment in the Bell System of AT&T:

• *In 1977, the Bell System had to process and interview thirty applicants in order to hire one new employee.*

• *In 1966, telephone operators represented about 24% of the phone company's work force. Ten years later, operators counted for only 17% of the work force.*

• *Between 1978 and 1980, employment in the central office will fall from 2,733 to 850 because of automation and technological advances.*

• *Between 1978 and 1983, about half (180) of the officers of the Bell System will have to be replaced.*

• *Nearly three-quarters of the company's operating expenses go to people-related costs.*

• *During the next twenty-five years, the Bell System will be serving about 28 million more households—a 50% increase.*

1. Assume that the Bell System is able to meet its increasing demand for services primarily through automation of clerical, operator, and technical positions without changing its total employment. What implications exist for meeting future staffing needs?

2. How might detailed staffing tables help the Bell System reduce the number of applicants that must be processed for each new employee hired?

REFERENCES

1. Bernard Taylor and Gordon L. Lippitt, *Management Development and Training Handbook*, New York: McGraw-Hill Book Company, 1975, p. ix.
2. George T. Milkovich and Thomas A. Mahoney, "Human Resource Planning Models: A Perspective," in James W. Walker (ed.), *The Challenge of Human Resource Planning: Selected Readings*, New York: Human Resource Planning Society, 1979, pp. 73–84.
3. Eddie C. Smith, "Strategic Business Planning and Human Resources: Part I," *Personnel Journal*, August 1982, pp. 606–610. (Part II appears in *Personnel Journal*, September 1982, pp. 680–682.)
4. Herbert Heneman and G. Seltzer, *Employer Manpower Planning and Forecasting* (Manpower Research Monograph No. 19), Washington: U.S. Department of Labor, 1970, p. 42.
5. Elmer H. Burack, *Strategies for Manpower Planning and Programming*, Morristown, N.J.: General Learning Press, 1972, pp. 1–8.
6. James W. Walker, "Linking Human Resources Planning and Strategic Planning," *Human Resource Planning*, Spring 1978, pp. 1–18.
7. Don Bryant, "Manpower Planning Models and Techniques," *Business Horizons*, April 1973, pp. 69–73. See also David J. Bartholomew, "Statistics in Human Resource Planning," *Human Resource Planning*, November 1978, pp. 67–77.
8. James W. Walker, "Evaluating the Practical Effectiveness of Human Resource Planning Applications," *Human Resource Management*, Spring 1974, p. 21.
9. David L. Chicci, "Four Steps to an Organizational/Human Resource Plan," *Personnel Journal*, June 1979, p. 392.
10. James W. Walker, "Human Resource Planning: Managerial Concerns and Practices," *Business Horizons*, June 1976, pp. 56–57.

11. Statistics Canada, *The Labour Force*, Catalogue No. 71-001, January 1984, Ottawa: Minister of Supply and Services, p. 70.
12. Ibid., p. 32.
13. Eli Ginzberg, *The Manpower Connection*, Cambridge, Mass.: Harvard University Press, 1975.
14. Kendrith M. Rowland and Scott L. Summers, "Human Resource Planning: A Second Look," *Personnel Administration*, December 1981, pp. 73–80. See also William H. Hoffman and L. L. Wyatt, "Human Resource Planning," *Personnel Administrator*, January 1977, pp. 19–23.
15. Dane Henriksen, "Outplacement: Guidelines that Ensure Success," *Personnel Journal*, August 1982, pp. 583–589. See also Joel A. Bearak, "Termination Made Easier: Is Outplacement Really the Answer?" *Personnel Administrator*, April 1982, pp. 63–71, 99; Jack Mendleson, "Does Your Company Really Need Outplacement?" *SAM Advanced Management Journal*, Winter 1975, pp. 4–12; Jack Mendleson, "What's Fair Treatment for Terminated Employees?" *Supervisory Management*, November 1974, pp. 25–34; and Donald H. Sweet, *Recruitment: A Guide for Managers*, Menlo Park, Calif.: Addison-Wesley Publishing Company, 1975.

Chapter *7*

Recruitment of Human Resources

It seems likely ... that by the mid-1980s the major constraint on corporate growth will not necessarily be a shortage of monetary or material resources, but rather a shortage of managerial resources....

John B. Miner[1]

CHAPTER OBJECTIVES

After studying this chapter, you should be able to:
1. **Explain** the constraints under which the recruitment process occurs.
2. **Identify** the appropriate recruiting methods for finding and attracting different types of recruits.
3. **Describe** the major employment-related services provided by Canada Employment Centres.
4. **Develop** an appropriate job application form.
5. **Diagram** the major features of the recruitment process.

Finding new employees for the organization is a continuing challenge for most personnel departments. Sometimes the need for new workers is known well in advance because of detailed human resource plans. At other times, the personnel department is faced with urgent requests for replacements that must be filled as quickly as possible. In either case, finding qualified applicants is a key activity.

Shirley Dodd was a junior mechanical engineer for Blakely Electronics when she quit to work for a competitor. Her resignation created a problem for the head of the mechanical engineering department, Sid Benson. As he expressed it, "She was doing an important job of developing the mechanical tolerances for our new electronic scale. It was all theoretical work, but it was going to save three months' worth of product development time. We must have a bright junior engineer to complete her work. I hope someone can be recruited."

Recruitment is the process of finding and attracting capable individuals to apply for employment. The process begins when new recruits are sought and ends when their applications are submitted. The result is a pool of job-seekers from which new employees are selected.

Responsibility for recruitment usually belongs to the personnel department. This responsibility is important because the quality of an organization's human resources depends upon the quality of its recruits. Since large
organizations recruit almost continuously, their personnel departments
use specialists in the recruiting process. These specialists are called *recruiters*.

Recruiters work to find and attract capable applicants. Their methods depend on the situation, since there is no one best recruiting technique. Normally, recruiters follow several steps. As Figure 7-1 illustrates, recruiters
identify job openings through human resource planning or requests by
managers. Then recruiters learn about the job's requirements from job
analysis information and talks with the requesting manager. The job's requirements influence the recruiter's methods of finding satisfactory applicants.

Figure 7-1
AN OVERVIEW OF THE RECRUITMENT PROCESS

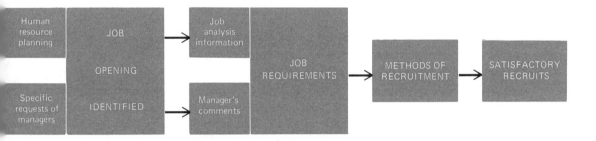

In recent years, primarily as a result of the recession, employers have
found that it is much easier to attract potential employees. In education, for
example, it is not uncommon to have hundreds of applicants for a vacancy.
However, this situation can lull the personnel department into a false sense
of security, for two reasons. First, the recession will—hopefully—not be
with us forever. As a result of the current ease of attracting applicants,
some personnel departments have become very lax in their recruitment efforts and may well end up paying the price for this laxness in years to come.
Second, recruitment, as will be discussed in this chapter, involves far more
than just getting people to apply for jobs. An effective recruitment process
involves all the aspects shown in Figure 7-1; therefore, success in recruiting
is not simply measured by the number of applications received. The right
type of applicants are far more important than the number of applicants.

*Sid Benson, head of mechanical engineering at Blakely Electronics, requested that
the personnel department find a new junior engineer. Charles Shaw, a recruiter, reviewed the job's requirements and discovered that applicants should have a basic
understanding of mechanical engineering concepts. No experience was required. This*

requirement of knowledge but not experience led Charles to seek applicants from among the graduating class of a small engineering-oriented university in the area.

This illustration makes several assumptions about Charles's role as a recruiter. It assumes that he knows the organizational and environmental constraints under which recruiting occurs at Blakely. It also assumes that he is aware of other sources of recruits but rejects those alternatives as inferior. Lastly, it assumes he will find people who are interested in applying for a job at Blakely Electronics.

These assumptions outline the key issues covered in this chapter: the constraints encountered in recruitment, the channels through which recruits are found and attracted, and the nature of application forms.

CONSTRAINTS ON RECRUITMENT

A successful recruiter must be sensitive to the constraints on the recruitment process. These limits arise from the organization, the recruiter, and the external environment. Although the emphasis may vary from situation to situation, the following list includes the most common constraints:

- Organizational policies
- Human resource plans
- Affirmative-action programs
- Recruiter habits
- Environmental conditions
- Job requirements

ORGANIZATIONAL POLICIES

Organizational policies are a potent source of constraints. Policies seek to achieve uniformity, economies, public relations benefits, and other objectives unrelated to recruiting. Those policies that may affect recruitment are highlighted below.

PROMOTE-FROM-WITHIN POLICIES. Promote-from-within policies are intended to give present employees the first opportunity for job openings. These policies are widespread. In a U.S. study, 76% of the organizations reported that they fill a majority of their openings internally.[2] Promote-from-within policies aid employee morale, attract recruits looking for jobs with a future, and help retain present employees. Although these policies reduce the flow of new people and ideas into different levels of the organization, the alternative is to pass over employees in favour of outsiders. By-passing current employees can lead to employee dissatisfaction and turnover. In the junior engineer example, Charles Shaw, the recruiter, should check with present employees—such as technicians who have been studying engineering at night school—before a new engineer is recruited.

COMPENSATION POLICIES. A common constraint faced by recruiters is pay policies. Organizations with personnel departments usually establish pay ranges for different jobs. If Charles Shaw finds a promising candidate, the pay range will influence the job seeker's desire to become a serious applicant. Recruiters seldom have the authority to exceed stated pay ranges. For example, when the market rate for junior engineers is $2,200 to $2,400 per month, satisfactory applicants will be few if Charles can offer only $1,800 to $2,000 per month.

EMPLOYMENT STATUS POLICIES. Some companies have policies restricting the hiring of part-time and temporary employees. Although there is growing interest in hiring these types of workers, such policies are common and can cause recruiters to reject all but those seeking full-time work. Limitations against part-time and temporary employees exclude many individuals from consideration. Likewise, policies against hiring employees who "moonlight" by having second jobs also inhibit recruiters. Prohibitions against holding extra jobs are intended to ensure a rested work force.

INTERNATIONAL HIRING POLICIES. Policies in some countries, including Canada, may also require foreign job openings to be staffed with local citizens. The use of foreign nationals, however, does reduce relocation expenses, lessen the likelihood of nationalization, and, if top jobs are held by local citizens, minimize charges of economic exploitation. Moreover, unlike relocated employees, foreign nationals are more apt to be involved in the local community and understand local customs and business practices.

HUMAN RESOURCE PLANS

The human resource plan is another factor recruiters consider. Through skills inventories and promotion ladders, the plan outlines which jobs should be filled by recruiting and which should be filled internally. The plan helps recruiters because it summarizes future recruiting needs. This foresight can lead to economies in recruiting.

At Blakely Electronics, Charles Shaw checked the human resource plan before recruiting a junior mechanical engineer. The plan indicated a projected need for five junior electrical engineers during the next three months. So Charles decided to recruit electrical engineering candidates at the same time he was looking for a junior mechanical engineer. If advertisements were to be placed in the university newspaper, there would be no additional cost for seeking both types of engineers. Travel costs, advertising costs, and the time devoted to a second recruiting trip would be saved. Since junior engineer is the lowest-level engineering position, it is unlikely that there would be any internal candidates identified in the human resource plan. However, if the opening had been for a more experienced worker, the human resource planning process may have identified potential candidates from within the company.

AFFIRMATIVE-ACTION PROGRAMS

Before recruiting for any position, Charles also checked the organization's voluntary affirmative-action program. The plan indicated a desire to recruit more women and minorities into professional jobs. So Charles had to consider what actions were needed to achieve these goals.

Blakely Electronics never pursued policies that intentionally discriminated against any group. But over the years, its sources of engineering recruits had been mostly white males who attended the small local university. To fulfill the intent of the affirmative-action plan, Charles decided to recruit engineering technicians at a large metropolitan university.

RECRUITER HABITS

A recruiter's past success can lead to habits. Admittedly, habits can eliminate time-consuming deliberations that reach the same answers. However, habits may also perpetuate past mistakes or obscure more effective alternatives. So although recruiters need positive and negative feedback, they must guard against self-imposed constraints.

Consider again the recruitment of the junior engineer at Blakely Electronics. Suppose that the engineering department expresses satisfaction with recruits from the nearby university. Such positive feedback encourages recruiters to make a habit of using this source for beginning engineers. Since all these engineers have a similar curriculum, they may also share strengths and weaknesses. As a result, the engineering department may suffer because of the educational uniformity of new recruits.

ENVIRONMENTAL CONDITIONS

External conditions strongly influence recruitment. Changes in the labour market and the challenges mentioned in Chapter 2 affect recruiting. The unemployment rate, the pace of the economy, spot shortages in specific skills, projections of the labour force by Statistics Canada, labour laws, and the recruiting activities of other employers—all of these affect the recruiter's efforts. Although these factors are considered in human resource planning, the economic environment can change quickly after the plan is finalized. To be sure that the plan's economic assumptions remain valid, recruiters can check three fast-changing measures:

LEADING ECONOMIC INDICATORS. Each month Statistics Canada announces the direction of the leading indicators. These economic indexes suggest the future course of the national economy. If these indexes signal a sudden downturn in the economy, recruiting plans may have to be modified.

PREDICTED VERSUS ACTUAL SALES. Since human resource plans are partially based upon the firm's predicted sales, variations between actual and predicted sales may indicate that these plans also are inaccurate. Thus recruiting efforts may need to be changed accordingly.

WANT-ADS INDEX. Statistics Canada and the Technical Service Council report the volume of want ads in major metropolitan newspapers. An upward trend in this index indicates increased competition for engineers and managers who are recruited on a nationwide basis. For clerical and production workers, who are usually recruited on a local basis, the personnel department may want to create its own index to monitor local changes in want ads.

As the economy, sales, and want ads change, recruiters also must adjust their efforts accordingly. Tighter competition for applicants may require more vigorous recruiting. When business conditions decline, an opposite approach is called for—as the following example illustrates.

As a major recreation centre was opening in Quebec, the leading economic indicators dropped. Although the human resource plan called for recruiting 100 workers a week for the first month, the employment manager set a revised target of 75. Lower recruiting and employment levels helped establish a profitable operation even though first-year admissions fell below the projections used in the human resource plan.

JOB REQUIREMENTS

Of course, the requirements of each job are a constraint. Highly specialized workers, for example, are more difficult to find than unskilled ones. Recruiters learn of a job's demands from the requesting manager's comments and job analysis information. Job analysis information is especially useful because it reveals the important characteristics of the job and applicants. Knowledge of a job's requirements allows the recruiter to choose the best way to find recruits, given the constraints under which the recruiter must operate.

"Find the best and most experienced applicant you can" is often a constraint that is imposed on recruiters as though it were a job requirement. At first this demand seems reasonable: all managers want to have the best and most experienced people working for them. But several potential problems exist with this innocent-sounding request. One problem in seeking out the "best and most experienced" applicant is cost. People with greater experience usually command higher salaries than less experienced people. If a high level of experience is not truly necessary, the recruit may become bored soon after being hired. Moreover, if the personnel department cannot show that a high degree of experience is needed, then experience may be an artificial requirement that discriminates against some applicants. Another point about experience is worth remembering: For some people in some jobs, ten years of experience is another way of saying one year of experience repeated ten times. Someone with ten years of experience may not be any better qualified than an applicant with only one year.[3]

CHANNELS OF RECRUITMENT

The ways of finding recruits are sometimes referred to as *channels*. Recruiters and applicants have historically contacted each other through a few typical channels which are summarized in Figure 7-2. As can be seen from the research reported in the figure, applying directly to the employer (72%) or to Canada Employment Centres (63%), asking friends about jobs where they work (60%), and answering local newspaper ads (49%) are the most commonly used methods. Managers also use job-hunting techniques similar to those shown in Figure 7-2.[4]

Figure 7-2
METHODS USED TO LOOK FOR WORK

Job Search Method	Percentage Who Used Each Method
Asked employer at place of business	72
Canada Manpower Centre or Quebec Employment Centre	63
Asked friends or relatives	60
Answered advertisements	49
Wrote letters of application	26
Checked with trade union or union hiring hall	10
Checked with placement offices	10
Used private employment agency	10

Source: Statistics Canada, *Job Search Patterns in Canada*, Ottawa: Minister of Industry, Trade, and Commerce, November 1975, p. 46.

Figure 7-3 shows that workers tend to use three or more channels to search for employment. However, there was some variation based on the prospective employees' education levels. The channels used by employers parallel those used by workers in order to match job seekers and job openings. Each of these channels is described below.

Figure 7-3
NUMBER OF METHODS USED TO FIND A JOB

Education Level	Mean Number of Methods Used
Elementary	2.8
Some Secondary	3.0
Secondary Complete	3.2
Post Secondary	3.6
All Jobseekers	3.1

Source: Statistics Canada, *Job Search Patterns in Canada*, Ottawa: Minister of Industry, Trade, and Commerce, November 1975, p. 51.

WALK-INS AND WRITE-INS
Walk-ins are jobseekers who arrive at the personnel department in search of a job. *Write-ins* are those who send a written inquiry. They normally are asked to complete an application form to determine their interests and abilities. Suitable applications are kept in an active file until an appropriate opening occurs or until the application is too old to be considered valid—usually six months.

EMPLOYEE REFERRALS

Present employees may refer jobseekers to the personnel department. Employee referrals have several unique advantages. First, employees with hard-to-find job skills may know others who do the same work. For example, a shortage of oilfield workers in Alberta was partially counteracted by having employees ask their friends to apply for the unfilled openings. Second, new recruits already know something about the organization from those employees who referred them. Thus referred applicants may be more strongly attracted to the organization than are walk-ins. Third, employees tend to refer friends who are likely to have similar work habits and work attitudes. Even if work values are different, these candidates may have a strong desire to work hard so that they do not let down the person who recommended them.

Employee referrals are an excellent and legal recruitment technique. However, recruiters must be careful that this method does not intentionally or unintentionally discriminate. The major problem with this recruiting method is that it tends to maintain the racial, religious, sex, and other features of the employer's work force. Such results can be viewed as discriminatory.

ADVERTISING

Advertising is another effective method of seeking recruits. Since it can reach a wider audience than employee referrals or unsolicited walk-ins, many recruiters use it as a key part of their efforts.

Want ads describe the job and the benefits, identify the employer, and tell those who are interested how to apply. They are the most familiar form of employment advertising. For highly specialized recruits, ads may be placed in professional journals or out-of-town newspapers located in areas with high concentrations of the desired skills. For example, recruiters in finance often advertise in Vancouver, Toronto, Montreal, and Halifax newspapers because these cities are major banking centres.

Want ads have some severe drawbacks. They may lead to thousands of job seekers for one popular job opening. Often the ideal recruits are already employed and not reading want ads. Finally, secretly advertising for a recruit to replace a current employee cannot easily be done with traditional want ads.

These problems are avoided with *blind ads*. A blind ad is a want ad that does not identify the employer. Interested applicants are told to send their résumé to a box number at the post office or to the newspaper. The *résumé* (or *vita*), which is a brief summary of the applicant's background, is then forwarded to the employer. These ads allow the opening to remain confidential, prevent countless telephone inquiries, and avoid the public relations problem of disappointed recruits.

As one writer observed, "Recruitment advertising should be written from the viewpoint of the applicant and his or her motivations rather than exclusively from the point of view of the company."[5] Since the cost of most classified advertising is determined by the size of the advertisement, short blurbs are the norm. These ads usually describe the job duties, outline minimum job qualifications, and tell interested readers how to apply. Short phrases and sentences, sometimes written in the second person, are the usual format. Figure 7-4 provides an example. However, some experts doubt that traditional approaches will remain sufficient, particularly when recruiting people with hard-to-find skills or whenever labour markets are tight. As one researcher suggested, want ads

> must contain not only information about the job but also information presented in a way that effectively portrays a message about the job and the company. This can't be done if the ad contains information that explains only what responsibilities the job includes, who can be qualified, where it is located, and how and when to apply. . . .[6]
>
> More important, in today's labour market, where increasing demands are being made for job relevance, quality of work life, and other job satisfaction factors, . . . the need for more descriptive job information and information concerning working environment, supervisory style and organizational climate are necessary.[7]

Figure 7-4
SAMPLE WANT AD

ENGINEERING GRADUATES

Blakely Electronics seeks junior mechanical and electrical engineering trainees for our growing team of engineering professionals. You will work with senior engineers in designing state-of-the-art electronic equipment for home and industry. Qualified applicants will be engineers graduating by the end of this term and wanting immediate employment. Send your résumé and transcripts to: Chuck Norris, Employment Office, Blakely Electronics, P.O. Box 473, Halifax, Nova Scotia B3H 3C3. Do it today for an exciting career tomorrow.

Advertisements for recruits through other media—billboards, television, and radio, for example—are seldom used because the results seldom justify the expense. However, these approaches may be useful when unemployment is low and the target recruits are not likely reading want ads.[8]

CANADA EMPLOYMENT CENTRES

Canada Employment Centres (CECs), through the ten regional offices of the Canadian Employment and Immigration Commission (CEIC) and a national network of four hundred CECs, offer a variety of programs and services for both employers and prospective employees.[9]

To match candidates with job openings, the process works as follows: When an employer has a job opening, the personnel department voluntarily notifies the CEC of the job and its requirements. Typically, the job opening information is then posted at the CEC's Job Information Centre. Here prospective employees can scan the job openings and discuss any vacancy with one of the centre's counsellors. When an applicant expresses interest in some particular job, the counsellors interview that person. Qualified applicants are then referred to the firm.

In larger metropolitan areas (e.g., Vancouver or Toronto) a Metropolitan Order Processing System (MOPS) has recently been established. This is a computerized system that automatically conveys information about vacancies listed with one centre to all other centres in the area. It allows employers to have their vacancy posted easily and quickly in more centres, thus improving their range of selection. On a national basis, CECs are linked via a telephone-computer system into the National Job Bank. Thus employers can make job information available across Canada. For workers who are willing to relocate or employers needing skills not available in their area, such a system provides yet another avenue for achieving their objectives.

Aside from the services already mentioned, most CECs also provide career and vocational counselling services, aptitude and skill assessments, training referrals, special services for women, native peoples, and the handicapped, and numerous other employment-related activities. They have also been involved with many "grant-type" programs such as Local Employment Assistance Programs (LEAP), Summer Youth Employment Programs (SYEP), and Canada Community Services Projects. These programs typically involved a cost-sharing arrangement between employers and the government; thus, through them, organizations were able to obtain funding to support employment of certain kinds of persons.

PRIVATE EMPLOYMENT AGENCIES

Private employment agencies—which now exist in every major metropolitan area—arose to help employers find capable applicants. Placement firms take an employer's request for recruits and then solicit jobseekers, usually through advertising or from walk-ins. Candidates are matched with employer requests and then told to report to the employer's personnel department. The matching process conducted by private agencies varies widely. Some placement services carefully screen applicants for their client. Others simply provide a stream of applicants and let the client's personnel department do most of the screening.

In most provinces it is either illegal for private employment agencies to charge the applicant a fee for placing him or her, or the fees charged are regulated. Most fees are paid by the agencies' clients, i.e. the prospective employers. The fees commonly equal either 10% of the first year's salary or one month's wages, but the fraction may vary with the volume of business provided by the client and the type of employee sought.

PROFESSIONAL SEARCH FIRMS

Professional search firms are much more specialized than placement agencies. *Search firms* usually recruit only specific types of human resources for a fee paid by the employer. For example, some search firms specialize in executive talent, while others use their expertise to find technical and scientific personnel. Perhaps the most significant difference between search firms and placement agencies is their approach. Placement agencies hope to attract applicants through advertising, but search firms actively seek out recruits from among the employees of other companies. Although they may advertise, the telephone is their primary tool for locating and attracting prospective recruits.

The Nelson Radar Company needed a quality control manager for its assembly line. After several weeks of unsuccessful recruiting effort, the personnel manager hired a search firm. The search firm reviewed the in-house phone directories of competing firms and telephoned the assistant quality control manager at one of Nelson's competitors. The phone call was used to encourage this assistant manager to apply for the position at the Nelson Company.

This brief example illustrates several important points. First, search firms have an in-depth experience that most personnel departments lack. Second, search firms are often willing to undertake actions that an employer would not do, such as calling a competitor. Third, it can be seen that some personnel professionals would consider search firms unethical because these firms engage in "stealing" or "raiding" among their clients' competitors. This last example shows why search firms are sometimes called "headhunters."[10]

EDUCATIONAL INSTITUTIONS

For beginning-level openings, educational institutions are another common source of recruits. Many universities, community colleges, and technical schools offer their current students and alumni placement assistance. This assistance helps employers and graduates to meet and discuss employment opportunities and the applicant's interest. Counsellors and teachers also may provide recruiters with leads to desirable candidates in high schools.

A view of what one group of university students sought in a recruiter is found in Figure 7-5. It shows that students desire well-informed and skilled campus recruiters. It also shows that candour among recruiters is an important characteristic.[11] Another study reports that the recruiter's title and age are important factors in creating a favourable impression on recruits.[12]

PROFESSIONAL ASSOCIATIONS

Recruiters find that professional associations also can be a source of job seekers. Many associations conduct placement activities to help new and experienced professionals get jobs; some have publications that accept classified advertisements. Professionals who belong to the appropriate associations are considered more likely to remain informed of the latest developments in their field, and so this channel of recruitment may lead to higher-quality applicants. Another advantage of this source of applicants is that it helps recruiters zero in on specific specialties, especially in hard-to-fill technical areas.

Figure 7-5
A PROFILE OF THE IDEAL RECRUITER

From a survey of second-year students in a university MBA program, the following profile of the ideal recruiter emerged.

The ideal recruiter:

1. was actually hiring for a specific position.
2. was very knowledgeable about and close to the job that was open.
3. knew the company well and could discuss both good and bad points.
4. didn't try to oversell the company.
5. had read the résumé before the interview.
6. found out how much the candidate knew about the job and the company.
7. was interested in the student as an individual.
8. was happy with the company and felt he or she was going places.
9. was personable, polite, on time, and sincere.
10. asked thought-provoking questions without being too direct or personal.
11. followed up promptly with feedback and evaluation.

Source: John E. Steele, "A Profile of the Ideal Recruiter," *Personnel Journal*, February 1977, pp. 58–59. Used by permission.

LABOUR ORGANIZATIONS

When recruiters want people with trade skills, local labour organizations have rosters of those people who are looking for employment. The local union of plumbers, for example, keeps a list of plumbers who are seeking jobs. In the construction industry, many contractors get their skilled workers from the local labour organizations. Since contractors often hire on a per-project basis, a union hiring hall is a convenient channel for attracting large numbers of pretrained recruits for new projects.

MILITARY PERSONNEL

Trained personnel leave the armed forces every day. Some veterans, such as those who have been trained as mechanics, welders, or pilots, have hard-to-find skills. Personnel departments that need skills similar to those found in the military often find nearby military installations a valuable source of recruits. Many of the technicians who maintain commercial jet airliners were first trained in the military, for example.

CANADA MANPOWER TRAINING PROGRAM

The Canada Manpower Training Program, a service provided under CEIC, supports both institutional (classroom) and industrial (on-the-job) training. In order to qualify for institutional training, an individual needs to be at least one year beyond the provincial school-leaving age (except for apprentices) and have been out of school for at least one year. Counsellors at the CECs are responsible for selecting people for this program. Persons selected for such training typically receive a training allowance or unemployment insurance benefits.

CEIC also assists employers with the training needs of their employees. Under the General Industrial Training Program, CEIC reimburses selected employers for a portion of the training costs and trainee wages. There are also other programs that encourage employers to train and hire women for jobs that have traditionally been held by men and, as well, one that supports training in high-level blue-collar skills.[13] Yet with the change in government in 1984, it is uncertain what new programs or modifications to existing programs will occur.

TEMPORARY-HELP AGENCIES

Most large cities have temporary-help agencies that can respond quickly to an employer's need for help. These agencies do not provide recruits. Instead, they are a source of supplemental workers. The temporary help actually work for the agency and are "on loan" to the requesting employer. For temporary jobs—during vacations, peak seasons, illnesses, etc.—these agencies can be a better alternative than recruiting new workers for short periods of employment. Besides handling the recruiting and bookkeeping tasks caused by new employees, these agencies can often provide clerical and secretarial talent on short notice—sometimes less than a day.[14] And when the temporary shortage is over, there is no need to lay off surplus workers, because "temporaries" work for the agency, not the company. Occasionally, temporary help are recruited to become permanent employees.

DEPARTING EMPLOYEES

An often overlooked source of recruits is among departing employees. These workers might gladly stay if they could rearrange their schedules or change the number of hours worked. Family responsibilities, health conditions, or other circumstances may lead a worker to quit when a transfer to a part-time job may retain valuable skills and training.[15] Even if part-time work is not a solution, a temporary leave of absence may satisfy the employee and some future recruiting need of the employer.

Buy-backs are a channel worthy of mention, although personnel specialists and workers tend to avoid them. A *buy-back* occurs when an employee resigns to take another job and the original employer outbids the new job offer. The following dialogue provides an example:

Employee: *I quit. I am going to work as a computer programmer for International Plastics.*
Manager: *You are too valuable for us to just let you walk out the door. How much is International offering?*
Employee: *They are offering me $3,000 a year more!*
Manager: *Stay and I'll make it $4,000.*
Employee: *No. I'm going.*
Manager: *How about $5,000?*
Employee: *Well, okay.*

Even when the authority to enter into a bidding war exists, the manager may discover that other workers expect like raises. Employees may reject a buy-back attempt because of the ethical issue raised by not reporting to a job that has already been accepted. Besides, what is to prevent the manager from using a blind ad to find a replacement? Then after International has filled its job in the example above, the employee is terminated.

OPEN HOUSE

A relatively new technique of recruiting involves holding an open house. People in the adjacent community are invited to see the company facilities, have refreshments, and maybe view a film about the company. This method has proved successful for recruiting clerical workers when people with office skills are in tight supply.

RECRUITMENT PROCESS SUMMARY

Figure 7-6 summarizes the recruiting process and identifies each of the commonly used channels of recruitment. As the figure indicates, the recruitment process ends when a recruit makes formal application, usually by completing an application form.

Figure 7-6
SUMMARY OF RECRUITING PROCESS

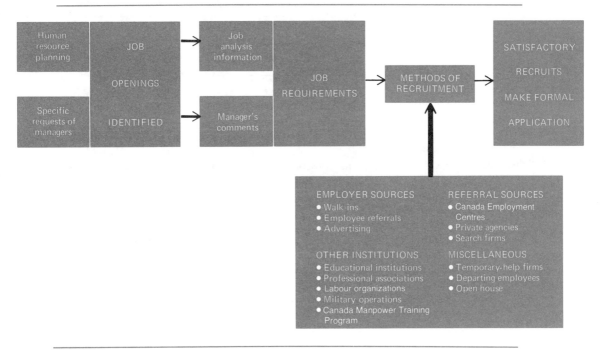

JOB APPLICATION FORMS

The *job application form* collects information about recruits in a uniform manner. Even when recruits volunteer detailed information about themselves, applications are often required so that the information gathered is comparable. Each personnel department generally designs its own form. Nevertheless, certain common features exist. Figure 7-7 provides a typical example of an application form and its major divisions. The remainder of this chapter reviews the major parts of such a form.

Figure 7-7
A TYPICAL APPLICATION FORM

BLAKELY ELECTRONICS, INC.
"An Equal-Opportunity Employer"
Application for Employment

Personal Data

1. **Name** _____
2. **Address** _____ 3. **Phone Number** _____

Employment Status

4. Type of employment sought _____ Full-time _____ Part-time
   _____ Permanent _____ Temporary
5. Job or position sought _____
6. Date of availability, if hired_____
7. Are you willing to accept other employment if the position you seek is unavailable?
   _____ Yes _____ No
8. Approximate wages/salary desired $_____ per month

Education and Skills

9. Circle the highest grade or years completed.
   | 9 10 11 12 13 | 1 2 3 4 | 1 2 3 4 |
   | High School | University | Graduate School |
10. Please provide the following information about your education. (Include high school, trade or vocational schools, and colleges.)
    a. School name _____ Degree(s) or diploma_____
       School address _____
       Date of admission _____ Date of completion _____
    b. School name _____ Degree(s) or diploma _____
       School address _____
       Date of admission _____ Date of completion _____
11. Please describe your work skills. (Include machines, tools, equipment, and other abilities you possess.) _____
    _____
    _____
    _____

Figure 7-7 (cont.)
A TYPICAL APPLICATION FORM

Work History

Beginning with your most recent or current employer, please provide the following information about each employer. (If additional space is needed, please use an additional sheet.)

12. a. Employer _____ Dates of employment _____
Employer's address _____
Job title _____ Supervisor's name _____
Job duties _____
Starting pay _____ Ending pay _____
b. Employer _____ Dates of employment _____
Employer's address _____
Job title _____ Supervisor's name _____
Job duties _____
Starting pay _____ Ending pay _____

Military Background

If you were ever a member of the Canadian Armed Forces, please complete the following:

13. Branch of service_____ Rank at discharge _____
Dates of service _____ to _____
Responsibilities_____
Type of discharge _____

Memberships, Awards, and Hobbies

14. What are your hobbies? _____
15. List civic/professional/social organizations to which you have belonged. _____
_____

16. List any awards you have received. _____
_____

References

In the space provided, list three references who are not members of your family.

17. a. Name _____ Address _____
b. Name _____ Address _____
c. Name _____ Address _____
18. Please feel free to add any other information you think should be considered in evaluating your application. _____
_____

By my signature on this application, I:
    a. Authorize the verification of the above information and any other necessary inquiries that may be needed to determine my suitability for employment.
    b. Affirm that the above information is true to the best of my knowledge.

_____ **Date** _____
           Applicant's Signature

PERSONAL DATA

Most application forms begin with a request for personal data. Name, address, and telephone number are nearly universal. But requests for some personal data such as place of birth, marital status, number of dependents, sex, race, religion, or national origin may lead to charges of discrimination. Since it is illegal to discriminate against applicants, an unsuccessful applicant may conclude that rejection was motivated by discrimination when discriminatory questions are asked. The personnel department must be able to show that these questions are job-related if it asks them.

Applications may solicit information about health, height, weight, handicaps that relate to the job, major illnesses, and claims for injuries. Here again, there may be legal problems. Discriminating against handicapped individuals is prohibited under the Canadian Human Rights Act of 1977. The burden of proof that such questions are job related falls on the employer.

EMPLOYMENT STATUS

Some questions on the application form concern the applicant's employment objective and availability. Included here are questions about the position sought, willingness to accept other positions, date available for work, salary or wages desired, and acceptability of part-time and full-time work schedules.

This information helps a recruiter match the applicant's objective and the organization's needs. Broad or uncertain responses can prevent the application from being considered. An example follows:

Inexperienced recruiter: *Under "position sought," this applicant put "any available job." Also, under "wages desired" the applicant wrote "minimum wage or better." What should I do with this application?*

Employment manager: *You are not a career counsellor. You are a recruiter. Put that application in the inactive file and forget about it.*

EDUCATION AND SKILLS

The education and skills section of the application form is designed to uncover the jobseeker's abilities. An understanding of the applicant's personality may be gained from this section too. Traditionally, education has been a major criterion in evaluating jobseekers. Educational attainment does imply certain abilities and is therefore a common request on virtually all applications. Questions about specific skills are also used to judge prospective employees. More than any other part of the application form, the skills section reveals the suitability of a candidate for a particular job.

WORK HISTORY

Jobseekers must frequently list their past jobs. From this information, a recruiter can tell whether the applicant is one who hops from job to job or is likely to be a long-service employee. A quick review of the stated job title, duties, responsibilities, and ending pay also shows whether the candidate is a potentially capable applicant. [16] If this information does not coincide with what an experienced recruiter expects to see, the candidate may have exaggerated job title, duties, responsibilities, or pay.

MILITARY BACKGROUND
Some applications request information on military experience. Questions usually include date of discharge, area of service, rank at discharge, and type of discharge. Such information clarifies the applicant's background and ability to function in a structured environment.

MEMBERSHIPS, AWARDS, AND HOBBIES
Recruits are more than potential workers. They are also representatives of the employer in the community. For managerial and professional positions, off-the-job activities may make one candidate preferable over another. Memberships in civic, social, and professional organizations indicate the recruit's concern about community and career. Awards show recognition for noteworthy achievements. Hobbies may reinforce important job skills and indicate outlets for stress and frustration, or opportunities for further service to the company.

When handed a pile of completed applications for manager of the car- and truck-leasing department, Frank Simmons (the personnel manager for a Toronto Ford dealership) sorted the completed applications into two piles. When asked what criteria were being used to sort the applications, he said, "I'm looking for golfers. Many of our largest car and truck accounts are sold on Saturday afternoons at the golf course."

REFERENCES
Besides the traditional references from friends or previous employers, applications may ask for other "referencelike" information. Questions may explore the jobseeker's criminal record, credit history, friends and relatives who work for the employer, or previous employment with the organization. Criminal record, credit history, and friends or relatives who work for the company may be important considerations if the job involves sensitive information, cash, or other valuables. Job-relatedness must be substantiated if these criteria disportionately discriminate against some protected group. Previous employment with the organization means there are records of the applicant's performance.

SIGNATURE LINE
Candidates are usually required to sign and date their applications. Adjacent to the signature line, a blanket authorization commonly appears. This authorization allows the employer to check with references; verify medical, criminal, or financial records; and undertake any other necessary investiga-

tions. Another common provision of the signature line is a statement that the applicant affirms the information in the application to be true and accurate as far as is known. Although many people give this clause little thought, falsification of an application form is grounds for discharge in most organizations.

Jim LaVera lied about his age to get into the police officers' training program. As he neared retirement age, Jim was notified that he would have to retire in six months, instead of thirty months as he had planned. When Jim protested, the lie he made years before came to the surface. Jim was given the option of being terminated or taking early retirement at substantially reduced benefits.

When the application is completed and signed, the recruitment process is finished. Its unanswered questions and implications continue to affect personnel management, as the Jim LaVera example illustrates.[17] In fact, the end of the recruitment process marks the beginning of the selection process, which is discussed in the next chapter.

SUMMARY

Recruitment is the process of finding and attracting capable applicants for employment. This responsibility normally is associated with specialists in the personnel department called recruiters. Before recruiters can solicit applicants, they should be aware of the constraints under which they operate. Of particular importance are such limitations as organizational policies, human resource plans, affirmative-action plans, recruiter habits, environmental conditions, and the requirements of the job.

At the recruiter's disposal are a variety of methods to find and attract job-seekers. Employer sources include walk-ins, write-ins, employee referrals, and direct solicitations through want-ads and other forms of advertisement. Applicants can be found through the referrals of Canada Employment Centres, private placement agencies, or search firms. Of course, recruits can be found through a variety of institutions, such as educational, professional, and labour organizations, the military, and government training programs. Some firms have reported success in converting temporary employees into permanent ones, on a full-time or part-time basis, and in inducing departing employees to remain. An open house may bring people into the facility and prompt them to submit applications.

The end of recruiting is a completed application form from ready, willing, and able candidates. Application forms seek a variety of answers from recruits, including personal, employment, educational, and work history information. Questions may be asked about hobbies, memberships, awards, and personal interests. References are usually solicited on the application form too. With a pool of recruits and the information contained in completed application forms, the personnel department is now ready to assist line managers in the process of selecting new employees, which is discussed in the next chapter.

TERMS FOR REVIEW

Recruitment	National Job Bank
Walk-ins	Metropolitan Order Processing
Blind ads	System (MOPS)
Résumé	Search firms
Canada Employment Centres	Canada Manpower Training Program
(CECs)	Buy-back

REVIEW AND DISCUSSION QUESTIONS

1. What background information should a recruiter have before beginning to recruit jobseekers?
2. Give three examples of how organizational policies affect the recruitment process. Explain how these influence a recruiter's actions.
3. Under what circumstances would a blind ad be a useful recruiting technique?
4. After months of insufficient recognition (and two years without a raise), you accept an offer from another firm which involves a $1,500-a-year raise. When you tell your boss that you are resigning, you are told how crucial you are to the business and are offered a raise of $3,250 per year. What do you do? Why? What problems might exist if you accept the buy-back?
5. Suppose you are a manager who has just accepted the resignation of a crucial employee. After you send your request for a replacement to the personnel department, how could you help the recruiter do a more effective job?
6. If at your company the regular university recruiter became ill and you were assigned to recruit at six universities in two weeks, what information would you need before leaving on the trip?
7. In small businesses, managers usually handle their own recruiting. What methods would you use in the following situations? Why?
   (a) The regular janitor is going on vacation for three weeks.
   (b) Your secretary has the flu.
   (c) Two more salespersons are needed: one for local customers and one to open a sales office in Victoria, B.C.
   (d) Your only chemist is retiring and must be replaced with a highly skilled person.
8. "If a job application omits important questions, needed information about recruits will not be available. But if a needless question is asked, the information can be ignored by the recruiter without any other complications." Do you agree or disagree? Why?

INCIDENT 7-1
BLAKELY ELECTRONICS EXPANSION

Blakely Electronics developed a revolutionary method of storing data electronically. The head of research and development, Guy Swensen, estimated that Blakely could become a supplier to every computer manufacturer in the world. The future success of the company seemed to hang on securing the broadest possible patents to cover the still-secret process.

The personnel director, Carol Kane, recommended that Swensen become a project leader in charge of developing and filing the necessary patent information. Swensen and Kane developed a list of specialists who would be needed to rush the patent applications through the final stages of development and the patent application process. Most of the needed skills were found among Blakely's present employees. However, after a preliminary review of skills inventories and staffing levels, a list of priority recruits was developed. It required the following:

• *An experienced patent attorney with a strong background in electronics technology.*

• *A patent attorney familiar with the ins and outs of the patent process and the patent office in Hull, Quebec.*

• *Twelve engineers. Three had to be senior engineers with experience in the latest computer technology and design. Four had to be senior engineers with experience in photographic etching reduction. Five junior engineers were also requested in the belief that they could handle the routine computations for the senior engineers.*

• *An office manager, ten typists, and four secretaries to transcribe the engineering notebooks and prepare the patent applications.*

Swensen wanted these twenty-nine people recruited as promptly as possible.

1. Assuming you are given the responsibility of recruiting these needed employees, what channels would you use to find and attract each type of recruit sought?

2. What other actions should the personnel department take now that there is the possibility of very rapid expansion?

INCIDENT 7-2
THE ETHICS OF "HEADHUNTING"

Darrow Thomas worked as a professional placement specialist for L. A. and D., Inc., an executive search firm. For the last three months Darrow had not been very successful in finding high-level executives to fill the openings of L. A. and D.'s clients. Not only did his poor record affect his commissions, but the office manager at L. A. and D. was not very pleased with Darrow's performance. Since Darrow desperately needed to make a placement, he resolved that he would do everything he could to fill the new opening he had received that morning.

The opening was for a director of research and development at a major food processor. Darrow began by unsuccessfully reviewing the in-house telephone directory of most of the large companies in this industry. Finally, he stumbled across the directory of a small food processor in the West. In the directory he found a listing for Suzanne Derby, assistant director of product development. He called her, and the following conversation took place.

Suzanne: *Hello. P.D. Department, Suzanne Derby speaking.*

Darrow: *Hello. My name is Darrow Thomas, and I am with L. A. and D. One of my clients has an opening for a director of research and development at a well-known food processor. In discussions with people in the industry, your name was recommended as a likely candidate. I was . . .*

Suzanne: *Who recommended that you call me?*

Darrow: *I'm awfully sorry, but we treat references and candidates with the utmost* *confidentiality. I cannot reveal that name. But rest assured, he thought you were ready for a more challenging job.*

Suzanne: *What company is it? What does the job involve?*

Darrow: *Again, confidentiality requires that the company name go unmentioned for now. Before we go any further, would you mind answering a few questions? Once I feel confident you are the right candidate, I can reveal my client.*

Suzanne: *Well, okay.*

Darrow: *Good. How many people do you supervise?*

Suzanne: *Three professionals, seven technicians, and two clerks.*

Darrow: *Approximately how large a budget are you responsible for?*

Suzanne: *Oh, it's about half a million dollars a year.*

Darrow: *What degreee do you hold, and how many years have you been assistant director?*

Suzanne: *My undergraduate degree and master's are in nutrition science. After I graduated in 1970, I came to work as an applications researcher. In 1975, I was promoted to chief applications researcher. In 1980, I was appointed assistant director of product development.*

Darrow: *Good career progress, two degrees, and managerial experience. Your background sounds great! This is a little personal, but would you tell me your salary?*

Suzanne: *I make $32,500 a year.*

Darrow: *Oh, that is disappointing. The opening I have to fill is for $46,500. That would be such a substantial jump that my client would probably assume your past experience and responsibility are too limited to be considered.*

Suzanne: *What do you mean?*

Darrow: *Well, the ideal candidate would be making about $35,000 a year. That figure would indicate a higher level of responsibility than your low salary. We could get around that problem.*

Suzanne: *How?*

Darrow: *On the data sheet I have filled out I could put down that you are making, oh, say $41,500. That sure would increase my client's interest. Besides, then they would know a salary of $46,500 was needed to attract you.*

Suzanne: *Wow! But when they checked on my salary history, they'd know that $41,500 was an inflated figure.*

Darrow: *No, they wouldn't. They wouldn't check. And even if they did, companies never reveal the salary information of past employees. Besides, my client is anxious to fill the job. I'll tell you what, let me send them the data sheet; I'm sure they'll be interested. Then we can talk about more of this. Okay?*

Suzanne: *Well, if you think it would mean a raise to $46,500, and they really need someone with my background, I guess I'd be interested.*

1. Although "headhunters" do not necessarily engage in the practice of "inflating" an applicant's wage, it does happen occasionally. What would you do in Suzanne's place? Would you allow your name to be used?

2. Since most "headhunters" receive a commission that is a percentage of the successful applicant's starting salary, what safeguards would you suggest to prevent "headhunters" from inflating salaries?

3. If Suzanne goes along with Darrow's inflated salary figure and she is hired, what problems may she face?

REFERENCES

1. John B. Miner, "The Real Crunch in Managerial Manpower," in Mary Green Miner and John B. Miner (eds.), *Policy Issues in Contemporary Personnel and Industrial Relations*, New York: The Macmillan Company, 1977, p. 81.
2. Herbert J. Sweeney and Kenneth S. Teel, "A New Look at Promotion from Within," *Personnel Journal*, August 1979, p. 535.
3. Gene E. Burton and Dev S. Pathak, "101 Ways to Discriminate Against Equal Employment," *The Personnel Administrator*, August 1977, pp. 42–45.
4. Lee D. Dyer, "Managerial Jobseeking: Methods and Techniques," *Monthly Labor Review*, December 1972, pp. 29–30. For a broad view of the methods used by a variety of workers, see Carl Rosenfeld, "Jobseeking Methods Used by American Workers," *Monthly Labor Review*, August 1975, pp. 39–42. See also Richard H. Coffina, "Management Recruitment Is a Two-Way Street," *Personnel Journal*, February 1979, pp. 86–89.
5. Van M. Evans, "Recruitment Advertising in the '80's," *Personnel Administrator*, 1978, p. 23.
6. James W. Schreier, "Deciphering Messages in Recruitment Ads," *Personnel Administrator*, March 1983, p. 35.
7. Ibid., p. 39.
8. Jo Bredwell, "The Use of Broadcast Advertising for Recruitment," *Personnel Administrator*, February 1981, pp. 45–49.
9. Employment and Immigration Canada, *Employment Programs and Services for Canadians*, Catalogue No. WH-7-092, Ottawa: Minister of Supply and Services Canada, 1981, p. 1.
10. John D. Erdlen, "Ethics and the Employee Relations Function," *The Personnel Administrator*, January 1979, pp. 41–43, 68.
11. Madalyn Freund and Patricia Somers, "Ethics in College Recruiting: Views from the Front Lines," *The Personnel Administrator*, April 1979, pp. 30–33. See also Joe Thomas, "College Recruitment: How to Use Student Perceptions of Business," *Personnel Journal*, January 1980, pp. 44–46.
12. Donald P. Rogers and Michael Z. Sincoff, "Favorable Impression Characteristics of the Recruitment Interviewer," *Personnel Psychology*, Autumn 1978, pp. 495–504.
13. Employment and Immigration Canada, op. cit., pp. 3–5.
14. Martin J. Gannon, "A Profile of the Temporary Help Industry and Its Workers," *Monthy Labor Review*, May 1974, pp. 44–49.
15. Barney Olmsted, "Job Sharing—A New Way to Work," *Personnel Journal*, February 1977, pp. 78–81. See also William B. Werther, Jr., "Part-Timers: Overlooked and Undervalued," *Business Horizons*, February 1975, pp. 13–20.
16. Bernard M. Bass, "Interface between Personnel and Organizational Psychology," in W. Clay Hamner and Frank L. Schmidt (eds.), *Contemporary Problems in Personnel*, Chicago: St. Clair Press, 1974, pp. 44–45.
17. Robert W. Ericson, "Recruitment: Some Unanswered Questions," *Personnel Journal*, February 1974, pp. 136–140, 147. See also Stephen J. Wilhelm, "Is On-Campus Recruiting on Its Way Out?" *Personnel Journal*, April 1980, pp. 302–304, 318.

Chapter 8

The Selection Process

The policy of "hire—then qualify" is replacing the old method of "hire qualified people."

George S. Odiorne[1]

CHAPTER OBJECTIVES

After studying this chapter, you should be able to:
1. **Explain** the dependency of personnel management activities on the selection process.
2. **Describe** the role of employment testing in the selection process.
3. **List** and explain each step in the selection process.
4. **Explain** the importance of validity and reliability in employee selection.
5. **Conduct** an employment interview and avoid the major pitfalls.
6. **Describe** the supervisor's role in the selection process and in realistic job previews.

Once a pool of suitable applicants is created through recruiting, the process of selecting applicants begins. This process involves a series of steps that add time and complexity to the hiring decision. Although important, it should be recognized that this time and complexity can lead to frustration among applicants who need jobs and operating managers who need their job openings filled. By way of introduction, consider an overview of the hiring process at Merrill Lynch, Pierce, Fenner & Smith Inc., one of the larger securities firms.

Applicants for the position of account executive at Merrill Lynch complete an application, take a written test, and undergo an interview. But none of these steps prepare them for the account-executive simulation test, which is just one step in Merrill Lynch's selection process. As described by a reporter for The Wall Street Journal, *the test can be unnerving.*

"Welcome to the Merrill Lynch account-executive simulation exercise, or, as dubbed by some, the Merrill Lynch stress test. It's a nail-biting three hours ... that leaves many longing for the good old days of calculus finals."

"The stakes are high, too. Those taking part in the simulation, except me, are applicants for the job of account executive, or stockbroker. . . . The simulation exercise is designed to gauge how they will perform under conditions similar to those that a real stockbroker faces."[2]

The test works by telling each applicant that he or she is replacing a stockbroker who has gone to another office. The stockbroker left the client book, which describes the accounts of each client. In addition, the applicants are given a variety of unanswered memos, letters, and telephone messages that they must sort through and decide what to do. In the background, recorded sounds of a brokerage office are played to add an air of confusing noises, shouts, telephone rings, and other unexpected distractions. During the three hours, fictitious clients call and other messages and reports are dropped on the applicant's "desk." As one applicant commented an hour after the simulation was over, "I just can't calm down. It was a real high."[3]

The point of this illustration is simply that the simulation exercise is only one part of Merrill Lynch's selection process. Other steps precede and follow it. Although most employers do not use this elaborate a screening device, all but the smallest employers put applicants through a variety of steps called the selection process. The *selection process* is a series of specific steps used to decide which recruits should be hired. The process begins when recruits apply for employment and ends with the hiring decision. The steps in between match the employment needs of the applicant and the organization. When these steps are not understood, selection seems like a stressful time and a bureaucratic process rather than the important function it is.

In many personnel departments, recruiting and selection are combined and called the *employment function*. In large personnel departments, the employment function is the responsibility of the employment manager. In smaller departments, personnel managers handle these duties.[4] Perhaps more than any other function, employment is associated closely with the personnel department. It is often the primary reason for creating the personnel department, since the selection process is central to personnel management. Improper selection causes the personnel department to fail at the objectives set forth in Chapter 1 and the challenges discussed in Chapter 2. Even worse, improper selection can crush individual hopes and violate antidiscrimination laws. Subsequent personnel activities (discussed later in the book) lose much of their effectiveness when they must contend with improperly selected workers. Therefore, it is not an exaggeration to say that selection is central to the success of personnel management and even to the success of the organization.

INPUTS TO SELECTION

Employment managers use the selection process to find new workers. As Figure 8-1 reveals, the selection process relies on three helpful inputs. Job analysis information provides the description of the jobs, the human specifications, and the performance standards each job requires. Human resource plans tell employment managers what job openings are likely to occur. These plans allow selection to proceed in a logical and effective manner. Finally, recruits are necessary so that the employment manager has a group of people from which to choose. These three inputs largely determine the effectiveness of the selection process. If job analysis information, human resource plans, and recruits are of high quality, the selection process should function well. At the same time, there are other inputs into the selection process that limit its success. To succeed, employment managers must grapple with a limited supply of labour, ethical considerations, organizational and equal-opportunity policies.

Figure 8-1
DEPENDENCY OF PERSONNEL MANAGEMENT ACTIVITIES ON THE SELECTION PROCESS

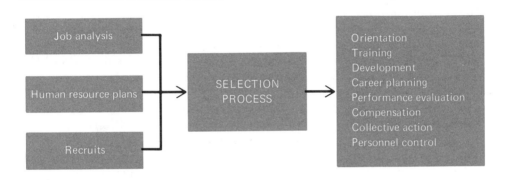

SUPPLY CHALLENGES

It is important to have a large, qualified pool of recruits from which to select applicants. But some jobs are so hard to fill that there are few applicants per opening. For example, Canadian business schools currently have over 200 vacancies which they are unable to fill, due to a shortage of qualified personnel. Thus when hiring, they have small selection ratios. A *selection ratio* is the relationship between the number of applicants hired and the total number of applicants available. A large selection ratio is 1:25; a small selection ratio is 1:2. A small selection ratio means there are few applicants from which to select. In many instances a small selection ratio also means a low quality of recruits. The ratio is computed as follows:

$$\frac{\text{Number of applicants hired}}{\text{Total number of applicants}} = \text{selection ratio}$$

Wes Klugh, an employment manager for a chain of motels, faced a low selection ratio for the third-shift desk clerk's job. Although it paid 25 cents an hour more than the day or evening clerk jobs, few people applied for it. Wes decided to redesign the job by enriching it. The job was expanded to include responsibility for completing the daily financial report and other bookkeeping tasks. The additional duties justified the substantial raise and new title—night auditor. The result was more applicants.

ETHICAL CHALLENGES

Since employment specialists strongly influence the hiring decision, that decision is shaped by their ethics.[5] Hiring a neighbour's relative, accepting gifts from a placement agency, and taking bribes all challenge the employment specialist's ethical standards. If those standards are low, new employees may not be properly selected.

Every summer, Athena Klemmer was told to find jobs for some of the executives' children. To disobey would affect her career. On the other hand, hiring some of them would be an admission that she selected people on criteria other than merit. Although many of her peers in the local personnel association thought employing the bosses' children was merely a benefit of the executive suite, Athena felt it was improper. Accordingly, she found summer jobs for them in other companies.

ORGANIZATIONAL CHALLENGES

The selection process is not an end; it is a means through which the organization achieves its objectives. Naturally, the organization imposes limits, such as budgets and policies, that may hinder the selection process. Without budget limitations, recruiting efforts and selection techniques could be refined. But without limits, employment expenses may be so high that organizational effectiveness would suffer.

Policies may expand existing challenges or simply add more constraints. Policies against discrimination reinforce external prohibitions, for example. Internal decrees may exceed legal demands from outside. For example, policies to hire ex-convicts further societal objectives but are not legally required. Yet such internal policies add still another challenge for employment specialists.

SELECTION: AN OVERVIEW

The selection process is a series of steps through which applicants pass. Sometimes the process can be made simple and effective, especially when selecting employees to fill internal openings.

At Citibank the selection process has been simplified and computerized in order to match present employees with internal openings. The "Jobmatch" selection system rests upon matching a profile of candidates for nonprofessional jobs and the jobs' task requirements. The specific tasks required of the job are programmed into the computer along with the specific abilities of employees. Those employees with the highest match for a given opening are then considered for the job. A major shortcoming of this computerized approach is that the matching process largely ignores behaviours not directly related to the job, such as attitudes, personality, and the like.[6]

To ensure that both task and nontask factors are considered, personnel departments commonly use a more involved sequence of steps, as shown in Figure 8-2. For internal applicants, there is seldom a need to provide a preliminary reception of applicants, verify references, or do a medical evaluation. But with external applicants, the steps in Figure 8-2 are common. The remainder of this chapter explains the selection process by examining each step in this figure.

Figure 8-2
STEPS IN THE SELECTION PROCESS

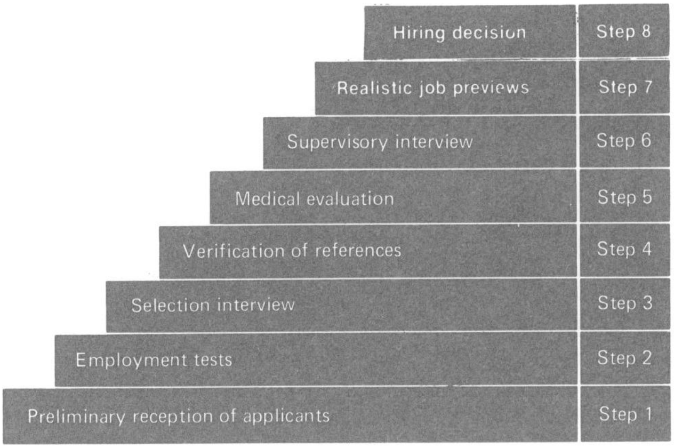

Hiring decision	Step 8
Realistic job previews	Step 7
Supervisory interview	Step 6
Medical evaluation	Step 5
Verification of references	Step 4
Selection interview	Step 3
Employment tests	Step 2
Preliminary reception of applicants	Step 1

PRELIMINARY RECEPTION: STEP 1

The selection process is a two-way street. The organization selects employees, and *applicants select employers*. From both views, selection begins with a visit to the personnel office or with a written request for an application. How this initial reception is handled affects the applicant's opinion of the employer.

When the applicant appears in person, a preliminary interview may be granted as a courtesy. This "courtesy interview," as it is often called, is simply a matter of good public relations. It also helps the personnel department screen out obvious misfits and get background information on potential recruits. A completed application is usually requested during this initial meeting. Later steps in the selection process verify this application information.

EMPLOYMENT TESTS: STEP 2

Employment tests are useful for obtaining relatively objective information which can be compared with that pertaining to other applicants and present workers. *Employment tests* are devices that assess the match between applicants and job requirements. Some are paper-and-pencil tests; others are exercises that simulate work conditions. A math test for a bookkeeper is an example of a paper-and-pencil test, and a manual dexterity test for an assembly worker is an example of a simulation exercise. These tests are used more frequently for jobs that pay an hourly wage than for salaried positions because hourly jobs usually call for a limited number of skills or activities that can be tested easily. Management and professional jobs are often too complex to be tested fairly and economically in this manner.

TEST VALIDATION

Testing became popular on a large scale during World War I when intelligence tests were given to army recruits. During the following sixty years, tests were developed for a wide range of employment uses, but many of these tests were assumed to be valid without sufficient proof.

For a test to be relied upon, it must be valid. *Validity* requires that the test scores significantly relate to job performance or some other relevant criterion. The stronger the relationship between test results and performance, the more effective the test is as a selection tool. When scores and performance are unrelated, the test is invalid and should not be used for selection.

An Ontario trucking company once gave all its applicants an extensive reading test. However, because the drivers received their instructions orally and were shown on a map where to go, the reading test had no relationship to job performance; it did not distinguish good drivers from bad ones. It only distinguished between those who could read English well and those who could not.

When an invalid test rejects people of a particular race, sex, religion, or national origin, it violates the Canadian Human Rights Act or related provincial legislation. However, test validity as it is related to discrimination has not received a great deal of attention in Canada. Given that many of the tests we use were developed in the United States, one wonders whether they are particularly valid, since they were developed for a different group of workers. A Toronto-based industrial psychologist has estimated that "only 3% of firms use properly validated selection tests."[7] If this estimate is correct, then an increased scrutiny of testing and its relationship to discrimination may well be a future trend in the personnel area.

To assure that its tests are valid, personnel departments should conduct *validation studies*. These studies compare test results with performance or traits needed to perform the job. Figure 8-3 summarizes the most common approaches to validation.

Empirical approaches rely on predictive or concurrent validity. Both methods attempt to relate test scores to some criterion, usually performance. The higher the correlation between test scores and the criterion, the more effective the test is. Empirical approaches are generally preferred because they are less subjective than rational methods.

Rational approaches include content and construct validity. These techniques are used when empirical validity is not feasible because the small number of subjects does not permit a reasonable sample upon which to conduct the validation study.

Regardless of which approach is used, testing experts advise separate validation studies for different subgroups, such as women and minorities. These separate studies for different subgroups are called *differential validity*. Without differential validity, a test may be valid for a large group (white male applicants) but not for subgroups of minorities or women.

Yet even when tests have been validated, the type of validation used is still important. Faulty procedures, no matter how well intentioned, cannot

Figure 8-3
AN EXPLANATION OF COMMON APPROACHES TO TEST VALIDATION

Empirical Approaches

Empirical approaches to test validation attempt to relate test scores with a job-related criterion, usually performance. If the test actually measures a job-related criterion, the test and the criterion exhibit a positive correlation between 0 and 1.0. The higher the correlation, the better the match.

• **Predictive validity** is determined by giving a test to a group of applicants. After these applicants have been hired and have mastered the job reasonably well, their performance is measured. This measurement and the test score are then correlated.

• **Concurrent validity** allows the personnel department to test present employees and correlate these scores with measures of their performance. This approach does not require the delay between hiring and mastery of the job.

Rational Approaches

When the number of subjects is too low to have a reasonable sample of people to test, rational approaches are used. These approaches are considered inferior to empirical techniques, but are acceptable validation strategies when empirical approaches are not feasible.

• **Content validity** is assumed to exist when the test includes reasonable samples of the skills needed to successfully perform the job. A typing test for an applicant that is being hired simply to do typing is an example of a test with content validity.

• **Construct validity** seeks to establish a relationship between performance and other characteristics that are assumed to be necessary for successful job performance. Tests of intelligence and scientific terms would be considered to have construct validity if they were used to hire researchers for a chemical company.

be relied on to prove a test's validity. An example of this point follows:

The Albemarle Paper Company, a U.S. firm, gave several black workers a battery of tests that had not been validated. The workers sued Albemarle, and so the company then implemented a validation study. But the study had several weaknesses, and the court ruled the tests as invalid and discriminatory.

The problem was that Albemarle:

• Used the tests that had been validated for advanced jobs, not the entry-level positions to which tests were being applied. Such validation does not prove tests are valid for entry-level jobs. Tests must be validated on those jobs to which tests are being applied.

• Validated the test on one group (white workers) and then applied the test to another group (black workers). Tests must be validated for all the groups to whom the test applies. [8]

Besides being valid, a test should also be reliable. *Reliability* means that the test yields consistent results. For example, a test of manual dexterity for assembly workers should give a similar score each time the same person takes the test. If the results vary widely with each retest because good scores depend on luck, the test is not reliable. When tests are not reliable, they may also be invalid.

TESTING TOOLS AND CAUTIONS

There are a wide variety of employment tests. But each type of test has only limited usefulness. The exact purpose of a test, its design, the directions for its administration, and its applications are recorded in the test manual, which should be reviewed before a test is used. The manual also reports the test's reliability and the results of validation efforts by the test designer. Today many tests have been validated on large populations. But personnel specialists should conduct their own studies to make sure a particular test is valid for its planned use. Each type of test has a different purpose. Figure 8-4 lists examples and a brief explanation of each of several different types of tests.

Psychological tests are those that measure personality or temperament. They are among the least reliable. Validity suffers because the exact relationship between personality and performance is unknown and perhaps nonexistent.

Knowledge tests are more reliable because they determine information or knowledge. Math tests for an accountant and a weather test for a pilot are examples. But personnel specialists must be able to demonstrate that the knowledge is needed to perform the job. The Ontario trucking company example is a case wherein the tested knowledge (reading at an advanced level) was not needed.

Performance tests measure ability of applicants to do some parts of the work for which they are to be hired. A typing test for typists is an obvious example. Validity is often assumed when the test includes a representative sample of the work the applicant is to do when hired. However, if the test discriminates against some minority group, personnel's assumption must be backed by detailed validation studies.

Graphic response tests are a more recent development that seek information about applicants in ways that cannot be distorted easily. The *polygraph* (or lie detector) is the most common, with over a fifth of all firms in one study reporting its use.[9] It measures physiological changes as a person responds to questions. When a person tells a lie, the conscience usually causes involuntary physiological reactions that are detected by the polygraph. At $25 to $50 per test, it is more economical than a detailed background check on applicants. In addition to ethical and public relations considerations, there are serious questions about the ability of most lie detector operators validly to administer and interpret the results.

Besides specific cautions associated with individual tests, personnel specialists should realize that testing is not always feasible. Even when tests can be developed or bought, their cost may not be justified for jobs that have low selection ratios or that are seldom filled. Examples include

Figure 8-4
EXAMPLES OF APPLICATIONS OF EMPLOYMENT-RELATED TESTS

Psychological Tests

Name	Application (Subjects)
Minnesota Multiphasic Personality Inventory	Measures personality or temperament (executives, nuclear power security)
California Psychological Inventory	Measures personality or temperament (executives, managers, supervisors)
Guilford-Zimmerman Temperament Survey	Measures personality or temperament (sales personnel)
Watson-Glaser Critical Thinking Appraisal	Measures logic and reasoning ability (executives, managers, supervisors)
Owens Creativity Test	Measures creativity and judgment ability (engineers)

Knowledge Tests

How Supervise?	Measures knowledge of supervisory practices (managers and supervisors)
Leadership Opinion Questionnaire	Measures knowledge of leadership practices (managers and supervisors)
General Aptitude Test Battery	Measures verbal, spatial, numeric, and other aptitudes and dexterity (jobseekers at unemployment offices)

Performance Tests

Stromberg Dexterity Test	Measures physical coordination (shop workers)
Revised Minnesota Paper Form Board Test	Measures spatial visualization (draftsman and draftswoman)
Minnesota Clerical Test	Measures ability to work with numbers and names (clerks)
Job Simulation Tests	Measures a sample of "on-the-job" demands (managers, professionals)

Graphic Response Tests

Lie Detector	Honesty and truthfulness (police, retail store workers)

technical, professional, and managerial jobs. Even when feasible, the use of tests must be flexible. They need not always be the first or last step in the selection process. Instead, personnel experts use tests during the selection process at the point they deem appropriate. Consider the comments of an experienced personnel manager for a chain of grocery stores.

Many personnel managers in other industries use testing only after other steps in the selection process. In the grocery business you must test first. Why waste time interviewing a grocery clerk who doesn't know that three for 88 cents is 30 cents apiece? Besides, when we take applications on Tuesdays, we may have 300 of them. Inter-

views would take 75 hours a week, and my staff consists of a clerk and myself. But through testing, we can test the entire group in an hour. Then we interview only those who score well.

Lastly, the employment test is only one of several techniques used in the selection process, because it is limited only to factors that can be tested and validated easily. Other items, not measurable through testing, may be equally important.

SELECTION INTERVIEW: STEP 3

The *selection interview* is a formal, in-depth conversation conducted to evaluate the applicant's acceptability. The interviewer seeks to answer two broad questions: Can the applicant do the job? How does the applicant compare with others who are applying for the job?

Selection interviews, or in-depth interviews as they are also known, are the most widely used selection technique. One study reports that 90% of all companies surveyed had more confidence in interviews than in any other source of selection information.[10] Their popularity stems from their flexibility. They can be adapted to unskilled, skilled, managerial, and staff employees. They also allow a two-way exchange of information: interviewers learn about the applicant and the applicant learns about the employer.

Interviews do have shortcomings. The most noticeable flaw is their reliability and validity. Good reliability means that the interpretation of the interview results should not vary from interviewer to interviewer. But it is common for different interviewers to form different opinions. Reliability is improved when identical questions are asked, especially if interviewers are trained to record responses systematically.[11] Validity is questionable because few personnel departments conduct validation studies on their interview results. However, proactive personnel departments are beginning to realize this problem and are comparing interview results with actual performance or other criteria, such as stability of employment.[12] More validation of interviews is needed because they may relate more to personal features of candidates than to the candidates' potential performance. For example, one study reported that two of the most important variables which influence an interview are fluency of speech and composure.[13] If these findings are applicable to most employment interviews, the results of the interviews may correlate with fluency and composure, instead of potential performance. However, whether validated or not, interviews persist because of their adaptability and believed effectiveness.

TYPES OF INTERVIEWS

Interviews are commonly conducted between the interviewer and the applicant on a one-to-one basis. Group interviews, however, are sometimes used. Variations of group interviews appear in Figure 8-5.

One form of group interview is to have applicants meet with two or more interviewers. This allows all interviewers to evaluate the individual on the

Figure 8-5
DIFFERENT COMBINATIONS OF INTERVIEWERS AND APPLICANTS

Number of Interviewers	Number of Applicants
Individual Interview	
1	1
Group interviews	
2 or more	1
1	2 or more
2 or more	2 or more

same questions and answers. Since the interviewers are more apt to reach the same conclusion, reliability is improved. Another major variation in the figure is to have two or more applicants interviewed together, by one or more interviewers. This saves time, especially for busy executives. It also permits the answers of different applicants to be compared immediately.

Whether a group interview or not, there are different interview formats, which depend on the type of questions that are asked. Questions can be structured, unstructured, mixed, problem-solving, or stress-producing. Figure 8-6 compares these different formats. And although the mixed format is most common in practice, each of the others has an appropriate role to play.

Figure 8-6
DIFFERENT QUESTION FORMATS IN INTERVIEWS

Interview Format	Types of Questions	Useful Applications
Unstructured	Few if any planned questions. Questions are made up during the interview.	Useful when trying to help interviewees solve personal problems or understand why they are not right for a job.
Structured	A predetermined checklist of questions, usually asked of all applicants.	Useful for valid results, especially when dealing with large numbers of applicants.
Mixed	A combination of structured and unstructured questions, which resembles what is usually done in practice.	Realistic approach that yields comparable answers plus indepth insights.
Problem-Solving	Questions are limited to hypothetical situations. Evaluation is on the solution and the approach of the applicant.	Useful to understand applicant's reasoning and analytical abilities under modest stress.
Stress-Producing	A series of harsh, rapid-fire questions intended to upset the applicant.	Useful for stressful jobs, such as handling complaints.

UNSTRUCTURED INTERVIEWS. As the summary in Figure 8-6 indicates, the unstructured interview allows personnel specialists to develop questions as the interview proceeds. The interviewer goes into topic areas as they arise, and the end result is more like a friendly conversation. Unfortunately, this unstructured method lacks the reliability of a structured interview because each applicant is asked a different series of questions. Even worse, this approach may overlook key areas of the applicant's skills or background.

STRUCTURED INTERVIEWS. Structured interviews rely on a predetermined set of questions. The questions are developed before the interview begins and are asked of every applicant. This approach improves the reliability of the interview process, but it does not allow the interviewer to follow up interesting or unusual responses. Here, the end result is an interview that seems quite mechanical to all concerned. The rigid format may even convey lack of interest to applicants who are used to more flexible interviews.

MIXED INTERVIEWS. In practice, interviewers typically use a blend of structured and unstructured questions. The structured questions provide a base of information that allows comparisons between candidates. But the unstructured questions make the interview more conversational and permit greater insights into the unique differences between applicants. Community college and university recruiters, for example, use mixed interviews most of the time.

PROBLEM-SOLVING INTERVIEWS. Problem-solving interviews focus on a problem or series of problems that the applicant is expected to solve. Often these are hypothetical interpersonal situations and the applicant is asked what should be done. Both the answer and the approach used by the applicant are evaluated. This interview technique has a very narrow scope. It primarily reveals the applicant's ability to solve the types of problems presented. Validity is more likely if the hypothetical situations are similar to those found on the job. The actual interview might consist of ten situations similar to the following:

Suppose you had to decide between two candidates for a promotion. Candidate A is loyal, cooperative, punctual, and hard-working. Candidate B is a complainer and is tardy and discourteous, but is the best producer in your department. Whom would you recommend for promotion to supervisor? Why?

The way the applicant reacts to the questions is noted. Since this type of interview produces modest amounts of stress, it gives an indication of how the applicant can function under moderately stressful situations.

STRESS INTERVIEWS. When the job involves much stress, a stress interview attempts to learn how the applicant will respond. Originally developed during World War II to see how selected recruits might react under stress behind enemy lines, these interviews have useful application in civilian employment. For example, applicants for police work are sometimes put through a stress interview to see how they might react to problems they encounter on the job. The interview itself consists of a series of harsh questions asked in rapid succession and in an unfriendly manner. Since stressful situations are usually only part of the job, this technique should be used in connection with other interview formats. Even then, negative public relations is likely to result among those who are not hired.

THE INTERVIEW PROCESS

The five stages of a typical employment interview are listed in Figure 8-7. These stages are interviewer preparation, creation of rapport, information exchange, termination, and evaluation. Regardless of the type of interview used, each of these steps must occur for a successful interview to result. They are discussed briefly to illustrate how the actual interview process occurs.[14]

Figure 8-7
STAGES IN THE TYPICAL EMPLOYMENT INTERVIEW

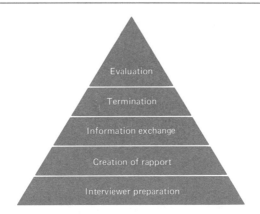

INTERVIEWER PREPARATION. Obviously, before the interview begins, the interviewer needs to prepare. This preparation requires that specific questions be developed by the interviewer. It is the answers to these questions that the interviewer will use in deciding the applicant's suitability. At the same time the interviewer must consider what questions the applicant is likely to ask. Since the interview is used to persuade top applicants to accept subsequent job offers, the interviewer needs to be able to explain job duties, performance standards, pay, benefits, and other areas of interest. A list of typical questions asked by recruiters and other interviewers appears in Figure 8-8. As can be seen from that list, these questions are intended to give the interviewer some insight into the applicant's interests, attitudes, and background. Specific or technical questions are added to the list according to the type of job opening.

Another action the interviewer should undertake before the interview is to review the application form. Research shows that the quality of the interviewer's decision is significantly better when the application form is present.[15] With or without the application form, interviewers seem to take about the same length of time to reach a conclusion—from four to ten minutes.[16] The longer the interview is scheduled to last and the better the quality of the applicants, the longer it takes interviewers to reach a decision.[17]

With the average cost of hiring new employees estimated to be as high as $4,000 for managerial and professional employees, the interviewer's preparation should be aimed at making the interview process efficient and comfortable for the applicant.[18] Often the interviewer is one of the first representatives of the company with whom the applicant has had an opportunity to talk. A strong and lasting impression of the company is likely to be formed at this stage.[19] If the interviewer does not show courtesy to the applicant, that impression is certain to be negative. If the applicant is a promising candidate for the job, he or she likely has other job prospects.[20]

Figure 8-8
SAMPLE QUESTIONS USED IN EMPLOYMENT INTERVIEWS

1. How do you spend your spare time? What are your hobbies?
2. What community or school activities have you been involved in?
3. Describe your ideal job. In what type of work are you interested?
4. Why do you want to work for our company?
5. What were your favourite classes? Why?
6. Do you have any geographic preferences?
7. What do you think a fair salary would be?
8. What do you think your salary should be in five years? Ten?
9. Why did you select your university major?
10. What do you know about our company's products or services?
11. Describe the ideal boss.
12. How often do you expect to be promoted?
13. What is your major weakness? Strength?
14. Why do you think your friends like you?
15. Do you plan to take additional university courses? Which ones?
16. What jobs have you had that you liked the most? Least?
17. Describe your least favourite boss or teacher.
18. What are your career goals?
19. If you could go back five years, what would you do the same? Differently?
20. Why should you be hired by our company?
21. Describe your last job.
22. How many hours do you think you will have to work at your job?
23. What job skills do you have?
24. Do you have a sample of your writing?
25. What is your favourite sport?

CREATION OF RAPPORT. Once the interview begins, the burden is on the interviewer to establish a relaxed rapport with the recruit. Without a relaxed rapport, the interviewer may not get a clear picture of the applicant's potential. Rapport is aided by beginning the interview on time and starting with nonthreatening questions such as, "Did you have any parking problems?" At the same time, the interviewer may use body language to help relax the applicant. A smile, a handshake, relaxed posture, and moving paperwork aside all communicate without words; such nonverbal communications maintain rapport throughout the interview session.[21]

INFORMATION EXCHANGE. The heart of the interview process is the exchange of information. To help establish rapport, some interviewers may begin by asking the applicant if there are any questions. This establishes two-way communication and lets the interviewer begin to judge the recruit by the type of questions asked. Consider the following dialogue. Which response creates the most favourable impression?

Interviewer: *Well, let's start with any questions you may have.*

Applicant 1: *I don't have any questions.*

Applicant 2: *I have several questions.˙How much does the job pay? Will I get two weeks' vacation at the end of the first year?*

Applicant 3: *What will the responsibilities be? I am hoping to find a job that offers me challenges now and career potential down the road.*

Each response creates a different impression on the interviewer. But only Applicant 3 appears concerned about the job. The other two applicants appear to be either unconcerned or interested only in what benefits they will receive.

In general, an interviewer will ask questions worded to learn as much as possible. Questions that begin with how, what, why, compare, describe, expand, or "Could you tell me more about . . ." are likely to solicit an open response, while questions that can be answered with a simple "yes" or "no" do not give the interviewer much insight.[22] As noted earlier, specific questions and areas of interest to an interviewer are suggested in Figure 8-8. Besides those questions, the interviewer may want more specific information about the applicant's background, skills, and interests.

TERMINATION. As the list of questions dwindles or available time ends, the interviewer must draw the session to a close. Here again, nonverbal communication is useful. Sitting erect, turning toward the door, glancing at a watch or clock all clue the applicant that the end is near. Some interviewers terminate the interview by asking, "Do you have any final questions?" At this point, the interviewer informs the applicant of the next step in the interview process, which may be to wait for a call or letter.

EVALUATION. Immediately after the interview ends, the interviewer should record specific answers and general impressions. Figure 8-9 shows a typical checklist used to record these impressions of the interviewer. Use of a checklist like the one in the figure can improve the reliability of the interview as a selection technique. As the checklist shows, the interviewer is able to obtain a large amount of information even from a short interview.

Figure 8-9
A POSTINTERVIEW CHECKLIST

EMPIRE INC.

"An Equal-Opportunity Employer"
Postinterview Checklist

Applicant's Name _____   Date _____
Position under Consideration _____   Interviewer _____

Interviewer's Comments

A. Rate the applicant on the following (1 = low; 10 = high):

_____ Appearance   _____ Ability to perform job
_____ Apparent interest   _____ Education/training
_____ Experience/background   _____ Timely availability
_____ Reasonable expectations   _____ Past employment stability

B. List specific comments that reveal the candidate's strengths and weaknesses for the job being considered:
  1. Attitude toward previous job _____
  2. Attitude toward previous boss _____
  3. Expectations about job duties_____
  4. Career or occupational expectations _____
  5. Other specific comments about applicant _____

  _____

Follow-up Actions Required

_____ None   _____ Follow-up interview with personnel
_____ Testing   _____ Applicant unacceptable (file)
_____ Supervisory interview   _____ Notify applicant of rejection
_____ Applicant unacceptable for job under consideration. Reconsider for job as

_____

INTERVIEWER ERRORS

Caution must be exercised to avoid some common pitfalls of the interviewer, summarized in Figure 8-10, that lower the effectiveness of the interview. When the applicant is judged according to the "halo effect" or personal biases, the results of the interview are misinterpreted. Applicants are accepted or rejected for reasons that may bear no relation to their potential performance. Likewise, leading questions and domination do not allow the interviewer to learn of the applicant's potential either. The evaluation of the applicant then becomes based on a guess with little or no substantiation. No matter which pitfall is involved, it reduces the validity and reliability of the interview. All the interview does when biases are presented is waste organizational resources and the applicant's time.

Figure 8-10
A SUMMARY OF TYPICAL INTERVIEWER ERRORS

"Halo Effect"

Interviewers who use limited information about an applicant to bias their evaluation of that person's other characteristics are subject to the *halo effect*.

Examples:
- An applicant who has a pleasant smile and firm handshake is considered a leading candidate before the interview begins.
- An applicant who wears blue jeans to the interview is rejected mentally.

Leading Questions

Interviewers who "telegraph" the desired answer by the way they frame their questions are using leading questions.

Examples:
- "Do you think you'll like this work?"
- "Do you agree that profits are necessary?"

Personal Biases

Interviewers who harbour prejudice against specific groups are exhibiting a personal bias.

Examples:
- "I prefer sales personnel who are tall."
- "Some jobs are for men and others for women."

Interviewer Domination

Interviewers who use the interview to oversell the applicant, brag about their successes, or carry on a social conversation instead of an interview are guilty of interviewer domination.

Examples:
- Spending the entire interview telling the applicant about company plans or benefits.
- Using the interview to tell the applicant how important the interviewer's job is.

VERIFICATION OF REFERENCES: STEP 4

What type of person is the applicant? Is the applicant a good, reliable worker? To answer these questions, employment specialists use references.

Many professionals have a very skeptical attitude toward references. *Personal references*—those that attest to the applicant's sound character—are usually provided by friends or family. Their objectivity and candour are certainly questionable. When a reference is in writing, the author usually emphasizes only positive points. Thus personal references are not commonly used.

Employment references differ from personal references because they discuss the applicant's work history. Many personnel specialists doubt the usefulness of these references because former supervisors or teachers may not be completely candid, especially with negative information. As a result, many employment references are little more than confirmation of prior employment.

This lack of candour has caused some personnel specialists to omit this step entirely from the selection process. Other specialists have substituted telephone inquiries for written references. Besides getting a faster response, often at lower cost, telephone inquiries have the advantage of directness: voice inflections or hesitation over blunt questions may tip off the interviewer to underlying problems. In practice, however, less than 22% of all reference checks seek negative information, according to one study.[23] The same study revealed that 48% of reference checks are used to verify application information and 30% are used to gather additional data.

MEDICAL EVALUATION: STEP 5

The selection process may include a medical evaluation of the applicant before the hiring decision is made. Normally, the evaluation is a health checklist that asks the applicant to indicate health and accident information. The questionnaire is sometimes supplemented with a physical examination by a company nurse or physician. The medical evaluation may:

• Entitle the employer to lower health or life insurance rates for company-paid insurance.

• Be required by provincial or local health officials—particularly in food-handling operations where communicable diseases are a danger.

• Be useful to evaluate whether the applicant can handle the physical or mental stress of a job.

Many employers have done away with this step because of the costs involved. Also, if an applicant is rejected, charges of discrimination under the Canadian Human Rights Act or related provincial legislation may be brought. A congenital health condition may be considered a disability, and failure to hire may be seen as discrimination against the qualified applicant. If the employer wants a medical evaluation, it may be scheduled after the hiring decision.

SUPERVISORY INTERVIEW: STEP 6

The immediate supervisor is ultimately responsible for newly hired workers. Since that responsibility is ever-present, supervisors should have input into the final hiring decision. The supervisor is often better able to evaluate the applicant's technical abilities than is the personnel department. Likewise, the immediate supervisor can often answer the interviewee's specific job-related questions with greater precision. As a result, one study reported that in over three-quarters of the organizations surveyed, the supervisor had the authority to make the final hiring decision.

When supervisors make the final decision, the role of the personnel department is to provide the supervisor with the best applicants available. From these two or three applicants, the supervisor decides whom to hire. Some organizations leave the final hiring decision to the personnel department, especially when applicants are hired into a training program instead of for a specific job. If supervisors constantly reject particular groups of applicants, such as minorities or women, the personnel department may be given final hiring authority to avoid future charges of discrimination.

Regardless of who has the final hiring authority, the personal commitment of supervisors is generally higher when they participate in the selection process. Their participation is best obtained through the supervisory interview. Through a variety of structured and nonstructured questions, the supervisor attempts to assess the technical competency, potential, and overall suitability of the applicant. The supervisory interview also allows the recruit to have technical, work-related questions answered. Often, the supervisory interview is supplemented with a realistic job preview that better enables the employee to comprehend the job before being hired. A review of realistic job previews caused one authority to conclude that they are effective ways to minimize turnover among employees who are eventually hired.[24]

When the supervisor recommends hiring an individual, he or she has made a psychological commitment to assist the new employee. If the candidate turns out to be unsatisfactory, the supervisor is then more likely to accept some of the responsibility for failure.

REALISTIC JOB PREVIEWS: STEP 7

Often, the supervisory interview is supplemented with a realistic job preview. A *realistic job preview* (RJP) allows the potential employee to understand the job and the job setting before the hiring decision is made—often by showing him or her the type of work, equipment, and working conditions involved.

Unmet expectations about a job probably contribute to initial job dissatisfaction. The realistic job preview attempts to prevent job dissatisfaction by giving the newcomer an insight into the job.[25] Recently hired employees who have had a realistic job preview are less likely to be shocked by the job or the job setting on the first day they report to work after being hired. Two writers concluded the following:

> The RJP functions very much like a medical vaccination. . . . The typical medical vaccination injects one with a small, weakened dose of germs, so that one's body can develop a natural resistance to that disease. The RJP functions similarly by presenting job candidates with a small dose of "organizational reality." And, like the medical vaccination, the RJP is probably much less effective after a person has already entered a new organization.[26]

Research on the effectiveness of realistic job previews has shown that in nine out of ten studies, employee turnover was higher when the job previews were not used. The average of these studies was 28.8% higher.[27] Clearly, realistic job previews are an effective way to reduce turnover;[28] however, as two other researchers concluded:

> Telling prospective employees about unpleasant working conditions may improve the probability that they will remain on the job in comparison to those who are not told about the conditions. However, . . . those who are told about less pleasant conditions will be no more satisfied with them once they are experienced than will those who are not told. To improve satisfaction and the quality of work, ultimately some changes must be made in those aspects of the work environment with which employees are dissatisfied.[29]

HIRING DECISION: STEP 8

Whether made by the supervisor or the personnel department, the final hiring decision marks the end of the selection process. From a public relations standpoint, other applicants should be notified that they were not selected. Employment specialists may want to consider rejected applicants for other openings, since these recruits have already gone through various stages of the selection process. Even if no openings are available, applications of candidates not hired should be kept on file for future openings. Retaining these applications can be useful if the employer is charged with employment discrimination.

The applications of those hired should be retained also. The application form begins the employee's personnel file and contains useful information for studies that the personnel department may conduct to learn about the source of its applicants, their age, sex, race, or other work-related characteristics. If some recruits prove unsatisfactory after they are hired, for example, personnel specialists may be able to reconstruct the selection process beginning with the application. In their reconstruction, they may uncover invalid tests, improperly conducted interviews, or other flaws in the selection process.

OUTCOMES AND FEEDBACK

The final outcome of the selection process is the people who are hired. If the preselection inputs are considered carefully and the major steps of the selection process have been followed correctly, then new employees are likely to be productive. And productive employees are the best evidence of an effective selection process.

To evaluate both new employees and the selection process requires feedback. Feedback on successful employees is sometimes hard to find for employment managers, since supervisors usually claim responsibility for their successes. Feedback on failures is ample. It can include displeased supervisors, growing employee turnover and absenteeism, poor performance, low employee satisfaction, union activity, and legal suits.

More constructive feedback is obtained through specific questions. How well does the new employee adapt to the organization? To the job? To the career of which the job is a part? And lastly, how well does the employee perform? Answers to each of these questions provide feedback about the employee and the selection process. The following chapters examine each of these questions in depth.

SUMMARY

The selection process depends heavily upon inputs such as job analysis, human resource plans, and recruits. These inputs are used within the challenges of the external environment, ethics, and guidelines established by the organization.

With these inputs and challenges, the selection process takes recruits and puts them through a series of steps to evaluate their potential. These steps vary from organization to organization and from one job opening to another. In general, the selection procedure relies on testing for many hourly jobs and on interviews for virtually every opening that is to be filled. References and medical evaluations are steps commonly found in the selection process of most employers.

The supervisor's role should include participation in the selection process, usually through an interview with job candidates. Through participation, the supervisor is more likely to be committed to the new worker's success.

Growing research evidence supports the use of realistic job previews (RJPs). After considerable expense and effort to recruit and select employees, the use of realistic job previews seems well advised as a means of reducing turnover among new employees.

TERMS FOR REVIEW

Selection process
Employment function
Selection ratio
Employment tests
Validity
Reliability

Selection interview
Structured interviews
Stress interviews
"Halo effect"
Employment references
Realistic job preview (RJP)

REVIEW AND DISCUSSION QUESTIONS

1. What information should the employment specialist review before beginning the selection process?
2. Suppose you are an employment specialist. Would you expect to have a large or small selection ratio for each of the following job openings?
   (a) Janitors
   (b) Nuclear engineers with five years' experience designing nuclear reactors
   (c) Clerk-typists
   (d) Supervisors
   (e) Elementary school teachers in the Yukon
   (f) Elementary school teachers in the Atlantic provinces

3. List and briefly describe each of the steps in the selection process.
4. If an employment manager asked you to streamline the firm's selection process for hourly paid workers, which steps described in this chapter would you recommend cutting? Why?
5. The typical employment interview has five stages to it. What are those stages? Briefly explain each.
6. Why should employment tests be validated?
7. As you begin interviewing a job applicant, you notice this person is very nervous. Yet your evaluation of the applicant indicates that this applicant is highly qualified. What should you do to put the person at ease in order to establish rapport?
8. Some people believe that personnel should have the authority to decide who is hired because personnel are the experts on hiring. Others say that the immediate supervisor, being responsible for employee performance, should have the final authority. Explain your reasons for accepting one argument or the other.

INCIDENT 8-1
A SELECTION DECISION AT EMPIRE INC.

At Empire Inc., the turnover rate is very high among assembly workers. Supervisors in the production department have told the personnel department that they do not have time to conduct a supervisory interview with the large number of applicants who are processed to fill assembly-line openings. As a result, the personnel department's employment specialists make the final hiring decisions.

The profiles of three typical applicants are presented below.

	Applicant A	**Applicant B**	**Applicant C**
Years of Experience	4	7½	1
Education	1 year of university	Finished eighth grade	High school diploma
Age	24	43	32
Test Score	76/100	73/100	85/100
Medical Evaluation	OK	OK	OK
Job Knowledge	Very good	Excellent	Fair/good
Work History	Limited data	Stable	Stable
Ranking by:			
Interviewer 1	1	2	3
Interviewer 2	3	2	1
Apparent Eagerness	Moderate	Strong	Weak/average
Availability	4 weeks	2 weeks	Immediately

The nature of the assembly jobs is rather simple. Training seldom takes more than an hour or two. Most people master the job and achieve an acceptable level of production during the second full day on the job. The tasks involve very little physical or mental effort. The test is valid, but has only a weak relationship between scores and actual performance.

1. What information would you consider irrelevant in the preceding selection profiles?
2. Are there any changes you would recommend in the selection process?
3. Which of the three candidates would you select, given the limited knowledge you possess? Why?

INCIDENT 8-2
NATIONAL FOOD BROKERS SELECTION PROCESS

National Food Brokers buys carload orders of nonperishable food products for resale to food wholesalers. Phone-sales personnel take orders from major food wholesalers, write up the orders, and send them to the appropriate food producers. Nearly 90 of National's 130 employees work in the phone-sales department. Since the job requires long hours on the phone to different accounts, the work is not very pleasant and turnover is high.

The manager of the phone-sales department, Carol Decinni, made the following observations in the presence of the personnel manager, Craig Reems:

"Most of the people who work in the department fall into two groups. There are those who have been here for two or more years. They seem reasonably content and are the top sellers we have. The other group consists of people who have been here for less than two years. Most of our turnover comes from this group. In fact, we lose one of every three new employees during the first two months. When I talk with the people who are quitting, most of them tell me that they had no idea how much time they had to spend on the phone. I am generally pleased with the quality of recruits the personnel department provides. But we cannot continue with this high turnover. My supervisors are spending most of their time training new workers. Is there anything the personnel department can do to hire more stable workers?"

1. Suppose you are asked by the personnel manager to suggest some strategies for improving the selection process in order to hire more stable workers. What suggestions do you have for (a) preemployment testing and (b) reference checks?
2. Do you believe an interview with a supervisor in the department would help applicants understand the work better?
3. What do you think the supervisors should do to give the applicants a realistic understanding of the job before they are hired?

REFERENCES

1. George S. Odiorne, *Programmed Learning Aid for Personnel Administration: A Management by Objectives Approach*, Homewood, Ill.: Richard D. Irwin Inc., 1973, p. 71.
2. Lawrence Rout, "Going for Broker: Our Man Takes Part in Stock-Selling Test," *The Wall Street Journal*, April 4, 1979, p. 1.
3. Ibid.
4. American Society of Personnel Administrators, *The Personnel Executive's Job*, Englewood Cliffs, N.J.: Prentice-Hall Inc., 1977.
5. John D. Erdlen, "Ethics and the Employee Relations Function," *The Personnel Administrator*, January 1979, pp. 41–43, 68.
6. Paul Sheibar, "A Simple Selection System Called 'Job Match,'" *Personnel Journal*, January 1979, pp. 26–29, 53. See also Robert P. Delamontagne and James B. Weitzul, "Performance Alignment: The Fine Art of the Perfect Fit," *Personnel Journal*, February 1980, pp. 115–117, 131.
7. Martin Dewey, "Employers Take a Hard Look at the Validity and Value of Psychological Screening," *Globe and Mail*, February 7, 1981, p. B1.

8. James Leduinka and Lyle F. Schoenfeldt, "Legal Developments in Employment Testing: Albermarle and Beyond," *Personnel Psychology*, Spring 1978, pp. 1–13.
9. John A. Belt and Peter B. Holden, "Polygraph Usage among Major U.S. Corporations," *Personnel Journal*, February 1978, p. 82. See also "Business Buys the Lie Detector," *Business Week*, Feb. 6, 1978, pp. 100–191, 104; and Philip G. Benson and Paul S. Koris, "The Polygraph in Employment: Some Unresolved Issues," *Personnel Journal*, September 1979, pp. 616–621.
10. Bureau of National Affairs, *Personnel Policies Forum*, Survey No. 114, September 1976.
11. Robert N. McMurray, "Validating the Patterned Interview," *Personnel*, January 1947, pp. 263–272. See also Eugene Mayfield, "The Selection Interview—A Reevaluation of Published Research," *Personnel Psychology*, Autumn 1964, pp. 239–260; Edward C. Andler, "Preplanned Question Areas for Efficient Interviewing," *Personnel Journal*, January 1976, pp. 8–10; and Frederick S. Hills, "Job Relatedness vs. Adverse Impact in Personnel," *Personnel Journal*, March 1980, pp. 211–215, 229.
12. McMurray, op. cit.
13. James G. Hollandsworth, Jr. et al., "Relative Contributions of Verbal, Articulative, and Nonverbal Communication to Employment Decisions in the Job Interview Setting," *Personnel Psychology*, Summer 1979, pp. 359–367.
14. Jeffrey D. Latterell, "Planning for the Selection Interview," *Personnel Journal*, July 1979, pp. 466–467, 480.
15. William L. Tullar, Terry W. Mullins, and Sharon A. Caldwell, "Effects on Interview Length and Applicant Quality on Interview Decision Time," *Journal of Applied Psychology*, Vol. 64, No. 6, 1979, pp. 669–674.
16. D. H. Tucker and P. M. Rowe, "Consulting the Application Form Prior to the Interview: An Essential Step in the Selection Process," *Journal of Applied Psychology*, N.D., Vol. 62, 1977.
17. Tullar, Mullins, and Caldwell, op. cit.
18. Hall A. Acuff, "Quality Control in Employee Selection," *Personnel Journal*, July 1981, p. 565.
19. Scott T. Rickard, "Effective Staff Selection," *Personnel Journal*, June 1981, pp. 475–478.
20. Nancy J. Schweitzer and John Deely, "Interviewing the Disabled Job Applicant," *Personnel Journal*, March 1982, pp. 205–209.
21. Richard G. Nehrbass, "Psychological Barriers to Effective Employment Interviewing," *Personnel Journal*, December 1976, pp. 598–600. See also S. Trevor Michaels, "Seven Questions That Will Improve Your Managerial Hiring Decisions," *Personnel Journal*, March 1980, pp. 199–200, 224.
22. Michael H. Frisch, *Coaching and Counseling Handbook*, New York: Resource Dynamics, 1981.
23. George M. Beason and John A. Belt, "Verifying Applicants' Backgrounds," *Personnel Journal*, July 1976, p. 346. See also Jeremiah Bogert, "Learning the Applicant's Background through Confidential Investigations," *Personnel Journal*, June 1976, p. 272.
24. John P. Wanous, "Realistic Job Previews: Can a Procedure to Reduce Turnover Also Influence the Relationship between Abilities and Performance," *Personnel Psychology*, Summer 1978, pp. 249–258.
25. Lyman Porter and Richard Steers, "Organizational, Work, and Personal Factors in Employee Turnover and Absenteeism," *Psychological Bulletin*, Vol. 80, 1973, pp. 151–176.
26. Paula Popovich and John P. Wanous, "The Realistic Job Preview as a Persuasive Communication," *Academy of Management Review*, October 1982, p. 571.
27. Ibid., p. 572.
28. John P. Wanous, op. cit.
29. Bernard L. Dugoni and Daniel R. Ilgen, "Realistic Job Preview and the Adjustment of New Employees," *Academy of Management Journal*, September 1981, p. 590; see also James A. Breaugh, "Realistic Job Previews: A Critical Appraisal and Future Research Directions," *The Academy of Management Review*, October 1983, pp. 612–619.

Part 3

Development and Evaluation

Employees need help if they are to grow and be successful. The employer wants to help for its own benefit as well as theirs. It trains and develops them. It also helps them plan their careers for promotion and helps them learn to adjust to change. Finally, it appraises their performance so that both they and the company know how they are doing.

The next four chapters are about employee development and evaluation. As a student, you need to understand the personnel department's role in these activities. They affect you whether you work in a personnel department or elsewhere in an organization. Knowledge of these activities assists you to be a better employee or manager.

Chapter 9

Training and Development

It is no longer a question of whether we want to develop our human resources or whether we should develop our human resources. . . . It is a matter of survival for our society that we develop human resources.

James L. Hayes[1]

Our refusal to spend money on investing in a skilled work force shows up in large numbers of people who are unemployable.

Herbert E. Striner[2]

CHAPTER OBJECTIVES

After studying this chapter, you should be able to:
1. **Explain** the employee and organizational benefits of orientation programs.
2. **Distinguish** between training and development of human resources.
3. **Identify** the benefits of training to employees and the organization.
4. **Explain** different approaches to needs analysis in designing training and development programs.
5. **Describe** the major learning principles associated with each training technique.
6. **Identify** the equal-employment opportunity implications that surround training and development.
7. **Develop** an evaluation process to assess the results of a training and development program.

Newly hired employees are seldom capable of fully performing their job duties. Even experienced employees need to learn about the organization— its people, its policies, and its procedures. They may even need training in order to perform successfully. Although orientation and training cost time and money, most organizations find these costs to be a sound investment in human resources.

Manager: *Maybe you can tell me why our company needs a fancy orientation program* *and such a large training budget? The personnel department follows a very detailed selection process. Why can't we hire people who can be put right to work?*

Trainer: *No matter how well qualified applicants are when we hire them, they need to know the people with whom they work. They also need to understand our company's procedures and policies. And most need to be trained to do their job properly.*

Manager: *But that shouldn't require a half-day orientation program. While these people are in the orientation sessions, they are getting paid but do not contribute anything to the company.*

Trainer: *You're right. But the half-day orientation program speeds up the training process, and it lowers turnover among new recruits. It is more effective to spend a half-day in orientation and reduce training time by nearly two days.*

Manager: *I do not see how an orientation session speeds up training. What is the connection?*

Trainer: *The connection is that well-oriented employees can grasp what will be important to their job success. They spend less time trying to figure out if they will fit in, if they will like the company, if they will like the job, if they will be accepted by others, and if they have any future with our company.*

The gap between a new employee's abilities and the job's demands may be substantial. As Figure 9-1 suggests, orientation and training supplement the new worker's abilities. The hoped-for result is a balance between what the new employee can do and what the job demands. Although these efforts are time consuming and expensive, they reduce employee turnover and help new employees to be productive sooner.

Even long-service employees need training to avoid obsolescence and to do their present jobs better. When management wants to prepare employees for *future* job responsibilities, this activity is called human resource development. This distinction between training and development is primarily one of intent. *Training* prepares people to do their *present* jobs. *Development* prepares them for *future* jobs. Both training and development teach employees needed skills, knowledge, and attitudes. These activities are

Figure 9-1
THE BALANCE BETWEEN NEW EMPLOYEE CAPABILITIES AND JOB DEMANDS

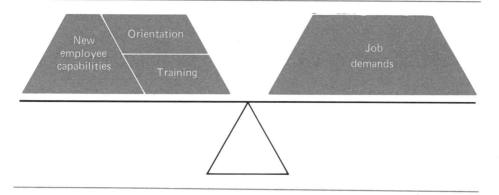

usually the responsibility of the personnel department and the immediate supervisor.

The rest of this chapter explains how orientation programs integrate new employees into the organization and make them more receptive to training. Then the major types of training and development are discussed, along with the underlying learning principles involved.

ORIENTATION PROGRAMS

Orientation programs familiarize new employees with their roles, with the organization, and with other employees. Figure 9-2 lists the topics typically covered during orientation. The program usually explains the organizational issues that new employees need to know. Often a film or slide show describes the history, products, services, and policies of the organization. Commonly, workers are given an *employee handbook* that explains key benefits, policies, and general information about the company. Personnel experts may also discuss pay rates as part of the program. The personnel department's role in the program often ends when employees meet their future supervisors or trainers.

Figure 9-2
TOPICS OFTEN COVERED IN EMPLOYEE ORIENTATION PROGRAMS

Organizational Issues	
History of employer	Product line or services provided
Organization of employer	Overview of production process
Names and titles of key executives	Company policies and rules
Employee's title and department	Disciplinary regulations
Layout of physical facilities	Employee handbook
Probationary period	Safety procedures and enforcement

Employee Benefits	
Pay scales and paydays	Insurance benefits
Vacations and holidays	Retirement program
Rest breaks	Employer-provided services to employees
Training and education benefits	Rehabilitation programs
Counselling	

Introductions	
To supervisor	To coworkers
To trainers	To employee counsellor

Job Duties	
Job location	Overview of job
Job tasks	Job objectives
Job safety requirements	Relationship to other jobs

Trainers or supervisors continue the orientation program by introducing the new employee to the other trainees and coworkers. Introductions are usually followed by a tour of the facilities and an explanation of the job, its objectives, and related information. At this point, training begins.

In organizations that hire large numbers of employees, the orientation program may take a half or even a whole day to discuss the topics in Figure 9-2. For employers that hire workers only occasionally and in small numbers, there may be no formal orientation program. Instead the employee is introduced to a senior worker who shows the new person around. These highly informal "buddy systems" are also used in large companies to help orient the new employee.

Formal programs explain orientation topics systematically. These programs are also more likely to create a favourable impression on new employees, which may explain why in a U.S. survey 72% of the firms had formal programs.[3] The experiences of two workers illustrate how orientation can affect new employees.

Caroline Mathau: *I reported to the personnel office ten minutes early. I was told to have a seat and that someone would "show me around." An hour later I was led to an interview room. After a few minutes the interviewer realized that I was not an applicant but a new employee. After apologies, I was taken to meet my supervisor. The supervisor screamed for a claims processor to show me around. While I was being introduced to other people, the claims processor, Irv Porter, complained about what a grouch the supervisor was all the time. At lunch, I asked personnel if I could get a transfer to another claims department. They told me that transfers were not permitted until after the three-month probation period. I am thinking about finding another job.*

Harvey Jackson: *My orientation was really super! When I arrived, I was shown to the auditorium. After coffee and pastry, we were given an employee handbook that explained most of the company's benefits and policies. We also received some forms to complete and a brief lecture about company policies. The lecture was followed by a really interesting film that explained the company's history, facilities, and how different jobs related to one another. The following hour was spent on questions and answers. We had a tour of the plant and then we were treated to lunch by the company. At lunch, our supervisors joined us to answer questions and tell us about their departments. Afterward, the supervisors introduced us to the people in my department and training began.*

If Caroline's experience is a typical one in her company, employees probably begin work with low motivation, poor morale, and a lot of anxiety. The company is "saving" the cost of an orientation, but it is paying a high cost in employee attitudes and performance.

RESPONSIBILITY FOR ORIENTATION

Responsibility for orientation is shared between the personnel department and the immediate supervisor.[4] Personnel departments usually orient employees to broad organizational concerns and benefits. Supervisors handle introductions and on-the-job training and help employees "fit in" with the work group.

The personnel department and the supervisor need to recognize several common pitfalls that detract from successful orientation programs.[5] Both are responsible to see that the employee is not:

- Overwhelmed with too much information to absorb in a short time.
- Given only menial tasks that discourage job interest and company loyalty.
- Overloaded with forms to fill out and manuals to read.
- Pushed into the job with a sketchy orientation under the mistaken philosophy that "trial by fire" is the best orientation.
- Forced to fill in the gaps between a broad orientation by the personnel department and a narrow orientation at the department level.

BENEFITS OF ORIENTATION PROGRAMS

Although research about orientation programs is limited, several benefits are commonly reported.[6] These benefits result from the orientation program's effect on employee behaviour.

Orientation lowers the employees' feelings of isolation, apprehension, and anxiety. They are able to become part of the organization quicker; they feel more secure and more like they belong. With less anxiety, they are better able to learn their new duties. Pressure from peers or criticism by supervisors can be kept in perspective since properly oriented workers have realistic job expectations. As a result, new employees need less attention from coworkers and supervisors, perform better, and are less likely to quit.[7]

At Texas Instruments in the U.S., one group of employees received an extended orientation program. The special program focused on the social adaptation problems usually encountered by employees at Texas Instruments. They were told that they had a high probability of success, that old employees might kid or haze them, that their supervisors were helpful people, and that as new employees they should initiate communications with supervisors if there were any questions.

The results of the specially oriented group showed that waste was reduced by 80%; training costs dropped by two-thirds; product costs were 15% lower; and training time, absenteeism, and tardiness were cut in half.[8]

These benefits occur because the orientation program helps an individual understand the social, technical, and cultural aspects of the new workplace. The process by which people adapt to an organization is called *socialization*. Socialization is a critical step toward acceptance by others in the organization. As new employees are accepted, they become a part of the social fabric of the organization. Orientation programs help speed up the socialization process and acceptance into the work group.

ORIENTATION FOLLOW-UP

Successful orientation programs include a built-in follow-up procedure. Follow-up is needed because new employees are often reluctant to admit that they do not recall everything they were told in the initial orientation.

Without follow-up, their questions go unanswered. The follow-up can be a prescheduled meeting or a simple checklist that asks the employee to critique the weaknesses of the orientation program. Weak areas, presumably, are topics about which an employee needs more information. The checklist also serves as feedback to the personnel department so that it can identify parts of the program that are good or bad. Poor orientation efforts by supervisors will also become apparent through feedback.

EMPLOYEE TRAINING AND DEVELOPMENT

Even after a comprehensive orientation, new employees seldom perform satisfactorily. They must be trained in the duties they are expected to perform. And experienced employees may need training to reduce poor work habits or to learn new skills that improve their performance.

Although *training* seeks to help employees do their present job, the benefits of training may extend throughout a person's entire career and help *develop* that person for future responsibilities.[9] Developmental activities, on the other hand, aim to help the individual handle future responsibilities with little concern for present job duties. As a result, the distinction between training and development often is blurred. What starts out as training commonly develops people into better workers or managers. Since the distinction between training and development is primarily one of intent, both are discussed together throughout the chapter, with significant differences noted where important. To illustrate the developmental impact of training, consider one personnel director's observations.

When I was first promoted to head all the job analysts in 1964, I did not know the first thing about supervising. So I was sent to a training program for new supervisors. In that seminar I learned a lot of things. But the section on delegation really impressed me. I have relied on that knowledge ever since. Probably the reason I head the personnel department today is because that training helped to develop me into a manager.

When looked at from the overall perspective of a corporate training and development effort, the distinction between training for a present job and development for future ones blurs even further. Consider an outline of the training program at one company.

At Corning Glass . . . we adopted a systematic approach in the development of a plant-wide training program. Our concept of training focuses on the individual. We . . . believe [that] all employees, regardless of salary grade, position or department assignment, can benefit from quality training.[10]

The training program at Corning has four phases. The first phase is individual training. Included here is an extensive orientation program for new employees and on-the-job training for those who have transferred to a new job. The second phase is departmental training. Hourly and management employees receive specialized courses that are intended to increase departmental productivity. These courses focus primarily on standard operation procedures used to run specific operations in the department. The third phase is plant/facilities training. It contains training of general interest to those at the plant. Safety training and courses for personal or professional development are included in this category. The final component of training is the corporate and outside training and development phase. This phase includes training and development efforts done by the corporate offices, private consultants, and universities. It tends to be more general and more developmental in nature.

To support these various levels of training, the plant training coordinator develops a master training schedule that is published monthly on a department-by-department basis. It shows the name, type, and appropriate audience for each training session to be held that month. This calendar is supplemented with a catalogue that shows whether the training subject is an operational, safety, departmental, or plant-wide session.[11]

This comprehensive array of learning opportunities includes some very specific training modules that teach people the company's standard operating procedure for doing a specific job. At the other end of the course spectrum are seminars on broad developmental issues that upwardly mobile managers at Corning can expect to face during their careers. Many of the other seminars may be training for some employees presently doing specified jobs while others are taking those courses to develop their skills and future job potential at Corning. Neither the training coordinator nor the students are much concerned whether a class is intended to be "training" or "development."

The more appropriate concern is whether the seminars help the employees and the organization. Corning obviously believes that their approach to training and development benefits both employees and the company. And judging from some of the results that Corning has been able to report, the training and development has had some identifiable payoffs in productivity and quality of work life.

As the personnel assistant and plant training coordinator at the Corning plant asked: "So, where have over two hundred various courses for our employees taken us? First, we have increased productivity."[12] In one department, record production runs were achieved following formalized on-the-job training by some departmental employees. Workplace practices also have become more standardized and employees have an in-plant means of self-improvement.[13]

Figure 9-3 summarizes some of the more common benefits of training and development. As can be seen in the figure, training helps the organization, the individual, and the human relations of the work group. Perhaps the easiest way to summarize these benefits is to consider training and development as an investment the organization makes in employees. That investment pays dividends to the employee, the organization, and other workers.

Figure 9-3
THE BENEFITS OF EMPLOYEE TRAINING

Benefits to the Organization

- Leads to improved profitability and/or more positive attitudes toward profit orientation.
- Improves job knowledge and skills at all levels of the organization.

Figure 9-3 (cont.)
THE BENEFITS OF EMPLOYEE TRAINING

- Improves the morale of the work force.
- Helps people identify with organizational goals.
- Helps create a better corporate image.
- Fosters authenticity, openness, and trust.
- Improves the relationship between boss and subordinate.
- Aids in organizational development.
- Learns from the trainee.
- Helps prepare guidelines for work.
- Aids in understanding and carrying out organizational policies.
- Provides information for future needs in all areas of the organization.
- Promotes more effective decision making and problem solving.
- Aids in developing promotions from within.
- Aids in developing leadership skill, motivation, loyalty, positive attitudes, and other traits that successful workers and managers usually display.
- Aids in increasing productivity and/or quality of work.
- Helps keep costs down in many areas, e.g., production, personnel, administration, etc.
- Develops in employees a sense of responsibility for being competent and knowledgeable.
- Improves labour-management relations.
- Reduces outside consulting costs by utilizing competent internal consulting.
- Stimulates preventive management, as opposed to "putting out fires."
- Eliminates suboptimal behaviour (such as hiding tools).
- Creates an appropriate climate for growth and communication.
- Aids in improving organizational communication.
- Helps employees adjust to change.
- Aids in handling conflict, thereby helping to prevent stress and tension.

Benefits to the Individual, Which in Turn Benefit the Organization

- Helps the individual toward better decision making and effective problem solving.
- Fosters a sense of recognition, achievement, growth, responsibility, and desire for advancement.
- Aids in encouraging and achieving self-development and self-confidence.
- Helps in handling stress, tension, frustration, and conflict.
- Provides information for improving leadership knowledge, communication skills, and attitudes.
- Increases job satisfaction and recognition.
- Moves the individual toward personal goals while improving interaction skills.
- Satisfies personal needs of the trainer (and trainee!).
- Provides trainee an avenue for growth and a say in his/her own future.
- Develops a sense of growth in learning.
- Helps a person develop speaking and listening skills—and writing skills when exercises are required.
- Helps eliminate fear of attempting new tasks.

Figure 9-3 (cont.)
THE BENEFITS OF EMPLOYEE TRAINING

Benefits in Personnel and Human Relations, Intra- and Intergroup Relations, and Policy Implementation

- Improves communication between groups and individuals.
- Aids in orientation for new employees and those taking new jobs through transfer or promotion.
- Provides information on equal opportunity and affirmative action.
- Provides information on other governmental laws and administrative policies.
- Improves interpersonal skills.
- Makes organizational policies, rules, and regulations viable.
- Improves morale.
- Builds cohesiveness in groups.
- Provides a good climate for learning, growth, and coordination.
- Makes the organization a better place in which to work.

Source: From M. J. Tessin, "Once Again, Why Training?" *Training*, February 1978, p. 7. Reprinted by permission.

To receive the benefits listed in Figure 9-3, personnel specialists and managers must assess the needs, objectives, content, and learning principles associated with training. Figure 9-4 plots the sequence of events to be followed before training and development begin. First, the person who is responsible for the training or development (usually a trainer) must assess the needs of the employee and the organization in order to learn what objectives should be sought. Once objectives are set, the specific content and learning principles are considered. Whether the learning process is to be guided by trainers in the personnel department or by first-level supervisors, these preliminary steps should be undertaken to create an effective program.

Figure 9-4
PRELIMINARY STEPS IN PREPARING A TRAINING AND DEVELOPMENT PROGRAM

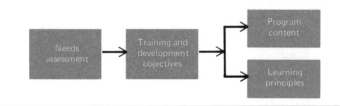

NEEDS ASSESSMENT

Although precise figures are not available, it is estimated that the cost of training and development in government and industry in Canada is between $7 and $8 billion.[14] An estimate of similar costs in the U.S. puts the figure at

$100 billion.[15] If organizations are to get maximum benefit from this staggering expenditure, then efforts must concentrate on people and situations that can benefit most.[16] To decide what approach to use, the trainer assesses the needs for training and development. *Needs assessment* diagnoses present problems and environmental challenges that can be met through training, or the future challenges to be met through long-term development. For example, changes in the external environment may present an organization with new challenges. To respond effectively, employees may need training to deal with the change. The comments of one training director illustrate the impact of the external environment.

After enactment of the human rights legislation, we had to train every interviewer in the personnel department. This training was needed to ensure that our interviewers would not ask questions that might violate federal or provincial laws. When managers in other departments heard of the training, they, too, wanted to sign up. What was to be a one-time seminar became a monthly session for nearly three years. We evaluated the requests of these other managers and decided that they interviewed recruits and that they should be trained also.

Sometimes a change in the organization's strategy can create a need for training. For example, new products or services usually require employees to learn new procedures. Xerox encountered this challenge when it decided to produce computers. Sales personnel, programmers, and production workers had to be trained to produce, sell, and service this new product line. Training can also be used when high accident rates, low morale and motivation, or other problems are diagnosed. Although training is not an organizational cure-all, undesirable trends may be evidence of a poorly prepared work force.

Regardless of these challenges, needs assessment must consider each person.[17] Needs may be determined by the personnel department, supervisors, or self-nomination. The personnel department may find weaknesses among those who are hired or promoted. Supervisors see employee performance daily, and so they are another source of recommendations for training. But their suggestions may be made to banish troublemakers, "hide" surplus employees who are temporarily expendable, or reward good workers. Since these are not valid reasons, the personnel department often reviews supervisory recommendations to verify the need for training. Likewise, the department also reviews self-nominations to determine whether the training is actually needed. In one research study, supervisors selected attendees for training programs more frequently than self-nominations.[18] Self-nomination appears to be less common for training situations but more common for developmental activities, such as getting an MBA under the employer's tuition reimbursement program.

Even when employees are allowed to nominate themselves for available training programs, training directors have little assurance that they are offering the correct mix of courses or that the courses have the right content. To better narrow the range of courses and define their content, more refined approaches to needs assessment are used. One approach is through task identification. Trainers begin by evaluating the job description to identify the salient tasks that the job requires. Then with an understanding of these tasks, specific plans are developed to provide the necessary training so that jobholders can perform the tasks.[19] The individual and departmental training phases of the Corning Glass Works' training program are an example of where a task identification approach would be appropriate.

Another approach is to survey potential trainees to identify specific topical areas that they want to learn more about.[20] The advantage of this method is that trainees are more likely to see the subsequent training programs as relevant, and thus they are more likely to be receptive to them. Of course, this approach to assessing training needs presumes that those surveyed know what training they need. For new employees needing specific individual or departmental training, this method is unlikely to be successful. In the case of more general training needs, however, group recommendations may be the best way to identify training needs. The groups' expertise may be tapped through a group discussion, questionnaire, a Delphi procedure (see Chapter 6, Human Resource Planning), or through a nominal group meeting.

The *Nominal Group Technique* (NGT) is a method of drawing out the ideas of a group of people on a specified topic.[21] It asks a group of ten to fifteen trainers, managers, or potential trainees to privately list all the training needs they can think of on a piece of paper. After the group has gone through this silent idea-generation phase, each person is asked to give one idea in round-robin fashion. This process of soliciting an idea from each person continues until each person has exhausted his or her ideas and "passes" when asked for another idea. The moderator (or scribe) lists every idea, without comment, until all ideas are listed. Comments are then clarified and duplications, if any, eliminated. Participants then vote for the five most important training needs. The votes are tabulated to determine which needs are regarded by the group as most pressing. Unlike brainstorming (where some people may not offer their ideas), NGT taps everyone's ideas and encourages the suggestions of others during the round-robin session, to stimulate even more ideas among the group members. The final "voting" ensures that the outcome reflects the group's collective wisdom.

Trainers are alert to other sources of information that may indicate a need for training. Production records, quality control reports, grievances, safety reports, absenteeism and turnover statistics, and exit interviews among departing employees may evidence problems that should be addressed through training and development efforts. Training needs may also become apparent from career planning and development discussions or performance appraisal reviews—both of which are treated in subsequent chapters.[22] Regardless of how needs assessment takes place, it is important because the success of the remaining steps in Figure 9-4 depends on an accurate assessment. If the trainer's assessment of need is not correct, it is unlikely that training objectives and program content will be appropriate.

TRAINING AND DEVELOPMENT OBJECTIVES

An evaluation of training needs results in training and development objectives. These objectives should state the desired behaviour and the conditions under which it is to occur. They serve as the standard against which individual performance and the program can be measured. For example, the objectives for an airline reservationist might be stated as follows:

1. Provide flight information to call-in customers within thirty seconds.

2. Complete a one-city, round-trip reservation in 120 seconds after all information is obtained from the customer.

Objectives like these give the trainer and the trainee specific goals that can be used to evaluate their success. If these objectives are not met, failure gives the personnel department feedback on the program and the participants.

PROGRAM CONTENT

The program's content is shaped by the needs assessment and the learning objectives. This content may seek to teach specific skills, provide needed knowledge, or try to influence attitudes. Whatever the content, the program must meet the needs of the organization and the participants. If company goals are not furthered, resources are wasted. And participants must view the content as relevant to their needs, or their motivation to learn may be low.

LEARNING PRINCIPLES

Although it is widely studied, little is known about the learning process. Part of the problem is that learning cannot be observed; only its results can be measured. From studies of learning, however, researchers have sketched a broad picture of the learning process and have developed some tentative principles of learning.

Perhaps the best way to understand learning is through the use of a *learning curve*, pictured in Figure 9-5. As the curve illustrates, learning takes place in bursts (from points *A* to *B*) and in plateaus (from points *B* to *C*). Trainers have two goals related to the shape of each employee's learning curve. First, they want the learning curve to reach a satisfactory level of performance. This level is shown as a dashed line in the figure. Second, they want the learning curve to get to the satisfactory level as quickly as possible. Although the rate at which an individual learns depends upon the person, the use of various learning principles helps speed up the learning process.

Learning principles are guidelines to the ways in which people learn most effectively. The more they are included in training, the more effective training is likely to be. The principles are: participation, repetition, relevance, transference, and feedback.

Figure 9-5
A TYPICAL LEARNING CURVE

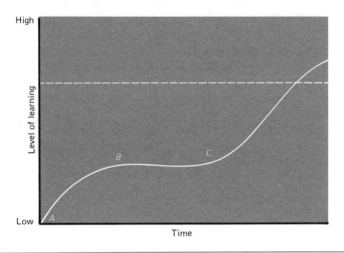

PARTICIPATION. Learning is usually quicker and more long-lasting when the learner can participate actively. Participation improves motivation and apparently engages more senses that help reinforce the learning process. As a result of participation, we learn quicker and retain that learning longer. For example, once they have learned, most people never forget how to ride a bicycle or drive a car.

REPETITION. Although it is seldom fun, repetition apparently etches a pattern into our memory. Studying for an examination, for example, involves memorization of key ideas to be recalled during the test. Likewise, most people learned the alphabet and the multiplication tables by repetition.

RELEVANCE. Learning is helped when the material to be learned is meaningful. For example, trainers usually explain the overall purpose of a job to trainees before explaining specific tasks. This explanation allows the worker to see the relevance of each task and the importance of following the given procedures.

TRANSFERENCE. The closer the demands of the training program match the demands of the job, the faster a person learns to master the job.[23] For example, pilots are usually trained in flight simulators because the simulators very closely resemble the actual cockpit and flight characteristics of the plane. The close match between the simulator and the plane allows the trainee to transfer quickly the learning in the simulator to actual flight conditions.

FEEDBACK. Feedback gives learners information on their progress. With feedback, motivated learners can adjust their behaviour to achieve the quickest possible learning curve. Without feedback, learners cannot gauge their progress and may become discouraged. Test grades are feedback on the study habits of test takers, for example.

TRAINING AND DEVELOPMENT TECHNIQUES

Before reviewing the various training and development techniques, it is important to remember that any method may be applied to both training and development. For example, a class on management techniques may be attended by supervisors and workers who are likely to be promoted to those positions.[24] For supervisors, the class covers how to do their present job better. In the case of workers who have no management responsibilities, the classes are intended to develop them into supervisors. The classroom instruction would be identical for both groups, but it has two different purposes: training for supervisors and development for workers.

In selecting a particular technique to use in training or development, there are several trade-offs. That is, no one technique is always best; the best method depends upon:

- Cost-effectiveness
- Desired program content
- Appropriateness of the facilities
- Trainee preferences and capabilities
- Trainer preferences and capabilities
- Learning principles

The importance of these six trade-offs depends upon the situation. For example, cost-effectiveness may be a minor factor when training an airline pilot in emergency manoeuvres. But whatever method is selected, it has certain learning principles associated with it. Figure 9-6 lists the most common training and development techniques and the learning principles each includes. As the figure reveals, some techniques make more effective use of learning principles than others. Even those approaches that use few learning principles, such as the lecture, are valuable tools because they may satisfy one of the other five trade-offs listed above. For example, lectures may be the best way to communicate some academic content in the most cost-effective manner, especially if the classroom is large and the room does not lend itself to other approaches. Although these six trade-offs affect the methods used, personnel specialists must be familiar with all the techniques and learning principles found in Figure 9-6.

JOB INSTRUCTION TRAINING

Job instruction training (also called on-the-job training) is received directly on the job and is used primarily to teach workers how to do their present

Figure 9-6

LEARNING PRINCIPLES IN DIFFERENT TRAINING AND DEVELOPMENT TECHNIQUES

	Participation	Repetition	Relevance	Transference	Feedback
On-the-Job Techniques					
Job instruction training	Yes	Yes	Yes	Yes	Sometimes
Job rotation	Yes	Sometimes	Yes	Sometimes	No
Apprenticeships	Yes	Sometimes	Yes	Sometimes	Sometimes
Coaching	Yes	Sometimes	Yes	Sometimes	Yes
Off-the-job Techniques					
Lecture	No	No	No	Sometimes	No
Video presentation	No	No	No	Yes	No
Vestibule training	Yes	Yes	Sometimes	Yes	Sometimes
Role playing	Yes	Sometimes	Sometimes	No	Sometimes
Case study	Yes	Sometimes	Sometimes	Sometimes	Sometimes
Simulation	Yes	Sometimes	Sometimes	Sometimes	Sometimes
Self-study	Yes	Yes	Sometimes	Sometimes	No
Programmed learning	Yes	Yes	No	Yes	Yes
Laboratory training	Yes	Yes	Sometimes	No	Yes

Source: From *Training in Industry: The Management of Learning,* by B. M. Bass and J. A. Vaughn. Copyright © 1966 by Wadsworth Publishing Company, Inc. Reprinted by permission of the publisher, Brooks/Cole Publishing Company, Monterey, Calif.

job. A trainer, supervisor, or coworker serves as the instructor. This method includes each of the five learning principles (participation, repetition, relevance, transference, and feedback) in a series of carefully planned steps.

First, the trainee receives an overview of the job, its purpose, and its desired outcomes, which emphasizes the relevance of the training. Then the trainer demonstrates the job to provide the employee with a model to copy. Since the employee is being shown the actions that the job actually requires, the training is transferable to the job. Next, the employee is allowed to mimic the trainer's example. Demonstrations by the trainer and the practice by the trainee are repeated until the job is mastered by the trainee. Repeated demonstrations and practice provide the advantage of repetition and feedback. Finally, the employee performs the job without supervision, although the trainer may visit the employee to see if there are any lingering questions.

JOB ROTATION

To cross-train employees in a variety of jobs, some trainers will move the trainee from job to job. Each move is normally preceded by job instruction training. Besides giving workers variety in their jobs, cross-training helps the organization when vacations, absences, and resignations occur. Learner participation and high job transferability are the learning advantages to job rotation.

APPRENTICESHIPS AND COACHING

Apprenticeships involve learning from a more experienced employee or employees. This approach to training may be supplemented with off-the-job classroom training. Most tradespeople, such as plumbers and carpenters, are trained through formal apprenticeship programs. Assistantships and internships are similar to apprenticeships. These approaches use high levels of participation by the trainee and have high transferability to the job.

Coaching is similar to apprenticeships in that the coach attempts to provide a model for the trainee to copy. Most companies use some coaching. It tends to be less formal than an apprenticeship program because there are few formal classroom sessions, and the coaching is provided when needed rather than being part of a carefully planned program. Coaching is almost always handled by the supervisor or manager and not the personnel department. Participation, feedback, and job transference are likely to be high in this form of learning.[25]

Someone who receives coaching by another person to assume that person's specific job is called an *understudy*. A senior executive may designate a replacement well before retirement so that that person can serve as an understudy.

Assignments to task forces or committees can also help to develop people in much the same way that apprenticeships and coaching do. Through periodic staff meetings or work with task forces and committees, a manager develops interpersonal skills, learns to evaluate information, and gains experience in observing other potential models.

LECTURE AND VIDEO PRESENTATIONS

Lecture and other off-the-job techniques tend to rely more heavily on communications rather than modelling, which is used in on-the-job programs. These approaches are applied in both training and development. Lecture is a popular approach because it offers relative economy and a meaningful organization of materials. However, participation, feedback, transference, and repetition are often low. Feedback and participation can be improved when discussion is permitted after the lecture.

Television, films, slides, and filmstrip presentations are comparable to lectures. A meaningful organization of materials and initial audience interest are potential strengths of these approaches. Interestingly, one survey of training directors revealed that they thought films were superior to lectures with questions.[26]

VESTIBULE TRAINING

So that training does not disrupt normal operations, some organizations use *vestibule training*. Separate areas or vestibules are set up with the same kind of equipment that will be used on the job. This arrangement allows transference, repetition, and participation. The meaningful organization of materials and feedback are also possible.

At the corporate training facilities of Best Western motels and hotels, vestibules exist that duplicate a typical motel room, a typical front counter, and a typical restaurant kitchen. This allows trainees to practise housekeeping, front counter service, and kitchen skills without disrupting the operations of any one property.

ROLE PLAYING

Role playing is a device that forces trainees to assume different identities. For example, a male worker and a female supervisor may trade roles. Then both may be given a typical work situation and told to respond in their new roles. The result? Usually participants exaggerate each other's behaviour. Ideally, they both get to see themselves as others see them. The experience may create greater empathy and tolerance of individual differences. This technique seeks to change attitudes of trainees, such as to improve racial understanding. It also helps to develop interpersonal skills.[27] Although participation and feedback are present, the inclusion of other learning principles depends on the situation.

The U.S. Navy has used role-playing exercises to reduce racial tensions between enlisted men aboard ships. Friction between sailors of different races within the limited confines of ships on extended patrol duty not only harmed morale and crew efficiency but also caused low rates of re-enlistment among highly trained personnel. High turnover impaired the navy's ability to function.

The role-playing exercises required small groups of black and white sailors to assume the role of opposite race. The role-playing leader gave each group an assignment and then directed them to carry it out as they thought members of the other race would do it. With the other group watching, each group in turn acted out the behaviour of the others. Through these exercises and the subsequent discussions, members of the different races were able to learn how their behaviour and attitudes affected each other. These role-playing exercises were an important step in reducing racial tensions.

Closely related to this form of role-playing is behaviour modelling. *Behaviour modelling* was described by two writers as follows:

> Modeling is one of the fundamental psychological processes by which new patterns of behavior can be acquired, and existing patterns can be altered. The fundamental characteristic of modeling is that learning takes place, *not* through actual experience, but through observation or imagination of another individual's experience. Modeling is a "vicarious process," which implies sharing in the experience of another person through imagination or sympathetic participation.[28]

Whether behaviour modelling is referred to as "matching" or "copying," "observational learning" or "imitation," ". . . all of these terms imply that a behavior is learned or modified through the observation of some other individual. . . ."[29] Employees may learn a new behaviour through modelling by observing a new or novel behaviour and then imitating it. The re-creation of the behaviour may be videotaped so that the trainer and trainee can review and criticize the behaviour. Often, when watching the ideal behaviour, the trainee also gets to see the negative consequences of not behaving in the ideal way. Observing both the positive and negative consequences of the taped behaviour gives the employee vicarious reinforcement to adopt the right behaviour. One area where this approach has been used successfully is in teaching supervisors the correct way to discipline employees.

In the supervisory training program of a large, unionized steel company, supervisors were put through a half-day disciplinary training session that used videotape-based behaviour modelling. After a short lecture on the principles of discipline, trainees were shown a brief tape of a supervisor conducting a disciplinary interview incorrectly and another where the discipline was handled properly. Then the supervisors were paired off and each one was told to "discipline" his or her partner using the correct method they just observed. These mock discipline sessions were filmed and played back—often to the horror of the participants. Each saw how others saw him or her when they conducted a disciplinary interview. After a brief and largely positive critique from the trainer, each supervisor conducted a second and a third "discipline session" that was followed by a critique. By the end of the morning, each supervisor was able to conduct a disciplinary interview in the correct manner. Whether this training was actually transferred to their day-to-day behaviour on the job was not evaluated by the training department nor the shop manager.

CASE STUDY
By studying a case, trainees learned about real or hypothetical circumstances and the actions others took under those circumstances. Besides learning from the content of the case, trainees can develop decision-making skills. When cases are meaningful and similar to work-related situations, there is some transference. There also is the advantage of participation through discussion of the case. Feedback and repetition are usually lacking. Research indicates that this technique is most effective for developing problem-solving skills.[30]

SIMULATION
Simulation exercises are in two forms. One form involves a mechanical simulator that replicates the major features of the work situation. Driving simulators used in driver's education programs are an example. This training method is similar to vestibule training, except that the simulator more often provides instantaneous feedback on performance.

Computer simulations are another technique. For training and development purposes, this method is often employed in the form of games. Players make a decision and the computer determines the outcome of the decision, given the conditions under which it was programmed. This technique is used most commonly to train managers, who otherwise might have to use trial and error in decision making.

SELF-STUDY AND PROGRAMMED LEARNING

Carefully planned instructional materials can be used to train and develop employees. These are particularly useful when employees are dispersed geographically or when learning requires little interaction. Self-study techniques range from manuals to prerecorded cassettes or videotapes. Unfortunately, few learning principles are included in this type of training.

The Pepsi Cola Management Institute is responsible for training bottlers all over the world. To contend with this dispersion, it created a network of videotape recorders and supplied bottlers with videotaped materials. The institute also uses other techniques.

Programmed learning materials are another form of self-study. Commonly, these are printed booklets that contain a series of questions and answers. After a question is read, the answer can be uncovered immediately. If the reader was right, he or she proceeds. If wrong, the reader is directed to review accompanying materials. Of course, computer programs with visual displays may be used instead of printed booklets.[31] Programmed materials do provide learner participation, repetition, relevance, and feedback; transference, however, tends to be low.

LABORATORY TRAINING

Laboratory training is a form of group training used primarily to enhance interpersonal skills. It, too, can be used to develop desired behaviours for future job responsibilities. Participants seek to improve their human relations skills by better understanding themselves and others. It involves sharing their experiences and examining the feelings, behaviour, perceptions, and reactions that result. Usually a trained professional serves as a facilitator. The process relies on participation, feedback, and repetition. One popular form of laboratory training is sensitivity training, which seeks to improve a person's sensitivity to the feelings of others.

HUMAN RESOURCE DEVELOPMENT

The long-term development of human resources—as distinct from training for a specific job—is of growing concern to personnel departments. Through the development of present employees, the personnel department reduces the company's dependence on hiring new employees. If workers are developed properly, the job openings found through human resource planning are more likely to be filled internally. Promotion and transfers also show employees that they have a career, not just a job. The employer benefits by increased continuity in operations and by employees who feel a greater commitment to the firm.

Human resource development is also an effective way to meet several challenges faced by most large organizations. These challenges include employee obsolescence, socio-technical changes, and employee turnover.[32] By meeting these challenges, the personnel department can help maintain an effective work force.

EMPLOYEE OBSOLESCENCE

Obsolescence results when an employee no longer possesses the knowledge or abilities to perform successfully. In fast-changing and highly technical fields, such as engineering and medicine, obsolescence can occur quickly. Among managers, the change may take place more slowly and be more difficult to determine. Other people in the organization may not notice obsolescence until it is advanced. Too often, favourable opinions about a manager, which are formed over years of association, prevent others from seeing telltale signs of obsolescence—such as inappropriate attitudes, poor performance, or incorrect or outdated procedures.

Although obsolescence may develop from some change in the individual, it is more likely to result from that person's failure to adapt to new technology, new procedures, or other changes. The more rapidly the environment changes, the more likely it is that employees will become obsolete.[33]

Some employers are reluctant to take strong action and fire obsolete employees, particularly those who have been with the company for a long time. Instead, they may be given a job where their obsolescence does not matter as much or where their skills are not as obsolete. For example, when top executives fail to perform satisfactorily, they sometimes are "promoted" to chair the board, where their primary role is to attend ceremonial functions such as banquets for retiring employees. For lower-level employees, the solution is often additional development programs.

To avoid the problem of obsolescence before it occurs is a major challenge for the personnel department. By periodically assessing the needs of employees and giving them programs to develop new skills, the department is using development programs proactively. If programs are designed reactively, after obsolescence occurs, they are likely to be less effective and more costly. For example, consider the situation faced by a personnel department of a regional airline:

Sam Oliver had been a ground crew chief in the Armed Forces for many of his twenty years in the service. After retirement, he joined a regional airline as a mechanic. Since he had extensive supervisory experience, he was promoted to ground crew chief with the airline. Sam had been successful in the Armed Forces by giving direct orders with little explanation, and he followed the same leadership style in his civilian job.

The personnel department realized something was wrong when an unusually large number of grievances were filed with the union by Sam's ground crew. To correct the problems, Sam was enrolled in an intensive sixteen-week supervisory training program at the local community college. Although he changed his approach after the program, Sam now showed resentment against those of his subordinates who had filed the grievances.

Had the personnel department undertaken proactive supervisory development before Sam was promoted rather than reacting to his obsolescence after problems arose, his resentment might have been avoided.

When an employee reaches a career plateau, obsolescence may set in. A *career plateau* occurs when an employee is in a position that he or she does well enough not to be demoted or fired, but not so well as to be promoted.[34]

When the employee realizes that he or she is at this plateau, the motivation to keep up with the times as a manager, professional, or technician may be reduced.[35]

One attempt to deal with obsolescence has been the continuing education offered by many companies to middle- and upper-level management. In one survey of over 10,000 companies in Canada, 26% reported to have training programs for executives, professionals, and managerial personnel.[36] Some large companies, like Alcan, Bell Canada, or Ontario Hydro, have their own programs, while most other firms allow their managers to attend continuing education courses offered by colleges and universities. Most of these companies pay all or part of the costs involved, usually depending on the degree of job relevance of the particular course.

Approximately 10% of the companies surveyed above offer extended leave of absence for educational purposes, often to acquire a university or professional degree or designation.[37]

SOCIO-TECHNICAL CHANGES

Social and technological changes also challenge the personnel department to maintain an effective work force. For example, cultural attitudes about women in the work force have caused many companies to redesign their development programs in order to meet societal pressures for equal employment:

Bell Canada redesigned an existing program for outside technicians to enable more women to qualify for outside jobs that previously had been dominated by men.

Likewise, rapid changes in technology require technology-based firms to engage in near-continuous development. Consider the technological changes that occurred during Frank T. Carey's career with IBM, for example:

Mr. Carey joined IBM in 1948 "because he liked its bright prospects in the office-equipment business."[38] Although IBM is a major producer of office equipment, most people think of IBM as the giant computer manufacturer. While Mr. Carey's career at IBM progressed up to chairman of the board, technology radically transformed IBM into the largest computer manufacturer in the world. Undoubtedly, his career, like many others' at IBM, was marked by near-continuous development activities in order to keep up with rapid technological change.

EMPLOYEE TURNOVER

Turnover—the movement of employees from one organization to another—creates a special challenge for human resource development. Since these departures are largely unpredictable, development activities must prepare present employees to succeed those who leave. Although research shows that leaders of very large industrial companies spend nearly all of their careers with one firm, the same research found that mobility is widespread among other managers.[39] Therefore, development programs must prepare other employees to replace departing managers. Sometimes an employer with excellent development programs finds that these programs actually *contribute* to employee turnover.

Ironically, the widely recognized development programs of such companies as the Royal Bank, Air Canada, Bell Canada, IBM Canada, and others partially cause some employee mobility. Their programs produce such high-quality results that recruiters from other companies are attracted to these employees.

EVALUATION OF TRAINING AND DEVELOPMENT

The implementation of training and development serves as a transformation process. Untrained employees are transformed into capable workers, and present workers may be developed to assume new responsibilities. To verify the program's success, personnel managers increasingly demand that training and development activities be evaluated systematically.

The lack of evaluation may be the most serious flaw in most training and development efforts.[40] Simply stated, personnel professionals too seldom ask "Did the program achieve the objectives established for it?" They often assume it had value because the content seemed important. Or trainers may rely on the evaluations of trainees who comment on how enjoyable the experience was for them but who cannot yet determine how valuable it is.

Evaluation of training and development should follow the steps in Figure 9-7. First, evaluation criteria should be established before training begins.[41] These criteria may be the same as the learning objectives set in Figure 9-4. Then participants should be given a pretest. That is, they should be tested to establish their level of knowledge before the program begins. Sometimes selection tests can serve this purpose. After training or development is completed, a posttest should reveal any improvement that may have resulted from the program. If the improvement is so significant that it did not likely result from chance, the program actually made a difference. The program is a success if the improvement met the evaluation criteria and is transferred to the job. Transference is best measured by improved job performance. Follow-up studies may be conducted months or even years later to see how well learning was retained.

Plagued by a disturbing number of accidents, a local home builder contracted with a management consulting firm to receive a safety training program. The training included a variety of techniques, but the builder wanted "proof" that it was effective without waiting to see if accidents declined. A safety quiz was given to the builder's

Figure 9-7
STEPS IN THE EVALUATION OF TRAINING AND DEVELOPMENT

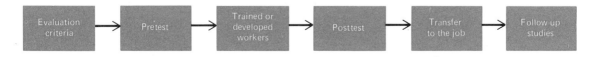

field employees. The average score was 39. After training, a posttest revealed that the average score was 67, a result that was not likely due to chance.

The management consultant claimed that the posttest proved that the training was successful. The builder's personnel manager correctly argued:

"The training is a qualified success. The posttest reveals that the training did increase the field personnel's knowledge of safety. But the only measure of success is whether that new knowledge results in behavioural changes—namely the lowering of the frequency and severity of accidents. We won't know if the training was successful until we get the quarterly accident reports in three months. In fact, I would like to run a follow-up study in a year to see how well the knowledge was retained."

As this example illustrates, posttests do not prove the success of the training. Success is best illustrated by behavioural changes. Therefore, the evaluation criteria should be stated in behavioural terms whenever possible. In the home builder's example, the learning objectives and the evaluation criteria might have read as follows:

• A reduction of the frequency of work-related accidents per 10,000 work-hours during the subsequent calendar quarter.

• A reduction of the severity of work-related accidents per 10,000 work-hours during the subsequent calendar quarter.

The posttest is still useful for determining if the information was communicated; it may also be useful for evaluating which applicants have failed to understand the materials. However, the success of a program must ultimately be measured by means of specific behavioural changes that occur on the job.[42]

SUMMARY

After workers are selected, they are seldom ready to perform successfully. They must be integrated into the social and work environment of the organization. Orientation programs help a worker begin this socialization process. The organization benefits because training time and costs are lowered, employee satisfaction is higher, and initial turnover is lower.

Even after employees are oriented, they may lack the necessary skills, attitudes, or knowledge to perform their jobs successfully. This deficiency is remedied through training, which begins with needs assessment. Then specific training objectives can be set. These objectives give direction to the training program and serve to evaluate the training program at its completion.

The content of the program depends upon the training objectives. The design of the training should consider such learning principles as participation, repetition, relevance, transference, and feedback.

Once training is completed, it should be evaluated. Evaluation includes a pretest, a posttest, measurement of how well the training content has been transferred to the actual job, and some form of follow-up studies to ensure that the learning has been retained.

TERMS FOR REVIEW

Orientation programs	Feedback
Employee handbook	Job instruction training
Socialization	Vestibule training
Needs assessment	Role playing
Nominal Group Technique (NGT)	Behaviour modelling
Learning curve	Laboratory training
Learning principles	Obsolescence
Repetition	Career plateau
Transference	Turnover

REVIEW AND DISCUSSION QUESTIONS

1. "If employees are properly selected, there should be no need for an orientation or training." Do you agree or disagree? Why?
2. What are the employee benefits from orientation programs? The organization benefits?
3. What are the common pitfalls of an informal orientation program?
4. Suppose your organization hired six new clerical workers. What types of orientation program would you design to help these workers become productive and satisfied?
5. For each of the following occupations, which training techniques do you recommend? Why?
   (a) A cashier in a grocery store
   (b) A welder
   (c) An assembly-line worker
   (d) An inexperienced supervisor
6. If you were directed to design a development program for managers that made use of all five learning principles, which two training techniques would you combine? Why?
7. Suppose you were a supervisor in an accounting department and the training manager wanted to implement a new training program to teach bookkeepers how to complete some new accounting forms. What steps would you recommend to evaluate the effectiveness of the training program?
8. Assume you were hired to manage a research and development department. After a few weeks you noticed that some researchers were more effective than others, and that the less effective ones received little recognition from their more productive counterparts. What forms of development would you consider for both groups?

INCIDENT 9-1

THE FOLLOW-UP ORIENTATION AT CHEVER'S CARPETS

During the first six months with Chever's Carpets, Oliver Talbot was promoted from supervisor to assistant warehouse manager. He also received two pay increases dur-

ing that time. Thus Leslie Coulter expected the follow-up orientation session with Oliver to be a short and pleasant experience. But when she asked Oliver what questions he had about Chever's operations, he replied:

"*For a business employing nearly 200 people, I am dumbfounded by the orientation and training new employees are provided with, or, more correctly, the lack of orientation and training. My orientation program consisted of being shuffled in to see Mr. Chever for fifteen minutes, over ten of which he spent on the phone. My encounters with other managers around here were equally unimpressive. Most spent the few minutes I had with them complaining of all of their problems. If the warehouse manager had not taken a couple of hours with me after work the first day to explain procedures and my job, I would have failed as a supervisor or quit.*

The training I received was essentially nonexistent. I was thrown in with drivers, forklift operators, and sales clerks and shown how to complete the necessary ordering and shipping forms. Three-quarters of that training applied to office procedures the salespeople are supposed to follow, not I.

I do not let new warehouse supervisors go to the training or orientation sessions. I may be new and have a narrow perspective, but I know they get a better orientation and better training from me than what I was given when I came here. This follow-up orientation is a nice idea, but it is six months too late. I hope my criticisms have been useful to you. I sure do not have any compliments about orientation and training around here."

1. On the basis of what Oliver Talbot said, what changes would you suggest in the orientation program? In the training program?
2. If you were Leslie Coulter, what specific questions would you want to ask Oliver Talbot?
3. What problems do you see in Oliver Talbot's conducting his own orientation and training programs?

INCIDENT 9-2
DEVELOPMENT OF HUMAN RESOURCES AT GENERAL HOSPITAL

Clayton Dahl was appointed director of human resource development at General Hospital. The hospital director, Andrea Hess, suggested that Clayton could best familiarize himself with the hospital's development needs by compiling a report about past development efforts.

In gathering the information for the report, Clayton made several interesting observations:

• *Development activities had been limited to preparing nonprofessionals to assume supervisory positions.*

• *Most department managers and staff directors took the attitude that it was easier to hire staff as it was needed than to develop present employees.*

• *Those managers who supervised professional hospital employees took the attitude that development is the responsibility of each professional.*

• *Most other managers viewed development programs as an admission of inability by those who took them voluntarily.*

• *During each of the last three years, the development budget had been cut by about 10%.*

1. What would you recommend if you were in Clayton's position?
2. What type of support should Clayton seek from the hospital administrator?

3. If a new development program is offered, what type of attendance policy should Clayton set? Why? What types of problems will that policy cause?

REFERENCES

1. James L. Hayes, "Human Resources—The Last Resource of a Frontier Society," *Training and Development Journal*, June 1976, p. 9.
2. Herbert E. Striner, "Retraining Displaced Workers: Too Little, Too Late?" *Business Week*, July 19, 1982, p. 178.
3. "ASPA-BNA Survey No. 32: Employee Orientation Programs," *Bulletin to Management, No. 1436*, Washington: Bureau of National Affairs, Inc., Aug. 25, 1977, p. 1.
4. Robert W. Hollmann, "Let's Not Forget about New Employee Orientation," *Personnel Journal*, May 1976, pp. 244–247, 250. See also Thomas LaMott, "Making Employee Orientation Work," *Personnel Journal*, January 1974, pp. 35–37, 44; and Walter D. St. John, "The Complete Employee Orientation Program," *Personnel Journal*, May 1980, pp. 373–378.
5. Ibid., p. 245.
6. "ASPA-BNA Survey No. 32: Employee Orientation Programs," op. cit., p. 5.
7. Earl R. Gomersall and M. Scott Myers, "Breakthrough in On-the-Job Training," *Harvard Business Review*, July–August 1966, pp. 66–72. See also Donald B. Summers, "Understanding the Process by Which New Employees Enter Work Groups," *Personnel Journal*, August 1977, pp. 394–397, 416.
8. Gomersall and Myers, op. cit.
9. Gale E. Newell, "How to Plan a Training Program," *Personnel Journal*, May 1976, pp. 220–224. See also Bonnye L. Matthes and Virginia Sweet Lincoln, "Try S.T.A.R.T.: The Systematic Training Aid Resource Tool," *Training*, January 1978, pp. 32–33; and S. D. Inderlied and D. L. Bates, "A Practical Approach to Determining Training Solvable Problems," *Personnel Journal*, January 1980, pp. 121–125. Also see Donald B. Miller, "Training Managers to Stimulate Employee Development," *Training and Development Journal*, February 1981, pp. 47–53.
10. John D. Dickey, "Training with a Focus on the Individual," *Personnel Administrator*, June 1982, p. 35.
11. Ibid., pp. 35, 37.
12. Ibid., p. 38.
13. Ibid., p. 7.
14. This figure is a composite derived from the following sources: Labour Canada, *Education and Working Canadians: Report of the Commission of Inquiry on Educational Leave and Productivity*, Ottawa, June 1979, and Employment and Immigration Canada, *Labour Market Development in the 1980's: Report of the Task Force on Labour Market Development*, Ottawa, 1981, p. 153. See also Ian Morrison and Paul Belanger (eds.), "Manpower Training at the Crossroads," proceedings of A Conference on Adult Education in Canada, Canadian Association for Adult Education, January 1976; and Roy T. Adams, "Toward a More Competent Labour Force," *Relations Industrielles*, 35 (1980) (3): 422–436.
15. Thomas F. Gilbert, "The High Cost of Knowledge," *Personnel*, March 1976, p. 23.
16. William C. Byham and James Robinson, "Building Supervisory Confidence—A Key to Transfer of Training," *Personnel Journal*, May 1977, pp. 248–250, 253.
17. John W. Lawrie, "A Guide to Customized Leadership Training and Development," *Personnel Journal*, September 1979, pp. 593–596.
18. "Employee Training," *Personnel Management: Policies and Practices*, Englewood Cliffs, NJ: Prentice-Hall Inc., 1979, p. 9.
19. Kenneth N. Wexley and Gary P. Latham, *Developing and Training Human Resources in Organizations*, Dallas, Texas: Scott, Foresman and Company, 1981, p. 35.
20. Mariless S. Niehoff and M. Jay Romans, "Needs Assessment as Step One toward Enhancing Productivity," *Personnel Administrator*, May 1982, pp. 35–39.
21. Andre Delbecq and A. Van de Ven, "A Group Process Model for Problem Identification and Program Planning," *Journal of Applied Behavioral Science*, August 1971, pp. 78–83. See also Mark Martinko and Jim Gepson, "Nominal Grouping and Needs Analysis," in Francis L. Ulschak (ed.), *Human Resource Development: The Theory and Practice of Needs Assessment*, Reston, VA: Reston Publishing Company, 1983, pp. 101–110.
22. Martinko and Gepson, op. cit.
23. Byham and Robinson, op. cit.
24. Ernest D. Jobe, W. Randy Boxx, and D. L. Howell, "A Customized Approach to Management Development," *Personnel Journal*, March 1979, pp. 150–153.
25. Joseph Yeager, "Coaching the Executive: Can You Teach an Old Dog New Tricks?" *Personnel Administrator*, November 1982, pp. 37–42.
26. Stephen J. Carroll, Frank T. Paine, and John M. Ivancevich, "The Relative Effectiveness of Training Methods—Expert Opinion and Research," *Personnel Psychology*, Autumn 1972, p. 499.
27. Ibid.
28. Henry P. Sims, Jr., and Charles C. Manz, "Modeling Influences on Employee Behavior," *Personnel Journal*, January 1982, p. 58.

29. Ibid.
30. See also John W. Newstrom, "Evaluating the Effectiveness of Training Methods," *The Personnel Administrator*, January 1980, pp. 55–60.
31. John R. Hinrichs, "Personnel Training," in Marvin D. Dunnette (ed.), *Handbook of Industrial and Organizational Psychology*, Chicago: Rand McNally & Company, 1976, pp. 850–851.
32. Edward J. Mandt, "A Basic Model of Manager Development," *Personnel Journal*, June 1979, pp. 395–400. See also Alfred W. Hill, "How Organizational Philosophy Influences Management Development," *Personnel Journal*, February 1980, pp. 118–120, 148.
33. Elmer Burack and Gopal Pati, "Technology and Managerial Obsolescence," *MSU Business Topics*, Spring 1970, pp. 49–56. See also Herbert Kaufman, *Obsolescence and Professional Career Development*, New York: AMACOM, 1974.
34. Christopher M. Dawson, "Will Career Plateauing Become a Bigger Problem?" *Personnel Journal*, January 1983, pp. 78–81.
35. Morley D. Glicken, "A Counseling Approach to Employee Burnout," *Personnel Journal*, March 1983, pp. 222–228. See also Jack Brewer and Carol Dubnicki, "Relighting the Fire with an Employee Revitalization Program," *Personnel Journal*, October 1983, pp. 812-818.
36. Labour Canada, "Education and Working Canadians," Report of the Commission of Inquiry on Educational Leave and Productivity, June 1979.
37. Weiermair, K., "Industrial Training and Industrial Excellence: Canada's Record in International Perspective," paper presented at the Ninth Annual Management Research Forum, Wilfrid Laurier University, September 1978.
38. "In the News," *Fortune*, Feb. 27, 1979, pp. 15–16.
39. William B. Werther, Jr., "Management Turnover Implications of Career Mobility," *The Personnel Administrator*, February 1977, pp. 63–66. See also Simeon J. Touretzky, "Changing Attitudes: A Question of Loyalty," *The Personnel Administrator*, April 1979, pp. 35–36.
40. Hermann F. Schwind, "Thoughts on Training Evaluation," *Canadian Training Methods*, 7(1) (June 1975): 14–15.
41. Hermann F. Schwind, "Issues in Training Evaluation: The Criterion," *Canadian Training Methods*, 7(4) (October 1975): 14–15.
42. Hermann F. Schwind, "Issues in Training Evaluation: The Methodology," *Canadian Training Methods*, 7(3) (August 1975): 22–25.

Chapter 10

Career Planning

Organizations are in a position to provide assessment and career planning programs for their employees so that more realistic and realizable aspirations are developed. These programs must also give due consideration to the personal life needs and goals. . . .

Ronald J. Burke and Tamara Weir[1]

In the search for miracle workers to turn their firms into giants, some crazed executives often hire and fire employees with great regularity.

Dr. Srully Blotnick[2]

CHAPTER OBJECTIVES

After studying this chapter, you should be able to:
1. **Advise** someone about the major points in career planning.
2. **Describe** how personnel departments encourage and assist career planning.
3. **Identify** the major advantages of career planning.
4. **Explain** the relationship between career planning and career development.
5. **List** the major actions that aid career development.

A *career* is all the jobs that are held during one's working life. For some people, these jobs are part of a careful plan. For others, their career is simply a matter of luck. These two extremes are illustrated in the following dialogue between a retired bank executive and an assistant manager of a branch bank.

Joe: *I didn't make it to executive vice president of a major bank by chance. I wanted to be a banking executive since I was a customer service clerk trainee. Sure I worked hard, but I also tried to plan my career.*

Joan: *Career planning is a waste of time. There are too many variables. Who knows which openings will occur? Besides, promotions are largely a matter of luck, a matter of being in the right place at the right time.*

Joe: *I agree, luck plays a part. But you would not be an assistant branch manager if you didn't have some university education.*

Joan: *Well, sure, that's true. But whether I make branch manager is mostly luck.*

Joe: *Is it? Don't you think you can control your future to some extent? Don't you believe that a promotion is more likely if you develop the background needed to func-*

tion as a branch manager? If your performance as a branch manager is superior to other branch managers, don't you think that your chances of promotion will be better? There are many things you can do to increase your chances of career success.

But merely planning a career does not guarantee career success. Superior performance, experience, education, and some occasional luck play an important part. But when people like Joan rely almost wholly on luck, they seldom are prepared for opportunities that arise. To be ready for career opportunities, successful people develop career plans and then take action to achieve their plans. Simply stated, a successful career needs to be managed through careful planning. If it is not, employees are seldom ready for career opportunities, and personnel departments find it extremely difficult to meet their internal staffing needs.[3]

Some people fail to manage their careers because they are unaware of the basic concepts of career planning described in Figure 10-1. They do not realize that goals can shape their career and yield greater success. As a result, their planning is left to fate and their development rests in the hands of others. Awareness of the concepts in the figure is no guarantee of action. But when awareness leads to goal setting, career planning is more likely to occur. For example, if Joan set a goal of becoming a branch bank manager in two years, that goal would lead her to the next question: How do I achieve the goal? If Joan answers that question by taking a special bank management course, she becomes better prepared to be a branch manager and her chances for promotion increase.

Figure 10-1
SELECTED CAREER PLANNING TERMS

- **Career.** A career is all the jobs that are held during one's working life.
- **Career path.** A career path is the sequential pattern of jobs that forms one's career.
- **Career goals.** Career goals are the future positions one strives to reach as part of a career. These goals serve as benchmarks along one's career path.
- **Career planning.** Career planning is the process by which one selects career goals and the path to those goals.
- **Career development.** Career development is the process by which one undertakes personal improvements to achieve a personal career plan.

Although every person's career is unique, a review of Joe's career in the banking industry shows how career planning works in practice. Joe's progress is summarized in Figure 10-2 and explained below.

- Four years after graduating from high school, Joe joined the Bank of New Brunswick as a customer service clerk trainee. At that point in his career his goal was to become a banking executive. He had no idea of the *career path* he would follow. But Joe realized that his first step would be to become a supervisor. This *career planning* caused him to enroll in the evening degree-program of a nearby university. During the next nine years he

Figure 10-2

CAREER PATH FOR A RETIRED SENIOR VICE PRESIDENT IN THE BANKING INDUSTRY

Job Number	Job Level	Job Title	Type of Change	Years on Job	Ending Age
1	Worker	Customer Service Clerk Trainee		$1/2$	22
2	Worker	Customer Service Clerk	Promotion	5	27
3	Supervising	Supervisor Customer Service	Promotion	2	29
4	Supervising	Loan Officer	Change in duties only	2	31
5	Management	Accounts Manager	Promotion and transfer	2	33
6	Management	Branch Manager	Promotion and transfer	2	35
7	Management	Branch Manager	Transfer	3	38
8	Management	District Manager	Promotion	5	43
9	Management	District Manager	Transfer (CGA)	6	49
10	Executive	Vice President (Finance)	Resignation and promotion	6	55
11	Executive	Senior V.P. (Finance)	Promotion	10	65

also entered some training programs organized by the local Board of Trade. These *career development* actions were the first of many that Joe undertook. He received two promotions and then at the age of thirty was made a loan officer.

• After he completed his degree, Joe was promoted to accounts manager and was transferred. Although the new job did not give him much of a salary raise in real terms (since the cost of living in the new city where he was to go was comparatively very high) Joe knew that some diversification in his background would increase his chances of becoming a senior manager someday.

• Two years after he became accounts manager, Joe was promoted to branch manager and transferred to a small branch in a suburban area. After two years, he was again transferred to a major city branch as its manager.

• Joe realized that without further qualifications his future career progress was likely to be quite slow. He therefore enrolled in the Certified General Accountant's Program. At the same time he began attending executive development seminars conducted by a nearby university. Three years later he was promoted to district manager, and five years later he was again transferred to a larger district.

• At the end of his fifth year in the new district, he had completed his Certified General Accountant's diploma. Since no promotion was forthcoming immediately, Joe left the Bank of New Brunswick a year later and joined the Ontario Dominion Bank as its vice president of finance. Six years later he was promoted to senior vice president (finance), in which position he remained for ten years.

As a review of Figure 10-2 indicates, Joe's career plan involved well-timed transfers and an educational leave. Figure 10-3 superimposes Joe's career changes on the organization charts of the two banks for which he worked. As the organization charts show, career progress is seldom straight up in an organization. Lateral transfers, leaves, and even resignations are used. When Joe started as a customer service clerk trainee at age twenty-one, there was no way he could have predicted the career path he would follow. But through periodic career planning, he reassessed his career progress and then undertook development activities to achieve intermediate career goals, such as becoming a supervisor. As a result of career planning and development, Joe's career consisted of a path that led him to his goal of becoming an executive in the banking industry.

CAREER PLANNING AND DEVELOPMENT OVERVIEW

During the forty years of Joe's career, personnel departments in banks and other large organizations gave relatively little support to career planning. When promotable talent was scarce, personnel departments usually reacted with crash training programs or additional recruitment. Human resource planning and career planning seldom occurred. Instead, organizations and employees reacted to new developments rather than seeking proactive solutions.

Viewed historically, this limited role for personnel departments was understandable, because career plans were seen largely as a personal matter.[4] Even when personnel managers wanted their department to provide assistance in career planning, they often lacked the resources to become involved. As a result, only a few (mostly large) organizations encouraged career planning by employees.

Today, an increasing number of personnel departments see career planning as a way to meet their internal staffing needs.[5] When employers encourage career planning, employees are more likely to set career goals. In turn, these goals may motivate employees to pursue further education, training, or other career development activities. These activities then improve the value of employees to the organization and give the personnel department a larger pool of qualified applicants from which to fill internal job openings.

Figure 10-3
A CAREER PATH DIAGRAM FOR AN EXECUTIVE VICE PRESIDENT IN THE BANKING INDUSTRY

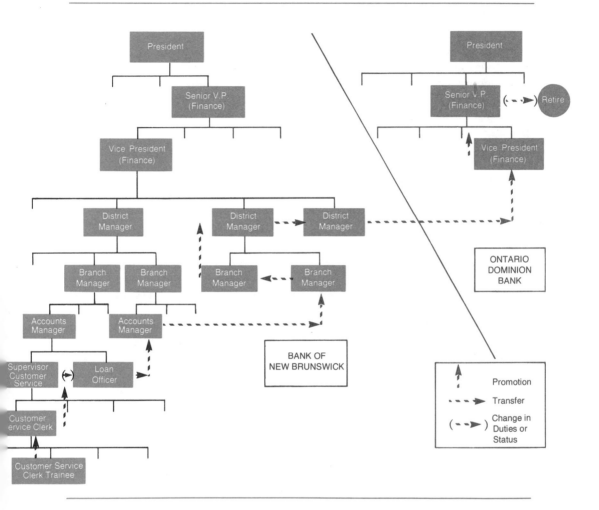

But what do employees want? A study of one group of employees revealed five areas of concern. These include:

• *Career equity.* Employees want to perceive equity in the organization's performance/promotion system with respect to career advancement opportunities.

• *Supervisory concern.* Employees want their supervisors to play an active role in career development and provide timely performance feedback.

• *Awareness of opportunities.* Employees want knowledge of the career advancement opportunities that exist in their organization.

• *Employee interest.* Employees need different amounts of information and have different degrees of interest in career advancement depending on a variety of factors.

• *Career satisfaction.* Employees have different levels of career satisfaction depending on their age and occupation.

Effective career planning and development programs must consider these different perceptions and wants of employees. What employees expect from the career programs developed by the personnel department will vary according to age, sex, occupation, education, and other variables. In short, whatever approach the personnel department takes toward career planning and development, it must be a flexible, proactive approach. As one personnel manager in a large corporation concluded:

Flexibility in career development programs is paramount if the goals of improved productivity, increased personal satisfaction, growth and ultimately increased organizational effectiveness are to be achieved. In many cases, this will require the modification of basic existing programs to address the specific needs of a particular group of employees.

PERSONNEL DEPARTMENTS AND CAREER PLANNING

Personnel departments should, and increasingly do, take an active interest in employee career planning.[6] Planning and managing human resources is emerging as an increasingly important determinant of organizational effectiveness.[7]

Personnel departments often handle career planning because their human resource plans indicate the organization's future employment needs and related career opportunities. In addition, personnel experts are more likely to be aware of training or other developmental opportunities. Of course, individual managers also should encourage career planning, as Joe did in the opening dialogue. But if personnel specialists leave career planning to managers, it may not get done. Not all managers take as strong an interest in their employees' careers as Joe appears to.

The involvement of personnel managers in career planning has grown during recent years because of its benefits. Here is a partial list of those benefits:

• *Develops promotable employees.* Career planning helps to develop internal supplies of promotable talent.

• *Lowers turnover.* The increased attention to and concern for individual careers generate more organizational loyalty and therefore lower employee turnover.

• *Taps employee potential.* Career planning encourages employees to tap more of their potential abilities because they have specific career goals.

• *Furthers growth.* Career plans and goals motivate employees to grow and develop.

• *Reduces hoarding.* Without career planning, it is easier for managers to hoard key subordinates. Career planning causes employees, managers, and the personnel department to become aware of employee qualifications.

• *Satisfies employee needs.* With less hoarding and improved growth opportunities for employees, individual needs for recognition and accomplishment are more readily satisfied, and self-esteem is boosted.

• *Assists affirmative-action plans.* Career planning can help members of protected groups prepare for more important jobs.

To realize these benefits, more personnel departments are following the lead of a few pioneers and supporting career planning. In practice, personnel departments encourage career planning in three ways: through career education, information, and counselling.

CAREER EDUCATION

Surprisingly, many employees know very little about career planning. Often they are unaware of the need for and advantages of career planning. And once made aware, they often lack the necessary information to plan their careers successfully. Personnel departments are suited to solve both of these shortcomings.

Personnel departments can increase employee awareness through a variety of educational techniques. For example, speeches, memoranda, and position papers from senior executives stimulate employee interest at low cost to the employer. If executives communicate their belief in career planning, other managers are likely to do the same.

Workshops and seminars on career planning increase employee interest by pointing out the key concepts associated with career planning.[8] Workshops help the employee set career goals, identify career paths, and uncover specific career development activities. These educational activities may be supplemented by printed or taped information on career planning.

Most of the employees in Trans Canada Harvester company had thirty or more years of service. Rapid growth caused many newcomers to join the company. These new employees had not developed the loyalty of their senior colleagues and were more prone to ask, "What is the company doing for my career?"

The personnel department of the company had taken the view that career planning and development is the responsibility of the employee. With this philosophy, a voluntary, four-hour career planning workshop was developed. Employees had to sign up to go to the workshop on their own time and did not receive any pay for attending. Instructors from the personnel department were not paid either; they volunteered to do the sessions which helped to reinforce the perspective that the department was interested in the participants as people, not just as employees.

The workshops typically began with participants being assigned to teams. This was followed by introductions and a discussion about the confidentiality of what they learn about each other's career interests. The groups then listed enjoyable and unpleasant activities as the first step in creating a personal inventory and identifying alternatives. Usually, discussions followed, centring on an internal staffing decision in which the teams were asked to fill a hypothetical job opening. These discussions were found to be extremely helpful in promoting acceptance of the management perspective on internal selection and promotion. Many participants realized for the first time that being passed over meant only that someone else was slightly better qualified—not that they were in disfavour with the company's management.

When the personnel department lacks the necessary staff to design and conduct educational programs, public programs conducted by local institutions or consultants may help.

One worldwide consulting firm, Towers, Perrin, Forster & Crosby, provides its clients with a four-step package. The packaged program develops (1) a strategy for the organization to solve its unique needs, (2) support systems based upon the present personnel management information system to give employees the data they need to plan their careers, (3) workbooks that allow employees to engage in career planning, and (4) a career resource centre that offers employees assistance with their career planning.

INFORMATION ON CAREER PLANNING

Regardless of the educational strategy the personnel department selects, it should provide employees with other information they need to plan their careers. Much of this information is already a part of the personnel department's information system. For example, job descriptions and specifications can be quite valuable to someone who is trying to estimate reasonable career goals. Likewise, personnel departments can identify future job openings through the human resource plan. Personnel specialists can also share their knowledge of potential career paths. For example, they are often keenly aware of the similarities between seemingly unrelated jobs. If this information is given to employees, it may reveal previously unseen career paths.

For example, consider the possible career paths faced by Leslie Stevens, who works in a newspaper. In this type of work, the jobs of typist, Linotype operator, and Teletype operator call for a similar characteristic: finger dexterity. But Leslie, a clerk-typist in the advertising department, may not realize that this skill applied to a Linotype machine may earn her three times as much as the other jobs.

When different jobs require similar skills, they form *job families*. Career paths within a job family demand little additional training since the skills of each job are closely related.[9] If personnel departments make information about job families available, employees can find feasible career paths. They can then assess these career paths by talking with those who already hold jobs along the path.

One problem with job families is that employees may want to skip over less pleasant jobs. To prevent employees from rejecting some jobs in a job family, the personnel department may establish a sequential progression of jobs. A *job progression ladder* is a partial career path where some jobs have prerequisites, as shown in Figure 10-4. The job progression ladder shown in the figure requires Leslie to become a Teletype operator before moving to the better-paying job of Linotype operator. This requirement assures the personnel department of an ample internal supply of Teletype operators because this job is a prerequisite for the well-paying position of Linotype operator.

Figure 10-4

THREE JOBS WITH SIMILAR REQUIREMENTS GROUPED INTO A JOB FAMILY

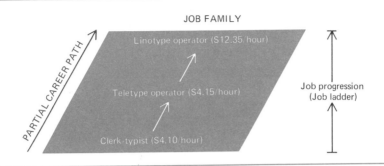

The personnel department can also encourage career planning by providing information about alternative career paths. Figure 10-5 shows that Leslie and other clerk-typists face several possible career paths. If a particular clerk-typist does not want to become a Teletype operator, personnel specialists can provide information about alternative careers not considered by the clerk-typist. In the newspaper example, Leslie might prefer a career in the editorial, secretarial, or advertising fields because those careers offer more long-term potential.

CAREER COUNSELLING

To help employees establish career goals and find appropriate career paths, some personnel departments offer career counselling by counsellors who are a source of competent advice. The counsellor may simply be someone who has the employee's interests in mind and provides the specific job-related information.[10] Or the counsellor may help employees discover their interests by administering and interpreting aptitude and skills tests.[11] Two tests in particular—the *Kuder Preference Record* and the *Strong Vocational Interest Blank*—are useful for guiding people into occupations that are likely to be of interest. Other tests are also available to measure individual abilities and interests in specific types of work. But to be truly successful, career counsellors must get employees to assess themselves and their environment.

EMPLOYEE SELF-ASSESSMENT. Career counsellors realize that a career is not the entirety of one's life. It may be a large part or even a central part; but career planning is only a part of one's *life plan*. A life plan is that often ill-defined series of hopes, dreams, and personal goals each person carries through life. For example, broad objectives to be happy, healthy, and successful combine with specific goals to be a good spouse, parent, student, citizen, neighbour, and manager. Together, these roles form one's life plan.

Figure 10-5
ALTERNATIVE CAREER PATHS AVAILABLE TO A CLERK-TYPIST IN A NEWSPAPER COMPANY

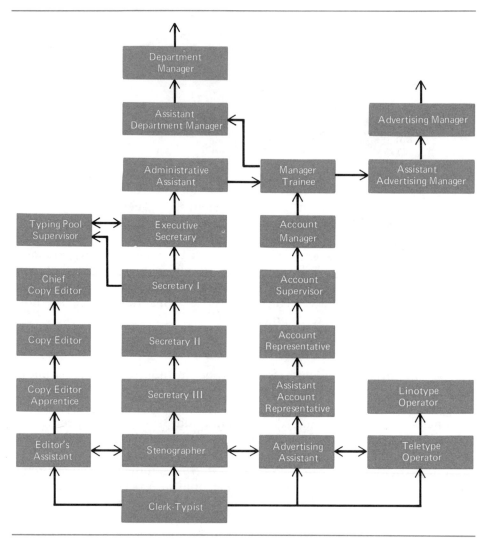

Ideally, a career plan is an integral part of one's life plan. Otherwise, career goals become ends (sometimes dead ends!) rather than means toward fulfilling a life plan. An example can be drawn from an overworked movie plot:

The husband struggles for decades to achieve a degree of career success. When that success is within reach, he realizes that his personal life—friendships, marriage, and paternal relationships—is in shambles. It is in shambles because career plans were pursued to the exclusion of all else; there was no integral life plan.

Why should people who are very successful in their careers develop feelings of personal failure? One research study[12] has suggested the following factors:

• *Contradictory life demands.* The realization that one has strived throughout one's life to attain goals that were irreconcilable.

• *Failure of expectations.* The realization that things one expected to happen will not ever happen and that one's beliefs about the work environment (e.g., the belief that rising in the organizational hierarchy will make one personally satisfied) are wrong.

• *Sense of external control.* The realization that one has been making too many of life's decisions in order to please others rather than oneself.

• *Loss of affiliative satisfactions.* A feeling of loneliness both at the workplace and at home.

In order to avoid this sense of personal failure, self-assessment coupled with life planning at the beginning of a career and at every major crossroads is crucial. Self-assessment includes a self-inventory. Components of a self-inventory are listed in Figure 10-6. If a career counsellor can get

Figure 10-6
A SELF-INVENTORY FOR CAREER PLANNING

Work Interests and Aptitudes	Low 1	2	3	4	High 5
Physical work (fixing, building, using hands)	—	—	—	—	—
Written work (writing, reading, using words)	—	—	—	—	—
Oral work (talking, giving speeches, using words)	—	—	—	—	—
Quantitative work (calculating, doing accounting, using numbers)	—	—	—	—	—
Visual work (watching, inspecting, using eyes)	—	—	—	—	—
Interpersonal work (counselling, interviewing)	—	—	—	—	—
Creative work (inventing, designing, ideas)	—	—	—	—	—
Analytical work (doing research, solving problems)	—	—	—	—	—
Managerial work (initiating, directing, coordinating)	—	—	—	—	—
Clerical (keeping records)	—	—	—	—	—
Outdoor work (farming, travelling, doing athletics)	—	—	—	—	—
Mechanical (repairing, fixing, tinkering)	—	—	—	—	—

Work Skills and Abilities

List below specialized skills, unique personal assets, enjoyable experiences, and major accomplishments. Then evaluate.	Physical	Written	Oral	Quantitative	Visual	Interpersonal	Creative	Analytical	Managerial	Clerical	Outdoor	Mechanical
_____	—	—	—	—	—	—	—	—	—	—	—	—
_____	—	—	—	—	—	—	—	—	—	—	—	—
_____	—	—	—	—	—	—	—	—	—	—	—	—
_____	—	—	—	—	—	—	—	—	—	—	—	—
_____	—	—	—	—	—	—	—	—	—	—	—	—

employees to complete a detailed and honest self-evaluation, it helps to focus their thinking about themselves. Then employees can match their interests and abilities on the self-inventory with the career information available to them from the personnel department. Likewise, they can match better their aptitudes and career paths with their personal life plan.

ENVIRONMENTAL ASSESSMENT. A career plan that matches employee interests with likely career paths may actually do a disservice to the employee if environmental factors are overlooked. Returning to the choices faced by Leslie Stevens at the newspaper provides an example.

The job family of clerk-typist, Teletype operator, and Linotype operator may appear to be a reasonable career path for Leslie since she already has the basic typing skills needed for all three jobs. But technological changes in the newspaper industry may reduce the need for Linotype operators in the future. Photographic and computer developments are quickly replacing the use of Linotype machines in newspaper printing. If career counsellors in the personnel department do not point out this development to Leslie, she may find her career stalled in the job of Teletype operator.

Regardless of the match between one's skills and the organization's career paths, counsellors need to inform employees of likely changes that will affect their occupational choices. Occupational information is readily available from publications of Employment and Immigration Canada and Statistics Canada. For example, Employment and Immigration Canada periodically publishes information relating to the demand and supply of various jobs in the *Ford Occupational Imbalance Listing* (FOIL). In another annual (sometimes biannual) publication entitled *Canada Occupational Forecasting Program* (COFOR), Employment and Immigration Canada provides forecasts on the demand for various types of jobs in the country. Some of the national daily newspapers and business magazines also provide useful information in this context. Figure 10-7 shows the growth potential of selected occupations in Canada for the 1980s. Finally, the National Job Bank of Employment and Immigration Canada provides up-to-date information on job openings to interested persons.

CAREER DEVELOPMENT

The implementation of career plans requires career development. *Career development* comprises those personal improvements one undertakes to achieve a career plan. These actions may be sponsored by the personnel department or undertaken independently by the employee. This section reviews tactics that employees may use to achieve their career plans and then discusses the department's role in career development.

INDIVIDUAL CAREER DEVELOPMENT

The starting point for career development is the individual. Each person must accept his or her responsibility for career development, or career

Figure 10-7
OCCUPATIONS OF THE FUTURE

Occupation	Percent Contribution to Overall Employment Growth in Canada		
	1972-79	1980-85	1986-90
Managers, administrators, and related occupations	8.2	5.2	5.6
Engineers, architects, systems analysts, occupations in physical & life sciences, mathematics, etc.	1.7	1.8	2.6
Occupations in the social sciences	1.8	1.5	1.7
Teaching	5.2	3.1	2.3
Doctors, dentists, veterinarians, etc.	1.2	0.7	0.6
Occupations in health (other than diagnosing)	5.2	5.0	2.9
Sales (skilled)	10.2	8.2	10.6
Highly skilled processing occupations	4.9	4.4	5.2

Source: Robert L. Perry, "Highly skilled occupations offer the best prospects," in a special report on "Careers and the Job Market," *The Financial Post*, September 26, 1981, p. 8. See also *Report of Task Force on Labour Market Development*, Ministry of Employment and Immigration, July 1981.

progress is likely to suffer. Once this personal commitment is made, several career development actions may prove useful. These actions involve:

- Job performance
- Exposure
- Resignations
- Organizational loyalty
- Mentors and sponsors
- Key subordinates
- Growth opportunities

JOB PERFORMANCE. The most important action an individual can undertake to further his or her career is good job performance. The assumption of good performance underlies all career development activities. When performance is substandard, regardless of other career development efforts, even modest career goals are usually unattainable. Individuals who perform poorly are excluded quickly by the personnel department and management decision makers. *Career progress rests largely upon performance.*

EXPOSURE. Career progress also is furthered by exposure.[13] Exposure means becoming known (and, it is hoped, held in high regard) by those who decide on promotions, transfers, and other career opportunities. Without exposure, otherwise good performers may not get a chance at the opportunities needed to achieve their career goals. Managers gain exposure primarily through their performance, written reports, oral presentations, committee work, community service, and even the hours they work. Simply put, exposure makes an individual stand out from the crowd—a necessary ingredient in career success, especially in large organizations. For example, consider how one management trainee gained some vital exposure early in her career:

Paula Dorsey noticed that two executives worked on Saturday mornings. As one of twelve new management trainees, she decided that coming to work on Saturday mornings would give her additional exposure to these key decision makers. Soon these two executives began greeting her by name whenever they passed in the halls. While still in the training program, she was assigned to the product introduction committee, which planned strategy for new products. At the end of the training program, Paula was made an assistant product manager for a new line of video recorders. The other eleven trainees received less important jobs.

In small organizations, exposure to decision makers is more frequent and less dependent upon reports, presentations, and the like. In some situations —especially in other nations—social status, school ties, and seniority can be more important than exposure.

RESIGNATIONS. When a person sees greater career opportunities elsewhere, a resignation may be the only way to meet one's career goals. Some employees—managers and professionals in particular—change employers as part of a conscious career strategy. If this is done effectively, they usually get a promotion, pay increase, and new learning experience. Resigning in order to further one's career with another employer has been called *leveraging.*[14] Astute managers and professionals use this technique sparingly because too many moves can lead to the label of "job hopper." Those who leave seldom benefit their previous organization, because they almost never return with their new experiences.

In a study of 268 mobile executives conducted by one of the authors, only 3% (seven of the executives) ever returned to an organization they left during their careers.[15] *This finding means that organizations seldom benefit from the return of managers who quit and go elsewhere.*

ORGANIZATIONAL LOYALTY. In many organizations, people put career loyalty above organizational loyalty. Low levels of organizational loyalty are common among recent university graduates (whose high expectations often lead to disappointment with their first few employers) and professionals (whose first loyalty is often to their profession).[16] Career-long dedication to the same organization complements the personnel department's objective of reducing employee turnover. However, if the following findings are applicable to other organizations, there may be few rewards for such dedication:

In a study conducted by one of the authors, it was found that a bare majority (51%) of the chief executives in the 100 largest industrial companies spent their entire careers with the same organization. The minority (49%) of presidents who changed employers at least once became chief executive officers at a younger age than those who spent their entire career with the same organization.[17]

MENTORS AND SPONSORS. Many employees quickly learn that a mentor can aid their career development. A *mentor* is someone who offers informal career advice. Neither the mentor nor the employee always recognizes that such a relationship exists; the junior worker simply knows that here is someone who gives good advice; the mentor sees the employee as simply someone who wants advice.

If the mentor can nominate the employee for career development activities, such as training programs, transfers, or promotions, the mentor becomes a sponsor. A *sponsor* is someone in the organization who can create career development opportunities for others. Often an employee's sponsor is the immediate supervisor, although others may serve as nominators.[18]

Many Japanese firms rely on senior managers to use their store of insight and wisdom to help junior managers with career development. In a relationship based on school ties or some other non-work-related factor, the senior manager serves as a career counsellor, mentor, and sponsor for the junior employee, who often works in a different department. In return, the senior manager's actions are reinforced by the respect he receives from other managers.

KEY SUBORDINATES. A successful manager relies on subordinates who aid his or her development and performance. The subordinates may possess highly specialized knowledge or skills that the manager may learn from them. Or the employees may perform a crucial role in helping a manager achieve good performance. In either case, employees of this type are *key subordinates*. They exhibit loyalty and dedication to their boss. They gather and interpret information, offer skills that supplement their manager's, and work unselfishly to further their manager's career. They benefit when the manager is promoted by also moving up the career ladder. Key subordinates also benefit by receiving important delegations that serve to develop their careers. These people complement personnel department objectives through their teamwork, motivation, and dedication. But when a manager resigns and takes a string of key subordinates along, the results can be devastating.

A small Ontario research firm had ten months' lead in developing a new type of memory component for computers. A major electronics company hired away the project manager, the chief engineer, and their key subordinates. With this loss, the small firm was forced to recruit replacements at a higher salary and at a cost of several months' delay.

As a career strategy, perceptive subordinates are careful not to become attached to an immobile manager. One researcher calls such immobiles "shelf-sitters."[19] Not only do shelf-sitters block promotion channels, but their key subordinates can become unfairly labelled as shelf-sitters too. Although working for a shelf-sitter may develop an employee's skills, it can also arrest one's career progress.

GROWTH OPPORTUNITIES. When employees expand their abilities, they complement the organization's objectives. For example, enrolling in a training program, taking noncredit courses, pursuing an additional degree, or seeking a new work assignment can contribute to employee growth. These growth opportunities aid both the personnel department's objective of developing internal replacements and the individual's personal career plan.

Rachael Holmes was the chief recruiter in the employment department of Brem Paper Products. Her department manager was 60 years old and had indicated that he planned to retire at age 65. At 37, with three years of experience as a recruiter, Rachael felt she was in a dead-end job. She obtained a transfer to the wage and salary department. Two years later the company planned a new facility and made Rachael the personnel manager for it. She was selected because of her broad experience in recruiting and compensation—two major concerns in starting the new operation.

Rachael initiated the transfer through self-nomination because she wanted to further her career development. But the real opportunity she obtained from the transfer was a chance to grow—a chance to develop new skills and knowledge.

Besides self-nomination to pursue growth opportunities, other groups outside the organization may help. For years, men have used private clubs and professional associations to form "old-boy networks," which afforded growth opportunities and often a fair amount of interaction among organizational decision makers. Now, however, many of these clubs have been forced to admit women, and increasingly, women are forming their own associations.

Halifax Women's Network aims to facilitate interaction among career-oriented women in the Halifax metropolitan area. Members of the network meet regularly in informal settings to disseminate professional and career-related information to other members. The network also holds sessions on a variety of job-related topics including money management, career search for women, etc.

PERSONNEL-SUPPORTED CAREER DEVELOPMENT

Career development should not rely solely on individual efforts, because they are not always in the organization's best interests. For example, employees may move to another employer, as in the Ontario research example. Or employees may simply be unaware of opportunities to further their careers and the organization's staffing needs. To guide career development so that it benefits the organization and employees, a personnel department often provides a variety of training and development programs for employees. In addition, departments should enlist the support of managers, provide feedback to employees, and create a cohesive work environment to improve the ability and desire of workers to undertake career development.

MANAGEMENT SUPPORT. Efforts by the personnel department to encourage career development have little impact unless supported by managers. Commitment by top management is crucial to gain the support of other managers. When support is lacking, managers are likely to ignore career development and devote their attention to their other responsibilities. Unlike Japanese employers, for example, North American and other western employers do not have a tradition of giving meaningful peer recognition to managers who voluntarily support employee development.

FEEDBACK. Without feedback about their career development efforts, it is difficult for employees to sustain the years of preparation sometimes needed to reach career goals. Personnel departments can provide this feedback in several ways. One way is to periodically tell employees how well they are performing their present job. To do this, many personnel departments develop performance evaluation procedures. If performance is poor, this feedback allows a worker to adjust his or her efforts or career development plan.

Another type of feedback concerns job placement. An employee who pursues career development activities and is passed over for promotion may conclude that career development is not worth the effort. Unsuccessful candidates for internal job openings should be told why they did not get the job they sought. This feedback has three purposes:

1. *To assure* bypassed employees that they are still valued and will be considered for future promotions, if they are qualified. Otherwise, valuable employees may resign because they think the organization does not appreciate their efforts.

2. *To explain* why they were not selected.

3. *To indicate* what specific career development actions should be undertaken. Care should be exercised not to imply that certain career development actions will automatically mean a promotion. Instead, the individual's *candidacy* for selection will be influenced by appropriate career development actions.

COHESIVE WORK GROUPS. For employees who want to pursue a career within an organization, they must feel that the organization is a satisfying environment. When they are a part of a cohesive work group, their career development efforts are more likely to be directed toward improving their opportunities within the organization.[20] But to create such a satisfying environment, personnel departments must deal with change and organizational development, the subject of the next chapter.

SUMMARY

Career planning and development are relatively new concepts to personnel specialists. In recent years, personnel departments have begun to recognize the need for more proactive efforts in this area. As a result, some (mostly large) departments provide career education, information, and counselling. But the primary responsibility for career planning and development rests with the individual employee.

Figure 10-8 illustrates an overview of career planning and development.

Figure 10-8
THE CAREER PLANNING AND DEVELOPMENT FRAMEWORK

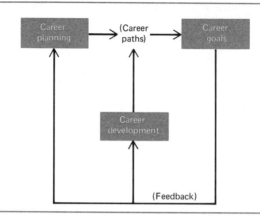

The planning process enables employees to identify career goals and the paths to those goals. Then through developmental activities the workers seek ways to improve themselves and further their career goals.

Even today, most developmental activities are individual and voluntary. Individual efforts include good job performance, favourable exposure, leveraging, building of alliances, and other actions. Personnel departments become involved by providing information and obtaining management support. The personnel department helps make career planning and development a success for both the employees and the organization.

Career planning does not guarantee success. But without it employees are seldom ready for career opportunities that arise. As a result, their career progress may be slowed and the personnel department may be unable to fill openings internally.

TERMS FOR REVIEW

Career	Career counselling
Career path	Life plan
Career planning	Exposure
Career development	Leveraging
Job families	Mentors and sponsors
Job progression ladder	Key subordinates

REVIEW AND DISCUSSION QUESTIONS

1. Why should a personnel department be concerned about career planning, especially since employee plans may conflict with the organization's objectives? What advantages does a personnel department expect to receive from assisting career planning?
2. In what ways can a personnel department assist career planning?

3. If you were interested in making a career out of your ability to play a musical instrument, what types of career goals would you set for yourself? How would you find out about the career prospects for musicians before you took your first job?

4. Suppose you are in a management training position after completing university. Your career goal is not very clear, but you would like to become a top manager in your firm. What types of information would you seek from the personnel department to help you develop your career plan?

5. After you develop your first career plan while employed by a bank, what career development activities would you pursue? Why?

6. Suppose you are assigned to develop a career planning and development program for the employees of a large city. How would you go about developing employee interest in career planning? How would you enlist the support of managers throughout the organization?

7. Why is employee feedback an important element of any organization's attempt to encourage career development?

8. Suppose a hard-working and loyal employee is passed over for promotion. What would you tell this person?

INCIDENT 10-1
CAREER PLANNING AND DEVELOPMENT AT IMMOBILE LTD.

Long-term employees at Saskatchewan Electric Company Ltd. nicknamed the company "Immobile Ltd." It seemed that the only time anyone received a promotion was when a manager retired or died. Even when job vacancies did occur, the personnel department frequently hired a replacement from some other electric utility, so that few employees received a promotion. Employee turnover was low partially because the jobs paid very well, provided high job security, and offered outstanding fringe benefits.

Top management became concerned about the negative attitude reflected by the nickname "Immobile Ltd." and hired a large Toronto consulting firm to develop a career planning program. After several months, the consultants revealed a detailed plan, complete with a special office of career counselling in the personnel department. Initially, employees responded favourably and made extensive use of the counselling and career information services available to them. But by the fourth month, the chief career counsellor asked the personnel manager for a transfer into any other part of the personnel department. When asked why, the counsellor said that employees were not using the service and the job of counsellor had become lonely and boring. The personnel manager gave the counsellor an assignment to discover why the program had failed and what might be done to revitalize it.

1. What explanations can you offer to explain the initial enthusiasm for career planning assistance followed by an almost total avoidance by employees?

2. Assuming part of the problem was a lack of support by middle and first-level management, what recommendations would you make? Could this company learn a lesson from the approach used by the Japanese?

INCIDENT 10-2
MOOSEHEAD TRANSPORT SYSTEM

Moosehead Transport System had been through some bad times. Year after year, losses had piled up. Finally, management decided that it must close down many of its operations in small towns that were not profitable. To ease the burden on long-term employees, a decision was made that no one with ten years of experience or more was to be laid off.

The personnel department developed a plan and notified each long-service employee in towns where the service was to be discontinued. Since many of the jobs were those of Depot Master and Assistant Depot Master, not enough comparable openings existed in other cities. While the personnel department sought a permanent solution, these long-service employees were transferred into any other openings that were available.

Many of the transferees complained that they were being demoted. The union thought it unfair that these workers were paid their old salary when other workers on the same jobs received considerably less.

1. Under these circumstances, would career planning be a useful tool for the personnel department to reduce the ill feelings of these long-service workers?
2. How do you think these long-term employees might react to career planning efforts by the personnel department? How do you think unaffected employees might react to a new career planning effort?

REFERENCES

1. Ronald J. Burke and Tamara Weir, "Career Success and Personal Failure Part II," *The Canadian Personnel & Industrial Relations Journal*, November 1980, p. 36.
2. Dr. Srully Blotnick, "How to Change Jobs and Live to Enjoy it," *Canadian Business*, August 1984, p. 83.
3. Harvey A. Thomson and Claude A. Guay, "Tapping Human Potential," *The Canadian Personnel & Industrial Relations Journal*, September 1978, pp. 21–26; Stephen L. Cohen, "Toward a More Comprehensive Career Planning Program," *Personnel Journal*, September 1979, pp. 611–615.
4. This individual/organizational dichotomy is useful for distinguishing between the role of the person and the role of the personnel department. For a more detailed discussion of this distinction, see Elmer H. Burack, "Why All of the Confusion about Career Planning?" *Human Resource Management*, Summer 1977, pp. 21–23. See also B. A. Keys, F. A. Thompson, and M. Heath, "Managerial Training and Development Practices of Selected Firms in Canada," *Meeting Managerial Manpower Needs*, Ottawa: Economic Council of Canada, 1971.
5. T. F. Hercus, "A Survey of Responses to Current Manpower," *The Canadian Personnel & Industrial Relations Journal*, January 1979, pp. 19–30. See also *The Financial Post*, "Urgent Priority to Job Training," January 16, 1982, p. 3.
6. William F. Rothenbach, "Career Development: Ask Your Employees for Their Opinions," *Personnel Administrator*, November 1982, pp. 43–46, 51. See also J. Thad Barnowe, "Influences of Personality, Organizational Experience, and Anticipated Future Outcomes on Choice of Career," Working Paper No. 537, Faculty of Commerce, University of British Columbia, December 1977.
7. C. W. Memeth and J. I. A. Rowney, "Professionalize or Perish," *The Canadian Personnel & Industrial Relations Journal*, January 1981, pp. 27–31.
8. Donald D. Bowen and Douglas T. Hall, "Career Planning for Employee Development: A Primer for Managers," *California Management Review*, Winter 1977, pp. 29–30. See also Douglas T. Hall, *Careers in Organizations*, Pacific Palisades, Calif.: Goodyear Publishing Company, Inc., 1976.
9. Elmer H. Burack and Nicholas Mathys, "Career Ladders, Pathing and Planning: Some Neglected Basics," *Human Resource Management*, Summer 1979, pp. 2–8. See also Philomena D. Warihay, "The Climb to the Top: Is the Network the Route for Women?" *The Personnel Administrator*, April 1980, pp. 55–60.
10. Ted R. Gambill, "Career Counseling: Too Little, Too Late?" *Training and Development Journal*, February 1979, pp. 24–29.
11. Hall, op. cit., pp. 27–28.

12. Ronald J. Burke and Tamara Weir, "Career Success and Personal Failure Part I," *The Canadian Personnel and Industrial Relations Journal*, October 1980, pp. 7–17. See also Laird W. Mealiea and Swee C. Goh, "An Empirical Evaluation of the Fear of Success Construct for Women Working in a Sex Stereotyped Job," *ASAC (Organizational Behaviour Division) Meeting Proceedings*, Vol. 2, Part 5, 1981, pp. 112–123.

13. Eugene E. Jennings, *The Mobile Manager*, New York: McGraw-Hill Book Company, 1967.

14. Jennings, op. cit.

15. William B. Werther, Jr., "Management Turnover Implications of Career Mobility," *The Personnel Administrator*, February 1977, pp. 63–66.

16. Simeon J. Touretzky, "Changing Attitudes: A Question of Loyalty," *The Personnel Administrator*, April 1979, pp. 35–38.

17. Werther, op. cit.

18. Verne Walter, "Self-Motivated Personnel Career Planning: A Breakthrough in Human Resource Management (Part I)," *Personnel Journal*, March 1976, pp. 112–115, 136. See also Part II in the April 1976 issue of *Personnel Journal*, pp. 162–167, 185–186.

19. Jennings, op. cit.

20. William A. Westley, "The Role of the Supervisor," *The Canadian Personnel & Industrial Relations Journal*, November 1980, pp. 10–23. See also Larry Earwood, "Employee Satisfaction through Career Development," *The Personnel Administrator*, August 1979, pp. 41–44; Kalburgi M. Srinivas, "The Superior-Subordinate Interface," Chapter 7 in K. M. Srinivas (ed.), *Human Resource Management: Contemporary Perspectives in Canada*, Toronto: McGraw-Hill Ryerson, 1984; Ron J. Burke and D. S. Wilson, "Effects of Different Patterns and Degrees of Openness in Superior-Subordinate Communication on Subordinate Job Satisfaction." *Academy of Management Journal*, 12, 3, 1969, pp. 319–326; Manfred F. R. Kets de Vries, "Crossed Signals: Dysfunctional Superior Subordinate Interaction Patterns," Working Paper No. 7911, Faculty of Management, Montreal: McGill University, Spring 1979; Ronald J. Burke, "Mentors in Organizations," *ASAC (Organizational Behaviour Division) Meeting Proceedings*, Vol. 3, Part 5, 1982, pp. 41–47.

Chapter **11**

Change and Organizational Development

It must be considered that there is nothing more difficult to carry out, nor more doubtful of success, nor more dangerous to handle, than to initiate a new order of things.

Niccolò Machiavelli[1]

CHAPTER OBJECTIVES

After studying this chapter, you should be able to:
1. **Explain** the personnel department's role in implementing change.
2. **Discuss** barriers and resistance to change.
3. **Describe** the organizational learning curve for change.
4. **Discuss** practices that support change.
5. **Describe** the characteristics of organizational development.
6. **Explain** steps necessary to implement organizational development.

The Mead Corporation faced some difficult decisions that required changes throughout several of its paper mills.[2] Its productivity was low and its competitive ability was declining. One of the company's major decisions to help overcome its decline was a broad program of organizational development in which the personnel department was heavily involved. According to the senior vice president for human relations, a key idea was to develop better work teams in each paper mill and encourage them to improve both product quality and quantity.

The move toward better quality and quantity required many small changes day by day until the company's whole organizational structure was changed. For example, all workers at one mill were put on salary rather than hourly wages. They were called members, not workers or employees. They were carefully trained in both human relations and technical skills so that they could work better as a team. Union involvement was required in order to change work rules to allow teamwork to develop. These changes and many others combined to build a strong spirit of teamwork and productivity.

Results of the program were significant. Costs of making paper cartons decreased by 20 to 30% in one plant. In another plant the labour hours required to make a ton of paper were reduced from 21 to 13, which was a reduction of 38% in two years. The company became more competitive and jobs were more secure because it had successfully responded to necessary changes.

Change such as that faced by Mead Corporation is normal and natural in every organization. It exists because the world both inside and outside the organization is dynamic, not static. Within a company, for example, people retire or problems develop that must be solved. Outside the company there are thousands of changes—ranging from new products to new government regulations. For example, when an employer installs industrial robots, hundreds of hours of time may be required for the personnel department to develop new work rules and negotiate them with the union. And employees may spend thousands of hours retraining for new jobs. There is no way for managers or employees to hide from change.

This chapter first discusses how change affects the whole organization and how the personnel department works to implement change. Then it focuses on organizational development, a major way to help an organization deal with change.

THE PERSONNEL DEPARTMENT AND CHANGE

Since an organization is a complex system in which all parts affect each other, a major change anywhere in the organization usually affects the personnel function. In addition, when a program for employees is changed, the personnel department becomes the agent of change. The following are examples of change and how they may affect the personnel department:

• *Production change.* Affects training, job descriptions, motivation, working conditions, and grievances.
• *New office computer.* Affects training, employee transfers, job descriptions, employment, pay, and quality of work life.
• *Company growth.* Affects career planning, employment, employee development, promotions, pay, and working conditions.

Before change is undertaken, managers and personnel specialists must recognize the trade-offs involved. Of particular concern are the costs and other effects of change on the organizational system. The personnel department must also work to reduce barriers to change. In the next few pages the costs, effects, and barriers to change are explored. Then the discussion centres on implementing change in an organization.

COSTS AND BENEFITS

The *change objective of the personnel department* is to manage change in ways that increase its benefits and reduce its costs. The approach is proactive rather than reactive, in order to make a positive contribution to the situation. The personnel department strives to provide a *net benefit*, as shown in Figure 11-1, which means that there will be a surplus of benefits after all costs are included. If a change produces more unfavourable results

Figure 11-1
NET BENEFITS AS THE SURPLUS OF BENEFITS ABOVE COSTS

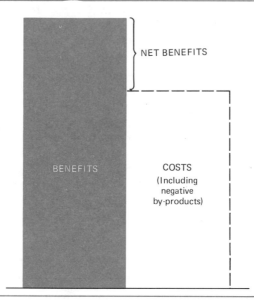

than favourable ones, then the change is probably undesirable and should not be implemented.

All changes are likely to entail some costs. For example, a new procedure may require the inconvenience of learning new practices, may disrupt work, or may temporarily reduce motivation. These conditions are costs, and they must be considered along with the potential benefits of the new procedure. The objective of personnel is to enhance the potential benefits while reducing costs, so that the net human and organizational benefits are increased.

One difficulty with introducing change is that different people are affected by it in different ways. Some may benefit while others suffer a loss. In these instances the personnel department works especially to assist those who will be affected negatively. In most instances it cannot prevent the costs, but perhaps it can encourage offsetting benefits in a related area, such as working conditions. In other instances it provides training to help employees adjust to change with the least possible disruption. It also builds communication to help employees understand the net benefit to the organization.

A provincial office introduced a new procedure as required by legislation. People throughout the office were affected in different ways, as follows:

• **Employees directly affected.** *A long-run cost because they performed more work without added benefits, and there was a temporary decline in job satisfaction.*

• **Accounting employees.** *A minor benefit, because they performed slightly less work.*

- **Other employees.** *No effect.*
- **Supervisor where change was made.** *A temporary cost of more problems during the change period.*
- **Other supervisors.** *No effect.*
- **Management.** *Minor temporary cost to plan and implement change.*
- **Personnel department.** *Intermediate-term costs to make job analysis and evaluation of jobs having new duties and to advise supervisor on problems of job satisfaction caused by change.*

In situations such as the one just described, there is no clear-cut 100% gain for the office. Rather, a series of separate costs and benefits must be managed on an individual basis. Other departments as well as the personnel department will become involved in working out these problems.

PSYCHIC COSTS OF CHANGE

Persons who experience change usually also experience some *psychic costs,* which are the stress, strain, and anxiety affecting the inner self during a period of change. Obviously, an undesirable, troublesome change may produce stress, but a desirable change—such as a promotion—may also be stressful. A promotion may require a person to learn new skills, develop new work contacts, and form new friendships; and all these requirements can be traumatic.

Glenda Cortez was promoted from a clerical job in the back office of a bank to the consumer loan department. She wanted the job and she looked forward to the opportunities it offered. In her new job she was required to learn new skills and make new friendships. She also had to discuss problems with customers, but her clerical background had given her little experience in customer contacts.

Glenda found these new experiences stressful, even though she wanted them for promotion and growth. Soon she sought the help of her supervisor and the personnel department in order to cope with the psychic costs of her new job.

After a number of employees had experienced stress similar to Cortez's, the personnel department developed a course on coping with change, in order to help employees adjust.[3] Employees who received a promotion were required to take the course, and other employees were encouraged to do so. The personnel department also improved its monitoring of promotions and transfers in order to assist individual employees when problems developed.

COSTS OF GEOGRAPHIC MOVES

Promotions and transfers tend to have especially high psychic costs when they require employees to move to another location. These changes involve the employee's family, and so coping may be more difficult. The children may not want to move from their friends and familiar surroundings. The spouse may have a job that he or she may not want to leave. Companies which require employees to relocate have found that they need thoughtful personnel policies to reduce the psychic costs involved. These policies are applied situationally so that each employee's individual needs can be considered.[4] Effective relocation policies often include an advance company-paid orientation trip to the new location for the employee and spouse, allowances for moving household goods, travel allowances to the new location, and assignment of one or more employees to help the new employee and family get acquainted after arrival. These policies greatly ease the stress of the move.

ENVIRONMENTAL EFFECTS ON CHANGE

Change is influenced partly by the environment in which an organization operates. Government, customers, labour unions, communities, and others initiate changes in organizations. For example, if union policy strongly favours seniority for promotion, then there will be pressures to change personnel policies in that direction. If customers want better product quality, then the personnel department will need to initiate training programs that upgrade labour skills. Each company's personnel policies and problems depend on the external environment in which the firm operates. Stable environments mean less change. Firms in dynamic industries encounter more change.

One study covered dynamic companies having an employee growth rate of 20% or more for at least four years.[5] Most of these companies were shown to have similar human resource problems, as follows:

- *A need to make quick decisions*
- *Rapidly changing jobs*
- *Large recruiting and employment demands*
- *Increased training needs*
- *Stress from frequent change, often unanticipated*
- *Strain on personnel resources*

BARRIERS TO CHANGE

Barriers to change are environmental factors that interfere with the acceptance and implementation of change. Among them are economic costs, difficulties in securing financing, problems with new technology, and lack of resources. However, usually the most difficult barrier, and the one of concern to the personnel department, is frequent employee opposition to change. This is called *resistance to change.* People sometimes stand like a wall against needed change. At other times they are responsive to it and cooperative with management. Their responses depend largely on their own values and interests, and so their responses are often different from management's.

As shown in Figure 11-2, employee resistance to change is of three different types. These may be expressed in three different uses of the word "logical," as follows:

- *Logical.* Based on rational reasoning
- Psycho*logical.* Based on emotions, sentiments, and attitudes
- Socio*logical.* Based on group interests and values

Logical-rational resistance arises from the time and effort required to adjust to change, including new job duties that must be learned. These are

Figure 11-2
TYPES OF EMPLOYEE RESISTANCE TO CHANGE

Logical; Rational

- Time required to adjust
- Extra effort to relearn
- Possible less desirable conditions, such as skill downgrading
- Costs of change
- Different assessment of the change

Psychological; Emotional

- Fear of the unknown
- Low tolerance of change
- Dislike of management or other change initiator
- Lack of trust in others
- Need for security; desire for status quo

Sociological; Group Interests

- Political coalitions
- Opposing group values
- Parochial, narrow outlook
- Vested interests
- Desire to retain existing friendships

true costs borne by the employees. Even though a change may be favourable for employees in the long run, these short-run costs must first be paid.

Psychological resistance is concerned with attitudes and feelings of individual employees about change. They may fear the unknown, mistrust management's leadership, or feel that their security is threatened. Even though management may believe there is no justification for these feelings, the feelings are real and must be recognized.

Yves Duguay was one of five skilled machine operators at St. Regis Company. His supervisor introduced a job change to provide a minor improvement in efficiency. For many years Yves had feared that any efficiency improvement would mean the loss of his job. Even though his job was not threatened in any way, fear caused him to fight the change.

Sociological resistance has more to do with group interests and values. There are political coalitions, opposing labour union values, and even different community values. On a small-group level there are work friendships that may be disrupted by changes. Social values are powerful forces in the environment, and so they must be carefully considered by personnel specialists.

The office manager reorganized departments in a way that moved Susan Maxwell to another department on a different floor of the building. The move was reasonable, and it would have given Susan more professional contacts for better training; however, she strongly resisted it. She was part of a closely-knit social circle in her department and did not want to leave it.

It can be seen that psychological resistance and sociological resistance are not illogical or irrational; rather they are logical according to different sets of values—they are based on the sound of a different drummer.

POSSIBLE BENEFITS OF EMPLOYEE RESISTANCE

Resistance interferes with management efforts to implement change; therefore, it is usually viewed by management as undesirable. On the other hand, it has some possible benefits. For example, resistance may encourage management to reexamine its change proposals so that it can be more sure of their appropriateness. In this way employees operate as a check and balance to ensure that management properly plans and implements a change. Not all changes are beneficial. Some have undesirable results in the long run, and if reasonable employee resistance causes management to screen more carefully its proposed changes, then employees have discouraged careless management decisions.

Resistance also may identify specific problem areas where a change is likely to have difficulty, so that management can take corrective action before a problem becomes serious. At the same time management may be encouraged to do a better job of communicating the change, an approach that in the long run should lead to better acceptance. Resistance also gives management information about the intensity of employee emotions on an issue, provides emotional release for pent-up employee feelings, and may encourage employees to think and talk more about a change so that they are better acquainted with it.

Personnel specialists become involved with change because they are seen as the "people" experts. Even when technical changes occur, managers may seek the advice of specialists in the personnel department. When managers draw on the personnel department's human resource expertise, barriers to change may be lowered and the change may be implemented more smoothly.

IMPLEMENTING CHANGE

The personnel department assists with change by increasing the supporting forces for change and reducing the forces that resist change. As shown in Figure 11-3, an organization at any time is a dynamic balance of forces supporting and resisting any practice. These practices will continue in a steady way until a change is introduced. However, the change is not likely to be accepted unless supporting forces are added to give it acceptance. Resisting forces also need to be removed to the extent possible. In this manner the old practice will be replaced by the desired change, because organizational forces support the change.

Both the number and the strength of supporting and resisting forces may be influenced by the personnel department. For example, a larger amount of feedback about quality of work should be a supporting force for it, and

Figure 11-3
A GENERAL MODEL FOR ORGANIZATIONAL CHANGE

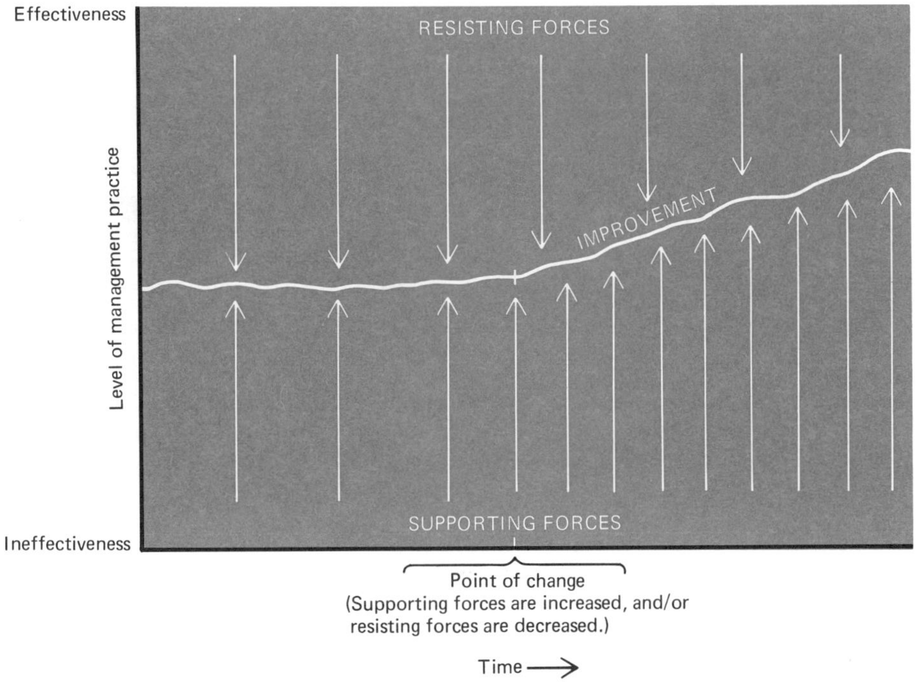

also more pride in work should support high quality. In the same situation, resisting forces may be reduced by decreasing high noise levels that interfere with work.

The Peerless Company was growing rapidly and needed more parking spaces for employees. The only space available was on the other side of the manufacturing-office building where all employees worked. One problem was that this new lot was farther from the building, so that employees might find it inconvenient and not use it. On the basis of advice from the personnel department, an additional supporting force was added in terms of a long covered walkway from the parking lot to the building. Since the weather in this area frequently was wet and the other lot had no covered walkway, employees were motivated to use the new lot.

THE ORGANIZATIONAL LEARNING CURVE FOR CHANGE

It takes people time to adapt to change. This period of adjustment and adaptation can be charted as the organization's *learning curve for change*. Figure 11-4 shows the learning curve for a change that was designed to reduce costs. As the figure shows, in the beginning costs increased rather than decreased, because of the difficulties people had adjusting to the change. This pattern is fairly typical with most changes. Procedures are upset and

Figure 11-4
TYPICAL ORGANIZATIONAL LEARNING CURVE FOR CHANGE

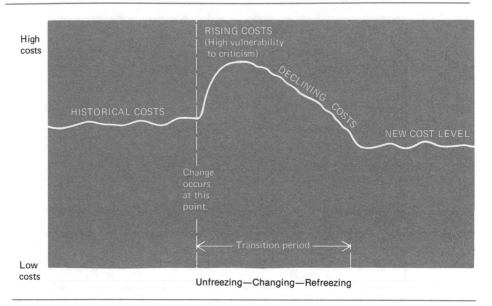

communication patterns are disrupted. Conflicts develop about the change and cooperation declines. Problems arise and time must be taken to resolve them. The result is that, as the saying goes, "things are likely to get worse before they get better."

During the transition period, when people are adjusting to a change, they may become discouraged because of the problems that develop. At this time the change is especially subject to criticism, attack, and even failure, because it appears not to be working. Only after the passage of time, when teamwork and efficiency have been restored, is the change likely to produce the results intended.

The learning curve shown in Figure 11-4 reflects three basic steps in the theory of change, as follows:

- *Unfreezing* (also *unlearning*). Casting aside old ideas and practices so that new ones can be learned.
- *Changing*. Learning new ideas and practices so that an employee can think and perform in new ways.
- *Refreezing*. Integrating what has been learned into actual practice.

All three steps are necessary to make a successful change.[6] For example, merely knowing a new practice is not enough. Unless the old practice is unfrozen, an employee tends to use an ineffective combination of both the old and new. Also, newly learned practices will be useless until an employee can refreeze them into actual practice.

PRACTICES THAT SUPPORT CHANGE

When a company faces change, it needs to develop practices that will support the change. Useful practices include planning, participation, communication, and supplementary rewards.

PLANNING. Careful planning is fundamental for the success of a change, and it is important for the personnel department to be involved in this planning from the beginning.[7] Often when other departments initiate change, they tend to plan independently and bring in the personnel department only after plans are well advanced. The result is that many human factors are overlooked and the change needs to be delayed while its human effects are reconsidered. In other instances, because the change is introduced hastily without giving enough thought to people, it fails.

Management in one large department introduced certain changes in work assignments. It was the management's intention to notify the personnel department after the changes became effective, so that new job evaluations could be made for the revised duties of some jobs. Employees, however, saw the change as a move that would give some of them secondary positions with reduced status.

When employees refused to go along with the change, there was a tardy call to the personnel department. At this point the situation was more difficult to handle than it would have been with the personnel department involved in the beginning. Personnel specialists also found that several personnel practices in addition to job evaluation were involved in the change—such as recruitment patterns, employment needs, career plans, training needs, and personnel policies.

PARTICIPATION. For many of the same reasons that the personnel department needs to be involved in change, employees also need to be involved. Participation is a key personnel practice that encourages employees to discuss, to communicate, to make suggestions, and to become interested in change.[8] Participation often operates through committees and task forces. It encourages commitment, rather than mere compliance with change. Commitment implies a motivation to support a change and to work to ensure that it operates effectively.

As shown in Figure 11-5, a general model of participation and change indicates that as participation increases, resistance to change tends to decrease. Resistance declines because employees have less cause to resist. Their needs are being considered and thus they feel secure in a changing situation. Participation produces security, cooperation, and feelings of personal worth.

As with the personnel department, it is essential for employees to participate in a change *before* it occurs, not after. When employees can be involved from the beginning, they feel protected from surprises and confident that their ideas are wanted. They begin themselves to see the need for change and to want to help management implement it.[9] On the other hand, employees are likely to feel that calling for their involvement after a change is nothing more than a selling device and manipulation by management.

Figure 11-5

A GENERAL MODEL OF PARTICIPATION IN RELATION TO RESISTANCE TO CHANGE

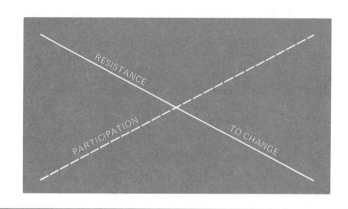

Many managers and supervisors think they alone are supposed to make decisions. So they unilaterally make decisions and deprive employees of an opportunity for participation. Figure 11-6 illustrates a time bar for two approaches to decision making. The bar on the left is labelled "Traditional." Here, managers believe their role is to make decisions. To do so efficiently, managers define their problems, identify alternatives, and select an alternative. Then they implement the decision—only to encounter resistance from employees who were not involved and have no "ownership" of the change because they did not participate in the decision-making process.

Participative decision makers frequently take longer to define problems, identify alternatives, and make a choice because employees are allowed to participate. As the longer time bar shows for steps 1, 2, and 3, these stages of decision making are time consuming. However, the next step, implementation, goes quicker because employees do not resist their own decisions. Additionally, since employees are likely to be more committed to those decisions in which they participate, the need for controls and follow-up by the manager are probably much less. The lower levels of resistance and control may mean that when all five steps are considered, the participative approach is not slow at all. As has been explained in Chapter 4, employee involvement in decision making also may lead to a higher quality of work life and more productivity.

Which employees should be involved? Essentially, any employees who are likely to be affected by a change should know about it and be involved in it. When large numbers of workers are affected, representatives of employees may be used to keep committees to a manageable size. Management seeks to involve both those who support a change and those who oppose it, because involvement tends to reduce opposition to change. Occasionally, management chooses a person opposed to change to chair a committee or task force implementing a change. In this way opponents are assured of a fair hearing, and the leader may develop a more balanced viewpoint as a result of intense involvement. Involvement does not always require official committees or task forces. When employees feel that there is open communication and that their ideas are wanted, change may be implemented through informal discussions.

COMMUNICATION. Communication, a major activity of the personnel department, encourages understanding. Employees are unlikely to give their support to any change that they do not understand. The personnel department needs to ensure that supervisors, managers, staff, and personnel specialists are fully aware of any impending change.

A textile plant faced a temporary increase in product demand. [10] *New manufacturing equipment could not be secured, and the plant was operating twenty-four hours a day for five days a week, so the only alternative was to use the plant on Saturdays and Sundays. The personnel department was assigned to implement the entire change in a manner that would gain the cooperation of employees.*

The department used communication to inform employees about the problem and seek their ideas. Communication revealed that employees did not want to work overtime or in a rotation with a fourth shift; so a solution appeared to be difficult. Over a period of time employee surveys and bulletins were used to inform employees and ask their reactions to different proposed solutions. Based on feedback, a task force finally

Figure 11-6
TRADITIONAL VS. PARTICIPATIVE APPROACHES TO DECISION MAKING

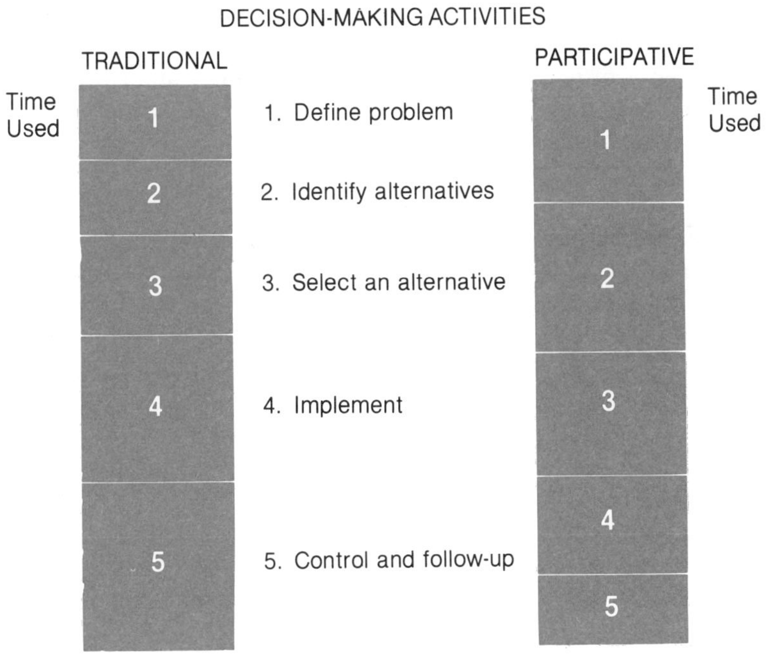

DECISION-MAKING ACTIVITIES

TRADITIONAL   PARTICIPATIVE

Time Used

1. Define problem
2. Identify alternatives
3. Select an alternative
4. Implement
5. Control and follow-up

Time Used

selected a separate part-time group to work only on Saturdays and Sundays. The plan was established, proved to be effective, and was well received by employees. It was evident that thorough two-way communication helped management make a correct decision and gained the support of employees.

Additional communication practices that are useful with change are discussed in Chapter 17, "Building Employee Communication."

SUPPLEMENTARY REWARDS. Another way to build employee support for change is to be sure that there are enough rewards for employees in the change situation. It is only natural for employees to ask, "What's in this for me?" If they see that a change brings them only losses and no gains, they can hardly be enthusiastic about it.

Rewards say to employees, "We care. We want you to benefit from this change as well as us." Rewards also give employees a sense of progress with a change. Both financial and nonfinancial rewards are useful. Employees appreciate a pay increase or promotion, but they also appreciate emotional support, training in new skills, and recognition from management.[11]

In one firm the personnel department held a "half-way banquet" when the group had implemented about half of the change. When the change was fully implemented, a "success banquet" was held and special recognition was given to key employees who had helped install the change. This additional recognition was a reward to employees for their extra effort, and it helped build their support for the change.

It can be seen that personnel practices such as those just discussed are a strong encouragement for employees to accept change. When these practices are added to those discussed in other chapters, such as training, the personnel department has a powerful kit of tools for implementing change.

When the environment is dynamic, the personnel department may also provide specialists in organizational development, as discussed in the next section.

ORGANIZATIONAL DEVELOPMENT

Organizational development has the potential to bring major improvements in cooperation, teamwork, and productivity. Its results can be impressive.

For example, an organizational development program at the Corning Glass Corporation produced significant gains.[12] Following its use in the glass shop, the productivity increase was 20% and in the instrument department the increase was 17%. Two other gains, even more impressive, were in the instrument department. The quality increase was about 50% and absenteeism was reduced 50%. While not all the improvements were the result of the program, at least a substantial part of them appeared to be.

DEFINITION OF ORGANIZATIONAL DEVELOPMENT

Organizational development (OD) is an intervention strategy that uses group processes to focus on the whole organization in order to bring about planned change. It seeks to change beliefs, attitudes, values, structures, and practices—in fact, the entire operational system—so that the organization can better adapt to change. It especially focuses on team building and group problem solving. An excellent by-product is human resource development as employees gain skills in coping with their common problems.[13]

A major reason for the growth of OD is that it builds support for changed behaviour and thus overcomes a limitation of traditional training. The problem with traditional training is that the reward structure on the job often fails to reinforce the training, and so there is excessive loss of training momentum in the transition from a classroom to a work situation.[14]

Margie Myers, shipping supervisor, returned from her course on supervisory effectiveness eager to try some of the new human relations practices she had learned. The first thing she did was plan some participative problem-solving meetings with her employees, but her manager rejected the idea. Then she attempted to make some schedule changes to fit the needs of her employees, but she could not get them approved. She planned some other changes to make her supervision more employee-centred, but she abandoned them when she found that her performance rating continued to emphasize mostly production and costs.

About the only long-run result of her training was that she became less happy with her job because the system discouraged efforts to try what was learned.

CHARACTERISTICS OF OD

OD has a number of characteristics that are implied in its definition. It can be seen that most of these characteristics are substantially different from those of a typical training program.

FOCUS ON THE WHOLE ORGANIZATION. OD attempts to develop the whole organization so that it can respond to change more uniformly and capably. It builds teamwork and cooperation. It also encourages more frequent and open communication. It seeks to build problem-solving capability by improving group relationships and problem confrontation. In short, it reaches into all parts of the organization in order to make it more humanly responsive.

SYSTEMS ORIENTATION. OD is concerned with interactions of various parts of the organization. It is concerned with intergroup relationships as well as interpersonal ones. It is concerned with structure and process as well as attitudes. The basic issue at which it is directed is: How do all these parts work together?

USE OF A CHANGE AGENT. OD uses one or more *change agents*, who are persons with the role of stimulating and coordinating change within a group.[15] Usually the primary change agent is a consultant from outside the company. In this way the agent can operate independently without ties to the hierarchy and politics of the firm. As shown in Figure 11-7, which presents an *OD change model*, the personnel director is the in-house change agent who coordinates the program internally with both management and

Figure 11-7
THE OD CHANGE MODEL

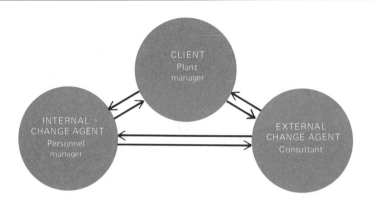

THE IN-HOUSE MANAGER'S SIDE

- Knowledge of specific sociotechnical systems
- Perspective limited to organization (local outlook)
- Dependency on organization for financial rewards
- Company-person career bond

WHAT THE CONSULTANT BRINGS

- Knowledge of OD techniques
- Experience in many organizations, variety of perspectives (cosmopolitan outlook)
- Independence
- No bond; easily dispensable relationship

Source: Reprinted by permission of the publisher, from Thomas H. Patten Jr., "Team Building, Part 1. Designing the Intervention," *Personnel*, January-February 1979, © copyright 1979 by AMACOM, a division of American Management Associations, p. 19. All rights reserved.

the external agent. The external agent also works with management, and so the result is a three-way relationship of the personnel director, management, and an outside consultant as they develop the OD program. In rare cases the organization has its own in-house professional who replaces the outside consultant and works with the personnel director and management. This in-house consultant is usually a specialist on the personnel staff.

PROBLEM SOLVING. OD emphasizes problem solving. It seeks to solve problems, rather than to discuss them theoretically as in a classroom. Because these problems are real problems that the participants face in their organization, they are stimulating and interesting. This focus on real, ongoing problems, not artificial ones, is called *action research*. It is such a key characteristic that OD is sometimes defined as organizational improvement through action research.

EXPERIENTIAL LEARNING. *Experiential learning* means that participants learn by experiencing in the training environment the kinds of behavioural problems they face on the job. Then they can discuss and analyze their own immediate experience and learn from it. This approach tends to produce more changed behaviour than traditional lecture and discussion methods in which people talk about abstract ideas. Theory is necessary and desirable, but the ultimate test is how one applies it in a real situation. OD helps to provide some of the answers. Participants work on real problems in real situations, and the experience helps to solidify their new learning.

GROUP PROCESSES. Another characteristic is group processes. There are group discussions, intergroup conflicts, confrontations, and team building. There is an effort to improve interpersonal relations, open communication channels, build trust, and encourage responsiveness to others.

FEEDBACK. OD relies heavily on feedback to participants so that they will have concrete data on which to make decisions. Feedback encourages them to understand a situation and take self-correcting action, rather than wait for someone else to tell them what to do. An example is a feedback exercise in one OD program:

Participants are separated into two groups representing two different departments in the organization. Both groups are asked to develop answers to the following questions:

- *What characteristics best describe our group?*
- *What characteristics best describe the other group?*
- *How will the other group describe us?*

After the two groups have prepared their answers, they come together and each group presents its answers to the other. They give concrete feedback about impressions each group has of the other. Usually there are major misunderstandings, but in this presentation no rebuttals are permitted. Questions are accepted only to clarify what the other group is saying.

Then the groups are again separated to discuss two other questions:

- *How did these misunderstandings occur?*
- *What can we do to correct them?*

Armed with this new feedback, the groups again meet to develop specific plans of action for solving their misunderstandings. In each instance feedback about themselves is the basis for their activities.

In summary, by focusing on the whole rather than the parts, OD tends to integrate the various activities of the firm that often go their separate ways. The result should be improved organizational performance.

The police force for a population of 170,000 persons was in difficulty. There was conflict between staff and law enforcement personnel, poor community relations, arbitrary decision making, and high employee turnover. An OD program was developed to help the group achieve better teamwork. Definite improvements followed. Employee relations improved and turnover declined from about 50% annually to less than 20%. Jail escapes declined from nine the first year to seven the next year, and then only one the following year.[16]

THE OD PROCESS
The *OD process* is a complicated one that tends to take a year or more in an organization and may continue indefinitely. For a program of this magni-

tude, top-management support is essential. There are many different approaches to OD, but a typical complete program includes the following steps.[17]

1. *Initial diagnosis.* Top management meets with the consultant to determine the type of OD program that is needed. During this phase the consultant may seek inputs by means of interviews with various people in the organization.

2. *Data collection.* Surveys may be made to determine organizational climate and behavioural problems. The consultant usually meets with groups away from work to develop information from questions such as:

- What kinds of conditions contribute most to your job effectiveness?
- What kinds of conditions interfere with your job effectiveness?
- What would you most like to change in the way this organization operates?

3. *Data feedback and confrontation.* Work groups are assigned to review the data collected, to mediate among themselves areas of disagreement, and to establish priorities for change.

4. *Action planning and problem solving.* Groups use the data to develop specific recommendations for change. Discussion focuses on real problems in their organization. Plans are specific, including who is responsible and when the action should be completed.

5. *Team building.* During the entire period of group meetings the consultant has been encouraging the groups to examine how they work together. The consultant helps them see the value of open communication and trust as prerequisites for improved group functioning. Team building is further encouraged by meetings of the natural group of manager and immediate subordinates to practise improved functioning with the guidance of the consultant.

6. *Intergroup development.* Following the development of natural teams, there may be development among larger groups comprising several teams.

7. *Evaluation and follow-up.* The consultant helps the organization evaluate the results of its OD efforts and develop additional programs in areas where additional results are needed. As an example of follow-up: in one organization, the consultant asked managers to provide tapes of committee meetings that they chaired subsequent to the program. The consultant analyzed these tapes and used them to discuss with managers how well each was applying what was learned in the OD program.

The steps in OD are part of a whole process; therefore, all of them need to be applied if a firm expects to gain the full benefits of OD. A firm that applies only two or three steps, such as diagnosis and team building, is likely to be disappointed with the results. However, the whole process can produce quite favourable results. In a manufacturing plant, for example, an OD program led to productivity increases of 22% in two years and 69% in four years.[18]

BENEFITS OF OD

When OD is successful, a number of variables may be improved. Three major areas of benefit are performance, job satisfaction, and self-change, as shown in Figure 11-8. However, the success rate for these areas is limited. Only 42% to 63% of the OD programs reported improved results for these areas.

Figure 11-8
PROPORTION OF OD PROGRAMS REPORTING IMPROVED RESULTS

Variable	Number of Studies	Percentage Reporting Improvement
Performance		
Individual	14	42
(Example: performance ratings)		
Group	8	63
(Example: quality of meetings)		
Organization	12	47
(Example: return on investment)		
General Job Satisfaction	7	43
Self-Change for Individual	10	62
(Example: openness to ideas and others)		

Source: Adapted from Jerry L. Porras and P. O. Berg, "The Impact of Organization Development," *Academy of Management Review*, April 1978, Tables 1 to 3, pp. 249–266.

PERFORMANCE. Performance benefits occur on three levels: individual, group, and organization. On the individual level, if the performance ratings of employees in the program improve, there is evidence that the OD program is associated with improved performance. The improvement may not have been *caused* by the OD program, but at least there is an *association*. The evidence is even stronger if there is a control group of nonparticipants and if this group fails to show any rating improvement during the same period.

There is a strong probability of improvement in group performance, since OD emphasizes group processes. Examples are improved cooperation and better meetings. In the long run these group improvements should be associated with broad organizational improvements such as lower unit costs of products and higher return on investment. These improvements are often called "bottom-line results" because they affect the bottom-line figure of profit on the profit-and-loss statement. They usually are the principal reason that management establishes an OD program.

JOB SATISFACTION. As shown in Figure 11-8, job satisfaction often increases following an OD program. Since teamwork, cooperation, and communication may improve, employees are likely to feel that they have a better place to work.

A supervisor, Gus Anka, participated in an OD program with supervisors from other departments. During this program the supervisors were encouraged to express conflicts and use a problem-solving approach on them. For three years Gus had an intense conflict with a supervisor in another department. During the OD meetings, this conflict was revealed and discussed. Gus felt that his conflict was adequately resolved in these meetings, so afterward he felt more accepted and involved. His job satisfaction substantially increased.

SELF-CHANGE. An important result of many OD programs is self-change. Participants learn to be more aware of their own feelings and of the feelings that others have toward them. They are encouraged to share their feelings with others, be more open in their communication, and become more co-operative. At least some of this new behaviour is likely to be carried back to the workplace and affect both self-perceptions and individual behaviour on the job.

PROBLEMS WITH OD

OD often is criticized because of several problems and weaknesses. As shown in Figure 11-9, an OD program is difficult and costly to apply. Some programs fail before completion, because employees dislike the methods used. OD also consumes much time as it continues through months or even years. Some of the techniques may invade privacy, and when they are misused, they can cause psychological damage to a participant.[19] For these reasons, management needs to assure itself that benefits will be clearly higher than costs, and the personnel director must be sure that the program is administered professionally.

Figure 11-9
TYPICAL PROBLEMS ASSOCIATED WITH OD

- Difficult to initiate; fails before completion
- Costly, including consultant and participant costs
- Slow and time-consuming, often requiring one to three years
- Possible psychological damage when misused
- Conceptual ambiguities
- Possible elitist, top-down imposition of values
- Narrow focus, mostly on people
- Antibureaucratic, at cross-purposes with authority systems

There are also a number of conceptual and philosophical questions about OD.[20] Some critics maintain that it has conceptual ambiguities that prevent it from being applied consistently. They also feel that it is an elitist, top-down program that tries to force humanistic values on people, even when they may not want these values. The values usually emphasize group processes and decisions, which may be contrary to the organization's authority structure. Some critics say that OD would be more effective if it were adjusted to have a better fit with authoritative organizations, instead of trying to revise the bureaucracy.[21]

In spite of the numerous weaknesses and problems of OD, it is an accepted practice in personnel management. It is widely used, and practitioners feel that its benefits are substantial in creating more humanly effective organizations.

SUMMARY

The personnel department is actively involved in most change because it affects people. The objective is to manage change in ways that increase its benefits and reduce its costs. The personnel department especially is concerned with barriers to change and the psychic costs associated with change. Major personnel practices that tend to support change include careful planning, participation, communication, and supplementary rewards to accompany change.

Organizational development (OD) is widely used to improve a firm's skills for working with change. OD is defined as an intervention strategy that uses group processes to focus on the whole organization in order to bring about planned change. It attempts to build the organization into a cooperative team. Although there are problems associated with OD, it is an accepted practice in personnel management because of its benefits.

TERMS FOR REVIEW

Psychic costs
Barriers to change
Resistance to change
Learning curve for change
Unfreezing
Refreezing

Organizational development (OD)
Change agents
OD change model
Action research
Experiential learning
OD process

REVIEW AND DISCUSSION QUESTIONS

1. Analyze your own responses to change during the last six months. What types of changes do you tend to accept more readily than others and why? Can you apply any of the change models in this chapter to help you understand your responses to change?
2. Discuss the relationship of costs and benefits of change. Can an organization implement a major change without costs? What are psychic costs?
3. Select a change that occurred within the classroom environment and discuss logical, psychological, and sociological resistance to it, if any.
4. If you were a supervisor in a government office and were required to make a major change in work methods, what practices would you use to support the change and why?

5. How are participation and resistance to change related?
6. Define and explain the characteristics of OD.
7. In which of the following situations would OD tend to be more effective and why?
   (a) Scientists in a product development laboratory
   (b) Workers on a television assembly line
8. What are potential benefits and problems of OD?

INCIDENT 11-1
CHARTERED BANK

Chartered Bank is a large bank with about eighty branches throughout the western provinces. For some months management has been considering a change in training evaluation procedures—a change that will affect both the personnel department and branch managers. The plan has been discussed with those who will be affected, and a number of them opposed the change. The training supervisor, Ramona Spelman, is one of the opposition.

After discussion with other bank officers, the vice president for personnel, Gary Reynolds, decided to adopt the change. He selected a task force to implement the change and chose Ramona as chairperson. When he asked her to accept, she did so, and then commented, "You knew I was opposed to this change. Why did you select me as chairperson?"

Gary replied, "Yes, we knew of your opposition. We chose you because we knew that if any flaws existed, you would find them. And we believed you could correct them." Nothing more was said.

1. Why would a manager such as Gary choose a leader of the opposition to implement a change? What models or basic ideas about change may have guided his thinking?
2. What degree of success do you predict for Ramona in implementing the change?

REFERENCES

1. Niccolò Machiavelli, *The Prince,* 1532.
2. Ralph E. Winter, "Firms' Recent Productivity Drives May Yield Unusually Strong Gains," *Wall Street Journal* (western edition), June 14, 1983, pp. 33 and 49.
3. For an example, see "Coping with Anxiety at AT&T," *Business Week,* May 28, 1979, pp. 95–106.
4. Lawrence W. Foster and Marilyn L. Liebrenz, "Corporate Moves—Who Pays the Psychic Costs?" *Personnel,* November–December 1977, pp. 67–75.
5. John P. Kotter and Vijay Sathe, "Problems of Human Resource Management in Rapidly Growing Companies," *California Management Review,* Winter 1978, pp. 29–36. A basic study of dynamic and stable environments is Paul R. Lawrence and Jay W. Lorsch, *Organization and Environment: Managing Differentiation and Integration,* Boston: Harvard Graduate School of Business Administration, 1967.
6. K. Lewin, "Frontiers in Group Dynamics I," *Human Relations,* Vol. 1, 1947, pp. 5–41; also (same issue) "Frontiers in Group Dynamics II," pp. 143–153.
7. For extensive discussion see Charles Margerison, *Influencing Organizational Change: The Role of the Personnel Specialist,* London: Institute of Personnel Management, 1978.
8. William P. Anthony, *Participative Management,* Reading, Mass.: Addison-Wesley Publishing Company Inc., 1978; Rensis Likert and Jane Gibson Likert, *New Ways of Managing Conflict,* New York: McGraw-Hill Book Company, 1976; and Alfred J. Marrow (ed.), *The Failure of Success,* New York: AMACOM, 1972.
9. Alexander Mikalachki, "Does Anyone Listen to the Boss?" *Business Horizons,* January–February 1983, pp. 18–24.
10. Richard C. Huseman et al., "Managing Change through Communication," *Personnel Journal,* January 1978, pp. 20–25.

11. John P. Kotter and Leonard A. Schlesinger, "Choosing Strategies for Change," *Harvard Business Review*, March–April 1979, pp. 106–114.

12. Edgar F. Huse and Michael Beer, "Eclectic Approach to Organizational Development," *Harvard Business Review*, September–October 1971, pp. 103–112; and William F. Dowling, "To Move an Organization: The Corning Approach to Organizational Development," *Organizational Dynamics*, Spring 1975, pp. 16–34.

13. Milan Moravec, "Is HRD Enough?" *Personnel*, January–February 1979, pp. 53–57.

14. Ronald H. Gorman and H. Kent Baker, "That's Okay in Theory, But . . . ," *Personnel*, July–August 1978, pp. 48–54. For a study of the perceived effectiveness of training methods as seen by training directors, see John W. Newstrom, "Evaluating the Effectiveness of Training Methods," *The Personnel Administrator*, January 1980, pp. 55–60.

15. For additional insights into the change agent in organizations, see Lee Grossman, *The Change Agent*, New York: AMACOM, 1974.

16. R. Wayne Boss, "The Not-So-Peaceful Incident at Peaceful Valley: A Confrontation Design in a Criminal Justice Agency," in Arthur G. Bedeian et al. (eds.), *Academy of Management Proceedings, 1975*, Auburn, Ala.: Auburn University, 1975, pp. 357–359.

17. For a more extensive discussion of the OD process, see John P. Kotter, *Organizational Dynamics: Diagnosis and Intervention*, Reading, Mass.: Addison-Wesley Publishing Company, Inc., 1978; and Glen H. Varney, *Organizational Development for Managers*, Reading, Mass.: Addison-Wesley Publishing Company Inc., 1977.

18. Rensis Likert and M. Scott Fisher, "MBGO: Putting Some Team Spirit into MBO," *Personnel*, January–February 1977, pp. 40–47. Other applications of OD are reported in a special section on OD in *Personnel*, March–April 1979, pp. 31–52, 62–68.

19. Morton A. Lieberman, Irvin D. Yalom, and Matthew B. Miles, *Encounter Groups: First Facts*, New York: Basic Books, Inc., Publishers, 1973.

20. A readable summary of criticisms is Patrick E. Connor, "A Critical Inquiry into Some Assumptions and Values Characterizing OD," *Academy of Management Review*, October 1977, pp. 635–644. A book reporting failures and problems is Philip H. Mirvis and David N. Berg (eds.), *Failures in Organization Development and Change: Cases and Essays for Learning*, New York: John Wiley & Sons Inc., 1977. Insights into the philosophy and processes of OD are provided in a special issue, entitled "Collaboration in Work Sessions," *Journal of Applied Behavioral Science*, 13 (1977) (3): 261–464.

21. Virginia E. Schein and Larry E. Greiner, "Can Organization Development Be Fine Tuned to Bureaucracies?" *Organizational Dynamics*, Winter 1977, pp. 48–61.

Chapter *12*

Performance Appraisal

The performance appraisal concept is central to effective management.
Harry Levinson[1]

CHAPTER OBJECTIVES

After studying this chapter, you should be able to:
1. **Identify** the issues that influence selection of a performance appraisal system.
2. **Explain** the uses of performance appraisals.
3. **Discuss** rater biases in performance appraisals.
4. **Describe** commonly used appraisal methods.
5. **Explain** how the results of performance appraisal affect personnel management.

Previous chapters discussed how employees are selected, developed, and formed into cohesive work groups. These are important activities. But the ultimate measure of a personnel department's success is employee performance. Both the personnel department and employees need feedback on their efforts. Unfortunately, managers in other departments may not understand the need for evaluating employee performance. Too often, they see performance appraisals as unnecessary conversation. The following discussion between Ellen, a line manager, and Sam, a personnel specialist, highlights these different views of performance appraisals:

Ellen: *Don't you think I know who the good performers are in my department? I know the strengths and weaknesses of every employee who works for me. So why do we need to have a formal performance evaluation program?*

Sam: *No one in the personnel department is questioning whether you know who the good performers are. In fact, we in personnel hope that all managers know who their best workers are. But we need a formal appraisal system to compare employees in different departments.*

Ellen: *Why is that so important?*

Sam: *We need that information for many reasons. We need to know who should receive additional training and development, who should be promoted, and who should* *get pay raises. Besides, employees need formal feedback on how they are doing their job.*

Ellen: *Well, I let my employees know how they are doing. And I do it without all the formality of a performance appraisal program.*

Sam: *Good managers, like yourself, always give employees feedback. The personnel department merely wants to formalize the process so that there is a written record of performance. Without such a record, we in the personnel department have no consistent way to compare employees when personnel-related decisions are made.*

Performance appraisal is the process by which organizations evaluate employee job performance. As the dialogue between Ellen and Sam indicates, appraisals expand the personnel department's information base. This knowledge can improve personnel decisions and the feedback employees receive about their performance.

The uses of performance appraisals are described in Figure 12-1. Accurate performance evaluations show employees where they are deficient. For

Figure 12-1
USES OF PERFORMANCE APPRAISALS

  • **Performance improvement.** Performance feedback allows the employee, the manager, and personnel specialists to intervene with appropriate actions to improve performance.

  • **Compensation adjustments.** Performance evaluations help decision makers determine who should receive pay raises. Many firms grant part or all of their pay increases and bonuses on the basis of merit, which is determined mostly through performance appraisals.

  • **Placement decisions.** Promotions, transfers, and demotions are usually based on past or anticipated performance. Often promotions are a reward for past performance.

  • **Training and development needs.** Poor performance may indicate the need for retraining. Likewise, good performance may indicate untapped potential that should be developed.

  • **Career planning and development.** Performance feedback guides career decisions about specific career paths one should investigate.

  • **Deficiencies in staffing process.** Good or bad performance implies strengths or weaknesses in the personnel department's staffing procedures.

  • **Informational inaccuracies.** Poor performance may indicate errors in job analysis information, human resource plans, or other parts of the personnel management information system. Reliance on inaccurate information may have led to inappropriate hiring, training, or counselling decisions.

  • **Job design errors.** Poor performance may be a symptom of ill-conceived job designs. Appraisals help diagnose these errors.

  • **Avoidance of discrimination.** Accurate performance appraisals that actually measure job-related performance ensure that internal placement decisions are not discriminatory.

  • **External challenges.** Sometimes performance is influenced by factors outside the work environment, such as family, finances, health, or other personal matters. If such influences are uncovered through appraisals, the personnel department may be able to provide assistance.

the personnel department, appraisals make compensation, placement, training, development, and career guidance decisions more effective. At the same time, the department obtains feedback on its development activities, staffing process, job designs, and external challenges. In short, performance appraisals serve as a quality control check on employee and personnel department performance.

Without an effective appraisal system, promotions, transfers, and other employee-related decisions become subject to trial and error. Career planning and human resource development suffer because there is no systematic performance feedback. And the personnel department lacks adequate information to evaluate its performance objectively. This lack of feedback can cause the personnel department to miss its objectives. Sometimes the consequences of this failure are severe:

A large agricultural cooperative association in the western provinces rated employees twice a year. But employees were evaluated on personality characteristics, such as attitude, cooperation, and other factors that were related only indirectly to actual performance. Employees that were well liked by their managers received higher ratings than others. As a result, promotions, pay raises, and other employee-related decisions were biased by personalities. Eventually, several employees filed charges against the cooperative, alleging racial and sexual discrimination. When company attorneys defended past decisions as unbiased, they lost the case because they could not show how the ratings related to job performance.

As this example emphasizes, an organization cannot have just *any* performance appraisal system. Figure 12-2 shows the elements of an acceptable appraisal system. The approach must identify performance-related criteria, measure those criteria, and then give feedback to employees and the personnel department. If performance measures are not job-related, the evaluation can lead to inaccurate or biased results.[2] Not only is performance feedback distorted, but errors in employee records can lead to incorrect personnel decisions, as happened in the example of the agricultural cooperative.

The personnel department usually develops performance appraisals for employees in all departments. One U.S. study found that the development of appraisal systems is the responsibility of the personnel department in over 80% of the firms surveyed.[3] This centralization is meant to ensure uniformity. With uniformity in design and implementation, results are more likely to be comparable among similar groups of employees. Although personnel may develop different approaches for managers and workers, uniformity within each group is needed to ensure useful results.

Even though the personnel department usually designs the appraisal system, it seldom does the actual evaluation of performance. Instead, research shows that the employee's immediate supervisor performs the evaluation 95% of the time.[4] Although others could rate performance, the immediate supervisor is often in the best position to make the appraisal.

So important is the evaluation of performance that 75% of large companies and 55% of medium-sized companies in one Canadian study used appraisals for their clerical, professional, supervisory, and management em-

Figure 12-2
KEY ELEMENTS OF PERFORMANCE APPRAISAL SYSTEMS

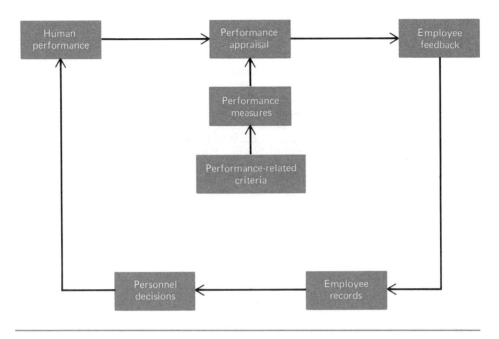

ployees.[5] To explain the importance of this widely used tool of personnel management, the rest of this chapter examines the preparation, methods, and implications of performance appraisals.

PERFORMANCE APPRAISAL PREPARATION

The appraisal should create an accurate picture of an individual's job performance. To achieve this goal, appraisal systems should be job-related, be practical, have standards, and use dependable measures. *Job-related* means that the system evaluates critical behaviours that constitute job success. If the evaluation is not job-related, it is invalid and probably unreliable. Without validity and reliability, the system may discriminate in violation of anti-discrimination laws. Even when discrimination does not occur, appraisals are inaccurate and useless if they are not job-related.

But a job-related approach also must be practical. A *practical* system is one that, first of all, is understood by evaluators and employees; a complicated, impractical approach may cause resentment and nonuse. The confusion can lead to inaccuracies that reduce the effectiveness of the appraisal. To be practical the procedure should also be standardized.

PERFORMANCE STANDARDS

Performance evaluation requires *performance standards*. They are the benchmarks against which performance is measured. To be effective, they should relate to the desired results of each job. They cannot be set arbitrarily. Knowledge of these standards is collected through job analysis. As discussed in Chapter 5, job analysis uncovers specific performance criteria by analyzing the performance of existing employees. As one pair of writers has observed:

> It is important that management carefully examine the characteristics of effective performance. Job analysis coupled with a detailed performance analysis of existing employees should begin to identify what characteristics are required by a job and which of those are exhibited by "successful" employees. It is possible that such an investigation may reveal that what management has used in the past to define successful performance is inadequate or misleading. This should not deter management from the task of defining the criteria, but should reinforce management for the "house cleaning" which is being undertaken. This must be a careful scrutiny with an eye to what the performance criteria should be in the future, rather than what criteria have been used in the past.[6]

From the duties and standards listed in the job description, the analyst can decide which behaviours are critical and should be evaluated. If it should happen that this information is lacking or unclear, standards may be developed from observation of the job or discussion with the immediate supervisor.

PERFORMANCE MEASURES

Performance evaluation also requires dependable *performance measures*. They are the ratings used to evaluate performance. To be useful, they must be easy to use, be reliable, and report on the critical behaviours that determine performance. For example, a telephone company supervisor must observe each operator's:

• Use of company procedures—staying calm, applying tariff rates for phone calls, and following company rules and regulations.
• Pleasant phone manners—speaking clearly and courteously.
• Call-placement accuracy—placing operator-assisted calls accurately.

These observations can be made either directly or indirectly. *Direct observation* occurs when the rater actually sees the performance. *Indirect observation* occurs when the rater can evaluate only substitutes for actual performance. For example, a supervisor's monitoring of an operator's calls is direct observation; a written test on company procedures for handling emergency calls is indirect observation. Indirect observations are usually less accurate because they evaluate substitutes for actual performance. Substitutes for actual performance are called *constructs*. Since constructs are not exactly the same as actual performance, they may lead to errors.

To test how well operators might respond to emergency calls, a provincial telephone company developed a paper-and-pencil test. The test was intended to determine if each operator knew exactly how to proceed when emergency calls were received for such requests as police, ambulance, or fire equipment. After several hundred opera-

tors were tested, it was noticed that fast readers scored better. The personnel department decided to scrap the test and use false emergency calls to evaluate the operators.

Another dimension of performance measures is whether they are objective or subjective. *Objective performance measures* are those indications of job performance that are verifiable by others. For example, if two supervisors monitor an operator's calls, they can count the number of misdialed ones. The results are objective and verifiable since each supervisor gets the same call-placement accuracy percentage. Usually, objective measures are quantitative. They typically include items such as gross units produced, net units approved by quality control, scrap rates, number of computational errors, number of customer complaints, or some other mathematically precise measure of performance.

Subjective performance measures are those ratings that are not verifiable by others. Usually, such measures are the rater's personal opinions. Figure 12-3 compares the accuracy of objective and subjective measures. It shows that subjective measures are low in accuracy. When subjective measures are also indirect, accuracy becomes even lower. For example, measurement of an operator's phone manners is done subjectively since supervisors must use their personal opinions of good or bad manners. Since the evaluation is subjective, accuracy is usually low even if the supervisor directly observes the operator. Accuracy is likely to be even lower when the rater uses an indirect measure, such as an essay test of phone manners. Whenever possible, personnel specialists prefer objective and direct measures of performance.

Figure 12-3
TYPES AND ACCURACY OF PERFORMANCE MEASURES

Types of Performance Measures	Relative Degree of Accuracy	
	Direct	Indirect
Objective	Very high	High
Subjective	Low	Very low

RATER BIASES

The problem with subjective measures is the opportunity for bias. *Bias* is the (mostly unintentional) distortion of a measurement. Usually it is caused by raters who fail to remain emotionally detached while they evaluate employee performance. The most common rater biases include:

- The halo effect
- The error of central tendency
- The leniency and strictness biases
- Personal prejudice
- The recency effect

THE HALO EFFECT. The halo effect (discussed in Chapter 8) occurs when the rater's personal opinion of the employee sways the rater's measurement of performance. For example, if a supervisor likes an employee, that opinion may distort the supervisor's estimate of the employee's performance. The problem is most severe when raters must evaluate their friends.

THE ERROR OF CENTRAL TENDENCY. Some raters do not like to judge employees as "effective" or "ineffective," so they avoid checking extremes —very poor or excellent—and instead place their marks near the centre of the rating sheet so that employees appear to be "average."[7] Thus the term *error of central tendency* has been applied to this bias. Personnel departments sometimes unintentionally encourage this behaviour by requiring raters to justify extremely high or low ratings.

THE LENIENCY AND STRICTNESS BIASES. The *leniency bias* occurs when raters are too easy in evaluating employee performance. The *strictness bias* is just the opposite: it results from raters' being too harsh in their evaluation of performance. Both errors more commonly occur when performance standards are vague.

PERSONAL PREJUDICE. A rater's dislike for a person or group may distort the ratings. For example, some personnel departments notice that male supervisors give undeservedly low ratings to women who hold "traditionally male jobs." Sometimes raters are unaware of their prejudice, which makes such biases even more difficult to overcome. Nevertheless, personnel specialists should pay close attention to prejudice in appraisals since it prevents effective evaluations and violates antidiscrimination laws.

THE RECENCY EFFECT. When using subjective performance measures, ratings are affected strongly by the employee's most recent actions. Recent actions—either good or bad—are more likely to be remembered by the rater.

When subjective performance measures must be used, personnel specialists can reduce the distortion from biases through training, feedback, and the proper selection of performance appraisal techniques. Training for raters should involve three steps. First, biases and their causes should be explained. Second, the role of performance appraisals in employee decisions should be explained to stress the need for impartiality and objectivity. Third, raters should be allowed to apply subjective performance measures as part of their training. For example, classroom exercises may require evaluation of the trainer or videotapes of various workers. Mistakes uncovered during simulated evaluations then can be corrected through additional training or counselling.

Once the use of subjective performance measures moves out of the classroom and into practice, raters should get feedback about their previous ratings.[8] When ratings prove relatively accurate or inaccurate, feedback helps raters adjust their behaviour accordingly.

Personnel departments also can reduce distortion through the careful selection of performance appraisal techniques.[9] For ease of discussion, these techniques are grouped into those that focus on past performance and those that focus on future performance.

PAST-ORIENTED APPRAISAL METHODS

The importance of performance evaluations has led academicians and practitioners to create many methods to appraise past performance. Most of these techniques are a direct attempt to minimize some particular problem found in other approaches. None is perfect; each has advantages and disadvantages.

Past-oriented approaches have the advantage of dealing with performance that has already occurred and, to some degree, can be measured. The obvious disadvantage is that past performance cannot be changed. But by evaluating past performance, employees can get feedback about their effects. This feedback may then lead to renewed efforts at improved performance. The most widely used appraisal techniques that have a past orientation include:

- Rating scale
- Checklist
- Forced choice method
- Critical incident method
- Behaviourally anchored rating scales
- Field review method
- Performance tests and observations
- Comparative evaluation methods

RATING SCALE

Perhaps the oldest and most widely used form of performance appraisal is the *rating scale*, which requires the rater to provide a subjective evaluation of an individual's performance along a scale from low to high. An example appears in Figure 12-4. As the figure indicates, the evaluation is based solely on the opinions of the rater. In many cases, the criteria are not directly related to job performance. Although subordinates or peers may use it, the immediate supervisor usually completes the form.

The form is completed by checking the most appropriate response for each performance factor. Responses may be given numerical values to enable an average score to be computed and compared for each employee. The advantages of this method are that it is inexpensive to develop and administer, raters need little training or time to complete the form, and it can be applied to a large number of employees.

Disadvantages are numerous. A rater's biases are likely to be reflected in a subjective instrument of this type. Specific performance criteria may be omitted to make the form applicable to a variety of jobs. For example, "maintenance of equipment" may be left off the form because it applies to only a few workers. But for some employees, that item may be the most important part of their job. This and other omissions tend to limit specific

Figure 12-4

A SAMPLE OF A RATING SCALE FOR PERFORMANCE EVALUATION

WESTERN FARM COOPERATIVE ASSOCIATION
Rating Scale

Instructions: For the following performance factors, please indicate on the rating scale your evaluation of the named employee.

Employee's Name _____   Department _____

Rater's Name _____   Date_____

	Excellent 5	Good 4	Acceptable 3	Fair 2	Poor 1
1. Dependability	___	___	___	___	___
2. Initiative	___	___	___	___	___
3. Overall Output	___	___	___	___	___
4. Attendance	___	___	___	___	___
5. Attitude	___	___	___	___	___
6. Cooperation	___	___	___	___	___
• •	•	•	•	•	•
• •	•	•	•	•	•
• •	•	•	•	•	•
20. Quality of Work Results	___	___	___	___	___
Totals	___	+ ___	+ ___	+ ___	+ ___ = ___

Total Score

feedback. Also, these descriptive evaluations are subject to individual interpretations that vary widely. And when specific performance criteria are hard to identify, the form may rely on irrelevant personality variables that dilute the meaning of the evaluation. The result is a standardized form and procedure that is not always job related.

CHECKLIST

The *checklist* rating method requires the rater to select statements or words that describe the employee's performance and characteristics. Again, the rater is usually the immediate superior. But unknown to the rater, the personnel department may assign weights to different items on the checklist, according to each item's importance. The result is called a *weighted checklist*. The weights allow the rating to be quantified so that total scores can be determined. Figure 12-5 shows a portion of a checklist. The weights for each item are in parentheses here but are usually omitted from the actual form. If the list contains enough items, it may provide an accurate picture of employee performance. Although this method is practical and standardized, the use of general statements reduces its job-relatedness.

Figure 12-5
AN EXAMPLE OF A WEIGHTED PERFORMANCE CHECKLIST

HATHAWAY DEPARTMENT STORES LTD.
Performance Checklist

Instructions: Check each of the following items that apply to the named employee's performance.

Employee's Name _____   **Department** _____
Rater's Name _____   **Date**_____

Weights		Check Here
(6.5)	**1.** Employee works overtime when asked.	_____
(4.0)	**2.** Employee keeps work station or desk well organized.	_____
(3.9)	**3.** Employee cooperatively assists others who need help.	_____
(4.3)	**4.** Employee plans actions before beginning job.	_____
•	• • •	•
•	• • •	•
•	• • •	•
(0.2)	**30.** Employee listens to others' advice but seldom follows it.	_____
100.0	**Total of All Weights**	

The advantages of a checklist are economy, ease of administration, limited training of raters, and standardization. The disadvantages include susceptibility to rater biases (especially the halo effect), use of personality criteria instead of performance criteria, misinterpretation of checklist items, and use of improper weights by the personnel department. Moreover, it does not allow the rater to give relative ratings. On item 1 in the figure, for example, employees who gladly work overtime get the same score as those who do so unwillingly.

FORCED CHOICE METHOD

The *forced choice method* requires the rater to choose the most descriptive statement in each pair of statements about the employee being rated. Often both statements in the pair are positive or negative. For example:

1. Learns quickly . . . . Works hard
2. Work is reliable and accurate . . . . Performance is a good example to
others
3. Absent too often . . . . Usually tardy

Sometimes the rater must select the best statement (or even pair of statements) from four choices. However the form is constructed, personnel specialists usually group the items on the form into predetermined categories, such as learning ability, performance, interpersonal relations, and the like. Then effectiveness can be computed for each category by adding up the number of times each category is selected by the rater. The results in each category can be reported to show which areas need further improvement. Again, the supervisor is usually the rater, although peers or subordinates may make the evaluation.

The forced choice method has the advantages of reducing rater bias, being easy to administer, and fitting a wide variety of jobs. Although practical and easily standardized, the general statements may not be specifically job-related. Thus it may have limited usefulness in helping employees to improve their performance. Even worse, an employee may feel slighted when one statement is checked in preference to another. For example, if the rater checks "learns quickly" in number 1 above, the worker may feel that his or her hard work is overlooked.[10] This method is seldom liked by either the rater or ratee because it provides little useful feedback.

CRITICAL INCIDENT METHOD

The *critical incident method* requires the rater to record statements that describe extremely good or bad employee behaviour related to performance. The statements are called critical incidents. These incidents are usually recorded by the supervisor during the evaluation period for each subordinate. Recorded incidents include a brief explanation of what happened. Several typical entries for a laboratory assistant appear in Figure 12-6. As shown in the figure, both positive and negative incidents are recorded. Incidents are classified (either as they occur or later by the personnel department) into categories such as control of safety hazards, control of material scrap, and employee development.

The critical incident method is extremely useful for giving employees job-related feedback. It also reduces the recency bias. Of course, the practical drawback is the difficulty of getting supervisors to record incidents as they occur. Many supervisors start out recording incidents faithfully, but lose interest. Then, just before the evaluation period ends, they add new entries. When this happens, the recency bias is exaggerated and employees may feel that the supervisors are building a case to support their subjective opinion. Even when the form is filled out over the entire rating period, employees may feel that the supervisor is unwilling to forget negative incidents that occurred months before.

BEHAVIOURALLY ANCHORED RATING SCALES

Behaviourally anchored rating scales (BARS) attempt to reduce the subjectivity and biases of subjective performance measures.[11] From descriptions of good and bad performance provided by incumbents, peers, and supervisors, job analysts or knowledgeable employees group these examples into performance-related categories such as employee knowledge, customer relations, and the like. Then specific examples of these behaviours are placed along a scale (usually from 1 to 7). Actual behaviours for a bank

Figure 12-6
CRITICAL INCIDENTS RECORD FOR A LAB ASSISTANT

HARTFORD CHEMICALS LTD.
Critical Incidents Worksheet

Instructions: In each category below, record specific incidents of employee behaviour that were either extremely good or extremely poor.

Employee's Name   Kay Watts   (lab assistant)   **Department**   Chemistry Lab

Rater's Name   Nat Cordoba   **Rating Period of**   10/1   **to**   12/31

Control of Safety Hazards

Date	Positive Employee Behaviour	Date	Negative Employee Behaviour
10/12	Reported broken rung on utility ladder and flagged ladder as unsafe	11/3	Left hose across storeroom aisle
10/15	Put out small trash fire promptly	11/27	Smoked in chemical storeroom

Control of Material Scrap

Date	Positive Employee Behaviour	Date	Negative Employee Behaviour
10/3	Sorted through damaged shipment of glassware to salvage usable beakers	11/7	Used glass containers for strong bases ruining glass
		11/19	Repeatedly used glass for storage of lye and other bases
			Poured acid into plastic container ruining counter top

branch manager are illustrated on the rating scale shown in Figure 12-7. Since the positions on the scale are described in job-related behaviour, an objective evaluation along the scale is more likely. And the form cites specific behaviours that can be used to provide performance feedback to employees. The BARS are job-related, practical, and standardized for similar jobs. But the rater's personal biases may still cause ratings to be high or low, although the specific behaviours that "anchor" the scale provide some criteria to guide the sincere rater.[12] If the rater collects specific incidents during the rating period, the evaluation is apt to be more accurate and more legally defensible, besides being a more effective counselling tool.[13] One serious limitation of BARS is that they only look at a limited number of performance categories, such as customer relations or personnel. Also, each of these categories has only a limited number of specific behaviours. Like the critical incident method, most supervisors are reluctant to maintain

Figure 12-7
BEHAVIOURALLY ANCHORED RATING SCALE FOR BANK BRANCH MANAGER

Bank of Ontario

Job Part: Personnel

Outstanding Performance	7	Can be expected to praise publicly for tasks completed well, and constructively criticizes in private those individuals who have produced less than adequate results.
Good Performance	6	Can be expected to show great confidence in subordinates, and openly displays this with the result that they develop to meet expectations.
Fairly Good Performance	5	Can be expected to ensure that personnel records are kept right up to date, that reports are written on time, and that salary reviews are not overlooked.
Acceptable Performance	4	Can be expected to admit a personal mistake, thus showing that he is human too.
Fairly Poor Performance	3	Can be expected to make "surprise" performance appraisals of subordinates.
Poor Performance	2	Can be expected not to support decisions made by a subordinate (makes exceptions to rules).
Extremely Poor Performance	1	Can be expected not to accept responsibility for errors and to pass blame to subordinates.

records of critical incidents during the rating period, which reduces the effectiveness of this approach when it comes time to counsel the employee. [14]

FIELD REVIEW METHOD

Whenever subjective performance measures are used, differences in rater perceptions cause bias. To provide greater standardization in reviews, some employers use the *field review method*. In this method, a skilled representative of the personnel department goes "into the field" and assists supervisors with their ratings. The personnel specialist solicits from the immediate supervisor specific information about the employee's performance. Then the expert prepares an evaluation based on this information. The evaluation is sent to the supervisor for review, changes, approval, and discussion with the employee who was rated. The personnel specialist records the rating on whatever specific type of rating form the employer uses. Since a skilled professional is completing the form, reliability and comparability are more likely. But the need for the services of skilled professionals may make this approach impractical for many firms.

PERFORMANCE TESTS AND OBSERVATIONS

With a limited number of jobs, performance appraisal may be based upon a test of knowledge or skills. The test may be of the paper-and-pencil variety or an actual demonstration of skills. The test must be reliable and valid to be useful. In order for the method to be job-related, observations should be made under circumstances likely to be encountered. Practicality may suffer when the cost of test development is high.

Pilots of all major airlines are subject to evaluation by airline raters and Transport Canada. Evaluations of flying ability are usually made both in a flight simulator and while being observed during an actual flight. The evaluation is based on how well the pilot follows prescribed flight procedures and safety rules. Although this approach is expensive, public safety makes it practical, as well as job-related and standardized.

COMPARATIVE EVALUATION METHODS

Comparative evaluation methods are a collection of different methods that compare one person's performance with that of coworkers. Usually, comparative evaluations are conducted by the supervisor. They are useful for deciding merit pay increases, promotions, and organizational rewards because they can result in a ranking of employees from best to worst. The most common forms of comparative evaluations are the ranking method, forced distributions, point allocation method, and paired comparisons. Although these methods are practical and easily standardized, they too are subject to bias and offer little job-related feedback.

Many large companies use an elaborate group evaluation method. This method reduces biases because multiple raters are used, and some feedback results when managers and professionals learn how they compared with others on each critical factor. However, these comparative results are often not shared with the employee because the supervisor and the personnel department want to create an atmosphere of cooperation among employees. To share comparative rankings may lead to internal competition instead of cooperation. Nevertheless, two arguments in favour of comparative approaches merit mention before discussing specific methods.

> Arguments for a comparative approach are simple and powerful. The simple part of it is that organizations do it anyway, all the time. Whenever personnel decisions are made, the performance of the individuals being considered is ranked and compared. People are not promoted because they achieve their objectives, but rather because they achieve their objectives *better* than others.
>
> The second reason (the powerful one) for using comparative as opposed to noncomparative methods is that they are far more reliable. This is because reliability is controlled by the rating process itself, not by rules, policies, and other external constraints.[15]

RANKING METHOD. The *ranking method* has the rater place each employee in order from best to worst. All the personnel department knows is that certain employees are better than others. It does not know by how much. The employee ranked second may be almost as good as the one who was first or considerably worse. This method is subject to the halo and recency effects, although rankings by two or more raters can be averaged to help reduce biases. Its advantages include ease of administration and explanation.

FORCED DISTRIBUTIONS. *Forced distributions* require raters to sort employees into different classifications. Usually a certain proportion must be put in each category. Figure 12-8 shows how a rater might classify ten subordinates. The criterion shown in the figure is for overall performance (but this method can be used for other performance criteria, such as reliability and control of costs). As with the ranking method, relative differences among employees are unknown, but this method does overcome the biases of central tendency, leniency, and strictness. Some workers and supervisors strongly dislike this method because employees are often rated lower than they or their supervisor/rater think to be correct. However, the personnel department's forced distribution requires some employees to be rated low.

Figure 12-8
THE FORCED DISTRIBUTION METHOD OF APPRAISAL OF TEN SUBORDINATES

CAPTONE FISHERIES LTD.
Forced Distribution Rating

Classification: Overall Performance

Best 10% of Subordinates	Next 20% of Subordinates	Middle 40% of Subordinates	Next 20% of Subordinates	Lowest 10% of Subordinates
A. Wilson	G. Carrs	B. Johnson	K. McDougal	W. Smythe
	M. Lopez	E. Wilson	L. Ray	
		C. Grant		
		T. Valley		

POINT ALLOCATION METHOD. The *point allocation method* requires the rater to allocate a fixed number of points among employees in the group, as shown in Figure 12-9. Better employees are given more points than poor performers. The advantage to the point allocation method is that the rater can recognize the relative differences between employees, although the halo effect and the recency bias are disadvantages that remain.

PAIRED COMPARISONS. *Paired comparisons* require raters to compare each employee with all other employees who are being rated in the same group. An example of paired comparisons appears in Figure 12-10. The basis for comparison is usually overall performance. The number of times each employee is rated superior to another can be summed up to develop an index. The employee who is preferred the most is the best employee on the

Figure 12-9

THE POINT ALLOCATION METHOD OF APPRAISAL

CAPTONE FISHERIES LTD.
Point Allocation Rating

Instructions: Allocate all **100** points to all employees according to their relative worth. The employee with the maximum points is the best employee.

Points	Employee
17	A. Wilson
14	G. Carrs
13	M. Lopez
11	B. Johnson
10	E. Wilson
10	C. Grant
9	T. Valley
6	K. McDougal
5	L. Ray
5	W. Smythe
100	

criterion selected. In the figure, A. Wilson is selected nine times and is the top-ranked employee. Although subject to halo and recency effects, this method counteracts the leniency, strictness, and central tendency errors because some employees must be rated better than others.

FUTURE-ORIENTED APPRAISALS

The use of past-oriented approaches is like driving a car by looking through the rearview mirror: you only know where you have been, not where you are going. Future-oriented appraisals focus on future performance by evaluating employee potential or setting future performance goals. Included here are four techniques used:

- Self-appraisals
- Psychological appraisals
- Management-by-objectives approach
- Assessment centre technique

SELF-APPRAISALS

Getting employees to conduct a self-appraisal can be a useful evaluation technique if the goal of evaluation is to further self-development. When employees evaluate themselves, defensive behaviour is less likely to occur. Thus self-improvement is more likely. When self-appraisals are used to determine areas of needed improvement, they can help users set personal goals for future improvement.

Obviously, self-appraisals can be used with any evaluation approach,

Figure 12-10

THE PAIRED COMPARISON METHOD OF EVALUATING EMPLOYEES

CAPTONE FISHERIES LTD.
Paired Comparison Rating

Instructions: Compare each employee on overall performance with every other employee. For each comparison, write the number of the employee who is best in the intersecting box. Each time an employee is found superior to another employee, the better employee receives one point. Employees then can be ranked according to the number of times each is selected as best by the rater.

Employee	2	3	4	5	6	7	8	9	10
1 G. Carrs	1	1	4	1	1	1	1	9	1
2 C. Grant		3	4	2	2	2	2	9	2
3 B. Johnson			4	3	3	3	3	9	3
4 M. Lopez				4	4	4	4	9	4
5 K. McDougal					6	5	8	9	10
6 L. Ray						6	8	9	10
7 W. Smythe							8	9	10
8 T. Valley								9	10
9 A. Wilson									9
10 E. Wilson									

past- or future-oriented. But the important dimension of self-appraisals is the employee's involvement and commitment to the improvement process.

At the Bechtel Company, the largest privately held construction and engineering firm in the world, their performance planning system involves the employee in a process of self-appraisal. The process starts with the supervisor telling the employee what is expected. Then the employee gets a worksheet and writes down his or her understanding of the job. Then, ten to fifteen days before a performance evaluation is to be done, the employee completes the worksheet by filling in the portions that relate to job accomplishments, performance difficulties, and suggestions for improvement. Not only does it get the employee involved in forming a self-appraisal of improvement areas, but the completed sheet indicates to the supervisor what he or she needs to do to ". . . eliminate roadblocks to meeting or exceeding job standards."[16]

PSYCHOLOGICAL APPRAISALS

Some, mostly very large, organizations employ full-time psychologists. When psychologists are used for evaluations, their role is primarily to assess an individual's future potential. The appraisal normally consists of in-depth interviews, psychological tests, discussions with supervisors, and a review of other evaluations. The psychologist then writes an evaluation of the employee's intellectual, emotional, motivational, and other work-related characteristics that may help predict future performance. The estimate by the psychologist may be for a specific job opening for which a person is being considered, or it may be a global assessment of an employee's future potential. From these evaluations, placement and development decisions may be made to shape the person's career. Because this approach is slow and costly, it is usually reserved for bright young managers who are thought to have considerable potential with the organization. The quality of these appraisals depends largely on the skills of the psychologists, and some employees object to evaluations by company psychologists.

MANAGEMENT-BY-OBJECTIVES APPROACH

The heart of the management-by-objectives (MBO) approach is that each employee and superior jointly establish performance goals for the future.[17] Ideally, these goals are mutually agreed upon and objectively measurable. If both conditions are met, employees are apt to be more motivated to achieve the goal since they have participated in setting it. Moreover, they can periodically adjust their behaviour to ensure attainment of the objectives if they can measure their progress toward the objective. But to adjust their efforts, performance feedback must be available on a regular basis.

When future objectives are set, employees gain the motivational benefit of a specific target to organize and direct their efforts. Objectives also help the employee and supervisor discuss specific developmental needs of the employee. When done correctly, performance discussions focus on the job's objectives and not on personality variables. Biases are reduced to the extent that goal attainment can be measured objectively.

In practice, MBO programs have encountered difficulties. Objectives are sometimes too ambitious or too narrow. The result is frustrated employees or overlooked areas of performance. For example, employees may set objectives that are measured by quantity rather than quality because quality, while it may be equally important, is often more difficult to measure. When employees and managers do focus on subjectively measured objectives, special care is needed to ensure that biases do not distort the manager's evaluation.

ASSESSMENT CENTRE TECHNIQUE

Assessment centres are another method of evaluating future potential, but they do not rely on the conclusions of one psychologist. Assessment centres are a standardized form of employee appraisal that relies on multiple types of evaluation and multiple raters. The assessment centre technique is usually applied to groups of middle-level managers who appear to have potential to perform at more responsible levels in the organization. Often the members of the group first meet at the assessment centre. During a brief stay at the facility, candidates are individually evaluated. The process subjects selected employees to in-depth interviews, psychological tests, personal background histories, peer ratings by other attendees, leaderless group discussions, ratings by psychologists and managers, and simulated work exercises to evaluate future potential. The simulated work experiences usually include in-basket exercises, decision-making exercises, computer-based business games, and other job-like opportunities that test the employee in realistic ways.

These activities are usually conducted for a few days at a location physically removed from the jobsite. During this time, the psychologists and managers who do the rating attempt to estimate the strengths, weaknesses, and potential of each attendee.[18] They then pool their estimates to arrive at some conclusion about each member of the group being assessed.

Assessment centres were first applied in business in 1956, by the director of human resources research at American Telephone and Telegraph. By the 1980s, more than 2,000 corporate-operated assessment centres were in existence in North America. This approach is both time consuming and costly: candidates are away from their jobs, travel and accommodation must be paid for, and evaluators are often company managers assigned to the assessment centre for short durations.[19] These managers are often supplemented by psychologists and personnel professionals who run the centre and make evaluations.[20] Some critics question whether the procedures used are objective and job-related, especially since rater biases are possible in forming the subjective opinions of attendees.[21] Nevertheless, assessment centres have gained widespread use and personnel researchers are finding ways to validate the process.

The results can be extremely useful for aiding management development and placement decisions. From the composite ratings, a report is prepared on each attendee. This information goes into the personnel management information system to assist human resource planning (particularly the development of replacement charts) and other personnel management decisions. Interestingly, research indicates that the results of assessment centres are a good prediction of actual on-the-job performance in 75% of all cases.[22] Unfortunately, this accurate method is expensive since it usually requires a separate facility and the time of multiple raters. Consider how the process works at Johnson Wax:

For years, the Consumer Products Division of S. C. Johnson & Son, Inc. ran a traditional assessment centre. Twice a year, selected managers from all over Johnson Wax attended the assessment centre for five days and were evaluated on a variety of skills. On the fourth day, the candidates attended a debriefing and career development session while the raters wrote their final evaluations. On the fifth day, attendees received a report of their performance and counselling. The assessment process was successful in helping management select sales representatives. However, the results of the centre

*tended to be overemphasized: people were seen to have "passed" or "failed" the pro-
cess. Those who "failed" became dissatisfied because they believed their career potential had been severely limited. Many people who attended the centre "failed" because
field management had few guidelines as to who should be sent and at what stage of
career development. Likewise, few programs existed to prepare people for the assessment centre process and no formal program existed to train people in management
skills.*

*To overcome these shortcomings, a project group was formed that included people
in personnel, field sales management, and a consultant. The group changed the thrust
of Johnson Wax's assessment centre by recommending that the centre's results be
given less importance and that they be used to identify strengths and weaknesses in
individual skills. The group also recommended that field management become more
involved in assisting management candidates with career planning and development
activities. The project group also made sure that field management knew what the
purpose of the centre was and gave them guidelines for recommending people to attend the centre. A voluntary program for skill development was also undertaken.
Even the name of the centre was changed to the Management Skill Identification
Center.[23]*

*Today, the MSI Center results are but one element in the 'management promotion
equation.' This equation consists of four weighted elements which are used by management to make a promotion determination: 1) the individual's record of performance on the job; 2) the individual's sales experience level; 3) the individual's previous job-related experience (i.e., previous employment experience, education experience, etc.); and 4) the individual's MSI Center results.[24]*

As the Johnson Wax example illustrates, the assessment centre results
must be kept in perspective. If they are the sole determinant of future
career progress in the organization, people will see the assessment process
as threatening. However, if they are used to appraise an individual's
strengths and weaknesses, and if the person has a way of improving areas of
deficiency, then the centre can be a positive force for developing future
talent within the organization.

To reduce the expense but still capture some of the benefits associated
with assessment centres, some companies use "mail-in" assessments. A
package of tests, exercises, and required reports are mailed to the individual, who mails them to the raters for subsequent evaluation.[25] Not only
are costs lower, but raters and employees do not spend time going to a centralized location.

IMPLICATIONS OF THE APPRAISAL PROCESS

Design of the appraisal system and its procedures are usually handled by
the personnel department. The specific approach is influenced by previous
procedures and the purpose of the new appraisal. If the goal is to evaluate
past performance to allocate rewards, comparative approaches may be
preferred. Similarly, other past-oriented methods may be best if the appraisal system exists primarily to give employees counselling about their
behaviour. Future-oriented appraisals may focus on specific goals, as is the
case with MBO techniques. Self-appraisals or assessment centres may seek
to uncover specific weakness or help with internal placement. Regardless

of the technique selected by the personnel department, however, the approach must be converted into an ongoing practice among the line managers. Except in the field review or psychological appraisal methods, raters are often unfamiliar with the procedures or the forms. And they may not be very interested in self-study to learn more, because the evaluation process may be seen as a project imposed by the personnel department and not something of immediate concern to those who supervise others.

Evaluation systems that involve others in their design may gain greater acceptance. Human rights legislation supports having employees involved in the design of the appraisal system. Involvement may increase interest and understanding of whatever performance appraisal system the personnel department eventually administers. However, to operate the performance appraisal system may require training for those who serve as raters.

TRAINING RATERS

Whether a simple comparative method or a sophisticated assessment centre is used, raters need knowledge of the system and its purpose. Just knowing whether the appraisal is to be used for compensation or placement recommendations may change the rater's evaluation of those being rated.

A major problem is rater understanding and consistency of evaluations. Some personnel departments provide raters with a rater's handbook that describes the employer's approach. Guidelines for conducting the evaluation or for providing ratees with feedback are often included in the handbook. Key terms—such as "shows initiative" or "provides leadership"—may also be defined in the handbook.

Companies like The Royal Bank, Air Canada, and others solve this knowledge gap through training. Training workshops are usually intended to explain to raters the purpose of the procedure, the mechanics of it, likely pitfalls or biases they may encounter, and answers to their questions. The training may even include trial-runs of evaluating other classmates just to gain some supervised experience. The Royal Bank and Air Canada use videotapes and role-playing evaluation sessions to give raters both experience and insight into the evaluation process. During the training, the timing and scheduling of evaluations are discussed. Typically, most companies do formal evaluations annually, around the time of the individual's employment anniversary. For new employees or those having performance problems, evaluations may be done more frequently as part of the personnel department's formal program or as the supervisor sees fit. Consider how one vice president and manager of human resources viewed the implementation of his firm's program:

> With the new appraisal process and related forms in place, the next major step was educating managers and supervisors in the use of the program. Mandatory one-day training workshops were given, providing each manager an opportunity to review, discuss and understand the objectives of the program. The appraisal forms were reviewed in detail with an explanation of

how to use the various sections in each form. A videotaped appraisal discussion was presented to demonstrate how performance appraisal worked. And finally, during the workshops, managers were given role-play situations using the new appraisal forms.[26]

Then on the bi-weekly payroll sheets that included everyone in the department or branch, the manager received a notification of who was due to be evaluated during the next month. If the review date was passed, a reminder would appear on the payroll sheets showing that the review date for the indicated employee was past due. As a result, managers knew how to complete the forms and few delinquencies occur. The human resource department also has valuable data that allow it to anticipate and respond to training needs and employee concerns.[27]

Once raters are trained, the appraisal process can begin. But the results of the appraisal process do little to improve employee performance unless employees receive feedback on their appraisals. This feedback process is called evaluation interviews.

EVALUATION INTERVIEWS

Evaluation interviews are performance review sessions that give employees feedback about their past performance or future potential. The evaluator may provide this feedback through several approaches: tell and sell, tell and listen, and problem solving.[28] The *tell-and-sell approach* reviews the employee's performance and tries to convince the employee to perform better. It is best used on new employees. The *tell-and-listen method* allows the employee to explain reasons, excuses, and defensive feelings about performance. It attempts to overcome these reactions by counselling the employee on how to perform better. The *problem-solving approach* identifies problems that are interfering with employee performance. Then through training, coaching, or counselling, efforts are made to remove these deficiencies, often by setting goals for future performance.

Regardless of which approach is used to give employees feedback, the guidelines listed in Figure 12-11 can help make the performance review session more effective.[29] The intent of these suggestions is to make the interview a positive, performance-improving dialogue. By stressing desirable aspects of employee performance, the evaluator can give the employee renewed confidence in her or his ability to perform satisfactorily. This positive approach also enables the employee to keep desirable and undesirable performance in perspective, because it prevents the individual from feeling that performance review sessions are entirely negative. When negative comments are made, they focus on work performance and not the individual's personality. Specific, rather than general and vague, examples of the employee's shortcomings are used, so that the individual knows exactly what behaviours need to be changed. The review session concludes by focusing on actions that the employee can take to improve areas of poor performance. In that concluding discussion, the evaluator usually offers to provide whatever assistance the employee needs to overcome the deficiencies discussed.

Figure 12-11
GUIDELINES FOR EFFECTIVE PERFORMANCE EVALUATION INTERVIEWS

1. **Emphasize** positive aspects of employee performance.
2. **Tell** each employee that the evaluation session is to improve performance, not to discipline.
3. **Conduct** the performance review session in private with minimum interruptions.
4. **Review** performance formally at least annually and more frequently for new employees or those who are performing poorly.
5. **Make** criticisms specific, not general and vague.
6. **Focus** criticisms on performance, not on personality characteristics.
7. **Stay** calm and do not argue with the person being evaluated.
8. **Identify** specific actions the employee can take to improve performance.
9. **Emphasize** the evaluator's willingness to assist the employee's efforts and to improve performance.
10. **End** the evaluation sessions by stressing the positive aspects of the employee's performance.

Since the evaluation interview provides employees with performance-related feedback, it is not surprising that 95% of the firms in one study require managers to discuss the appraisal with employees.[30] The study also reports that nearly 40% of these employers use appraisals at least annually.[31]

PERSONNEL MANAGEMENT FEEDBACK

The performance appraisal process also provides insight into the effectiveness of the personnel management function. Figure 12-12 summarizes the major concepts discussed so far in this book. As can be seen, performance appraisal serves as a "quality-control check." If the appraisal process indicates that poor performance is widespread, many employees are excluded from internal placement decisions. They will not be promoted or transferred. In fact, they may be excluded from the organization through termination.

Unacceptably high numbers of poor performers may indicate errors elsewhere in the personnel management function. For example, human resource development may be failing to fulfill career plans because the people who are hired during the selection process are screened poorly. Or the human resource plan may be in error because the job analysis information is wrong or the affirmative-action plan seeks the wrong objectives. Likewise, personnel may be failing to respond to the challenges of the external environment or job design. Sometimes the personnel function is pursuing the wrong human resource objectives. Or the appraisal system itself may be faulty because of management resistance, incorrect performance standards or measures, or a lack of constructive feedback.[32]

Wherever the problem lies, personnel specialists need to monitor carefully the results of the organization's performance appraisal process. It can

Figure 12-12
THE PERSONNEL MANAGEMENT PROCESS

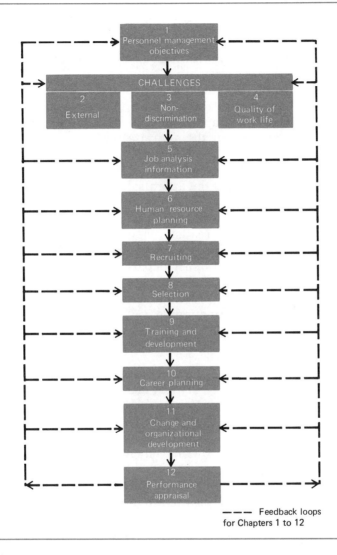

serve as a barometer of the entire personnel function. As will be explained in Part 4, performance appraisal serves as a guide to compensation and other personnel management activities too.

SUMMARY

Performance appraisal is a critical activity of personnel management. Its goal is to provide an accurate picture of past and/or future employee performance. To do this, performance standards are established. Standards are based on job-related criteria that best determine successful job perfor-mance. Where possible, actual performance then is measured directly and objectively. From a wide variety of appraisal techniques, personnel specialists select those methods that most effectively measure employee performance against the previously set standards. Techniques can be selected both to review past performance and to anticipate performance in the future.

The appraisal process is usually designed by the personnel department, often with little consultation from other parts of the organization. When it is time to implement a new appraisal approach, those who do the rating usually have little idea about the appraisal process or its objectives. To overcome this shortcoming, the department may design and deliver ap-praisal workshops to train managers.

A necessary requirement of the appraisal process is employee feedback through an evaluation interview. The interview tries to balance positive areas of performance and those areas where performance is deficient, so that the employee receives a realistic view of performance. Perhaps the most significant challenge raised by performance appraisals is the feed-back they provide about personnel department performance. Personnel specialists need to be keenly aware that poor performance, especially when it is widespread, may reflect problems with previous personnel manage-ment activities that are malfunctioning.

TERMS FOR REVIEW

Performance standards	Forced choice method
Performance measures	Critical incident method
Halo effect	Behaviourally anchored rating scales
Error of central tendency	Field review method
Leniency and strictness biases	Comparative evaluation methods
Recency effect	Management by objectives approach (MBO)
Rating scale	Assessment centres
Weighted checklist	Evaluation interviews

REVIEW AND DISCUSSION QUESTIONS

1. What are the uses of performance appraisals?
2. Suppose a company for which you work uses a rating scale. The items on the scale are general personality characteristics. What criticisms would you have of this method?
3. If you were asked to recommend a replacement for the rating scale, what actions would you take before selecting another appraisal technique?
4. If the dean of your faculty asked you to serve on a committee to develop a performance appraisal system for evaluating the faculty, what perfor-mance criteria would you identify? Of these criteria, which ones do you

think are most likely to determine the faculty members' success at your school? What standards would you recommend to the dean, regardless of the specific evaluation instrument selected?

5. Why are direct and objective measures of performance usually considered superior to indirect and subjective measures?

6. If your organization were to use subjective measures to evaluate employee performance, what instructions would you give evaluators about the biases they might encounter?

7. Describe how you would conduct a typical performance evaluation interview.

8. How do the results of performance appraisals affect other personnel management activities?

INCIDENT 12-1
MULTIPLE APPRAISAL FAILURES AT ROGET'S WATERWORKS

For two years, the employees at Roget's Waterworks were evaluated with the same performance appraisal method as other employees of the Roget Municipal Services Corporation (a company-operated city utility). The personnel manager decided that the duties at the waterworks were sufficiently different that a specially designed appraisal should be developed. A weighted checklist was decided on and was used for about one year. The personnel manager left, and the replacement disliked weighted checklists. Specialists then implemented behaviourally anchored rating scales. But no sooner was the method installed than top management decided to shift all evaluations at the Roget corporation to the critical incident method.

The critical incident method worked well in all phases of the corporation's operations except the waterworks. Supervisors in the waterworks would not keep a record of critical incidents until about a week before the incidents were due to be submitted to the personnel office. Training sessions were held for these supervisors, but little change in their behaviour resulted. To evaluate the supervisors, the company conducted a survey of employees at the waterworks. Most employees thought the supervision was fair to good in all dimensions except that supervisors showed too much favouritism. Thought was being given to other methods.

1. How would you suggest overcoming the resistance of the supervisors to using the critical incident method?

2. Should another evaluation method be tried?

3. What method would you recommend and why?

INCIDENT 12-2
THE MALFUNCTIONING REGIONAL PERSONNEL DEPARTMENT

For one month the corporate personnel department of Universal Insurance Ltd. had two specialists review the operations of their regional personnel department in Vancouver. The review of the regional office centred on the department's human resource information base. A brief summary of their findings listed the following observations:

A. *Each employee's performance appraisal showed little change from the previous year. Poor performers rated poor year in and year out.*

B. *Nearly 70% of the appraisals were not initialled by the employee even though company policy required employees to do so after they had discussed their review with the rater.*

C. *Of those employees who initialled the evaluations, several commented that the work standards were irrelevant and unfair.*

D. *A survey of past employees conducted by corporate office specialists revealed that 35% of them believed performance feedback was too infrequent.*

E. *Another 30% complained about the lack of advancement opportunities because most openings were filled from outside, and no one ever told these workers why they were unpromotable.*

The corporate and regional personnel directors were dismayed by the findings. Each thought the problems facing the regional office were different.

1. What do you think is the major problem with the performance appraisal process in the regional office?
2. What problems you do think exist with the regional office's (a) job analysis information, (b) human resource planning, (c) training and development, (d) career planning?

REFERENCES

1. Harry Levinson, "Appraisal of *What* Performance?" *Harvard Business Review*, July–August 1976, pp. 30–32, 34, 36, 40, 44, 46, 160.
2. John B. Miner, "Management Appraisal: A Review of Procedures and Practices," in W. Clay Hamner and Frank L. Schmidt (eds.), *Contemporary Problems in Personnel*, Chicago: St. Clair Press, 1977, p. 228.
3. Robert I. Lazer and Walter S. Wikstrom, *Appraising Managerial Performance: Current Practices and Future Directions*, New York: The Conference Board, 1977, p. 20.
4. Ibid., p. 26.
5. Royal Commission on Corporate Concentration, *Personnel Administration in Large and Middle-sized Businesses*, Study No. 25, Ottawa: November 1976, p. 61.
6. James M. McFillen and Patrick G. Decker, "Building Meaning into Appraisal," *The Personnel Administrator*, June 1978, pp. 78–79.
7. Miner, op. cit.
8. McFillen and Decker, op. cit., p. 80.
9. Bruce McAfee and Blake Green, "Selecting a Performance Appraisal Method," *The Personnel Administrator*, June 1977, pp. 61–64.
10. John B. McMaster, "Designing an Appraisal System That Is Fair and Accurate," *Personnel Journal*, January 1979, pp. 38–40.
11. L. Fogli, C. L. Hulin, and M. R. Blood, "Development of First-Level Behavioral Job Criteria," *Journal of Applied Psychology*, January 1979, pp. 3–8.
12. Craig Eric Schneir and Richard W. Beatty, "Developing Behaviorally-Anchored Rating Scales (BARS)," *The Personnel Administrator*, August 1979, pp. 59–68. See also Hermann F. Schwind, "Behavior Sampling for Effective Performance Feedback," in Judith W. Springer (ed.), *Job Performance Standards and Measures*, Madison: American Society for Training and Development, 1980, pp. 11–39.
13. Latham and Wexley, op. cit., pp. 52–54.
14. Ibid. See also Craig Eric Schneir and Richard W. Beatty, "Developing Behaviorally-Anchored Rating Scales (BARS)," *Personnel Administrator*, August 1979, pp. 59–68; Aharon Tziner, "A Fairer Examination of Rating Scales When Used for Performance Appraisal in a Real Organizational Setting," unpublished paper, 1982.
15. J. Peter Graves, "Let's Put Appraisal Back in Performance Appraisal: II," *Personnel Journal*, December 1982, p. 918.
16. Milan Moravec, "How Performance Appraisal Can Tie Communication to Productivity," *Personnel Administrator*, January 1981, pp. 51–52.
17. William B. Werther, Jr., and Heinz Weihrich, "Refining MBO through Negotiations," *MSU Business Topics*, Summer 1975, pp. 53–58.
18. John P. Bucalo, Jr., "The Assessment Center—A More Specified Approach," *Human Resource Management*, Fall 1974, pp. 2–13. See also William C. Byham, "Starting an Assessment Center," *The Personnel Administrator*, February 1980, pp. 27–32.
19. Ibid.
20. "How to Spot Hotshots," *Business Week*, October 8, 1979, pp. 62, 67.

21. Hubert S. Field and William H. Holley, "The Relationship of Performance Appraisal System Characteristics to Verdicts in Selected Employment Discrimination Cases," *Academy of Management Journal*, June 1982, pp. 392–406. See also George F. Dreher and Paul S. Sackett, "Some Problems with Applying Content Validity Evidence to Assessment Center Procedures," *Academy of Management Review*, October 1981, pp. 551–560; Steven D. Norton, "The Assessment Center Process and Content Validity: A Reply to Dreher and Sackett," *Academy of Management Review*, October 1981, pp. 561–566; Paul R. Sackett and George F. Dreher, "Some Misconceptions about Content-Oriented Validation: A Rejoinder to Norton," *Academy of Management Review*, October 1981, pp. 567–568.

22. Bucalo, op. cit., p. 11.

23. Leland C. Nichols and Joseph Hudson, "Dual-Role Assessment Center: Selection and Development, *Personnel Journal*, May 1981, pp. 380–386.

24. Ibid., p. 382.

25. "How to Spot the Hotshots," *Business Week*, October 8, 1979, pp. 62, 67.

26. William J. Birch, "Performance Appraisal: One Company's Experience," *Personnel Journal*, June 1981, pp. 456–460.

27. Ibid.

28. Norman R. F. Maier, *The Appraisal Interview: Three Basic Approaches*, La Jolla, CA: University Associates, 1976.

29. Miner, op. cit., p. 249.

30. Lazer and Wikstrom, op. cit., p. 31.

31. Ibid., p. 24.

32. Kenneth S. Teel, "Performance Appraisal: Current Trends, Persistent Progress," *Personnel Journal*, April 1980, pp. 296–301. See also "Appraising the Performance Appraisal," *Business Week*, May 19, 1980, pp. 153–154.

Part 4

Performance, Compensation, and Protection

A successful company needs a motivated and satisfied work force. This responsibility is part of every manager's job. But the personnel department can help. It can advise managers about useful motivation techniques. It can also help indirectly with compensation, benefits, and services. Often the department assists managers with safety and communications programs. When employee problems do recur, personnel helps with counselling and discipline.

Each of these topics is discussed in Part 4. They are important management tools for personnel specialists and managers alike. Regardless of your job, you will find that these tools are helpful ways to ensure effective performance.

Chapter **13**

Employee Motivation and Satisfaction

In golf and work, goals are a major component of motivation!
William H. Mobley[1]

Organization behavior is a function of its consequence.
Fred Luthans and Robert Kreitner[2]

CHAPTER OBJECTIVES

After studying this chapter, you should be able to:
1. **Explain** how the personnel function helps with motivation and job satisfaction.
2. **Discuss** how employee needs may affect motivation.
3. **Interpret** differences among models of motivation.
4. **Analyze** employee performance in terms of models of motivation.
5. **Explain** the relationship between job satisfaction and performance.
6. **Describe** the implications of low levels of job satisfaction.

An organization's productivity is determined by many factors. Employee motivation and satisfaction are just two of these, but they are important factors in any organization.[3] Personnel departments affect employee motivation and satisfaction through almost every activity they perform: training and development; performance and compensation; benefits and services; security, safety, and health.[4] Personnel professionals also serve as human resource consultants to managers in other departments. More and more well-managed personnel departments want other managers to use the department as a source of employee relations expertise. When these other managers seek assistance with human resource problems, they often want personnel professionals to suggest ways to motivate employees to perform more productively. So for both the manager and the personnel professional, understanding employee motivation and satisfaction is an important topic.

But understanding employee motivation and satisfaction is more than a handful of theories or some specific set of activities done by personnel specialists. Motivation and satisfaction are affected by virtually every aspect of the organization—many of which the personnel department cannot directly control, such as supervisory treatment of employees, promotions, merit raises, and other personnel actions normally reserved for line managers. Personnel specialists can contribute to employee motivation and satisfaction, however, by assisting these decision makers. Given the commitment and leadership of top management, personnel specialists can help the organization achieve high levels of productivity and quality through a motivated and satisfied work force.[5] An interesting example comes from a Sharp Corporation plant in the United States:

When plans were announced to build the facility in Memphis, Tennessee, many people thought Sharp had made a bad decision. As the Wall Street Journal *observed: "After all, RCA Corp. had built a TV plant in Memphis in 1966—and shut it down five years later. That facility had suffered just about every labor management affliction imaginable: wildcat strikes, union-authorized strikes, apparent sabotage of the product and a series of layoffs that took the payroll from 4,200 workers down to 1,600. At times, so many hundreds of defective TV sets clogged the assembly-line aisles that technicians had difficulty repairing them. Finally, RCA pulled the plug, shipped most of the machinery and work off to Taiwan. . . ."[6]*

Paul Hogusa, the president of Sharp Manufacturing Company of America, did not think it was labour problems that closed the RCA plant. He thought it was RCA's poor product quality from that factory. At a rate of a quarter-million high-quality TV sets and microwave ovens per year, Sharp has proved the skeptics wrong. Sharp's success was not caused by special machinery or automation; its competitors use the same equipment. Instead, Sharp's management focused on producing quality products while making employees feel that they are an important member of the "Sharp family." Management demands high standards of employees and is constantly pushing for improvements in quality or productivity. But at the same time, the organization has managed to create a work environment that is motivating and satisfying to the employees. Although all their Memphis employees do not sing the company song, dress in uniforms, or exercise before work (as they do in Japan), the American workers at this Japanese-owned plant produce high-quality products at high levels of productivity.

What makes the difference between RCA's plant in the 1960s and Sharp's plant in the 1980s? Many factors are different. Mr. Hogusa attributes it all to ". . . the quality of the people."[7] However, since Sharp recruits in the same labour pool that RCA used for its assemblers, the real difference must be the day-to-day management of human resources.

People make the difference. If a personnel department can contribute toward the motivation and satisfaction of an organization's employees, then the department can make a meaningful contribution toward the organization's productivity. In fact, a growing recognition among managers, consultants, and professors that people are the key to organizational success has led to a parade of popular books that share this theme.[8]

This chapter discusses the basic framework within which the personnel function operates to influence motivation and job satisfaction. Then it discusses different models for motivating employees and how motivation and job satisfaction are related.

HOW PERSONNEL INFLUENCES MOTIVATION AND SATISFACTION

The personnel function has both a direct and an indirect influence on employee motivation and satisfaction. As Figure 13-1 illustrates, the personnel function makes direct contact with employees and supervisors in ways that influence them. For example, orientation, training and development, career planning, and counselling activities may directly motivate employees through one-to-one or group meetings. At the same time, these activities may help a supervisor do a better job of motivating employees.[9]

Personnel policies and practices also influence motivation and satisfaction indirectly. Rigorously enforced safety and health policies, for example, can give employees and supervisors a greater sense of safety from accidents and industrial health hazards. Likewise, compensation policies may motivate and satisfy employees through incentive plans, or they may harm motivation and satisfaction if worthwhile contributions are not recognized. The motivation and satisfaction of employees act as feedback on the organizational climate and the personnel function's day-to-day activities.

ORGANIZATIONAL CLIMATE

Personnel policies and activities have a major impact on an organization's climate for people. *Organizational climate* is the favourableness or unfavourableness of an organization's environment for its employees. Some organizations "live by the rules" and are bureaucratic; other firms are friendly and easy-going. Some companies emphasize work; others em-

Figure 13-1
INFLUENCE OF THE PERSONNEL FUNCTION ON MOTIVATION AND SATISFACTION   *insendative*

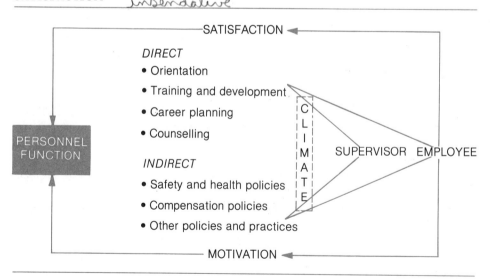

phasize teamwork. The difference between work and teamwork may appear small, but it is significant in the climate of an organization.

One study compared the relationship between organizational climate and job satisfaction.[10] *The study covered 695 employees in a large utility. Climate was studied along with such dimensions of satisfaction as attitudes toward pay and supervision. The results show a significant relationship between organizational climate and job satisfaction. When the climate was favourable, satisfaction was high; when the climate was unfavourable, satisfaction was low.*

DAY-TO-DAY ACTIVITIES

The policies and activities of the personnel department affect all employees in a number of ways, and personnel has daily opportunities to strengthen or weaken the organization in the eyes of employees. Almost by itself, personnel can "make" or "break" the humanness of an organization. Since personnel's influence on the climate is widespread and important, personnel specialists need to ask themselves day by day as they do their work:

- Do we show people that we care?
- Are we seen as a help to people or as a problem?
- Do we encourage the growth of cooperation and teamwork?
- Do we encourage the growth of people?

To illustrate the importance of these questions, we will examine some basic ideas about motivation and job satisfaction to see how personnel activities relate to these issues.

MOTIVATION

Motivation is a complex subject. It involves the unique feelings, thoughts, and past experiences within each of us as we share a variety of relationships within and outside the organizations of which we are members. To expect a single motivational approach to work in every situation is probably unrealistic. In fact, even the theorists and researchers take different points of view about motivation. Nevertheless, some basic guidelines do exist for improving motivation under some circumstances.

Motivation is a person's drive to take an action because he or she wants to do so. If people are pushed, they are merely reacting to pressure and acting because they feel that they have to. However, if they are motivated, they make the positive choice to do something because they see the act as meaningful to them. Therefore, motivation can be simply defined as goal-oriented behaviour.

CONTENT THEORIES OF MOTIVATION

Content theories of motivation describe the human needs or desires that initiate behaviour. Figure 13-2 compares three of the most common content theories. Each of these theories is discussed in the following pages.

Figure 13-2
A COMPARISON OF CONTENT THEORIES OF MOTIVATION

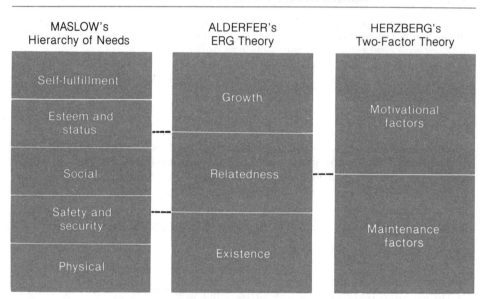

MASLOW's Hierarchy of Needs	ALDERFER's ERG Theory	HERZBERG's Two-Factor Theory
Self-fulfillment	Growth	Motivational factors
Esteem and status		
Social	Relatedness	
Safety and security		Maintenance factors
Physical	Existence	

✳ **MASLOW'S HIERARCHY OF NEEDS.** One model of motivation is Maslow's hierarchy of needs.[11] Since all needs cannot be expressed at once, there tends to be some priority in the way they find expression. That is, people have different levels of needs, as shown in Figure 13-3. Lower-order needs claim priority. Once they begin to be satisfied, then higher-order needs become more important and gradually tend to dominate a person's behaviour. As each successive level of needs becomes reasonably satisfied, the next level of needs becomes more important. This model does not apply to all people all of the time. It is possible to suppress some needs in favour of others, and some people have greater or lesser needs at each level in the hierarchy of needs. However, even with its limitations, the theory is believed to apply to large numbers of people in normal situations.

Lower-order needs include both the physical level of needs and the safety and security level of needs shown in Figure 13-3. *Physical (or physiological) needs* are those which maintain life and the physical aspects of well-being: food, clothing, accommodation, and adequate pay, vacation, and benefits. *Safety and security needs* concern the longer-run maintenance of life and well-being. They include freedom from workplace hazards, the presence of appropriate disability and retirement benefits, fair treatment, and proper supervision. Lower-order needs are useful only in limited quantities. For example, one can have too much food, clothing, and consumer goods.

Higher-order needs, on the other hand, are not so easily oversupplied. Satisfaction of *social needs*, such as belonging and love, is difficult to overdo. Likewise, the need for *esteem*, which is met by the recognition of others

Figure 13-3
HIERARCHY OF NEEDS ACCORDING TO MASLOW

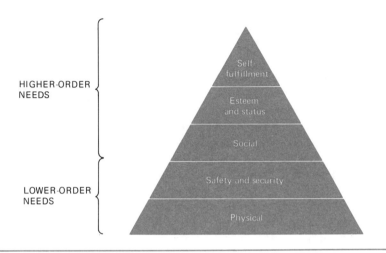

or by a personal sense of growth and achievement, is seldom oversatisfied. Money will satisfy lower-level needs by buying food, clothing, hospital care, etc., but it is less useful as a means to secure most higher needs, such as self-esteem and status. Essentially, higher needs relate more to feelings and values than to material objects. The highest need is *self-fulfillment*, also called self-actualization. It is met when people become all that they are capable of becoming. In this manner they find inner fulfillment. This state of mind is achieved only rarely, and it usually does not assume priority until after other needs are reasonably satisfied.

ALDERFER'S ERG THEORY. Alderfer's theory is similar to Maslow's except that it condenses Maslow's hierarchy into three categories: existence (E), relatedness (R), and growth (G).[12] Figure 13-2 shows these categories in comparison with Maslow's approach.

Existence needs include those desires that meet Maslow's lower-order needs (physical, safety and security). *Relatedness* needs encompass interpersonal relationships and include the sense of acceptance, belonging, and security that comes from the approval of those in the organization. This division of Alderfer's model parallels Maslow's social needs but overlaps slightly with his security and self-esteem levels. *Growth* needs are those that challenge the individual's capabilities and cause personal growth on the job. Included here are the esteem, status, and self-fulfillment needs found in Maslow's model.

The ERG theory rests on three suppositions:
1. The desired satisfaction for each need will be stronger the less the need is satisfied.

2. The strength of desire for higher-level needs goes up the more lower-level needs are satisfied.
3. The more frustration one finds in meeting higher-level needs, the more lower-level needs will be desired.

Unlike Maslow's theory, which is based on a progression of satisfaction up the hierarchy, Alderfer's ERG theory includes a "frustration-regression" pattern. In circumstances where higher-order needs remain unsatisfied, frustration occurs and the individual "regresses" to fulfilling more basic needs. Also unlike Maslow, Alderfer's model acknowledges that more than one need may be operative at any one time. The common element in both approaches is that people have needs, and each need varies in its intensity depending on how well it and other needs are being satisfied.

HERZBERG'S TWO-FACTOR THEORY. Herzberg and his associates have developed a model of motivation based on motivational and maintenance needs. They interviewed employees to determine what conditions led to strong positive or negative feelings about their jobs. The result was that most employees named different types of causes for their good and bad feelings. That is, if recognition led to a good feeling, lack of recognition seldom led to a bad feeling.[13]

The conclusion was that some factors primarily increase motivation and satisfaction, but their absence is not strongly negative. These elements are called *motivational factors*, motivators, or satisfiers, because they tend to motivate and satisfy. They give the employee a built-in generator that provides an internal drive toward better performance. Ideally, the job itself—the actual work the person does—should provide this source of internal motivation.

Another set of factors primarily lower motivation when they are absent, but their presence does not provide strong motivation. They are called *maintenance factors*, hygiene factors, or dissatisfiers. An example is fringe benefits. Employees can be quite unhappy when they lack them, but their presence is not strongly motivating. For many years personnel people had been wondering why generous fringe benefits did not increase employee motivation. The concept of maintenance factors explained why. Fringe benefits are needed to maintain an employee (prevent dissatisfaction), but they are not by themselves strong motivators.

As shown in Figure 13-4, each of the two factors operates primarily, but not always, in one direction. Since each of the two is different, the Herzberg model is often called a *two-factor model of motivation*.

Figure 13-5 shows the factors reported in the original Herzberg study. The motivational factors mostly occur in direct connection with the job, so that performance of the work becomes self-rewarding. Employees obtain this reward for themselves. On the other hand, the maintenance factors occur mostly in the environment that surrounds the job. Employees typically have minimal control over these conditions.

Figure 13-4
MOTIVATIONAL FACTORS COMPARED WITH MAINTENANCE FACTORS

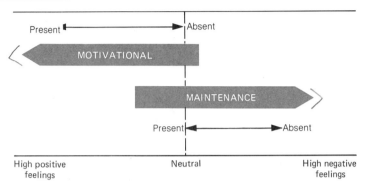

The Herzberg model has been strongly criticized, because a number of studies do not support the idea of two separate factors in motivation.[14] In spite of criticism, however, it remains a popular model because it helps managers and personnel specialists label conditions as likely to either motivate employees or to dissatisfy them.

EQUITY THEORY
Although needs-oriented theories may explain what factors motivate employees, they offer little insight as to why people behave as they do. *Equity theory* suggests that people are motivated to close the gap between their efforts and the amount of rewards they receive.[15] When rewards are perceived as insufficient, greater rewards are sought or less effort is expended. These issues are most likely to arise through comparisons with other people in the organization or with people who do similar work out-

Figure 13-5
MOTIVATIONAL AND MAINTENANCE FACTORS

Motivational Factors	Maintenance Factors
Work itself	Status
Achievement	Relationships with supervision
Possibility of growth	Relationships with peers
Advancement	Relationships with subordinates
Recognition	Supervision: technical
	Company policy and administration
	Job security
	Working conditions
	Salary
	Personal life

side the organization. When an employee compares his or her job inputs (performance, effort, skills, or education) with those of another person, comparable inputs should have comparable results. If the other person receives more pay, recognition, status, promotions or other favourable outcomes with no more inputs, the situation is seen to be inequitable. When inequity exists between inputs and outcomes, the person is motivated to reduce the inequity by obtaining an increase in the rewards (a raise or a promotion, for example) or by decreasing the inputs (being less productive, for example) or some combination of both.

The research on equity theory supports the contention that people will be motivated to reduce the inequities that result from insufficient rewards. The research on rewards that represent overpayments, however, is less clear.[16] Nevertheless, the theory does emphasize to personnel professionals the need to scrutinize diligently an organization's reward structure to ensure equity. Otherwise, inequities may lead to turnover, absenteeism, or even strikes.

Reconsider the comparison between Sharp and RCA in their efforts to make television sets in Memphis, Tennessee. Even if RCA had had an equitable pay structure, employees would have sensed inequities because unionized workers typically receive different benefits than do non-unionized employees, particularly managers. The result can sometimes be an "us-versus-them" syndrome. Since workers can do little to increase their rewards until the next union contract is negotiated, some of them may have elected to reduce their quantity or quality of work as a way to reduce the perceived inequities of the reward system.

✳ EXPECTANCY THEORY

A more sophisticated view of motivation is found in Vroom's expectancy theory. *Expectancy theory* states that motivation is a result of the outcomes one seeks and one's estimate that action will lead to these desired outcomes.[17] In more straightforward terms, if a person wants something strongly enough, and if the path looks sufficiently open to get it, that person will go for it.

Peter LeBlanc, a clerk in an x-ray laboratory, strongly wanted the outcome of promotion to x-ray technician. As he assessed the situation, he saw that the present technicians had medical or technical backgrounds. Since he lacked either, he saw little chance of promotion and so was not motivated to try for promotion. Regretfully, the hospital sought technicians and would have considered him for training, but its objectives and his needs were not mutually communicated, and so he remained unmotivated.

VALENCE AND EXPECTANCY. The strength of a person's preference for one outcome in relation to others is called *valence*. Since a person also may desire not to have an outcome, valence may range from -1 to $+1$.

The strength of a person's belief that an act will lead to a particular outcome is called *expectancy*. If an employee is certain that an act has no chance of leading to an outcome, then expectancy is zero. At the opposite end of the scale, if an employee is sure that an act will lead to an outcome, expectancy is +1. The result is that expectancy may range anywhere from zero to +1. In short, valence is one's *desire* for an outcome and expectancy is the *probability* that action will achieve the outcome. When valence and expectancy are multiplied, the product is a person's approximate state of motivation. The equation is as follows:

$$\text{Valence} \times \text{expectancy} = \text{motivation}$$
$$(\text{or}) \, \text{Desire} \times \text{probability} = \text{motivation}$$

APPLICATION OF THE EXPECTANCY MODEL. The expectancy model suggests that people use their experience and judgment to determine which kinds of desired outcomes are available, and then they judge which ones they have the best probability of reaching. What they perform is a type of cost-benefit analysis to determine whether a reward is worth its costs. If the reward is enough to justify the cost of more effort, then they tend to apply more effort.

A criticism of the model is its inapplicability for use by personnel professionals. The model can be extremely complex. Although that complexity may reflect the complexity of motivation, few personnel practitioners can apply this complex model to everyday motivational situations. Furthermore, the probabilities used are subjective. An employee's estimate of a particular outcome may be very inaccurate because the probabilities that someone assigns vary from person to person. And little evidence suggests that employees become motivated through careful assignment and multiplication of probabilities.

Even with these criticisms, a personnel department can reduce costs and increase benefits for employees whose motivation is shaped by a careful reflection of desired outcomes (valence) and their likelihood of attainment (expectancy). Personnel may be able to increase employee motivation through counselling, training, compensation, and other activities that stimulate employee desires for rewards such as promotions. Likewise, personnel's efforts may strengthen an employee's belief that training, hard work, and other efforts lead to wanted rewards (outcomes). This approach is a *path-goal personnel strategy*, in which the personnel department improves the path toward the goal (such as by reducing red tape) and then tries to improve the outcomes at the end of the path (such as by developing an award program for suggestions). In this way the personnel function is building a better organizational climate for motivation.

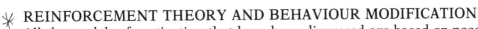 REINFORCEMENT THEORY AND BEHAVIOUR MODIFICATION

All the models of motivation that have been discussed are based on needs determined internally by each person. They are called *cognitive models of motivation*, because they depend on the thinking and feeling (that is, cognition) of each individual. They relate to the internal psychological self and a personal view of the world.

The problem with cognitive models is that they are not subject to precise scientific measurement and observation. We can never be sure whether needs really exist as we see them, because we can only infer them from what people say and do. It is argued that we could understand motivation better if we gave more attention to models that are more subject to scientific analysis. The principal model of this type is behaviour modification, which has evolved from the work of Skinner and others.[18]

Behaviour modification states that behaviour depends on its consequences. While cognitive models argue that *internal* needs lead to behaviour, behaviour modification states that *external* consequences tend to determine behaviour. We no longer have to figure out what is in a person's mind, because we can affect a person's behaviour by modifying the consequences.

Since behaviour depends on its consequences, the *law of effect* states that people learn to repeat behaviour that has favourable consequences and avoid behaviour that has unfavourable consequences. Thus favourable consequences are used to reinforce desired behaviour so that one tends to repeat it.

Brent Parks discovered that nearly every time he tried to use his own judgment or take initiative on the job, he received support and recognition from his supervisor. For example, his supervisor commended him for making an operating decision "on the spot." Brent liked these favourable consequences and so he worked hard to improve his competence and increase his on-the-job judgment and initiative.

Figure 13-6 illustrates the law of effect. An antecedent or cue in the environment triggers a behaviour and that behaviour has a favourable consequence, which reinforces that behaviour and makes it more likely to occur

Figure 13-6
THE LAW OF EFFECT

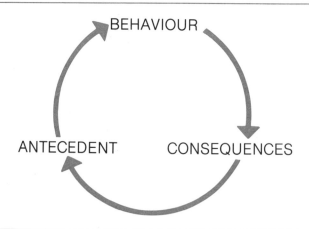

when the appropriate antecedent occurs again. For example, if people notice that it is lunchtime (the antecedent), they eat lunch (behaviour), which has the favourable outcome of reducing hunger (consequence).

REINFORCEMENT SCHEDULES. Reinforcement may be given in different ways, called *reinforcement schedules. Continuous reinforcement* follows each desired behaviour. For example, each time an agent sells an automobile, the agent earns a commission. *Intermittent reinforcement* does not follow every desired behaviour. Instead, the timing of reinforcers follows one of four schedules:

- *Fixed interval.* After a certain period of time, such as a weekly paycheque.
- *Variable interval.* After a random or varied number of time periods.
- *Fixed ratio.* After a certain number of correct responses, similar to a piece-rate system of pay.
- *Variable ratio.* After a random or varied number of correct responses; lotteries are an example of this.

Variable-ratio reinforcement tends to be the most powerful motivator among the four schedules. For example, slot machines in gambling casinos pay on a variable-ratio schedule. It is difficult for gamblers to leave them because payoffs are unpredictable and players keep hoping to beat the odds. However, since work situations are more complex than slot machines, variable-ratio schedules are not always the most successful form of reinforcement in a work situation.

INTERPRETING BEHAVIOUR MODIFICATION. Behaviour modification is criticized as being manipulative, because it controls one's environment and largely ignores one's internal needs. It is seen as a threat to the classical concepts of human dignity and autonomy. Others claim that it is an oversimplified explanation of a complex situation.

Application of behaviour modification is somewhat limited. In addition to objections to its use, there are numerous difficulties in installing it so that it applies a specific reinforcement for specific correct behaviours. On the other hand, when the behaviour-and-reinforcement connection is rather direct, behaviour modification is successful.[19] An example is control of absences.

A small electronics plant had trouble with employee absences, and so it developed a lottery for those who had no absence or tardiness during each month.[20] Winners of each lottery received $10 cash. In addition, all eligible employees had their names posted on the bulletin board.

The result was that absences were reduced. For sick leave alone there was a savings of $3,125 the first year. In comparison, the reinforcement cost was $120 cash ($10 monthly for twelve months).

Some managers have problems using positive reinforcement to motivate employees because it is a long-run approach. To use positive reinforcement

Figure 13-7
A HYPOTHETICAL RANGE OF EMPLOYEE PERFORMANCE

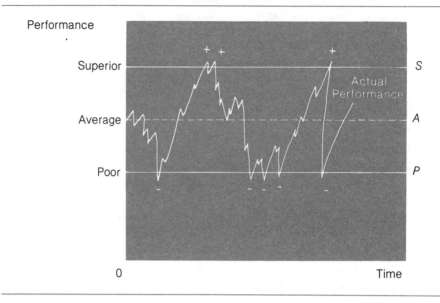

once or twice is not likely to change an employee's behaviour patterns. Figure 13-7 illustrates the problem. Dashed line *A* represents an employee's average performance. (The actual performance varies, being both good and bad.) Whenever an employee's performance is unacceptable, it falls below line *P* and the employee is disciplined. The discipline may be no more than a corrective comment or it may be as severe as several days off without pay— or worse. After discipline (shown as a minus), performance improves in most cases. The manager learns that discipline apparently improves performance. Therefore, the manager is reinforced to use discipline when poor employee performance is observed, because the consequences of using discipline lead to improved employee performance.[21] However, improvement may have occurred without discipline, because poor performance is well below the employee's average or normal efforts.

Where many managers go wrong is that they do not put in an upper threshold (line *S*) to signify superior performance. Even when managers do reward superior performance, outstanding results may not occur the next time, because the high-level performance is also an exception to the employee's normal level of performance. The manager observes that the superior performance received some positive reinforcement (shown as a plus) and then it subsequently drops. The consequences of using rewards for the manager seems to be a return to lower levels of performance. After several tries at reinforcing performance and having it drop back toward the average, many managers stop using positive reinforcement. However, if they continued using it, episodes of superior performance would become more frequent and the average level of performance would increase.

A REWARD-PERFORMANCE MODEL ✳

All the models of motivation have their strengths and weaknesses. No model is perfect, but each one adds something to our understanding of motivation. A model that combines strengths from others is the *reward-performance model*. It is shown as a wheel in Figure 13-8 because it is a circular relationship that regularly reinforces performance so that it will continue.

As the figure shows, employee motivation occurs in an environmental system that consists of the following factors:

- The job itself
- Small groups
- The organization
- The external environment

These four factors make up the *environmental system for motivation*. As shown in the figure, all these factors are interacting together in a complex system relationship. Each factor must be considered when planning a motivational action. The personnel department's task is to help build a repetitive system of rewards so that performance continues for a long period of time. If the proper rewards can be developed, they reinforce performance, provide satisfaction of needs, and build self-image.[22]

Figure 13-8
A REWARD-PERFORMANCE MODEL OF MOTIVATION

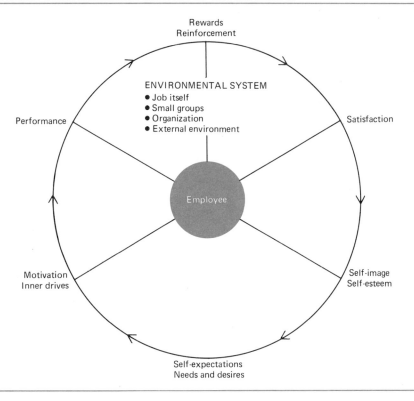

Enhanced self-image is a key in the motivational sequence. People must have an acceptable self-image in order to function effectively. A favourable self-image releases the creativity and potential that are in everyone and thus encourages growth. It helps people cope with the world around them and encourages them to make decisions and accept responsibility for their own actions. A favourable self-image leads to higher self-expectations about one's performance, which means that expectancy is increased, further encouraging employee drive. Motivation is built up and released in the form of performance to accomplish desired results. At this point, rewards and reinforcement occur, and the reward-performance sequence repeats itself.

The model shows that suitable rewards must continue if motivated performance is to be maintained. But what are suitable rewards? Rewards that meet the employee's self-expectations and fulfill his or her needs are appropriate. However, built into the model are other sources of rewards that are not readily apparent. For example, most people will be motivated to perform at a level that is consistent with their self-image. When that level of performance is achieved, it reaffirms the individual's self-image and sense of self-esteem, which further reinforces the person's self-expectations about future performance. If the environmental system continues to provide reinforcement, the person's self-image is likely to grow and the person will be motivated by higher self-expectations to function at a higher level of performance. This higher level of performance is, therefore, congruent with the stronger self-image and self-esteem that have been developed. In turn, if suitable rewards are received at the higher level of performance, self-image, self-expectations, motivation, and performance are all likely to increase again.

✳ JOB SATISFACTION

Job satisfaction is the favourableness or unfavourableness with which employees view their work. As with motivation, it too is affected by the environmental system shown in Figure 13-8. The job itself imparts satisfaction through its design, as discussed in Chapter 5. Jobs that are rich in behavioural elements such as autonomy, variety, task identity, task significance, and feedback contribute to an employee's satisfaction. Likewise, an employee's acceptance into the small work group and the organization is important for high levels of satisfaction. Also, Chapter 2 outlined some of the major environmental challenges that can directly affect a personnel department and indirectly affect an organization's human resources. In short, each element of the environmental system can add to—or detract from—job satisfaction.

As was shown in Figure 13-1, the personnel function is substantially concerned with job satisfaction. It monitors job satisfaction closely, because satisfaction affects turnover, absences, grievances, and other vital personnel issues. In many organizations personnel specialists periodically conduct job satisfaction surveys and study other indexes of satisfaction in order to be aware of employee feelings. In addition, satisfaction is affected by the way that personnel specialists administer personnel activities. Bureaucratic, rules-oriented personnel departments in the past have been the source of much employee dissatisfaction. In contrast, more helpful, humane personnel departments build employee motivation, growth, and satisfaction.

In 1977, the Canadian Institute of Public Opinion asked a random sample of working Canadians 18 years or over: "How do you feel about the work you are doing—do you find it very interesting for you personally, fairly interesting, or not interesting at all?" As shown in Figure 13-9, most Canadians (92%) found their jobs to be fairly or very interesting. Only 7% felt they were not interesting at all. However, this 7% does represent over 500,000 Canadian workers. Although men appeared to be slightly more interested in their work, the difference between males and females was not great. [23]

Figure 13-9
LABOUR FORCE JOB INTEREST

	"How do you feel about the work you are doing?"			
	Very Interesting	**Fairly Interesting**	**Not at All Interesting**	**Undecided**
Both Sexes	57%	35%	7%	1%
Men	58%	34%	7%	2%
Women	53%	37%	9%	1%

Source: "Over Five Hundred Thousand Find No Interest in their Work," *The Gallup Report*, Toronto: Canadian Institute of Public Opinion, May 28, 1977, p. 2.

JOB SATISFACTION AND PERFORMANCE

Are high job satisfaction and high performance related? If so, what is the relationship? Historically, it was assumed that more satisfied workers performed better. There often are positive relationships between high satisfaction and improved performance, but most of these are not large. [24] There are many satisfied workers who are not high producers. They remain content to perform only an average job. Satisfaction by itself is not a strong motivator, but it may maintain employees so that they are more receptive to a motivational environment when it is provided. This relationship probably accounts for the connection often found between satisfaction and performance.

Georgia Moore liked her employer and was satisfied with her job, but her performance was average. However, when the personnel department developed a program that increased her participation in job issues and encouraged small work teams, Georgia was receptive and developed strong motivation. During the next few months her performance improved substantially.

A basic issue is whether satisfaction leads to better performance or better performance leads to satisfaction. Which comes first? The relationship between satisfaction and motivation or performance is not as straightforward as might be expected. Various studies have shown that high *and* low performance can be associated with *either* high *or* low job satisfaction. This lack of causation may not be as strange as it first seems. The fact that workers are satisfied does not mean that they are motivated. It only means that they are satisfied. They may be satisfied because they do not have to work hard and yet they have an environmental system that is very favourable to them personally. Conversely, employees who work very hard are not always highly satisfied. They may be working diligently because they fear discipline or because they personally hold high work standards. The reason for the apparently uncertain relationship between performance and satisfaction is because rewards intervene between performance and satisfaction, as shown at the top of Figure 13-8. Whether satisfaction is going to be improved depends on whether the rewards at the top of the diagram match the expectations, needs, and desires held by the employee at the bottom of the figure. If better performance leads to higher rewards and if these rewards are seen as fair and equitable, then improved satisfaction results. It results because employees feel that they are receiving rewards in proportion to their performance.[25] If, on the other hand, rewards are seen as inadequate for one's level of performance, dissatisfaction tends to occur. In either case, one's level of satisfaction becomes feedback that affects one's self-image and motivation to perform. The total performance-satisfaction relationship is a continuous system, making it difficult to assess the impact of satisfaction on motivation or performance, and vice versa.

A doctor in a remote hospital may be very dissatisfied by the long working hours or the remote location. However, that same doctor may be motivated by a self-image of doing a good job and expectations of working hard, regardless of the rewards or level of satisfaction. However, if the doctor gets appropriate rewards (extra or long vacations, for example), satisfaction may climb. For the personnel specialists at the hospital, however, job satisfaction is an important determinant of whether the doctors will stay.[26]

JOB SATISFACTION, TURNOVER, AND ABSENCES

Although research has been unable to specify the exact relationship between satisfaction and performance, personnel professionals should be very concerned about job satisfaction. Research has shown that there is a strong relationship between job satisfaction and employee turnover and absenteeism.[27] And, as RCA discovered at its television plant in Memphis, Tennessee, extreme employee dissatisfaction can lead to union activity, strikes, and other causes of disruption.

Turnover and absences, two important concerns for the personnel function, are influenced by job satisfaction, although it is only one of the many influences on them.[28] As might be expected, when job satisfaction goes up, turnover declines. The reverse is also true. As shown in Figure 13-10, those employees who have lower satisfaction usually have higher turnover. They are more likely to leave their employer and seek greener pastures elsewhere, while their more satisfied associates remain.

Figure 13-10
GENERAL MODEL RELATING JOB SATISFACTION TO TURNOVER AND ABSENCES

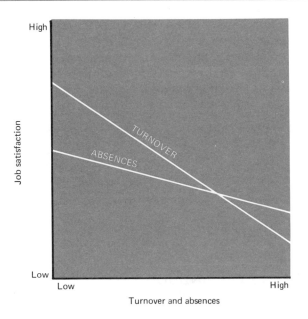

A similar relationship applies to absences. Those employees who have less satisfaction tend to be absent more often. They do not necessarily plan to be absent, but when some reason for absence arises, they find it easier to respond to that reason. As shown by the steepness of the lines in the figure, job satisfaction may not have quite as strong an effect on absences as it does on turnover. Personnel costs for turnover and absences can be rather easily calculated:

A bank calculated that each turnover cost $4,500 for records, recruitment, and training of a replacement. When a job satisfaction problem developed in one of its branches, three clerks resigned. The personnel department calculated a direct cost of $13,500 ($4,500 × 3) and used this cost as leverage to persuade the branch manager to improve branch practices.

As one group of writers observed about absenteeism:

Imaginary illnesses are especially likely to occur in those organizations which have a paid sick leave program. A common behavioral outcome of such a program might be labeled Parkinson's Law of Sick Leave Abuse: the days lost due to sickness expand to equal the number of paid sick days allowed.[29]

Perhaps the only sure way for personnel to repeal this version of Parkinson's Law is to provide high levels of job satisfaction.

AGE AND JOB SATISFACTION

As workers grow older, they tend to become more satisfied with their jobs. There are a number of reasons for their satisfaction, such as lowered expectations and better adjustment to their work situation because of experience with it. Younger workers, on the other hand, tend to be less satisfied because of higher expectations, less adjustment, and other causes. There may be exceptions, but a correlation of higher job satisfaction and age is shown by most studies. This general relationship is shown in Figure 13-11. The trend applies to both men and women, and both managers and workers.[30]

One study of 510 Canadian workers showed steadily rising job interest with advancing age.[31] The age groups and how they found their jobs were as follows:

	Very Interesting	Fairly Interesting	Not at All Interesting	Undecided
Under 30 Years	49%	38%	12%	1%
30–49 Years	57%	37%	5%	2%
Over 50 Years	66%	27%	5%	1%

OCCUPATIONAL LEVEL AND JOB SATISFACTION

Figure 13-11 also shows that people with higher-level occupations tend to be more satisfied with their jobs. Because they usually have better pay and

Figure 13-11
GENERAL MODEL RELATING JOB SATISFACTION TO AGE AND OCCUPATIONAL LEVEL

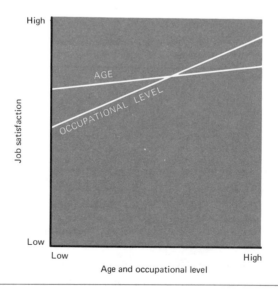

better working conditions, and their jobs make fuller use of their abilities, they have good reasons to be more satisfied. The result is that managers and professionals usually are more satisfied than skilled workers, who tend to be more satisfied than semiskilled and unskilled workers. The steepness of the lines in the figure shows that occupation is more strongly related to job satisfaction than age. Those who work in high occupational levels are considerably more satisfied than unskilled workers.

ORGANIZATION SIZE AND JOB SATISFACTION

Organization size tends to be inversely related to job satisfaction. As organizations grow larger, job satisfaction tends to decline moderately unless corrective action is taken to offset the trend.[32] Without corrective action large organizations tend to overwhelm people and disrupt supportive processes such as communication, coordination, and participation. Employees begin to feel that they are losing control over the events that affect them, because decision-making power is so far removed. The work environment also loses elements of personal closeness, friendship, and small-group teamwork that are important to the satisfaction of many people.

The term "organization size" refers to the size of an operating unit, such as a branch plant, rather than an entire corporation or governmental unit. For example, a large manufacturer could operate with thirty decentralized units, all of small size. Other things being equal, each of the decentralized units should be able to maintain high job satisfaction, even though the entire corporation is large.

Because of the size-satisfaction relationship, the personnel function in larger organizations may have a more difficult job in maintaining employee satisfaction. Large size puts a personnel department on notice that it needs to give more attention to job satisfaction issues. Satisfaction is more difficult to provide in large organizations because people feel that they are not as important an element of the organization as they would be in a small unit. Personnel specialists can help people feel more satisfied through effective communication. Subsequent chapters address the personnel department's role in organizational communication.

SUMMARY

The personnel function is directly and indirectly involved with organizational climate, motivation, and job satisfaction. Organizational climate is the favourableness or unfavourableness of the work environment for employees. Personnel policies and programs have a major effect on organizational climate.

Motivation is a person's drive to take an action because he or she wants to do so. It is a complex system of relationships that are affected by forces inside and outside the organization. Major frameworks for understanding motivation include a hierarchy of needs, ERG needs, motivation and maintenance factors, equity theory, expectancy theory, and behaviour modification. They may be combined into a reward-performance model that responds to needs within an environment of the job, small groups, the organization, and the external environment. The model is portrayed in a circular manner to show that it rewards and reinforces desired behaviour on a regular basis. It builds satisfaction, self-image, and self-expectations, so that motivation is encouraged to continue.

Job satisfaction is the favourableness or unfavourableness with which employees view their work. The personnel function tries to develop and monitor job satisfaction because of its close association with certain measures of performance. It is inversely related to turnover, absences, and organization size. On the other hand, it is positively related to age and occupational level.

TERMS FOR REVIEW

Organizational climate	Valence
Motivation	Expectancy
Hierarchy of needs	Path-goal personnel strategy
Lower-order needs	Cognitive models of motivation
Higher-order needs	Behaviour modification
Existence-Relatedness-Growth (ERG) theory	Law of effect
Motivational factors	Reinforcement schedules
Maintenance factors	Reward-performance model
Equity theory	Environmental system for motivation
Expectancy theory	Job satisfaction

REVIEW AND DISCUSSION QUESTIONS

1. In what ways is the personnel function involved with organizational climate, motivation, and job satisfaction?
2. Discuss similarities and differences among cognitive models of motivation. Do you see any major differences among them?
3. Are you personally motivated by higher-order or lower-order needs? Think about this issue and discuss it.
4. In relation to the expectancy model, think of a situation in which someone had strong desires for an outcome, but low expectancy frustrated that person. Discuss corrective action that could have been taken.
5. Explain why the application of positive reinforcement by managers sometimes fails. If you had to use behaviour modification, which reinforcement schedule would you use?
6. Explain how Alderfer's ERG theory differs from Maslow's hierarchy of needs.
7. Why should a personnel manager be concerned about the level of job sat-

isfaction in the plant? Explain the consequences of low levels of job satisfaction.

8. Interview two employees in large organizations and two others in small organizations. Do you find differences in their job satisfaction that may be related to organization size? Discuss your findings.

INCIDENT 13-1
EMPIRE MACHINERY COMPANY

Marge Jones, 45, is a machinist in a small factory. She has been there for six months. She had not been in the job market prior to her training to become a machinist at a trade school a year ago.

Marge Jones's quality of work had been borderline during the last several weeks, and so Paul Bunyan, her supervisor, decided to have a conference with her. After routine discussion of other matters, Paul asked her how she felt about her quality of output during the last few weeks. Marge replied, "I know that I haven't been doing as good work as I should. I have thought about this a great deal; and, though I regret to tell you this, my conclusion is that you are the cause of my poor work! The problem is the way you talk to me and the others in this department. You talk to all of us so gruffly and in such a loud voice that I am upset all day long. I just can't get motivated."

Paul was visibly upset by Marge's comments, because he realized he was gruff and talked in a loud voice, but that was his normal personality.

1. Can Maslow's hierarchy of needs help Paul understand this situation? Can the idea of motivational and maintenance factors help? What about the expectancy model? Discuss.
2. What action do you recommend Paul to take? Discuss.

INCIDENT 13-2
HEALTH-MORE FOODS CORPORATION

Health-More Foods Corporation of Vancouver, B.C., has been growing at a compounded rate of 30% for the last seven years. It entered the vitamin and health food business at a time when many people were concerned about natural foods and vitamins, and it sells high-quality products. It has captured a dominant position in its regional market and now has about 150 employees.

Because of its growth it has had difficulty maintaining trained clerical employees. Billing errors have been 9% and accounts payable errors have been 8%. The new personnel director was asked to recommend corrective action, and he proposed and installed a simple two-step program. First, supervisors and employees in each work unit met to discuss and set goals for improvement. Then supervisors regularly praised employees who had fewer errors than standard, and results for each work unit were charted daily. Within one month the error rates for both billing and accounts payable declined to less than 1% and remained there.

1. Discuss the two-step program and its results in terms of each of the models of motivation presented in this chapter.
2. How many of the models apply? Does one apply better than others? Discuss.

REFERENCES

1. William H. Mobley, "Where Have All the Golfers Gone?" *Personnel Journal*, July 1977, p. 340.
2. Fred Luthans and Robert Kreitner, *Organizational Behavior Modification*, Glenview, Ill.: Scott, Foresman and Company, 1975.
3. David Macarov, *Worker Productivity*, Beverly Hills, Ca.: Sage Publications, 1982.
4. Erwin S. Stanton, "A Critical Reevaluation of Motivation, Management, and Productivity," *Personnel Journal*, March 1983, pp. 208–214.
5. Edward E. Lawler III and Gerald E. Ledford, Jr., "Productivity and the Quality of Work Life," *National Productivity Review*, Winter 1981–82, pp. 23–36.
6. L. Erik Calonius, "Factory Magic: In a Plant in Memphis Japanese Firm Shows How to Attain Quality," *Wall Street Journal* (Western Edition), April 29, 1983, p. 1. Reprinted by permission of the *Wall Street Journal* © Dow Jones & Company, Inc. 1983. All rights reserved.
7. Ibid., p. 12.
8. See for example, Kenneth Blanchard and Spencer Johnson, *The One Minute Manager*, New York: William Morrow and Company, Inc., 1982; William G. Ouchi, *Theory Z, How American Business Can Meet the Japanese Challenge*, New York: Avon, 1981; and Thomas J. Peters and Robert H. Waterman, Jr., *In Search of Excellence, Lessons from America's Best-Run Companies*, New York: Harper & Row Publishers, Incorporated, 1982.
9. Stanton, op. cit.
10. Paul M. Muchinsky, "Organizational Communication: Relationships to Organizational Climate and Job Satisfaction," *Academy of Management Journal*, December 1977, pp. 592–607.
11. A. H. Maslow, "A Theory of Human Motivation," *Psychological Review*, Vol. 50, 1943, pp. 370–396; and A. H. Maslow, *Motivation and Personality*, New York: Harper & Row Publishers, Incorporated, 1954.
12. Clayton P. Alderfer, *Existence, Relatedness, and Growth*, New York: Free Press, 1972.
13. Frederick Herzberg, Bernard Mausner, and Barbara Snyderman, *The Motivation to Work*, New York: John Wiley & Sons, Inc., 1959. See also Clifford E. Jurgensen, "Job Preferences (What Makes a Job Good or Bad?)," *Journal of Applied Psychology*, June 1978, pp. 267–276; and Frederick Herzberg, *The Managerial Choice*, revised edition, Salt Lake City, 1982.
14. Gerald R. Salancik and Jeffrey Pfeiffer, "An Examination of Need-Satisfaction Models of Job Attitudes," *Administrative Science Quarterly*, September 1977, pp. 427–456. This article also criticizes other need-satisfaction models, such as Maslow and Alderfer.
15. J. Stacy Adams, "Toward an Understanding of Inequity," *Journal of Abnormal and Social Psychology*, November 1963, pp. 422–436.
16. M. R. Carrell and J. E. Dettrich, "Equity Theory: The Recent Literature, Methodological Considerations, and New Directions," *Academy of Management Review*, April 1978, pp. 202–210. See also Richard A. Cosier and Dan R. Dalton, "Equity Theory and Time: A Reformulation," *Academy of Management Review*, April 1983, pp. 311–319.
17. Victor H. Vroom, *Work and Motivation*, New York: John Wiley & Sons, Inc., 1964.
18. B. F. Skinner, *Science and Human Behavior*, New York: The Macmillan Company (The Free Press), 1953; and B. F. Skinner, *Contingencies of Reinforcement*, New York: Appleton-Century-Crofts, 1969. See also Luthans and Kreitner, op. cit.
19. Charles A. Snyder and Fred Luthans, "Using OB Mod to Increase Hospital Productivity," *Personnel Administrator*, August 1982, pp. 67–68, 70–73.
20. Jerry A. Wallin and Ronald D. Johnson, "The Use of Positive Reinforcement to Reduce the Costs Associated with Employee Absenteeism," *Proceedings of the Twenty-Eighth Annual Winter Meeting*, Madison, Wis.: Industrial Relations Research Association, 1976, pp. 41–46.
21. Arthur C. Beck and Ellis D. Hillman, "The Power of Positive Management," *Personnel Journal*, February 1983, pp. 126–131; see also Philip C. Grant, "Why Employee Motivation Has Declined in America," *Personnel Journal*, December 1982, pp. 905–909.
22. J. H. Kerr Inkson, "Self-Esteem as a Moderator of the Relationship between Job Performance and Job Satisfaction," *Journal of Applied Psychology*, April 1978, pp. 243–247.
23. "Over Five Hundred Thousand Find No Interest in their Work," *The Gallup Report*, Toronto: Canadian Institute of Public Opinion, May 28, 1977, p. 2.
24. Lawler and Ledford, op. cit., p. 26.
25. See Edward E. Lawler III, and Lyman W. Porter, "The Effect of Performance on Job Satisfaction," *Industrial Relations*, October 1967, pp. 20–28.
26. Lyman W. Porter and Edward E. Lawler, *Managerial Attitudes and Performance*, Homewood, Ill.: Irwin, 1968.
27. Lyman W. Porter and Richard M. Steers, "Organizational, Work, and Personal Factors in Employee Turnover and Absenteeism," *Psychological Bulletin*, August 1973, pp. 151–176. See also Richard T. Mowday, Lyman W. Porter, and Richard M. Steers, *Employee-Organization Linkages*, New York: Academic Press, 1981.
28. Richard M. Steers and Susan R. Rhodes, "Major Influences on Employee Attendance: A Process Model," *Journal of Applied Psychology*, August 1978, pp. 391–407; William H. Mobley, Stanley O. Horner, and A. T. Hollingsworth, "An Evaluation of Precursors of Hospital Employee Turnover," *Journal of Applied Psychology*, August 1978, pp. 408–414; and Richard T. Mowday and Daniel G. Spencer, "The Influence of Task and Personality Characteristics on Employee Turnover and Absenteeism Incidents," *Academy of Management Journal*, September 1981, pp. 634–642.

29. Richard E. Kopelman, George O. Schneller IV, and John J. Silver, Jr., "Parkinson's Law and Absentee-ism: A Program to Rein in Sick Leave Costs," *Personnel Administrator*, May 1981, p. 28.
30. Timothy J. Keaveny, John H. Jackson, and John A. Fossum, "Are There Sex Differences in Job Satisfac-tion?" *The Personnel Administrator*, March 1978, pp. 55–58.
31. *The Gallup Report.*
32. Keith Davis, *Human Behavior at Work*, 6th ed., New York: McGraw-Hill Book Company, 1981, pp. 87–88; and Lyman W. Porter, Edward E. Lawler III, and J. Richard Hackman, *Behavior in Organizations*, New York: McGraw-Hill Book Company, 1975, pp. 248–252.

Chapter *14*

Compensation Management

Management's challenge is to create an environment which stimulates people in their jobs and fosters company growth, and a key aspect of the environment is compensation.

Milton L. Rock[1]

... something happened on the road to the 20th century. Employees became "wage earners"—pure and simple—not concerned about the overall success of the business because they did not have a direct *stake in profits or ownership.*

Bert L. Metzger[2]

CHAPTER OBJECTIVES

After studying this chapter, you should be able to:
1. **Discuss** the consequences of mismanaged compensation programs.
2. **Explain** the objectives of effective compensation management.
3. **Describe** how wages and salaries are determined.
4. **Identify** the major issues that influence compensation management.
5. **Evaluate** the advantages and disadvantages of incentive systems.
6. **Explain** the major approaches to group incentive plans.

One way the personnel department improves employee performance, motivation, and satisfaction is through compensation. *Compensation* is the money employees receive in exchange for their work. Whether it be in the form of hourly wages or periodic salaries, the personnel department usually designs and administers employee compensation. When compensation is done correctly, employees are more likely to be satisfied and motivated toward organizational objectives. And the department is more likely to achieve its objective of an effective work force. But when employees perceive their compensation to be inappropriate, performance, motivation, and satisfaction may decline dramatically, as the following dialogue illustrates.

Joan Swensen walked into Al Jorgeson's office, slammed down her clipboard, and said, "I quit!"

"What is the matter, Joan?" Al questioned. "You've been here two years, and I've never seen you so mad."

"That's just the problem. I've been here two years, and this morning I found out that the new man you hired last week, Kurt, is making the same pay that I am," Joan said.

"Well, he does the same work, he works the same hours, and he has the same responsibilities. Would it be fair to pay him less?" Al asked.

"Doesn't experience count for anything around here? When you brought him into the shop, you told me to show him the ropes. So not only did I have more experience, but I am also responsible for training him," Joan responded.

"Okay, okay, I'll talk with personnel this afternoon and see if I can get you a raise," Al conceded.

"Don't bother. I'm quitting," Joan asserted. "If this company doesn't want to do what is right voluntarily, I'd rather work someplace else."

Compensation programs maintain an organization's human resources. When wages and salaries are not administered properly, the firm may lose employees and the money spent to recruit, select, train, and develop them. Even if workers do not quit, as Joan did in the opening illustration, they may become dissatisfied with the company.

Dissatisfaction arises because employee needs are affected by absolute and relative levels of pay, as shown in Figure 14-1. When the total, or *absolute*, amount of pay is too low, employees cannot meet their physiological or security needs. In industrial societies, the absolute level of pay usually is high enough to meet these basic needs, at least minimally. A more common source of dissatisfaction centres on *relative pay*, which is an employee's pay compared with that of other workers. For example, Joan's concern was over the *relative* amount of her salary in comparison with the new, less experienced employee, Kurt. Her additional experience and training responsibilities were not reflected in her pay as compared with Kurt's pay. Her esteem needs were affected because she did not get the recognition she thought she deserved.

Figure 14-1
ABSOLUTE AND RELATIVE PAY LEVELS IN RELATION TO EMPLOYEE NEEDS

Pay Levels	Employee Needs Primarily Served
Absolute	Physiological and security needs
Relative	Social and esteem needs

Absolute and relative pay levels also may hold negative consequences for the organization.[3] The implications of pay dissatisfaction are diagrammed in Figure 14-2. In severe cases, the desire for more pay can lower performance, increase grievances, or lead employees to search for new jobs. The lower attractiveness of their jobs can cause job dissatisfaction, absenteeism, or other undesirable outcomes. Even overpayment of wages and

Figure 14-2
MODEL OF THE CONSEQUENCES OF PAY DISSATISFACTION

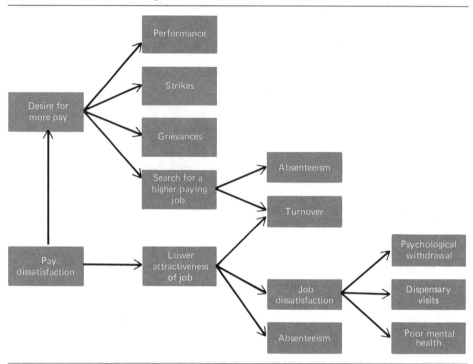

Source: Edward E. Lawler, III, *Pay and Organizational Effectiveness: A Psychological View*, New York: McGraw-Hill Book Company, 1971, p. 233. Used with permission of the McGraw-Hill Book Company.

salaries can harm the organization and its people. Overpaid employees may feel anxiety, guilt, and discomfort.[4] High compensation costs can reduce the firm's competitiveness and lessen its future ability to provide attractive jobs. This balance between pay satisfaction and the organization's competitiveness underlies most of the personnel department's compensation efforts.

Since compensation affects the organization and its employees, this chapter examines the requirements for an effective compensation system.[5] The chapter also discusses the objectives and procedures used to administer compensation. Then it concludes with a review of financial incentives.

OBJECTIVES OF COMPENSATION ADMINISTRATION

The administration of compensation must meet numerous objectives. Sometimes the ones listed in Figure 14-3 conflict with each other and trade-offs must be made.[6] For example, to retain employees and ensure equity, wage and salary analysts pay similar amounts for similar jobs. But a recruiter may want to offer an unusually high salary to attract a qualified recruit. At this point the personnel manager must make a trade-off between the recruiting and consistency objectives.

Figure 14-3
**OBJECTIVES SOUGHT THROUGH EFFECTIVE COMPENSATION
ADMINISTRATION**

- **Acquire qualified personnel.** Compensation needs to be high enough to attract applicants. Since companies compete in the labour market, pay levels must respond to the supply and demand of workers. But sometimes a premium wage rate is needed to attract applicants who are already employed in other firms.
- **Retain present employees.** When compensation levels are not competitive, some employees quit. To prevent employee turnover, pay must be kept competitive with that of other employers.
- **Ensure equity.** The administration of wages and salaries strives for internal and external equity. **Internal equity** requires that pay be related to the relative worth of jobs. That is, similar jobs get similar pay. **External equity** involves paying workers at a rate equal to the pay that similar workers receive in other companies.
- **Reward desired behaviour.** Pay should reinforce desired behaviours. Good performance, experience, loyalty, new responsibilities, and other behaviours can be rewarded through an effective compensation plan.
- **Control costs.** A rational compensation program helps an organization to obtain and retain its work force at a reasonable cost. Without a systematic wage and salary structure the organization could overpay or underpay its employees.
- **Comply with legal regulations.** As with other aspects of personnel management, wage and salary administration faces legal constraints. A sound pay program considers these constraints and ensures compliance with all government regulations that affect employee compensation.
- **Further administrative efficiency.** In pursuing the other objectives of effective compensation management, wage and salary specialists try to design the program so that it can be efficiently administered. Administrative efficiency, however, should be a secondary consideration compared with other objectives.

Other objectives of compensation are to reward desired behaviour and to control costs. These objectives can conflict, too. For example, a department manager may want to reward outstanding performance with a raise, but every raise adds to costs. Here again, the personnel manager must decide between two conflicting goals.

Regardless of the trade-offs, an overriding objective is to maintain legal compliance. For example, the Canada Labour Code requires employers to pay minimum wages and time and a half for overtime. Periodically, federal and provincial governments raise minimum wages, and employers must comply regardless of other objectives being sought.

Compensation objectives are not rules. They are guidelines. But the less these guidelines are violated, the more effective wage and salary administration can be. To meet these objectives, compensation specialists evaluate every job, conduct wage and salary surveys, and price each job. Through these steps, the appropriate pay level for each job is determined.

Figure 14-4 depicts these three major phases of compensation management. Each phase is discussed in the following sections.

Figure 14-4
MAJOR PHASES OF COMPENSATION MANAGEMENT

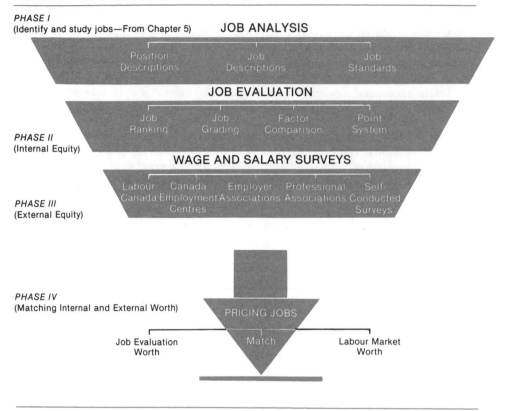

JOB EVALUATION

Job evaluations are systematic procedures to determine the relative worth of jobs. Although there are several different approaches, each one considers the duties, responsibilities, and working conditions of the job. The purpose of job evaluation is to identify which jobs should be paid more than others.

Since evaluation is subjective, it is conducted by specialists, or a group of specialists called a *job evaluation committee*.[7] They begin with a review of job analysis information to learn about the duties, responsibilities, and working conditions that shape their evaluation. With this knowledge, the relative worth of jobs is determined by selecting a job evaluation method. The most common ones are job ranking, job grading, factor comparison, and the point system.

JOB RANKING

The simplest and least precise method of job evaluation is *job ranking*. Specialists review the job analysis information for each job. Then each job is ranked subjectively according to its importance in comparison with other jobs. These are overall rankings, although raters may consider the responsibility, skill, effort, and working conditions of each job. It is quite possible that important elements of some jobs may be overlooked while unimportant items are weighted too heavily. What is even more damaging, these rankings do not differentiate the relative importance of jobs. For example, the job of janitor may be ranked as 1, the secretary's job may get a 2, and the office manager is ranked as a 3. But the secretarial position may be three times as important as the janitorial job and half as important as the job of office manager. The job ranking approach does not allow for these relative differences between jobs. Pay scales based on these broad rankings ensure that more important jobs are paid more. But since the rankings lack precision, the resulting pay levels may be inaccurate.

JOB GRADING

Job grading, or job classification, is a slightly more sophisticated method than job ranking, but it, too, is not very precise. It works by having each job assigned a grade, as explained in Figure 14-5. The standard description in

Figure 14-5
A JOB CLASSIFICATION SCHEDULE FOR USE WITH THE JOB GRADING METHOD

EMPIRE MACHINE SHOP
Job Classification Schedule

Directions: To determine appropriate job grade, match standard description with job description.

Job Grade	Standard Description
I	Work is simple and highly repetitive, done under close supervision, requiring minimal training and little responsibility or initiative. **Examples:** Janitor, file clerk
II	Work is simple and repetitive, done under close supervision, requiring some training or skill. Employee is expected to assume responsibility or exhibit initiative only rarely. **Examples:** Clerk-typist I, machine cleaner
III	Work is simple, with little variation, done under general supervision. Training or skill required. Employee has minimum responsibilities and must take some initiative to perform satisfactorily. **Examples:** Parts expediter, machine oiler, clerk-typist II
IV	Work is moderately complex, with some variation, done under general supervision. High level of skill required. Employee is responsible for equipment or safety; regularly exhibits initiative. **Examples:** Machine operator I, tool and die apprentice
V	Work is complex, varied, done under general supervision. Advanced skill level required. Employee is responsible for equipment and safety; shows high degree of initiative. **Examples:** Machine operator II, tool and die specialist

the figure that most nearly matches the job description determines the grade of the job. Once again, more important jobs are paid more. But the lack of precision can lead to inaccurate pay levels. The largest user of this approach has been the Canadian Public Service Commission, which is gradually replacing this approach with more sophisticated methods.

FACTOR COMPARISON

The *factor comparison* method requires the job evaluation committee to compare critical job components. The critical components are those factors common to all jobs being evaluated. The most widely used ones are responsibility, skill, mental effort, physical effort, and working conditions.[8] Each of these factors is compared, one at a time, against the same factor for other jobs. This evaluation allows the committee to determine the relative importance of each job. The factor comparison method involves five steps, as follows:

STEP 1: DETERMINE THE CRITICAL FACTORS. Analysts must first decide which factors are common and important in a broad range of jobs. The critical factors shown in Figure 14-6 are most commonly used. Some organizations use different factors for managerial, professional, sales, or other types of jobs if the factors in the figure are considered inappropriate.

Figure 14-6
THE APPORTIONMENT OF WAGES FOR KEY JOBS

Critical Factors	Key Jobs				
	Machinist	Forklift Driver	Secretary	Janitor	File Clerk
Responsibility	$ 4.40	$ 3.60	$ 2.40	$ .80	$1.90
Skill	8.00	3.00	3.20	1.20	2.40
Mental Effort	4.00	1.60	2.60	.60	1.80
Physical Effort	4.00	2.20	1.40	3.40	1.40
Working Conditions	1.40	1.20	1.20	3.00	1.20
Total	$21.80	$11.60	$10.80	$9.00	$8.70
Wage Rate	$21.80	$11.60	$10.80	$9.00	$8.70

STEP 2: DETERMINE KEY JOBS. *Key jobs* are those that are common in the organization and are common in the employer's labour market. Common jobs are selected because it is easier to discover the market rate for them. Ideally, these jobs should include those with a wide variety of critical factors to be evaluated.

STEP 3: APPORTION PRESENT WAGES FOR KEY JOBS. The job evaluation committee then allocates a part of each key job's wage rate to each critical factor, as shown in Figure 14-6. The proportion of each wage assigned to the different critical factors depends on the importance of the factor.

For example, a janitor receives $9.00. This amount is apportioned in Figure 14-6 as follows: $.80 for responsibility, $1.20 for skill, $.60 for mental effort, $3.40 for physical effort, and $3.00 for working conditions. In apportioning these wage rates, two comparisons must be made. First, the amount assigned to each factor should reflect its importance when compared with the other factors of that job. For example, if $8.00 is assigned to skill and $4.00 to physical effort for the machinist, this implies that the skill factor is two times as important as physical effort. Second, the amount allocated to a single factor should reflect the relative importance of that factor among different jobs. For example, if responsibility of the secretary is three times that of the janitor, then the money allocated to the secretary for responsibility ($2.40) should be three times that of the janitor ($.80).

STEP 4: PLACE KEY JOBS ON FACTOR COMPARISON CHART. Once the wage rates are assigned to the critical factors of each key job, this information is transferred to a factor comparison chart like the one in Figure 14-7. The titles of key jobs are placed in the columns according to the amount of wages assigned to each critical factor. In the responsibility column, for example, the secretary title is placed next to the $2.40 rate to reflect how much the secretary's responsibility is worth to the organization. This job also appears under the other critical factors according to the relative worth of those factors in the job of secretary. The same assignment process takes place for every other key job.

STEP 5: EVALUATE OTHER JOBS. The titles of key jobs in each column of Figure 14-7 serve as benchmarks. Other non-key jobs are then evaluated by fitting them on the scale in each column.

For the job of senior maintenance mechanic to be evaluated, the job evaluation committee compares the responsibility of the mechanic with that involved in other key jobs already on the chart. It is decided subjectively that the mechanic's responsibility is between that of the forklift driver and the secretary. And since the mechanic's job requires about three-quarters of the machinist's skills, the skill component of this job is placed below that of the machinist in the skill column. This procedure is repeated for each critical factor. When completed, the committee can determine the worth of the mechanic's job, which is:

Responsibility	$ 2.90
Skill	6.00
Mental effort	5.40
Physical effort	2.80
Working conditions	2.60
	$19.70

By using the same procedure applied to the mechanic's job, every other job in the organization is then evaluated. When the evaluations are completed, the job evaluation committee can rank every job according to its relative worth as indicated by its wage rate. These rankings should be reviewed by department managers to verify their appropriateness.[9]

Figure 14-7
FACTOR COMPARISON CHART

Rate	Responsi-bility	Skill	Mental Effort	Physical Effort	Working Conditions
8.00		— Machinist			
7.00					
6.00		— **Mechanic**			
			— **Mechanic**		
5.00					
	— Machinist				
4.00			— Machinist	— Machinist	
	— Forklift				
				— Janitor	
		— Secretary			
3.00	— **Mechanic**	— Forklift			— Janitor
				— **Mechanic**	
			— Secretary		— **Mechanic**
	— Secretary	— File clerk			
				— Forklift	
2.00	— File clerk				
			— File clerk		
			— Forklift		
				—{Secretary / File clerk}	— Machinist
		— Janitor			—{Forklift / Secretary / File clerk}
1.00					
	— Janitor				
			— Janitor		
0.00					

POINT SYSTEM

Research shows that the *point system* is used more than any other method.[10] It evaluates the critical factors of each job. But instead of using wages, as the factor comparison method does. points are used. Although it is more difficult to develop initially, it is more precise than the factor comparison method because it can handle critical factors in more detail. This system requires six steps to implement. It is usually done by a job evaluation committee or an individual analyst.

STEP 1: DETERMINE CRITICAL FACTORS. The point system can use the same factors as the factor comparison method, but it usually adds more detail by breaking those factors down into subfactors. For example, Figure 14-8 shows how the factor of responsibility can be broken down into:

a. Safety of others
b. Equipment and materials

c. Assisting trainees
d. Product/service quality

Figure 14-8
POINT SYSTEM MATRIX

	Levels			
Critical Factors	Minimum I	Low II	Moderate III	High IV
1. Responsibility				
a. Safety of others	25	50	75	100
b. Equipment and materials	20	40	60	80
c. Assisting trainees	5	20	35	50
d. Product/service quality	20	40	60	80
2. Skill				
a. Experience	45	90	135	180
b. Education/training	25	50	75	100
3. Effort				
a. Physical	25	50	75	100
b. Mental	35	70	105	150
4. Working conditions				
a. Unpleasant conditions	20	40	60	80
b. Hazards	20	40	60	80
	Total points			1000

STEP 2: DETERMINE LEVELS OF FACTORS. Since the extent of responsibility, or other factors, may vary from job to job, the point system creates several levels associated with each factor. Figure 14-8 shows four levels, although more or fewer may be used. These levels help analysts to reward different degrees of responsibility, skills, and other critical factors.

STEP 3: ALLOCATE POINTS TO SUBFACTORS. With the factors listed down one side and the levels placed across the top of Figure 14-8, the result is a point system matrix. Points are then assigned to each subfactor to reflect the relative importance of different subfactors. Analysts start with level IV and weight each subfactor with the number of points they think it deserves. This allocation allows them to give very precise weights to each element of the job. For example, if safety is twice as important as assisting trainees, it is assigned twice as many points (100) as assisting trainees (50).

STEP 4: ALLOCATE POINTS TO LEVELS. Once the points for each job element are satisfactory under column IV, analysts allocate points across each row to reflect the importance of the different levels. For simplicity, equal point differences are usually assigned between levels, as was done for "Safety of others" in Figure 14-8. Or point differences between levels can be variable, as shown for "assisting trainees." Both approaches are used depending on how important each level of each subfactor is.

STEP 5: DEVELOP THE POINT MANUAL. Analysts then develop a point manual. It contains a written explanation of each job element, as shown in Figure 14-9 for responsibility of equipment and materials. It also defines what is expected for the four levels of each subfactor. This information is needed to assign jobs to their appropriate level.

Figure 14-9
POINT MANUAL DESCRIPTION OF "RESPONSIBILITY: EQUIPMENT AND MATERIALS"

1. **Responsibility**
   b. **Equipment and Materials.** Each employee is responsible for conserving the company's equipment and materials. This includes reporting malfunctioning equipment or defective materials, keeping equipment and materials cleaned or in proper order, and maintaining, repairing, or modifying equipment and materials according to individual job duties. The company recognizes that the degree of responsibility for equipment and material varies widely throughout the organization.

   Level I.   Employee reports malfunctioning equipment or defective materials to immediate superior.
   Level II. Employee maintains the appearance of equipment or order of materials and has responsibility for the security of such equipment or materials.
   Level III. Employee performs preventive maintenance and minor repairs on equipment or corrects minor defects in materials.
   Level IV. Employee performs major maintenance or overhauls of equipment or is responsible for deciding type, quantity, and quality of materials to be used.

STEP 6: APPLY THE POINT SYSTEM. When the point matrix and manual are ready, the relative value of each job can be determined. This process is subjective. It requires specialists to compare job descriptions with the point manual for each subfactor. The match between the job description and the point manual statement reveals the level and points for each subfactor of every job. Once completed, the points for each subfactor are added to find the total number of points for the job. An example of this matching process for Machine Operator I appears below:

The job description of Machine Operator I states ".... operator is responsible for performing preventive maintenance (such as cleaning, oiling, and adjusting belts) and minor repairs." The sample point manual excerpt in Figure 14-9 states "Level III: ... performs preventive maintenance and minor repairs. ..." Since the job description and the point manual match at Level III, the points for the equipment subfactor are 60. Repeating this matching process for every subfactor yields the total points for the job of Machine Operator I.

After the total points for each job are known, the jobs are ranked. As with the job ranking, job grade, and factor comparison systems, this relative ranking should be reviewed by department managers to ensure that it is appropriate.

Beyond the four job evaluation methods discussed in this section, many other variations exist. Large organizations often modify standard approaches to create unique in-house variations.

The "Hay Plan," for example, is one variation widely used by Canadian and U.S. firms. This proprietary method is marketed by a large consulting firm, Hay and Associates, and relies on a committee evaluation of critical job factors to determine each job's relative worth. Although other job evaluation approaches exist, all effective job evaluation schemes attempt to determine a job's relative worth to ensure internal equity.

WAGE AND SALARY SURVEYS

All job evaluation techniques result in a ranking of jobs based upon their relative worth. This assures *internal* equity. That is, jobs that are worth more will be paid more. But how much should be paid? What constitutes *external* equity?

To determine a fair rate of compensation, most firms rely on *wage and salary surveys*. These surveys discover what other employers in the *same* labour market are paying for specific key jobs. The *labour market* is the area from which the employer recruits. Generally, it is the local community in which the employer is located. However, the firms may have to compete for some workers in a labour market that extends beyond the local community. Consider how the president of one large university viewed the market:

Our labour market depends on the type of position we are trying to fill. For the hourly paid jobs such as janitor, clerk, typist, and secretary, the labour market is the surrounding metropolitan community. When we hire professors, our labour market is Canada. We have to compete with universities in other provinces to get the type of faculty member we seek. When we have the funds to hire a distinguished professor, our labour market is the whole world.

SOURCES OF COMPENSATION DATA

Wage and salary data are benchmarks against which analysts compare compensation levels. This survey information can be obtained in several ways. One source is Labour Canada. It conducts surveys in major metropolitan labour markets periodically. Sometimes, these surveys are out of date in a fast-changing labour market, and so other sources may be needed. Many consultants provide this service for their clientele. Canada Employment Centres also compile wage and salary information for distribution to employers. When compiled frequently by the centre consulted, this information may be current enough for use by compensation analysts. A fourth source of compensation data may be an employer association, which surveys member firms. Employer associations—or a fifth source, professional associations—may be the only source of compensation data for highly specialized jobs.

The major problem with all these published surveys is their varying comparability. Analysts cannot always be sure that their jobs match those reported in the survey. Matching just job titles may be misleading. Federal, provincial, and association job descriptions may be considerably different, even when the jobs have the same title. Since most published surveys rely on the *Canadian Classification and Dictionary of Occupations* (CCDO), any job description should be compared with descriptions in the CCDO.

SURVEY PROCEDURE

To overcome the limitations of published surveys, some personnel departments conduct their own wage and salary survey.[11] Since surveying all jobs is cumbersome and expensive, usually only key jobs are used. Then a sample of firms from the labour market is selected. Finally, these organizations are contacted by phone or mail to learn what they are paying for the key jobs. Most companies are willing to cooperate since they, too, need this information. Contacts through professional associations, such as the Canadian Manufacturers' Association and its local affiliates or provincial personnel associations, can further aid this process. Again, it is important to make sure that the comparisons are between similar jobs and not just similar titles.

At this point, all jobs are ranked according to their relative worth, as a result of the job evaluation process. Through wage and salary surveys, the rate for key jobs in the labour market is also known. This leaves the last phase of wage and salary administration, pricing the jobs.

PRICING JOBS

Pricing jobs includes two activities: establishing the appropriate pay level for each job and grouping the different pay levels into a structure that can be managed effectively.

PAY LEVELS

The appropriate pay level for any job reflects its relative and absolute worth. A job's relative worth is determined by its ranking through the job evaluation process. The absolute worth of a job is controlled by what the labour market pays similar jobs. To set the right pay level means combining the job evaluation rankings and the survey wage rates.

This information is combined through the use of a graph called a *scattergram*. As Figure 14-10 shows, its vertical axis is pay rates. If the point system is used to determine the ranking of jobs, the horizontal axis is in points. The scattergram is created by plotting the total points and wage level for each *key job*. Thus each dot represents the intersection of the point value and the wage rate for a particular key job. For example, Key Job A in Figure 14-10 is worth 500 points and is paid $8.00 an hour.

Through the dots that represent key jobs, a *wage-trend line* is drawn as close to as many points as possible. (This line can be done freehand, or more accurately, by a statistical technique called the *least squares method*.)[12]

The wage-trend line helps to determine the wage rates for non-key jobs. There are two steps. First, the point value for the non-key job is located on the horizontal axis. Second, a line is traced vertically to the wage-trend line, then horizontally to the dollar scale. The amount on the vertical scale is the appropriate wage rate for the non-key job. For example, non-key job B is worth 700 points. By tracing a vertical line up to the wage-trend line and then horizontally to the vertical (dollar) scale, it can be seen in Figure 14-10 that the appropriate wage rate for job B is $10.00 per hour.

Figure 14-10
THE DEVELOPMENT OF A WAGE-TREND LINE

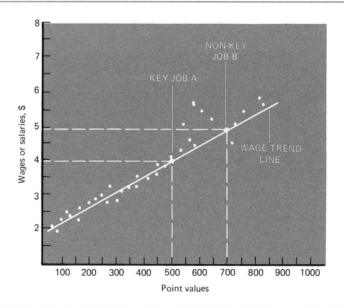

THE COMPENSATION STRUCTURE

A medium-sized organization with 2,000 workers and 325 separately identifiable jobs would present the wage and salary analyst with complex problems. The existence of 325 separate wage rates would be meaningless
because the differences in wages between each job might be no more than a
few cents.

Compensation analysts find it more convenient to lump jobs together into
job classes. In the job grade approach, jobs are already grouped into
predetermined categories. With other methods, the grouping is done by
creating job grades based on the previous ranking, pay, or points. In the
point system, for example, classifications are based on point ranges: 0 to
100, 101 to 150, 151 to 200, and so forth. This grouping causes the wage-
trend line to be replaced with a series of ascending dashes, as shown in
Figure 14-11. Thus all jobs in the same class receive the same wage rate. A
job valued at 105 points, for example, receives the same pay as a job with
145 points. Too many grades defeat the purpose of grouping; too few groupings result in workers with jobs of widely varying importance receiving the
same pay.

The problem with flat rates for each job class is that exceptional performance cannot be rewarded. To give a worker a merit increase requires moving the employee into a higher job class. This upsets the entire balance of internal equity developed through job evaluations. To solve these problems,
most firms use rate ranges for each class. [13]

Rate ranges mean simply a pay range for each job class. For example, suppose the wage-trend line indicates that $10.00 is the average hourly rate for

Figure 14-11
THE IMPACT OF JOB CLASSES ON THE WAGE-TREND LINE

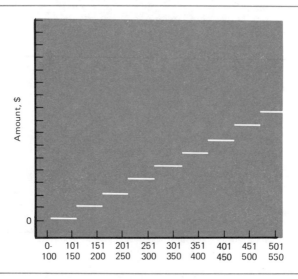

Figure 14-12
VARYING WAGE RATES FOR JOB CLASSES

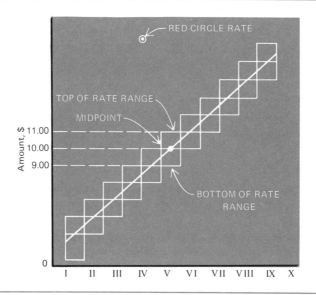

a particular job class. Every employee in that class gets $10.00 if a flat rate is paid. With a rate range of $2.00 for each class, a marginal performer can be paid $9.00 at the bottom of the range, as indicated in Figure 14-12. Then an average performer is placed at the midpoint in the rate range, $10.00. When performance appraisals indicate above-average performance, the employee may be given a *merit raise* of, say, $.50 per hour for the exceptional performance.[14] If this performance continues, another merit raise of $.50 can be granted. Once the employee reaches the top of the rate range, no more wage increases will be forthcoming. Either a promotion or a general across-the-board pay raise needs to occur for this worker's wages to exceed $11.00. An across-the-board increase moves the entire wage-trend line upward.[15]

As new jobs are created, the wage and salary section performs a job evaluation. From this evaluation, the new job is assigned to an appropriate job class. If the rate ranges are used, the new employee will start at the bottom of the range and receive raises, where appropriate, to the top of the rate range.

CHALLENGES AFFECTING COMPENSATION

Even the most rational methods of determining pay must be tempered by several challenges. The implications of these contingencies may cause wage and salary analysts to make further adjustments to employee compensation.

PREVAILING WAGE RATES

Some jobs must be paid more than is indicated by their relative worth because of market forces. In the late 1960s, there was a scarcity of computer specialists. Fitting these jobs onto a wage-trend line often resulted in a wage rate below their prevailing wage rate. Since demand outstripped supply, market forces caused wage rates for these specialists to rise above their relative worth when compared with other jobs. Firms that needed these talents were forced to pay a premium. Diagrammatically, these rates appear on a wage chart as a *red-circle rate*, as seen in Figure 14-12. The term arises from the practice of marking out-of-line rates with a red circle on the chart.

UNION POWER

When unions represent a portion of the work force, they may be able to use their power to obtain wage rates out of proportion to their relative worth. For example, wage and salary studies may determine that $14.00 an hour is appropriate for a truck driver. But if the union insists on $18.00, the personnel department may believe paying the higher rate is less expensive than a strike. Sometimes the union controls most or all of a particular skill, such as carpentry or plumbing. This enables the union actually to raise the prevailing rate for those jobs.

PRODUCTIVITY

Companies must make a profit to survive. Without it, the company cannot attract the investors necessary to remain competitive. Therefore, a company cannot pay workers more than they contribute back to the firm through their productivity. When this happens (because of scarcity or union power), companies usually redesign those jobs, train new workers to increase their supply, or automate.

WAGE AND SALARY POLICIES

Most organizations have policies that cause wages and salaries to be adjusted. One common policy is to give nonunion workers the same raise as that received by unionized workers. Some companies have a policy of paying a premium above the prevailing wages to minimize turnover or to recruit the best workers. Also, some companies have automatic cost-of-living clauses that give employees automatic raises when the Statistics Canada cost-of-living index increases. Raises or policies that increase employee compensation move the wage-trend line upward.

GOVERNMENT CONSTRAINTS

Canada is a nation of wage earners. What people earn bears a direct relationship to the economy and general welfare of the population. Since the 1930s, the federal government has regulated some aspects of compensation.

The Canada Labour Code in its revised version of 1971 is the most comprehensive law affecting compensation rights for organizations under federal jurisdiction. It sets requirements for minimum wage, overtime pay, equal pay, child labour, and record-keeping. The minimum-wage and over-time provisions require employers to pay at least a minimum hourly rate of pay regardless of the worth of the job. (When the minimum is increased by law, it may mean adjusting upward the wages of those who already earn above the minimum. If those just above minimum wage do not also get raises, wage differentials will be squeezed together.[16] This is called *wage compression*.) For every covered job, the organization must pay one and a half times the employee's regular pay rate for all hours over forty per week. Executive, administrative, professional, and other employees are exempt from the overtime provisions. Laws involving similar regulations have been enacted by each province for organizations under their jurisdiction.

In 1977 the Canada Labour Code, Part I, was repealed and replaced by the Canadian Human Rights Act. Since this act prohibits, among other things, discrimination because of sex, it is illegal for companies to pay women less than men if their jobs involve equal skills, effort, responsibilities, and conditions.[17] As explained more fully in Chapter 3, the government enforces these provisions by requiring wrongdoers to equalize pay and make up past discrepancies:

The Ste. Anne de Bellevue Veterans Hospital near Montreal had to increase a woman's salary by $10,000 and pay $14,262 in back wages for past discrimination.[18]

The law also creates standards for employment of children. These regulations apply to minors under the age of seventeen and limit the use of children in hazardous occupations. They also determine the minimum wages for children.

The record-keeping requirements mean that employers must maintain detailed records of hours worked, pay rates, amounts of overtime, deductions and additions to pay, and other information related to compensation. These records must be kept for at least thirty-six months after the work is performed and must be available at all reasonable times for examination by an inspector.

EQUAL PAY FOR WORK OF EQUAL VALUE VS. EQUAL PAY FOR EQUAL WORK

As first mentioned in Chapter 3, an important issue in compensation management and equal opportunity is *equal pay for work of equal value*. Equal pay for equal value is the idea that jobs of comparable worth to the organization should be equally paid. This idea goes beyond equal pay for equal work. The equal pay concept has been enacted into law and requires an employer to pay men and women the same wage or salary when they do the same work. Exceptions to equal pay are allowed when a valid seniority or merit system exist. Employers can pay more for seniority or to workers who perform better and merit higher pay. Exceptions also are allowed when pay is determined by the employee's production, such as sales commissions.

The equal pay for work of equal value concept, however, takes a slightly different perspective. It would require employers to pay equal wages for jobs of comparable value. For example, if a nurse and an electrician both received approximately the same number of job evaluation points under the point system, they would have to be paid the same wage or salary, regardless of market conditions. This approach to compensation is sought by some people as a means of eliminating the historical gap between the income of men and women, which results in women in Canada earning about 60% as much as men. This gap exists in part because women have traditionally found work in lower-paying occupations—teaching, retailing, nursing, and other areas. Part of the difference results from women often leaving the work force to have and care for children. And part of the difference may result from discrimination. Although the equal value approach may reduce the gap, this compensation theory ignores marketplace realities. If, in the previous example, nurses were paid $20,000 a year and electricians were paid $30,000, the equal value concept would require paying the nurses $30,000 a year even though wage and salary surveys showed the market rate to be $20,000. (To pay the electricians $20,000 would be appropriate under the equal pay for work of equal value doctrine but impractical if their market rate was $30,000 a year.)

In Canada the equal pay for work of equal value concept is already part of the federal Human Rights Act. However, as may be recalled, federal labour and human rights laws apply to only 10% of the Canadian labour force. At the provincial level, only Quebec has enacted a similar law, but it is almost certain that other provinces will follow. For organizations under federal jurisdiction and in Quebec, the equal pay for work of equal value concept poses a major challenge. It requires a restructuring of their wage and salary plans to comply with the law while trying to obtain, maintain, and retain an optimal and cost-effective work force. They may find it more difficult to recruit for certain jobs because demand may exceed supply and rates could not easily be adjusted because of legal restraints.[19]

FINANCIAL INCENTIVE SYSTEMS

Incentive systems provide the clearest link between compensation and performance. Employees who work under a financial incentive system find that their performance determines, in whole or part, their income.

One of the most significant benefits of financial incentives is that better performance is reinforced on a regular basis. Unlike raises and promotions, the reinforcement is generally quick and frequent—usually with each paycheque. Since the worker sees the results of the desired behaviour quickly, that behaviour is more likely to continue. The employer benefits because wages are given in proportion to performance, not for the indirect measure of time worked. And if employees are motivated by the system to expand their output, recruiting expenses for additional employees and capital outlays for new work stations are minimized. As one economist observed:

> With fixed wages individual workers also have little incentive to cooperate with management or to take the initiative in suggesting new ideas for raising productivity. At the level of the individual worker, higher productivity has no immediate payoff—wages are fixed for the length of the contract. The immediate effect of higher productivity is, in fact, negative. Less labor is needed, and the probability of layoffs rises.
>
> The higher productivity growth rates of the Japanese may also be due to their bonus system that encourages labor to take a direct interest in raising productivity.[20]

Offsetting these advantages are significant problems. The administration of an incentive system can be complex. As with any control system, standards have to be established and results measured. For many jobs, the standards and measures are too imprecise or too costly to develop. This means that the incentive system may result in inequities. Some incentive systems require less effort than other systems that pay the same. Sometimes workers make more than their supervisors, who are on salary. Another problem is that the employee may not achieve the standard because of uncontrollable forces, such as work delays or machine breakdowns.

Unions often resist incentive systems because they fear management will change the standard and workers will have to work harder for the same pay. This fear of a speedup often leads to peer pressure against anyone who exceeds the group's output norms. The advantages of the incentive system are essentially lost when group pressures restrict output. And incentives tend to focus efforts on only one aspect (output, sales, or stock prices), sometimes to the exclusion of other dimensions (quality, service, and long-term objectives).

Some of the more common incentive systems follow.

PIECEWORK

Piecework is an incentive system that compensates the worker for each unit of output. Daily or weekly pay is determined by multiplying the output in units times the piece rate per unit. For example, in agricultural labour, workers are often paid a specific amount per bushel of produce picked. Piecework does not always mean higher productivity, however. Group norms may have a more significant impact if peer pressure works against higher productivity. And in many jobs, it may be difficult to measure the person's productive contribution (for example, a receptionist), or the employee may not be able to control the rate of output (for example, an assembly-line worker).

PRODUCTION BONUSES

Production bonuses are incentives paid to workers for exceeding a specified level of output. They are used in conjunction with a base wage rate or salary. Under one approach, the employee receives a predetermined salary or wage. Through extra effort that results in output above the standard, the base compensation is supplemented by a bonus, usually figured at a given rate for each unit of production over the standard. Another variation rewards the employee for saving time. For example, if the standard time for replacing an automobile transmission is four hours and the mechanic does it in three, the mechanic may be paid for four hours. A third method combines production bonuses with piecework by compensating workers on an hourly basis, plus an incentive payment for each unit produced. In some cases, the employee may get a higher piece rate once a minimum number of units are produced. For example, the employee may be paid $6.00 an hour plus $.25 per unit for the first thirty units each day. Beginning with the thirty-first unit, the bonus may become $.35.

COMMISSIONS
In sales jobs, the salesperson may be paid a percentage of the selling price or a flat amount for each unit sold. When no base compensation is paid, the salesperson's total earnings come from commissions. Real estate agents and car salespeople are often paid this form of straight commission.

MATURITY CURVES
What happens when technical or scientific employees reach the top of their rate range? Generally, still higher increases can be achieved only by promotion into a management position. To provide an incentive for technical people, some companies have developed *maturity curves*. Employees are rated on productivity and experience. Outstanding contributors are assigned to the top curve in Figure 14-13. Good, but less outstanding, performers are placed on the next-to-top curve. Through this technique, high-performing professionals continue to be rewarded for their efforts without being forced into a management position to keep increasing their earnings.

EXECUTIVE INCENTIVES
Executive incentives vary widely. Young and middle-aged executives are likely to want *cash bonuses* to meet the needs of a growing or maturing family. As they get older, the need for present income is offset by retirement considerations. Here, bonuses may be deferred until the executive reaches the lower tax rates of retirement.

Executives are sometimes granted stock options—the right to purchase the company's stock at a predetermined price. This price may be set at, below, or above the market value of the stock. Thus the executive has an incentive to improve the company's performance in order to enhance the value of the stock options. Generally, it is considered appropriate to give stock options only to those executives who can have a significant effect on company profits.

Figure 14-13
MATURITY CURVES FOR PROFESSIONALS WITH VARYING DEGREES OF PERFORMANCE

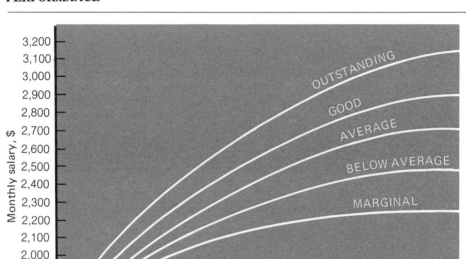

Other forms of executive incentives exist, including incentive systems that allow executives to design their own compensation package. The common element in most executive incentive plans, however, is their relation to the performance of the organization. When these systems do not relate the incentive to performance, no matter what they are called, they are not incentive plans. And, executive incentives are increasingly being geared to promote long-term performance.[21]

GROUP INCENTIVE PLANS

Performance is often a group effort. In recognition of this fact, several plans have been developed to provide incentive for teamwork. Most fall into one of the following categories: production incentives, profit sharing, or cost-reduction plans.

PRODUCTION INCENTIVE PLANS. These plans allow groups of workers to receive bonuses for exceeding predetermined levels of output. They tend to be short-range and related to very specific production goals. A work team may be offered a bonus for exceeding predetermined production levels. Or it may receive a per-unit incentive which results in group piece rate.

One well-publicized example comes from Nucor Corporation, a U.S. steel company.

Nucor's management transformed the company into a steel producer in the late 1960s when the North American steel industry was beginning to face strong competition from European and Japanese producers. Nucor's strategy was to ".... build plants economically and run them very efficiently with high productivity."[22] One of Nucor's tactics was an incentive plan.

Nucor's non-union production workers earned a base wage below that of workers in the United Steelworkers union. But they could supplement their weekly pay with bonuses of 100 to 200% of their base wage if they could reach progressively higher production targets. If production did not reach the target, no bonuses were paid, regardless of the reasons for the production shortfall.

The results? Workers are motivated to work as a team and find improvements. Production employees who do not do their share receive considerable peer pressure to work harder. Employees earn about 20% more than their unionized counterparts and about 250% more than the average hourly-paid production worker in South Carolina, the home of Nucor's flagship steel mill. The company has been able to add mills in Texas, Nebraska, and Utah while producing steel at prices equal to or below foreign producers.[23]

PROFIT-SHARING PLANS. Profit sharing plans share company profits with the workers. The effectiveness of these plans may suffer because profitability is not always related to the employee's performance; a recession or new competitors may have a more significant impact. Even when outside sources do not seriously affect results, it is difficult for employees to perceive their efforts as making much difference. Some companies further reduce the effectiveness of the incentive by diverting the employee's share of profits into retirement plans. Thus the immediate reinforcement value of the incentive is reduced because the incentive is delayed. However, when these plans work well they can have a dramatic impact on the organization, because profit-sharing plans can create a sense of trust and a feeling of common fate among workers and management. One example comes from a leading Canadian producer of steel, Dofasco Inc.

Located in Hamilton, Ontario, Dofasco is one of the largest manufacturers of steel in Canada. Within a very competitive and technologically fast-changing industry Dofasco has become a model of economic efficiency and effectiveness through the development of a "people-oriented" organization.

The company has experienced great success through the mechanisms of a profit-sharing plan (on top of high wages relative to the industry average) and open, sincere, personal communications based upon a healthy and cooperative management-employee relationship. Since the company was founded in 1912 it was never unionized, despite several efforts by the United Steelworkers of America, and since the introduction of its profit-sharing plan in 1938 it has never had an unprofitable year. Employees contribute a maximum of $200 a year to the Employees Savings and Profit-Sharing Fund. The company contributes 11% of its pretax profits, paid out in two ways:

1. For every $1 the employee contributes to the fund, Dofasco pays in $3.00. This contribution is made even if the company must exceed the 11% ceiling, but the deficit is made up from the fund the following year.

2. Once the three-for-one payout is made, any funds remaining up to that ceiling of 11% of pretax profits are divided equally among all fund members. Employees can take the money as cash or put it in a deferred profit-sharing plan to postpone paying tax until retirement. Most opt for cash. Since 1973 the average cash payout has been $913. Last year (1983) it was $2140. Some long-service blue collar workers who let the savings accumulate collected over $200,000 upon retirement.

John Sheppard, executive vice president, concedes that in terms of costs per employee Dofasco is not better off than other steelmakers. If the cost of all the frills are added (recreation program, the famous Christmas party for 35,000 employees and their families) the costs are probably higher. But according to Sheppard, the benefits outweigh the costs. The benefits include the absence of work stoppages, a lower turn-over rate than the industry average, and no fear of strikes. In addition, there are no union demarcation rules. "There is nothing that stops our people from pitching in and helping with something that is not their particular defined job," says Sheppard. "An electrician is allowed to hammer a nail into a piece of wood."[24]

William (Bill) Tinsley, vice president of personnel, puts the profit sharing concept into perspective. "Profit sharing alone," he says, "will not do it. There has to be a compatible atmosphere, trust between management and employees, and a good line of communication. Then it works."[25]

It should be mentioned that the Liberal government under Pierre Trudeau in the 1984 budget speech proposed a tax incentive scheme for employers to implement profit-sharing plans. Starting in January 1985, companies were to get a tax credit of 10%, shared 60/40 between employer and employees, on profits placed in a registered Employee Profit Participation Plan (EPPP). A key point in the EPPP proposal was the requirement to set up an employee-management committee to determine the definition of profits, verify their measurement, and monitor the plan's operation. At the time of the revision of this book (Fall 1984) the new Conservative government had just come into power, leaving the proposal in limbo.

COST-REDUCTION PLANS. Some critics of group incentive plans argue that profit-sharing schemes, such as those found at Dofasco, do not always reward the employees' efforts if profits fall for reasons beyond the employees' control. For example, the average bonus received by workers at Lincoln Electric, a U.S. company with a cost-reduction plan, fell from $22,690 one year to $15,460 the next because of a slowdown in the economy during the early 1980s. Although $15,460 is a considerable bonus, the bonus is influenced by forces outside the employees' control.

Another approach is to reward employees for something they can control: labour costs. Most cost-reduction plans seek to tap employee effort and ideas for ways to reduce costs. Many times, a committee of employees will be formed to open new lines of communications that allow employee ideas to be heard, while the plan allows greater psychological and financial participation in the firm's day-to-day operations. Perhaps the best known of these approaches is the *Scanlon Plan*, which bases bonuses on improvements in labour costs, as compared with historical norms.[26] Under a Scanlon Plan group incentive, employees aim to reduce costs and then they share in those savings. If, for example, employee productivity increases at the Canadian Valve and Hydrant Manufacturing Company, the ratio of payroll costs to net sales revenue improves. These savings are then shared with employees in the form of a bonus. *Rucker* and *Improshare* Plans are similar to the Scanlon approach, but they differ in how bonuses are calculated and in other administrative matters. All three of these approaches differ from profit-sharing in that they focus on something the employee can influence (costs), and not on something which the employees may control only indirectly (profitability).

Compensation consists of more than wages, salaries, and bonuses. Remuneration includes an ever-growing list of fringe benefits and services. Although these benefits are referred to as non-cash compensation, they are a significant part of most employee's total labour costs. The next chapter describes the range of fringe benefits and services offered by employers.

SUMMARY

Employee compensation, if properly administered, can be an effective tool to improve employee performance, motivation, and satisfaction. Pay programs that are mismanaged may lead to high turnover, high absenteeism, more grievances, poor performance, and job dissatisfaction.

For compensation to be appropriate, it must be internally and externally equitable. Through job evaluation techniques, the relative worth of jobs is determined. This assures internal equity. Wage and salary surveys are used to determine external equity. With knowledge of the relative worth of jobs and external pay levels, each job can be properly priced.

The process of wage and salary administration is influenced by several challenges, including union power, the productivity of workers, the company's compensation policies, and government constraints on pay. The Canada Labour Code is the major federal law affecting compensation management. It regulates minimum wages, overtime, and child labour. The Human Rights Act seeks to eliminate sex-based pay differentials. All provinces have similar laws., i.e. labour codes and human rights legislation, for their jurisdictions. (A good example of government constraints on pay is wage and price controls. In 1975 the federal government introduced such a program in order to fight inflation. Pay and price increases were limited to a certain percentage and were controlled by an anti-inflation board. The program was abolished in 1978.)[27]

Another dimension of compensation management is financial incentives. Individual incentives attempt to relate pay to productivity. Group plans have the same objectives, but the relationship is often not as direct or obvious to workers. Some approaches pay a bonus for reaching a production target, others share the company's profits with workers, and still others share savings in labour costs.

TERMS FOR REVIEW

Job evaluations
Job ranking
Job grading
Factor comparison method
Key jobs
Point system
Wage and salary surveys
Rate range
Merit raise

Red-circle rate
Canada Labour Code
Equal pay for work of equal value
Piecework
Production bonuses
Maturity curves
Profit sharing
Scanlon Plan

REVIEW AND DISCUSSION QUESTIONS

1. Suppose you manage a small business with thirty employees. You discover that some people are much motivated by money and others by security. For those who want more money you provide an incentive plan in which their income is determined by their results. The other employees have a fair salary. What problems might arise?
2. Why is job analysis information, discussed in Chapter 5, necessary before job evaluations can be performed?
3. Suppose that when you interview new employees, you ask them what they think is a fair wage or salary. If you hire them, you pay them that amount as long as it is reasonable and not below minimum-wage laws. What problems would you expect?
4. Assume your company has a properly conducted compensation program. If a group of employees ask you why they receive different hourly pay rates even though they perform the same job, how would you respond?
5. Why are the factor comparison method and the point system more widely used than the job ranking or the job grading approaches to job evaluation?
6. If you are told to find out what competitors in your area are paying their employees, how would you get this information without conducting a wage and salary survey?
7. Even after jobs are first priced using a wage-trend line, what other challenges might cause you to adjust some rates upward?
8. Since financial incentives give employees feedback for good performance and they relate pay to performance, why do most companies pay wages and salaries rather than financial incentives?

INCIDENT 14-1
COMPENSATION ADMINISTRATION AT REYNOLDS PLASTIC PRODUCTS

The Reynolds Plastic Products Corporation was recently purchased by a much larger organization, International Plastics Ltd. The personnel director of International

Plastics is concerned that the wage and salary policies are irrational and in some cases actually violate the law. To evaluate the compensation system of the Reynolds Plastic subsidiary, a recent personnel management graduate, Thea Silverstein, was assigned to make an investigation. The key points of her report are summarized below.

A. *The wage range for hourly employees is from $5.70 per hour to $13.96.*

B. *The amount of overtime paid by Reynolds is very modest; overtime is paid for all hours over 180 per month.*

C. *The wage rates for different workers vary widely even on the same job; those employees who are heads of households receive approximately 18% more than those workers who are not heads of households. Most of the heads of households are men.*

D. *On highly technical jobs, the firm pays a rate that is 20% above the prevailing wage rate for these jobs. All other jobs are paid an average of 15% below the prevailing rate.*

E. *Turnover averages a modest 12%. However, in technical jobs turnover is less than 2%; in nontechnical jobs turnover is nearly 20%. Absenteeism follows the same pattern.*

1. What laws are probably being violated?
2. Develop a step-by-step plan of actions you would take and the order in which you would undertake them if you were made personnel director of the Reynolds subsidiary.

INCIDENT 14-2
INCENTIVES AT KARMA RECORDS

Joe Karma owned and operated Karma Records since its founding in 1979. Joe was often heard to say, "I believe in paying people for what they do, not for how many hours they work." This management philosophy was expressed through a variety of incentive plans that Joe designed himself. Although he was firmly committed to the use of incentives, he hired a management consulting team to make recommendations about his compensation programs.

To help the consultants, Joe wrote down the major features of each incentive program. His notes were as follows:

A. *Executives do not own any stock, but they each get $1,000 for each dollar the stock price goes up from the previous year.*

B. *Every time sales go up 10%, all the hourly employees get a day off with pay or can work one day at double-time rates.*

C. *Production workers get paid $.18 for each record they press and $.03 for each record they package.*

D. *Sales personnel get a $50 savings bond each time a new record store or department store starts stocking Karma Records.*

1. What problems do you see with the incentives for (a) executives, (b) hourly workers, (c) production workers, (d) salespeople?
2. If you were a member of the consulting team, what incentives would you recommend for each group?

REFERENCES

1. Milton L. Rock, *Handbook of Wage and Salary Administration*, New York: McGraw-Hill Book Company, 1972, p. xiii.

2. Bert L. Metzger, *Profit Sharing: A Natural for Today's Changing Work Force/Economy*, Evanston, Illinois: Profit Sharing Research Foundation, 1982, p. 7.
3. Edward E. Lawler III, *Pay and Organizational Effectiveness: A Psychological View*, New York: McGraw-Hill Book Company, 1971, p. 71.
4. Ibid., p. 244.
5. David W. Belcher, "Pay Equity or Pay Fairness," *Compensation Review*, Second Quarter 1979, pp. 31–37. See also Elaine Wegener, "Does Competitive Pay Discriminate?" *The Personnel Administrator*, May 1980, pp. 38–43, 66.
6. Thomas M. Hestwood, "Ensuring the Effectiveness of Compensation Programs," *Compensation Review*, First Quarter 1979, p. 14. See also Robert J. Greene, "Thoughts on Compensation Management in the '80s and '90s," *The Personnel Administrator*, May 1980, pp. 27–28.
7. Allan N. Nash and Stephen J. Carroll, Jr., *The Management of Compensation*, Monterey, Calif.: Brooks/Cole Publishing Company, 1975, pp. 109–111; and Richard I. Henderson, *Compensation Management*, Reston, Va.: Reston Publishing Company, 1976, pp. 158–159.
8. Nash and Carroll, op. cit., p. 132.
9. Eugene J. Benge, "Using Factor Methods to Measure Jobs," in Milton L. Rock (ed.), op. cit., pp. 242–256.
10. Nash and Carroll, op. cit., p. 128.
11. Edward Perlin, Irwin Bobby Kaplan, and John M. Curcia, "Clearing Up Fuzziness in Salary Survey Analysis," *Compensation Review*, Second Quarter 1979, pp. 12–25.
12. The least squares method is explained in most introductory statistics books.
13. William A. Evans, "Pay for Performance: Fact or Fable," *Personnel Journal*, September 1970, p. 731.
14. Douglas L. Fleuter, "A Different Approach to Merit Increases," *Personnel Journal*, April 1979, pp. 225–226, 262. See also James T. Brinks, "Is There Merit in Merit Increases?" *The Personnel Administrator*, May 1980, pp. 59–64.
15. Stephen H. Appelbaum and John B. Millard, "Engineering a Compensation Program to Fit the Individual, Not the Job," *Personnel Journal*, March 1976, pp. 121–124.
16. Michael N. Wolfe and Charles W. Candland, "The Impact of the Minimum Wage on Compression," *The Personnel Administrator*, May 1979, pp. 24–28, 40. See also Allen Flamion, "The Dollars and Sense of Motivation," *Personnel Journal*, January 1980, pp. 51–52, 61.
17. Robert F. Johnston, "Equal Pay for Work of Equal Value," *The Canadian Personnel & Industrial Relations Journal*, 18(2) (March 1981): 59–65.
18. Theresa Chruscinski, "Equal Pay Front Pushes Forward," *Financial Post*, April 8, 1981.
19. Hermann F. Schwind, "Equal Pay for Work of Equal Value," *Commercial News*, a publication of the Halifax Board of Trade, July 1981, pp. 28–31.
20. Lester Thurow, "Productivity Pay," *Newsweek*, May 3, 1982, p. 69.
21. Pearl Merey, "Executive Compensation must Promote Long-Term Commitment," *Personnel Administrator*, May 1983, pp. 37–38, 40, 42. See also Carl J. Loomis, "The Madness of Executive Compensation," *Fortune*, July 12, 1982, pp. 42–46.
22. Richard I. Kirkland, Jr., "Pilgrims' Profits at Nucor," *Fortune*, April 6, 1981, p. 44.
23. Ibid., 43–44, 46. See also John Savage, "Incentive Programs at Nucor Corporation Boost Productivity," *Personnel Administrator*, April 1981, pp. 33–36, 49.
24. Andrew Weiner, "In the Family Way", *Canadian Business*, November 1980, pp. 113–124.
25. Personal communication.
26. Robert J. Schulhop, "Five Years with the Scanlon Plan," *Personnel Administrator*, June 1979, pp. 55–60, 62, 92. See also John Hoerr, "Why Labor and Management Are Both Buying Profit Sharing," *Business Week*, January 10, 1983, p. 84; and Richard I. Henderson, "Designing a Reward System for Today's Employee," *Business*, July–August 1982, pp. 2–12.
27. Allan M. Maslow and Gene Swimmer, *Wage Controls in Canada 1975-78: A Study of Public Decision Making*, Toronto: The Institute for Research on Public Policy, 1982.

Chapter *15*

Employee Benefits and Services

In many respects Canada's position in the area of fringe benefits is unique, striking a balance between the situation prevailing in the U.S. and that in Europe.

Bill Megalli[1]

CHAPTER OBJECTIVES

After studying this chapter, you should be able to:
1. **Describe** the objectives of indirect compensation.
2. **Identify** policies that minimize fringe benefit costs.
3. **Explain** the key issues in designing pension plans.
4. **Identify** the administrative problems of employee benefits and services.
5. **Explain** how benefits and services can be better administered.
6. **Cite** benefits and services that are likely to become more common in the future.

To many people, compensation means pay. Anything else an employer might provide is often considered so minor that it is called a "fringe benefit." But since World War II, benefits and services have become a major part of employee compensation. No longer are benefits and services on the "fringe" of employee compensation.

"Did you receive another job offer?" Carla asked her brother.

"Yes. I received a letter yesterday from a bank in Vancouver. That's my problem; I don't know which to accept," Ed responded. "The pay, working conditions, and job duties are almost identical. The people I met at both banks seem equally pleasant."

"What about fringe benefits?" Carla asked.

"What about them? They are only the extras. They don't make much difference," Ed answered.

"They don't make much difference? Are you kidding?" Carla questioned. "Some companies spend half as much on fringe benefits as they do on wages."

"Now who is kidding? They're just fringes," Ed asserted.

"I'm not kidding. Let me give you an example. Suppose one bank pays all your supplementary health and life insurance and the other pays half. At a cost of $1000 a year,

you would be $600 better off with the bank that pays all of your benefits," Carla said confidently.

Ed interrupted, "You mean $500."

"Don't forget taxes," Carla added. "To pay your half of the $1000 you will have to come up with $500, true. But to have $500, you would probably have to earn $600 before taxes. And that is $50 a month."

"Maybe I should find out more about their fringe benefits before I decide," Ed pondered.

When employees like Ed ignore benefits and services, they exclude from consideration all other forms of compensation except pay. Admittedly, pay is a major concern to employees. But since the typical organization spends a considerable share of its labour costs on benefits and services, ignorance like Ed's raises questions about the role of pay and benefits. Simply put, what is the difference between pay and benefits?

Pay is called *direct compensation* because it is based on critical job factors or performance. Benefits and services are *indirect compensation* because they are usually extended as a condition of employment and are not directly related to performance. They include insurance, security, time off, and scheduling benefits, in addition to educational, financial, and social services.

To explain the broad scope of benefits and services, this chapter discusses the objectives in indirect compensation. Then common benefits and services are described. The chapter concludes with an examination of benefit administration. Legally required benefits and services are covered in the following chapter.

THE ROLE OF INDIRECT COMPENSATION

Employee benefits and services seek to satisfy several objectives. These include societal, organizational, and employee objectives.

SOCIETAL OBJECTIVES

Industrial societies have changed from rural nations of *independent* farmers and small businesses to urban nations of *interdependent* wage earners. This interdependence was illustrated forcefully by the mass unemployment of the Great Depression of the 1930s. Since that time, industrial societies have sought group solutions to societal problems.

To solve social problems and provide security for interdependent wage earners, governments rely on the support of employers. Through favourable tax treatment, employees can receive most benefits tax-free, while employers can deduct the cost of benefits as a regular business expense. The result has been a rapid growth in indirect compensation since World War II.

Today, benefits and services give many employees financial security against illness, disability, and retirement. In fact, the growth of fringe benefits since World War II means that the average employer spends over one-third of its payroll costs on benefits and services. No longer are benefits those "little extras" or "fringes." These outlays are a major and growing cost of doing business. As seen in Figure 15-1, the importance of such outlays has grown dramatically during the last twenty years. If this trend continues, benefits and services could amount to over one-half of most firms' payroll costs in the 1990s.

Figure 15-1

BENEFITS AND OTHER NONWAGE AND SALARY COST COMPARISONS FOR CANADIAN COMPANIES FROM 1954 TO 1980*

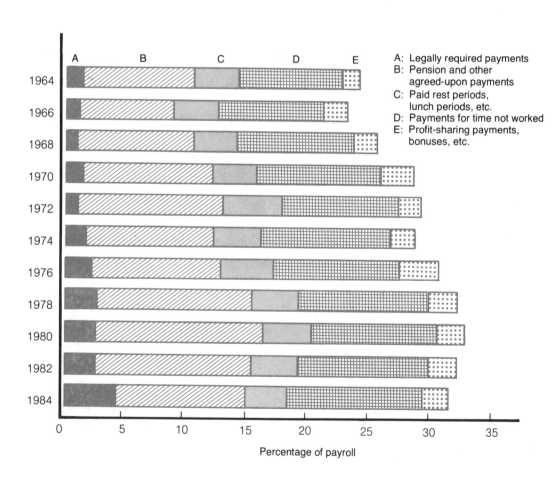

Source: Thorne Stevenson & Kellogg, "Employee Benefits in Canada," *Annual Surveys from 1954–1984.* Used with permission.
Graphic: Hermann F. Schwind.

ORGANIZATIONAL OBJECTIVES

From these large outlays for fringe benefits, what do employers gain? Companies must offer some fringe benefits if they are to be able to recruit successfully in the labour market. If a company did not offer retirement plans and paid vacations, recruits and present employees would work for competitors who would offer these "fringes." Similarly, many employees will stay with a company because they do not want to give up benefits, so employee turnover is lowered by benefits. For example, employees may stay to save pension credits or their rights to the extended vacations that typically come with greater seniority.

Vacations, along with holidays and rest breaks, help employees reduce fatigue and may enhance productivity during the hours the employees do work. Similarly, retirement, health care, and disability benefits may allow workers to be more productive by freeing them from concern about medical and retirement costs. Likewise, if these benefits were not available to employees, they might elect to form a union and collectively bargain with the employer. (Although collective action is legal, many nonunion employers prefer to remain nonunion.) Therefore, it is accurate to state that indirect compensation may:

- Reduce fatigue
- Discourage labour unrest
- Satisfy employee objectives
- Aid recruitment
- Reduce turnover
- Minimize overtime costs

EMPLOYEE OBJECTIVES

Employees usually seek employer-provided benefits and services because of lower costs and availability. For example, company insurance benefits usually are less expensive because the employer may pay some or all of the costs. Even when the workers must pay the entire premium, rates are often lower because group plans save the insurer the administrative and selling costs of many individual policies. With group plans, the insurer also can reduce the *adverse selection* of insuring just those who need the insurance. Actuaries—the specialists who compute insurance rates—can pass these savings on to policyholders in the form of lower premiums.

Lower income taxes are another employee objective. For example, an employee in a 20% tax bracket has to earn $1,000 to buy an $800 policy. But for $1,000, the employer can buy the same insurance policy and give the worker a $200 raise. After taxes, the employee can keep $160 and the policy, while the employer is no worse off. And in many cases, the "buying power" of the company can allow it to negotiate a lower cost for the insurance policy. So the policy might cost only $600 instead of $800. Added to the $200 raise, the employer's outlays are only $800. By paying the employee to buy his or her own policy, the cost would have been $1,000.

When the employer pays for a benefit, the employee achieves the benefit of partially being protected from inflation. For example, a two-week paid vacation is not reduced in value by inflation. The employee still gets two weeks off with pay. Or if a completely employer-paid insurance premium rises from $800 to $900, the worker is protected (although pay raises may be smaller since the employer has less money available for pay).

For some employees, the primary objective may be to obtain benefits and services—especially supplementary health and life insurance. Without employer-provided insurance, these policies may not be obtainable if the employee has a pre-existing medical condition.

The objectives of society, organizations, and employees have encouraged rapid growth of benefits and services. This growth has affected all areas of fringe benefits and services, including insurance, security, time-off, and scheduling benefits.

INSURANCE BENEFITS

Insurance benefits spread the financial risks encountered by employees and their families. These risks are shared by pooling funds in the form of insurance premiums. Then, when an insured risk occurs, the covered employees or their families are compensated.

LIFE INSURANCE

Life insurance was the first form of insurance offered to workers by employers. As a result, "group life insurance has become a practically universal element in corporate employee benefit programs."[2] In a recent survey which covered 171 large and small companies in Canada, 98.8% of the companies reported that they provide a group life insurance program for all of their employees.[3]

In the majority of firms, the amount of life insurance is a multiple of the employee's salary. For example, if the multiple is 2, a $20,000-a-year worker has $40,000 of coverage. A few firms provide a flat amount for all workers. Employer-provided life insurance is typically not extended to the worker's family members. Most personnel managers and benefits experts reason that life insurance is to protect the family from the loss of the worker's income. However, since group life insurance is considerably cheaper than most private policies, supplemental life insurance may be available; these policies allow employees to increase their coverage or include dependants. But employees must pay for this coverage.

HEALTH-RELATED INSURANCE

In Canada all citizens are covered by provincial health care programs which pay for basic hospital care and offer comprehensive coverage for medically required services of physicians, surgeons, and other qualified health professionals. For this reason, employers in Canada offer only supplementary health insurance plans. This is in contrast to the U.S., where health insurance is the most common form of coverage.[4]

SUPPLEMENTARY HEALTH INSURANCE PLANS. The purpose of supplementary health insurance plans is to provide coverage for health care costs that are not included in provincial health care plans, such as private or semiprivate rooms. Some supplementary plans provide for the payment of any amount in excess of the maximum coverage for a particular benefit as stipulated by the provincial plans. Other plans specify either some maximum overall coverage or some maximum coverage for specified services. Most employers bear the total cost of supplemental health plans; approximately one-third pay between 50% and 100%.[5]

DENTAL INSURANCE. Dental insurance plans are one of the fastest-growing additions to the total benefit package.[6] According to the latest survey, 86% of the employers who responded offered dental plans.[7] Such plans, most of which are custom-designed, are usually provided at three levels: (1) simple fillings, x-rays, and extractions; (2) major restorative work such as bridgework, dentures, and crowns; (3) orthodontic work. Provincial dental plans cover emergency dental services required as a result of accidents. In addition, many provinces provide a limited dental care program for children.

SALARY CONTINUATION PLANS. If an employee misses a few days because of illness, it is usually not crucial from a financial point of view, since most employers grant paid sick leave for a limited time. It becomes more of a problem when an employee becomes disabled for a longer period of time or even permanently. Canadian companies offer short-term disability and long-term disability plans.

SHORT-TERM DISABILITY PLANS. Short-term disability plans comprise a variety of arrangements which provide sick or injured employees, temporarily incapable of working, with some form of income. The most common arrangement is the formal paid-sick-leave plan, financed and administered by the employer. Such a plan usually involves crediting or allocating a certain number of days to an employee, to be used as sick leave for nonoccupational accidents or illnesses. Sick-leave credits may be cumulative or noncumulative. A plan is cumulative if insured credits earned during one year may be transferred to the following year; it is noncumulative when the employee's entitlement is reviewed on a yearly basis or after each illness. In one survey all of the participating 171 companies offered paid-sick-leave plans.[8]

Another arrangement is the sickness indemnity insurance plan. This is an insured income protection plan provided through an insurance company or outside agency. The employer pays either all or part of the premiums. The typical plan will cover benefits only over a specified time interval and has a waiting period for illness which is waived in cases of accident. Benefits paid are usually expressed as a percentage of weekly earnings. Some companies offer a combination of formal paid-sick-leave and sickness indemnity insurance plans.

LONG-TERM DISABILITY PLANS. For workers who are disabled for a prolonged time, employers offer some form of long-term disability insurance. Such plans generally have a long waiting period (six months is very common), and they pay the employee only a fraction (usually 50 or 60%) of the income that working would have earned. Under most plans these payments, if necessary, are made until the normal retirement age is reached.[9]

OTHER INSURANCE PLANS

The economics of group plans has led a few companies to provide a variety of other insurance programs. Some employers offer group homeowners' and group automobile insurance. Since individual rates vary widely, and not all employees have homes or cars, employers seldom contribute to the cost of these premiums. More common is liability insurance which protects employees from legal action resulting from the performance of their normal duties. In contrast to the group insurance plans mentioned above, employers contribute to the cost of liability insurance.

A new benefit that is more likely to become widespread is group legal services. Under these plans employees gain access to low-cost legal services. "The basic premise is akin to group medical programs. By pooling prepaid amounts, organized group members can obtain legal assistance that might not be readily available to individuals."[10] Personnel departments usually control these costs through maximum dollar limits on total services received per year, or a dollar limit on each type of legal service, such as selling a house, handling a divorce, or drawing up a will. At present, the major force encouraging these plans is unions through their negotiations with employers.

EMPLOYEE SECURITY BENEFITS

In addition to insurance, there are noninsurance benefits that enhance employee security. These benefits seek to ensure an income before and after retirement.

EMPLOYMENT INCOME SECURITY

Discharges or layoffs may entail severe economic consequences for an employee; the impact, however, can be cushioned by employer-provided benefits. If employees have not been given at least two weeks' notice and if the dismissal was not for just cause, then according to the Canada Labour Code they are entitled to *severance pay* equal to two weeks' regular wages. For executives, who usually work on a contract basis, severance pay can reach six months' or a year's compensation.

Layoffs may be eased by accrued vacation pay. A few companies go so far as to provide a *guaranteed annual wage* (GAW). These plans assure the worker of receiving some minimum amount of work or pay. For example, employees may be promised a minimum of 1,500 hours of work or pay a year (compare this with the "normal" fifty-two forty-hour weeks for a total of 2,080 hours). Some employers guarantee thirty hours per week. Even on layoff, the employees draw some income.

The auto industry is a leader in another method, *supplemental unemployment benefits* (SUB). When employees are out of work, unemployment insurance benefits are supplemented by the employer from monies previously paid to the SUB fund. This assures covered employees an income almost equal to their previous earnings for as long as the SUB fund remains solvent.

Alfredo Sedona was put on indefinite layoff. Under the SUB plan, he is entitled to 95% of his previous take-home pay, less $22.00 that would otherwise go for commuting, lunches, and other work-related expenses.

Alfredo typically took home $260 a week. Therefore, he will get $225 [($260 × 0.95) − $22.00]. Since unemployment insurance benefits will pay Alfredo $156 a week, the SUB plan will pay him $69.00 a week ($225 − 156 = $69.00). Alfredo will get $225 until the SUB fund is depleted, he finds another job, or he is called back to work.

Although SUB plans are expensive, personnel specialists find that a very high percentage of workers are available for work when recalled. This high return rate occurs because few auto workers find jobs that pay as much as they are receiving while on layoff.

RETIREMENT SECURITY

Retirement plans were originally designed to reward long-service employees. Through employer generosity and union pressure, retirement plans have grown in scope and coverage, so that in Canada the average firm spends 6.3% of its total payroll costs on government and private pension plans alone.[11]

PRIVATE PENSION PLANS (PPP). Approximately 40% of all Canadian employees are covered by PPP. Most employers contribute to such plans. *Integrated PPP*—which make up approximately two-thirds of all PPP—take into account benefits received from the Canada Pension Plan.[12] (See the discussion in the following chapter.)

DEVELOPING A RETIREMENT PLAN. When a personnel department decides to develop a retirement plan, several critical questions must be answered. One is: Who will pay for it? In a *noncontributory plan*, the employer pays the entire amount. *Contributory plans* require both the employee and the employer to contribute.

Another question is: When will the pension rights vest? *Vesting* gives the workers the right to pension benefits even if they leave the company. Pension rights usually vest after several years of service. If an employee leaves before pension benefits are vested, the worker has no rights except to regain his or her contributions to the plan. Some pensions have *portability clauses*. They allow accumulated pension rights to be transferred to another employer.

A third question is: How will the firm meet its financial obligations? Some companies pay pensions out of current income when employees retire. This is called an *unfunded plan*. *Funded plans* require the employer to accumulate monies in advance so that the employer's contribution plus interest will cover the pension obligation.

Another important question is: Will the plan be *trusted* or *insured*? The trusted plan calls for all monies to be deposited into a trust fund, usually with a trust company. The company manages and protects the funds. It does not guarantee that the employer's pension liabilities will be met. These guarantees are provided by provincial or federal legislation covering pensions. With an insured plan, the pension monies are used to buy employee annuities from the insurer. Each annuity represents an insurance company's pledge to pay the worker a given amount per month upon retirement.

Two significant problems have developed in the administration of pension plans. First, some employers go out of business, leaving the pension plan unfunded or only partially funded. Second, some companies minimize their pension costs by having very long vesting periods. Thus an employee who quits or is fired often has no pension rights. Since both of these problems may impose hardships on employees and on the nation's welfare burden, Parliament has passed the *Pension Benefits Standards Act*.

PENSION BENEFITS STANDARDS ACT. This act regulates pension plans in industries under the jurisdiction of the Government of Canada, such as banks, railways, shipping companies, and radio and other communication companies. In addition, six provinces (Alberta, Saskatchewan, Manitoba, Ontario, Quebec, and Nova Scotia) have enacted their own pension benefits acts which in content are similar to the federal act. Pension plans in the remaining provinces, to qualify for tax deductions, must conform to certain standards set forth in the federal legislation. The Pension Benefits Standards Act requires that pension funds be held in trust for members, and that the funds not be held under the complete custody and control of either the employer or the employees. To accomplish this the funding of a private pension plan must be carried out by one or more of the following means:

• an insurance contract with a company authorized to conduct a life insurance business in Canada;

• a trust in Canada whose trustees are either a trust company or a group of individuals, at least three of whom live in Canada and one of whom must be independent of the employer and employees;

• a corporate pension society;

• an arrangement administered by the Government of Canada or a provincial government.

EARLY RETIREMENT. As retirement plans mature, companies tend to liberalize them. Increasingly, this has meant early retirement provisions, which allow workers to retire before age sixty-five. Benefits are normally reduced for early retirement, because statistically the employee draws benefits longer and the employer has less time to fund its share of the pension. Some pensions—those used by the military, for example—pay the retiree an amount based on years of service, regardless of age.

RETIREMENT COUNSELLING. As part of the retirement program, some employers conduct pre-retirement and post-retirement counselling. The primary purpose of *pre-retirement counselling* is to encourage the employee to plan for retirement. The sooner counselling occurs, the more able the worker is to prepare emotionally and financially. These sessions are also used to explain the nature of the employee's retirement program and indicate the likely adjustments a retiree may face.

Post-retirement counselling is designed to ease the transition from worker to retiree. The retiree is made aware of community and company programs for retired people. Retired employees of Ontario Hydro, for example, can join an organization of other retired Hydro employees. This type of association provides social contacts, community projects, and recreational opportunities.

PAID TIME-OFF BENEFITS

Time periods during which the employee is not working but is getting paid are the result of time-off benefits. Although time-off benefits may seem minor, according to one survey they were the costliest major category, comprising 14.9% of gross annual payroll.[13] (See Figure 15-1).

ON-THE-JOB BREAKS

Some of the most common forms of time-off benefits are those found on the job. Examples include rest breaks, meal breaks, and wash-up time. Through a break in the physical and mental effort of a job, productivity may be increased. The major problem for personnel and line managers is the tendency of employees to stretch these time-off periods.

When one personnel manager was confronted by a supervisor with the problem of stretched breaks, she suggested a simple solution. Each employee was assigned a specific break time—from 9:15 to 9:30 A.M., or 9:30 to 9:45 A.M., for example—but could not leave for break until the preceding employee returned. Since each clerk was anxious to go on break, the peer group policed the length of breaks and the stretched breaks ended.

PAID SICK LEAVE

Absences from work are unavoidable. Today, most companies pay workers when they are absent for medical reasons by granting a limited number of days of sick leave per year. Unfortunately, this is one of the most abused fringe benefits; many workers take the attitude that these are simply extra days off. If the personnel policies prohibit employees from crediting unused sick leave to next year's account, absences increase near the end of the year. To minimize abuses, some companies require medical verifications of illness or pay employees for unused sick leave.

A few firms avoid the abuse question by granting "personal leave days." This approach allows an employee to skip work for any reason and get paid, up to a specified number of days per year. *Sick leave banks* allow employees to "borrow" extra days above the specified number when they use up their individual allocation. Then when they earn additional days, the days are repaid to the sick leave bank.

HOLIDAYS AND VACATIONS

The average company grants eleven holidays. Like sick leave, however, this benefit is subject to abuse. Employees sometimes try to stretch the holiday by missing the work day before or after the holiday. Personnel policies that require attendance the day before and after the holiday as a condition of holiday pay lessen this problem.

Vacations are usually based on the employee's length of service, but federal and provincial laws specify a two- (in Saskatchewan three-) week minimum vacation entitlement. In some regions this increases to three weeks (in Saskatchewan four) after five, six, or ten years of service.

Policies for vacations vary widely. Some companies allow employees to use vacation days a few at a time. Other companies insist that the worker take the vacation all at once. A few employers actually close down during designated periods and require vacations to be taken during this period. Still other companies negate the reason for vacations completely by allowing employees to work and receive vacation pay as a bonus.

LEAVES OF ABSENCE

Leaves of absence are often granted for pregnancy, extended illness, accidents, summer military camps, jury duty, funeral services, and other reasons specified in a company's personnel policies. Extended leaves are normally without pay. Shorter absences—especially for jury duty or funerals of close relatives—are often with pay.

WORK SCHEDULING BENEFITS

The length of the typical workweek has declined significantly since the early days of the Industrial Revolution, as illustrated by Figure 15-2. A norm of a five-day, forty-hour workweek remained relatively unchanged from the 1930s to the early 1970s. During the 1970s, however, several new approaches to scheduling work gained popularity: the shorter workweek, flextime, and job sharing.[14]

Figure 15-2
A TYPICAL WORK SCHEDULE 100 YEARS AGO

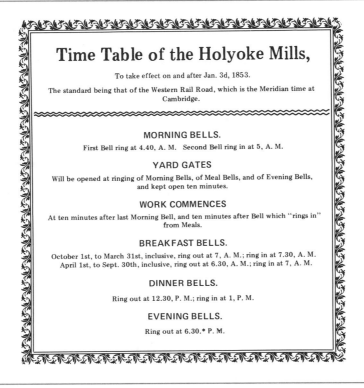

Source: *Labor's Long, Hard Road*, Air Line Employees Association, International, p. 4. Used by permission.

SHORTER WORKWEEKS

A shorter workweek compresses forty hours of work into less than five full days. Some plans even shorten the workweek to less than forty hours. The most popular version has been forty hours of work compressed into four days. Figure 15-3 summarizes the major advantages and disadvantages commonly associated with shorter workweeks. The rankings of these factors are based on a U.S. survey of 223 firms.

The idea for a shorter workweek developed in 1973 in western Canada when the Oil, Chemical and Atomic Workers' International Union bargained for and was granted reduced working hours for 10,000 petrochemical and petroleum industry workers. Soon afterwards it suggested to management that workers be allowed to complete their thirty-seven and one-third hours in four days, giving them a free Friday. After a trial period, this feature became permanent. Although some companies are reluctant to change their schedules, employees generally seem to enjoy the greater opportunity for leisure activities. A survey in Ontario covered 10,600 employees in 175 com-

Figure 15-3
PERCEIVED ADVANTAGES AND DISADVANTAGES OF THE
SHORTER WORKWEEK

Perceived Advantages of the Shorter Workweek

Rank Order	Percentage of Responses	Potentially Advantageous Factors
1	18.8	Less total time would be lost due to startup, washup, breaks, and cleanup.
2	15.8	Absenteeism and turnover rates will be lower.
3	13.2	Efficiency would increase through better utilization of our equipment.
4	12.9	Employee morale and loyalty will be higher.
5	8.1	It would be good public relations and create a progressive image.
6	7.9	It will stimulate employee motivation and higher productivity.
7	7.2	More employees could be scheduled at peak workload days or times.
8	6.2	It would be easier to recruit a large supply of good workers.
9	5.7	It would provide an opportunity to implement other important changes.
10	4.1	It would fulfill the firm's social responsibility to our employees.

Perceived Disadvantages of the Shorter Workweek

Rank Order	Percentage of Responses	Potentially Disadvantageous Factors
1	22.1	Customers or suppliers would be inconvenienced.
2	20.3	It would create too many scheduling and communications problems.
3	12.9	Productivity would be lower once the novelty wore off.
4	12.1	All hours over eight per day would probably have to be paid as overtime.
5	9.7	The long hours would be boring, monotonous, and tiresome for employees.
6	7.7	Too many employees would be fatigued from moonlighting on second jobs.
7	7.2	If it fails, returning to the five-day workweek will be difficult.
8	4.0	Absenteeism and/or turnover would be greater under a shorter workweek.
9	3.1	Employees would dislike and resist the idea.
10	0.9	We might get bad publicity because as yet the program is not widely accepted.

Source: John W. Newstrom and William B. Werther, Jr., "Managerial Perceptions of the Shorter Workweek," *Arizona Business*, February 1973, pp. 10, 11. Used by permission.

panies where the short workweek had been implemented. The majority of employees reported improved employee morale, greater continuity in the work process, higher productivity, and lower absenteeism.[15]

FLEXTIME

Flextime abolishes rigid starting and ending times for the workday. Instead, employees are allowed to report to work at any time during a range of hours. For example, starting time may be from 7 A.M. to 9 A.M., with all employees expected to work the core hours of 9 A.M. to 3 P.M.. The workday usually remains unchanged at eight hours. Therefore, the end of the workday is variable also.

The outcome of a flextime program, however, is contingent upon the nature of the firm's operations. For example, the major disadvantage of flextime is the difficulty in meeting minimum staffing needs early and late in the day. Assembly-line and customer service operations find this problem to be especially significant. But in many operations users have reported noteworthy successes.[16]

JOB SHARING

A third approach to employee scheduling that gained popularity during the 1970s is job sharing. *Job sharing* involves one or more employees doing the same job but working different hours, days, or even weeks. Most commonly, two people handle the duties of one full-time job.

Karen and Bob Rosen both taught English at Queen Elizabeth High School. After Karen had her first child one summer, Karen, Bob, and their principal agreed to a job-sharing arrangement. Bob taught three classes of Engligh literature and composition in the morning. He then drove home, gave Karen the car, and she returned to school and taught three English classes in the afternoon. The school benefitted because teachers normally had five classes and a planning period. With job sharing, the school received six classes of English instruction. Also, Bob and Karen were able to share in raising their child with neither of them completely giving up a career.

The major advantage claimed for job sharing is increased productivity from workers who are not fatigued. Problems arise from the increased paperwork and administrative burden associated with two employees' doing the job of one. Another problem is that of fringe benefits. Personnel specialists are forced to decide whether job sharers should be given benefits equal with other employees or benefits that are scaled down in proportion to the employee's hours.[17]

EMPLOYEE SERVICES

Some companies go beyond pay and traditional benefits. They also provide educational, financial, and social services for their employees.

EDUCATIONAL ASSISTANCE

Tuition refund programs are among the more common employer services. These programs partially or completely reimburse employees for furthering their education. They may be limited only to courses that are related to the employee's job, or the employer may reimburse workers for any educational expenditure. In the future, more companies may follow the lead of Kimberly-Clark Corporation in the U.S.:

Kimberly-Clark created an educational savings account for employees and their dependents. The company gives employees credits for each year of service. Then when an employee or dependent wants to go to college, he or she can be reimbursed partially from the educational savings account established by the company.

FINANCIAL SERVICES

Probably the oldest service is employee discount plans. These programs—common among retail stores and consumer goods manufacturers—allow workers to buy products from the company at a discount.

Credit unions are another well-established employee service. The interest collected by the credit union on loans and investments is distributed to members in the form of dividends. The dividends (interest payments) are allocated in proportion to the amount employees have in their share (savings) account. The lower interest rate on loans, the higher interest on deposits, and payroll deductions for savings or loan repayment are the major employee advantages.

Stock purchase programs are another financial service. These plans enable employees to buy company stock—usually through payroll deductions. In some stock purchase programs, employee outlays may be matched by company contributions.

Profit sharing, increasingly popular in the United States, has attracted relatively little interest in the Canadian business community; a recent study included only eighty-three companies, in contrast to more than 300,000 in the U.S.[18] Three types of profit sharing plans exist in Canada:

1. *Current distribution* plans, which distribute a share of a company's profits to all employees in direct cash payments or company stock.

2. *Deferred payout* plans of two kinds: (*a*) employee profit sharing plans (EPSP) and (*b*) deferred profit sharing plans (DPSP), as defined in Sections 144 and 147 of the Income Tax Act. Both plans allow for deferred tax payments until the profits are actually paid out.

3. *Combination* plans, wherein plans 1 and 2 may be combined.

SOCIAL SERVICES

A wide range of social services is provided by employers. At one extreme are simple interest groups such as bowling leagues and softball teams. At the other extreme are comprehensive *employee assistance programs* designed to assist employees with personal problems.

A large bank had a high turnover rate among its entry-level workers. After study, it appeared that many new workers had transportation, housing, child-care, and other problems. These difficulties were sometimes insurmountable for employees, and they would quit. To combat this situation, the bank created its "Contact" program. Each employee was informed of the program and given the telephone number to call whenever a work or non-work-related problem occurred. Then when employees had child-care or transportation difficulties, they would call the Contact number. The Contact staff provided individual counselling or a referral service by informing employees of groups in the community that could help them. The program was not limited to just new employees, however. To help build better employee relations, the Contact staff tried to assist with all types of employee problems. This involved the staff in resolving employee quarrels, advising managers of employee complaints, and even helping workers solve family disputes.

Although employee assistance programs like the one at this bank are rare, personnel managers realize that employee problems affect company performance. Employer services that can lessen these problems offer potential dividends in employee performance, loyalty, and turnover.

One employer service with a growing record of success is alcoholic and drug rehabilitation. For example, personnel experts formerly recommended the discharge of alcoholic workers. During the last ten years, however, an increasing number of personnel departments have implemented *alcohol and drug rehabilitation programs*. This service has saved many otherwise good employees in companies such as Canadian National Railways and General Motors of Canada, Ltd. When rehabilitation has been effected, the company usually gains a hardworking, loyal employee.

Canadian National Railways (CNR) spends $300,000 to run an employee assistance program (EAP), 85% of which is devoted to employees having alcohol-related or drug-related problems. CNR has twelve trained counsellors who deal with 400 problem drinkers annually. The company estimates that 80% of the 3,000 workers referred to its EAP were rehabilitated, saving the company approximately $5 million.[19]

Relocation programs are the support in dollars or services a company provides to its transferred or new employees. At a minimum, this benefit includes payment for moving expenses. Some employees receive fully paid house-hunting trips with their spouse to the new location before the move, subsidized home mortgages, placement assistance for working spouses, and even family counselling to reduce the stress of the move. A transferred employee also may be able to sell his or her home to the employer for the appraised value in order to avoid having to sell it.[20]

Additional employee assistance activities are discussed in Chapter 18, in connection with counselling.

ADMINISTRATION OF BENEFITS AND SERVICES

A serious shortcoming of personnel management has been poor administration of indirect compensation. Even in otherwise well-managed personnel departments, benefits and services have grown in a haphazard manner.

Those costly supplements were introduced in response to social trends, union demands, employee pressures, and management wishes, and so personnel departments seldom established objectives, systematic plans, and standards to determine the appropriateness of benefits and services. This patchwork of benefits and services has caused several problems.

PROBLEMS IN ADMINISTRATION

The central problem in supplementary compensation is a lack of employee participation. Once a fringe benefit program is designed by the personnel department and the labour union (if there is one), employees have little discretion. For example, pension and maternity benefits usually are granted to all workers equally. Younger employees see pensions as distant and largely irrelevant; older workers find maternity benefits are not needed. This uniformity fails to recognize individual differences and wishes. Admittedly, uniformity leads to administrative and actuarial economies; but when employees receive benefits they neither want nor need, these economies are questionable.

Since employees have little choice in their individual benefit package, most workers are unaware of all of the benefits to which they are entitled.

Two researchers designed a study to learn how knowledgeable selected workers were about their benefits. In two different plants—one with a union and one without—they asked employees to list all the benefits that they could recall. The average employee could not recall 15% of the employer-provided benefits.[21]

Ignorance and the inability to influence the mix of benefits often lead to pressure from employees for more benefits to meet their needs. For example, older workers may request improved retirement plans, while younger workers seek improved insurance coverage of dependents. Often the result is a proliferation of benefits and increased employer costs. These costs, which represented 15.10% of an employee's gross annual payroll in 1953, have escalated to 32.5% in 1984, an increase of 115%.[22] Still, employee ignorance and confusion can lead to complaints and dissatisfaction about their fringe benefit package.

TRADITIONAL REMEDIES

The traditional remedy to benefit problems has been to increase employee awareness, usually through publicizing employee benefits. This publicity starts with orientation sessions that explain the benefit programs and provide employee handbooks. Company newspapers, special mailings, employee meetings, bulletin-board announcements, and responses to employee questions are also used to further publicize the organization's benefit package.

William M. Mercer Ltd., a large consulting firm specializing in compensation and benefit issues, with branches in twelve cities in Canada, offers seminars to recipients of benefits and training courses to compensation officers. Interested employees of a client may ask for an individual assessment and for recommendations on more effective coverage.

Publicizing the benefits and services attacks only the symptoms of the problem: lack of employee interest. Moreover, this reactive approach further adds to the costs of administration through increased "advertising" expenses.

A PROACTIVE SOLUTION: CAFETERIA BENEFITS

Cafeteria benefit programs, or variable fringe benefit programs, allow employees to select benefits and services that match their individual needs. Workers are provided a benefit and services account with a specified number of dollars in the account. Through deductions from this account, employees shop for specific benefits from among those offered by the employer. The types and prices of benefits are provided to each employee in the form of a computer printout. This cost sheet also describes each benefit. Then, as illustrated in Figure 15-4, employees select their package of benefits and services for the coming year.

Figure 15-4
HYPOTHETICAL BENEFIT SELECTION OF TWO DIFFERENT WORKERS

Worker A		Worker B
Age 27, female, married with one child. Husband in graduate school.		Age 56, male, married with two grown and married children. Wife does not work.
	Supplemental health insurance:	
$245	Maternity	0
935	$100 deductible	0
0	Prescription drug coverage	$625
	Life insurance:	
100	$20,000 for worker	100
150	$10,000 for spouse	0
600	Vacations	900
300	Holidays	300
200	Pension plan	1,270
0	Jury duty pay	0
100	Disability insurance	100
870	Weekly income benefit	205
$3,500	Total	$3,500

Figure 15-4 indicates how two different workers might spend the $3,500 the company grants each worker. Workers A and B select two different sets of benefits because their personal situations differ dramatically. Worker A is a young parent who is supporting a family and her husband. If they were to have another child or if they had some other health-related expense, it might seriously affect their plans, so they have elected to be well insured for pregnancy and supplemental health costs. Worker B can more easily *afford unexpected medical expenses, so he bought less supplemental health insurance and allocated fewer dollars for weekly income benefits. Instead, he put a large portion of his benefit monies into the company pension plan.*

Although this approach creates additional administrative costs and an obligation for the personnel department to advise employees, there are several advantages. The main advantage is employee participation. Through participation, employees come to understand exactly what benefits the employer is offering. And employees can better match their benefits with their needs.[23]

SUMMARY

Employee benefits and services are the fastest-growing component of compensation. Employers have sought to expand them to discourage labour unrest, respond to employee pressures, and remain competitive in the labour market. Employees have desired to obtain benefits and services through their employer because of the low costs, tax advantages, and inflation protection they provide.

Benefits are classified into four major types: insurance, security, time-off, and scheduling benefits. Services include educational, financial, and social programs. This diversity contributes to several serious administrative problems. The most significant problem is the orientation of managers and personnel specialists toward cost savings. In pursuit of administrative and actuarial economies, most companies and unions do not allow individualized benefit packages in indirect compensation programs.

TERMS FOR REVIEW

Long-term disability insurance
Severance pay
Guaranteed annual wage (GAW)
Supplemental unemployment
 benefits (SUB)
Vesting
Portability clauses

Canada Pension Plan
Contributory plans
Pension Benefits Standards Act
Shorter workweek
Flextime
Job sharing
Cafeteria benefit programs

REVIEW AND DISCUSSION QUESTIONS

1. What factors have contributed to the rapid growth of fringe benefits since World War II?
2. Suppose you are a benefits administrator at Air Canada and you discover that health-care costs had increased from $0.15 to $0.90 per hour in recent years. What actions would you recommend to control these rising costs?
3. Suppose you are requested to explain why employees are better off receiving pay and benefits rather than just getting larger paycheques that include the monetary value of benefits. What arguments will you use?

4. Briefly describe the benefits that an organization might give employees to provide them with greater financial security.
5. Why was the Pension Benefits Standards Act needed? What are its major provisions?
6. For each of the following groups of employees, what types of problems are likely to occur if a company goes from a five-day, forty-hour week to a four-day, forty-hour week: (a) working mothers, (b) labourers, (c) assembly-line workers?
7. What are the common problems you would expect to find with the benefits and services program of a large company?
8. If you were asked to increase employee awareness of fringe benefits, what actions would you take without changing the way the company provides benefits? If you could change the entire benefits program, what other methods would you use to increase employee awareness?

INCIDENT 15-1
SOAP PRODUCERS AND DISTRIBUTORS LTD.

Soap Producers and Distributors Ltd. faced a severe employee turnover problem. The company's annual turnover rate was nearly 40% among technical and white-collar workers. Among hourly paid employees, the rate was nearly 75%.

Wage and salary surveys repeatedly showed that company's pay levels were 10 to 12% above comparable jobs in the labour market. The fringe benefit program was not as impressive, but management thought it was competitive. Employees received supplementary health and life insurance, paid vacations and holidays, and a Christmas bonus of $100. Although some employees complained about the company's benefits, complaints varied widely and no one benefit or lack of benefit seemed to be the key issue.

To make Soap Producers and Distributors' problems worse, they operated in a tight labour market, which meant jobs sometimes took weeks to fill. To hire specialized workers almost always meant recruiting them from other cities and paying their moving expenses.

1. What additions do you think should be made to the company's fringe benefit program?
2. What problem in the incident might be solved by a cafeteria approach?
3. To overcome the company's recruitment problems, what other changes do you suggest?

INCIDENT 15-2
INTERNATIONAL SEA PRODUCTS' PENSION PLAN

In 1962 International Sea Products Ltd. established a private, noncontributory pension plan for all workers who had twenty years of service with the company. After the twenty years, workers were eligible for a pension beginning at the age of sixty-five. The pension plan was funded by putting 2½% of each year's payroll into a trust fund administered by the company's vice president of finance. Although employees were told that there was an employer-paid pension fund, little explanation of the plan was offered. Whenever questioned, the president of the company would only state: "This company takes care of loyal employees."

1. What changes should be made in this company's pension plan to comply with the Pension Benefits Standards Act?
2. What other changes would you recommend to increase the effectiveness of the pension plan in improving employee morale?

REFERENCES

1. Bill Megalli, "The Fringe Benefit Debate," *Labour Gazette*, July 1978, p. 313.
2. Mitchell Meyer and Harland Fox, *Profile of Employee Benefits*, New York: The Conference Board, Inc., 1974, p. 22.
3. Pay Research Bureau, *Benefits and Working Conditions*, Vol. 1, Ottawa: Public Service Staff Relations Board, January 1, 1980.
4. *Employee Benefits 1975*, Washington: Chamber of Commerce of the United States, 1976, p. 17. See also John J. Miller, "Trends and Practices in Employee Benefits," *The Personnel Administrator*, May 1980, pp. 48–51, 57.
5. Pay Research Bureau, op. cit.
6. Robert English, "Smiles All Round," *The Financial Post*, December 22, 1979, p. 55. See also Brent King, "Dental Plan Trend Something to Smile About," *The Financial Post*, May 9, 1981, p. 42.
7. *Employee Benefit Cost in Canada, 1984*, Toronto: Thorne Stevenson & Kellogg, p. 13.
8. Pay Research Bureau, op. cit., p. 76.
9. Ibid., p. 114.
10. Dave Stack, "Legal Services: An Evolving Union Benefit," *The American Federationist*, January 1975, p. 18. See also Pay Research Bureau, op. cit., p. 68.
11. *Employee Benefit Cost in Canada*, p. 20.
12. Pay Research Bureau, op. cit., p. 123.
13. *Employee Benefit Cost in Canada*, p. 22.
14. John W. Newstrom and Jon L. Pierce, "Alternative Work Schedules: The State of the Art," *The Personnel Administrator*, October 1979, pp. 19–23.
15. Gordon Robertson and Peter Ferlejowski, "Effects of the Shorter Work Week on Ontario Firms," Ontario Ministry of Labour, 1975.
16. Geoff FitzGibbon, "Flexible Working Hours: The Canadian Experience," *The Canadian Personnel & Industrial Relations Journal*, January 1980, pp. 28–33.
17. R. W. Growly, "Worksharing and Layoffs," *Relations Industrielles*, 34 (1972) (2): 329–334. See also Dorothy Dearborn, "Pioneer Worksharing Fact," *The Financial Post*, December 3, 1977, p. 9.
18. Donald V. Nightingale, "*The Profit Sharing Handbook*," Profit Sharing Council of Canada, Don Mills, 1983. See also Donald V. Nightingale, "Profit Sharing: Meeting Today's Business Challenges," *The Business Quarterly*, Spring 1980, pp. 74–81.
19. Peter Silverman, "United Effort to Beat Alcoholism," *The Financial Post*, May 23, 1981, p. 25.
20. Craig C. Pinder, "Comparative Reactions of Managers and their Spouses to Corporate Transfer Policy Provisions," *Relations Industrielles*, 1978, Vol. 37, pp. 654–665. See also Craig C. Pinder and H. Das, "Hidden Costs and Benefits of Employee Transfers," *Human Resource Planning*, Vol. 2.3, 1979, pp. 135–145.
21. William H. Holley, Jr. and Earl Ingram II, "Communicating Fringe Benefits," *Personnel Administrator*, March–April 1973, pp. 21–22. See also Robert Krogman, "What Employees Need to Know about Benefit Plans," *The Personnel Administrator*, May 1980, pp. 45–47.
22. *Employee Benefit Cost in Canada*, p. 10.
23. William B. Werther, Jr., "A New Direction in Rethinking Employee Benefits," *MSU Business Topics*, Winter 1974, pp. 36–37. See also "Labour Letter," *Wall Street Journal*, Western ed., January 30, 1979, p. 1.

Chapter 16

Security, Safety, and Health

The existence of laws and regulations is not enough on its own. The regulations tend to become minimum standards whereby companies meet legal requirements. What is required on the part of business management is a comprehensive accident prevention and health program that is ongoing. Such a program not only involves tangible elements such as physical conditions but also has intangible elements such as the attitudes of employees and employers toward the problem.

Robert Sexty[1]

CHAPTER OBJECTIVES

After studying this chapter, you should be able to:

1. **Explain** how government furthers employee security.
2. **Describe** the major Canadian laws relating to employee security and safety.
3. **Identify** the implications of employee security programs.
4. **Summarize** the safety and health responsibility of employers and employees.

There are two types of benefits and services: those that an employer voluntarily gives and those that are legally required. Chapter 15 described the benefits and services that are voluntarily granted. This chapter examines the legally required ones.

Legally required benefits and services are imposed upon organizations by the government. As a result, employers must comply with the law and its procedures. Sometimes compliance may even lead to actions against employees. Consider, for example, why one supervisor had to fire a good worker.

"Hi, I'm Ted McDonald. I work in personnel and handle the unemployment compensation claims for the company. I need some information about Charlene Crays," Ted told Charlene's former supervisor.

"Sure. What do you need?" Len Podski responded.

"Charlene's termination slip says that she was fired for failure to follow safety regulations. Can you explain that to me?" Ted questioned.

"She would not wear safety shoes. I even sent her home without pay, twice. She said her safety shoes were uncomfortable and ugly," Len added.

"What brought about the firing itself? Was it safety?" Ted probed.

"You bet. After two warnings we had a big argument about her not wearing the safety shoes. She said they were 'her feet.' I told her that the company was responsible for her safety. Since it was her third offence, I fired her. I hated to do it. She was a nice person and a good worker. But I have to enforce safety rules. Why the sudden interest from personnel?" Len inquired.

"She has filed for unemployment insurance compensation. From what you've told me, she was terminated for cause. I'm here to determine whether we should object to her claim," Ted added as he left.

Most legally required benefits and services are designed to help employees. But when an individual worker, like Charlene, refuses to comply, management must take action. Otherwise, the company may be held in violation of the law. For example, if Charlene had had an on-the-job accident and injured her foot, the government would have held the employer responsible for not enforcing safety laws.

Both provincial and federal governments require certain benefits and services of employers to achieve societal objectives. For example, safety and health laws are imposed on most employers to meet society's objective of having safe and healthy workplaces. Still other requirements are imposed on organizations to meet different societal objectives. In general, government seeks to ensure minimum levels of financial and physical security for the nation's work force.

The nature and sources of this security are summarized in Figure 16-1. It shows that the objective of providing financial security is to ease the mone-

Figure 16-1
SOURCES OF FINANCIAL AND PHYSICAL PROTECTION FOR WORKERS

Protection for Workers	Sources of Protection	Legislating Government
Financial Security		
Fair remuneration	Minimum wage acts	Federal and provincial
Retirement	Canada Pension Plan	Federal (except in Quebec)
Involuntary unemployment	Unemployment insurance	Federal
Industrial accidents	Workmen's compensation acts	Federal and provincial
Medical care	Health insurance plans	Provincial
Child sustenance	Family Allowances	Federal
Physical Security		
Working conditions	Canada Labour Code	Federal
	Labour standards codes	Provincial
	Occupational health regulations	Provincial

tary burdens of retirement, death, long-term disability, unemployment, and injury. The loss of income from these causes is cushioned by these security provisions. The financial problems of involuntary employment are lessened by unemployment compensation. And job-related injuries and death are compensated under workmen's compensation laws. None of these programs fully reimburses the affected workers; nevertheless, each worker does get a financial floor upon which additional protection can be added.

The objective in providing physical security is to protect employees from unhealthy environments and injury-causing situations. These goals are partially achieved through health and safety legislation.

Legally required benefits and services are important to the personnel department for two reasons. First, top management holds the personnel department responsible for meeting these legal obligations. If the department is to meet this responsibility, it must keep the firm in compliance. Second, if the obligations are improperly handled, the result can be severe fines, more taxes, or higher insurance premiums for the company. None of these outcomes contribute to the organization's objectives.

Perhaps on an even more fundamental basis, government objectives usually parallel the goals of the personnel department and the needs of employees. Most personnel departments want to provide employees with financial security and safe work environments. For example, the wide range of benefits and services discussed in the previous chapter attests to this near-universal concern for employee well-being.

This chapter extends the study of indirect compensation begun in Chapter 15 by focussing on government-required benefits and services. Specifically, it discusses the implications for personnel management of government programs that concern the financial and physical security needs of workers.

FINANCIAL SECURITY

A large majority of Canadians are financially dependent on their monthly paycheques. Only a small percentage of the population is self-employed; most others work for another person or organization. To protect the well-being of society, governmental regulations on fair remuneration, retirement plans, and disability compensations are imperative. The major legal provisions on the above matters will be discussed below. It should be emphasized that in Canada (unlike in the U.S. or in some other western countries) many of these regulations are provincially administered. To suit the specific work environments, many of these statutes and provisions vary from province to province in Canada.

MINIMUM WAGES

All the provinces have minimum wage legislation that applies to most classes of workers, other than farm labourers and domestic servants. The legislation provides for a board to set minimum wage rates, and these rates are imposed by means of minimum wage orders which are periodically issued.[2] Wide discretion is given to all provincial boards for determination of the classes of employees for which minimum wages are to be established. The general minimum wage rates at the provincial and federal levels are given in Figure 16-2. The rates shown are typical for persons eighteen years of age and over. For employees under eighteen the rates are somewhat lower.

Figure 16-2
MINIMUM HOURLY WAGE RATES AS OF JULY 1, 1984

Federal (all employees 17 years of age and over)	$3.50
Alberta (all employees 18 years of age and over)	$3.80
British Columbia (all employees 18 years of age and over)	$3.65
Manitoba (all employees 18 years of age and over)	$4.00
New Brunswick (no special rates with respect to age)	$3.80
Newfoundland (all employees 16 years of age and over)	$3.75
Northwest Territories (all employees 17 years of age and over)	$4.25
Nova Scotia (all employees 18 years of age and over)	$3.75
Ontario (all employees 18 years of age and over)	$3.85
Prince Edward Island (all employees 18 years of age and over)	$3.75
Quebec (all employees 18 years of age and over)	$4.00
Saskatchewan (all employees 18 years of age and over)	$4.25
Yukon Territory (all employees 17 years of age and over)	$3.60

Source: Ministry of Labour (Research and Planning Division), Halifax, Nova Scotia.

The federal government passed the Minimum Wages Act in 1935, pursuant to one of the three conventions adopted by the International Labour Organization. However, under the British North America Act, minimum wages legislation comes under provincial jurisdiction. The federal Minimum Wages Act currently applies to all government agencies, Crown corporations, and some selected industries as mentioned in Chapter 3.

CONTRACTS WITH THE GOVERNMENT. The Fair Wages and Hours of Labour Act applies to contracts made with the Government of Canada for all types of work. It is mandatory on the part of contractors dealing with the Government of Canada to pay fair wages and establish an eight-hour work day during all such work.[3]

PERSONNEL RECORDS. The Canada Labour Code requires every employer in those industries falling under federal jurisdiction to furnish information relating to wages of employees, their hours of work, general holidays, annual vacation, and conditions of employment whenever the Ministry of Labour demands it. Similar provisions exist in the provincial legislation. Accurate records are also to be kept on maternity leave, severance pay, etc. relating to all employees. This is to ensure that all provisions of the legislation relating to minimum wages, maximum weekly hours, overtime payments, etc. are strictly adhered to by each employer.

CRITICISMS OF MINIMUM WAGE REGULATION. It has been pointed out by some that minimum wage regulations increase the cost of production in Canada. This may eventually work against the workers rather than for them.

> In recent years, minimum wages across Canada have risen more than the average increase in manufacturing wages. And some economists are suggesting ... [that] ... it could lead to an intolerable increase [in unemployment] and cause the major burdens to fall precisely on the workers it was designed to help.[4]

Increases in minimum wages are usually accompanied by increases in unemployment figures of low-skilled and young persons in the work force. It is also pointed out by some that continual increases in minimum wage rates may actually contribute to the inflationary trends in the economy.[5] There is, however, no conclusive evidence on the matter one way or the other at this time. Figure 16-3 shows the average hourly wages paid in different Canadian industries for the years 1979–81. As can be seen, there has

Figure 16-3
AVERAGE HOURLY WAGE, BY INDUSTRY, 1979–1981

Manufacturing	1979	1980	1981
Food & Beverages	$6.96	$7.65	$8.62
Rubber Products	7.38	8.22	9.37
Leather Products	4.91	5.35	5.97
Textile Products	5.80	6.44	7.07
Clothing	4.95	5.31	5.68
Wood Products	7.95	8.86	9.63
Furniture, Fixtures	5.86	6.37	6.99
Paper and Products	8.93	9.77	11.25
Printing, Publishing	8.21	8.98	9.97
Primary Metals	8.73	9.56	10.93
Metal Fabricating	7.72	8.52	9.58
Machinery	8.01	8.83	9.92
Transportation Equipment	8.45	9.33	10.39
Electrical Products	6.57	7.35	8.17
Non-metallic Mineral Products	8.92	8.92	10.05
Petroleum and Coal Products	10.04	11.12	12.53
Chemicals and Chemical Products	7.67	8.50	9.54
All Manufacturing	7.44	8.19	9.97
Other Industries:			
Mining and Milling	9.66	10.80	13.30
Construction:			
Building	11.24	12.47	14.07
Engineering	10.68	11.41	13.04
Urban Transport	8.55	9.44	10.44
Highway, Bridge Maintenance	7.13	7.79	8.69
Laundries, Cleaners, and Pressers	4.46	4.76	5.24
Hotels, Taverns, and Restaurants	4.23	4.50	4.89

Source: *Quick Canadian Facts*, 36th Annual Edition, B.C.: Can Expo Publishers Inc., 1983, p. 221.

been a steady increasing trend in all industries. When all manufacturing industries are taken together, the average wages have gone up by approximately 34% in just two years.

THE CANADA PENSION PLAN AND THE QUEBEC PENSION PLAN (CPP AND QPP)

The Canada Pension Plan (Quebec Pension Plan in the province of Quebec), which came into effect on January 1, 1966, is a mandatory plan for all self-employed persons and employees in Canada. Both plans are contributory, i.e., both the employer and the employee pay part of the costs. The plans are portable in Canada, i.e., pension rights are not affected by changes of job or residence. The plans are also tied to cost-of-living changes.

CPP and QPP pay retirement pensions, disability pensions, and pensions for surviving spouses. They also pay lump-sum death benefits to eligible applicants, benefits to children of disabled contributors, and orphan's benefits where applicable. At present, employers and employees each pay 3.6% of the total employee earnings as their contribution to the pension fund. The requirement for receiving a pension in Canada, for a person sixty-five or over, is forty years of residence in Canada or ten years' residence including the year prior to retirement.

CURRENT BENEFITS. In 1977 1,163,858 persons in Canada received benefits from CPP and QPP.[6] (This figure does not pertain to death benefits paid in lump sum to the estate on application.) These persons represented 11.3% of the labour force then, whereas the figure was 0.1% ten years back. Monthly retirement pensions were approximately $80 in 1977 and $9 in 1968. In addition to this, in 1977 death benefits were paid to about 44,000 persons and disability pensions to approximately 78,000 persons. It should be noted that it is possible for one person to draw more than one pension. For example, widowers and widows who have contributed to CPP or QPP may be entitled to a retirement or a disability pension in their own right. When this is the case, pensions are combined and in the case of CPP the combined total may not exceed the current maximum retirement pension amount.

Since CPP and QPP provides retirees with only 25% of their average pensionable earnings as pension benefits, supplementary payments are available from the federal government through Old Age Security (OAS) and Guaranteed Income Supplements (GIS). OAS is a monthly benefit paid to all persons sixty-five years of age and over; it is not necessary to be retired to be eligible for OAS. GIS was set up mainly for those who retired prior to the enactment of the CPP and were therefore ineligible for CPP. It is a basic supplement to other over sixty-five income. GIS and OAS are tied to the cost of living and will increase with the consumer price index. These additional benefits are designed to provide retirees with a guaranteed minimum income. To increase their pension benefits further, employees have to turn to private pension plans.

EVALUATION. Whether the government or private industry should plan and administer pensions is a question that has been debated for some time. It has been pointed out by some that compulsory national pension plans add to the costs of production, thus making Canadian goods uncompetitive in the international markets.[7] However, any welfare society has to take care of its old, disadvantaged, and poor. It should also be noted that CPP is much greater in scope than an old-age pension plan and provides for other contingencies not usually covered by common pension plans. On these dimensions CPP and QPP have indeed played a crucial role in the past.[8]

UNEMPLOYMENT INSURANCE (UI)
In 1940 Canada started a program to help alleviate people's monetary problems during the transition from one job to another. The Unemployment Insurance Act of 1971 significantly changed and added to the program. Since 1971 there have been several modifications to eligibility criteria and payment schedules.

Most salaried and hourly workers who are employed for at least twenty hours a week are covered by UI. Other workers who are paid on commission or by piecework must make at least $79.50 a week (since 1979) to be covered. The self-employed are not eligible for benefits under the present regulations.

Jobs covered by UI are called *insurable employment*. All persons holding insurable employment are required to pay premiums to the Unemployment Insurance Commission (UIC). UIC premiums are deducted automatically from an employee's pay. All the premiums, along with employers' contributions, are deposited together in the *unemployment insurance account*, out of which the final payments are made to persons who are temporarily out of their jobs.

Under the present regulations there are two kinds of payments: *regular* and *special*. To receive regular benefits the applicant should have had an interruption of earnings for at least seven days. Further, the applicant must have worked in insurable employment for a certain number of weeks in the past fifty-two weeks. The number of weeks an applicant needs to have worked varies from ten to fourteen, depending on the unemployment rate in the economic region, and hence this period is called the *variable entrance requirement*. Special benefits are paid if the person is sick, injured, pregnant, or in quarantine. There is also a special one-time payment when a person reaches the age of sixty-five. To get special benefits a person needs to have worked at least twenty weeks immediately prior to the claim date.

BENEFITS. In 1980, the average weekly payment was $120,[9] and total unemployment benefits paid to claimants exceeded $4.3 billion, in contrast to $2.1 billion in 1974. On average, approximately 510,000 persons received either partial or full UI benefits each month; added to these were sickness payments (23,400 persons), maternity benefits (34,700 persons), retirement pensions (2,400 persons), and training and fishing benefits (12,000 persons).

The benefit rate is 60% of the average weekly insurable earnings of an employee. As of January 1, 1983, the maximum weekly benefit is $231.00. Maximum weekly payment by employee is $8.86, while employers pay a maximum of $12.40 per week. Unemployment insurance benefits are given for a maximum of fifty weeks at present. During the time that a person receives UI, he or she is expected to report details of all other earnings to the UIC. Figure 16-4 shows the procedure for calculating UI benefits in those situations.

Figure 16-4
EARNING MONEY WHILE ON UNEMPLOYMENT INSURANCE (UI)

Anyone claiming regular UI benefits can earn up to 25 percent of their weekly benefit rate (before deductions) through part-time or temporary work. Regular benefits are paid to eligible people who are unemployed because they can't find work. (If you are getting illness or maternity benefits *all* money you earn from a job will be deducted from your benefits.)

Any money you earn over 25 percent of your regular weekly benefit and all earnings in your waiting period will be deducted from your UI cheque. You must report your total gross earnings.

Let's look at an example. If your UI benefit rate is $100 a week, you can earn up to $25 before any money is deducted from your cheque. Suppose you earn $30 one week at a part-time job. We will deduct $5 from your benefit payment for that week. This will leave you with $95 from UI, plus the $30 you earned. Your total income for the week is $125.

We figure it out this way. If, for example, you get
$100 a week UI benefit rate
$ 30 a week earnings from part-time work
$ 25 a week allowed earnings
    (25% of $100)
How much is deducted?
      $30 earnings
minus 25 allowed earnings
      $ 5 excess earnings deducted from benefit payment
How much is your cheque?
      $100 UI
minus   5 excess earnings
      $ 95 benefit payment before tax
Don't forget, though—report the whole $30. We'll work it out for you.

Source: Canada Employment and Immigration, *How Unemployment Insurance Works For You*, Ottawa, pp. 4–5.

EVALUATION. A large part of the increase in UI payments in the past has been attributed to the "loose" manner in which the system is administered.

Charlie Brown is upset. He's been trying—without success—for the past six months to hire two steady waiters or waitresses for his Toronto beer hall. "The system has me beat," Brown says. "I guess it's only natural that people would rather draw pogy (unemployment insurance) than work, but I don't feel very good about the present situation.

"About 50% of my customers are on unemployment, and they would probably take their business elsewhere if you used my name," he explains.

So, while Brown is having difficulty getting staff—he'll even settle for untrained workers—he benefits from the unemployment payments his customers get.

Still, he's unhappy about what he calls the "unemployment rip-off" and believes changes should be made to make it more difficult for people to collect.

"The government thinks it is dealing with naive people," Brown says. "This is not the case. These guys (his customers) should be awarded Ph.D.'s for their knowledge of the unemployment insurance system. They understand exactly how long they have to work before they can collect, how long they can collect and how much job hunting effort they have to exert to fool the government official handling their cases. . . ."[10]

Like Brown, many others believe that UI rules should be tightened. Some suggestions have been to extend the minimum work period before a person can collect UI payments and to reduce the benefits as well as the benefit period (currently a maximum of fifty-two weeks). It is also contended by some that UI takes away all incentive to work. One writer points out that the rewards for a person who is unemployed may be quite comparable (if not higher in real terms) than those for someone who is actually working.[11] (See Figure 16-5). According to Clare, when a person works and earns a gross weekly wage of $220 but is only $47.84 ahead of a person who is unemployed, then the total taxation on that person's income is $172.16 or 78%. To put it another way, the person loses $44.06 or 20% (i.e., the sum of the UIC premium, the CPP contribution, and income tax) as deductions and, further, loses (or has to work for) $128.10 of employment insurance. With a job paying 10% less, the total loss would be even greater (as a proportion of income). In another survey by *The Financial Times of Canada*, evidence of widespread abuse of the UIC system was found.[12] Since then some efforts have been made by the government to plug some of the loopholes in the system.

Figure 16-5
HOW UI STACKS UP FOR THE SINGLE WORKER

	Unemployment	Working, paid average industrial wage	Working, paid 90% of average industrial wage
Gross Income	$147.00	$220.00	$198.00
Less:			
UIC Premium	nil	−3.30	−3.30
CPP Contribution	nil	−2.91	−2.91
Income Tax	18.90	−37.85	−31.70
Net Income to Spend	$128.10	$175.94	$160.09

Source: James L. Clare, "Taxing Question: How Hard to Work When There's UIC?" *The Financial Post*, November 12, 1977, p. 52.

WORKMEN'S COMPENSATION ACTS

All ten provinces, the Northwest Territories, and the Yukon have some act or other (usually called "Workmen's Compensation Act" *or* "Ordinance") which entitles workers to compensation in the event of personal injury by accident during their regular work. The administration of the act is done provincially and all the provincial acts are of the "collective liability" type: that is, compensation is payable by employers collectively. The industries covered by the act are classified into groups according to their special hazards, and all employers in each group are collectively liable for payment of compensation to all workers employed in that group. The annual contribution rate (a percentage of payroll) is determined on the basis of an employer's total annual payroll figures. However, an employer can also be charged a higher rate of contributions if there are many workmen's compensation claims.

BENEFITS. Various types of benefits are available under the workmen's compensation legislation: protection against accidents as a result of accident prevention activities of the Workmen's Compensation Board or employer's associations; first aid and all necessary medical aid, including hospitalization, cash benefits during the period of disablement (typically 75% of wages subject to an annual wage ceiling), rehabilitation (physical and vocational), and a pension available for life for any resulting permanent disability. When disablement is slight a lump-sum payment is made.[13] In the case of a fatal accident, cash benefits are provided for the spouse and dependent children of the deceased employee. Figure 16-6 shows a summary of present benefit scales in the province of Nova Scotia. The figures for other Canadian provinces are similar, with some minor variations.

The right of an employee to compensation is not affected by the employer's neglect or refusal to furnish information or to pay its assessment, or by its insolvency.[14] Also, the employee's right to compensation may not be assigned without Board approval and it cannot be waived or attached. All claims for compensation are received and adjudicated by the Workmen's Compensation Board, whose decision is final (except in the four Atlantic provinces, where appeals are allowed).

EMPLOYER'S LIABILITY. All the provincial acts and those of the Yukon Territory are of the "collective liability" type: that is, compensation is payable by employers collectively. However, an individual liability act is still in force in the Northwest Territories. In addition to the collective liability laws, there are laws of individual liability which provide for payment of compensation by particular employers. For all types of employment in the shipping industry, for example, the Merchant Seamen Compensation Act assigns responsibility to individual employers. Similarly, while most industries in Ontario and Quebec are under the collective liability system, certain large corporations are individually liable to pay compensation. Part II of the acts in British Columbia, Manitoba, New Brunswick, Nova Scotia,

Figure 16-6
SUMMARY OF WORKMEN'S COMPENSATION BENEFIT SCALES IN
NOVA SCOTIA AS OF AUGUST 1, 1984

The maximum yearly earnings compensated on,
   and the maximum for assessment premium purposes $19,000.00
The maximum weekly earnings compensated on . . . . $ 365.38
The maximum weekly compensation. . . . . $ 274.04
The minimum weekly compensation . . . . $ 112.50
The rate of compensation 75%

Spouse's pension . . . . $ 536.00 per month
Spouse's remarriage allowance $2,745.00
Widow's/widower's special allowance following
   loss of spouse, in addition to pension $1,000.00
Funeral expenses paid to . . . . $ 750.00
Transportation of body . . . . $ 300.00
Children's pension . . . . $ 140.00 per month each and no
                                      limit as to number of
                                      children
Orphan's pension . . . . $ 140.00 per month each and no
                                      limit as to number of
                                      children
Other dependants' pension . . . . $ 171.00 one dependant
                                        $ 223.00 more than one dependant

Source: Workmen's Compensation Board of Nova Scotia, Halifax, Nova Scotia.

Ontario, and Prince Edward Island specify industries wherein individual employer liability exists. Finally, compensation for federal government employees is covered under a separate enactment, the Government Employees Compensation Act.

There is a trend in most provinces to remove health and safety provisions from the Workmen's Compensation Board and place them under a separate industrial safety or occupational health and safety division. British Columbia, Prince Edward Island, and the Yukon, however, continue to place occupational health and safety under the compensation board. In almost all cases the occupational health and safety jurisdiction of the board comes under the heading "accident prevention." In Nova Scotia, Newfoundland, and the Northwest Territories, concurrent powers are shared between the board and the occupational health and safety authorities. While compensation boards have played an active role in all provinces, there is a feeling among at least some workers that more should be done by the compensation boards in the areas of safety inspection, instruction, and other preventive actions. In one survey of 618 claimants of British Columbia's Workers' Compensation Board, the question was asked: "Is there anything that the Compensation Board should be doing in the area of accident prevention?" Their responses, shown in Figure 16-7, indicate that much more needs to be done by the boards in preventing accidents.[15]

Figure 16-7

WHAT INJURED WORKERS BELIEVE THE COMPENSATION BOARD SHOULD DO

		Specified Comments	
Safety Inspections	103	More inspections	88
		Inspect small employers	10
		Unannounced inspections	2
		Safety committee members accompany inspectors	2
		Stop pleasing employers	1
Safety Instruction	42	Talks by WCB to workmen	24
		Distribute more signs, posters, and pamphlets	9
		More instruction from employers	7
		Seminars for handicapped	2
Safety Procedures	30	Enforcement of safety rules	16
		Provision of proper clothing, equipment by employers	8
		Stretchers, first aid kits	4
		Two or more men working together	2
Specific Hazards	11	Lifting too much weight	7
		Dust, lighting	4
Miscellaneous	6	Hire WCB staff from working ranks	2
		Rewards for safe shops	2
		Require knowledge of English	1
		More WCB advertising	1
Total	192		

Source: Keith Mason, *Industrial Accident Survey*, Vancouver, B.C.: Workers' Compensation Board of B.C., June, 1973.

HEALTH INSURANCE PLANS

As was mentioned in Chapter 15, Canada's health and medical insurance is provided by provincial governments with assistance from the federal government.[16] In April 1972 the scope of the Medical Care Act of 1966 was widened to include all of Canada. Since then, a major part of the cost of medical care has been paid for by taxes collected at the federal level.

In addition to the provincial health insurance, group life and disability insurance is widely provided as an employee benefit in Canada. Health insurance takes care of cost of hospitalization (room and board and hospital service charges), surgery, and other major medical goods and services. Some firms still offer major medical insurance for their employees whenever they travel outside the province or country. Increasingly, many organizations have also been providing dental insurance to their employees. In many cases, the cost of health and dental premiums is shared between the employer and the employee.

FAMILY ALLOWANCES

In 1944, through an act of Parliament, the family allowance scheme was inaugurated in Canada. Under this act, all Canadian children under sixteen years of age were to be given monthly payments for their sustenance and education. Under the original act, school attendance for children was required, although this was dropped in 1974. Currently, the average monthly payments are about $20 per child (compared to $5 in 1944), although variations across provinces exist. The family allowance payments are now taxable, except when the child is in a special institution or foster home.

IMPLICATIONS FOR PERSONNEL MANAGEMENT

The implications of financial security plans for personnel departments are several. First, personnel managers should make sure that the firm adheres to all provisions relating to minimum wages and pension deductions. For example, the Canada Labour Code requires every employer to furnish, from time to time, information relating to the employees' wages, hours of work, general holidays, annual vacations, and conditions of employment. As well, the Canada Labour Standards regulations require that the employee's social insurance number, sex, and occupational classification be recorded and kept ready for inspection. Accurate records of maternity leave, overtime, and termination should also be maintained.

Second, to avoid duplication, personnel managers need to consider CPP and other health benefits available to employees when designing their firm's own benefit and service plans. In many provinces, some of the items included in private group insurance plans are already covered under the workers' compensation and health insurance plans.

Often, workers are only vaguely aware of these compensation laws and even less aware of their rights. Consider the comments one employee made to a personnel specialist:

It really came as a shock to learn that the province would only pay me 75% of my wage while I was unable to work. On top of that the province paid nothing for the first seven days I was out. I guess I am lucky that the disability wasn't permanent or my weekly benefit would have been even lower.

As this example illustrates, employees are sometimes shocked by workers' compensation rules that pay only a fraction of the regular paycheque. For example, every province pays disabled claimants only part of their regular pay to discourage self-inflicted accidents or malingering. Another common provincial rule provides for waiting periods to lessen claims for trivial accidents. Payments are eventually reduced—or even discontinued—to encourage the permanently disabled to seek rehabilitation.

The inadequacy of workers' compensation coverage has two related implications for personnel departments. First, workers need to be informed by the personnel department of the limited financial security provided by these laws. Second, gaps in the employee's financial security need to be closed with supplemental disability and death insurance. By responding to these needs, personnel departments can show a genuine concern for employee welfare.

Personnel specialists also need to be concerned about reducing accidents in order to lower the cost of workers' compensation. These costs are directly related to the claims made against the company by employees. The more that must be paid to these employees, the greater the cost. Yet even aside from cost considerations, many managers feel a moral obligation to provide a safe working environment.

George Fitzgerald, the new personnel manager in a machine shop, was appalled when he learned that in the past two years one employee was totally blinded and another lost an eye while operating a grinding machine. Mr. Fitzgerald posted a sign that said, "Any employee who runs the grinding machine without safety goggles will be fired!" After fifteen years (and several new signs) not one eye injury (or safety-related discharge) has occurred in the shop. A by-product of Mr. Fitzgerald's concern was that his workers' compensation premiums declined by 42%.

Unfortunately, too few personnel departments achieve such a dramatic success. As a result, government interest in the physical security of workers has increased and safety laws have been enacted.

As mentioned already, unemployment insurance payments have been increasing rapidly in the past few years. There are several things that personnel managers can do to improve the situation. First, they can institute human resource planning, which minimizes overhiring and subsequent layoffs. With such planning, shortages and surpluses of personnel are anticipated. Then retraining or attrition can lead to proper staffing levels without layoffs. Second, they can educate other decision makers—particularly production planners and schedulers. Production specialists may not realize that "hire, then lay off" policies increase payroll costs, which in turn raise production costs and selling prices. Third, personnel can review all discharges to make sure that they are justified. Unjustified dismissals by supervisors can be reversed or changed into intracompany transfers in order to prevent the higher payroll taxes that can result from dismissals or layoffs.[17]

A fourth approach is to challenge all unjustified claims for unemployment compensation made against employers. Those claims that are successfully challenged may reduce the costs in the future.

Kevin Hirtsman was fired for stealing from the company, since the employee manual stated that stealing was grounds for immediate dismissal. When his claim for unemployment insurance was sent to the company for its comments, the personnel manager wrote back that Kevin was terminated for cause. Kevin's claim for unemployment compensation was denied.

PHYSICAL SECURITY

Workers' compensation programs have a serious defect: they are after-the-fact efforts. They attempt to compensate employees for accidents and illnesses that have already occurred. Many early supporters of these laws had hoped that costs would force employers to become more safety-conscious. Yet even with greater efforts by employers, accidents continued to grow along with economic activity. In addition, toxins and unhealthy work environments continue to create new health hazards.

An edger operator was struck by a kickback from a piece of lumber that was being processed. The edger in question was not equipped with an anti-kickback device for reasons of original design features. There were no violations of the Industrial Safety Act and Regulations. The company was directed to look into the possibility of having the manufacturer of the equipment incorporate some mechanical means of preventing a kickback from the edger. [18]

An explosion occurred in the hold of a car ferry that was in a shipyard for hull maintenance. Propane was being used to dry out areas in a hold that was being prepared for painting. An employee was blown out of the hold, suffered multiple injuries and died in hospital some days later. The use of monitoring equipment and proper ventilation procedures was ordered to be carried out when propane is used for drying purposes. The employer was also directed to instruct his employees in the safe use of propane. [19]

Similar accidents occur every day. Labour Canada estimates that for every one hundred employees, approximately five disabling injuries occur each year. Figure 16-8 shows some statistics of workplace fatalities in Canada. As may be noted, the number of fatal injuries has been decreasing overall; however, many problems still exist in occupational health and safety administration. Nor are accidents a phenomenon unique to the manufacturing sector:

Kate McDonald has been working in a dentist's office in Winnipeg for the last several years. About four years back she found that she had continual spells of headaches,

Figure 16-8
FATALITIES IN CANADA

Sector	Number of Fatal Injuries			
	1967	1970	1976	1981
Agriculture	30	16	16	6
Forestry	106	94	58	67
Fishing	33	25	26	21
Mining	183	157	143	132
Manufacturing	187	183	161	117
Construction	223	195	167	149
Transport	237	187	197	183
Trade	64	62	52	62
Finance	5	4	7	7
Services	55	57	52	71
Public Administration	35	81	47	41
Other (unspecified)	—	—	—	15
Total	1,158	1,061	926	871

Source: The 1967, 1970 & 1976 figures are from *The Labour Gazette*, December, 1977, p. 557; The 1981 figures are from Labour Canada: *Canadian Employment Injuries and Occupational Illnesses*, 1982.

nausea, fainting, and overall lethargy. When repeated use of pain killers and sympto-matic treatments did not improve the situation, she went to a specialist. Her illness was diagnosed as prolonged mercury poisoning.

Nor is Canadian industry very safe when compared to other industrialized nations. Figure 16-9 shows the fatal accident rates in Canada, Great Britain, Ireland, United States, Germany, and Japan.[20]

Figure 16-9
FATAL ACCIDENT RATES BY COUNTRY AND INDUSTRY FOR THE YEAR 1975

	Manufacturing	Construction	Railways	Mining & Quarrying
Canada	15	96	25	198
Great Britain	4	18	19	37
Ireland	9	8	40	45
U.S.	3	16	10	33
Germany	16	35	26	46
Japan	2	13	4	61

Source: Adapted from Charles E. Reasons, Lois L. Ross, and Craig Paterson, *Assault on the Worker,* Toronto: Butterworth, 1981, p. 145.

The figures suggest that in Canada more workers are killed by their jobs: Canada had the highest number of fatalities for the construction and mining industries, second highest for manufacturing, and third highest for railways.

By and large, work accidents are caused by a complex combination of unsafe employee behaviour and unsafe working conditions.[21] Some of the key dimensions of the problem are shown in Figure 16-10. Unless solutions are found to all these issues, no significant reduction in industrial accidents may be achieved.

SAFETY REGULATIONS
Part IV of the Canada Labour Code (Safety of Employees) incorporates the provisions of the Canada Safety Code of 1968. It details the elements of an industrial safety program and provides for regulations to deal with various types of occupational safety problems. However, the actual administration of the safety programs comes mainly under provincial jurisdiction. Each province has legislated specific programs for the various industries and occupations within it. Examples from Nova Scotia are the Industrial Safety Act and Regulations, the Occupational Health Regulations, the Nova Scotia Construction Safety Act, the Steam Boiler and Pressure Vessel Act, the Elevators and Lifts Act, the Engine Operators Act, and the Amusement Devices Safety Act.

SAFETY ENFORCEMENT. All industrial units are inspected at least once a year to confirm their safe operation. Depending on the unit's accident

Figure 16-10
REASONS FOR THE COMPLEXITY OF THE SAFETY PROBLEM

- The effects of some industrial diseases do not show up for years.
- Industrial health problems may extend to families (as when contaminants are brought home on clothing or in vehicles) and to consumers who use the final products.
- Employers may not adequately monitor or disclose health hazards.
- Employers often "clean up" the situation just before the inspector arrives; problem identification hence becomes difficult.
- The medical profession is generally ignorant about, or not interested in, occupational health.
- Personal habits of employees, e.g. smoking, add to the problem.
- Strict safety guidelines may force an employer out of business because of increased costs.
- In collective bargaining, unions give higher priority to wages than to safety conditions.
- Workers often ignore safety regulations.

Source: Adapted from Robert W. Sexty, *Issues in Canadian Business*, Scarborough, Ontario: Prentice-Hall of Canada, 1979, p. 104.

record and its size, the safety inspectors may visit more or less frequently. For the purposes of such inspection a safety officer may at any reasonable time enter any property or place used in connection with the operation of any business or undertaking. To carry out their duties effectively, the safety inspectors are given a wide range of powers. Section 91(2) of the Canada Labour Code, Part IV, details these powers:

A safety officer may, in the performance of his duties,

(a) inspect and examine all books and records relating in any way to conditions of work that affect the safety or health of any person employed upon or in connection with the operation of any federal work, undertaking or business;

(b) take extracts from or make copies of any entry in the books and records mentioned in paragraph (a);

(c) require an employer to make or furnish full and correct statements, either orally or in writing in such form as may be required, respecting the conditions of work affecting the safety or health of all or any of his employees, and the materials and equipment used by them in their employment;

(d) require any person employed upon or in connection with the operation of any federal work, undertaking or business to make full disclosure, production and delivery to him of all records or documents or copies thereof, or other information, orally or in writing, that he has in his possession or under his control and that in any way relate to the conditions of work affecting his safety or health, or that of his fellow workers, in his or their employment; and

(e) take or remove for purposes of analysis samples of materials and substances used or handled by employees, subject to the employer or his representative being notified of any samples or substances taken or removed for such purpose.

There is no written list of priorities used in conducting safety and health inspections in Canada. However, the priorities of the Occupational Safety and Health Administration (OSHA) in the United States are in general also applied in Canada.

1. *Imminent danger.* The compliance officer, who determines if any OSHA standards have been violated and how similar events can be avoided in the future, gives first priority to any condition likely to lead to death or a serious injury if allowed to continue. Included are situations that could cause severe bodily damage, disability, or life-shortening illness. Improperly shored ditches, machines with open gears, and toxic fumes and dust are examples. Compliance officers must seek an immediate voluntary solution or obtain a court order to correct any imminent dangers.

2. *Catastrophes and fatal accidents.* Catastrophes, deaths, or accidents resulting in hospitalization of five or more employees are the second priority of compliance officers.

3. *Employee complaints.* When employees complain to OSHA about safety violations or unsafe or unhealthy conditions, these allegations receive OSHA's third priority. Employees have the right under OSHA to request an inspection when they believe improper safety and health conditions exist. Should complaints of imminent danger be made, the employee's name is withheld from the employer if the employee wishes.

4. *Special emphasis programs.* Occupations, industries, or substances that lead to high levels of accidents or illnesses receive special attention and extra inspections under OSHA. Meatcutting, sheet metal working, logging and their associated industries are examples of target occupations and industries. Asbestos and lead are examples of hazardous health substances.

5. *Random inspections.* To encourage all employers to comply with the act, inspections are conducted randomly in all industries, in all size firms, and in all parts of the country.

6. *Reinspections.* Employers who have been cited for violations of OSHA are reinspected to ensure hazards have been corrected and compliance is maintained.

The occupational health regulations in each province set standards relating to gases, vapours, mists, fumes, smoke, dust, and other chemical substances or physical agents associated with industrial activities. The "Threshold Limit Values" for chemical substances and physical agents are established and periodically revised. Figure 16-11 shows some adopted threshold limit values for a normal forty-hour workweek. It should be noted that these are used only as general guides in the control of health hazards.

IMPLICATIONS FOR PERSONNEL MANAGEMENT
The Canada Labour Code requires that an employer:

> (1) operating or carrying on . . . business shall do so in a manner that will not endanger the safety or health of any person employed thereupon or in connection therewith;

Figure 16-11
THRESHOLD LIMIT VALUES FOR SOME COMMON SUBSTANCES

	mg/m^3*
Carbon monoxide	55
Coal dust	4
Chlorine	3
Graphite	5
Mica	6
Mercury	0.05
Lead	0.15
Ozone	0.20
Phosphorus	0.10
Silicone (tetrahydride)	0.70

* approximate milligrams of substance per cubic metre of air

Source: American Conference of Governmental Industrial Hygienists, *Threshold Limit Values for Chemical Substances in Workroom Air*, Cincinnati, Ohio: 1977, pp. 12–54.

(2) shall adopt and carry out reasonable procedures and techniques designed or intended to prevent or reduce the risk of employment injury in the operation.[22]

Likewise, the act imposes a duty on employees to take all reasonable and necessary precautions to ensure their own safety and the safety of their fellow employees, and at all appropriate times to use such devices and wear such articles of clothing as are intended for employees' protection. This means that the personnel managers should (1) obtain organization-wide compliance, (2) maintain adequate records, (3) seek consistent enforcement of all rules and procedures, and (4) honour workers' rights to safety at the workplace.

Organization-wide compliance requires a detailed safety program. To be effective, the program should have several characteristics. Top management support is crucial to the personnel department's plans. Without such backing, other managers often fail to make the necessary commitment of time and resources. With this support, the personnel department needs to conduct a self-inspection so that health and accident hazards can be eliminated and unsafe practices corrected. Then training should include safety awareness programs for employees and supervisors, whose support is essential. Firm enforcement of safety rules by the supervisor quickly establishes a safety-conscious work environment. Supervisory commitment also requires that rewards (such as pay increases and promotions) depend on a good safety record. Finally, personnel must communicate directly with employees about safety. Not only do communications elevate safety awareness, but they reinforce supervisory actions. Some companies develop safety-slogan contests or offer rewards to employees to increase safety awareness.

The personnel manager should also ensure consistent enforcement of all safety and health rules. If personnel policies let one worker violate safety rules, others may follow. If an accident results, it is the employer that is fined by the government. By being firm—even if this means discharge of a valued employee—management quickly convinces employees that safety is important.

The law also permits employees to refuse to work when working conditions are unsafe. In such instances the employee should report the circumstances of the matter to his or her boss or to the boss's superior, and to the safety committee (if any) in the firm. Figure 16-12 shows a summary of comments made by 184 injured workers during a survey on what should be done to prevent accidents.[23]

Figure 16-12
WHAT INJURED WORKERS BELIEVE SHOULD BE DONE TO PREVENT ACCIDENTS

		Specified Comments	
Machinery, Equipment	54	New equipment, machinery	30
		Better maintenance of machinery	12
		Better safety features on machinery	11
		Machines for left-handers	1
Working Environment	48	Better housekeeping	25
		Ventilation, lighting, heating	12
		Chemical fumes	4
		Nails in logs	4
		Too much noise	3
Production	26	Reduce pace of production	14
		More staff	12
Instruction	23	Better job training	21
		More warning signs	2
Safety Procedures	17	Hire qualified employees	5
		Competent safety officers	4
		Reduce lifting loads	4
		Two or more men working together	4
Personal Safety Equipment	14	Compulsory hard hats, safety boots	6
		Safety glasses, shields (grinders)	4
		General safety equipment	4
Miscellaneous	2	Reduce boredom, routine	1
		Design safety outfit, tight but not restricting	1
Total	184		

Source: Keith Mason, *Industrial Accident Survey*, Vancouver, B.C.: Workers' Compensation Board of B.C., June 1973.

Health and safety programs have begun to receive more attention in recent years. However, the demands on the safety programs are also likely to be much greater in the future as changing technology has led to new hazards, such as radioactive materials and nuclear devices. Research has also indicated that many of the past safety standards may no longer be acceptable today.[24] In view of the complex nature of the problem, a more concerted effort by employers, employees, and the government may be necessary in the future.[25]

SUMMARY

To further societal objectives, the Canadian government has instituted compulsory programs that provide citizens with certain benefits and services.

Financial security is achieved partially through such benefits as the Canada Pension Plan, unemployment insurance, and workers' compensation. The Canada Pension Plan provides income at retirement or upon disability. It also provides the family members of a deceased worker with a death benefit and a survivor's annuity, under certain conditions.

Unemployment insurance pays the worker a modest income to reduce the hardships of losing a job. These payments go to employees who are involuntarily separated from their jobs. Payments last until the worker finds suitable employment or until the worker receives the maximum number of payments permitted by the government.

Workers' compensation pays employees who are injured in the course of their employment. The payments are made to prevent the employee from having to sue to be compensated for injuries. If an employee dies, benefits are paid to the employee's survivors.

The government has tried to provide physical security through various safety and health acts. These acts impose a duty on employers to provide a safe and healthy place of employment. Violations of this law, which can lead to serious injuries or industrial diseases, are subject to severe penalties.

Organizations rely on other techniques to motivate and satisfy employees. The next chapter examines the use of employee communications to build an effective, satisfied, and motivated work force, and the subsequent chapter explores counselling and discipline.

TERMS FOR REVIEW

Minimum wages
Canada Pension Plan (CPP)
Unemployment Insurance
Regular and special unemployment
   benefits
Workers' compensation

Health insurance
Family Allowances
Industrial safety program
Imminent danger
Occupational health regulations

REVIEW AND DISCUSSION QUESTIONS

1. Why has government been interested in providing financial security to workers through laws? What areas do you think are likely to receive government attention in the future, to ensure employee financial security?

2. Some people believe that unemployment insurance has over a period of time worked against workers rather than for them. What is your opinion of unemployment insurance? Why?

3. Suppose a friend of yours contracted lead poisoning on the job. What sources of income could this person rely on while recovering during the next two months? What if it took two years for your friend to recover? Are other sources of income available?

4. If you worked at the same lead processing plant as your ill friend, what actions would you take?

5. Besides retirement income, what other benefits are provided through the Canada Pension Plan?

6. Since minimum wage regulations sometimes give rise to unemployment, is it wise to continue to enforce them? Why?

7. What changes should be made to the unemployment insurance system to eliminate its present weaknesses?

8. What specific actions should be taken by a personnel manager to ensure employee safety at the workplace?

INCIDENT 16-1
SAFETY AT CANADA CHEMICALS LIMITED

Canada Chemicals Limited is a large wholesaler of industrial chemicals in Ontario. It handles swimming pool supplies, industrial solvents, fertilizers, and special lubricants. The sales and clerical operations caused few safety worries, but the warehouse facilities caused Sam Peterson sleepless nights. Sam's title was manager of safety and security. He had worked in the personnel department since his job was created in 1971.

His biggest problem was the warehouse manager, Garfield McKenney. Gar simply did not appreciate safety. Nearly every action Sam took to improve safety resulted in objections from Gar, especially if it meant warehouse workers were to be slowed or delayed in their jobs. Most of the workers liked Sam, but they paid more attention to Gar. The only time employees wore their safety goggles, shoes, and acid-resistant gloves was when Sam was around. They knew Gar did not care and would not discipline good workers for safety violations unless company property was damaged.

One day a case of sulfuric acid was dropped, badly burning a new employee. The employee recovered after four weeks and two plastic surgery operations. Immediately after the accident, Sam requested a meeting with Gar, the personnel manager, and the general manager.

1. If you were the general manager, what would you do to gain greater co-operation on safety from (a) Gar and (b) the workers under him?

2. Should Sam be given authority to discipline those who violate safety rules?

INCIDENT 16-2
NIGHT WORK IN A HOSPITAL

Ann LeBlanc is a laboratory technician in one of the city hospitals in Halifax. As a technician she has to work two day and three night shifts every week. She has been working at the hospital for the last eight years.

"This job is beginning to get to me," says Ann. "Night work is getting really harder and harder. I don't sleep or eat well on the three days when I have to work at night. I feel groggy most of the time."

Ann is one of four employees in the laboratory, three of whom have to work at night on a rotating basis. "All three of us have the same kinds of problems," Ann adds. "We all feel that our mental balance is lost at times. Sleep during the daytime does not help at all. It doesn't have the same depth as sleep at night. We also don't get a chance to spend time with our family most of the week. I would have quit a long time ago, but with the kids going to school we need the money."

"We are so sleepy at night that on several occasions we have been close to making serious mistakes. One day I mistook water for glycerine.... And Jackie almost fell down the stairs one day."

1. Can night work be called a health hazard? Why?
2. What can be done to eliminate the problems of night work?

REFERENCES

1. Robert W. Sexty, "Working Conditions." *Issues in Canadian Business*, Scarborough, Ontario: Prentice-Hall of Canada, 1979, pp. 102–104.
2. *Canadian Labour Law Reports*, Toronto: CCH Canadian Limited, 1981, p. 771.
3. Ibid.
4. *The Labour Gazette*, March 1976, pp. 155–156.
5. Clayton Sinclair, "Minimum Wage Increase 25% in Two Years," *The Financial Times of Canada*, January 10, 1977, p. 3.
6. Statistics Canada, *Social Security: National Programs*, 1978, Bulletin No. 4-2003-501 (86-201), March 1978.
7. Donald Coxe, "Pensions: Up to Government or Business?" *The Canadian Business Review*, Spring 1973, pp. 36–40.
8. See, for example, Roy LaBerge, "Canadian Retirement Policies," *The Labour Gazette*, June 1976, pp. 316–319; Donald Neelands, "Twin Threats to Pension Funds," *The Canadian Business Review*, Summer 1974, pp. 43–45.
9. Statistics Canada, *Statistical Report on the Operation of the Unemployment Insurance Act*, Report No. 73-001, 1980.
10. *The Financial Post*, November 16, 1974, p. 4.
11. James L. Clare, "Taxing Question: How Hard to Work When There's UIC?" *The Financial Post*, November 12, 1977, p. 52.
12. *Canadian Labour Law Reports*, Toronto: CCH Canadian Limited, 1980, p. 1903.
13. *The Financial Times of Canada*, February 3, 1975, p. 11.
14. Canada Department of Labour, *Workmen's Compensation in Canada*, Ottawa: Information Canada, 1971.
15. Keith Mason, *Industrial Accident Survey*, Vancouver, B.C.: Workers' Compensation Board of B.C., June 1973.
16. For a more complete discussion, see Amanda Benett, "Canada's National Health Plan," *The Wall Street Journal*, December 13, 1976; and T. Marmor et al., "National Health Insurance: Some Lessons from the Canadian Experience," *Policy Sciences*, 6 (1975) (4): 447–466.
17. Kathleen Classen-Ut Soff, "Unemployment Insurance: What Does It Really Do?" *Business Horizons*, February 1979, pp. 53–56.
18. Nova Scotia Department of Labour, *Annual Report*, March 31, 1980, Halifax, N.S.: Queen's Printer, 1980, p. 28.
19. Ibid.
20. Charles E. Reasons, Lois L. Ross, and Craig Paterson, *Assault on the Worker*, Toronto: Butterworth, 1981, p. 145. See also Jean Surry, *Industrial Accident Research: A Human Engineering Approach*, Toronto: Ontario Ministry of Labour, March 1979; Keith Mason, *Industrial Fatalities to Fathers of Young*

Children, Vancouver, B.C.: Workers' Compensation Board of B.C., April 1972; Keith Mason, 1973, op. cit.; Lloyd Tataryn, *Dying for a Living*, Ottawa: Deneau and Greenberg, 1979; Elliott Layton, *Dying Hard*, Toronto: McClelland and Steward, 1975; *Canadian Occupational Health and Safety News*, Vol. 2, no. 18, September 3, 1979.

21. Sexty, op. cit. See also Keith Mason, *Accident Patterns by Time of Day and Day of Week of Injury Occurrence*, Vancouver, B.C.: Workers' Compensation Board, September 1975; "Workers' Fall Blamed on Faulty Scaffolding," *The Calgary Herald*, March 3, 1981; Jean Surry, op. cit.; "Investigation, Tighter Standards Sought," *Canadian Occupational Health and Safety News*, April 14, 1980, p. 1; Robert Morgan, "Tracing Causes of Industrial Illness," *Canada Labour*, Vol. 23, no. 1, March 1978, p. 19; Linda McQuaig, "Occupational Death," *Macleans*, May 19, 1980, p. 45; Ray Sentes, *Hazards in the Work Place: Responses and Recommendations of Alberta's Unionized Workers*, Edmonton: Alberta Federation of Labour, 1981; "Utility Admits to Misleading Public," *The Calgary Herald*, July 22, 1980.

22. Canada Labour Code, Part IV, as amended in 1978.

23. Keith Mason, 1973, op. cit.

24. Sexty, op. cit. See also G. B. Reschenthaler, *Occupational Health & Safety in Canada: The Economics and Three Case Studies*, Toronto: Institute for Research on Public Policy, 1979.

25. See George Odiorne, *Personnel Administration by Objectives*, Homewood, Illinois: Richard D. Irwin, 1971, Chapter 14, for a discussion of the development of safety management programs by objectives. See also Charles E. Reasons, Lois L. Ross and Craig Paterson, op. cit.; Joan C. Brown, "Occupational Health and Safety—The Right to Know," *Labour Gazette*, February–March 1978, p. 75; Pran Manga, Robert Broyles, and Gil Reschenthaler, *Occupational Health and Safety: Issues and Alternatives*, Technical Report No. 6, Ottawa: Economic Council of Canada, March 1981; Economic Council of Canada, *Reforming Regulation*, Ottawa: Supply & Services Canada, 1981.

Chapter *17*

Building Employee Communication

If we believe that the company and the employees are mutually dependent, then there is a clear requirement to share knowledge— knowledge about the company's goals, operations and policies— particularly those which have a bearing on the welfare and the future of the employees. . . .

John Troyer[1]

A healthy communication climate cannot prevail without resolving organizational tensions.

Herman Roodman & Zelda Roodman[2]

CHAPTER OBJECTIVES

After studying this chapter, you should be able to:
1. **Explain** the personnel function's communication job.
2. **Describe** the communication process.
3. **State** guides for improved listening.
4. **Discuss** barriers to communication.
5. **Interpret** how the grapevine works.

Leonard, Isabel, and Heinz were on their way to work at the main office of Vancouver Insurance Company. The office employed about 500 persons.

Leonard: *Did you read in the morning paper about the new expansion of our building? It sounds like our company is growing.*

Isabel: *The paper said this will add about 100 new jobs.*

Heinz: *I wonder why we didn't learn about this at the office? Why do we have to read about it in the paper? Did either of you know about it earlier?*

Leonard and Isabel: *No.*

Heinz: *Why doesn't management tell us what is happening? I'm interested. Others are interested. Management only communicates with us when there is some crisis. The rest of the time they ignore us.*

Isabel: *I could do a better job if I knew how my work relates to everybody else's. They don't tell us enough.*

Lack of adequate communication is a problem that most organizations face. Managers and other employees often do not realize how important it is for them to share information with others in their organization. An organization is a team, and all members of the team need to know what the team is doing so that the members can work together better.

A major objective of the personnel function is to build, develop, and support improved communication. It seeks to keep all employees informed, and it accomplishes this activity in a number of ways. It has its own communication programs, such as employee magazines, suggestion programs, and meetings. It also works with managers and employees to encourage them to improve their own communication. One way that it goes about this is to provide training programs for better communication, but there also are less evident ways that it works.

In one factory, a personnel specialist analyzed grievance data and found that two supervisors were having an unusual amount of grievances in their departments. Further analysis showed that most of the grievances of one supervisor arose from misunderstandings and lack of information. Apparently the supervisor was not communicating adequately with her people. At this point the personnel department, working through the supervisor's immediate manager, intervened in the situation to help the supervisor improve communication:

- *Causes of past grievances were analyzed and discussed with the supervisor.*
- *A personnel specialist made a survey of the supervisor's employees to determine where communication breakdowns existed.*
- *Counselling was provided to encourage a more positive communication attitude.*
- *Planning sessions were held to help the supervisor develop better communication techniques.*
- *The supervisor was encouraged to attend a communication training program at a later date.*

A personnel department is significantly involved in building better communication in an organization.

THE NEED FOR COMMUNICATION

Information is the engine that drives organizations.[3] Information about the organization—its environment, its products and services, and its people—is essential to management and workers. Without information, managers cannot make effective decisions about markets or resources, particularly human resources. Likewise, insufficient information may cause stress and dissatisfaction among workers. This universal need for information is met through an organization's communication system. *Communication systems* provide formal and informal methods to move information through an organization so that appropriate decisions can be made. This chapter discusses the personnel department's role in managing the human resource communication system. Our focus is upon organization-wide communication efforts, rather than the primarily individual, one-to-one communications of employee counselling and discipline discussed in the following chapter.

The *human resource communication system* includes formal and informal procedures used to acquire and distribute information about an organization's human resources. All organizations have human resource communication systems. In small or unsophisticated ones, communications may be informal and subject to little management intervention. In large, multi-billion dollar enterprises, specialists may serve as employee communications directors, whose responsibility is to manage and improve employee communications. Most organizations use a blend of the formal, systematically-designed communications efforts and informal, ad hoc arrangements. Consider, for example, just a few parts of IBM's human resource communication system.

Top management at IBM long ago realized that IBM's future success rested with the people who developed its technology and sold its products. One example of that commitment has been a 1940s policy against laying off full-time, permanent employees. That policy has remained in effect since then. Another example is its continued commitment to the development of its employees. IBM also relies heavily on employee communication, including extensive career planning information and assistance, attitude surveys, suggestion systems, open-door policies, daily newspapers at some sites and near-daily bulletins on educational opportunities and promotions. Beyond these formal methods, personnel specialists and line managers informally communicate with employees. This "management by walking-around" is known at IBM as "trolling for open doors." IBM has an open-door policy whereby employees are free to walk into any manager's office with their problems.

These informal approaches—combined with formal, systematic communications efforts—enhance other aspects of the personnel department's efforts at IBM. By creating an atmosphere of informed employees, a sense of trust and commitment is likely to develop. In turn, trust and commitment help further motivation and satisfaction (as discussed in Chapter 13) while reducing job-related stresses for managers and employees (as discussed in Chapter 18). Effective communication does not guarantee a successful personnel department or organization. However, neither the department nor the organization are likely to achieve high levels of productivity and quality of work life without effective human resource communication.

Following an overview of communication concepts, the remainder of this chapter focuses on ways the personnel department can improve human resource communication in organizations.

COMMUNICATION FUNDAMENTALS

Communication is the transfer of information and understanding from one person to another person. It is a way of reaching others with ideas, facts, thoughts, and values. It is a bridge of meaning among people so that they can share what they feel and know.

Organizations cannot exist without communication. If there is no communication, employees cannot know what their associates are doing, management cannot receive information inputs, and management cannot give instructions. Coordination of work is impossible, and the organization will collapse for lack of it. Cooperation also becomes impossible, because people cannot communicate their needs and feelings to others. We can say with some confidence that *every act of communication influences the organization in some way.*

THE COMMUNICATION PROCESS

The *communication process* is the method by which a sender reaches a receiver. It consists of six steps, as shown in Figure 17-1. Step 1 is to *develop the idea* or thought that the sender wishes to transmit. This is the key step, because unless there is a worthwhile message, all the other steps are somewhat useless. This step is represented by the sign sometimes seen on office or factory walls, "Be sure brain is engaged before putting mouth in gear."

Step 2 is to *encode* the idea into suitable words, charts, or other symbols for transmission. At this point the sender determines the method of transmission so that the words and symbols may be organized in suitable fashion for the type of transmission. For example, back-and-forth conversation usually is not organized the same way as a written memorandum.

When the message is finally developed, step 3 is to *transmit* it by the method chosen. Transmission allows another person to *receive* the message, which is step 4. At this point the message becomes the receiver's responsibility. If the message is not received, no communication has occurred.

Mabel Corrigan called across the aisle to Thelma Bates to ask her a question about a production order. Thelma was preoccupied with her own job, and so she did not hear the request. Communication did not occur.

Figure 17-1
THE COMMUNICATION PROCESS

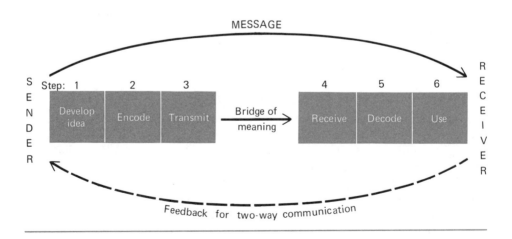

Step 5 is to *decode* the message so that it can be understood. The sender wants the receiver to understand the message exactly as it was sent. For example, if the sender transmits the equivalent of a square and the decoding step produces a circle, then a message has been communicated, but not much understanding has taken place. Even with the best of intentions, situations and ideas in organizations are so complex that a receiver may not understand *exactly* what a sender intended. The best that senders can hope for in most situations is substantial understanding of the message sent.

When the message is received and understood, then step 6, the receiver's use of the message, can occur. This step completes the communication process.

FEEDBACK AND TWO-WAY COMMUNICATION

Even though a communication from sender to receiver has been completed, the sender usually wants some type of feedback to assure that the message has been understood. Feedback initiates a new communication that must pass through the same six steps as the original communication. The result is a completed communication circuit known as two-way communication.

Two-way communication means that a sender and a receiver are exchanging messages so that a regular flow of communication is maintained. For example, a supervisor develops effective two-way communication with an employee, or management and employees develop better two-way communication. An important job of the personnel function is to help management and employees build two-way communication so that they can work together better. To aid in the establishment of two-way communication, personnel specialists need to understand the roles of listening, nonverbal communication, and barriers in the two-way communication process.

In the customer service department of a large financial organization, the number of customer calls and their average time to resolve each one are recorded. This information is communicated through charts posted on the walls for each team. The posters show the trend-line in call volume and average duration. Management uses this tool to decide on staffing levels and evaluate supervisory performance. The employees benefit from being able to see how they are doing each week compared with previous ones.

LISTENING

Listening is a receiver's positive effort to receive and understand a message transmitted by sound. It has many benefits. For example, it helps receivers get true messages, not false ones. Misunderstanding is reduced, and this situation creates a better organizational climate for all concerned. Good listening also helps receivers understand the feelings, emotions, and needs of communicators, so that the receivers can better relate to the sender.

Good listening is good manners, because it shows others that we care and are interested in them and their ideas. In turn, their attitudes toward us improve, and so they are likely to be more receptive to what we have to say.

For example, supervisors who listen effectively are judged to be better supervisors, better communicators, and more interested in their people.

From a manager's point of view, good listening provides inputs for better decision making. Managers who do not know what is happening in their organization are unlikely to make sound decisions. Perhaps they can learn basic facts from reports, but they will not understand the needs and feelings of their employees without two-way oral communication in which they practise effective listening. Good listening often can be the difference between a successful manager and an unsuccessful one.

Since good listening is of major importance, personnel activities try to encourage it. Personnel specialists conduct training programs to improve listening among their own staff, other professional staff, and managers. Company magazines include articles about listening, and sometimes bulletins are issued that offer guidelines for improving it, such as the guides shown in Figure 17-2. The goal is to convince managers that listening is important and that it requires active, interested effort. This goal is difficult to sell, because most of us would rather speak our own ideas than listen to ideas from others.

Figure 17-2
LISTENING GUIDES FOR DISPLAY AT THE WORKPLACE

---

1. Stop talking. You cannot listen if you are talking.
2. Put the talker at ease.
3. Show the talker that you want to listen.
4. Remove distractions.
5. Empathize. See the situation from the other person's point of view.
6. Be patient.
7. Hold your temper.
8. Go easy with argument and criticism. When you argue, even if you win, you lose.
9. Ask questions to show interest and encourage response.
10. Stop talking. This is first and last because all other guides depend on it.

- Nature gave people two ears but only one tongue, which is a gentle hint that they should listen more than they talk.
- Listening requires two ears, one for meaning and one for feeling.
- Decision makers who do not listen have less information for making sound decisions.

Studies of the amount of time managers spend listening show that listening takes more managerial time than any other form of communication. One study covered forty-six managers for a number of working days.[4] Most of the managers were middle managers, and they reported that their communication time was spent as follows:

Listening	33%	Reading	19%
Speaking	26%	Writing	22%

Listening was the main communication activity during both morning and afternoon, and for all five days of the week. It clearly was a regular and important part of their jobs.

NONVERBAL COMMUNICATION

People often do not realize that their actions communicate as well as their words. In fact, the message received from action is often stronger than the one from words. As the saying goes, "Actions speak louder than words." Actions that communicate are called *nonverbal communication.*[5] This kind of communication is a part of almost all that a manager does—or fails to do, because *lack of action also communicates.*

Martin Carnes, an office supervisor, often said that he wanted suggestions from employees. He mentioned this fact in departmental meetings, and he even issued a bulletin calling for suggestions. However, his actions indicated otherwise. He became angry when employees offered suggestions, rejected useful ones, and "lost" some suggestions in his files. His employees believed his actions, not his words.

Another part of nonverbal communication is *body language*, which is communication by body movements during face-to-face communication. There are many subtle movements, and some not so subtle, that people make when they are talking with each other: smiles, frowns, eye movements, wringing of hands, and countless other body movements communicate to others. A weak handshake may mean lack of interest, and a bowed head may mean worry. All employees need to be aware of how body movements are used to communicate, so that they can interpret these movements effectively.

BARRIERS TO COMMUNICATION

Even when the receiver gets the message and makes a genuine effort to decode it, a number of interferences may limit the receiver's understanding. These interferences are known as *barriers to communication*, and they may entirely prevent a communication, filter part of it out, or give it incorrect meaning. The three types of barriers are personal, physical, and semantic, as shown in Figure 17-3.

Figure 17-3
OPERATION OF COMMUNICATION BARRIERS

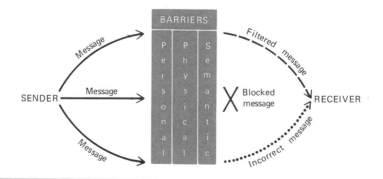

PERSONAL BARRIERS. *Personal barriers* are communication interferences that arise from human emotions, values, and limitations. They are the most common type in work situations and include poor listening habits and emotions. We all have experienced how our personal feelings can inhibit our communication with other people, and these situations happen at work just as they do in private life.

A personnel specialist tried to explain the company promotion policy to an employee who had been bypassed for a promotion. The employee was unhappy because she had been bypassed, and so she emotionally did not want to hear what the real policy was. She let her own emotions block her understanding of the policy.

PHYSICAL BARRIERS. *Physical barriers* are communication interferences that occur in the environment in which the communication takes place. A typical physical barrier is a distracting noise of some type. Other physical barriers include distances between people, walls, or static that interferes with radio messages.

A personnel specialist named Carey McGraw was presenting a training program in the Blue Room. Just as he came to a key point in his presentation, a tardy trainee entered the room. The employee was perspiring from rushing to the training session, and so he left the door open for better ventilation. The loud talking outside the door caused several trainees in the back of the room not to hear the key point, and so later the trainer discovered that it was necessary to repeat that point.

SEMANTIC BARRIERS. *Semantic barriers* arise from limitations in the symbols with which we communicate. Words are our main form of communication, but they have so many different meanings that they are often misunderstood. For example, the word "pipe" has more than a dozen meanings, some of which are shown in Figure 17-4. We often think that a pipe is a cylinder that carries liquid, but there are a number of other meanings. The different meanings place an obligation on the sender to create a total environment (context) that pinpoints only one meaning for key words that are used.

Figure 17-4
SELECTED MEANINGS OF THE WORD "PIPE"

- A tube for liquid, as a water pipe
- A cask for liquid, such as wine or oil
- The call of a bird
- A device for smoking
- A musical instrument
- Something that is easy, such as a course that is a pipe
- The opening for lava in the crater of a volcano
- To trim with piping, as to pipe a dress
- To give orders by signals, as to pipe a crew aboard

An electric utility crew was constructing a substation about 100 kilometres from the company warehouse. The workers needed certain supplies quickly, and so they called the warehouse on their radio. The supply superintendent wrote out the list of supplies and handed it to a new warehouse loader-truck driver with the comment, "Here, take this to our crew in Brown Valley. They are waiting for it." The driver hurriedly drove to Brown Valley with the list, *not the supplies.*

BARRIERS IN MANAGEMENT-WORKER COMMUNICATION
Communication barriers are especially evident in two-way management-worker communication. The chain of command creates some distance between the two parties, and this distance is intensified by other conditions, such as different interests, job conditions, and backgrounds. Managers seek performance goals, but these are not necessarily the main interests of employees. A high proportion of managers are university graduates, but usually fewer workers have any degree. Managers have secretaries or clerks to help prepare their communications, but few workers have the benefit of this kind of help.

The result of these barriers is that as communications move up or down the chain of command, they lose some of their information content and meaning, and so they become less effective. As shown in Figure 17-5, the number of correct message units that arrive at the end of the chain is substantially reduced. Assuming a 15% loss from barriers at each level, only about half of the original message units reach the fifth level or return to the first level.

Communication loss between individuals may be somewhat less than in downward-upward communications, but this is not necessarily so. For example, an engineer and an accountant have different interests and job languages, and so they may have difficulty communicating job information.

Figure 17-5
CORRECT MESSAGE UNITS REACHING EACH LEVEL IN DOWNWARD AND UPWARD COMMUNICATION, ASSUMING A 15% LOSS FROM BARRIERS AT EACH LEVEL

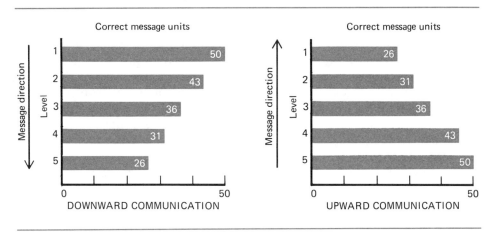

In general, we can say that communication difficulties increase with:

- Different interests, job languages, and backgrounds
- Distance in job levels
- The rate of change (because change upsets communication patterns)
- The amount of information involved
- The complexity of the situation

Since there is substantial communication loss in organizations, the personnel function uses a number of approaches to improve communication, as is discussed in the remainder of the chapter.

ENCOURAGING OPEN COMMUNICATION

The personnel department is a service department, and all its communication activities merely supplement the most important communication program, which is between supervisors and employees. Within this environment the personnel department works to encourage open communication throughout the organization. *Open communication* occurs when people feel free to communicate all relevant messages. An environment that fosters open communication tends to improve job satisfaction and effectiveness in organizations.[6]

COMMUNICATION ATTITUDES

It is essential for employers to have positive communication attitudes that encourage them to communicate freely. If managers have the attitude, "I'll tell them what I want them to know," then the communication climate will be poor. If managers say, "I'll wait until they ask me before I tell them," then communication will be limited. And if managers say, "If you don't understand me, you should tell me," then there will be much misunderstanding. All organizations need a positive, proactive communication environment.

COMMUNICATION QUALITY VERSUS QUANTITY

In all its communication activities the personnel department applies the guide of *quality, not quantity.* It is possible to accomplish the goal of improved understanding with less total communication, provided it is of higher quality. In the past some personnel departments operated with the philosophy that more is better, and so they published enormous amounts of employee materials; but they found that employees merely felt overwhelmed with data; understanding was not improved. What happened was a *communication overload,* which occurs when employees receive more communication inputs than they can process or than they need. The employee fringe benefit report shown in Figure 17-6 is short, but it probably communicates better than five pages of detailed explanations about fringe benefits. It exhibits quality of communication, not quantity.

Figure 17-6
EMPLOYEE FRINGE BENEFIT REPORT

Fringe Benefit	Your Annual Contribution	Company's Annual Contribution
Canada Pension Plan	$240	$ 240
Life insurance	20	60
Vacation plan	none	600
Dental plan	none	92
Paid holidays	none	1,660
Group medical insurance	302	302
Legal insurance	none	75
Total benefit value	$562	$ 3,029
Annual salary		$10,000
Total value of pay package		$13,029

Miscellaneous benefits, such as released time for funerals and pay during jury duty, are not included, nor are payments by the company for workers' compensation and unemployment compensation.

READABILITY

One way to improve quality of communications is to improve their *readability*, which means that language and style are simplified.[7] Specialists tend to communicate in technical language that may not be understood by nonspecialists, and so there is a need to simplify. Better readability reduces word count, word length, and sentence length. It also uses more popular words and simplifies organization and style.

Figure 17-7 shows an example of low readability compared with improved readability for a sentence taken from a company bulletin. The improvement reduced the number of words from 35 to 11 and simplified the thought. Without question, the improved sentence should communicate the message better than the original.

Figure 17-7
AN EXAMPLE OF IMPROVED READABILITY

Low Readability	Improved Readability
Should the supply of the banners which were sent to you prove to be insufficient to meet your requirements, application should be made to this office for additional ones in whatever quantities you think desirable.	If you need more banners, write us how many you want.

DOWNWARD COMMUNICATION SYSTEMS

The personnel department operates a large communication system in order to keep people informed. To do that, personnel specialists must be aware that barriers to communication may exist in any type of message. What personnel departments try to do is create in-house approaches that overcome as many of these barriers as possible.[8] Although the goal is to facilitate an open, two-way flow of information, most messages in organizations are top-down ones. *Downward communication* is information that begins at some point in the organization and proceeds down the organization hierarchy to inform or influence others in the organization. Top-down methods are necessary for decision makers to have their decisions carried out. These communications also help give employees knowledge about the organization and feedback on how their efforts are perceived.

Organizations use a variety of downward communications. The reason for this diversity is the need to use different methods or channels of communication, since messages that use multiple channels are more likely to overcome barriers and reach the intended receivers. Some common examples of downward communication approaches include company magazines (house organs), information booklets, employee bulletins, television and films, jobholder reports, and meetings. Each of these techniques will be discussed in the following sections before concluding this chapter with a discussion of upward communication systems.

COMPANY MAGAZINES (HOUSE ORGANS)

Many organizations publish company magazines, newspapers, or bulletins for employees. These publications are also called *house organs*. Their purpose is to inform employees about current developments and to build long-run understanding about company activities and goals.[9] Large organizations are able to publish well-designed magazines and/or newspapers, while small organizations may have only a weekly personnel information bulletin. Employees are encouraged to take employee magazines and newspapers home so that family members also may develop a better understanding of the organization. Frequently there are articles about company bowling teams, discount theatre tickets, and hobbies of employees that are designed to appeal to family members as well as employees.

Saint Mary's University in Halifax publishes a monthly paper called The Times, *where details of the activities of the university faculty, staff, and students, as well as regional and national educational trends are recorded. For instance, details of faculty research, publications, and community involvements, staff and student activities, and information about government announcements are listed in each issue, thus enabling every member of the university and its alumni to know what is going on in and around the university. This is supplemented by other student newspapers, general circulars, bulletin board announcements, etc., all aiming to increase organizational communication.*

Editors of in-house magazines and newspapers occasionally make readership surveys to determine what parts of their publication are being read and what additional information readers desire. In this way they can improve content, readability, and other features for better communication.

Samples of questions asked on readership surveys are as follows:

- What sections do you read regularly? (A list with check-boxes follows.)
- What articles did you read in the July issue? (A list of the articles, with check-boxes, follows.)
- What article in the July issue did you like most?
- What additional subjects would you like information about?

INFORMATION BOOKLETS

Personnel departments often distribute information booklets on various subjects to their employees. A well-known booklet is the employee hand-book given to new employees to inform them about regulations and benefits. Other booklets are distributed on specialized subjects relating to personnel work, such as suggestion programs, wage incentives, retirement, and fringe benefits. When benefits such as life and medical insurance are purchased through an insurance company, that firm usually supplies the booklets. The following are examples of information booklets distributed by personnel departments:

- *How to Read Your Future* (the retirement program)
- *You've Got Something There* (the suggestion program)
- *Steps to Security* (programs for employee security)
- *The Employee Supplemental Health Insurance Plan*

EMPLOYEE BULLETINS

Personnel departments publish a number of bulletins that concern their day-to-day operations. Usually these are placed on employee bulletin boards and copies are sent to each manager. For example, job openings are announced so that all employees have an equal opportunity for them. Holidays are announced, along with the regulations that govern payment and absences before and after holidays. Announcements are made about awards, retirements, and similar events. As a service activity it is the personnel function's responsibility to keep employees informed about all events relevant to their employment.

TELEVISION AND FILMS

Since the public is conditioned to watching television sets, some organizations tape their own television programs for later replay to employees. These programs are viewed on television screens in company lunchrooms and other locations. Large firms with branch operations especially use this approach to keep their branch employees informed about corporate developments or to assist with training. Other firms prepare information films for the same kind of use. As was noted by one manager:

> The importance of video as a means of communication has been recognized by a number of organizations in Canada . . . on the employee communica-

tions side such networks are used for training, induction, orientation, explaining salary and benefit plans and so on. . . .[10]

Some organizations use recorded telephone messages to present the latest information. Employees can dial a certain number from any telephone, and a recorded message is played to them. In a typical program the message takes one minute, and a new one is prepared daily.

JOBHOLDER REPORTS AND MEETINGS

A few organizations give *jobholder reports* to employees.[11] These are reports to employees about a firm's economic performance. The reasoning is that company economic information is just as important to employees as it is to shareholders, and so the firm should report this information. The report is presented in the same style as the annual report, except that the jobholder report shows how the annual economic results affect jobholders.

Some organizations follow the jobholder reports with jobholder meetings that are organized and conducted in the same way as shareholder meetings. Top management attends the meetings, and all employees are invited. Management presents its reports, and employees are invited to question management and make proposals in the same way that owners do in stockholder meetings. These meetings improve communication and give jobholders a stronger feeling of belonging.

UPWARD COMMUNICATION SYSTEMS

Personnel professionals need to understand the communication process, the role of feedback, barriers to communication, and the downward communication process. With that knowledge, personnel experts can help improve their organization through more effective upward communications systems.[12] Perhaps no area of communications is more in need of improvement in most organizations than upward communications.

Upward communication consists of information initiated by people who seek to inform or influence those higher up in the organization's hierarchy. The cornerstone of all such messages is the employee and the supervisor.[13] When a free flow of information travels between an employee and the supervisor, informal day-to-day communications are often sufficient for most situations. When open communications do not exist, or exist only for a limited range of issues, other tactics are needed. For example, an employee may have a good, open relationship with the supervisor about job-related matters such as supplies, work performance, quality of outputs and the like. However, that same employee and supervisor may not be able to discuss effectively interpersonal issues such as peer relations, relations between the employee and his or her supervisor, or issues pertaining to the conditions and the leadership style of the supervisor. A discussion follows of several programs and processes that facilitate upward communication.

LIVING WITH THE GRAPEVINE

There are two types of communication systems in an organization: the formal system and the informal one. The latter is usually called the "grapevine." A formal communication system is the one established by the organization for the official conduct of its activities. Examples of formal communications are job instructions, surveys, reports, and bulletins. *Grapevine communication* is an informal system that arises spontaneously from the social interaction of people in the organization.[14] It is the people-to-people system that arises naturally from human desires to make friends and share ideas. When two employees chat at the water cooler about their trouble with a supervisor, that is a grapevine communication.

The personnel department has a major interest in the grapevine for several reasons:

- The grapevine affects motivation and job satisfaction.
- The grapevine reflects breakdowns in communication.
- The grapevine provides valuable feedback of personnel information.
- Supervisors tend to have poor understanding of the grapevine, and training is a personnel activity to improve understanding.

GRAPEVINE PATTERNS. Management did not establish the grapevine and cannot control it. This means that the grapevine can fly across chains of command or between departments as quickly as a telephone call or a chance meeting in the hallway. It is impossible to control these freewheeling communications. Even if control were possible, it is not desirable, because grapevines help satisfy social needs. Whenever normal people are together, they are going to share their ideas. All that management can do is learn to live with the grapevine. Management perhaps can influence it, but control is impossible.

Figure 17-8 shows how a grapevine moves easily across chains of command in an organization. It also can bypass levels of authority and even move to and from the community as it runs its course. Employee J originated the communication, which was interesting gossip about the love affair of employee H. The grapevine network then developed as follows:
J told I at the same organizational level.
I told L, a subordinate.
L told his wife, who did not work for the organization.
The wife told a friend, E, who was two levels higher than her husband.
E told C, an associate.
C told K two levels lower.

It is evident that the people involved in this grapevine could ignore chains of command, because they were communicating on the basis of their interests and friendships, not the organization structure.

GRAPEVINE FEEDBACK FROM EMPLOYEES. The grapevine provides a large amount of useful off-the-record feedback from employees. There are many opportunities for feedback, because personnel specialists are in regular contact with employees as they discuss fringe benefits, counsel employees, and perform other functions. Employees feel somewhat free to talk with personnel specialists, because the occupation of personnel management is oriented toward human needs and resources. In addition,

Figure 17-8
A GRAPEVINE NETWORK COMPARED WITH A CHAIN OF COMMAND

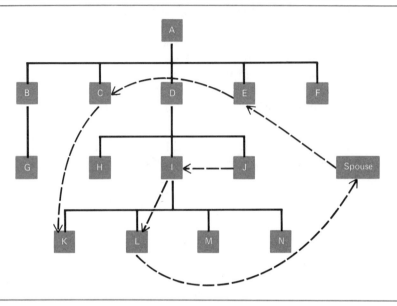

employees feel safe to express their feelings, because personnel specialists do not directly supervise employees in other departments. The result is a large amount of useful input, provided the personnel department is prepared to listen, understand, and interpret the information. Some of the types of grapevine feedback that come to the personnel department are shown in Figure 17-9.

If the personnel department shows that it is responsive and can handle off-the-record information in confidence without putting the communicator

Figure 17-9
TYPES OF GRAPEVINE FEEDBACK TO THE PERSONNEL DEPARTMENT

- Information about the problems and anxieties that employees have.
- Incorrect feedback that is evidence of breakdowns in communication.
- Insights into goals and motivation of employees.
- Identification of job problems that have high emotional content, because intense feelings encourage grapevine communication.
- Information about the quality of labour relations, including grievance settlements.
- Information about the quality of supervision. Complaints about supervision are often brought informally to the attention of personnel specialists with the hope that they will do something.
- Information about areas of job dissatisfaction.
- Feedback about acceptance of new policies and procedures.

in jeopardy, then open communication is further encouraged. There are risks in this kind of communication, because supervisors may feel threatened by disclosures about their departments, but usually the benefits of more complete information are greater than the disadvantages.

A further point is that even when personnel specialists know that a grapevine input is incorrect, they should still listen, because the input may be helpful. Incorrect inputs tell management that there are communication breakdowns that need to be remedied. A useful guide to follow is: Always listen to the grapevine; it may be trying to tell you something.

IN-HOUSE COMPLAINT PROCEDURES

How does an employee solve a complaint if the supervisor is not receptive? In some organizations, the employee has no other option except to go talk with the supervisor's superior. Although that may seem reasonable, most people in organizations are very reluctant to do that because they do not want to create negative feelings between themselves and their supervisor. To lessen the burden of "going over the boss's head" some organizations have installed in-house complaint procedures.

In-house complaint procedures are formal methods through which an employee can register a complaint. Normally these procedures are operated by the personnel department and require the employee to submit the complaint in writing. Then an employee relations specialist investigates the complaint and advises its author of the results. In some companies, the employee's name is known only by the employee relations investigator. However, if a supervisor is questioned about the issue, it is sometimes obvious who filed the complaint—so the person's anonymity is lost.

IBM's program is called "Speak Up!" It is a confidential form designed as a pre-paid envelope. On the inside the employee completes a home address section and then writes up the complaint, opinion, or question. When the "Speak Up!" administrator receives the item, the name and address section are removed and the issue investigated. Once an answer is found, it is mailed to the employee's home address. No one but the "Speak Up!" administrator knows who submitted the form. If the employee does not provide a name and address, the issue and the response may be printed in the company newspaper. If the employee is not satisfied with the answer, an interview with an executive from corporate headquarters will be arranged, regardless of where the employee's job site is located.

Managers at IBM "troll for open doors" to avoid "Speak Ups!" that cause an executive to visit a disgruntled employee. If that employee is dissatisfied with some improper management action and talks with an executive about it, that manager's career with IBM may be affected adversely. What makes IBM's complaint procedure and open communications so effective is that IBM executives support the program with their actions; they are willing to get on an airplane and fly to a meeting with a dissatisfied employee. That level of commitment from top managers causes lower-level managers to pay close attention to employee communications. An *open-door policy* exists when employees are encouraged to come to their manager or even to higher management with any matter that concerns them. Probably the most effective open door is one that managers walk through to get out among their people. In this way they can learn more than they ever would sitting in their offices.

The director of a large hospital reversed the usual "open door" by walking through all departments nearly every day. In this way he saw people he would not otherwise see, and he was able to observe operations directly. Over a period of time he developed personal contacts with many employees at different levels of the hospital. He discussed matters of interest with them and learned much more about his organization than if he had remained in his office. The result was low employee turnover and strong feelings of teamwork to accomplish the hospital's goals of quality medical care and personal concern for people.

RAP SESSIONS

Closely related to in-house complaint procedures are rap sessions. *Rap sessions* are meetings between managers and groups of employees to discuss complaints, suggestions, opinions, or questions. These meetings may begin with some information sharing by management to tell the group about developments in the company. However, the primary purpose of these meetings is to encourage upward communications, often with several levels of employees and lower level management in attendance at the same time. When these meetings are face-to-face, informal discussions between a higher manager and rank-and-file workers, the process is called *deep-sensing* because it attempts to probe in some depth the issues that are on the minds of employees.[15] These meetings also are called *vertical staffing meetings*, because they put higher managers directly in touch with employees.[16] Attendance at rap sessions varies according to how the meetings are planned. In small facilities, it may be possible to get all the employees together annually or semiannually. In other large units different formats may be needed.

One plant manager runs a "birthday club." All employees who have a birthday during the month meet with the manager and the personnel manager to have coffee and birthday cake. The occasion is used to discuss what changes these people think are needed.

Consider another example:

One major bank's Open Meeting Program arranges meetings of about a dozen employees at a time. Meetings are held with different groups until at least one in five employees from each department attends. Employees are selected randomly and may decline to participate if they wish. A personnel specialist coordinates each meeting and develops the group report on a newsprint sheet in open discussion with the group. No employee names are used on the report, which becomes the basis of action plans with management. The program is repeated annually, and it has materially improved upward communication.

Two common problems often arise from these meetings. First, the top manager must be careful not to undermine other managers by countermanding orders without all the facts. Sometimes employees present a compelling case that does not contain all the facts. If the top manager reacts too quickly, a bad decision may result. Second, initial meetings tend to focus on employee complaints, such as pay, working conditions, fringe benefits, and the like. Many managers and personnel specialists become discouraged with the lack of constructive ideas and sometimes abandon these approaches too quickly. Personnel departments that have responded to employee complaints promptly and continued the rap sessions into a second year often find that complaints become constructive suggestions for improvement in operations policies and practices. Sometimes, constructive suggestions emerge in the early meetings, as the president of a major hotel chain discovered:

In an eight-month period, he held a dozen meetings with the hotel employees. Sometimes he heard serious problems that required immediate attention. More often, he heard seemingly trivial complaints—but they concerned matters that can make day to day life miserable. "Every time I had one of these meetings, I realized that it's the little things that most often affect morale. . . . This is a way to make the employee feel like we care."

EMPLOYEE LETTERS AND QUESTION-ANSWER PROGRAMS

Some firms encourage employee letters, questions, and complaints, which are processed anonymously by a personnel specialist. The personnel specialist works with the appropriate manager to secure a reply that is prepared and signed by the manager. If a reply is of general interest, it may be published in the company newspaper or in a bulletin. All replies are routed back through the personnel specialist to the person who originally asked the question.

The R.S.V.P. program of the Royal Bank of Canada encourages employee questions on special forms that are available throughout the bank. All letters are retyped in order to keep the employee's name confidential. A personnel specialist then discusses the retyped letter with those who can resolve the matter. The specialist has access to all management, including the president, and so full support for the program is assured. About 800 letters a year are received.

Instead of using letters, another company uses a telephone number that employees can call to leave their comments on a tape. The message is transcribed and processed by the vice president of industrial relations in a manner similar to that of the Royal Bank of Canada.

SUGGESTION SYSTEMS

Suggestion systems are a formal method for generating, evaluating, and implementing employee ideas. If only one of these three elements—generating, evaluating, or implementing—is missing, the suggestion plan fails. All three are crucial to a successful suggestion system.

Figure 17-10 shows the key steps in successful suggestion systems. It begins with the employee's idea and a discussion with the supervisor. Once the suggestion form is completed, the supervisor reviews and signs the form, indicating awareness of the suggestion but not necessarily approval.

Figure 17-10
SUGGESTION SYSTEM STEPS

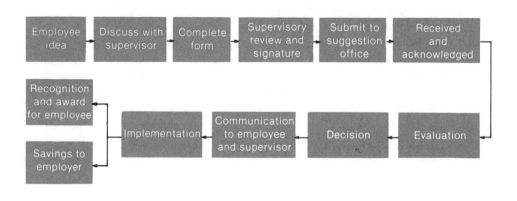

The suggestion system office or committee receives the idea and acknowledges it to the employee through company mail. The idea is then evaluated and the decision is communicated to the employee. If it is a good idea, implementation follows with the employee receiving recognition and usually some award.[17] (Typically, awards are equal to 10% of the first year's savings.) The savings from the idea accrue to the organization.

Success is likely if management provides prompt and fair evaluations, supervisors are trained to encourage employee suggestions, and top management actively supports the program. Unfortunately, this source of upward communications is not very effective in many companies because evaluations often take months or supervisors see suggestions as more work for them with few personal benefits. As a result, many company suggestion plans exist on paper, but are not very effective.[18]

Although most suggestion systems pay employees a percentage of the first year savings, some companies pay a flat dollar amount in order to minimize the need for precision in evaluating the suggestion's exact dollar savings. This approach means that employees receive feedback about their suggestions much faster.

In a large, multinational electronics corporation, the supervisors' performance is evaluated in part by the effectiveness of the suggestion system among their employees. Obviously, this approach causes supervisors to encourage employee suggestions. Another organization gives $25 to the supervisors for each employee suggestion that has been found viable.

An airline company went a step further in encouraging employee feedback:

The company gave its supervisors the authority to make "quick look" awards. Supervisors were authorized to issue cheques for $10 immediately on receiving an idea that *seemed useful. If the formal evaluation procedure rejected the idea, the employee could still keep the $10. This procedure facilitated quick feedback to the employees and encouraged them to generate good ideas.*

Not all organizations have suggestion programs, because problems can develop unless they are administered carefully. Some employees feel that their award is not enough, and others resent the fact that their suggestion is not accepted. Other employees may object to a suggestion because it changes their jobs. They show their feelings by retaliation against the suggestor, who is discouraged from offering further ideas. In spite of the problems, suggestion programs offer an opportunity for management to explain job improvement needs to employees and for them to offer ideas to management. This exchange of ideas builds two-way communication, improves the organization's productivity, and can further the quality of work life for employees.[19]

ATTITUDE SURVEY FEEDBACK

What do employees think about the organization? Do they have problems or concerns? Do they understand the personnel department's fringe benefit plan? Compensation program? Career planning efforts? Answers to these and many other questions can make a useful addition to the personnel department's human resource information system.[20]

Attitude surveys are systematic methods of determining what employees think about their organization. These surveys may be conducted through face-to-face interviews, but usually are done through questionnaires that employees complete anonymously. An attitude survey typically seeks to learn what employees think about working conditions, supervision, and personnel policies. New programs or special concerns to management also may be a source of questions. The resulting information can be used to evaluate specific concerns, such as how individual managers are perceived by their employees.

Attitude surveys can be a frustrating experience for employees if they do not see any results. It is only natural that people would like to know what the survey questionnaire uncovered. Otherwise the survey has little meaning to them, especially if it is readministered in the future. Therefore, a summary of upward communication should be provided to employees for their reaction. When this feedback loop is closed, the overall process is called *attitude survey feedback*. However, feedback is not enough. Action is needed. Employees need to see that the survey results caused problems to be solved. Feedback of the results and action on the problem areas make attitude survey feedback a powerful communication tool. However, providing feedback in a constructive manner may require considerable assistance from the personnel department, especially for first-level supervisors who may have little experience in running meetings and listening to employee criticisms.

Maple Leaf Automotive Products has for several years relied on employee surveys as a method of facilitating organizational communication. Supervisors in the company are given a workbook to analyze survey results. Trained internal facilitators help the supervisors to interpret the survey results. Then the facilitators conduct a role-playing exercise with the supervisors to prepare them for the questions that employees are likely to ask.

After the role-playing, the supervisor meets with the employees and presents the results. Together, problems are identified and solutions sought. From this meeting a prioritized list of action items emerges with dates for their completion. The result of all these efforts is not only that employees know what others in the organization feel, but it also helps the organization to develop an action plan to resolve its immediate and potential problems.

Whether attitude survey feedback is appropriate for an organization depends on several factors. Is top management truly willing to take action based on the results of the survey feedback process? Are resources available to conduct the survey, train facilitators that might be needed, and follow-up on the prioritized action items? But the key question may be whether the organization and its leadership are ready for change. Dealing with change as a means of developing a more productive and satisfying organization is an ongoing concern of most proactive personnel departments.

SUMMARY

Communication is the transfer of information and understanding from one person to another. It is a bridge of meaning among people. The sender of a message develops an idea, encodes it, and transmits it. The receiver takes the message, decodes it, and uses it. When the receiver replies to the sender, two-way communication is established. It is difficult to establish because there are personal, physical, and semantic barriers that must be overcome.

The personnel department's role in organizational communication is to create an open, two-way flow of information. Part of the foundation of any organizational communication effort is the view held by management of employees. If that view is one that sincerely strives to provide an effective downward and upward flow of information, the personnel department can help develop and maintain appropriate communication systems.

Downward communication approaches include house organs, information booklets, employee bulletins, television and films, and jobholder reports and meetings. Multiple channels are used to help ensure that each message reach the intended persons.

Perhaps the greatest difficulty in organizational communication is to provide an effective upward flow of information. In-house complaint procedures, rap sessions, suggestion systems, and attitude survey feedback are commonly-used tools to facilitate upward communications.

In both downward and upward communication, the personnel department provides a major service to the entire organization and helps improve organizational effectiveness by establishing and maintaining good communication channels.

TERMS FOR REVIEW

Communication	House organs
Communication process	Upward communication
Two-way communication	Grapevine communication
Nonverbal communication	In-house complaint procedures
Body language	Open-door policy
Barriers to communication	Rap sessions
Semantic barriers	Vertical staffing meetings
Open communication	Suggestion systems
Downward communication	Attitude survey feedback

REVIEW AND DISCUSSION QUESTIONS

1. After reading this chapter, what actions do you recommend the personnel department take to prevent the kind of problem Leonard, Isabel, and Heinz had in the example at the beginning of the chapter?
2. Using your own judgment, develop a list of reasons why two-way communication usually is better than one-way communication.
3. Think of a situation in which you did not listen adequately and misunderstanding developed. Analyze and discuss this incident.
4. Prepare a list of the ways others have communicated to you nonverbally during the last twenty-four hours. Discuss. What could you do to improve your awareness of nonverbal communication signals?
5. Discuss different barriers to communication and how each of them interferes with communication.
6. Discuss how grapevines work in an organization and what kinds of feedback management can learn from them.
7. Think of a situation in which you learned some new information from the grapevine and took action on the basis of that information. Discuss.
8. List and discuss different programs that the personnel department manages in order to improve communication.
9. Describe why the best open-door policy is one where "The manager gets up from behind the desk and goes through the door to talk with employees."
10. Most organizations have a significant accounting department to collect data about the organization and its performance. However, very few organizations have even one full-time person whose responsibility is collecting information about employee attitudes. Why do you think this lack of a full-time person is common?
11. What reasons can you list that might explain why many suggestion systems do not work or do not work very well?

INCIDENT 17-1
LABORATORY EXERCISE: ONE-WAY COMMUNICATION AND THE GRAPEVINE

The instructor selects a short newspaper article of from three to five sentences and fifteen to thirty "message units," such as the following:

Melody Wilcox of the Radiology Department will be married to August Lindberg of the Computer Department on May 18 at St. Paul's Anglican Church on Broadway Street. Reverend William Merrihue will officiate at the double-ring ceremonies at 4:30 P.M. The couple plans a honeymoon in Niagara Falls with a stopover in Montreal.

Students A, B, C, and D are selected, and instructed to do their best to receive and communicate the message, which will come to them through a simulated grapevine chain from the instructor to A to B to C to D. Only one-way communication can be used, and the message can be given only once to each person.

Students B, C, and D are sent out of the room, and the instructor reads the message to student A. Then B is called into the room, and A states the message as completely as possible, only once. The process is repeated so that B tells C, C tells D, and D finally tells the class the message received.

1. When you performed this experiment, how did the final message differ from the original? Discuss. What barriers were evident?
2. Does this exercise indicate any weaknesses in one-way oral communication and in grapevine chains? Discuss.

INCIDENT 17-2
LABORATORY EXERCISE: ONE-WAY COMMUNICATION

The instructor prepares a sheet of paper that shows an arrangement of rectangles and triangles somewhat like the following:

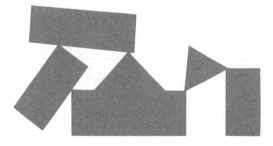

Students A and B are selected as message receivers. All other students are given a copy of the sheet of paper with the figures on it. Student B is sent out of the room for later recall. Then one of the students acts as instructor to tell student A how to draw the figures on the chalkboard. Only one-way communication can be used. Student A cannot ask questions. In addition, the instructor cannot tell student A whether the drawing is correct or incorrect until it is completed.

Then student B is called into the room, and the process is repeated with student B, except that two-way communication is allowed.

1. What kinds of communication problems developed in this exercise? Within the limitations of the assignment, was there any way the instructor could have improved the message? Did the receivers practise good listening?
2. Was better understanding achieved with two-way communication? Discuss.

REFERENCES

1. John Troyer, "The Use of Television in Employee Communications," *The Canadian Personnel & Industrial Relations Journal*, January 1975, p. 38.
2. Herman Roodman and Zelda Roodman, *Management By Communication*, Toronto: Methuen Publications, 1973.
3. Everett M. Rogers and Rekha Agarwala Rogers, *Communication in Organizations*, N.Y.: Free Press, 1976, p. 26. See also Jean M. Guiot, "The "Small World" Method and Organizational Communication," *ASAC (Organizational Behaviour Division) Meeting Proceedings*, Vol. 2, Part 5, 1981, pp. 52–60.
4. J. Donald Weinrauch and John R. Swanda, Jr., "Examining the Significance of Listening: An Exploratory Study of Contemporary Management," *The Journal of Business Communication*, Fall 1975, pp. 25–32.
5. See *The Journal of Communication*, December 1972 (a special issue on nonverbal communication), pp. 339–477; and Mark L. Knapp, *Nonverbal Communication in Human Interaction*, 2nd ed., New York: Holt, Rinehart and Winston, Inc., 1978.
6. Troyer, op. cit., pp. 36–39. See also Paul M. Muchinsky, "Organizational Communication: Relationships to Organizational Climate and Job Satisfaction," *Academy of Management Journal*, December 1977, pp. 592–607. See also Jacob P. Siegel, "Searching for Excellence: Company Communications as Reflections of Culture," *ASAC (Organizational Behaviour Division) Meeting Proceedings*, Vol. 5, Part 5, 1984, pp. 1–8; H. Broms & H. Gahmberg, "Communication to Self in Organizations and Cultures," *Administrative Science Quarterly*, Vol. 28, 1983, pp. 482–495.
7. Classic books on readability are Rudolf Flesch, *The Art of Plain Talk*, New York: Harper & Row Publishers, Incorporated, 1946; and idem, *The Art of Readable Writing*, New York: Harper & Row Publishers, Incorporated, 1949.
8. Walter D. St. John, "In-House Communications Guidelines," *Personnel Journal*, November 1981, pp. 872–878.
9. For example, see Roger M. D'Aprix, "The Believable House Organ," *Management Review*, February 1979, pp. 23–28. American Express Company publications for employees are summarized in "How Amex Employees Learn What's Happening," *Management Review*, February 1980, pp. 48–49.
10. Troyer, op. cit., p. 39. See also "TV that Competes with the Office Grapevine," *Business Week*, March 14, 1977, pp. 49–54.
11. "Spreading the Word about the Facts of Life in the Corporation," *Personnel*, May–June 1976, pp. 4–5.
12. For discussion of upward and downward communication programs, see the special section on communication in *The Personnel Administrator*, July 1979, pp. 23–55. See also Nancy Z. Reynolds, "Improving Upward Communication," *Management Review*, October 1977, p. 21. See also the Bank of America Open Line program in *Harvard Business Review*, January–February 1980, pp. 101–114.
13. Walter D. St. John, "Successful Communications between Supervisors and Employees," *Personnel Journal*, January 1983, p. 73.
14. See Keith Davis, *Human Behavior at Work: Organizational Behavior*, 6th ed., New York: McGraw-Hill Book Company, 1981, pp. 335–346.
15. "Deep Sensing: A Pipeline to Employee Morale," *Business Week*, Jan. 29, 1979, pp. 124–128.
16. "Vertical Staffing Meetings Open Lines of Communication at Rocketdyne Plant," *World of Work Report*, April 1979, pp. 27–28. See also Adri A. Boudewyn, "The Open Meeting—A Confidential Forum for Employees," *Personnel Journal*, April 1977, pp. 192–194.
17. "Employee Recognition: A Key to Motivation," *Personnel Journal*, February 1981, pp. 103–106.
18. *The "Key Program"*, Chicago: National Association of Suggestions Systems, 1983.
19. Lee A. Graf, "Suggestion Program Failure: Causes and Remedies," *Personnel Journal*, June 1982, pp. 450–454.
20. William J. Rothwell, "Conducting an Employee Attitude Survey," *Personnel Journal*, September 1982, pp. 689–691.

Chapter 18

Stress, Counselling, and Discipline

My problems are just as important to me as the president's problems are to him.

An employee

CHAPTER OBJECTIVES

After studying this chapter, you should be able to:
1. **Explain** causes of stress and how it affects performance.
2. **Define** employee counselling and the major types of counselling.
3. **Interpret** differences between directive and nondirective counselling.
4. **Explain** how progressive discipline works.
5. **Interpret** differences between preventive and corrective discipline.

Barbara Nichols, an office employee, walked into the office of her supervisor, Patricia Burnside.
Barbara: *Pat, may I see you for a moment?*
Patricia: *Come right in, Barb. What's on your mind?*
Barbara: *I'll get right to the point. I can't keep my mind on my work. I have so many problems at home that I get to thinking about them. My stomach's been upset for a week, and I guess you noticed yesterday that I got angry with Marvin about a trivial problem. Later I regretted what I did, but I couldn't help it. I was so upset.*
Patricia: *Yes, I did notice, and I was hoping you would come by to talk with me. Tell me more about how you have been feeling.*
Patricia *[After some discussion]: Perhaps we can help you, Barb. Our personnel department has working relationships with a number of community service organizations that can give professional help to people with problems like yours. And the service is always confidential. Is it all right if I call Dorothy Nance in the personnel department and make an appointment for you?*
Barbara: *Maybe I should give it a try.*

The worries and problems of Barbara Nichols are not unusual. All of us from time to time face difficulties, problems, and emotional upsets; and frequently another person can help us cope with them. Some difficulties occur off the job, and others are job-related. In either case, they may affect performance on the job and be of concern to management.

The first section of this chapter discusses stress, which is one of the major conditions that create a need for counselling. The next section explains counselling programs and how they are applied. If counselling is not successful and an employee continues with inadequate performance, some form of disciplinary action may be necessary, as will be discussed in the final section.

EMPLOYEE STRESS

Stress both on and off the job creates a major need for counselling. *Stress* is a condition of strain that affects one's emotions, thought processes, and physical condition. Excessive amounts of stress can threaten one's ability to cope with the environment.[1] As a result, employees develop various symptoms of stress that can harm their job performance. As shown in Figure 18-1, these symptoms involve both mental health and physical health. Persons who are stressed may become nervous and develop chronic worry. They are easily provoked to anger and are unable to relax. They may even develop stress-related physical ailments, such as stomach upsets. These conditions also occur from causes other than stress, but they are common symptoms of stress.

Figure 18-1
TYPICAL SYMPTOMS OF STRESS

• Nervousness and tension	• Excessive use of alcohol and/or tobacco
• Chronic worry	• Sleep problems
• Digestive problems	• Uncooperative attitudes
• High blood pressure	• Feelings of inability to cope
• Inability to relax	• Anger and aggression

CAUSES OF STRESS

The basic theory of stress, often called a *person-environment fit*, states that "when the resources and demands of the work environment do not fit the needs and abilities of the worker, the worker will develop symptoms of strain."[2] These eventually can lead to problems with job performance, physical health, and mental health. Conditions that tend to cause stress are called *stressors*. Although major distress can occur from only one stressor, usually stressors combine to affect an employee in a variety of ways until distress develops.

Bill felt that he was doing well, but then he failed to get a promotion that he had sought. At about the same time two of his key employees quit, and he had difficulty replacing them. Then his son got into trouble in high school, and the transmission failed on an automobile that he had planned to trade for a new one the next week. So many different problems were hitting Bill that he began to show signs of stress. He became easily upset, less considerate of employees, and less successful in meeting his deadlines.

JOB CAUSES OF STRESS

Almost any job condition may cause stress, depending upon an employee's reaction to it. For example, one employee will accept a new work procedure, while another employee rejects it. There are, however, a number of job conditions that frequently cause stress for employees. Major ones are shown in Figure 18-2.

Figure 18-2
TYPICAL CAUSES OF STRESS ON THE JOB

- Work overload
- Time pressures
- Poor quality of supervision
- Insecure political climate
- Insufficient performance feedback
- Inadequate authority to match responsibilities
- Role ambiguity
- Frustration
- Interpersonal and intergroup conflict
- Differences between company and employee values
- Change of any type

Work overload and time deadlines put employees under pressure and lead to stress. Often some of these pressures arise from supervision, and so a poor quality of supervision can cause stress. For example, the following stressful conditions are mostly created by supervision: an insecure political climate, lack of performance feedback, and inadequate authority to match one's responsibilities. Managers especially report that these conditions cause them to feel job stress.[3]

Another cause of stress is *role ambiguity*.[4] In situations of this type, superiors and coworkers have different expectations of an employee's responsibilities in a job, and so the employee does not know what to do and cannot meet all expectations. In addition, the job is often poorly defined, and so the employee has no official model on which to depend.

Frustration is a result of a motivation being blocked to prevent one from reaching a desired goal, and it is a major cause of stress.[5] If you are trying to finish a report before quitting time, you are likely to become frustrated by repeated interferences that prevent you from reaching your goal. You may become irritable, develop an uneasy feeling in your stomach, or have some other reaction. These reactions to frustration are known as *defense mechanisms*, because you are trying to defend yourself from the psychological effects of the blocked goal.

Both interpersonal and intergroup conflicts may cause stress. As people with different backgrounds, points of view, needs, and personalities interact there occur disagreements and other conflicts which may cause stress.

A further cause of stress is important differences between company values and employee values. In a sense, these differences "tear the employee apart" with mental stress as an effort is made to meet the requirements of both values.[6] For example, a salaried employee may value home life and regular quitting time. But that worker's manager may expect salaried employees to work overtime to meet department objectives. The company values employee loyalty, but the employee's loyalty may be family-centred.

A general and widely recognized cause of stress is change of any type, because it requires adaption by employees. It tends to be especially stressful when it is major, unusual, or frequent.

A sales representative named Dorothy Wang developed job stress as a result of certain management changes. During the last twelve months she had had three different sales managers, each with a different leadership style. As soon as Dorothy had adjusted to the style of one manager, she was forced to learn how to live with another. She felt insecure and under constant pressure. She longed for the day when she would have only one sales manager for two or three years and a measure of stability would return to her world.

A final source of stress on workers that is not listed in the above figure, but which is increasingly becoming important, is sexual harassment on the job. Sexual harassment is typically aimed at women by males who are in positions of power. It can range from unwanted comments or suggestions to attempted physical contact or actual rape, and includes subtle acts like sexual jokes or requests for dates.[7] No matter how subtle it is, sexual harassment is real and often extremely stressful.

OFF-THE-JOB CAUSES OF STRESS

Causes of stress off the job are the full range of problems that can occur to people, but certain causes are fairly common. As shown in Figure 18-3, managers report that their primary causes of stress off the job are financial worries, problems with children, physical problems, marital problems, and change in residence. The problem most reported was financial worries, with 38% of top managers and 52% of middle managers reporting this problem.

Other studies have reported that the most stressful personal problems are the death of a spouse or other close family member, divorce, marital

Figure 18-3
THE TOP FIVE OFF-THE-JOB CAUSES OF MANAGERIAL STRESS

- Financial worries
- Problems with children
- Physical problems
- Marital problems
- Change in residence

Source: Adopted from Ari Kiev and Vera Kohn, *Executive Stress*, New York: AMACOM, 1979, p. 35.

separation, and major injury or illness.[8] At these times the personnel department needs to be especially helpful with its personnel policies, counselling, and other programs.

BURNOUT

Burnout is a condition of mental, emotional, and sometimes physical exhaustion that results from substantial and prolonged stress. It can occur for any type of employee—whether one is a manager, professional, clerk, or factory worker. Even human resource managers may experience it.[9] Burned-out employees tend to feel used up, worn out, and "at the end of their rope."

People with burnout tend to have a variety of symptoms, such as depression and a low self-image.[10] They may become withdrawn and detached from interpersonal contacts and day-to-day activities. They tend to be irritable and blame others for their difficulties, and they may develop health problems, such as sleep disorders and excessive use of alcohol. They eventually can become so emotionally exhausted that they go through the motions of work but accomplish very little. As one employee described a burned-out associate, "His body is here today, but his mind stayed home."

With regard to burnout, the personnel department's role is a proactive one to help employees prevent burnout before it occurs. For example, the personnel department can train supervisors to recognize stress and rearrange work assignments to reduce it. Jobs may be redesigned, personnel conflicts resolved, counselling provided, and temporary leaves arranged. Many other approaches to stress reduction are discussed throughout this book. The popular statement that "prevention is better than curing" definitely applies to burnout, because it has high human and economic costs. Weeks or months of rest, reassignment, and/or treatment may be required before recovery occurs. Some emotional or health damage can be permanent.

One large paper and forest products firm was faced with problems of employee absenteeism, a large number of accidents, and poor employee morale. After trying other methods which did not yield any great success, the company decided to make a counselling program available to all its employees. Most counselling problems related to the job, alcohol and drug abuse, marital relations, family problems, and personal finances. One year after the counselling program was started, there was a 43% reduction in absences and a 70% reduction in the number of accidents.

STRESS AND JOB PERFORMANCE

Stress can be either helpful or harmful to job performance, depending upon the amount of it. Figure 18-4 presents a *stress-performance model* that shows the relationship between stress and job performance. When there is no stress, job challenges are absent and performance tends to be low. As stress increases, performance tends to increase, because stress helps a person call up resources to meet job requirements. It is a healthy stimulus to encourage employees to respond to challenges. Eventually it reaches a pla-

Figure 18-4
A STRESS-PERFORMANCE MODEL

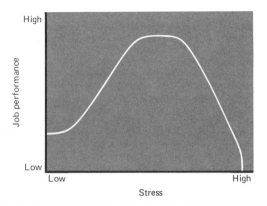

teau that represents approximately a person's top day-to-day performance capability. At this point additional stress tends to produce no more improvement.

Finally, if stress becomes too great, performance begins to decline, because stress interferes with it. An employee loses the ability to cope, becomes unable to make decisions, and is erratic in behaviour. If stress increases to a breaking point, performance becomes zero, because the employee has a breakdown, becomes too ill to work, is fired, quits, or refuses to come to work to face the stress.

STRESS THRESHOLDS

People have different tolerances of stressful situations. The level of stressors that one can tolerate before feelings of stress occur is one's *stress threshold*. Some persons are easily upset by the slightest change or emergency. Others are calm, cool, and collected, partly because they have confidence in their ability to cope. They feel very little stress unless a stressor is major or prolonged.

Mabel Kelly worked at the driver's licence desk in a provincial government office. She faced a variety of problems, complaints, angry citizens, and red tape during the day, but it did not seem to trouble her. On the other hand, Malcolm Morgan, her associate at an adjoining desk, had difficulty with the complaints, anger, and abuse that he received. He began taking longer breaks and then extra breaks. He seemed nervous. Finally, he asked for a transfer to another office.

The two employees had different stress thresholds.

TYPE A AND TYPE B PERSONS

Reactions to stressful situations are often related to Type A and Type B persons.[11] *Type A persons* are those who are aggressive and competitive, set high standards, and put themselves under constant time pressures. They even make excessive demands on themselves in recreational sports and leisure activities. They often fail to realize that many of the pressures they feel are of their own making, rather than in their environment. Because of the constant stress that they feel, they are more prone to physical ailments related to stress, such as heart attacks. A group of Canadian researchers has suggested that company environment, job conditions, and individual characteristics all combine to generate Type A behaviour (see Figure 18-5).

Type B persons are more relaxed and easygoing. They accept situations and work within them, rather than fighting them competitively. They are especially relaxed regarding time pressures, and so they are less prone to problems associated with stress.

Figure 18-5
THE PATHWAYS OF TYPE A BEHAVIOUR

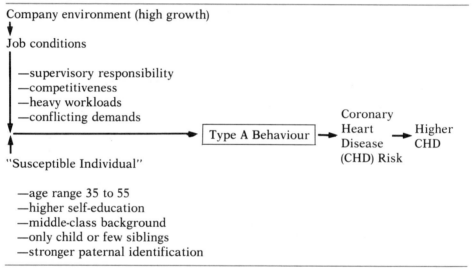

Source: John H. Howard, Peter A. Rechnitzer & David A. Cunningham, "Childhood Antecedents of Type A Behaviour," *ASAC (Organizational Behaviour Division) Meeting Proceedings*, Vol. 2, Part 5, 1981, p. 62.

RECOVERY FROM STRESS

Some persons recover from stressful situations easily. For example, some recover away from the job daily and return to work the next day refreshed. Others can recover over a weekend. Although stress builds up during the week, they return to work the next week ready to absorb more stress. Other persons allow stress to build up, and it is these persons who are of special concern to the personnel department.

Figure 18-6 shows the stress responses of three employees to the same job. Employee A showed moderate stress in the beginning but adapted rapidly. Employee B showed higher stress. There was some recovery over weekends, but stress built up again dur-

Figure 18-6
STRESS RESPONSES OF THREE EMPLOYEES TO THE SAME JOB

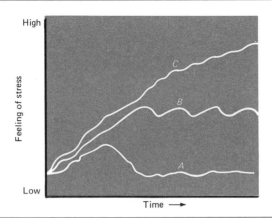

ing the week. In the case of employee C the stress was cumulative, becoming higher and higher. Each employee responded individually to stress.

PERSONNEL ACTIONS TO REDUCE STRESS

A desirable way to respond to stress is to try to remove or reduce its causes. For example, one option is to escape the stress, and the personnel department can help by arranging a transfer to another job, a different supervisor, and different work associates. Training and career counselling can be provided to qualify an employee for a new job.

Another way to reduce stress is to redesign jobs so that employees have more decision choices and authority to match their responsibility.[12] Job design can also reduce work overload, time pressures, and role ambiguity. Communication can be improved to give more performance feedback, and participation can be expanded.[13]

The personnel department also helps employees improve their ability to cope with stress. Better communication improves an employee's understanding of stressful situations, and training courses can be provided on the subject of coping with stress.[14] But counselling services may be the most effective way to help employees deal with stress.

Figure 18-7 shows some of the specific actions that the human resource department should take to reduce employee stress and burnout.

EMPLOYEE COUNSELLING

Counselling is discussion of a problem with an employee, with the general objective of helping the employee cope with it better. The basic purpose of counselling is to help employees solve their problems so that they can become more effective persons.

Figure 18-7
PERSONNEL ACTIONS TO REDUCE STRESS AND BURNOUT

- Develop a basic stress management policy for company approval.
- Communicate the policy to all employees in a sensitive, caring way. Then continue communication so that employees are always aware of the programs that are available to help them.
- Train managers to be sensitive to the early symptoms of stress so that they can take corrective action before it becomes severe. For example, an employee with signs of distress may be given less demanding work, encouraged to take a vacation, or referred to a counsellor.
- Train employees to recognize and cope with stress.
- Improve communication and participation throughout the organization so that employees understand what is affecting them and feel that they have a useful role in dealing with it.
- Monitor company activities to discover any conditions that unnecessarily lead to stress.
- Improve job and organization design to avoid stressful jobs.
- Provide counselling and other employee assistance programs to help employees in stressful situations.

The definition of counselling implies a number of characteristics that make counselling a useful activity in the personnel department. As shown in Figure 18-8, counselling requires two people, both a counsellor and a counsellee. It is their exchange of ideas that creates a counselling relationship, and so counselling is an act of communication. Counselling can improve organizational performance, because the employee is more cooperative, worries less about personal problems, or makes progress in some other way. It also helps the organization be more humane and considerate because it deals with people problems.

Figure 18-8
CHARACTERISTICS OF COUNSELLING

- Requires two people, a counsellor and a counsellee.
- Is an action of communication.
- Helps employees cope.
- Reduces employee problems and emotional upsets.
- Improves organizational performance.
- Helps an organization be more humane and considerate.
- Is performed by both professionals and nonprofessionals.
- Is usually confidential.
- Involves both job and personal problems.

One company has a slogan: "Our employees can handle just about any problem—except their own." Its counselling program is available to employees and their families. It maintains a twenty-four hour hot-line for contact any time and it uses both company counsellors and community agencies. The service is strictly confidential. A study of alcoholic employees who used this service reported a remarkable 85% reduction in lost work hours, a 47% reduction in sick leave, and a 72% reduction in sickness and accident benefit payments.

Counselling may be performed by both professionals and nonprofessionals. For example, both a personnel specialist in counselling and a supervisor who is not trained in counselling may counsel employees. Company physicians also counsel employees, and even the friends of an employee may provide counselling.

Counselling is usually confidential so that employees will feel free to talk openly about their problems. Counselling involves both job and personal problems, since both types of problems may affect an employee's performance on the job.[15]

NEED FOR COUNSELLING

Counselling programs emerged in response to problems caused by change and social unrest. In the 1970s many community counselling services were available, so companies expanded their use of these services as an extension of their own counselling programs. For example, family counselling and drug abuse counselling are available in most major cities. Firms refer their employees to these services and cooperate with them.

The need for counselling arises from a variety of employee problems. When these problems exist, employees need understanding and help of the type that counselling can provide. For example, an employee feels insecure about retirement, and so counselling is necessary. Another employee is hesitant to take the risk required by a promotion, so the employee ceases growing on the job. In other cases, family and financial problems develop. Employees themselves recognize that personal problems cause performance changes such as absenteeism. Figure 18-9 shows the percentage of employees who knew someone in their unit who was absent because of the personal problems listed. Marital problems led the list, with 15% knowing a fellow worker who was absent, but psychological problems were not far behind.

Figure 18-9
EMPLOYEES KNOWING COWORKERS WHO MISSED WORK FOR PERSONAL PROBLEMS LISTED

Problem	Percentage
• Marital problems	15
• Psychological problems	12
• Alcohol habit	9
• Overweight	6
• Smoking habit	3
• Drug habit	2

Source: Adapted from James A. Finkelstein and James T. Ziegenfuss, Jr., ''Diagnosing Employees' Personal Problems,'' *Personnel Journal*, November 1978, p. 635.

Many problems that require counselling are emotional in origin. Emotions are a normal part of life. But emotions can get out of control and cause workers to do things that are harmful to their own best interests and those of the firm. They may leave the firm because of a trifling conflict that seems large to them, or they may undermine morale in their department. Managers want their employees to maintain reasonable emotional balance and to channel their emotions along constructive lines so that they will work together effectively. Counselling is a useful tool to help accomplish this goal.

Counselling usually is performed by both professionally trained counsellors and nonprofessionals. For example, both personnel specialists in counselling and supervisors engage in counselling activities.

A study of supervisors in seven companies reported that they spent an average of 2.5 hours a week discussing moderately serious personal problems with their employees. The most frequently discussed problems were work related, such as difficulties with associates; but more personal subjects, such as marital problems, were discussed. The researchers' conclusion was that most supervisors "felt positively about being cast in the interpersonal helper role and considered that to be an important part of their job."[16]

Some firms, however, advise managers to avoid giving personal, nonjob advice to employees because the managers are not professionally qualified to do so. There is a chance that they will give inappropriate or wrong advice that aggravates an employee's problem.

COUNSELLING FUNCTIONS

Counselling functions are the activities performed by counselling. Major counselling functions are as follows:

• *Advice.* Counsellors often give advice to counsellees in order to guide them toward desired courses of action.

• *Reassurance.* The counselling experience often provides employees with reassurance, which is confidence that they are following a suitable course of action and have the courage to try it.

• *Communication.* Counselling is a communication experience. It initiates upward communication to management, and also it gives the counsellor an opportunity to interpret management problems and give work insights to employees.

• *Release of emotional tension.* People tend to get emotional release from their tensions when they have an opportunity to discuss them with someone else.

• *Clarified thinking.* Serious discussion of problems with someone else helps a person to think more clearly about these problems.

• *Reorientation.* Reorientation involves a change in an employee's basic self through a change in goals and values. Deeper counselling of the type practised by psychologists and psychiatrists often helps employees reorient values. For example, it helps them recognize their own limitations.

TYPES OF COUNSELLING

When we look upon counselling in terms of the amount of direction that a counsellor gives a counsellee, we see that it is on a continuum from full direction (directive counselling) to no direction (nondirective counselling), as shown in Figure 18-10. Between the two extremes is cooperative counselling. These three counselling types will be discussed in order to show how counsellors may vary their direction of a counsellee in a counselling situation.

Figure 18-10
COUNSELLING TYPES ACCORDING TO AMOUNT OF DIRECTION COUNSELLORS PROVIDE COUNSELLEES

DIRECTIVE COUNSELLING. *Directive counselling* is the process of listening to an employee's emotional problems, deciding with the employee what should be done, and then telling and motivating the employee to do it. Directive counselling mostly accomplishes the counselling function of *advice*, but it may also reassure, communicate, give emotional release, and to a minor extent clarify thinking. Reorientation is seldom achieved in directive counselling.

Most everyone likes to give advice, counsellors included, and it is easy to do. But is it effective? Does the counsellor really understand the employee's problem? Does the counsellor have the knowledge and judgement to make a "right" decision? Even if the decision is right, will the employee follow it? The answer to these questions often is "no," and this is why advice may not be helpful in counselling. On other occasions an employee welcomes guidance because of a counsellor's broader knowledge and contacts in a situation.

Ronald Clark came to a personnel counsellor, Vince Mardian, to discuss a conflict he was having with an employee in another department, Margie DeLaval. Ronald alleged that Margie reduced his incentive earnings by delivering products late from her department. He said that several loud arguments had developed. Vince offered some insights into interdepartmental difficulties so that Ronald could see that his problem was not unique. Vince advised, "Sit tight and don't rock the boat while I check this with the people involved."

Vince discovered that the problem resulted from some misunderstood instructions that caused Margie to deliver the products after her lunch rather than before. She also was upset by the conflict and was glad to try to settle it. Instructions were changed to provide delivery before lunch, and the problem was easily solved.

NONDIRECTIVE COUNSELLING. *Nondirective, or client-centred counselling* is at the opposite end of the continuum. It is the process of skillfully listening and encouraging a counsellee to explain bothersome problems, understand them, and determine appropriate solutions. It focusses on the counsellee rather than on the counsellor as judge and advisor; hence it is "client-centred." Some variation on this type of counselling usually is practised by professional counsellors.

Professionals often accomplish four of the six counselling functions. Communication occurs both upward and downward through the counsellor. Emotional release takes place, even more effectively than with directive counselling, and clarified thinking tends to follow. The unique advantage of nondirective counselling is its ability to encourage the employee's reorientation. It emphasizes changing the person, instead of dealing only with the immediate problem in the usual manner of directive counselling. Here is the way nondirective counselling typically works.

Harold Pace comes to a counsellor, Janis Peterson, for assistance. Janis attempts to build a permissive relationship that encourages Harold to talk freely. At this point Janis defines the counselling relationship by explaining that she cannot tell Harold how to solve his problem, but that she may be able to help him understand his problem and deal satisfactorily with it.

Harold then explains his feelings, while Janis encourages their expression, shows interest in them, and accepts them without blame or praise. Eventually the negative feelings are drained away, giving Harold a chance to express tentatively a positive feeling or two, a step that marks the beginning of Harold's emotional growth. Janis encourages these positive feelings and accepts them without blame or praise, just as she did the negative feelings.

Harold at this point begins to get some insight into his problem and to develop alternative solutions to it. As he continues to grow, he is able to choose a course of positive action and see his way clear to try it. He then feels less need for help and recognizes that the counselling relationship should end.

COOPERATIVE COUNSELLING. Nondirective counselling by employers is limited because it requires professional counsellors and is costly. Directive counselling often is not accepted by modern, independent employees. This means that the type of counselling used by many supervisors and personnel department employees is between the two extremes of directive and nondirective counselling. This middle ground is called cooperative counselling, because it uses the cooperative efforts of both the counsellor and the counsellee.[17]

Cooperative counselling is a mutual counsellor-employee relationship that establishes a cooperative exchange of ideas to help solve an employee's problems. It is neither wholly counsellor-centred nor wholly counsellee-centred. Rather, the counsellor and counsellee mutually cooperate to apply their different knowledge, perspectives, and values to problems. It integrates the ideas of both participants in the counselling relationship. It is, therefore, a balanced compromise that combines many advantages of both directive and nondirective counselling, while throwing off most of their disadvantages.

Cooperative counselling starts by using the listening techniques of nondirective counselling; but as the interview progresses, cooperative counsellors may play a more active role than a nondirective counsellor plays. They may offer bits of knowledge and insights that they have. They may discuss the situation from their broader knowledge of the organization, thus giving an employee a different view of the problem. In general, cooperative counsellors apply the four counselling functions of reassurance, communication, emotional release, and clarified thinking.

Mario Ponti came to see his supervisor about the insecurity he was feeling on his job. Because of technological changes in the type of work he did, he was losing confidence in his ability to retain his job. His supervisor did not tell Mario what to do (directive approach) and he did not merely listen to Mario (nondirective approach). Instead, the supervisor listened, offered some advice, communicated some ideas about training opportunities, and gave Mario reassurance that he could overcome his problem. The result was that Mario developed clarified thinking about a proper course of action.

COUNSELLING PROGRAMS

If a problem is one that a company can help, it usually provides counselling because of its long-run interest in working with employees. However, when a problem is a personal one such as a marital problem, the employee may be referred to community agencies. They are more prepared to work with these types of problems, and they have full-time professional counsellors. Referral also avoids questions about the employer's prying into the private lives of employees.

An example in the U.S. of an outside referral program for personal problems is Control Data Corporation's Employee Advisory Resource (EAR) program.[18] One of the program's slogans is: "Employees are bright and well-trained enough to handle just about any problem—except their own."

The program applies only to personal problems such as alcoholism. It uses a noncompany diagnostic and referral agency to do a diagnosis and refer each employee to the proper community agency. The diagnostic agency maintains a twenty-four-hour hot-line for contact at any time. The service is strictly confidential. There was no union opposition to it when it was introduced.

During one year over 4,000 employees used the service. Many successes were reported, although the program was unable to solve every employee's problem. A more specific study of alcoholic employees by Control Data reported a remarkable 85% reduction in lost work hours, a 47% reduction in sick leave, and a 72% reduction in sickness and accident benefit payments.

DISCIPLINE

Discipline is management action to enforce organizational standards. It is of two types, preventive and corrective.

PREVENTIVE DISCIPLINE

Preventive discipline is action taken to encourage employees to follow standards and rules so that infractions are prevented. The basic objective is to encourage self-discipline among employees. In this way the employees maintain their own discipline, rather than having management impose it.

Management has the responsibility for building a climate of preventive discipline. In doing so, it makes its standards known and understood. If employees do not know what standards are expected, their conduct is likely to be erratic or misdirected. Employees will better support standards that they have helped create. They will also give more support to standards stated positively instead of negatively, such as "Safety first!" rather than "Don't be careless!" They usually want to know the reasons behind a standard so that it will make sense to them.

The personnel department has major responsibility for preventive discipline. For example, it develops programs to control absences and grievances. It communicates standards to employees and encourages employees to follow them. It also gives training programs to explain the reasons behind standards and to build a positive spirit of self-discipline. On other occasions, it develops employee participation in setting standards in order to build commitment to them. Effective discipline is a system relationship, and so the personnel department needs to be concerned with all parts of the system.[19]

CORRECTIVE DISCIPLINE

Corrective discipline is an action that follows a rule infraction and seeks to discourage further infractions so that future acts are in compliance with standards. Typically the corrective action is a penalty of some type and is called a *disciplinary action.* Examples are a warning or suspension without pay.

The objectives of disciplinary action are as follows:

- To reform the offender
- To deter others from similar actions
- To maintain consistent, effective group standards

The objectives of disciplinary action are positive. They are educational and corrective, rather than a negative slapping back at employees who have done wrong. The goal is to improve the future rather than punish the past. A negative, punishing approach introduces too many undesirable side effects, such as emotional relations, apathy, absences, and fear of the supervisor.[20]

The corrective disciplinary interview often follows a "sandwich model," which means that a corrective comment is sandwiched between two positive comments in order to make the corrective comment more acceptable. An example is: "Your attendance is excellent, Roy (a positive comment), but your late return from coffee breaks disrupts our repair operations (negative). Otherwise, your work is among the best in our department (positive)."

The most drastic disciplinary action is *discharge,* which is separation from the company for cause. It has been said that every employee discharge is evidence of management and personnel department failure, but this view is not realistic. Neither managers nor employees are perfect; so some problems cannot be solved regardless of how hard people try. Sometimes it is better for an employee to go somewhere else. There are limits to how much effort an organization can devote to retain a poor employee.

RESTRICTIONS ON CORRECTIVE DISCIPLINE

In general, discipline is substantially restricted by unions and government and the rules, laws, and regulations that have grown up around them. Corrective discipline is an especially sensitive subject with unions. They see it as an opportunity to protect employees from unreasonable management authority and to show employees that the union leadership cares for their interests. Employees also are sensitive about disciplinary issues, because these issues can be a threat to employee pay and jobs. If there is a hint of unfairness in a disciplinary action, it can lead to a prolonged, costly dispute and eventual arbitration.[21] Walkouts and strikes can occur, and new bargaining issues about discipline may develop for the next bargaining session. The personnel department's job is to reduce chances for conflict by working with supervisors and union representatives to assure that corrective discipline is fairly and uniformly applied, and that employees and unions will accept such discipline as appropriate.

Government is increasing its regulation of discipline, making it more difficult to justify. The historical employer right to terminate an employee at any time without cause (the *termination-at-will doctrine*) is increasingly getting restricted.[22] For example, an employee cannot be disciplined or dismissed for union activities (as determined by law), conditions controlled by human rights legislation (such as race, sex, religion, etc.) or refusing to perform very hazardous or unsafe or unlawful activities. Other employment restrictions may also apply, depending on the circumstances and on the laws in the provinces concerned.

In all cases, *due process* for discipline may be required of the employer by courts of law, arbitrators, and labour unions. Due process means that established rules and procedures for disciplinary action are followed and that employees have an opportunity to respond to charges made against them.[23] It is the personnel department's responsibility to ensure that all parties in a disciplinary action follow the correct rules and procedures so that due process will be used.

If a disciplinary action is challenged, the personnel department also must have sufficient documentation to support the action; therefore, personnel policy usually requires proper documentation for all employer disciplinary actions.[24] Proper documentation should be specific, beginning with the date, time, and location of an incident. It also describes the nature of the undesirable performance or behaviour and how it relates to job and organizational performance. Specific rules and regulations that relate to the incident are identified. Documentation also states what the manager said to the employee and how the employee responded, including specific words and acts. If there were witnesses, they should be identified. All documentation needs to be recorded promptly, while the supervisor's memory is still fresh.

It should be objective, based on observations and not impressions. Documentation need not be lengthy, but it should be complete, precise, and accurate. If a supervisor follows these practical documentation guidelines, then the employer is reasonably protected in case of challenges by employees, unions, regulatory bodies such as the Human Rights Commission, and lawsuits.

THE HOT-STOVE RULE

A useful guide for corrective discipline is the hot-stove rule, as shown in Figure 18-11. The *hot-stove rule* states that disciplinary action should have the same characteristics as the penalty a person receives from touching a hot stove. These characteristics are that discipline should be with warning, immediate, consistent, and impersonal.

Figure 18-11
THE HOT-STOVE RULE FOR DISCIPLINE

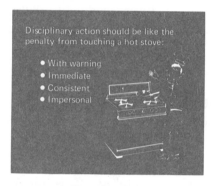

Warning is essential. It requires communication of the rules to all employees. If an employee can show that management failed to give adequate notice of rules, management will have difficulty justifying the discipline before a union or arbitrator.

Dorothy Settler was given a one-day suspension for smoking in a restricted area. She was able to show that there was not any "No Smoking" sign, and that she had had no other notice that smoking in the area was a fire hazard. The arbitrator revoked the penalty and ordered one day of back pay for Dorothy.

Discipline also should be *immediate*. When the discipline quickly follows an infraction, there is a connection between the two events in the employee's mind, and there is less probability for a future infraction.

Consistent discipline is required, because consistency is an important part of fairness. Lack of consistency causes employees to feel discriminated against. On the other hand, occasional exceptions can be justified.[25]

Walter Miller, who had worked eighteen years without a disciplinary infraction, came to work slightly intoxicated three weeks after the death of his wife. Different treatment for him was justified, compared with the penalty for Betina Rouse, who had only two years of seniority, had been warned twice about coming to work intoxicated, and then again came to work slightly intoxicated.

The hot-stove rule also requires *impersonal* discipline, just as a stove burns men and women, young and old, equally. The supervisor's like or dislike of an employee is not relevant to disciplinary action. Effective discipline condemns the employee's wrongful act, not the employee as a person. There is a difference between applying a penalty for a job not performed and calling an employee a lazy loafer. (Of course, managers should be personal and considerate enough of employee feelings to administer discipline in private.)

PROGRESSIVE DISCIPLINE

Most employers apply a policy of *progressive discipline*, which means that there are stronger penalties for repeated offences. The purpose of this is to give an employee an opportunity to take corrective action before more serious penalties are applied. Progressive discipline also gives management time to work with an employee to help correct infractions.

When Margaret Stoner had two unauthorized absences, the personnel department provided counselling. It also arranged for her to join a ride pool that allowed her to leave home thirty minutes later than with public transportation. Eventually her unauthorized absences stopped.

A typical progressive discipline system is shown in Figure 18-12. The first infraction leads to a verbal reprimand by the supervisor. The next infraction leads to a written reprimand, with a record placed in the files. Further infractions build up to stronger discipline, leading finally to discharge. Usually the personnel department becomes involved at Step 3 or sooner, in order to assure that company policy is applied consistently in all departments.

Figure 18-12
A PROGRESSIVE DISCIPLINE SYSTEM

1. Verbal reprimand by supervisor
2. Written reprimand, with a record in personnel file
3. One- to three-day suspension from work
4. Suspension for one week or longer
5. Discharge for cause

Some progressive systems allow minor offences to be removed from the record after one to three years, allowing each employee to return to Step 1. But specified serious offences, such as fighting or theft, are usually not dealt with by means of progressive discipline. An employee who commits these offences may be discharged on the first offence.

A COUNSELLING APPROACH TO DISCIPLINE

Most organizations use counselling in connection with discipline, but a few firms have moved a step further and taken a counselling approach to the entire procedure. In this approach, an employee is counselled rather than progressively penalized for the first few breaches of organizational standards. Here is how the program works in one organization.[26]

The philosophy is that violations are employee malfunctions that can be constructively corrected without penalty. The first violation results in a private discussion with the supervisor. The second violation brings further discussion with the supervisor with a focus on correcting causes of the behaviour. A third violation leads to counselling with the immediate supervisor and the shift supervisor to determine roots of the employee's malfunction. For example, does the employee dislike the job and want a transfer? Is the employee prepared to abide by the standard? The result of the discussion is given to the employee in a letter.

A fourth infraction within a reasonable time, such as a year, results in final counselling with the superintendent. The offender is released from duty with pay for the remainder of the day to consider willingness to abide by standards. The offender is told that a further violation, regretfully, will result in termination, because it shows that the employee is unable or unwilling to work within the standards of the organization.

The counselling approach is fact-finding and guiding, instead of retaliatory. In this manner the employee's self-image and dignity are retained and the supervisor-employee relationship remains cooperative and constructive.

SUMMARY

Counselling is sometimes necessary for employees because of job and personal problems, many of which are associated with stress. Major causes of stress include work overload, time pressures, role ambiguity, financial problems, and family problems. Stress affects both physical and mental health. The stress-performance model indicates that excessive stress reduces job performance, but a moderate amount may help employees respond to job challenges. Type A persons tend to show more stress compared with Type B persons. Personnel department programs to help reduce stress include job design, communication, training, and counselling.

Counselling is discussion of a problem with an employee to help the employee cope with it better. It is performed by the personnel department as well as supervisors. Major counselling functions are advice, reassurance, communication, release of emotional tension, clarified thinking, and reorientation. The most appropriate type of counselling for day-to-day problems is usually cooperative counselling. Counselling programs include both job and personal problems, and there is extensive cooperation with community counselling agencies.

Discipline is management action to enforce organizational standards, and it is both preventive and corrective. The hot-stove rule is a useful general guide for corrective discipline. Most disciplinary action is progressive, with stronger penalties for repeated offences. Some disciplinary programs emphasize a counselling approach.

TERMS FOR REVIEW

Stressors	Counselling functions
Role ambiguity	Directive counselling
Burnout	Nondirective counselling
Stress-performance model	Cooperative counselling
Stress threshold	Preventive discipline
Type A persons	Corrective discipline
Type B persons	Hot-stove rule
Counselling	Progressive discipline

REVIEW AND DISCUSSION QUESTIONS

1. Think of a part-time or full-time job that you have had. What stressors did you experience on the job?
2. Discuss how stress and job performance are related.
3. Do you feel that you are a Type A or Type B person? Do you have a high or low stress threshold? How would you rate your best friend on these items, and what are your reasons for choosing these ratings?
4. Discuss what the personnel department can do to help people cope with stress.
5. Explain the three types of counselling and ways in which they differ.
6. Discuss differences between preventive and corrective discipline. What examples of each were applied to you on the last job you had?
7. Marvin Katz became angry and used loud and abusive language with his supervisor in the data processing office. This was unusual behaviour for Katz. Do you recommend preventive or corrective discipline for Katz, or both?
8. Discuss different restrictions on an employer's right to discipline or dismiss an employee "at will," and explain why each of these restrictions probably exist.

INCIDENT 18-1
THE MACHINIST'S ABUSIVE COMMENTS TO THE SUPERVISOR

William Lee, a machine operator, worked as a machinist for Horace Gray, a supervisor. One day Horace told William to pick up some garbage that had fallen from William's work area, and William replied, "I won't do the janitor's work."

Horace replied, "When you drop it, you pick it up," and William became angry and abusive, calling Horace a number of uncomplimentary names in a loud voice and refusing to pick up the garbage. All employees in the department heard William's comments.

The situation was as follows: Horace had been trying for two weeks to get his employees to pick up garbage in order to have a cleaner workplace and prevent accidents. He had talked with all employees in a weekly department meeting and to each employee individually at least once; he had stated that he was following instructions of the superintendent. Only William objected with the comment, "I'm not here to do janitor's work. I'm a machinist."

William had been in the department six months and in the company three years. Horace had spoken to him twice about excessive horseplay, but otherwise his record was good. He was known to have a quick temper.

When William had finished with his abusive outburst, Horace told him to come to the office and suspended him for one day for insubordination and abusive language to a supervisor. This discipline was within company policy, and similar acts had been disciplined in this manner in other departments.

When William walked out of Horace's office, Horace called the personnel director, reported what he had done, and said that he was sending a copy of his action for William's file.

1. As a personnel director, what comments would you make?
2. What follow-up actions should the personnel director take or recommend that Horace take? For example, would you recommend counselling for William? Would you reconsider existing disciplinary procedures and policies?

INCIDENT 18-2
A COUNSELLING PROGRAM FOR DRUG ABUSE

Windsor Electronics, a growing electronics manufacturing firm, has increasingly faced problems with employees who abused alcohol and other drugs. Supervisors had previously been dealing with these employees in whatever ways seemed appropriate; however, both the supervisors and the personnel director now agreed that drug abuse problems were serious enough to require a company policy and a procedure to implement it. They also believed that the company needed a consistent, dependable policy to protect itself from possible human rights complaints of discrimination in counselling or treatment.

The personnel director asked his assistant, Carolyn Stevens, to prepare a policy and procedure for working with employees when drug abuse was suspected. Carolyn had been in the personnel department for three years following her graduation with a major in personnel management from a nearby university.

1. Form teams of three to five members and develop an appropriate drug abuse policy and procedure for Carolyn. Be sure to include specific steps covering who will work with drug abusers and what they should do. Then present your report to the entire classroom group and compare it with statements by other teams.

REFERENCES

1. For an expanded discussion, see Dennis W. Organ, "The Meanings of Stress," *Business Horizons*, June 1979, pp. 32–40; and Terry A. Beehr and John E. Newman, "Job Stress, Employee Health, and Organizational Effectiveness: A Facet Analysis, Model, and Literature Review," *Personnel Psychology*, Winter 1978, pp. 665–699. See also Hans Selye, *The Stress of Life*, rev. ed., New York: McGraw-Hill Book Company, 1976; and Hans Selye, *Stress Without Distress*, Philadelphia: J. B. Lippincott, 1974; R. L. Payne, T. D. Jick and R. J. Burke, "Whither Stress Research? An Agenda for the 1980s," *Journal of Occupational Behaviour*, 1982, 3, pp. 131–145; Robert Sass, "Stress: The Tolerated Bedfellow," *Canadian Dimension*, June 1980, p. 30; Robert Sass, *Stressors and Work Populations*, Regina: Occupational Health and Safety Branch, 1979.
2. "Coping with Job Stress," *ISR Newsletter* (Institute for Social Research, University of Michigan), Winter 1982, p. 4, referring to work by John R. P. French Jr., and others at the Institute.
3. John Howard, "To Reduce Stress Get Yourself a Senior Manager's Job," *The Canadian Personnel & Industrial Relations Journal*, 23(1), January 1976, pp. 27–31; Ari Kiev and Vera Kohn, *Executive Stress*, N.Y.: AMACOM, 1979, pp. 20–23.

4. Gene Deszca, Ronald Burke and Victor N. MacDonald, "Organizational Correlates of Role Stress of Administrators In the Public Sector," *ASAC (Organizational Behaviour Division) Meeting Proceedings*, Vol. 3, Part 5, 1982, pp. 100–109; Lyons, R., "Role Clarity, Need for Clarity, Satisfaction, Tension and Withdrawal," *Organizational Behaviour and Human Performance*, 1971, 6, pp. 99–110. See also V. V. Baba and M. J. Harris, "Strain and Absence: A Study of White-Collar Workers in Quebec," Working Paper #83-010, Montreal: Concordia University, Faculty of Commerce, 1983.

5. Ari Kiev and Vera Kohn, 1979, op. cit. See also Muhammad Jamal, "Hours of Work, Use of Leisure Time, Physical and Psychological Health Problems, and Work Performance: A Study in Work and Leisure," *ASAC (Organizational Behaviour Division) Meeting Proceedings*, Vol. 1, Part 4, 1980, pp. 38–47; James S. Manuso, "Executive Stress Management," *The Personnel Administrator*, November 1979, pp. 23–26, and the model of frustration reported in Paul E. Spector, "Organizational Frustration: A Model and Review of Literature," *Personnel Psychology*, Winter 1978, pp. 815–829.

6. Kurt R. Student, "Personnel's Newest Challenge: Helping to Cope with Stress," *The Personnel Administrator*, November 1978, pp. 20–24. See also John Howard, 1976, op. cit.; Gene Deszca, Ronald Burke and Victor N. MacDonald, 1982, op. cit.

7. Farida Shaikh, "Sexual Harassment: The Social Disease and How To Fight It" C.U.P.E.: *The Facts*, Vol. 2, March 1980, p. 107. See also "Harassment Exaggerated, Say Men", *The Calgary Herald*, February 18, 1981.

8. T. H. Holmes and R. H. Rahe, "The Social Readjustment Rating Scale," *Journal of Psychosomatic Research* November 1968, pp. 213–218.

9. A. R. Cahoon and J. I. A. Rowney, "The Three Phases Model of Burnout: A Comparison by Sex and Level of Management Responsibilities," paper presented at the ASAC (Organizational Behaviour Division) meeting, University of Guelph, Ontario, May 29, 1984. Oliver L. Niehouse, "Burnout: A Real Threat to Human Resources Managers," *Personnel*, September/October 1981, pp. 25–32. For books on burnout, see Robert L. Veninga and James P. Spradley, *The Work Stress Connection: How to Cope with Job Burnout*, Boston: Little, Brown, 1981; and Herbert J. Freudenberger, with Geraldine Richelson, *Burn-Out: The High Cost of High Achievement*, New York: Anchor Press/Doubleday, 1980.

10. For discussion see Harry Levinson, "When Executives Burn Out," *Harvard Business Review*, May–June 1981, pp. 73–81; Susan E. Jackson and Randall S. Schuler, "Preventing Employee Burnout," *Personnel*, March–April 1983, pp. 58–68; and Morley D. Glicken and Katherine Janka, "Executives under Fire: The Burnout Syndrome," *California Management Review*, Spring 1982, pp. 67–72.

11. John H. Howard et al., "Childhood Antecedents of Type A Behaviour," *Proceedings of the Administrative Sciences Association of Canada*, May 23–24, 1981, Halifax: Dalhousie University, 1981. See also Meyer Friedman and Ray H. Rosenman, *Type A Behavior and Your Heart*, New York: Alfred A. Knopf, Inc., 1974, and Karl Albrecht, *Stress and the Manager: Making It Work for You*, Englewood Cliffs, N.J.: Prentice-Hall, Inc., 1979; John M. Ivancevich, Michael T. Matheson and Cynthia Preston "Occupational Stress, Type A Behaviour and Physical Well Being," *Academy of Management Journal*, June 1982, pp. 373–391.

12. Robert A. Karasek, Jr., "Job Demands, Job Decisions Latitude, and Mental Strain: Implications for Job Redesign," *Administrative Science Quarterly*, June 1979, pp. 285–308. General strategies for handling stress are summarized in John E. Newman and Terry A. Beehr, "Personal and Organization Strategies for Handling Job Stress: A Review of Research and Opinion," *Personnel Psychology*, Spring 1979, pp. 1–43. See also Muhammad Jamal, 1980, op. cit.

13. "Redesigning the Workplace," *The Financial Times of Canada*, November 14–20, 1977, p. 11. See also John M. Ivancevich, "An Analysis of Participation in Decision Making among Project Engineers," *Academy of Management Journal*, June 1979, pp. 253–269. See also Saroj Parasuraman and Joseph A. Alutto, "An Examination of Organizational Antecedents of Stressors at Work," *Academy of Management Journal*, March 1981, pp. 48–67; and James B. Shaw and John H. Riskind, "Predicting Job Stress Using Data from the Position Analysis Questionnaire," *Journal of Applied Psychology*, May 1983, pp. 253–261.

14. Charles R. Stoner and Fred L. Fry, "Developing a Corporate Policy for Managing Stress," *Personnel*, May–June 1983, pp. 66–76. The article also has two excellent lists of corrective policies and action programs for reducing stress. See also Morley D. Glicken, "A Counselling Approach to Burnout," *Personnel Journal*, March 1983, pp. 222–228.

15. The beginning and early history of modern counselling are reported in F. J. Roethlisberger and William J. Dickson, *Management and the Worker*, Cambridge, Mass.: Harvard University Press, 1939, especially pp. 189–205, 593–604. Surveys of counselling practices are reported in Helen LaVan, Nicholas Mathys, and David Drehmer, "A Look at the Counseling Practices of Major U.S. Corporations," *Personnel Administrator*, June 1983, pp. 76ff.; Hermine Zagat Levine, "Employee Counseling Services," *Personnel*, March–April 1981, pp. 4–11; and Robert C. Ford and Frank S. McLaughlin, "Employee Assistance Programs: A Descriptive Survey of ASPA Members," *Personnel Administrator*, September 1981, pp. 29–35.

16. Elizabeth M. Kaplan and Emory L. Cowen, "Interpersonal Helping Behavior of Industrial Foremen," *Journal of Applied Psychology*, October 1981, pp. 633–638. See also, Ronald J. Burke, "Mentors in Organizations" *ASAC (Organizational Behaviour Division) Meeting Proceedings*, Vol. 3, Part 5, 1982, 41–48.

17. A participative counselling program is discussed in Stephen H. Appelbaum, "A Human Resource Counselling Model: The Alcoholic Employee" *Personnel Administrator*, August 1982, pp. 35–44.

18. Information supplied by Control Data Corporation; David Robison, "Social Responsibility Projects Make Business Sense at Control Data Corporation," *World of Work Report*, November 1976, pp. 1, 6–7; and "Outer Ear," *Wall Street Journal*, Western ed., Feb. 21, 1978, p. 1. For another approach, see Hana Ros-

tain, Peter Allan, and Stephen Rosenberg, "New York City's Approach to Problem-Employee Counseling," *Personnel Journal*, April 1980, pp. 305–309, 321.

19. James A. Belohlav and Paul O. Popp, "Making Employee Discipline Work," *The Personnel Administrator*, March 1978, pp. 22–24. See also Ira G. Asherman, "The Corrective Discipline Process" *Personnel Journal*, July 1982, pp. 528–531; Frank E. Kumits, "No Fault: A New Strategy for Absenteeism Control," *Personnel Journal* May, 1981, pp. 387–390.

20. Henry P. Sims, Jr., "Tips and Troubles with Employee Reprimand," *The Personnel Administrator*, January 1979, pp. 57–61; and idem, "Further Thoughts on Punishment in Organizations," *Academy of Management Review*, January 1980, pp. 133–138.

21. Laurence J. Stybel, Robin Cooper, and Maryanne Peabody, "Planning Executive Dismissals: How to Fire a Friend," *California Management Review*, Spring 1982, pp. 73–80; and Stanley J. Schwartz, "How to Dehire: A Guide for the Manager," *Human Resource Management*, Winter 1980, pp. 22–25; and Robert Coulson, "The Fine Art of Informing an Employee: You're Fired!" *Management Review*, February 1982, p. 37. Jeffrey C. Pingpank and Thomas B.. Mooney, "Wrongful Discharge: A New Danger for Employers," *Personnel Administrator*, March 1981, pp. 31–35.

22. Maria Leonard, "Challenges to the Termination-at-Will Doctrine," *Personnel Administrator*, February 1983, pp. 49–56; and Edward Mandt, "Employee Termination: Proceed with Care," *Management Review*, December 1980, pp. 25–28. For a general discussion of restrictions on the right to dismiss, see David W. Ewing, *Do It My Way or You're Fired!* New York: Wiley, 1983; Edward L. Harrison, "Legal Restrictions on the Employer's Authority to Discipline" *Personnel Journal*, February 1982, pp. 136–141; David W. Ewing, "Your Right to Fire," *Harvard Business Review*, March–April 1983, pp. 33–42. See also John Huberman, " 'Discipline without Punishment' Lives," *Harvard Business Review* July–August 1975, pp. 6–8.

23. David W. Ewing, "Due Process: Will Business Default?" *Harvard Business Review*, November–December 1982, pp. 114–122; and Bryan P. Heshizer and Harry Graham, "Discipline in the Nonunion Company: Protecting Employer and Employee Rights," *Personnel*, March–April 1982, pp. 71–78.

24. Ira G. Asherman and Sandra Lee Vance, "Documentation: A Tool for Effective Management," *Personnel Journal*, August 1981, pp. 641–643.

25. For differences between disciplinary policies for professional and nonprofessional employees see Irene Unterberger and S. Herbert Unterberger, "Disciplining Professional Employees," *Industrial Relations*, October 1978, pp. 353–359.

26. John Huberman, 1975, op. cit., Richard C. Grote, "Positive Discipline: Keeping Employees in Line Without Punishment," *Training* October 1977, pp. 42–44; James A. Belohlav and Paul O. Popp, "Making Employee Discipline Work," *The Personnel Administrator*, March 1978, pp. 22–24.

Part 5

Labour- Management Relations

Employees sometimes form unions. This action changes the framework of employee relations. It forces the personnel department to deal with the challenges of union organizing and bargaining. Then the collective agreement needs to be administered.

The next three chapters explain the challenges that you can expect when employees join unions. Your job is likely to be affected whether or not you are in the personnel department. But by understanding labour-management relations, you can avoid serious errors that may harm your career success.

Chapter 19

The Union-Management Framework

The principles which underlie the Canadian Industrial Relations system are reflected in Canada's heritage of fundamental Western values, in the liberal democratic system adopted in this country and in the modified capitalistic or mixed enterprise economy that has developed.

Task Force on Labour Relations[1]

CHAPTER OBJECTIVES

After studying this chapter, you should be able to:
1. **Explain** the relationship between unions, employers, and government.
2. **Describe** the nature and priorities of union objectives.
3. **Identify** illegal management and union activities.
4. **Distinguish** between various government agencies that enforce labour laws.
5. **Discuss** the major reasons why workers join unions.
6. **Describe** how unions affect the personnel management environment.

When employees are dissatisfied, they may band together and form a *union*. This does not mean the end of an organization's success. Many successful companies have one or more unions among their employees. But the use of collective action puts new limits on the role of personnel management. Many times, operating managers find these new limitations hard to accept. Consider the views of one plant manager in the following dialogue:

"As plant manager, I don't think we need to worry about unions. Our company pays good wages and has a sound benefit program," argued Dave Weldon.

"Sure our pay and benefits are fair. But a union could promise our employees even more. Besides, workers don't always join unions for higher pay or better benefits. They may want a union as a protest of company policies or simply because they feel unfairly treated," Stan commented.

"Well, if any supervisor is treating workers unfairly, they could tell me. I would

take action quickly. Since management at this plant takes care of workers, I don't think workers should want to join a union. If they did, I would try to stop it before it got out of hand," Dave added with little thought.

"When your boss does something you don't like, do you complain to the company president?" Stan questioned. "Most workers are probably reluctant to complain to you about their supervisors. And workers have a legally protected right to join a union!"

The union-management framework consists of three principal actors: workers and their representatives (unions); managerial employees (management); and government representatives.[2] Each of these parties depends upon the others, as shown in Figure 19-1. For example, the union relies on management for jobs and on the government for protection of workers' rights. Government protection is why Dave Weldon legally cannot fire employees who want to start a union. Managers depend on the union to honour its contract obligations. Government needs both unions and management to provide productive organizations that meet society's needs.

Although each party depends on the other, the parties are not equals. Government is the dominant force because it defines the roles of management and unions through laws. Within these laws, unions and management may use their respective powers to shape their relationship. For example, a powerful union may force management to make concessions in order to avoid a crippling strike. Likewise, when the union is weak, management can get concessions from the union because the threat of an effective strike is remote. The power of each side depends on the capacity of each to influence or threaten the other.

Figure 19-1
THE INTERDEPENDENCE OF UNIONS, MANAGEMENT, AND GOVERNMENT

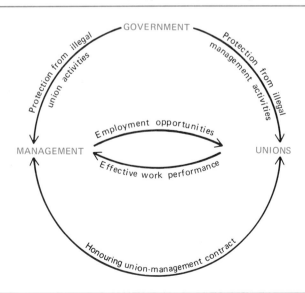

Durability is another characteristic of the labour-management framework. The process of collective bargaining between employers and unions has survived in its present form since the 1930s. Admittedly, the framework has undergone continuous refinements in law and practice. And unions, management, and the government have grown more sophisticated. But the three-way relationship has shown considerable stability, while remaining flexible enough to adjust to countless legal, social, and economic challenges.

This chapter explains the labour-management framework. It begins with a look at the goals, structure, and impact of unions on the work environment. Then the government's role is discussed. The chapter ends by examining the challenges that unions hold for personnel management.

LABOUR UNIONS AND PERSONNEL MANAGEMENT

Labour unions do alter the work environment. Their presence changes the relationship between employees and the organization, especially the role of supervisors and the personnel department. As seen through the eyes of one veteran supervisor, the personnel department's response to unions is not always well received by lower levels of management:

When I started working here in 1962, supervisors had it made. We handled our own discipline, hiring, and firing. We had clout around here. Then we got a union. Immediately, the personnel department grew and got involved in everything we did. We had training in how to deal with the union, training in the labour laws, training in what the contract meant, and training in all the new rules we had to follow.

Even worse, the personnel department started to have a bigger part in hiring, firing, and discipline. At the same time, I had to deal with the union representative. Of course, my manager still expected me to meet my department's objectives and its budget. Supervising sure is less satisfying than it used to be before the union and the personnel department made all these changes.

As this supervisor's comments indicate, unions have a major effect on the work environment, but in many other ways the environment remains unchanged. Supervisors and managers retain their primary responsibility for employee performance. Profit objectives and budgetary goals are not usually shared with the union. Nor do unions reduce the need for effective personnel procedures. In short, management must still manage; and the union does not assume the responsibilities of the personnel department.

To understand how and why unions influence human resource management, it is necessary to examine their goals and structure.

UNION GOALS AND PHILOSOPHY

Like other organizations, unions are social systems that pursue objectives. Their objectives are influenced internally by the wishes of their members, aspirations of their leaders, and the financial and membership strength of the union. And like other organizations, unions are open social systems that are affected by their external environment. The financial condition of the employer, the gains of rival unions, the inflation and unemployment rates, and government policies influence the union's objectives.

Yet among all these internal and external considerations, there does exist a common core of widely-agreed-upon objectives. According to one prominent labour leader, the mission for the labour movement is to protect workers, increase their pay, improve their working conditions, and help workers in general.[3] This approach has become known as *business unionism*, primarily because it recognizes that a union can survive only if it delivers a needed service to its members in a businesslike manner. But some unions have chosen to address broader social issues of politics and economics when such concern is in the best interests of their members. This second kind of union, engaged in what is called *social* (or *reform*) *unionism*, tries to influence the economic and social policies of government at all levels— municipal, provincial, and federal.[4] In practice, union leaders pursue the objectives of social unionism by speaking out for or against government programs. For example, many union leaders rejected federal government wage and price control in 1975 because it seriously impeded the collective bargaining process.[5]

Business and social unionism present unions with multiple, and sometimes conflicting, objectives. Figure 19-2 explains these trade-offs. For example, when the union bargains with management, it seeks high pay and good working conditions. But higher costs may cause the company to hire fewer workers or encourage management to use more automation. The social unionism trade-offs are less obvious.

Figure 19-2
TRADE-OFFS FACED BY UNIONS UNDER BUSINESS AND SOCIAL UNIONISM

Philosophical Approaches	Trade-Offs between Union Objectives		
Business Unionism	Maximize number of employed members.	OR	Maximize pay and benefits of members.
Social Unionism	Maximize welfare of members.	OR	Maximize welfare of working people.

Examples of this would be the unions' support of industrial safety acts. These acts improve the safety and health of all working people. But the cost of compliance may lessen the ability of union employers to provide pay raises. Thus social unionism causes labour organizations to face the trade-off of maximizing the well-being of all workers without minimizing the welfare of its members.[6]

Personnel management is influenced by both business and social unionism goals. The growth of fringe benefits discussed in Chapter 15 has resulted partly from union pressure. Even nonunionized employers have added many benefits in order to remain competitive in the labour market or to forestall unionization among their employees. Social unionism goals affect personnel management through such union-supported actions as the Canada Pension Plan and others. Consider how one personnel department responded to the business and social goals of unions.

A large foreign tire company had two plants in Nova Scotia, employing over 4,000 workers. To prevent the employees from seeking unionization, management paid wages significantly above those of other unionized companies in the region. Since some unions were able to negotiate dental plans with their employers, the management of the tire company offered its employees free dental insurance coverage as an extra inducement not to unionize.

UNION STRUCTURE AND FUNCTIONS

Some writers believe that employees lost direct contact with the owners as employers grew large, and so unions emerged to help workers influence workplace decisions.[7] Through unions, workers were able to exert control over "their jobs" and "their work environment."[8] Then when attempts were made by employers to cut wages, the employees relied on their unions to resist these actions.[9]

Early attempts to control the work environment were merely local efforts, because most employers were small local operations. As employers, particularly the railway companies, began to span municipal and then provincial boundaries, some labour organizations created national unions composed of locals all over the country; other locals either became affiliated with or were directly organized by strong U.S. unions, thus forming international unions. When social problems affected several national or international unions at once, they joined together and formed multiunion associations like the Canadian Labour Congress (CLC) or the American Federation of Labor and Congress of Industrial Organizations (AFL-CIO). In Canada there are several such associations, but the CLC is the most influential. A brief review of these four levels—the locals, the nationals, the internationals, and the multiunion association as represented by CLC and AFL-CIO—will illustrate the functions and structure of the unions that personnel departments encounter.[10]

QUEBEC. The development of the labour movement in Quebec is relatively independent of its development in the rest of Canada. Perhaps the most active role in organizing workers in Quebec was played by the clergy of the Roman Catholic Church. In 1921, there were enough unions to form the first national confederation, the Canadian and Catholic Confederation of Labour (C.C.C.L.). Because of their religious nature the unions in the C.C.C.L. strongly opposed the international unions, whom they perceived as antireligious and too materialistic. Only after World War II did the religious character of the C.C.C.L. change, and the change became official by 1960, when the organization adopted its present name, the Confederation of National Trade Unions (CNTU). Although the CLC's Quebec arm, the Quebec Federation of Labour (QFL), with about 275,000 members, represents most of the province's unionized workers, the CNTU is the largest independent labour federation in Quebec, with about 175,000 members. A number of large unions have chosen not to affiliate with either the AFL or the CNTU, e.g. the 80,000 teachers organized in the Centrale de l'Enseignement du Québec, and 30,000 provincial civil servants, members of the Syndicat des Fonctionnaires Provinciaux du Québec.

LOCAL UNIONS. For personnel administrators, the *local unions* are the most important part of the union structure.[11] They provide the members, the revenue, and the power of the entire union movement. There are three types of local unions: craft, industrial, and mixed local. *Craft unions* are composed of workers who possess the same skills or trades; these include, for example, all the carpenters who work in the same geographical area. *Industrial unions* include the unskilled and semiskilled workers at a particular location. When an employer has several locations that are unionized, employees at each location are usually represented by a different local union. Members of the United Automobile Workers are an example. A *mixed local* combines both unskilled and skilled employees. This arrangement is common, for example, in the electric utility industry, where the International Brotherhood of Electrical Workers includes skilled, semiskilled, and unskilled workers.

Figure 19-3 shows the structure of a typical local. The *steward* is usually

Figure 19-3
STRUCTURE OF A TYPICAL LOCAL UNION

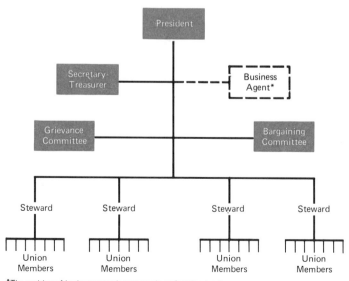

*The position of business agent is common in craft union locals.

elected by the workers and helps them present their problems to management. If the steward of an industrial or mixed local cannot help the employee, the problem is given to the *grievance committee*, which takes the issue to higher levels of management or to the personnel department. [12] In craft unions, the steward, who is also called the representative, usually takes the issue directly to the *business agent*, who is a full-time employee of the union.

This process of resolving employee problems, called the *grievance procedure*, limits personnel specialists and line managers because it challenges their decisions. If the challenge is successful, the result may serve as a precedent that limits future decisions.

Christine Rae was a department manager in a large retail store. Whenever she needed someone to work overtime, she asked the first employee she saw. One employee, Ian George, filed a formal grievance which complained that overtime was not granted fairly to all employees. Eventually the problem reached the regional personnel manager and the union president. They agreed that in the future overtime would be rotated among all departmental employees. The solution of this grievance set a precedent that other managers of union workers must follow in granting overtime.

An even more important limitation on supervisors and personnel specialists is the collective agreement. It normally specifies wages, hours, working conditions, and related issues such as grievance procedures, safety standards, probationary periods, and benefits. It is usually negotiated between the local union's *bargaining committee* and the personnel or industrial relations department.

NATIONAL UNIONS. Most local unions are part of a larger association called the *national union*. It exists to organize and help local unions. It also pursues social objectives of interest to its members.

Most national unions maintain a staff that assists the local unions with negotiations, grievance handling, and expert advice. Among the craft unions, the national tends to leave many key decisions to the locals. Mixed and industrial nationals are more likely to be involved with their locals. For example, a national union may require that locally bargained contracts receive its approval. Sometimes the national union may actually bargain an industry-wide contract, as the United Automobile Workers union does in the automobile industry.

INTERNATIONAL UNIONS. There are approximately as many national as international unions in Canada (ninety-eight and ninety-four). [13] An international union provides services similar to those of a national union, the major difference being that the international union operates in Canada *and* the U.S. and has headquarters in the U.S. Since international unions are usually stronger financially, they are in better condition to support locals in a prolonged strike. [14]

CLC. The CLC represents most of the unions in Canada, and has a total

Figure 19-4
STRUCTURE OF THE CANADIAN LABOUR CONGRESS

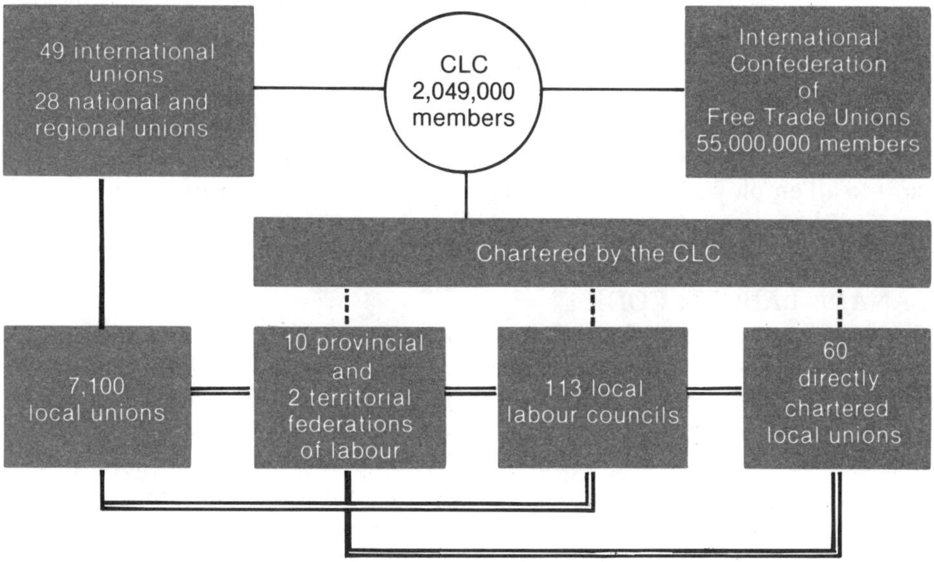

Source: Canadian Labour Congress, "The Structure of Labour in Canada," *Notes on Unions*, Ottawa: CLC, 1983, p. 2.

membership of over two million.[15] It is primarily a service organization composed of seventy-seven national and international unions who finance the CLC through dues based on the size of their membership. Figure 19-4 illustrates the structure of the CLC.

One of the major objectives of the CLC is to influence legislation and promote programs which are relevant to the labour force. It achieves these objectives through lobbying, education, and research.

AFL-CIO. The AFL-CIO is the U.S. counterpart of the CLC. The two organizations operate independently, but since most international unions in the AFL-CIO are also members of the CLC, a certain degree of common interest exists. Most international unions are dues-paying members of both organizations.

GOVERNMENT AND PERSONNEL MANAGEMENT

Government shapes the union-management framework through laws and their interpretation. The federal government's role comes from its obligation to protect the welfare of society and from the authority found in Section 91 of the British North America Act which states that the Canadian Parliament shall have the power to "make laws for the Peace, Order, and Good Government of Canada," in relation to those matters not assigned exclusively to the provinces. The latter part of this statement is quite significant for personnel practitioners, because the Canadian Parliament is restricted in its jurisdiction over labour relations matters to organizations involved in interprovincial trade and commerce, e.g. banks, airlines, railways, and federal government agencies. All other organizations fall under the jurisdiction of the provinces. It has been estimated that only about 10% of the Canadian labour force comes under federal jurisdiction, in contrast to about 90% in the United States.[16] Nevertheless, a number of federal laws are relevant to all employees in Canada. Those laws, and the appropriate provincial laws, will be discussed in the following sections.

CANADA LABOUR CODE

The backbone of Canadian labour legislation has been—and still is, with modifications—the Industrial Disputes Investigation Act of 1907, now the Canada Labour Code, in effect since 1971. Two major components make this legislation unique as compared to similar laws in the United States and the United Kingdom: the creation of a tripartite Labour Relations Board and the delay of the right to strike or to lockout until conciliation efforts have failed. Otherwise, the law gives employees the right to organize without interference by employers. It also requires any party to a collective agreement to bargain in good faith.

To prevent employers from interfering with employee rights, the law prohibits specific *unfair labour practices* by management. These legal prohibitions are summarized in Figure 19-5. They require that management neither interfere with nor discriminate against employees who undertake collective action. These unfair labour practices also make firing these employees illegal and outlaw "blacklisting" and "yellow dog" contracts.

Figure 19-5
UNFAIR LABOUR PRACTICES BY MANAGEMENT

The Canada Labour Code makes it an unfair labour practice for members of management to:
   1. Suspend, transfer, lay off, or otherwise discriminate against employees who want to unionize.
   2. Impose any condition in a contract of employment that restricts an employee's rights under the code.
   3. Suspend, discharge, or impose any penalty on an employee for refusing to perform the duties of another employee who is participating in a legal strike.
   4. Deny pension rights or accrued benefits to an employee because of involvement in a legal strike.
   5. Intimidate or threaten an employee to compel that person to refrain from becoming or cease to be a member, officer, or representative of a trade union.
   6. Bargain collectively with a trade union if another trade union is the bargaining agent of that bargaining unit.

Before the Canada Labour Code was passed, a common personnel policy was to require new employees to sign a "yellow dog" contract. This employment contract meant that if an employee assisted a union in any way, that person could be fired. Those who agreed to these contracts were often called "yellow dogs." And anyone who supported unions might be "blacklisted" by the previous employer's giving a negative reference. [17]

The Canada Labour Code also makes company-dominated unions illegal. In the past, some employers believed that if they could not prevent their employees from organizing, the next best thing would be to encourage a union they could dominate. Through threats, bribes, or infiltration, some companies tried to control union activities. For example:

Robin Hood Multi-Foods Inc. in Ontario arranged for an employee to infiltrate the Service Employees International Union, take part in its deliberations, and report back to general management about its activities. The Ontario Labour Relations Board issued a "cease and desist" order and required the company to post a notice in the plant explaining the board's order and making it clear that the company would not engage in any of a long, specified list of unfair labour practices. [18]

The law also prohibits employers from discriminating against anyone who brings charges against a company for violating the law. And to make the result of unionization meaningful, employers must bargain with the union in good faith over wages, hours, and working conditions.

Unfair labour practices by unions are also prohibited. Such practices are described in Figure 19-6.

To illustrate how few constraints unions faced before this law was passed, consider how one powerful union arranged for a large number of its unemployed members to

Figure 19-6
UNFAIR LABOUR PRACTICES BY UNIONS

The Canada Labour Code makes it an unfair labour practice for a trade union to:

1. Seek to compel an employee to bargain collectively through it if the trade union is not the bargaining agent of a unit which includes that employee.

2. Bargain collectively with an employer if the trade union knows or ought to know that another trade union is the bargaining agent for the unit of employees.

3. Participate in or interfere with the foundation or administration of an employers' organization.

4. Attempt, at the workplace and during working hours, to persuade an employee to become a union member—except with the consent of the employer.

5. Require an employer to discharge an employee because he or she has been expelled or suspended by the trade union for reasons other than failure to pay membership dues.

6. Expel or suspend an employee from membership, or deny membership, by applying union membership rules in a discriminatory manner.

7. Intimidate, coerce, or penalize a person because he or she has filed a complaint or testified in any proceedings pursuant to the code.

picket a small trucking firm. The pickets so severely interfered with deliveries that the owner was forced to recognize the union against the wishes of his employees.

When negotiations on the first contract began, the union leader refused to meet with the company's lawyer. The owner was told to pick someone else to represent the firm. The owner, having no legal remedies and fearing more disruption, hired a new attorney. Then the union presented the lawyer with a completed contract and said, "Sign or we strike." There was no negotiation, and the company signed.

Although most unions do not abuse their power, isolated cases like this one contributed to legal restrictions on unions.

The law makes it illegal for unions to force employees into a union or to interfere with an employer's selection of its collective-bargaining representative. It also requires unions to bargain with management in good faith.

As has been mentioned before, federal legislation like the Canada Labour Code is relevant only to employees and employers under federal jurisdiction, whereas most employees and employers are governed by provincial legislation. Fortunately for the personnel practitioner, the content of provincial laws is similar to that of the federal law. Nevertheless, for specific legal problems the relevant jurisdiction and appropriate laws have to be determined.

Despite the fact that Canada has eleven independent jurisdictions affecting employee-employer relations, it is possible to distinguish some common characteristics, which are outlined in Figure 19-7.

Figure 19-7
COMMON CHARACTERISTICS OF FEDERAL AND PROVINCIAL LABOUR LEGISLATION

---

1. All jurisdictions create labour relations boards to decide who has the right to participate in collective bargaining and what bargaining unit should be permitted to represent those who are organized.

2. All jurisdictions (except Saskatchewan) prohibit strikes during the life of an agreement.

3. All jurisdictions (except Saskatchewan and British Columbia) contain regulations which delay strike action until a conciliation effort has been made and has failed.

4. All jurisdictions require that a collective agreement be in force for at least one year.

5. All jurisdictions specify and prohibit certain "unfair practices" by management and unions.

LABOUR RELATIONS BOARDS

To enforce the Canada Labour Code at the federal level and related legislation in the provinces, the federal and all provincial governments have created their own Labour Relations Boards (LRB). These agencies investigate violations of the law and have the power to determine: (1) whether a person is an employee for the purposes of the law; (2) whether an employee is a member of a trade union; (3) whether an organization is an appropriate bargaining agent for bargaining purposes; (4) whether a collective agreement is in force; and (5) whether or not any given party is bound by it. The enforcement procedures of an LRB are summarized in Figure 19-8.

Figure 19-8
LRB PROCEDURES FOR REDRESSING UNFAIR LABOUR PRACTICES

1. The aggrieved individual or organization contacts the appropriate LRB office (federal or provincial) and explains the alleged violation.

2. If the case appears to have merit, the LRB informs the other party of the complaint and asks for a response.

3. The LRB gives the parties involved the opportunity to present evidence and to make representations. If the complaint cannot be solved informally, the LRB conducts an official hearing with the interested parties present and usually represented by legal counsel.

4. On the basis of the evidence, the board will either dismiss the case or, if one party is found guilty of a violation, issue a cease-and-desist order. In the event of non-compliance, this order is enforceable in a court of law.

5. It is up to the board to decide whether a verdict can be appealed or not. In any case, an appeal can be made in matters of jurisdiction, failure to pursue legitimate complaints, and procedural irregularities.

In comparison to traditional courts of law, LRBs are more flexible in their procedures for solving a conflict. They may rely on expert testimony instead of looking for precedents, suggest a compromise, or even impose a solution upon the parties. In all jurisdictions, the boards' decisions are final and binding and cannot be appealed except on procedural matters. On the other hand, the boards may revise, rescind, or override any of their decisions.

When charges have been filed against an employer, the personnel department usually assists the company's attorney in preparing the case. The department compiles performance appraisals, attendance records, and other documents that help the company prove its case. Sometimes the department's investigation reveals that the company is guilty. At this point, time and legal costs are saved by admitting guilt and accepting the LRB's proposed settlement.

Personnel departments also become involved when the LRB holds an employee election. This other function of the LRB comes into play when a union applies for certification as a bargaining unit. The election is held to determine if a majority of the employees want a union.

In cases where a substantial number of employees (usually between 50 and 60%, depending on jurisdiction) have signed union cards, the LRB may certify the unit without an election. However, if the number of signed union cards is less than the majority but over some figure between 35 and 45% (again depending on jurisdiction), an election is mandatory. A secret ballot is taken under the supervision of the LRB at the employees' place of business. If the union loses, another election among the same employees cannot be held for one year. If the union wins, then the personnel department must prepare to bargain with the union and reach a collective agreement.

CONCILIATION AND MEDIATION. In their legislation, all jurisdictions provide for conciliation and mediation services. Actually (with the exception of Saskatchewan and British Columbia), no strike action is permitted before a conciliation effort has been made and has failed. The terms conciliation and mediation are often used interchangeably, but in Canada some jurisdictions give them different definitions. "Conciliation" usually implies a relatively passive role by the third party (conciliator) involved, the major purpose being to bring the parties together and keep them talking. "Mediation" connotes a more active involvement of the third party. A mediator may make suggestions and recommendations after having determined the positions of the parties. Often a mediator will meet separately with each bargaining team, especially when the negotiations take place in a hostile atmosphere. Effective mediation requires a high degree of sensitivity, patience, and expertise in the psychology of negotiation. An example will illustrate how a skillful mediator enabled deadlocked negotiations to get moving again.

> I had a case where the union had asked for a 15 per cent increase in a one-year contract. Their spokesman told me he would go to 10, but not now—not until the company indicated some movement. The company was holding at 5, but said to me they would go to 7, if the union would come down a little. Both of the parties convinced me that they would go no further, and a strike seemed certain.
>
> In some cases, if I knew the parties well, I would tell them exactly what the other said. However, in this case I simply indicated to each bargaining team in separate meetings that there was some flexibility in the other's position, but I didn't know how much. Then I said to the union: "I'd like to see you get 10 per cent or even 15, but I don't believe the company will go that high. In my opinion the most you can get is 7 or 8 per cent. I may be mistaken, but if you hold to the 10 per cent figure I think you'll have a strike."
>
> Then I went to the company and said: "If you hold to the 5 or 7 per cent figure I can almost assure you that you'll have a strike. Now the decision is yours, and it's not for me to tell you how to spend your money, but in my opinion the settlement will eventually be 10 per cent, and I think 10 per cent might do it now. You might have to go as high as 13. If you want me to explore 7 per cent I'll give it a try, because, as I've said, the union has indicated some flexibility. But I don't think 7 per cent will get a settlement."[19]

Conciliators and mediators are appointed by the federal or provincial ministers of labour, at the request of either one or both of the parties involved or at the discretion of the ministers. A conciliator is requested to submit a report to the minister within a specified time period. If conciliation fails, strikes or lockouts can legally commence, usually two weeks after the submission of the conciliator's report. A mediator is not required to write a report on the legality of a strike or lockout and in fact has no influence in this matter.

ARBITRATION. All jurisdictions, with the exception of Saskatchewan, require that collective agreements include a provision for final settlement by arbitration, without stoppage of work, of all differences concerning the interpretation or administration of a contract. This means that as long as a collective agreement is in force, any strike or lockout is illegal. An arbitrator is selected from a list furnished by the appropriate ministry of labour, and the choice must be approved by both parties. If this is not possible, an arbitrator is appointed by the minister of labour. The arbitrator's decision is final and cannot be changed or revised, except in cases wherein corruption, fraud, or a breach of natural justice has been proven.

CORPORATIONS AND LABOUR UNIONS RETURNS ACT. In the 1960s and early 1970s, Parliament created a number of royal commissions and study groups that investigated many aspects of organized labour and labour-management relations. The investigations were largely fact-finding exercises, conducted in hopes of providing information and recommendations which would be useful in the drafting of new legislation. Of considerable concern to the federal government and the public were reports of mismanagement of funds and corruption by officials of national and international unions. Based upon the results of some investigations, Parliament in 1962 passed the Corporations and Labour Unions Returns Act, designed primarily to gather information on the activities and financial dealings of international unions and corporations. The act requires unions and corporations to submit annual reports containing statements of assets and liabilities, income and expenditures, and other more detailed information relating to financial matters. This information is published annually (in summary form to maintain anonymity) by Statistics Canada and is available to interested parties.[20]

PUBLIC SERVICE STAFF RELATIONS ACT

When Parliament passed the Public Service Staff Relations Act (PSSRA) in 1967, it essentially gave federal civil servants bargaining rights similar to those granted workers in the private sector: usually the right to bargain for wages, hours, and certain working conditions. More importantly, it also gave them the right to strike. This is in contrast to civil servants in the United States, who since 1962 have had the right to bargain collectively, but not to withhold their services. The PSSRA created the Public Service Staff Relations Board (PSSRB), a body equivalent to the Canada Labour Relations Board in the private sector. However, the PSSRB possesses a wider range of responsibilities than the CLRB. The reason for this lies mainly in the conflict-of-interest situation that arises with the federal government having to protect the public welfare on the one hand and being in the role of an employer on the other. Like the CLRB in the private sector, the PSSRB is responsible for certification of unions as bargaining agents for appropriate groups of employees. The methods of conflict resolution, however, are different. Before a bargaining agent can give notice that it wishes to bargain, a decision must be made whether a conciliation-strike procedure or a binding-arbitration procedure will be used should a deadlock occur. Once that decision is made and the PSSRB has been informed, the employer must accept it. The union has the right to choose different procedures for each subsequent collective agreement. If the strike route has been chosen, conciliation procedures must be followed before a strike can begin. The chairman of the PSSRB will appoint a conciliation officer at the request of either party. Once the officer has submitted his or her report, the chairman of the PSSRB will decide whether or not to appoint a conciliation board. If a board is not appointed, or if an appointed board is unsuccessful in settling the dispute, the union may initiate strike action.

Another difference from the private sector is that the law allows the employer to designate certain employees as performing essential services, thus divesting them of the right to strike. The union, however, may challenge the list of "designated employees," in which case the PSSRB makes the final decision. This latter function gives the board a certain responsibility for the safety and security of the public, since in a strike of civil servants it must decide which services are essential.

PROVINCIAL LEGISLATION. A comparison of the federal and provincial legislation for public service labour relations reveals little uniformity of treatment across Canada. In Saskatchewan the public sector is treated the same as the private sector (meaning there is no special legislation), whereas in Alberta, Ontario, Nova Scotia, and Newfoundland, there are different legal frameworks for the public and the private sectors, with severe restrictions on or even total prohibition of strikes. The remaining provinces are somewhere in between. It can be said, however, that the general trend is toward granting public sector employees the same rights as private employees.

THE CHALLENGE TO PERSONNEL MANAGEMENT

Today, many personnel managers and union leaders perceive government intervention as a threat to the traditional freedoms they both have enjoyed. Their common concern rises out of the fear of more government laws that will control their affairs. And since existing laws are enforced by agencies with the power to "make laws" by their interpretation of existing ones, regulations are bound to grow.

Closer union and management cooperation to improve labour relations is a major way to slow the growth of government regulations. This does not mean that either party must abandon its constituents: rank-and-file members and stockholders. On the contrary, both sides must continue to perform. What is needed is a realization that cooperation, not legalistic advocacy, represents the shortest route away from additional government constraints. Otherwise, political expediency and public welfare will demand, for better or worse, further legislative action, new agency decisions, and more government constraints.[21]

PERSONNEL'S PROACTIVE RESPONSE

Unions cause changes in the behaviour of managers and in the operation of the personnel function. In nonunionized facilities, an implicit objective of personnel management is often to remain nonunion. Since the Canada Labour Code prohibits the use of coercion or discrimination, management must rely on a proactive approach. That is, it must use *effective* personnel practices that discourage unionization, if that is the company's policy. For example, this approach requires that personnel specialists (within the constraints of organizational effectiveness and efficiency, law, technology, and other challenges) carefully do the following:

- *Design* jobs that are personally satisfying to workers.
- *Develop* plans that maximize individual opportunities while minimizing the possibility of layoffs.
- *Select* workers who are qualified.
- *Establish* fair, meaningful, and objective standards of individual performance.
- *Train* workers and managers to enable them to achieve expected levels of performance.
- *Evaluate* and reward behaviour on the basis of actual performance.

In other words, personnel managers need to apply actively the ideas discussed in earlier chapters of this book! Failure to implement sound personnel policies and practices provides the motivation *and* justification for workers to form unions.

PERSONNEL MANAGEMENT IMPLICATIONS

When unions are present, the personnel function is changed. Organizationally, the personnel department is expanded by the addition of a labour relations section. This section allows labour specialists to deal with such critical areas as negotiations and contract administration, while personnel professionals attend to their more traditional roles. In fact, personnel and labour relations may form two equal divisions within a broader department, typically called *industrial relations*.

Operationally, the personnel section seeks sound employee relations through effective policies. "Open door" policies and in-house complaint procedures are two examples. The labour relations section has a complementary role. It wants to minimize the restrictions on management by diligent negotiations and fair administration of the union contract. Or to use a sports analogy, personnel serves as the offensive team and labour relations as the defensive team.[22]

Unions can cause greater centralization of employee record keeping and discipline to ensure uniformity. This change can mean that line managers lose some of their authority to the personnel department. They also find their jobs more difficult because of the new rules imposed by the contract. In other words, line managers may become dissatisfied because their authority diminishes while their responsibility increases. These added responsibilities are likely to be imposed at the request of personnel administrators, who now need more information from the line managers. To illustrate, the line manager may have to compile new reports on absenteeism, tardiness, productivity, and comments voluntarily made by workers about the union. Often these demands on supervisors create a fertile ground for friction between line managers and personnel staff members.

Besides the high costs for record keeping, additional staff, negotiations, and occasional strikes, management has less freedom to make unilateral changes. No longer can a manager decide what is desirable and then make a change. Instead, union-management agreements and the labour laws must also be considered.

A large manufacturing company was losing money on the company cafeteria in one of its plants. Although the company never expected to make money from this operation, it certainly wanted to break even. To correct the deficit, the company raised prices slightly without discussing this with the union. The union threatened to file an unfair labour practice charge unless management reduced the prices and agreed to negotiate the matter.

Although this incident is relatively minor, every year there are thousands of unfair labour practice cases. And even more significant than the time and costs of such legal actions are the inefficiencies caused when unilateral decisions must be reversed. The processes used to create a bilateral relationship will be discussed in the next chapter.

SUMMARY

The labour-management framework consists of unions, governments, and management. Although each union is unique, unions share the common objectives of protecting and improving their members' wages, hours, and working conditions. To further these objectives, the union movement has created local, national, and international structures, plus federations at the provincial and federal levels. Moreover, most unions are loosely incorporated into the Canadian Labour Congress (CLC).

In Canada the federal government has jurisdiction in labour relations matters over only Crown corporations, airlines, most railways, communication companies, and federal government agencies—or approximately 10% of the labour force. All other organizations fall under the jurisdiction of the provinces, who have enacted separate but similar legislation. Every jurisdiction has its own labour relations board which is responsible for the enforcement of the law in that jurisdiction.

Management's role is to integrate resources to meet society's needs within an environment substantially shaped by union and government constraints. Although unions may represent the employees, management remains ultimately responsible for obtaining organizational performance and effectively utilizing the human resources. Only through proper utilization of human resources can management fulfill its labour-management role.

TERMS FOR REVIEW

Business unionism   Canadian Labour Congress (CLC)
Social unionism   Canada Labour Code
Local unions   Labour Relations Board
Craft unions   Unfair labour practices
Industrial unions   Conciliation and mediation
National unions   Public Service Staff Relations Act (PSSRA)
International unions   Public Service Staff Relations Board (PSSRB)
Corporations and Labour Unions Returns Act
American Federation of Labor and Congress of Industrial Organizations (AFL-CIO)

REVIEW AND DISCUSSION QUESTIONS

1. In your own words, summarize the primary objectives of unions.
2. What distinguishes craft, industrial, and mixed unions from each other?
3. Suppose an employee in your department is an active member of the union but is performing improperly. After several sessions with the employee, performance is still unacceptable. What type of support would you want to gather before you terminated that employee? What legal complications might result from your action?
4. What roles does the Labour Relations Board serve in labour-management relations?
5. Why are sound personnel policies necessary even when no union is present?
6. If you work in the personnel department of a small company that is suddenly unionized, what changes would you expect to occur in the personnel department?
7. What role do you think federal and provincial governments will play in future labour-management relations? What actions can unions and management take to reduce the probability of future government involvement?

INCIDENT 19-1
UNION PRESSURES AT HALBY LTD.

After the employees at Halby Ltd. won the Labour Relations Board election, they selected Tom York to be the local union president. Tom had no experience in the role of union president, but he was well liked by the other employees and was largely responsible for starting the local union.

About two weeks after the election, the personnel manager, the company lawyer, Tom, and the union's vice president began negotiating the contract. Among the union's demands, Tom listed the following:

- *A 75-cent-an-hour raise to be given all employees in the union*
- *The removal of the company lawyer from negotiations, since the union had no lawyer and could not afford one*
- *The termination of Hal Sinkin and Francis Ellison because they had fought against the union's representation of the workers*
- *The discharge of all employees who do not join the union before the contract is signed*
- *Free supplementary medical insurance for all employees in the union*

Although Tom had other demands, he said these were the ones that were most important.

1. Do any of Tom's demands violate the labour laws? Which ones?
2. If Tom insisted on each of these demands, what legal action could the company take?

INCIDENT 19-2
A ROUTINE DISCHARGE AT ITC

On October 2, 1984, Pete Ross was discharged from ITC. The supervisor requested that the personnel department discharge Pete Ross because he was caught drinking in the employees' locker room. Drinking on company property was prohibited, as it had been since publication of the ITC Employees' Handbook *in 1971.*

All employees of ITC were given a copy, and whenever new employees joined, as had Pete Ross in 1980, they too were given one. The handbook stated in part: "The consumption of alcoholic beverages on company premises is grounds for immediate termination. . . ."

The discharge appeared rather routine to personnel and to the plant manager. Although drinking violations were uncommon, the plant manager believed clear-cut violations of company policy should be punished. Besides, he was frequently heard to say, "We must support our first-line managers."

Pete's fellow machinists did not see it as a "routine discharge." John Briggs, a fellow machinist, summed up the group's feelings:

Pete was a darn good machinist. He was seldom tardy, never absent, and always did a first-class job. If Pete did it, it was done right! That bugged George (the supervisor) because George would pressure Pete to get out the work and say, "Don't worry about the quality; they only measure quantity." But Pete wasn't slow. He'd turn out a quality product as fast as some people turned out junk. I don't think George liked Pete. I don't know if Pete took a belt before leaving the plant Wednesday evening, but I think George just wanted to can Pete.

The following Monday, October 8, 1984, John Briggs spent his rest breaks and lunch hour talking with the other machinists, telling them that "If we don't want to end up like Pete, we'd better get a union." He even had cards from the International Association of Machinists Union. By Monday evening, Briggs had thirty-two signed cards. (There were thirty-nine machinists in the shop.)

On Tuesday morning John Briggs was called into the supervisor's office. The plant manager and the supervisor grilled him. They asked him if he had been distributing authorization cards, who had signed them, and how many he had obtained. Briggs simply replied by saying, "That is none of your business." The plant manager adjourned the meeting without saying a word.

On Thursday (payday at ITC), Briggs received a termination notice with his pay-cheque. The notice was effective immediately. The notice said termination was for low productivity and excessive absences during the previous twelve months.

1. What unfair labour practices may have occurred?
2. Should management offer reinstatement to Pete Ross or John Briggs? Why?
3. Was Briggs correct when he answered "That is none of your business," to the questions about the authorization cards?

REFERENCES

1. *Canadian Industrial Relations*, the Report of Task Force on Labour Relations, Ottawa: Privy Council Office, December 1968, p. 9.
2. Alton W. T. Craig, "A Model for the Analysis of Industrial Relation Systems," in Harish C. Jain (ed.), *Canadian Labour and Industrial Relations*, Toronto, McGraw-Hill Ryerson Limited, 1975.
3. Samuel Gompers, *Labour and the Common Welfare*, Freeport, N.Y.: Books for Libraries Press, 1919, p. 20.
4. An editorial in *Canadian Labour*, June 1968, p. 5.
5. Ed Finn, "Collective Bargaining under Wage Controls Seen as a Charade," *Toronto Star*, January 26, 1976.
6. J. W. Miller, Jr., "Power, Politics, and the Prospects for Collective Bargaining: An Employer's Viewpoint," in Stanley M. Jacks (ed.), *Issues in Labor Policy*, Cambridge, Mass.: MIT Press, 1971, pp. 3–10.
7. Frank Tannenbaum, *The Labor Movement, Its Conservative Functions and Consequences*, New York: Alfred A. Knopf, Inc., 1921.
8. Selig Perlman, *A Theory of the Labor Movement*, New York: The Macmillan Company, 1928.
9. Charles Lipton, *The Trade Union Movement in Canada 1827–1959*, Montreal: Canadian Social Publications Ltd., 1967, p. 4.
10. See Charles Lipton, op. cit.; John Crispo, *The Canadian Industrial Relations System*, Toronto: McGraw-Hill Ryerson Limited, 1978; Gerald E. Phillips, *The Practice of Labour Relations and Collective Bargaining in Canada*, Toronto: Butterworth and Co. (Canada) Ltd., 1977; and Stuart Jamieson, *Industrial Relations in Canada*, 2nd ed., Toronto: Macmillan of Canada, 1973.
11. Leonard Sayles and George Strauss, *The Local Union*, New York: Harcourt, Brace & World, 1967.
12. Phillips, op. cit., pp. 143–145.
13. *Labour Organizations in Canada*, Ottawa: Supply and Services Canada, 1975, p. 23.
14. John Crispo, *International Unionism—A Study in Canadian-American Relations*, Toronto: McGraw-Hill of Canada Limited, 1967.
15. Canadian Labour Congress, "The Structure of Labour in Canada," *Notes on Unions*, Ottawa: CLC, 1983, p. 2.
16. R. M. Lyon, M. Reiner, and E. R. Teple (eds.), *The Labor Relations Law of Canada*, Washington, D.C.: Bureau of National Affairs, 1977, p. 18.
17. Jack Williams, *The Story of Unions in Canada*, T. M. Dent & Sons (Canada) Ltd., 1975.
18. Wilfred List, "Food Processing Firm Used Employee as Spy, Board Certifies Union," *Globe and Mail*, July 30, 1981, p. 2.
19. David A. Peach and David Kuechle, *The Practice of Industrial Relations*, Toronto: McGraw-Hill Ryerson Limited, 1975, p. 165.
20. *Annual Report of the Minister of Supply and Services Canada under the Corporations and Labour Unions Returns Act, Part II: Labour Unions*, Ottawa: Minister of Supply and Services, published annually.
21. William B. Werther, Jr., "Government Control v. Corporate Ingenuity," *Labor Law Journal*, June 1975, pp. 360–367.
22. John R. Bangs, *Collective Bargaining*, New York: Alexander Hamilton Institute, Inc., 1964, pp. 29–34.

Chapter 20

Union Organizing and Collective Bargaining

Collective bargaining may be described as a joint endeavour on the part of workers to bring their combined pressure to bear on their employers in order to persuade them to better their wages, fringe benefits, and other conditions of employment.

John Crispo[1]

CHAPTER OBJECTIVES

After studying this chapter, you should be able to:
1. **Discuss** the major reasons why workers join unions.
2. **Identify** conditions that indicate unionization may occur.
3. **Describe** how personnel departments respond to unionization attempts.
4. **Explain** the key steps in negotiating a union contract.
5. **Define** the major topics of collective bargaining.

Unions do not just happen. They are usually caused by some management action or inaction that seems unfair to the workers. For example, consider how two people viewed the discharge of their coworker Pete Ross.

John Briggs: *Our supervisor finally found an excuse to fire Pete. All Pete did was take a drink in the locker room after his work shift ended. He wasn't even on company time.*

Kate Vander: *I know, and it really scares me. I have a family to support. If the supervisor ever decided to fire me, my family would suffer a lot.*

John Briggs: *It frightens me too, especially since the personnel department approved the discharge without an investigation. Everybody in the shop knew the supervisor didn't like Pete's happy-go-lucky attitude.*

Kate Vander: *If the supervisor had liked Pete, the drinking in the locker room would have been overlooked. It is all a matter of favouritism around here. But what can we do?*

John Briggs: *Well, if we had a union, at least we might get a fair hearing. A union can stand up to management. I wonder if we can start a union?*

Whether John and Kate can start a union depends on the support they get from other workers. If others feel a need to join together, then a union can be organized successfully. Once it is created, the union and management may negotiate a contract that defines their roles. These two actions of organizing and bargaining create the union-management relationship.

Each relationship between a union and an employer is unique. To explain why, this chapter examines the causes of unions and the methods used to organize them. It also discusses the negotiation process and its goals.

CAUSES OF UNIONS

The reasons for joining a union vary from person to person. Even workers in the same organization may have different reasons for joining a union because of their different perceptions. For example, consider the views of two bank tellers at a recently organized branch bank.

Maria Tomas: *I decided to join the union for many reasons. I'm not even certain which one was the main reason. One thing for sure, the branch manager now must prepare work schedules fairly. Before the union, we never had any say about them. The manager told us what hours we worked, and it was final. Now we can appeal to the union. Sure, I could have complained to the personnel department at head office. But then the manager might have become angry. That sure would reduce my chances for a merit raise or promotion. I supported the union, and I am proud of it.*
Paul Anglin: *I really don't know why so many people wanted a union at this branch. This is the best job I have ever had, and the boss is really nice. All the union means is dues, rules, and maybe even a strike. I simply can't afford to miss a paycheque over some strike. To me, we were better off without a union.*

Although it is hard to believe, both tellers have the same boss, work in the same bank branch, receive the same pay, and have the same job. The big difference between Maria and Paul is their views of the bank and the union. Had someone at the bank realized Maria's dissatisfaction and reacted favourably, she might agree with Paul's feelings. But when employees like Maria think they are treated unfairly and believe that personnel is unable to help, union membership may seem desirable.[2]

Since individual perceptions vary, there is no single force that motivates people to join unions. Instead, perceptions are shaped by a variety of reasons. Some of the more important ones are shown in Figure 20-1, according to the types of unions that may result. A further discussion of the figure explains why some people join unions and others do not.

CRAFT UNIONS

As described in Chapter 19, craft unions exist to organize workers who have similar skills, such as carpenters or plumbers. People join these unions for practical reasons. They hope to learn a useful skill through the union's apprenticeship program, which offers them both a job and training.

Workers who already have a trade often use craft unions to find jobs. In the construction industry (where many skilled tradespeople are employed), craft workers are hired on a per-project basis. When the project is over, the

Figure 20-1
WORKERS' MAJOR REASONS FOR JOINING OR NOT JOINING UNIONS

Type of Organization (and Workers)	Major Reasons for Joining	Major Reasons for Not Joining
Craft Unions (Blue-collar workers)	• Learn a trade • Find employment through union • Receive union benefits • Acquire collective power	• Dislike unions • Possess steady employment • Receive fair treatment
Industrial Unions (Blue- and white-collar workers)	• Seek change in management practices • Dislike supervision • Receive peer pressure • Required by union shop • Want benefits promised during organizing drive	• Want a management position • Afraid of strikes • Dislike dues • Dislike unions • Receive fair treatment
Professional Associations (White-collar workers)	• Seek professional contacts • Dislike supervisory practices • Resolve professional issues • Want better pay	• Reject as unprofessional • Unions not needed for self-employed • Want a management position • Receive fair treatment

contractor lays them off. Then workers typically ask the union for a referral to another contractor who has requested their skills. Thus membership in a craft union makes it easier to find a job.

Craft unions also offer other services. The union may provide supplemental health insurance, life insurance, pension plans, and other benefits to members. Besides the employment service and benefits, the union's collective bargaining power can mean favourable wages and working conditions.

Some skilled workers do not join craft unions, however. Aside from those who dislike unions, most nonmembers have acceptable management, personnel policies, employment security, and fringe benefits.

INDUSTRIAL UNIONS

If the workers of a single employer decide to organize without regard to individual skill, the result is an industrial union. Workers usually form these unions when personnel policies or supervisors cause mistreatment.

Personnel policies guide managers in their treatment of employees. Policies that affect discipline, layoffs, compensation, job design, and communications are especially important. When these policies are ignored or do not address employee needs, a union may be formed by workers to make changes.

Possibly even more important than policies are first-level supervisors. These people serve as the link between employees and management. If supervisors do not provide fair treatment, employees may look to unions for protection.

As manager of CGKS TV and Radio Station Ltd., Lily Konna had to cut expenses since sales of advertisements had declined 10%. She ordered a freeze on all hiring, a stop to the annual cost-of-living raise, and a 10% layoff. Kevin DeFleur, the personnel manager, suggested a policy of keeping 90% of the workers that had been with the company the longest.

Lily responded, "Are you kidding? Those are the highest-paid workers and not necessarily the best ones. Besides, layoffs allow supervisors to get rid of their dead-wood. Let the supervisors decide whom to keep."

"You're going to open us up to charges of favouritism," Kevin argued.

"I doubt it." Lily added, "My order stands!"

Four months later, the Communications Workers of Canada organized a union among the remaining workers. The union's organizing slogan was "End favouritism, join the CWC."

Once a union exists, members may pressure their peers to join. This *peer pressure* is most effective on new workers, who are often uncertain of their roles and want to "feel like I belong." This pressure also can cause other employees (who might otherwise be indifferent) to join the union.

Labour leaders and management may also agree to a *union shop*. Under this agreement, all workers are obligated to join the union to keep their jobs. If they fail to join, management must fire those workers. Union shops are allowed in all provinces.[3]

Reasons for nonmembership are equally diverse. Workers who want to become managers may believe union membership damages their chances for promotion. Other employees view unions as "just another boss" that leads to extra costs, such as union dues or lost wages from strikes. Like-wise, past experiences or isolated stories of union wrongdoing may cause some people to form a negative opinion of collective action.[4] Or, more simply, personnel policies and supervisory treatment may be fair, so that employees lack motivation to join a union.

PROFESSIONAL ASSOCIATIONS

Most professionals do not join unions. Instead, they belong to *professional associations* that are designed to further their knowledge and improve the image of the profession. But when professionals are also employees, their association may become more like a union.[5]

Some professional groups—provincial education associations and pro-vincial nurses' associations, for example—have evolved into unions. This change usually results from poor treatment by management. These "unions" emerge when supervisory practices, personnel policies, or profes-sional issues are unacceptable. For example, a few years ago the Nova Scotia Registered Nurses Association complained bitterly about poor management and unpleasant working conditions in Nova Scotia hospitals. A short time later the first union for nurses was certified.

There are several reasons why professionals do not join unions. Those who are self-employed would receive few benefits from such membership. Even those who work for an employer have little to gain if their treatment is professionally favourable. And many professionals view unions as de-grading and inappropriate.

UNION ORGANIZING

It is worth remembering that a union begins only when workers create it.[6] Though this is a simple observation, it is a key to understanding the process of unionization. While unions use professional organizers, the outcome of the organizing drive depends primarily upon the employee. As George Meany, the first president of the AFL-CIO in the U.S., once commented:

> Despite the well-worn trade union phrase, an organizer does not organize a plant. Now, as in the beginning, the workers must organize themselves. The organizer can serve only as an educator; what he organizes is the thinking of the workers.[7]

Union organizers educate the workers by explaining how the union can reduce mistreatment. These professionals only assist workers; they do not cause workers to join a union. Organizers are less successful when confronted by a proactive personnel department because there is little that a union can offer. Even the most experienced organizers find it difficult to organize a truly well-managed and growing company. IBM provides an appropriate example:

> In more than thirty-five years, IBM claims the company has never laid off a worker for economic reasons. Instead, it retrains workers unneeded in one job and assigns them to another. Since 1970 it has retrained and physically relocated 5,000 employees as part of the most extensive corporate education program in the U.S.
>
> Not surprisingly, IBM has never been the target of a major union organizing drive in the U.S. . . . "I don't know what a union at IBM would do," says one salesman, incredulously, when asked if he would join a union.[8]

SIGNS OF ORGANIZING ACTIVITY

Personnel departments can estimate the chances of union organizing by looking for the proper signs. One set of signs is found in the work environment. Figure 20-2 lists specific questions that can alert a personnel department to union activity. The higher the number of "yes" answers to the questions in the figure, the more likely it is that union activity will occur. The external factors shown in the figure are largely outside the personnel department's control. But external developments can cause personnel to pay greater attention to the internal factors over which it has influence.

When the federal government and some provinces changed the labour laws to allow employees of organizations run by federal or provincial governments to participate in the collective bargaining process, many personnel managers under their jurisdiction realized that union organizing would become more likely. Rather than wait for a union drive to begin, some personnel managers began an assessment of the internal factors over which they had control. This prompt, proactive action gave them a wide range of options for improving the work environment. Their counterparts who did not respond to this external sign had less flexibility once union activity had started.

Another set of signs comes from changes in employee behaviour that suggest a union drive may be under way. Figure 20-3 indicates the type of behaviour to which supervisors and personnel specialists should be alert.

Figure 20-2
ENVIRONMENTAL FACTORS THAT MAY LEAD TO UNIONIZATION

External Factors

• Have there been recent changes in the labour laws that affect your industry which might cause interest in your firm by union organizers?

• Has there been a sudden increase in unionization activity in your community or industry?

• Is your company planning a major increase in its work force that might stimulate union interest in organizing the firm before it becomes larger and more expensive to organize?

Internal Factors

• Has your organization failed to resolve systematically the union complaints made during previous, unsuccessful organizing attempts?

• Are employee turnover and absenteeism rates worse than the norms for your industry or community?

• Has the company failed to conduct job satisfaction surveys? Or, if they have been conducted, do they reveal a trend toward dissatisfaction?

• Are pay and fringe benefits below the average for the industry, community, or unionized firms?

• Is the company's procedure for resolving employee complaints largely not used by workers?

Again, a high number of "yes" answers may mean unionization is occurring. It is important to remember that these are only indications, not proof.

One manager who observed some suspicious activities notified the personnel depart-ment. A few days later she was embarrassed "pleasantly" when the employees presented her with a gift certificate and a card as a Christmas present. What this manager saw was a group of employees passing around a card and collecting con-tributions for a gift. She thought they were signing up to join a union.

Figure 20-3
EMPLOYEE BEHAVIOUR THAT SUGGESTS UNIONIZATION ACTIVITY

• Do some employees seem to be suddenly popular?

• Are workers making unusual inquiries about fringe benefits, wage levels, raises, promotions, grievance procedures, or other employee-related matters?

• Do criticisms of management decisions and policies seem more vocal?

• Have employee directories been disappearing at a high rate?

• Are employees asking about management's reaction to unions?

• Are questions being asked about company rules on solicitation?

• Have employees discussed past or future group meetings?

• Are there strangers in the cafeteria or parking lots?

• Do employees exclude supervisors from their conversations?

• Are cards or handbills being distributed?

LIMITS ON MANAGEMENT'S RESPONSE

Once a union drive begins, management's choice of responses becomes limited in several important ways. First, Labour Relations Boards (LRB) protect workers' rights from management reprisals. For example, the discipline of union supporters can result in legal violations, unless the employer can prove the wrongdoer received the same punishment as other employees normally receive.[9] Even an *increase* in wages or fringe benefits during an organizing drive may be considered a violation because the employer is trying to ''buy'' employee support.

When the Union of Bank Employees tried to organize branches of the Canadian Imperial Bank of Commerce, bank management granted pay increases to all employees except where the union had already been certified or where certification was pending. Management contended that any salary adjustment for unionized employees was a matter of future negotiations. The Canadian Labour Relations Board declared this action to be unfair labour practice and ordered the bank to compensate employees who had not received an increase.[10]

Another limit results when a *union organizing committee* is present.[11] This committee consists of those workers who are leading the union drive. Their responsibility is to convince other employees to join the union. To do this, they use handbills, speeches, conversations, and even home visits. The committee's goal is to get workers to sign *authorization cards*, which evidence the employees' interest in the union. Once a certain percentage of the employees sign cards, the committee can ask an LRB to conduct a representative election or grant certification of the union. During this process, the organizing committee may raise questions about management actions that affect employees, even if management's actions are fair.

After the Blue Water Swimming Pool Company fired Reed Creaseman for stealing, the organizing committee mailed a letter to each employee's home. The letter never questioned Reed's guilt or innocence. Instead, the union raised questions about the swimming pool company's discipline procedures. One paragraph of the letter read as follows:

''Have you ever taken home a pen or pencil from work? If you have, you might be fired like Reed Creaseman. He took home some company tools and the maintenance yard guard stopped him. Will a guard stop you with company property? Will you get fair treatment, or will you end up like Reed? Fired! Before you are next, sign an authorization card. Join the union for your own protection.''

A third limit during unionization is the actions of management. Personnel administrators should stress to every manager, from supervisor to chief executive officer, the following two cautions:

- Will management actions be ruled as unfair labour practices?
- Will management actions provide fuel for the organization drive?

When an unfair labour practice is committed by any member of management, it can lead to expensive, time-consuming lawsuits. What is equally damaging, the organizing committee can point to violations as further justification for a union. Even when management actions are legal, union leaders may claim credit for new policies favourable to employees.

The personnel manager and president of a small insurance company were surprised by what happened after they gave a 10% raise during a union organizing campaign. The day after the pay raise was announced, the union circulated handbills that read as follows:

"Beware! Management is trying to trick you. They gave you a 10% raise to con you into voting against the union next week. What will happen if the union loses? Will it take another drive to get a raise? Isn't it odd that with the union here, management suddenly cares about your pay? Don't be tricked! Vote for the Teamsters Union! Show management that you are smarter than they think. ..."

Even worse than the union's counterattack was the LRB's charging the employer with an unfair labour practice. The union then promptly circulated another handbill titled "LRB Catches Company Breaking Labour Laws." The union won the election thirty-seven to fourteen.

MANAGEMENT'S CAMPAIGN

Most employers mount a careful campaign to counteract a union drive. Normally, the personnel department is responsible for fending off the union, although outside consultants and labour lawyers often help.

The campaign usually begins by getting needed information. The most important information is top management's attitude toward unionization.[12] Although management officials usually oppose unions, the personnel department must determine what response, if any, top management wants to make. Assuming management wants to keep the company nonunion, the personnel department collects data about the (proposed or campaigning) union. Personnel specialists learn about the union's dues, strike record, if any, salaries of officers, and any other relevant facts that might cause workers to reject the union.

Armed with this detailed information, the personnel department arranges for speeches to workers about the need to stay nonunion. Speeches are usually supplemented with group meetings, handbills, letters to employees, and articles in the company newspaper.

To coordinate these activities, an *information clearing office* may be established in the personnel department. This office provides information to supervisors about the need to stay nonunion, and answers their questions. Sometimes telephone "hot lines" are installed so that supervisors and employees can get quick answers to questions raised during the organizing drive. The personnel department uses the clearing office to remind employees of the company's good points while refuting the union's claims. Ideally, the employer's case is presented in a factual, honest, and straightforward manner. However, the personnel department's success is determined only partially by its campaign. More important is the treatment employees have received before the organizing drive began.

COLLECTIVE BARGAINING

When a union wins an election, the LRB requires both the union and management to bargain in good faith. The failure of either party to do so can lead to unfair labour practice charges. Clearly, it is important for management to bargain in good faith. Should it needlessly postpone negotiations, refuse to meet with the union, fail to discuss relevant issues, or undertake any other action that represents a failure to bargain in good faith, the results can be costly. Besides the cost of legal expenses, the workers are free to strike. If the strike is caused by management's refusal to bargain or other illegal activities, the strikers can get their jobs back *plus* the wages they would have earned.

The editor of a now-defunct newspaper found out the hard way what "bargaining in good faith" means. He had decided to automate by installing computerized typesetting machines. When he told the president of the local typographical union, the president said, "Let's talk about it."

"No! I've made up my mind and my decision is final. I own this newspaper, and I'll do with it what I want," the editor concluded.

"Well, I guess we are at an impasse. I'm going to call a strike. We'll end the strike after we settle this automation nonsense," added the union president.

The union charged the newspaper with refusal to bargain. Thirty months later a court of appeals upheld the LRB and ordered the owner to pay thirty months' back wages, with interest, to every striker. The total bill was $374,000.

The process of collective bargaining has three overlapping phases. Preparation for negotiations is the first and the most critical stage. The success of the second stage, face-to-face negotiations, largely depends on how well each side has prepared. The third phase involves the follow-up activities of contract administration. To conduct these new duties, a labour relations department may be added to personnel.

PREPARATIONS FOR NEGOTIATIONS

The purpose of negotiations is to achieve a *collective agreement*. The agreement specifies the rights and responsibilities of management and the union.

Detailed preparations are required if the agreement is to achieve a balance of rights and responsibilities.[13] Figure 20-4 shows the major stages of collective bargaining. As can be seen, several steps are required before actual negotiations begin.

MONITOR THE ENVIRONMENT. Collective bargaining does not occur in a vacuum. Labour relations specialists need to monitor the environment to find clues about likely union concerns. These clues can be found in several ways. First, the labour department must be sensitive to the inflation rate and the gains made by other unions. Since union leaders are elected, they seldom accept wage increases that are less than those of rival unions. Otherwise, they may be voted out of office. Acceptable increases usually exceed the inflation rate by a few percentage points, unless the employer cannot afford the usual pattern. For example, the United Auto Workers allowed Chrysler Corporation in Canada and the U.S. to give a smaller wage increase in 1979, because of its weaker financial position in comparison with General Motors and Ford.

Figure 20-4
THE STAGES OF COLLECTIVE BARGAINING

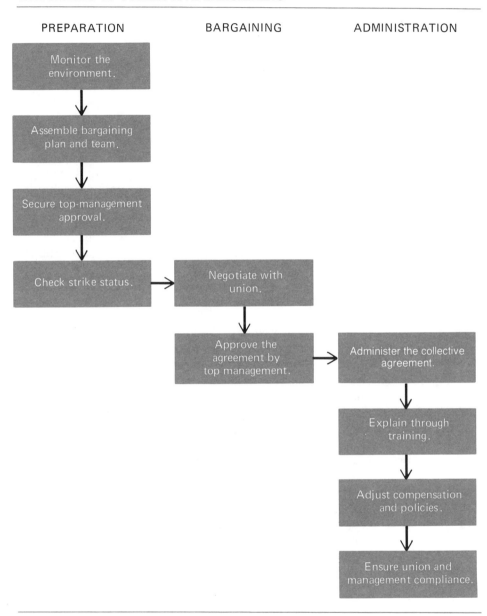

PREPARATION   BARGAINING   ADMINISTRATION

A second class of clues can be found among union promises made during the organizing drive or among unmet demands from previous negotiations.

During an organizing drive at an electronics company in the Maritimes the union promised to make day-care facilities for children of employees the key issue for the first negotiations. The majority of the employees were women who several times before had put forward similar requests to management, to no avail. The union won the election by a 155-to-28 margin, although the year before it had failed to get a majority.

During the following negotiations, management again refused to consider day-care facilities, but relented when 95% of the employees voted for strike action. A day-care centre was organized on a trial and cost-sharing basis. When the agreement expired and was renegotiated the following year, the union demanded that the company should accept the full cost of the centre. Since management had just secured a lucrative supply contract and could not afford a strike, it agreed to the demand.

A third source of bargaining issues is *management rights*. These rights are the freedoms that supervisors and managers need to do their jobs effectively.[14] They often include the right to reassign employees to different jobs, to make hiring decisions, and to decide other matters important to management. If these rights are not protected in the contract, the union may hinder management's effectiveness. For example, supervisors may want all job descriptions to include the phrase "and other duties assigned by management." This clause prevents workers from refusing to do work because it is not in their job description. The clause also gives supervisors greater freedom in assigning employees. Labour relations specialists in the personnel department discover which rights are important on the basis of discussions and surveys among supervisors and managers.[15]

ASSEMBLE A BARGAINING PLAN. After monitoring union demands and management rights, this information is compiled into a *bargaining book*. The "book," or more commonly a computer tape, contains estimates of likely union demands and management's counterproposals. It represents the employer's plan for the upcoming negotiations.

To implement the plan, a bargaining team is assembled. The team is usually led by the director of labour relations or an attorney. The team also may include specialists in wages and benefits and line managers familiar with company operations.

SECURE TOP-MANAGEMENT APPROVAL. Top management should approve the overall bargaining plans and goals since it is responsible for the organization's success. These goals serve as controls that enable top management to gauge the bargaining team's effectiveness. Knowledge of the controls also may help the bargaining team because it knows the limits on its authority to bargain with the union.

CHECK STRIKE STATUS. Most contracts are negotiated without a strike. But labour specialists usually plan for a possible strike to strengthen their bargaining position. Their preparations depend upon the likelihood of a strike. If employees strongly support union demands, a strike is more likely and plans are more thorough.

The goal of labour specialists is to reduce the damage from a strike if it occurs. Their efforts include special arrangements with important buyers and suppliers. If operations are to be stopped during a strike, close-down and start-up plans are made. When top management seeks to continue production or service, work schedules for managers and nonstriking employees are developed. These preparations signal to union leaders that the employer is ready for a strike. This signal may cause union leaders to rethink their demands and agree to a negotiated settlement without a strike.

BARGAINING

After preparations, the second phase of collective bargaining is face-to-face negotiations with the union. Discussions usually start sixty to ninety days before the end of the present contract. If the negotiations are for the first time, they begin after the union is recognized by the employer or wins an LRB election.

NEGOTIATE WITH THE UNION. Negotiations cover wages, hours, and working conditions. These three areas are interpreted broadly. *Wages* mean all forms of compensation such as pay, insurance plans, retirement programs, and other benefits and services. *Hours* include the length of the workday, breaks, holidays, vacations—in fact, any component of the work schedule. *Working conditions* involve safety, supervisory treatment, and other elements of the work environment.[16]

Once face-to-face bargaining begins, it is important to follow the techniques listed in Figure 20-5. Otherwise confusion may develop that can cause needless delays or even a strike.[17]

General Electric in the U.S. used to follow an approach called Boulwarism.[18] *Instead of following the suggestions in the figure, GE simply presented the union with its final offer at the beginning of negotiations. This approach created confusion because the unions did not know that GE's first offer was also its last. Politically, the union leaders did not dare accept this offer. If they did, members might question the need for leaders who merely accepted the company's first offer. As a result, bitter strikes occurred between GE and its unions. Eventually, the U.S. National Labor Relations Board ruled this approach to be illegal because GE was not really bargaining. It only made an offer on a take-it-or-leave-it basis.*

Successful bargaining usually begins with easy issues to build a pattern of give-and-take. This give-and-take occurs in private, since off-the-record comments may be embarrassing to either side when repeated out of context. This way management does not have to worry about what stockholders may think of its bargaining comments, and union leaders can focus on bargaining without guarding against member reactions.

When deadlocks do occur, several tactics can keep negotiations moving toward a peaceful settlement. By settling easy issues first, bargainers can often point to this progress and say, "We've come too far to give up on this impasse. Surely, we can find a solution." This sense of past progress may increase the resolve of both sides to find a compromise.

Figure 20-5
GUIDELINES FOR NEGOTIATIONS

The "Dos" of Negotiations

---

1. Do seek more (or offer less) than you plan to receive (or give).
2. Do negotiate in private, not through the media.
3. Do let both sides win; otherwise the other side may retaliate.
4. Do start with easy issues.
5. Do remember that negotiations are seldom over when the agreement has been signed; eventually it will be renegotiated.
6. Do resolve deadlocks by stressing past progress, another point, or counterproposals.
7. Do enlist the support of the federal or provincial conciliator if a strike seems likely.

The "Don'ts" of Negotiations

---

1. Do not make your best offer first; that is so uncommon that the other side will expect more.
2. Do not seek unwanted changes; you may get them.
3. Do not say "no" absolutely, unless your organization will back you up absolutely.
4. Do not violate a confidence.
5. Do not settle too quickly; union members may think a quick settlement is not a good one.
6. Do not let the other side bypass your team and go directly to top management.
7. Do not let top management actually participate in face-to-face negotiations; they are often inexperienced and poorly informed.

Compromises may be achieved by offering counterproposals that take into account the objections of the other party. Sometimes progress is made by simply dropping the issue temporarily and moving on to other items. Further progress on other issues may lead to compromises regarding earlier impasses. If no progress results, bargainers may request the assistance of federal or provincial mediators or conciliators, as discussed in Chapter 19.

The suggestions in Figure 20-5 also imply common bargaining strategies. For example, most management teams will exclude top executives. They are kept out of negotiations because top managers are often not experienced in collective bargaining. But their exclusion also gives management bargainers a good reason to ask for a temporary adjournment when the union produces demands that require a careful review. Rather than refusing the union's suggestions, management bargainers may ask for a recess to confer with top management.

Experienced management bargainers also realize that the union must "win" some concessions. If the employer is powerful enough to force an unacceptable contract on the union, union leaders may seek revenge by refusing to cooperate with management once the collective agreement goes into effect. They may encourage slowdowns and other uncooperative actions. Or when the agreement is renegotiated, the union may be strong enough to cause a long strike. Besides, an unfavourable agreement may not be ratified by union members. If it is rejected, many union constitutions require the parties to resume collective bargaining.[19]

APPROVE THE PROPOSED AGREEMENT. The negotiation stage of collective bargaining is completed when the agreement has been approved. Often final approval for the employer rests with top management, although the bargaining team may have the authority to commit the company.

Negotiations are not complete until the union also approves the proposed agreement. Union bargainers usually submit the proposal to the membership for ratification. If a majority of the members vote for the proposal, it replaces the prior arrangements. When members reject it, union and management bargainers reopen negotiations and seek a new compromise. Administration of the agreement begins when both sides sign it.

ADMINISTRATION OF THE COLLECTIVE AGREEMENT

Once the agreement is accepted by union members and top management, the personnel department normally explains it by means of training programs and also adjusts pay, fringe benefits, and policies to conform with it. At this point, the agreement needs to be administered to ensure union and management compliance with its provisions. Chapter 21 explains this third stage of collective bargaining more fully.

SUMMARY

A union-management relationship occurs when workers perceive the need for a union. Their perceptions depend upon many factors. However, treatment by management is the single most important factor in most cases.

Union organizing usually begins with a small group of dissatisfied workers. Cases of an outside organizer's suddenly appearing and gaining widespread employee support seldom occur. Even when this happens, this is because of basic dissatisfactions among the work force.

The organizing process finds workers (with or without a professional organizer) trying to convince others to join the union. Management's response is limited severely by laws and employee reactions. The employer's primary defence is sound personnel policies implemented by competent supervisors *before unionization begins.*

If workers form a union, the federal or provincial Labour Relations Boards require management and the union to bargain in good faith. The success of the personnel department at the bargaining table is affected by its actions before negotiations begin. Labour relations specialists must monitor changes in the collective bargaining environment and assemble a detailed bargaining plan. Then after top management approval and strike preparations, bargainers begin to negotiate. Negotiations with the union result in an agreement that must be approved by union members and top management. Once negotiated, the agreement is administered by the union and management.

TERMS FOR REVIEW

Union shop	Information clearing office
Professional associations	Collective agreement
Union organizers	Management rights
Union organizing committee	Bargaining book
Authorization cards	Boulwarism

REVIEW AND DISCUSSION QUESTIONS

1. What conditions must be met before a labour-management relationship comes into existence?
2. In your own words, summarize the reasons why workers join (a) craft unions, (b) industrial unions, and (c) professional associations.
3. "Unions do not happen, they are caused—by management." Do you agree or disagree with that statement? Why?
4. The major role of personnel departments occurs before union organizing begins. In what major ways does the personnel department influence employee decisions to unionize?
5. In preparing to negotiate an agreement with a union, what types of information would you gather before arriving at the bargaining table?
6. If you were asked to explain why various types of people are on the employer's bargaining team, what reasons would you give for (a) the company lawyer, (b) the director of industrial relations, (c) a wage and salary specialist, (d) a benefit specialist, and (e) the assistant plant manager?
7. If you had to advise the manager of a small chain of bakeries how to prepare for a possible strike, what would you suggest?
8. Suppose you decide to make the union the best offer you could to begin negotiations. What problems might you expect?

INCIDENT 20-1
DECORATIVE MAIL BOXES LTD.

During the past three years, Decorative Mail Boxes Ltd. had received contracts from Sears and Eaton's to supply large quantities of decorative mailboxes. This rapid expansion left Amy and Chuck Minor with little time to create a personnel department. Their wage and salary clerk did a good job of keeping wages in line with local pay scales and benefit programs. But little was done about the workers' complaints of poor supervisory practices.

One day, several employees stormed into Chuck's office and threatened to get a union unless he fired two supervisors. Not wanting a union, Chuck transferred the two supervisors. About a month later, the same group of employees said they wanted to change the company's policy on vacations and holidays. Chuck refused to discuss these policies with the group, but said that he was willing to talk with each person in-dividually. From these discussions, Chuck learned that:

• *Employees were tired of ten-hour days and work on Saturday, even though they received overtime pay for hours over forty in a week.*
• *Employees were fed up with having orders yelled at them by supervisors.*
• *Employees felt that the shop area should be cleaned more regularly.*

Although other problems were mentioned, these issues seemed to be the main ones. So Chuck began to solve each problem as time permitted.

1. By using a reactive approach to employee complaints, what impression is Chuck leaving with employees?
2. If a union drive began at Decorative Mail Boxes and Chuck suddenly solved all the problems that employees had mentioned, how do you think the union organizing committee would react?
3. If you were hired as personnel manager, what would be your first action?

INCIDENT 20-2
NICHOLSON AND SONS LTD.

Nicholson and Sons Ltd., a large fish-product manufacturer in Atlantic Canada, experienced a serious drop in fresh fish supplies when the local fishermen preferred to sell their catches to Russian fishing ships, who paid higher prices. Management of Nicholson and Sons Ltd. asked the government to regulate the amount of fish local fishermen could sell to foreigners. The Minister of Fisheries and Ocean Resources promised to study the issue.

In the meantime the collective agreement with the Seafood Workers' Union was close to expiration. The president and the personnel manager of the company met to discuss their bargaining plans. According to the information available to the person-nel manager, the union would probably ask for 30% wage increases, two more holi-days, and a dental plan.

The president was shocked. It was obvious that the company could not afford to meet the union demands, at least not until the situation had improved. And if it did not improve, the company would either have to reduce its volume of business con-siderably or shut down completely.

The three managers then decided to ask the union to forgo any pay or benefit in-creases during the term of the next agreement. To make this idea more acceptable, the personnel manager was told to offer the union a one-year agreement instead of the traditional two-year one. The president said: "Tell the union bargaining committee we'll make it up to them if business improves. For us to give any more to the workers would aggravate our losses and may mean more layoffs. I'm sure they don't want that to happen. Also tell them that if they want to strike, it would be fine with us; we prob-ably could reduce our losses if we shut down the plant until we secure more supplies."

1. What action would you take before negotiations begin if you were the personnel manager?
2. Suppose that the situation improves after the collective agreement has been signed. What action do you think the union may take under these circumstances?

REFERENCES

1. John Crispo, *The Canadian Industrial Relations System*, Toronto: McGraw-Hill Ryerson Limited, 1978, pp. 378–383.
2. Randall Brett, "No Need for a Union Today," *The Personnel Administrator*, March 1979, pp. 23–24. See also James H. Hopkins and Robert D. Binderup, "Employee Relations and the Union Organizing Campaigns," *The Personnel Administrator*, March 1980, pp. 57–61.
3. International Labor Law Committee, Section of Labor Relations Law, American Bar Association, *The Labor Relations Law of Canada*, Washington, D.C.: Bureau of National Affairs, Inc., 1977, p. 97.
4. Joseph W. R. Lawson, II, *How to Meet the Challenge of the Union Organizer*, Chicago: The Dartnell Corporation, 1972, pp. 7–24.
5. Hermann F. Schwind and Vance F. Mitchell, "Attitudes of Canadian Middle Managers toward Unionization," *Proceedings of the Administrative Science Association of Canada*, microfiche, Edmonton, 1975.
6. George Meany, "Organizing: A Continuing Effort," *The American Federationist*, July 1976, p. 1.
7. Ibid.
8. "How IBM Avoids Layoffs through Retraining," *Business Week*, November 10, 1975, pp. 110, 112.
9. International Labor Law Committee, p. 156.
10. Canada Labour Relations Board, "Union of Bank Employees and Canadian Imperial Bank of Commerce," *Reasons for Decisions*, No. 202, *di 35*, November 30, 1979, pp. 105–112.
11. Edward S. Haines and Alan Kistler, "The Techniques of Organizing," *The American Federationist*, July 1967, pp. 30–32. See also James F. Rand, "Preventative-Maintenance Techniques for Staying Union-Free," *Personnel Journal*, June 1980, pp. 497–499.
12. Lawson, op. cit., pp. 25–45.
13. Gerard I. Nierenberg, *The Art of Negotiating*, New York: Cornerstone Library Publications, 1968, pp. 47–61.
14. Crispo, op. cit., pp. 378–383.
15. George E. Constantino, Jr., "Defining Line and Staff Roles in Collective Bargaining," *Personnel Journal*, October 1979, pp. 689–691, 717.
16. David A. Peach and David Kuechle, *The Practice of Industrial Relations*, Toronto: McGraw-Hill Ryerson Limited, 1975, pp. 94–117.
17. George E. Constantino, Jr., "The Negotiator in Collective Bargaining," *Personnel Journal*, August 1975, pp. 445–447.
18. See Herbert R. Northrup, *Boulwarism*, Ann Arbor: Bureau of Industrial Relations, Graduate School of Business, The University of Michigan, 1964. For an excellent discussion of negotiation see Richard E. Walton and Robert B. McKersie, *A Behavioral Theory of Labor Negotiations*, New York: McGraw-Hill Book Company, 1965, pp. 13–46. See also Nierenberg, op. cit., pp. 7–12.
19. Crispo, op. cit., pp. 244–245.

Chapter 21

Collective Agreement Administration

The most important aspect of industrial relations involves day-to-day administration of the collective bargaining agreement.

David A. Peach and David Kuechle[1]

CHAPTER OBJECTIVES

After studying this chapter, you should be able to:

1. **Explain** how a collective agreement limits personnel management.
2. **Describe** the major provisions of a collective agreement.
3. **Discuss** common techniques to resolve disputes.
4. **Identify** the personnel department's role in handling grievances and in arbitration.
5. **Suggest** ways to build union-management cooperation.

The outcome of organizing and negotiating is the *collective agreement*, or contract. This agreement limits management's flexibility. For example, labour contracts often specify how work assignments, promotions, wages, benefits, and other employee matters are to be handled. In other words, the agreement is an important challenge to managers and personnel specialists.

Fran Harper manages the sporting goods department of a large department store. After the store and the Retail, Wholesale and Department Store Union negotiated their first contract, Fran received a copy. Since she was busy with the new work schedule, the contract was set aside. Shortly after the schedule was posted on the bulletin board, one of Fran's best salesmen, Jake Renna, complained that the schedule was wrong.

Jake said, "I'm the most senior salesman; I should be able to pick the schedule I want."

"You know we don't do things that way around here," Fran firmly responded.

"You're wrong!" Jake shouted. "You haven't heard the end of this."

Fran said, "What do you mean?"

"The new collective agreement says that senior employees in each department get first choice of schedules," Jake added. "I want off on Mondays, or I'll file a complaint with the union."
"But I need you to help with inventory on Mondays," Fran argued.
"I don't care. The collective agreement says I get first choice," Jake angrily replied.

Even under the most restrictive contracts, managers, like Fran, must still manage. Decisions are made; orders are given. When a manager violates the agreement, employees like Jake may demand their rights. If their rights are denied, these employees may call on the union to help them.

The ideal is for the union and management to act cooperatively. Through cooperation, management can become more effective and can better meet the union's demands. But the extent of cooperation is shaped by the day-to-day administration of the contract. If properly administered, the contract is the basis for a cooperative relationship. Otherwise, violations lead to employee complaints that may reduce the organization's effectiveness.

This chapter describes the scope of contract administration and the resolution of complaints. It concludes with a discussion of union-management cooperation.

THE SCOPE OF CONTRACT ADMINISTRATION

Once ratified by union members and approved by management, the contract must be carried out. As Figure 21-1 shows, the agreement affects many areas of personnel management. As a result, its administration often limits personnel practices in a number of ways. These limitations come from the contract's terms, past practices, and resolution of disputes.

Figure 21-1
SOURCES OF CONTRACT LIMITATIONS ON PERSONNEL MANAGEMENT

Source of Constraints	Means of Achievement	Major Areas Affected
Contract Provisions	Negotiations	Personnel practices and policies; costs; discipline; management, union, and employee rights; promotions; layoffs, work assignments; overtime; pay; benefits
Past Practices	Management and union actions while administering the contract	Personnel practices and policies; costs; discipline; management, union, and employee rights
Dispute Resolution	Decisions made while resolving disputes between union and management	Personnel practices and policies; costs; discipline; management, union, and employee rights

CONTRACT PROVISIONS

Every labour agreement contains specific terms and provisions. The most common ones are listed in Figure 21-2. These clauses are important because they define the rights and obligations of the employer and the union. Since nearly every provision affects the management of human resources, these clauses merit the attention of personnel specialists.

Whether the collective agreement contains all the provisions found in Figure 21-2 depends on the parties. For example, the employer is never required by law to grant a union security clause. Management bargainers may agree to a *union shop* or *checkoff* provision when it leads to a lessening of other demands. Often these security clauses are given in return for a provision that protects important management rights.

With the exception of clauses on management rights, most clauses in the agreement limit personnel actions. Some of these limitations are minor and similar to the self-imposed policies of well-managed organizations. For example, even without a union, most employers provide competitive wages, benefits, and working conditions. The collective agreement merely formalizes these obligations. But other contract terms may change the policies used before the contract was negotiated. Seniority and discipline clauses are two constraints that are commonly added.

SENIORITY. Unions typically prefer to have employee-related decisions determined by the length of the worker's employment, called *seniority*. Seniority assures that promotions, overtime, and other employee concerns are handled without favouritism. But as the following example illustrates, seniority may limit management's flexibility in making personnel decisions.[2]

Three weeks before the retirement of the senior clerk in the parts department, the manager of the Anderson Buick dealership sought a replacement. The collective agreement stated that "all job openings must be posted on the employee bulletin board for one week. Interested employees must submit their bids during the one-week open period. After the open period, the most senior, qualified employee will be selected from among those who submitted job bids." Accordingly, this was done.

Two workers applied. One, Jacob Marls, had been with the car agency for almost three years. His performance as a junior clerk was efficient and courteous. In fact, many parts customers asked for Jacob by name. John Abbott also submitted a bid. He had been with the dealership for three years and two months. John was dependable, but sometimes he was moody in dealing with customers. The general manager wanted to reward Jacob's good performance. But the contract required that the promotion go to John since he was qualified and had the most seniority.

Seniority also is used to decide overtime and layoff rights. As with promotions, merit cannot always be rewarded. For example, suppose that a supervisor needs three subordinates to finish a job. Since seniority must be honoured, the supervisor cannot select the best employees. Likewise, when a company plans a layoff, the most recently hired workers are the first to go. Those who are left probably get higher wages if there is a premium for

Figure 21-2
COMMON PROVISIONS IN UNION-MANAGEMENT AGREEMENTS

• **Union recognition.** Normally near the beginning of a contract, this clause states management's acceptance of the union as the sole representative of designated employees.

• **Union security.** To ensure that the union maintains members as new employees are hired and present employees quit, a union security clause is commonly demanded by the union. Forms of union security include:

　　a. Union shop. All new workers must join the union shortly after being hired.

　　b. Agency shop. All new workers must pay to the union an amount equal to dues.

　　c. Checkoff. Upon authorization, management agrees to deduct the union dues from each union member's paycheque and transfer the monies to the union.

• **Wage rates.** The amount of wages to be paid to workers (or classes or workers) is specified in the wage clause.

• **Cost of living.** Increasingly, unions are demanding and receiving automatic wage increases for workers when price levels go up. For example, a common approach is for wages to go up by one cent an hour for each 0.3 or 0.4% increase in the consumer price index.

• **Insurance benefits.** This section specifies which insurance benefits the employer provides and how much the employer contributes toward these benefits. Frequently included benefits are life and supplemental hospitalization insurance, and dental plans.

• **Pension benefits.** The amount of retirement income, years of service required, penalties for early retirement, employer and employee contributions, and vesting provisions are described in this section if a pension plan exists.

• **Income maintenance.** To provide workers with economic security, some contracts give guarantees of minimum income or minimum work. Other income maintenance provisions include severance pay and supplements to unemployment insurance.

• **Time-off benefits.** Vacations, holidays, rest breaks, wash-up periods, and leave-of-absence provisions typically are specified in this clause.

• **Seniority clause.** Unions seek contract terms that cause personnel decisions to be made on the basis of seniority. Often senior workers are given preferential treatment in job assignments, promotions, layoffs, vacation scheduling, overtime, and shift preferences.

• **Management rights.** Management must retain certain rights to do an effective job. These may include the ability to require overtime work, decide on promotions into management, design jobs, and select employees. This clause reserves to management the right to make decisions that management thinks are necessary for the organization's success.

• **Discipline.** Prohibited employee actions, penalties, and disciplinary procedures are either stated in the contract or included in the agreement by reference to those documents that contain the information.

• **Dispute resolution.** Disagreements between the union and management are resolved through procedures specified in the contract.

• **Duration of agreement.** Union and management agree on a time period during which the collective agreement is in force.

longevity. Thus the higher-paid employees are retained, even though the layoff was probably needed to reduce costs. And these layoffs may undermine the company's affirmative-action plan, since employees hired through the program may have low seniority.

DISCIPLINE. Unions often challenge any discipline of a union member. Therefore, discipline must abide by the contract and be backed with evidence. The need for proof requires management to document employee discipline, which means more (not necessarily productive) paperwork. Even when discipline is done correctly, the union may argue that special circumstances should be considered.

One Monday, Georgia Green was late for work. She explained to her supervisor that her son was sick and so child-care arrangements delayed her. Sally, Georgia's supervisor, said, "Okay, but get here on time from now on. You know how strict my boss is." The following three days Georgia was late. The contract stated, "Any employee late four days in one month is subject to a two-day layoff without pay." On Thursday morning, Sally told Georgia to go home, citing the contract clause.

Georgia told the union what had happened. The union complained that Georgia's sick child should be grounds for an exception. The personnel manager disagreed. When the union representative asked to see Georgia's personnel file, it was discovered that Sally did not give Georgia a written warning after the second tardiness. Again, the contract was specific: "No worker can be given a layoff for tardiness or absenteeism unless a written notice is given after the second occurrence." The company had to pay Georgia for the two days she was off because the contract's procedure was not followed.

PAST PRACTICES
The actions of managers and union officials sometimes change the meaning of the agreement. Consider again the incident involving Georgia Green. Suppose the supervisor had failed to discipline Georgia. Or suppose that personnel management had been sympathetic to Georgia's problem and decided against approving the layoff. The result might have been to set a precedent.

A *precedent* is a new standard that arises from the past practices of either party. Once a precedent results from unequal enforcement of disciplinary rules, the new standard may affect similar cases in the future. Then any other tardy employee with child-care problems might demand special treatment too. In time, it may become difficult for management to control tardiness because precedents have created exceptions to the rules. If the personnel manager felt that an exception in Georgia's case was appropriate, the union and the company can sign a letter stating that this exception is not a binding precedent. Then other employees cannot rely on Georgia's case to win exceptions from the rules.

The fear of past practices usually causes two changes in personnel procedures. First, employee-related decisions are often centralized in the personnel department. Supervisors are stripped of their authority to make decisions on layoffs, discipline, and other employee matters. Instead, supervisors are required to make recommendations to the personnel department to ensure uniformity and prevent precedents.

The other change is to increase the training of supervisors in the administration of the contract. The training is needed to ensure that supervisors administer the remaining portions of the contract uniformly. For example, if each supervisor applies a different standard to tardiness, some employees may get discipline while others with more lenient supervisors may escape discipline. In time, the union might argue that unequal treatment makes it unfair to discipline those who are late. The enforcement of the contract terms by supervisors then can lead to damaging precedents. Through centralization and training, personnel departments create a more uniform enforcement of the contract to avoid such damaging precedents.

In addition to contract provisions and past practices, a third constraint is dispute resolution, which is discussed in the following section.

THE RESOLUTION OF DISPUTES

Constraints on management during contract administration also come from the resolution of disputes with the union. Since in Canada the use of strikes as a weapon is limited—strikes are illegal when a collective agreement is in force—disputes have to be settled through *grievances*. A grievance is defined as a complaint by an employee or employer which alleges that some aspect of a collective agreement has been violated. Almost every collective agreement in Canada contains some type of formalized procedure for resolving disputes. All jurisdictions (with the exception of Saskatchewan) require that a grievance which cannot be solved between the parties be submitted to an arbitrator or arbitration board whose decision will be final and binding.

GRIEVANCE PROCEDURES

Either management or the union may file a grievance when the contract is violated. But since most decisions are made by management, there are few opportunities for the union to break the agreement and cause a grievance to be initiated by management. More commonly, unions file grievances because of an alleged violation by management.

The *grievance procedure* consists of an ordered series of steps. Figure 21-3 describes the steps through which an employee's grievance typically passes. An example further explains how grievances arise and are settled.

Hanson Environment Services had an opening for the job of service representative. The job required making house calls to repair home air conditioners and heaters sold by the company. Only two employees applied for the job. The contract with the International Brotherhood of Electrical Workers stated: "Promotions are made on the basis of seniority, provided ability is equal." Mr. Hanson, the owner, selected the second most senior employee for the promotion.

When Rick West found out he did not get the job even though he had more seniority, he talked with his supervisor. The supervisor said, "It is Mr. Hanson's decision.

Figure 21-3
TYPICAL STEPS IN A UNION-MANAGEMENT GRIEVANCE PROCEDURE

- **Preliminary discussion.** The aggrieved employee discusses the complaint with the immediate supervisor with or without a union representative.
- **Step 1.** The complaint is put in writing and formally presented by the shop steward to the first-level supervisor. Normally, the supervisor must respond in writing within a contractually specified time period, usually two to five days.
- **Step 2.** The chief steward takes the complaint to the department superintendent. A written response is required, usually within a week.
- **Step 3.** The complaint is submitted to the plant manager/chief administrative officer by the union plant or grievance committee. Again, a written response is typically required.
- **Step 4.** If Step 3 does not solve the dispute, arrangements are made for an arbitrator or an arbitration board to settle the matter.

But you didn't get the job because you use profanity. We can't have you swearing in some customer's home. We would lose too much business."

Together, Rick and the union representative wrote up a formal grievance and submitted it to the supervisor. Although the supervisor had two days to review the complaint before making a written decision, he handed it back to Rick immediately with "Denied" written across it. Then the union submitted the complaint to the shop manager, which was the next step in the procedure. The result was the same. Finally, the grievance was taken to Mr. Hanson. He explained his fear of losing business over Rick's profanity and denied the grievance.

Finally, the union requested that the issue be submitted to arbitration and that a single arbitrator be chosen. Management agreed to that. The arbitrator ruled that management had no evidence that Mr. West ever used profanity in the presence of customers, and that the mere assumption he would do so was not sufficient grounds for denying his promotion.

The number of steps in the grievance procedure and the personnel involved at each step will vary from organization to organization. The purpose of a multistep grievance procedure is to allow higher-level managers and union representatives to look at the issue from different angles and to assess the consequences of alternative further actions. This approach will increase the chance that the dispute gets resolved without submission to arbitration.

TYPES AND CAUSES OF GRIEVANCES. Even though the personnel department may not handle grievances in their early stages, it plays an important role. Each supervisor sees only a small number of complaints. But personnel has an organization-wide view from which it can identify the types and causes of grievances. With this information, personnel can create programs to improve grievance handling.[3]

Grievances can be classified into three types: legitimate, imagined, and political. *Legitimate grievances* occur when there is reasonable cause to think there has been a contract violation. Even in a cooperative environment, contract clauses may have different meanings to different people. In the Hanson Environment Services example, the union thought the contract meant that promotions were decided on the basis of seniority if workers were technically qualified. Mr. Hanson, the owner, used a different perspective. He thought that "qualified" included both technical and personality variables. Misunderstanding of the agreement caused a legitimate grievance.

Imagined grievances occur when employees believe that the agreement has been violated even though management is exercising its contract rights reasonably. Again, misunderstanding is the primary cause of these grievances. A cooperative union can help settle such complaints quickly by explaining management's rights. Otherwise, when a manager says the complaint is without merit, the worker may feel that management is trying to save face for a bad decision.

Political grievances are the most difficult to solve. They occur when a complaint is pursued to further someone's political aspirations. For example, a union representative may be reluctant to tell union members that their grievances are without merit. To do so may mean a loss of political support in the next union election. Instead, the union leader may process a worthless grievance. Likewise, management also files political grievances.[4]

Jake Renna filed a grievance against his manager, who had failed to abide by the contract. Jake's grievance demanded that he get first choice of work schedules since he was the most senior employee in the sporting goods department. The store manager wanted to show his support for the department manager, Fran Harper, and so he denied Jake's grievance without even reviewing the contract. The corporate personnel department agreed that Jake was right and directed that he get first selection of work schedules. The personnel manager also sent a memo to the store manager and Fran telling them that their refusal to follow the contract may lead to other grievances and employee dissatisfaction.

HANDLING GRIEVANCES. Once a grievance has been submitted, management should seek to resolve it fairly and quickly. Failure to do so can be seen as a disregard for employee needs. In time, morale, motivation, performance, and company loyalty may be damaged.[5]

In adjusting grievances, several precautions should be followed.[6] Most importantly, grievances should be settled on their merits. Political considerations by either party weaken the grievance system. Complaints need to be carefully investigated and decided on the facts, not emotional whim. Otherwise, damaging precedents may result. Second, the cause to each grievance should be recorded. Many grievances coming from one or two departments may indicate personality conflicts or a poor understanding of the contract. Third, employees should be encouraged to use the grievance procedure. Problems cannot be solved unless management and union officials know what they are. But before employees can use the grievance process, it must be explained through meetings, employee handbooks, or bulletin-board notices. Lastly, whatever the final solution, it needs to be explained to those affected. Even though union leaders usually do this, management should not fail to explain *its* reasoning to the worker.[7]

ARBITRATION

Arbitration is the submission of a dispute to a neutral third party. The arbitrator acts in the role of a judge and hears both sides to the dispute. Based on the facts, the arbitrator renders a binding decision.

In Canada, federal and provincial legislation (except in Saskatchewan) requires that every collective agreement contain a provision for final settlement, by arbitration or otherwise, without work stoppage, of all differences concerning its interpretation, application, administration, or alleged violations. Although the law permits the use of means other than arbitration for settlement, unions and management so far have not found a viable alternative.[8]

Arbitration holds two potential problems for personnel administrators: costs and unacceptable solutions. Although the employer and the union usually share expenses, a case may cost from several hundred to several thousand dollars.

Another potential problem occurs when an arbitrator renders a decision that is against management's best interests. Since the ruling is binding, it may alter drastically management's rights. Suppose, for example, that management lays off several hundred workers, and the union convinces an arbitrator that management did not follow the contract's layoff procedure. The arbitrator may rule that all workers get their jobs back with back pay. Or if an arbitrator accepts the union's argument of extenuating circumstances in a disciplinary case, those extenuating circumstances may be cited in future cases. For example, consider what happened in a chain of convenience markets:

The Quick Foods Market had a policy that stealing from the company was grounds for immediate discharge. Sam Sample, a new employee, took a sandwich from the cooler and consumed it without paying. He was fired when caught by the store manager. The union argued that Sam should get a second chance since he was a new employee. The arbitrator upheld management. But he added that discharge for such a minor theft might be too harsh a penalty if Sam had not been a probationary employee.

This ruling implies that the judgement may have been different had a senior employee been caught stealing. The union may then use this argument to argue that discharge is an inappropriate penalty. There is a possibility that a different arbitrator may agree.

It is important for personnel specialists to seek a solution with the union before arbitration. In this manner they avoid additional costs, delays, and the possibility of an unsatisfactory decision. When arbitration is unavoidable, personnel specialists should follow the guidelines in Figure 21-4. These suggestions offer the best chance of winning a favourable decision. If these guidelines reveal serious flaws with the employer's case, a compromise solution with the union before arbitration is usually advisable.

FORM OF ARBITRATION. In Canada most arbitration cases are decided by an arbitration board, in contrast to the U.S., where the majority of cases are handled by individual arbitrators.[9] The interested parties each appoint one

Figure 21-4

PREPARATION GUIDELINES FOR ARBITRATION HEARINGS

1. Study the original grievance and review its history through every step of the grievance machinery.

2. Determine the arbitrator's role. It might be found, for instance, that while the original grievance contains many elements, the arbitrator is restricted by the contract to resolving only certain aspects.

3. Review the collective bargaining agreement from beginning to end. Often, other clauses may be related to the grievance.

4. Assemble all documents and papers you will need at the hearing. Where feasible, make copies for the arbitrator and the other party. If some of the documents you need are in the possession of the other party, ask in advance that they be brought to the arbitration.

5. Make plans in advance if you think it will be necessary for the arbitrator to visit the plant or job site for on-the-spot investigation. The arbitrator should be accompanied by representatives of **both** parties.

6. Interview all witnesses. Make certain that they understand the whole case and the importance of their own testimony within it.

7. Make a written summary of what each witness will say. This serves as a useful checklist at the hearing to make certain nothing is overlooked.

8. Study the case from the other side's point of view. Be prepared to answer the opposing evidence and arguments.

9. Discuss your outline of the case with others in your organization. A fresh viewpoint will often disclose weak spots or previously overlooked details.

10. Read as many articles and published awards as you can on the general subject matter in dispute. While awards by other arbitrators for other parties have no binding precedent value, they may help clarify the thinking of parties and arbitrators alike.

Source: *Labor Arbitration Procedures and Techniques*, New York: American Arbitration Association, 1972, pp. 15–16. Used with permission.

of the three-member body. These two members, in turn, select a neutral chairman. The advantage of using a board lies in the fact that representatives of the parties are directly involved in the decision-making process. The disadvantage is that boards usually take more time to make their decisions, not to mention the higher costs involved when there are three arbitrators instead of one.[10]

UNION-MANAGEMENT COOPERATION

Although dispute resolution techniques stop most complaints from erupting into a strike, they are after-the-fact measures. Even the "winner" of a favourable arbitration decision loses the time and money it took to argue the case. Through cooperation, both parties can replace reactive measures with proactive approaches. Proactive efforts benefit the union and the company by saving time and expenses. These savings can mean higher profits for the employer and better contracts for the union.

As personnel manager for the East Coast Logging Company Ltd., Joe VonKampen spent about 40% of his time on some phase of dispute resolution. Although the Teamsters represented only 125 of the employees, there were usually 275 to 300 grievances a year. About 10% of these cases went to arbitration. These costs seriously affected the company's profitability, which forced the union to accept the lowest wage rates in the area. To change the situation, which was uncovered by research into the company's grievance records, the town's mayor offered to help.

The mayor devised a training program that involved the union leader's and the personnel manager's taking turns reading the contract to an audience of supervisors and union representatives. After each paragraph, the personnel manager and the union president both summarized what the paragraph meant. The mayor did not let them go on to the next paragraph until both agreed on the meaning of the previous one. After several sessions, the entire contract was reviewed. Lower-ranking union and management officials learned what the contract meant and that they were expected to cooperate with each other. The following year, fourteen grievances were filed and only one went to arbitration. The company's profitability improved dramatically, and the local union obtained its largest wage increase in the next negotiations.

UNION-MANAGEMENT ATTITUDES

Severe conflicts between a company and union often can be traced to the attitudes each holds about the other.[11] In the East Coast Logging example, supervisors felt that the union was intruding on their rights. When supervisors denied workers their rights, the union had to fight back with grievances. Sometimes members of a union get so upset that they conduct a *wildcat strike*. These strikes are spontaneous acts that take place in violation of the contract, regardless of the objections raised by union leaders. Even after such a strike is over, the underlying problems still have to be settled.

If the attitudes between the parties remain hostile, the organization suffers poor performance. Serious disruptions can affect even the very survival of the organization and the union.[12] Sometimes extreme disruptions may require the two parties to cooperate in preventing bankruptcy and mass layoffs.

BUILDING COOPERATION

Proactive personnel departments cannot wait for disaster before they attempt to build cooperation with the union. They realize that cooperation is not automatic and must be initiated by human resource specialists. However, there are several obstacles to cooperation.

OBSTACLES TO COOPERATION. Personnel specialists often seek union cooperation to improve the organization's effectiveness. But effectiveness is usually far less important to union leaders. Quite naturally, these officials are more concerned about the welfare of their members and winning reelection to union office. So when cooperation fails to be attractive politically, union leaders have little incentive to cooperate. In fact, if leaders do cooperate, they may be accused by workers of forgetting the union's interests. These accusations can mean defeat by political opponents within the union. Thus cooperation may not be in the leader's best interest.

For many years, negotiations in the U.S. steel industry were marked by strikes and threats of strikes. The result was lower profitability and even a loss of markets to foreign producers. In turn, many members of the United Steel Workers union were put on layoff. Both the union and the steel companies were being damaged.

The unions and major steel producers reached a cooperative arrangement called the Experimental Negotiations Agreement. *This agreement called for concessions from the producers and no nationwide strikes by the union against the steel industry. This cooperative move was intended to benefit both the union and employers. But some members saw it as a loss of rights, particularly the right to strike. In the union's national elections, a splinter group was able to make a serious challenge to the established leadership by attacking this cooperative agreement.*

Besides political obstacles, union leaders may mistrust the personnel department. For example, bitter remarks during the organizing drive may convince union officials that personnel specialists are antiunion. Within this climate, cooperative gestures may be seen as tricks against the union. If cooperative proposals threaten the members or leaders, mistrust increases and cooperation usually fails.

COOPERATIVE METHODS. Once personnel specialists realize the political concerns and suspicions of union leaders, several cooperative methods can be tried. These techniques are summarized in Figure 21-5 and are explained in the following paragraphs.

Figure 21-5
METHODS OF BUILDING UNION-MANAGEMENT COOPERATION

Managers and personnel specialists can build cooperation between the employer and the union through:

- **Prior consultation** with union leaders to defuse problems before they become formal grievances.
- **Sincere concern** for employee problems and welfare even when management is not obligated to do so by the collective agreement.
- **Training programs** that objectively communicate the intent of union and management bargainers and reduce biases and misunderstandings.
- **Joint study committees** that allow management and union officials to find solutions to common problems.
- **Third parties** who can provide guidance and programs that bring union leaders and managers closer together to pursue common objectives.

One of the most basic actions is *prior consultation* with the union. Not every management decision must be approved by the union. But actions that affect the union or its leaders may cause a grievance unless explained before the action is taken. Consider once more the Hanson Environment Services example given earlier in this chapter. Suppose personnel had explained to the union leaders that the use of profanity by the most senior worker could mean a loss of valuable business and jobs for union members; perhaps the union leader would have accepted the promotion of the junior worker. At least politically, the union president would be less likely to challenge the promotion decision of Mr. Hanson. Some managers even call on union leaders to talk with problem employees before management takes action that might lead to a grievance. For example, Mr. Hanson could have asked the union leader to talk with Rick West about his profanity.

Personnel specialists can also build cooperation through a *sincere concern* for employees. This concern may be shown through the prompt settlement of grievances, regardless of who wins. Or management can bargain sincerely with the union to reduce the need for a strike. Even when a strike occurs, management can express its concern for workers. For example, during the 1970 strike at General Motors in the U.S. and Canada, GM continued to pay the strikers' insurance premiums to prevent a lapse in their insurance coverage.

Training programs are another way to build cooperation. After a new contract is signed, the personnel department usually trains just managers. The union does the same for its leaders. The result is that both sides continue their biases and misunderstandings. If personnel sponsors training for both the union and management, a common understanding of the contract is more likely to be brought about. The training can be as simple as taking turns paraphrasing the contract, as done in the East Coast Logging Company example. Or outside neutrals can be hired to do the training. Either way, supervisors and union officials end the training with a common understanding of the contract and a new basis for cooperation.

When a complex problem confronts the union and employer, *joint study committees* are sometimes formed.[13] For example, the three largest automobile companies have agreed to create separate committees with the United Auto Workers union to study health-care costs. If the idea is successful, costs will grow more slowly and there will be more money available for other benefits.[14]

A final method of building cooperation is through *third parties*, such as consultants or government agencies, who may act as catalysts to cooperation. In Canada, this is the most common approach, since parties to a collective agreement are required by law to ask for conciliation before any strike or lockout action can be taken.

There is no single best approach to building cooperation. Since each relationship is unique, the methods used will depend upon the situation. But if personnel administrators can build more cooperative relations with their unions, the employer gains higher productivity. In turn, there are more resources against which the union and its members can make demands. Improving union-management relations, therefore, is a potentially significant role that can be played by personnel departments in unionized organizations.

SUMMARY

Contract administration begins after union organizing and contract negotiations. In administering the agreement, personnel specialists face several
challenges. First, contract clauses place limits on management. Second,
day-to-day administration of the contract can lead to precedents. Third,
limitations often result from the dispute resolution procedures: grievance
handling and arbitration help interpret the contract, sometimes in ways
that limit management.

Yet managers still must manage in spite of these constraints. Only
through increased cooperation between the company and the union can
these limitations be lessened. Responsibility for improving the relationship
must be assumed by the personnel department, if political barriers and mistrust are to be overcome. Through prior consultation, concern for employees, training programs, or joint committees, personnel specialists can lay
the foundations of a cooperative union-management relationship.

TERMS FOR REVIEW

Collective agreement   Political grievances
Seniority   Arbitration
Precedent   Wildcat strikes
Grievance procedure   Cooperative methods

REVIEW AND DISCUSSION QUESTIONS

1. In your own words, explain why most grievances are usually filed by
   unions.
2. What are the major sources of constraints on personnel management
   during the administration of a collective agreement?
3. During one union organization drive, a plant manager told employees:
   "A union means less flexibility in dealing with your individual problems.
   With a union present, the company must follow the collective agreement." Explain how this loss of freedom might be to the employees' disadvantage.
4. Suppose one of your unionized employees wanted to leave work early to
   see her child play in the minor hockey league. Further, suppose she offered to work through her lunch hour so no loss of work or production
   would occur. If you agreed to her suggestions, what problems might
   result?
5. Since grievance procedures are found in most contracts, both managers
   and unions must want them. Explain why both managers and unions
   want grievance procedures.
6. Suppose several supervisors said they had hoped to create enough problems for the union to cause it to go away. What advice would you give
   them?
7. What are the disadvantages of using arbitration as a last step in the
   grievance procedure?

8. Suppose your union and company had very hostile relations. What steps would you recommend to the personnel manager?

INCIDENT 21-1
THE REINDEER LAKE PAPER MILL

The Reindeer Lake Paper Mill in Saskatchewan has been plagued with numerous problems since it began operations in 1980. In 1981, the Canadian Paperworkers Union was successful in organizing the workers and negotiating a three-year collective agreement. After two years of operation under the agreement, personnel problems were growing worse. In 1983, there were several illegal walkouts by small groups of workers to protest unresolved grievances. Management decided not to prosecute the employees although the wildcat strikes disrupted production.

Now, the personnel director expects a strike at the expiration of the collective agreement, because of low wages and unpleasant working conditions. The workers are claiming that inflation has exceeded the wage increases granted in the 1980 agreement. In addition, although working conditions meet federal and provincial health and safety regulations, the workers complain that heat, smell, and humidity in the plant make working very uncomfortable, especially during the summer months.

1. This incident suggests several changes that should be made in the next collective agreement, given the company's past experiences. What changes do you think the personnel department should recommend?
2. What actions could the personnel department undertake immediately to reduce the problems that exist between workers and the company?
3. If management decided to implement the changes you suggest, what actions should be taken to win the support of union leaders?

INCIDENT 21-2
IN-FLIGHT FOOD SERVICES COMPANY

The In-Flight Food Services Company provides prepared meals for several airlines at a major airport in the East. Food handlers cook and package meals to be reheated in airplane galleys for service to passengers while in flight. Most of the 535 food handlers belong to the Independent Food Handlers Union, which has represented these employees for over five years.

Each year, the industrial relations department has noticed that the number of grievances filed by members of the union increases by about 15%. The time spent by union representatives, employees, and supervisors was affecting productivity in the company's cafeteria. The general manager was concerned that the company's costs and low productivity could lead to a loss of several key contracts with major airlines.

The industrial relations department studied all the grievances during the past year and provided the following analysis.

Total grievances filed	*803*
Number settled at:	
First-level supervision	*104*
Second-level supervision	*483*
General manager level	*205*
Arbitration	*11*

Although some grievances involved more than one issue, most of them were single-

issue matters. When the industrial relations department classified the grievances, the following results were reported:

Grievance issues:

Tardiness or absence control	*349*
Overtime disputes	*265*
Other discipline or discharge	*77*
Incorrect job schedules	*75*
Multiple-issue disputes	*37*

1. Assuming the industrial relations director asked you to design a training program to reduce the high number of grievances, who do you think should attend the training sessions?
2. What topics would you cover in the training?
3. If you felt that many of the grievances resulted from poor wording in the contract, what could you do to make changes before the expiration of the contract?

REFERENCES

1. David A. Peach and David Kuechle, *The Practice of Industrial Relations*, Toronto: McGraw-Hill Ryerson Limited, 1975, p. 181.
2. Gerald E. Phillips, *Labour Relations and Collective Bargaining in Canada*, Toronto: Butterworth and Co. (Canada) Ltd., 1977, pp. 160–161.
3. William B. Werther, Jr., "Reducing Grievances through Effective Contract Administration," *Labor Law Journal*, April 1974, pp. 211–216.
4. Ross Stagner and Hjalmar Rosen, *Psychology of Union-Management Relations*, Belmont, Calif.: Wadsworth Publishing Company, Inc., 1965, pp. 110–111.
5. Jeffrey Gandz, "Grievance Initiation and Resolution: A Test of the Behavioural Theory," *Relations Industrielles*, 34 (1979) (4): 790.
6. Thomas F. Gideon and Richard B. Peterson, "A Comparison of Alternate Grievance Procedures," *Employee Relations Law Journal*, Autumn 1979, pp. 222–223. See also "The Antiunion Grievance Ploy," *Business Week*, February 12, 1979, pp. 117, 120.
7. James C. McBrearty, *Handling Grievances: A Positive Approach for Management and Labor Representatives*, Tucson: Division of Economics and Business Research, University of Arizona, 1972, pp. 3–6. See also George W. Bohlander, "Fair Representation: Not Just a Union Problem," *The Personnel Administrator*, March 1980, pp. 36–40, 82.
8. Peach and Kuechle, op. cit., p. 284.
9. Ibid., p. 243.
10. Ibid., p. 244.
11. Joseph Tomkiewicz and Otto Brenner, "Union Attitudes and the 'Manager of the Future,'" *The Personnel Administrator*, October 1979, pp. 67–70, 72.
12. Richard E. Walton and Robert B. McKersie, *A Behavioral Theory of Labor Negotiations*, New York: McGraw-Hill Book Company, 1965, pp. 184–221.
13. Edger Weinberg, "Labor-Management Cooperation: A Report on Recent Initiatives," *Monthly Labor Review*, April 1976, p. 13.
14. "A Joint Look at Cutting Health Care Costs," *Business Week*, November 17, 1975, p. 49.

6

Personnel Management in Perspective

A personnel department cannot become content with its performance. It must search for new ways to help its firm and its people. One way is through an audit of its activities. Audits point to changes that can improve the department's performance. Another way to improve is by attention to the future. By anticipating new challenges, the department can be more proactive.

As a manager or personnel specialist, you need to understand audits and future challenges. They affect you. They can change the procedures you use and the way you manage employees.

Chapter 22

The Personnel Audit

Personnel audits measure the effectiveness of personnel departments in terms of their professional development and the degree to which they are meeting their client departments' needs.

Terry Hercus and Diane Oades[1]

CHAPTER OBJECTIVES

After studying this chapter, you should be able to:
1. **Identify** the benefits of a personnel audit.
2. **Explain** the scope of personnel audits.
3. **Describe** the most common approaches to personnel audits.
4. **List** the research tools used in a personnel audit.
5. **Define** the components of a successful personnel audit report.

Personnel departments cannot assume everything they do is correct. Errors do occur and policies become outdated. By checking its activities, the personnel department can find problems before they become serious. If the evaluation is done correctly, it can build support between the department and operating managers. For example, consider the following conversation between a manager and a member of the personnel department.

"As manager of the underwriting department, I know we make mistakes. Most errors are caught and corrected before any damage is done. But sometimes outside auditors catch our mistakes for us, so I am glad that you are auditing the personnel procedures. I was beginning to wonder if your department thought it was above outside review," commented Linda Desmarais.

"We realize that there is room for improvement. In fact, the reason we are doing this review is to check our methods and learn how we can better serve managers like yourself," Fred Nolin reacted.

"What do you hope to discover?" Linda asked.

"First, we want to see if our present procedures are being followed. We need uniformity in our selection, career planning, compensation, and other activities. If there is a lack of consistency, we want to find out why. Maybe people do not understand our procedures. Or maybe our methods are not practical and should be changed. Second, we are checking to ensure compliance with employee relations laws such as human rights, safety, and others. This audit is not a 'witch hunt.' We are simply trying to improve our performance," Fred concluded.

A *personnel audit* evaluates the personnel activities used in an organization. The audit may include one division or an entire company. It gives feedback about the personnel function to operating managers and personnel specialists. It also provides feedback about how well managers are meeting their human resource duties. In short, the audit is an overall quality control check on personnel activities in a division or company.

As the opening dialogue indicates, several benefits result from a personnel audit. Figure 22-1 lists the major ones. An audit reminds managers like Linda of the department's contribution.[2] It also creates a more professional image of the department among managers and personnel specialists. And the audit helps clarify the department's role and leads to greater uniformity. Perhaps most importantly, it uncovers problems and ensures compliance with a variety of laws. These benefits explain the increasing interest in personnel audit by major Canadian firms in recent years.

Figure 22-1
BENEFITS OF A PERSONNEL MANAGEMENT AUDIT

- **Identifies** the contributions of the personnel department to the organization.
- **Improves** the professional image of the personnel department.
- **Encourages** greater responsibility and professionalism among members of the personnel department.
- **Clarifies** the personnel department's duties and responsibilities.
- **Stimulates** uniformity of personnel policies and practices.
- **Finds** critical personnel problems.
- **Ensures** timely compliance with legal requirements.
- **Reduces** human resource costs through more effective personnel procedures.
- **Creates** increased acceptance of needed changes in the personnel department.
- **Includes** a thorough review of the department's information system.

This chapter examines the scope, approaches, and tools used to conduct audits. Although the audit is usually done by personnel experts, their findings affect both the personnel function and operating managers.

THE SCOPE OF PERSONNEL AUDITS

The scope of an audit extends beyond just the personnel department's actions. The department does not operate in isolation. Its success depends on how well it performs *and* how well its programs are carried out by others in the organization. For example, consider how supervisors at the Atlantic Lobster Company reduced the effectiveness of the performance appraisal process.

To appraise performance, Atlantic Lobster Company used a critical-incident procedure, which means supervisors had to record both positive and negative incidents as they occurred. To become a section supervisor an employee needed three years of good or superior performance evaluations. However, in practice, supervisors stressed employee mistakes when they recorded incidents; as a result, few employees received the three years of good ratings needed to qualify for a promotion. Many of them blamed the personnel department's appraisal process for their lack of promotions.

An audit uncovered this misuse of the program and led to additional training for supervisors in the use of the critical-incident method. If the audit had not uncovered this problem, employee dissatisfaction might have grown worse.

As the example of the Atlantic Lobster Company illustrates, personnel problems are seldom confined to just the personnel department. Thus these audits must be broad in scope to be effective. They should evaluate the personnel function, the use of personnel procedures by managers, and the impact of these activities on employee goals and satisfaction.

AUDIT OF THE PERSONNEL FUNCTION

Audits should logically begin with a review of the personnel department's work.[3] Figure 22-2 lists the major areas they cover. An audit touches on vir-

Figure 22-2

MAJOR AREAS COVERED BY A PERSONNEL FUNCTION AUDIT

Personnel Management Information System

Human rights legislation
• Information on compliance

Human resource plans
• Supply and demand estimates
• Skills inventories
• Replacement charts and summaries

Job analysis information
• Job standards
• Job descriptions
• Job specifications

Compensation administration
• Wage and salary levels
• Fringe benefit package
• Employer-provided services

Staffing and Development

Recruiting
• Sources of recruits
• Availability of recruits
• Employment applications

Selection
• Selection ratios
• Selection procedures
• Human rights legislation compliance

Training and orientation
• Orientation program
• Training objectives and procedures
• Learning rates

Career development
• Internal placement success
• Career planning program
• Human resource development effort

Organization Control and Evaluation

Performance appraisals
• Standards and measures of performance
• Performance appraisal techniques
• Evaluation interviews

Labour-management relations
• Legal compliance
• Management rights
• Dispute resolution problems

Human resource controls
• Employee communications
• Discipline procedures
• Change and development procedures

Personnel audits
• Personnel function
• Operating managers
• Employee feedback on personnel

tually every topic discussed in this book. A review of only a few aspects of the personnel management system may ignore topics that affect the department's effectiveness. For each item in the figure, the audit team of personnel specialists should:

- *Identify* who is responsible for each activity.
- *Determine* the objectives sought by each activity.
- *Review* the policies and procedures used to achieve these objectives.
- *Sample* the records in the personnel information system to learn if policies and procedures are being followed correctly.
- *Prepare* a report commending proper objectives, policies, and procedures.
- *Develop* a plan of action to correct errors in objectives, policies, and procedures.
- *Follow up* on the plan of action to see if it has solved the problems found through the audit.[4]

Admittedly, an audit of every personnel activity is time consuming. As a result, very large organizations have full-time audit teams similar to those who conduct financial audits. These teams are especially useful when the personnel department is decentralized into regional or field offices. Through the use of audits, the organization can maintain consistency in its practices even though there are several personnel offices in different locations. And the mere existence of an audit team encourages compliance and self-audits between visits by the audit team.

Cliff Robertson, a regional personnel manager, realized that his chances for promotion to the corporate headquarters in Toronto depended on how well his region's personnel offices performed. The company's personnel audit team reviewed his region's performance every June. So in preparation for the audit, Cliff had each personnel office in the central region conduct a self-audit in April. Then in early May the personnel administrators from the three branches met in Winnipeg to review the results of the audit, and during May errors uncovered through the audit were corrected, if possible. Thus when the corporate audit team completed its own review in June, they always gave Cliff's region high marks for compliance with company policies and with laws.

AUDIT OF MANAGERIAL COMPLIANCE

An audit also reviews how well managers comply with personnel policies and procedures. If managers ignore personnel policies or violate employee relations laws, the audit should uncover these errors so that corrective action can be taken. Compliance with laws is especially important, for when human-rights, safety, compensation, or labour laws are violated, the government holds the company responsible.

The manager of a fast-food restaurant hired two high school students to do janitorial work on a part-time basis. The two boys were glad to earn $3.00 an hour. But one boy's father complained to the government that the restaurant was paying below minimum wage. Not only was the parent company found guilty of violating the minimum wage *laws, but the complaint triggered an investigation of the pay and overtime practices of the firm's other restaurants. Had this company used an internal personnel audit, the error could have been corrected before formal government action was taken.*

Besides assuring compliance, the audit can improve the personnel department's image and contribution to the company. Operating managers may gain a higher respect for the department when an audit team seeks their views. If the comments of managers are acted upon, the department will be seen as more responsive to their needs. And since it is a service department, these actions may improve its contribution to organizational objectives. For example, consider what one audit team learned when it talked with managers of local claims offices:

After several interviews with claims office managers, the audit team discovered a pattern to their comments. Most managers believed that although the personnel department filled job vacancies quickly, it did not train recruits before assigning them to a claims office. Day-to-day pressures in the claims offices caused training to be superficial and led to many errors by new adjusters. The managers felt that the training should be done at the regional office by the personnel department.

After reading the team's report, the regional personnel manager was pleased to learn that the selection process was satisfactory, and to solve the problem of field training, she created a one-week training program for claims adjusters with her next budget increase.

AUDIT OF EMPLOYEE SATISFACTION

Effective personnel departments meet both company objectives and employee needs. When employee needs are not met, turnover, absenteeism, and union activity are more likely. To learn how well employee needs are met, the audit team gathers data from workers. The team collects information about wages, benefits, supervisory practices, career planning assistance, and the feedback employees receive about their performance.

The audit team of an automobile parts distributor received one common complaint from employees: they felt isolated because they worked in retail stores or warehouses located all over Canada. They had little sense of belonging to the large company of which they were a part. To bolster sagging morale and to help employees feel that they were members of a fast-growing and dynamic company, the personnel department started a biweekly "Payroll Action Newsletter." The two-page letter was stuffed in every pay envelope each payday. It gave tips on new developments at headquarters and different field locations. In this way, the department used the audit to make the firm more responsive to its employees' needs.

RESEARCH APPROACHES TO AUDITS

Personnel activities are evaluated through research.[5] Several research approaches are used because the scope of audits includes the personnel function, operating managers, and employees. Sometimes the "research" is little more than an informal investigation or fact-finding effort. At other times, the approach may be advanced and rely on sophisticated research designs and statistics.[6] Whether informal or rigorous, this research seeks to improve the personnel activities of the organization. These applications-oriented efforts are called *applied research*. The most common forms of applied personnel research are summarized in Figure 22-3 and explained in the following paragraphs.[7]

Figure 22-3
RESEARCH APPROACHES OF PERSONNEL AUDITS

- **Comparative approach.** The personnel audit team compares its firm (or division) with another firm (or division) to uncover areas of poor performance. This approach commonly is used to compare the results of specific personnel activities or programs. It helps to detect areas of needed improvement.
- **Outside authority approach.** The audit team relies on the expertise of a consultant or published research findings as a standard against which personnel activities or programs are evaluated. The consultant or research findings may help diagnose the cause of problems.
- **Statistical approach.** From existing records, the audit team generates statistical standards against which activities and programs are evaluated. With these mathematical standards, the team may uncover errors while they are still minor.
- **Compliance approach.** By sampling elements of the personnel information system, the audit team looks for deviations from laws and company policies or procedures. Through their fact-finding efforts, the team can determine whether there is compliance with company policies and legal regulations.
- **MBO approach.** When a management-by-objectives (MBO) approach is applied to the human resource area, the audit team can compare actual results with stated objectives. Areas of poor performance can be detected and reported.

Perhaps the simplest form of research is the *comparative approach*. It uses another division or company as a model. The audit team then compares their results or procedures with those of the other organization. The comparative approach is often used to compare absence, turnover, and salary data. This approach also makes sense when a new procedure is being tried for the first time. For example, if a company installs an alcoholic rehabilitation program, it may copy a similar program at another firm or division. Then the results of the two programs are compared.

Alternatively, the personnel department may rely on an *outside authority approach*. Standards set by a consultant or from published research findings serve as benchmarks for the audit team. For example, the consultant or industry-wide research may indicate that the personnel budget is usually about three-quarters of 1% of gross sales. This figure then serves as a rough guidepost when evaluating the personnel department's overall budget. At present, external comparison is one of the most popular approaches to evaluating personnel activities and services.

A third approach is to develop statistical measures of performance based on the company's existing information system. For example, research into the company's records reveals its absenteeism and turnover rates. These data indicate how well personnel activities and operating managers control these problem areas. This *statistical approach* is usually supplemented with comparisons against external information, which may be gathered from other firms. This information is often expressed as ratios that are easy to compute and use. For example, an employer that averages two hundred employees during the month and has twelve quit finds that its turnover rate is 6%.[8]

$$\frac{\text{Number of separations} \quad (12)}{\text{Average number of employees} \ (200)} \times 100 = 6\%$$

Likewise, if eight employees miss work on a particular day, the absenteeism rate is 4%.

$$\frac{\text{Number of employees absent} \quad (8)}{\text{Total number scheduled to work} \ (200)} \times 100 = 4\%$$

The *compliance approach* is another personnel audit strategy. This method reviews past practices to determine if those actions followed company policies and procedures. Often the audit team reviews a sample of employment, compensation, discipline, and employee appraisal forms. The purpose of the review is to ensure that field offices and operating managers comply with internal rules and legal regulations.

An internal audit of the selection process used at Bio-Genetics Ltd. revealed that the employment manager followed the correct procedures. But the audit team noticed that many applications had comments written in the margins. These comments were added by operating managers who also interviewed applicants. Most of their notes referred to personal data that were not asked on the form, such as sex, age, marital status, ages of dependents, and race. Managers did this to help them remember individual candidates. But if some applicant was not hired, these comments could lead to charges of discrimination on the basis of age, sex, or race.

A final approach is for personnel specialists and operating managers to set objectives in their area of responsibility. This *MBO* (management by objectives) *approach* creates specific objectives against which performance can be measured.[9] Then the audit team researches actual performance and compares it with the previously set objectives. For example, operating managers may set a goal of resolving a higher percentage of grievances before they reach arbitration. Then the audit evaluates the trends in this area. This is also a popular approach to evaluating personnel function.

No one of these audit approaches can be applied to all parts of personnel management. More commonly, audit teams use several of these strategies, depending on the specific personnel activities under evaluation. Then, as Figure 22-4 suggests, the audit team selects specific research tools to collect audit information. This information serves as feedback on personnel activities to the personnel function, operating managers, and employees. Unfavourable feedback leads to corrective action that improves the contribution of personnel activities.

Figure 22-4
AN OVERVIEW OF THE PERSONNEL MANAGEMENT AUDIT PROCESS

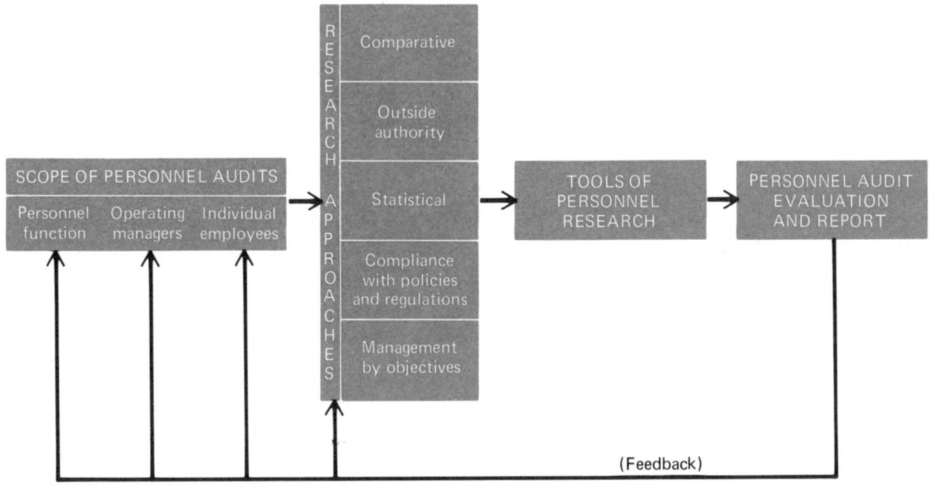

TOOLS OF PERSONNEL RESEARCH

Regardless of the audit team's approach, it must collect data about the firm's personnel activities. To collect the data, several techniques serve as information-gathering tools for them. Each tool provides partial insights into the firm's personnel activities. If these tools are used skillfully, the team can weave these insights into a clear picture of the organization's personnel activities. These tools include:

- Interviews
- Questionnaires and surveys
- Record analysis
- External information
- Personnel experiments

INTERVIEWS

Interviews with employees and managers are one source of information about personnel activities. Their comments help the audit team find areas that need improvement. Criticisms by employees may pinpoint those actions that the department should take to meet their needs. Likewise, suggestions by managers may reveal ways to provide them with better service. When their criticisms are valid, changes should be made. But when it is the personnel department who is right, it may have to educate others in the firm by explaining the procedures being questioned.

Bob Gordon served as a member of the audit team at Canadian Furniture Company. He interviewed various managers, who complained that the frequent transfer of managerial staff was a problem. Bob understood their concerns. He explained that the unique type of furniture the company dealt with led to too many fluctuations in market demand for the company's products. Unless senior managers were frequently transferred to faraway branches, the sales of these branches could not be pulled up. Although many managers still disliked the situation, the audit interview helped them understand the need for the frequent transfers of managers.

Another useful source of information is the exit interview.[10] *Exit interviews* are conducted with departing employees to learn their views of the organization. Figure 22-5 shows the typical questions asked during the interview. It is done separately from the personnel audit, and the employees' comments are recorded. Then during the audit these answers are reviewed to find the causes of employee dissatisfaction and other personnel management problems.

Figure 22-5
AN EXIT INTERVIEW FORM

SASKATOON KITCHEN APPLIANCES LTD.
Exit Interview Form

Employee's name _____   **Date hired** _____

Interviewed by _____   **Interviewed on** _____

Supervisor's name_____   **Department** _____

1. Were your job duties and responsibilities what you expected? _____
   If not, why?_____
2. What is your frank and honest opinion of:
   a. Your job? _____
   b. Your working conditions? _____
   c. Your orientation to your job? _____
   d. Your training provided by the company?_____
   e. Your pay? _____
   f. Your company-provided benefits and services?_____
   g. Your treatment by your manager?_____
3. What is your major reason for leaving the company? _____
   _____
4. What could we have done to keep you from leaving? _____
   _____
5. What could be done to make Saskatoon Kitchen Appliances a better place to work? _____
   _____

QUESTIONNAIRES AND SURVEYS

Many personnel departments supplement interviews with questionnaires and surveys. These tools are used because interviews are time consuming, costly, and usually limited to only a few people. Through surveys of employees, a more accurate picture of employee treatment can be developed. Also, questionnaires may lead to more candid answers than face-to-face interviews.

One common questionnaire is an *attitude survey*. These multipage paper-

and-pencil tests are used to learn how employees view their manager, their job, and the personnel department. Sometimes several hundred questions are asked. These questions seek answers to the critical issues listed in Figure 22-6. Then the answers are grouped into areas of analysis to find out where employee attitudes are high and where low. Further analysis may identify problems with specific supervisors, jobs, or benefits.

Figure 22-6
CRITICAL CONCERNS TO BE ANSWERED BY ATTITUDE SURVEYS

Employee Attitudes about Supervisors

- Are some supervisors' employees exceptionally satisfied or dissatisfied?
- Do specific supervisors need training in supervisory and human relations skills?
- Have attitudes improved since the last survey?

Employee Attitudes about Their Jobs

- What are common elements of jobs that cause negative attitudes? Positive attitudes?
- Can jobs that cause poor attitudes be redesigned to improve satisfaction?
- Can jobs that cause poor attitudes be given alternative work schedules (such as shorter workweeks or flextime)?

Perceived Effectiveness of the Personnel Department

- Do employees think they work for a good or bad employer?
- Do employees think they have a career or merely a job?
- Do employees feel they have some place to turn in order to solve their problems, besides to their immediate superior?
- Do employees feel informed about company developments?
- Do employees know what is expected of them in their jobs?
- Are employees satisfied by the amount and type of feedback they get about their performance?
- Are employees satisfied with their pay? Benefits?

After an attitude survey, the manager of a small steel mill found that the detailers in the design department were dissatisfied. Their dissatisfaction stemmed from their jobs, supervision, and medical insurance.

Detailers are typically responsible for executing detailed drawings. However, at the mill some detailers specialized in doing the drawings, while others labelled the blueprints. Also, they worked under a supervisor who rigidly enforced company rules and was very autocratic. Finally, they were upset at the personnel department because it usually took nearly two months for them to be reimbursed for claims against the supplementary dental insurance plan.

The mill manager, the personnel manager, and the design department supervisor met to discuss the attitude problem among the detailers. They agreed to redesign the jobs so that each detailer was responsible for all phases of a drawing. The personnel and mill managers convinced the supervisor to implement flexible working hours and move these workers from hourly pay to salary. The supervisor also agreed to enroll in the company's sixteen-week human relations training program. Since dissatisfaction with dental expenses reimbursement existed throughout the company, the personnel manager arranged for all employees to send their claims directly to the insurance company. The next survey revealed that this problem no longer existed.

As the example shows, attitude surveys give valuable feedback. Operating managers can learn where changes in jobs or supervision are needed. The personnel department learns how its efforts are viewed by employees. And when surveys are conducted periodically, the audit team can identify trends. Perhaps more importantly, changes made after an attitude survey show employees management's commitment to their welfare.

RECORD ANALYSIS

Not all problems are revealed through employee attitudes. Sometimes problems can only be found by studying personnel records. These reviews are done to ensure compliance with company procedures and laws. The records normally reviewed by an audit team are listed in Figure 22-7 and discussed in the following paragraphs.

Figure 22-7
RECORDS COMMONLY REVIEWED AS PART OF A PERSONNEL AUDIT

Safety and Health Records

• Determine differences before and after personnel programs aimed at lowering turnover or absenteeism.

Grievance Records

• Are there patterns to grievances arising from specific contract clauses or supervisors?
• Are there sections of the agreement that are unclear to union or management officials?

Compensation Studies

• Are wages externally and internally equitable?
• Are fringe benefits understood by employees?
• Does the fringe benefit package compare favourably with those of local firms and national competitors?

Human Rights Plans

• Is the firm in compliance with all human rights laws?
• Should there be an affirmative-action plan to address those areas where the firm is not in compliance?
• Has the firm made acceptable progress toward meeting its human rights goals?

Program and Policy Studies

• Does each personnel program meet its stated goals?
• Are personnel policies and procedures being followed by the personnel department and line managers?

Figure 22-7 (cont.)
RECORDS COMMONLY REVIEWED AS PART OF A PERSONNEL AUDIT

Scrap Rates

- Determine if training, bonuses, or other personnel programs have reduced scrap rates.

Turnover/Absenteeism

- Are there patterns or discernible causes? By age? Sex?
- How do these records compare with those of other employers?
- Determine differences before and after personnel programs aimed at lowering turnover or absenteeism.

Pretest/Posttest Scores

- Determine if orientation or training programs improve test scores or job performance.
- How well do test scores relate to job performance?

Internal Placement Records

- What percentage of jobs are filled internally?
- How well do internally promoted candidates perform?
- Do replacement charts/summaries indicate sufficient promotable talent?

Selection Records

- Is the performance of recruits better according to the source from which they were recruited?
- Are recruitment and selection costs comparable with those of other firms?

Employee Files

- Are employee files in order and properly completed?
- Do records contain accurate, up-to-date information that is useful for making employee decisions?
- Is this employee making reasonable career progress?
- Is this employee a source of discipline or interpersonal problems?

Special Programming Reports

- Are special programs achieving the desired results?

SAFETY AND HEALTH AUDITS. An analysis of safety and health records may reveal violations of provisions of the Canadian Labour Code and other provincial safety and health regulations. Under the record-keeping requirements of the Canada Labour Code, Part IV, accurate records of all matters coming under the jurisdiction of the Safety and Health Committee should be kept by every organization. A personnel audit can help to document the firm's compliance with safety and health requirements in each province.

GRIEVANCE AUDITS. The audit team may also be able to uncover a pattern in employee grievances. Patterns may emerge by jobs, supervisors, union representatives, age groups, or contract provisions. If patterns are detected, personnel specialists seek out the underlying causes and take corrective action to reduce the causes of these complaints. Interviews with supervisors and union officials may reveal the underlying causes of grievances. And if union officials participate in finding patterns of grievances, they may support management's suggested changes.

A grievance audit at the Kelowna Logging Company indicated that supervisors and managers were spending too much of their time dealing with grievances. In fact, the lost production time by workers and costs of arbitration were seriously reducing the company's profitability. Low profitability meant that the union had to accept the smallest wage increases in the area.

The audit team asked the two top union officials to help review the causes of grievances. The union leaders thought the problem was a poor understanding of the contract by both supervisors and union representatives. The audit team's analysis fit the union leaders' comments. As a result, the company asked the town's part-time mayor to help train both sides. The training led to a noticeable drop in grievances.

COMPENSATION AUDITS. Audit teams carefully review the personnel department's compensation practices.[11] Primarily, they study the level of wages, benefits, and services that are provided. If jobs have been priced properly through job evaluations and salary survey, pay levels will be fair. Benefits and services are also studied, to learn if they are competitive with those of other employers and in compliance with government regulations.

HUMAN RIGHTS COMPLIANCE AUDITS. Although several large companies employ one or more persons to monitor the company's compliance with Canadian human rights legislation, the audit team serves as a further check on compliance. The team usually concentrates its attention on hiring, placement, and compensation of all minority groups; if discriminating practices exist, it informs management of the need for corrective action.

PROGRAM AND POLICY AUDITS. Besides safety, grievance, compensation, and human rights corrective action programs, audits evaluate many other personnel programs and policies. The purpose of these audits is to determine whether other programs and policies are doing what was intended.

Two years after Seafood Canners Ltd. adopted a "promotion from within" policy, most supervisors were still recruited from outside the firm. Few workers applied for supervisory openings, even though these jobs were posted throughout the plant and employees were encouraged to apply. The audit team learned that during peak seasons, production workers earned more money than supervisors because of overtime pay and the incentive system. Many employees viewed supervisory jobs as entailing more responsibility and less pay. To remedy the problem, supervisors were given a percentage of their department's production bonus. A year later, 90% of the supervisory openings were being filled internally.

As the Seafood Canners example illustrates, policies ("promote from within") may conflict with other programs (the incentive system). And legal requirements (overtime pay) may conflict with the department's goals. Virtually every personnel policy and program affects at least one other. Thus a thorough audit needs to include all the major personnel policies and programs and how they relate to each other.

Figure 22-7 also identifies other typical records reviewed by audit teams. These records are evaluated to find areas of poor performance and conflicts between policies, programs, and employee relations laws. The use of these records in an audit is wide-ranging, as suggested by the questions raised in the figure.

EXTERNAL INFORMATION

Another tool of the audit team is external information.[12] Research that is limited to just the organization's internal attitudes and records may uncover unfavourable trends. But outside comparisons also give the audit team a perspective against which their firm's activities can be judged. Some needed information is available readily, while other data may be difficult to find.

Most of the external information is available from the publications of Statistics Canada and Labour Canada. These agencies regularly publish information about future employment opportunities, employee turnover rates, work-force projections, area wage and salary surveys, severity and frequency rates of accidents, and other data that can serve as benchmarks for comparing internal information. Statistics Canada, Labour Canada, Employment and Immigration Canada, and provincial labour and manpower offices provide information that can also be used for comparative purposes. Work-force demographics—age, sex, education, and national-ethnic composition—are commonly available from provincial agencies.

Industry associations and boards of trade usually make available to members specialized data related to the industry. Of most use to audit teams are statistics on industry norms—such as turnover rates, absenteeism rates, standard wage rates, growth rates, standardized job descriptions, accident rates, fringe benefit costs, and sample union-management agreements.

Professional associations often provide similar information to members of the profession. Studies conducted by the association may include salary and benefit surveys, demographic profiles, and other data that can serve as standards against which the personnel department's efforts are measured.

Consultants and university research bureaus may be able to provide other needed information through research.

PERSONNEL EXPERIMENTS

A final tool available to personnel departments and audit teams is research experiments. The ideal research design is a *field experiment* that allows the personnel department to compare an experimental and a control group under realistic conditions. For example, the personnel department may implement a safety training program for half of the department supervisors. This half is the experimental group. The control group is the supervisors who are not given training. Then the subsequent safety records of both groups are compared several months after the training is completed. If the experimental group has significantly lower accident rates, this is evidence that the safety training program was effective.

Experimentation does have some drawbacks. Many managers are reluctant to experiment with only some workers because of morale problems and potential dissatisfaction among those who were not selected. Those involved may feel manipulated. And the experiment may be confounded by changes in the work environment or simply by the two groups' talking with each other about the experiment.

These problems are lessened by using a research design that involves two organizations, as did one school board:

The personnel department of a rural school district gave all the elementary school teachers of one school a special two-day training program. The teachers at another school thirty kilometres away did not receive the training. At the end of the year, the school board's audit team compared the teacher evaluations and pupil scores on province-wide tests to assess the success of the development program.

This design reduced the likelihood of the experimental and control groups' discussing the training. It also prevented the problem of principals' having half of their faculty in each group. Of course, the difficulty with this design is that it assumes that the two organizations, their teachers, and their students were comparable before the experiment began.

AUDIT REPORT

Research approaches and tools are used to develop a picture of the organization's personnel activities. For this information to be useful, it is compiled into an audit report. The *audit report* is a comprehensive description of personnel activities, which includes both commendations for effective practices and recommendations for improving practices that are ineffective. A recognition of both good and bad practices is more balanced and encourages acceptance of the report.

Often an audit report is in three parts. One part is for operating managers, another for managers of specific personnel functions, and the third for the personnel manager.

REPORT FOR OPERATING MANAGERS

The audit report for operating managers summarizes their personnel objectives and responsibilities. Their goals may seek to reduce absenteeism or turnover, further employee development, improve union relations, or achieve other objectives. Specific duties of line managers also may be included. These duties may involve interviewing applicants, training employees, evaluating performance, motivating workers, and satisfying employee needs.

The report also identifies personnel problems. Violations of personnel policies and employee relations laws are highlighted. Poor management practices are revealed in the report along with recommendations where appropriate. For example, consider an excerpt of a report received by the manager of a bottling plant.

Employee turnover. *Overall, the turnover rates in the Sydney Bottling Plant compare favourably with turnover rates in the community and the industry. Plant management appears to be sensitive to the needs of long-service employees.*

Turnover among recently hired employees tends to be very high. Attitude surveys and exit interviews reveal two problems. First, new employees sometimes quit because their job duties were not what they had expected. Second, among those new employees who stay, many report feelings of isolation and not being part of the "team." If applicants were given realistic job previews by showing them the actual duties and working conditions, fewer of them would resign during the ninety-day probationary period. It is also recommended that each supervisor start a departmental orientation program. This program should introduce new hires to the people, facilities, and policies of their department. Then new employees should be assigned to a senior worker to create a "buddy system" that will help them become part of the work team and the informal organization.

REPORT TO PERSONNEL SPECIALISTS

Those specialists who handle employment, training, compensation, and other personnel activities also need feedback. The audit report they receive isolates specific areas of good and poor performance. For example, one audit team observed that many jobs did not have qualified replacements. This information was given to the manager of training and development along with the recommendation for more programs to develop promising supervisors and managers.

The report may also provide these specialists with other feedback, such as attitudes of operating managers about the specialists' efforts. Sometimes comparative data are included to show what other companies are doing and to provide standards of comparison.

REPORT TO PERSONNEL MANAGER

The personnel manager's report contains all the information given to line managers and specialists within the personnel department. In addition, the personnel manager gets feedback about:

• Attitudes of operating managers and employees about the personnel department's benefits and services.

• A review of the department's objectives and its organization to achieve them.

• Human resource problems and their implications.

• Recommendations for needed changes, which may be stated in the priority seen by the audit team.

With the information contained in the audit report, the personnel manager can take a broad view of the personnel function. Instead of solving problems in a random manner, the manager now can focus on those areas that have the greatest potential for improving the department's contribution to the firm.[13] Emerging trends can be studied and corrective action taken while the problems are still minor. Prompt response to the problems of operating managers may earn added support among them. Even morale and motivation within the personnel department may be increased—for example, through timely congratulations to those who have performed well.

Perhaps most importantly, the audit serves as a map for future efforts and a reference point for future audits. With knowledge of the department's present performance, the manager can make long-range plans to upgrade crucial activities. These plans identify new goals for the department. And these goals serve as standards—standards that future audit teams will use to evaluate the firm's personnel management activities.

SUMMARY

A personnel audit evaluates the personnel activities used in an organization. Its purpose is to ensure that operating managers and personnel specialists are following personnel policies and maintaining an effective work force.

The scope of the audit involves personnel specialists, operating managers, employees, and the external environment. Inputs are sought from all four sources because each has a unique perspective. And to be truly effective, personnel activities cannot meet just the wishes of personnel experts. They also must meet the needs of employees and operating managers and the challenges from the environment.

The audit team uses a variety of research approaches and tools to evaluate personnel activities. Along with internal comparisons, audit teams need to compare their firm's efforts against those of other companies or against standards developed by external authorities and internal statistics. Or their approach may evaluate compliance with laws or with objectives set by management.

Data are gathered through interviews, questionnaire surveys, internal records, external sources, or experimentation. Through these tools, the audit team is able to compile an audit report. The audit report gives feedback to top management, operating managers, personnel specialists, and the personnel manager. Armed with this information, the personnel manager then can develop plans to ensure that personnel activities better contribute to the organization. If personnel management is to be responsible, it needs to review its past performance through audits and research. At the same time, it needs a future orientation to anticipate upcoming challenges. Finally, a proactive view encourages personnel to contribute to both people and company goals.

TERMS FOR REVIEW

Personnel audit
Audit team
Applied research
Research approaches
MBO approach

Exit interviews
Attitude survey
Field experiment
Audit report

REVIEW AND DISCUSSION QUESTIONS

1. In your own words, what are the benefits of a personnel audit to an organization?
2. Why does a personnel audit go beyond just the actions of personnel specialists?
3. If you were asked to conduct a personnel audit on the compensation function (or any other function within the personnel department), what steps would you follow?
4. If you had to conduct an audit of employee job satisfaction, what tools would you use?
5. What research approach do you think should be followed for each of the following areas of concern to the personnel audit team: (a) evaluation of a new company-sponsored drug rehabilitation program, (b) an analysis of employee tardiness patterns, (c) the appropriateness of present recruiting costs?
6. Why are exit interviews an effective source of insight into employee problems in the organization?
7. How would you design a field experiment to evaluate the advantages of two different employee compensation programs?
8. What types of information should be put in an audit report for (a) the employment manager, (b) the assistant plant manager, and (c) the personnel director?
9. In the last two decades, many cultural values have changed—some rather drastically. Briefly describe how personnel management might be affected by (a) a trend toward smaller families, (b) increased participation of women in the work force, (c) increased acceptability by society of divorce.
10. Explain why a personnel department should be proactive in its approach.

INCIDENT 22-1

MARITIME COAL INDUSTRIES LIMITED

Maritime Coal Industries ran two underground coal mines and a coke oven for converting coal into industrial coke. The locations were about sixty kilometres distant from one another, and so each operation had a branch personnel office. The branch offices did their own hiring, administration of employee benefits, safety programs, and labour relations with the local union. After reading an article about the merits of a personnel management audit, the personnel director at Maritime, Gabe Robertson, discussed the need for an audit with the three branch personnel officers. Their individual reactions are summarized below:

Tony Masone: *We don't need an audit. It will take weeks to conduct, and it won't change a thing. Each of us branch personnel managers does the best job we know how. Besides, most of our actions are audited daily by the union. If we make a mistake in employee treatment, pay, benefits, safety, or most of the traditional audit areas, the union lets us know promptly. When you have a union, an audit is not needed.*

Joyce McDonald: *I disagree with Tony. The union would complain if we made an error against their members. But if our error were detrimental to the best interests of Maritime, I doubt the union would say anything. Besides, in the matters of recruiting, selection, orientation, and training, the union has little say or interest. An audit might even reveal areas where each branch might improve. I for one welcome an audit and a chance to see how my office compares with the other two.*

Duke Cush: *Joyce makes a good case for an audit, but if we were having problems in training, selection, or the other areas she mentions, we'd know it. We have gotten along for years without an audit; I see no need to put in a lot of overtime and disrupt everything else just to compile a report that will tell us what we already know.*

1. Assuming you agree with Joyce, what other arguments would you add to justify the overtime and disruption that worries Duke?
2. Even though the union contract specifies many areas in detail, briefly describe the possible benefits from an audit of Maritime's (a) compensation program, (b) safety program, (c) grievance process, and (d) labour relations training for supervisors.
3. Do you think Tony and Duke would have a different attitude if they and Joyce were assigned to the audit team? Why?

INCIDENT 22-2
EMPLOYEE ATTITUDES AT ANKO LTD.

Anko Ltd. rents sports equipment. Its main business is renting out ski equipment and snowmobiles. During the winter, the number of employees ranges between fifty and sixty at five locations in various winter resort areas. Al Anko, the owner, hired a management consultant to evaluate employee satisfaction and attitudes. After interviewing nearly twenty employees and supervisors, the consultant developed an attitude survey that was mailed to all employees. From the interviews and attitude surveys, the consultant made the following observations:

• Nearly two-thirds of the employees felt little loyalty to the firm because they considered their jobs temporary.

• Many employees applied to work at Anko because they were interested in skiing.

• Although the firm gave few benefits, many employees commented about the reduced rental rates on equipment as an important "extra" of their jobs.

• Every supervisor mentioned that the most important selection criterion was whether an applicant knows how to fit and adjust ski bindings.

• Over half of the employees worked split shifts from 7 to 10 A.M. and from 4 to 7 P.M., which were the hours most skis were rented and returned. Some employees liked those hours because they could ski during the day. However, employees who lived in the resort area all year long generally disliked the hours.

• *Employee turnover was very low. But many employees indicated that they would quit if they could find a better-paying job.*

• *Several employees who had worked for Anko in previous years thought it was unfair that they received the same hourly wage as new employees.*

1. If you were the consultant, what recommendations would you make to the owner about (a) the use of split shifts, (b) the types of people recruited, and (c) the treatment of employees who have worked for Anko more than one season?
2. Should Anko treat employees who permanently live in the resort areas differently from those who move there just for the ski season? If so, what differences in treatment would you recommend?

REFERENCES

1. Terry Hercus and Diane Oades, "A Diagnostic Instrument to Evaluate Personnel Practices," *The Canadian Personnel & Industrial Relations Journal*, September 1980, pp. 24–32.
2. Ibid.; Eugene Schmuckler, "The Personnel Audit: Management's Forgotten Tool," *Personnel Journal*, November 1973, pp. 977–980; Walter R. Mahler, "Auditing Pair," in Dale Yoder and Herbert G. Heneman, Jr. (eds.), *Planning and Auditing Pair*, Washington: Bureau of National Affairs, Inc., 1976, pp. 2–92.
3. Hercus and Oades, loc. cit.; Mahler, loc. cit.
4. Dean F. Berry, *The Politics of Personnel Research*, Ann Arbor: Bureau of Industrial Relations, Graduate School of Business Administration, University of Michigan, 1967, pp. 89–103.
5. Fred Crandall, "Personnel Research for Problem-Solving," *The Personnel Administrator*, September 1978, pp. 13–16.
6. Fred Luthans and Terry L. Maris, "Evaluating Personnel Programs through the Reversal Technique," *Personnel Journal*, October 1979, pp. 692–697.
7. George Odiorne, "Evaluating the Personnel Program," in Joseph Famularo (ed.), *Handbook of Modern Personnel Administration*, New York: McGraw-Hill Book Company, 1972, Ch. 8. See also Walter R. Mahler, op. cit.; Vytenis P. Kuraitis, "The Personnel Audit," *Personnel Administrator*, November 1981, pp. 29–34.
8. Thomas F. Cawsey and William C. Wedley, "Labor Turnover Costs: Measurement and Control," *Personnel Journal*, February 1979, pp. 90–95, 121; Joseph Lowman and Tom Snediker, "Pinpointing Avoidable Turnover with 'Cohort Analysis,'" *Personnel Journal*, April 1980, pp. 310–315.
9. Odiorne, loc. cit.
10. Wanda R. Embrey, R. Wayne Mondy, and Robert M. Noe, "Exit Interview: A Tool for Personnel Management," *The Personnel Administrator*, May 1979, pp. 43–48.
11. Carl H. Driessnack, "Financial Impact of Effective Human Resources Management," *The Personnel Administrator*, January 1976, pp. 22–26.
12. Richard W. Beatty, "Research Needs of PAIR Professions in the Near Future," *The Personnel Administrator*, September 1978, pp. 17–20. See also Jac Fitz-Enz, "Measuring Human Resource Effectiveness," *The Personnel Administrator*, July 1980, pp. 33–36.
13. Dennis C. King and Walter G. Beevor, "Long-Range Thinking," *Personnel Journal*, October 1978, pp. 542–545; William C. Byham, *The Uses of Personnel Research*, American Management Association Research Study 91, New York: American Management Association, 1968.

Chapter 23

Future Challenges in Personnel

Personnel has the opportunity to help ... in ways that will both increase productivity and enhance the quality of working life.

Fred K. Foulkes[1]

CHAPTER OBJECTIVES

After studying this chapter, you should be able to:
1. **Explain** the major challenges facing personnel practices in the future.
2. **Identify** the emerging forces in society that will challenge personnel management.
3. **Describe** how third parties cause changes in personnel management.
4. **List** major workplace innovations that are likely to occur by the year 2000.
5. **Explain** why careers in personnel management affect most managers.

As one view of the future, consider the lunchtime conversation between a personnel manager, a new trainee, and a management consultant:

Trainee: *Both of you have worked in the personnel field for a long time. You must have some opinions about its future.*

Manager: *Well, I don't have a crystal ball, but some of the trends of the 1960s and 1970s are likely to continue. I expect, and hope, most women will continue to enter the work force. We are going to need high participation rates of women to offset the low birthrates of the 1960s.*

As traditional values about family and work continue to change, those of us in personnel are going to have to be more innovative. We are going to have to find new ways to meet employee and company needs. Undoubtedly, we will see more moves toward professionalism. Unfortunately, I fear we will also see more government intervention during the next couple of decades.

Consultant: *Even if government involvement should lessen, special-interest groups and unions will pressure for change. But the big change that must come in personnel is convincing top managers to use a human resource approach.*

Trainee: *What do you mean?*

Consultant: *Few operating managers are convinced that sound personnel policies, practices, and programs directly benefit the company.*

Manager: *I think many believe it, but we sometimes fail to demonstrate the dollars-and-cents payoff of our personnel programs. Too often we promise more than we can deliver. So when a line manager faces a choice between investing in people or equipment, the equipment decision is sometimes more certain.*

Consultant: *Or worse, we suggest programs that benefit the employee with little regard for the impact on profitability. Don't misunderstand me. Someone in the organization must consider employees' needs, but those needs must be balanced by the organization's objectives.*

Trainee: *But through personnel management audits and research, aren't ineffective programs uncovered?*

Manager: *Sure, audits and research weed out mistakes and poor programs. But mistakes will be fewer from top management's viewpoint if we consider the impact on both employees* and *the bottom line.*

Personnel management must seek a balance between company objectives and employee needs. To be responsible, personnel cannot just audit itself, as discussed in the last chapter. Audits are necessary, but they are backward-looking. They uncover only the results of past decisions. Although past performance should be evaluated, personnel departments also should look to the future in order to be more proactive.[2]

A proactive approach requires personnel managers and their staff to develop a *future orientation*. They must constantly scan their professional and social environment for clues about the future. New developments may mean new challenges. For example, high divorce rates may lead to more employer-provided child-care facilities and flexible work schedules so that working parents can fulfill their parental duties.

Without a future orientation, the personnel department becomes reactive, not proactive. And reactive approaches allow minor problems to become major ones. The area of succession planning provides an appropriate example.

Several top managers of West Coast Paper Products, Ltd. seldom took more than a one-week vacation. They felt that no one else was qualified to take their place for longer than a week. When one mill manager quit, the replacement problem became a crisis for several weeks until a new manager was found. Even then, the mill had problems for months until the new manager had learned the company's policies.

Had the personnel office used human resource planning, replacement could have been developed ahead of time. Even without human resource planning, a future-oriented personnel manager would have questioned the lack of replacements.

But a proactive approach is insufficient by itself. A systems orientation also is needed. Personnel specialists must view company objectives and employee needs as parts of the total system. When managers fail to keep this perspective in mind, they may misuse human resources to achieve company objectives. Likewise, if personnel specialists forget this relationship, they may pursue employee needs to the exclusion of company objectives.[3] The appropriate focus is a proactive, human resource approach to personnel management within a systems framework. As explained in Chapter 1:

• *Proactive approach* means having a future orientation in order to anticipate challenges before they arise. Therefore, personnel management needs to be sensitive to emerging trends.

• *Human resource approach* means that employees should be treated with importance and dignity. Since the standards of fair treatment and dignity change through time, personnel management should be sensitive to future developments.

• *Systems approach* means that personnel management takes place within a larger context, the organization and its environment. Personnel management can be evaluated only with respect to its contribution to the organization. And since organizations are open systems, personnel management needs to relate to the external environment.

By applying these three approaches, personnel departments are better able to meet the future challenges discussed in this chapter.[4] These challenges arise from the department's day-to-day practices and from the external challenges it faces.

CHALLENGES TO PERSONNEL PRACTICES

Although personnel practices have matured rapidly in recent years, improvements still are needed to meet future challenges.[5] Many challenges are unique to individual employers. But demands for an expanded contribution, modern information systems, and professionalism are likely to touch all personnel departments.

CONTRIBUTION TO OBJECTIVES

Personnel departments need to increase their contribution to organizational objectives. But this expanded contribution requires the support of line managers, particularly top management. And many operating managers question the department's contribution to the firm's objectives. Too often, top managers see personnel experts as worrying about records, employee rights, and laws—instead of costs, performance, and profitability. This difference between operating and personnel managers is shown in Figure 23-1. Line managers often view people's needs as important only to the extent that profitability is affected.

Perhaps the biggest challenge facing personnel managers is convincing line managers that personnel practices do contribute to overall performance.[6] That is, personnel specialists need to evaluate their efforts against the company objectives in Figure 23-1. To gain management support, personnel experts need to emphasize cost, performance, and profitability.

This challenge requires more than just a change in the personnel mana-

Figure 23-1
TRADITIONAL CONCERNS OF OPERATING AND PERSONNEL MANAGERS

Operating Managers and Organizational Objectives	Personnel Managers and Human Resource Needs
• Control cost.	• Improve employee satisfaction.
• Improve efficiency.	• Lower employee turnover.
• Improve performance.	• Meet employee needs.
• Increase profitability.	• Raise employee morale.
• Help the organization grow.	• Provide job security.
• Comply with legal requirements.	• Comply with legal requirements.
• Improve earnings per share.	• Improve reputation as an employer.

ger's vocabulary. Personnel specialists must realize that company performance sometimes assumes priority over employee needs.[7] Ideally, personnel practices can benefit employees *and* the organization. But the ideal is not always attainable, as the following dialogue illustrates:

Joe: *As personnel manager, I cannot support the layoff of 3,200 workers. Consider what that means to all those families. This close to Christmas, we are going to look like Scrooge reborn. Besides, imagine the impact on the Hamilton area. We should cancel the layoff altogether, or at least put it off until after the Christmas holidays.*

Bob: *Put it off? Are you kidding? Every week we wait, it costs nearly $1 million in added wages. This division isn't so profitable that we can afford to absorb costs like that for seven weeks. I am sorry for those who are put on layoff. I truly am. But your suggestion might cause headquarters to close the entire division. Consider the impact of 8,000 people being unemployed. What would that do to the local economy? As plant manager, I need to take the broad perspective.*

This conflict between Joe, the personnel manager, and Bob, the plant manager, can be explained by viewing Figure 23-2. Joe's concern is for the employees. Bob's focus is the organization's survival. Since Joe's efforts were directed at employee needs only, they were not supported by the plant manager. In fact, Joe's comments probably convinced the plant manager that Joe is a humane person, but not a good businessman.[8]

If personnel managers are to contribute meaningfully, they must show how organizational objectives are furthered by meeting employee needs. For example, the personnel manager might get the layoff postponed if he stressed profits and costs. Suppose Joe had said:

The division cannot afford this layoff if it is only for a few weeks. It will raise our unemployment tax for the next three years; it will renew employee interest in unions; and it will cost nearly a half-million dollars in layoff and recall expenses. Our best employees—particularly engineers—will be recruited by competitors. Besides, wages won't fall for two weeks since most employees will use their vacation time. Our studies in the personnel department show that if the layoff lasts for more than three weeks, savings will exceed the direct costs. When employee morale, community reactions, and the loss of key employees are considered, I would recommend against the layoff if it is to be less than five weeks. I recommend we consider a reduced workweek for a period of time. We should be able to get employee support for it during this season.

Figure 23-2
AREA OF OVERLAP BETWEEN ORGANIZATIONAL OBJECTIVES AND EMPLOYEE NEEDS

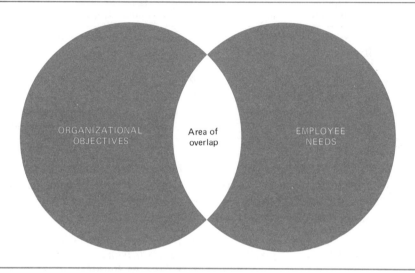

ORGANIZATIONAL
OBJECTIVES

Area of
overlap

EMPLOYEE
NEEDS

PERSONNEL MANAGEMENT INFORMATION SYSTEMS

To contribute to the organization, personnel specialists need a modern *personnel management information system*, which is the total of all personnel data and plans. The department is a staff function that exists in part to advise management. Its role cannot be more effective than the information it makes available to line managers.

To provide useful advice, large personnel departments have computerized much of their information base.[9] Smaller departments are likely to do so in the future as the price of computers declines. The challenge in both large and small organizations is to provide personnel information that is useful to management. At present, personnel records are often organized for ease of use by personnel specialists, rather than managers, and so their use is limited. For example, personnel staff members often complain that line managers do not consider the employees in their decisions. Yet those same managers complain that personnel offers only generalities, not specific figures. If the department provides cost, profit, and performance data, then managers are more likely to consider both the organizational *and* employee implications of their decisions.

Personnel specialists also find that a modern information system can help prove the value of the personnel department's contribution.

As director of personnel research at United Chemical, Ltd., Ruben Krigsman was assigned to improve the morale and productivity of one of its manufacturing plants. After extensive surveys, he made changes in job designs and started a training program. In time, productivity increased by 25% and absenteeism dropped from 5 to 3%, and much of it appeared to be the result of the personnel improvements. Without a

good information system, Krigsman would have been unable to demonstrate the per-
sonnel department's contribution to the company's profitability.

PROFESSIONALISM

Another challenge is professionalism. As mentioned in Chapter 2, personnel activities are too important to be carried out by the untrained. To ensure competency within the field, many provincial personnel associations have created certification programs. The Personnel Association of Ontario (PAO), for example, which presently has over 4,000 members, offers a certification program which requires the completion of eight courses related to the personnel field. These credits, plus a minimum of three years of managerial experience as a personnel manager or personnel professional, are the preconditions for full membership in the association.[10] Although certification does not elevate the personnel field to the professional standing of medicine or law, it is an important first step.

Professionalism may lead to more widely accepted standards within the personnel field. As standards in employment, development, and other activities become widespread, more firms are likely to upgrade their personnel practices accordingly.

Professionalism also created a need to stay informed about advances in the personnel field.[11] This need causes self-renewal through reading, seminars, and work with professional associations of personnel experts. These renewal efforts can also produce a greater awareness of external challenges. It should be mentioned that almost all personnel associations in Canada offer a variety of seminars, lectures, or complete courses on personnel-related topics to improve the management skills of current personnel officers and managers.

EXTERNAL CHALLENGES TO PERSONNEL MANAGEMENT

Changes in society also affect personnel management. Many of those changes will challenge personnel management during the 1980s and beyond. They arise from changes in demographics, values, pressures from third parties, and other sources. These challenges are likely to stimulate many innovations in personnel management over the next couple of decades. Some of the more important challenges are listed in Figure 23-3 and discussed further in the following paragraphs.

Figure 23-3
SELECTED CHALLENGES FACING PERSONNEL MANAGEMENT IN THE 1980s AND 1990s

• **Demographic changes.** The birthrate decline that started in the 1950s means the average age in the work force will rise. Employee productivity may go up as workers gain experience. But those same people are likely to seek more job security and improved pensions.

Figure 23-3 (cont.)
**SELECTED CHALLENGES FACING PERSONNEL MANAGEMENT IN THE
1980s AND 1990s**

• **Changing values.** Cultural and work values change through time. These
changes affect the attitudes of people toward work, retirement, loyalty,
attendance, tardiness, and work effort. In turn, these changes shape the demands
placed on personnel management. Providing employee motivation and satisfaction
during periods of changing values is a significant challenge.

• **Third-party interests.** Government, unions, and special-interest groups make
demands on organizations and personnel activities. As a result, personnel
activities must take place within many constraints. However, as the needs of
society grow, the interests of third parties may grow closer to those of
organizations.

• **Innovation.** Coping with the many challenges facing personnel managers and
specialists will require continued innovation in order to meet both employee
needs and company goals.

• **Canada Pension costs.** As the work force grows older, the burdens on the
government pension system will grow. Government may need employers to
shoulder more of the burden with private pension plans.

• **Portable pensions.** Workers are mobile. Since people change jobs, even
careers, during their life, personnel departments may see a greater need to make
pensions portable. Portable pensions will allow employees who go to another
employer to take their accrued pension benefits with them to ensure a comfortable
retirement.

• **Retirement programs.** As larger numbers of workers approach retirement in
coming years, they may seek improved pensions and other retirement-related
services. Preretirement counselling will grow in popularity, and more firms will
be expected to provide postretirement benefits to meet the social and insurance
needs of the employees.

• **Immigration.** The number of immigrants to Canada has generally been
decreasing in the past few years. However, international upheavals may result in
large numbers of immigrants arriving in a relatively short period of time.
Because of their different social and cultural backgrounds, the effective
integration of such employees into the work force will be a challenge for
personnel specialists.

• **Technological changes.** Remarkable changes in electronic technology are
likely to mean radical changes in the types of jobs and skill levels needed by
organizations in the 1980s and 1990s. Training, development, and career planning
activities are areas of tremendous growth potential within the personnel field as
employers try to adjust the work force to technological change.

• **Privacy legislation.** With the growth of computerized personnel information
systems, companies maintain ever-growing data banks on employees. The need to

Figure 23-3 (cont.)
SELECTED CHALLENGES FACING PERSONNEL MANAGEMENT IN THE 1980s AND 1990s

ensure privacy of employees against abuses of this information may cause greater attention to be paid to the privacy of employee records.

• **Women workers.** The higher participation rates of women in the work force will create demands for greater equality in pay or career advancement opportunities. The limited number of women in top management means many women will be unable to find the mentors that are more available to men. Personnel departments may be expected to respond with more extensive career planning assistance.

• **Dual-career families.** With the increased participation of women in the work force, personnel departments will become involved more with helping spouses find suitable employment as a condition of employment transfers.

• **Employee rewards.** Inflation has caused many firms to put less emphasis on merit increases and more emphasis on "across-the-board" raises to adjust wages for inflation. Inflation and strong demand for skilled workers have caused "wage compression" where the gap between the pay of new and senior workers has narrowed. As a result, wage and salary differentials offer small rewards for experience and loyalty. If these trends continue, employee rewards may focus more and more on noncash compensation.

• **Quebec.** The uncertain political situation in Quebec has resulted in the exodus of many English-speaking managers and professionals as well as the relocation of some businesses. Depending on how these issues are resolved, interprovincial migration patterns may be altered and this will have an impact on the supply of qualified personnel.

• **The Constitution.** What the actual effect of the repatriated Constitution with a federal charter of rights will be, is unknown. However, it could have a significant impact on personnel departments, especially in the area of employee discrimination.

DEMOGRAPHIC CHANGES

The work force of the future has already been born. Only the number of people who will seek jobs is unknown. This rate of participation in the labour force determines the size and composition of the work force. Although these rates are unknown, Statistics Canada does make projections of the work force available based on low and high estimates. One projection appears in Figure 23-4. An examination of that figure indicates that, in general, the number of workers between fifteen and nineteen years old will decline during the 1980s. Likewise, between 1983 and 1989, the availability of twenty- to twenty-four-year-olds will also drop. These trends are good news for government officials and sociologists who have anticipated high unemployment rates among these groups. But for personnel administrators who work for restaurant chains, retail outlets, and other large employers of young workers, recruiting and retention programs may become more important than ever.

Figure 23-4
PROJECTED RATE OF CHANGE IN POPULATION LEVELS (IN %)

Age	Low-Growth Projection			High-Growth Projection		
	1983 to 1989	1989 to 1995	1995 to 2001	1983 to 1989	1989 to 1995	1995 to 2001
15 years and over	5.30	4.15	3.74	7.80	7.07	7.52
15 to 19 years	− 14.89	− 0.31	4.66	− 11.40	7.20	15.37
20 to 24 years	− 16.02	− 12.18	2.65	− 13.47	− 8.13	11.26
25 to 34 years	9.11	− 8.29	− 15.52	12.41	− 5.53	− 11.22
35 to 44 years	19.63	11.48	4.70	23.61	15.81	7.18
45 to 54 years	8.41	25.25	16.94	9.81	27.74	21.12
55 to 64 years	3.13	0.43	14.35	3.77	1.29	15.86
65 and over	16.13	11.84	6.58	18.07	12.74	7.35
Total Population	4.40	2.91	1.46	8.48	7.12	5.54

Source: Developed from data provided in Statistics Canada, *Population Projections for Canada and the Provinces 1976–2001*, Catalogue 91-520, Ottawa: Industry, Trade and Commerce, 1979.

CHANGING VALUES

Changing cultural and work values confront personnel experts with future challenges.[12] To return to Figure 23-4, some of these changes are already evident in the demographic trends. For example, as a result of a declining birth rate that began about twenty years ago, the work force will become proportionately older and older. The 1983-to-1989 projections for fifteen-to-nineteen and twenty-to-twenty-four age categories vividly show this decline. As a result, the overall values of the work force may well change as the proportion of older employees increases. Likewise, although it is not shown in Figure 23-4, the percentage growth of women over fifteen in the labour force is higher than for men over fifteen. These projections show an increase in the participation rate of women in the work force. This trend, coupled with growing demands for women's rights, will continue to challenge personnel specialists to find meaningful employment opportunities for women.

Many personnel professionals believe that mandatory retirement at any age will be abolished nationwide by the 1990s. Here, the challenge for personnel is to honour the rights of senior workers while providing promotional opportunities for younger workers (whose promotion rates may be slowed by older employees who elect to work rather than retire).[13]

Some experts suggest that work may become a less important aspect of people's lives in the future. Jobs may not be as central to the lives of some people. Extended periods of education, flexible lifestyles, changes in traditional male-female roles, and improved welfare benefits may cause a decline in work-force participation rates. Some knowledgeable researchers even suggest that rapidly growing technology may lead to shorter work-weeks and job sharing, as the benefits of electronics and automation spread through society. In this environment, personnel departments may find it exceedingly difficult to attract and retain workers with anything less than an ideal work environment. As a result, consider one possible scenario:

In the 1990s, we may see life patterns undergo major revisions. The traditional education-work-retirement pattern that became popular with the Industrial Revolution may become less common. Although all three elements are likely to be present, their sequence may be more jumbled. For example, education may be followed by work for a few years. Then "retirement" might be elected for five years followed by education and work. These elements—education, work, and retirement—may be interchanged throughout one's life without a formal or permanent retirement.[14]

If values and the workplace change as radically as suggested by this scenario, human resource planning, career counselling, and human resource development will all have to be rethought carefully.

THIRD-PARTY INTERESTS

As discussed throughout the book, government, unions, and special-interest groups are concerned with the employment relationship. And since jobs are likely to remain the primary way most people earn their livelihood, third parties will continue to be an important force in shaping the practice of personnel management.

Although pressures from these third parties add complexity to personnel management, greater cooperation in the future may be possible.[15] As more people realize that the well-being of society is tied to the health of its organizations, especially its business firms, pressures may mount for increased government-business cooperation. Regulations may become fewer, or at least grow more slowly. Those rules that remain are more likely to be designed with both employer *and* employee interests in mind.

Unions, too, show signs of growing more cooperative.[16] As other nations become more effective competitors in world markets, union leaders increasingly recognize the benefits of greater cooperation with the employer. Of course, their goals are likely to remain focussed on employee welfare; but when competition threatens firms or entire industries, their interests and the employers' may parallel more closely.[17]

Although demands from special-interest groups will undoubtedly grow during coming decades, personnel departments have an established record of meeting the needs of such groups and the objectives of the employer. Even with this record of success, personnel specialists must remain sensitive to demands for equality and improved community relations.

OTHER CHALLENGES TO PERSONNEL MANAGEMENT

Changes in society and business practices mean that there will be many other challenges facing personnel management in the future. Figure 23-3 mentions those that are likely to stimulate innovations in personnel management. Each of these challenges holds unseen implications. And as this list grows in coming years, the role of personnel management will grow and become more dynamic.

The need for innovation will be the greatest challenge of all. Personnel managers and specialists will have to be creative, dedicated, and hardworking. They will have to find new ways to meet the demands of employees that contribute to their organization's success. Many of these innovations involve the job and the job setting.[18]

WORKPLACE INNOVATIONS IN THE FUTURE

Future challenges to personnel management will require workplace innovations. Some of these will develop in response to increased professionalism and more advanced human resource information systems. Others will be intended to meet the challenges of changing demographics, values, and external pressures.

Although it is impossible to list all the innovations that are likely to occur by the end of the century, several trends appear likely to affect personnel management. Among these trends are improved employee participation, security, assistance, and work schedules.

EMPLOYEE PARTICIPATION

Throughout western Europe—especially in Scandinavia—employees are gaining rights to participate in the decisions that affect them. As described in Chapter 4, these rights may include participation in decisions through their involvement in autonomous work groups. In these groups, employees are often responsible for the day-to-day decisions that produce goods or services. Although the motivation behind these programs appears to be the improvement of the quality of work life, North American versions may seek to improve productivity.

Also in Europe, codetermination laws require employee representation on supervisory boards and in other top-management decision-making groups. These employee (usually union) representatives have the right to vote on key management decisions that affect employees. Although most North American union leaders claim no interest in codetermination, its continued use in Europe may create interest among workers, unions, and politicians on this side of the ocean. For example, in the U.S., Chrysler Corporation installed the president of the United Automobile Workers union on the board of directors to win collective bargaining concessions.

EMPLOYEE SECURITY

The desire to participate in management decisions may come from a desire for greater employment security. Generally speaking, workers in western Europe and Japan have higher levels of employment security than their Canadian or American counterparts. In those overseas countries, employers give high priority to maintaining stable employment even during recessions. Besides extensive unionization, government pressure, and different economies, the higher level of security may result from greater employee participation in decision making.

North American workers may seek greater employment security and rights, especially if international events or technology lead to major changes in the nature of industry. The pressure for security likely will come through traditional avenues such as unions or legislation or both. Some experts believe it will take the form of an employee "bill of rights," which will grant workers increased civil liberties on their job. It may include guarantees of free speech, job security, and outside review of disciplinary actions.[19] If these changes do evolve, the role of personnel management will grow, and employee satisfaction and motivation may move to even higher levels throughout industry.

EMPLOYEE ASSISTANCE

A clear trend since World War II has been growing employer assistance to employees. During the 1980s and 1990s, more employers are likely to provide help through *employee assistance programs* that follow the pioneering work done by Control Data Corporation and others.

Control Data's efforts to help employees solve their problems have been formalized into an employee assistance program. Its purpose is to provide employees with a broad range of counselling and other professional services. It includes career guidance services, drug and alcoholic rehabilitation programs, outplacement assistance, and referrals to community groups that can provide help with housing, food, medical, marital, and other employee problem areas.

When employee assistance programs are combined with the more common insurance and time-off benefits, workers find the employer as a source of solutions to personal, financial, and family problems. Although lifetime employment security, company housing, vacation resorts, and employer-operated schools are not as common as in Japan, the trend toward "womb-to-tomb" care seems well advanced in most developed countries and is likely to expand.

A continuation of this trend may appear in the form of flexible compensation programs. Under these plans, employees are allowed to select the mix of fringe benefits they want from among those the employer provides. This cafeteria approach recognizes human differences. It also allows employees to maximize their satisfaction from the employer's fringe benefits. Although these programs present administrative, actuarial, and tax problems to employers, they may be a logical continuation of ever-expanding benefit programs.[20]

EMPLOYEE WORK SCHEDULES

The trend toward flexible work schedules began in earnest during the 1970s. During that decade a variety of different schedules gained increased use. Many of these innovations were not new but were given exposure to large numbers of people for the first time.

The common element of these schedules is that they avoid the traditional eight-hour, five-day workweek with fixed starting and ending times for fifty weeks a year.[21] One variation is called the *compressed workweek*. It shortens the workweek to less than five days; four days at ten hours each is a common type of compressed workweek schedule. *Flextime* may involve five days a week, but it gives the employee some control over when the workday starts and ends. *Flexyear* is a newer variation that allows employees to work only part of the year, which is helpful in seasonal businesses.

The most common variation and perhaps the oldest is part-time employment. It merits mention because of its growing popularity and flexibility. Some employers are allowing two part-time workers to team up to handle a full-time job. Often called *job sharing*, this practice may grow as employees seek different lifestyles. In Scandinavia, job sharing is popular among new parents because it allows them to share job and parental responsibilities more fully. In the United States, part-time employment appears to be used as a recruiting tool to better utilize plant and equipment or to meet peak demands in retailing.

A Honeywell plant in the Boston area adopted a "mothers' shift" as a means of recruiting additional workers. These shifts coincide with school hours, so that working mothers can attend to parental duties by arriving at work after the children have gone to school and getting home when school ends each day. During the summer, these employees are replaced by college students.

DuPont wanted to make greater use of a chemical plant near the University of Georgia, so it created a weekend shift staffed largely by college students.

AN OVERVIEW OF PERSONNEL MANAGEMENT

As mentioned earlier, future challenges require that personnel activities be considered as a system of connected activities, each of which may be affected by the others and the external environment. The numbered circles in Figure 23-5 represent the different parts of this book, which are summarized in the following paragraphs.

For personnel specialists to be successful, they must balance the human, societal, personnel, and organizational objectives that form the core of every personnel department. At the same time, personnel specialists need to be aware of the challenges they face. These challenges come from the environment and the design of jobs. Within these challenges, personnel experts must collect human resource information. Information about jobs is a key

Figure 23-5
AN OVERVIEW OF PERSONNEL MANAGEMENT

I
FOUNDATIONS
AND CHALLENGES
● Environmental
● Nondiscrimination
● Quality of work life

VI
PERSONNEL MANAGEMENT
IN PERSPECTIVE
● Personnel audit
● Future challenges

II
PREPARATION
AND SELECTION
● Job analysis
● Human resource planning
● Recruitment
● Selection

Personnel

Human

OBJECTIVES

Societal

Organization

V
LABOUR-MANAGEMENT
RELATIONS
● Union management framework
● Organizing and bargaining
● Collective agreement administration

III
DEVELOPMENT
AND EVALUATION
● Training and development
● Career planning
● Change and organizational
  development
● Performance appraisal

IV
PERFORMANCE,
COMPENSATION,
AND PROTECTION
● Motivation and satisfaction
● Compensation
● Benefits and services
● Security, safety, and health
● Communications
● Counselling and discipline

input for human resource plans. These plans then serve as the basis for external and internal staffing activities.

External staffing is based on the recruitment needs estimated in the human resource plan. Applicants are recruited; selection begins. The selection process screens out those who are unqualified and selects those who possess the potential to perform. Orientation and training then translate potential into ability.

Internal staffing prepares present employees to assume future duties. In a growing number of companies, the internal staffing process begins with career planning. Employees also are urged to pursue development activities that further both their career and the organization's staffing needs. Along the way, personnel must contend with change and organizational development. To verify the internal staffing process and previous personnel activities, employees are evaluated with performance appraisals.

But personnel activities do not end with staffing. Once a staff is assembled, it must be motivated and satisfied. A major aspect of motivation and satisfaction is compensation. Wages and salaries must be paid in exchange for employee performance. Today that exchange includes numerous fringe benefits and employee services.

Personnel specialists also need to maintain communications with employees. It is through communications that management controls its human resources. When that control fails, counselling or discipline may be necessary.

If employees are not satisfied with the treatment they receive from the organization, they may form a labour organization. Unions mean new limits on personnel management. The collective bargaining relationship limits the roles of management and employees through a collective agreement and its administration.

Responsible personnel management also requires an audit of personnel policies, practices, and programs. Only through research can the personnel department uncover areas in need of improvement. However, responsible personnel management means more than just evaluating past actions. It requires a future orientation if people are to be managed proactively within a systems framework.

Without a future orientation, the most creative inventions of our time— organizations—will fail. But with a proactive outlook, our organizations will benefit from the contributions of personnel management and human resources.

SUMMARY

If personnel management is to be responsible, its practitioners need to review their past performance through audits and research. At the same time, they need a future orientation that causes them to anticipate upcoming challenges.

A proactive view encourages personnel to contribute to both people and company goals. But to be proactive requires modern information systems and increased professionalism. Otherwise, personnel will not be able to meet the challenges of changing demographics, values, and third-party pressures. These evolving challenges will cause personnel managers to find new approaches. Some possible new approaches are suggested by overseas employers, particularly in Europe and Japan. Likely developments include more employee participation, security, assistance, and work schedule flexibility.

With all the challenges facing personnel management, its role is sure to grow in scope and importance. The key to this growth is unlocking the contribution that people make to organizations. It is through this contribution that organizations prosper. And it is through our life-giving and life-sustaining organizations that we prosper as individuals and as a society.

TERMS FOR REVIEW

Employee assistance programs   Flexyear
Compressed workweek   Job sharing

REVIEW AND DISCUSSION QUESTIONS

1. How do personnel specialists prepare for the future?
2. In some firms the personnel manager is not considered a key part of the top-management team. In other firms personnel managers are considered important executives. In your own words, what may be the causes of this different perception?
3. How do you think the growing professionalism of the personnel management field will affect the preparation and performance of personnel specialists?
4. Several times in this book, demographics have been mentioned as an area of concern to personnel managers. Why should personnel managers be concerned with population demographics?
5. In the last two decades, many cultural values have changed, some rather drastically. Briefly describe how personnel management might be affected by these values: (a) a trend toward smaller families, (b) increased participation of women in the work force, (c) increased acceptability to society of divorce.
6. "With the average employer paying over 30% of payroll costs for employee fringe benefits and with the long list of fringe benefits now available to workers, it is unlikely that fringe benefits will experience much change during the 1980s and 1990s." Do you agree or disagree? Discuss.
7. What are some of the reasons why employers might adopt more flexible work schedules? Discuss which type of work schedule you would prefer.

INCIDENT 23-1
FUTURE SCENARIOS LTD.

Future Scenarios Ltd. is a West Coast "think tank" that accepts contracts from business and government to research possible trends in the future. One recent contract required a broad estimate of the future of work. A summary of their report appears below:

> *Excluding the possibility of a global energy crisis, ecological disaster, or war, we at Future Scenarios hold a realistically optimistic view of the world of work. Slow but continually increasing productivity during the 1980s and 1990s will lead to a much improved work environment. The design of jobs will reflect the needs of workers more fully. Unpleasant jobs will be the focus of major innovations in auto-*

mation, which will all but eliminate the monotonous assembly-line jobs of the industrial era. Some menial tasks will be left in the service area; restaurant, retail, and clerical jobs will absorb the bulk of young, inexperienced, or undereducated workers.

Employees will be able to set their own hours of work in most establishments. Those people still working an average workweek will be employed thirty-two hours a week. Most people will work more hours per week, but they will work less than the normal forty-four week workyear. About one-third of the work force will work part-time, which means less than twenty-five hours per week.

Fringe benefits will amount to nearly 65% of most employers' payroll costs, and employees will be able to select the mix of fringe benefits they want. Moreover, benefit costs will be rising quickly because of the growing demand by workers for more time off with pay.

Participation rates by men and women will be essentially equal, when adjusted for maternity and paternity leave. Pay differentials between males and females and between white and minority workers will be narrowed considerably. Statistical differences will be explained primarily by educational differences and by the greater concentration of women in teaching, nursing, and clerical positions.

Growing numbers of workers will be working into their seventies and eighties. This trend will be encouraged by extended leaves at partial pay during one's working lifetime. These leaves will be financed by a deduction from employee retirement accounts. The greater participation of people over seventy years old in the work force will greatly reduce the pressures on the social insurance system and underfunded employer pension plans.

Although unions still will carry on their traditional roles of collective bargaining and representing employees to members of management, they will begin to copy the union patterns now found in Europe. Union leaders will sit on company boards of directors and will become much more cooperative with management. Union leaders will spearhead company productivity improvement programs and will often be given the position of chairperson of the employer's productivity committee.

1. Assuming this seemingly unlikely scenario occurs, what implications does it hold for the future of personnel management?
2. Do you think these predicted developments will increase or decrease the importance of the personnel function in most organizations? Why?
3. What other changes do you think might occur?

REFERENCES

1. Fred K. Foulkes, "The Expanding Role of the Personnel Function," *Harvard Business Review*, March–April 1975, p. 84.
2. For a discussion of the issues of the next decade, see R. Gordon Cassidy and E. H. Neave, "Management Issues in the 1980s," *Proceedings of the Atlantic Schools of Business* Conference, Sydney, N.S.: College of Cape Breton, 1980.
3. Walter R. Nord and Douglas E. Durand, "What's Wrong with the Human Resources Approach to Management?" *Organizational Dynamics*, Winter 1978, pp. 13–25.
4. For a discussion of some of the emerging trends, see "Labour movement unsure about its public image," *The Globe and Mail*, November 5, 1979, p. B5; "Right to strike gets heat from business," *The Financial Post*, August 15, 1981, p. 3; "Workers in Management," *Alberta Report*, June 13, 1980, p. 21; Donald V. Nightingale, *Workplace Democracy: An Inquiry into Employee Participation in Canadian Work Organizations*, Toronto: University of Toronto Press, 1982; "Manpower—A High Technology Problem," *Canada Commerce*, special supplement, 1982, pp. 20–21; James Bagnell, "Urgent Priority to Job Training," *The Financial Post*, January 16, 1982, p. 3; *Work for Tomorrow: Employment Opportunities for the '80s*, Report of the Parliamentary Task Force on Employment Opportunities for the '80s, Ottawa: Speaker of the House of Commons, Cat. No. XC2-321/4-OIE, 1981; Marilyn Goneau, "Discrimination is still Part of

the Work Place," *The Financial Post*, November 21, 1981, p. 27; Solomon Barking, "Troubled Worker Militancy," *Relations Industrielles*, Vol. 38, no. 4, 1983, pp. 713–727; Robert L. Perry, "Pointing the Way Ahead," in a Special Report on Careers and the Job Market, *The Financial Post*, September 26, 1981.

5. George S. Odiorne, "Personnel Management for the '80s," *The Personnel Administrator*, August 1977, pp. 20–24. See also James C. Toedtman, "A Decade of Rapid Change: The Outlook for Human Resources Management in the '80s," *Personnel Journal*, January 1980, pp. 29–35.

6. Carl H. Driessnack, "The Financial Impact of Effective Human Resources Management," *The Personnel Administrator*, January 1976, pp. 22–26.

7. Nord and Durand, op. cit., p. 15.

8. Erwin S. Stanton, "Last Chance for Personnel to Come of Age," *The Personnel Administrator*, November 1975, pp. 14–16, 49. See also "Reflections on the Profession and ASPA," *The Personnel Administrator*, June 1980, pp. 51–54; and Fred R. Edney, "The Greening of the Profession," *The Personnel Administrator*, July 1980, pp. 27–30, 42.

9. Sidney H. Simon, "Personnel's Role in Developing an Information System," *Personnel Journal*, November 1978, pp. 622–625, 640. See also Michael N. Wolfe, "Computerization—It Can Bring Sophistication into Personnel," *Personnel Journal*, June 1978, pp. 325–326, 336; A. J. Walker, "The 10 Most Common Mistakes in Developing Computer Based Personnel Systems," *The Personnel Administrator*, July 1980, pp. 39–42.

10. Dan. A. Ondrack, "P/IR Professional Certification in Ontario: The PAO Model," paper presented at a symposium on professional education in P/IR, Canadian Industrial Relations Association, Dalhousie University, Halifax, N.S., May 1981.

11. "The New Personnel Professional," *Personnel Journal*, January 1979, pp. 17–19.

12. Daniel Yankelovich, "The New Psychological Contracts at Work," *Psychology Today*, May 1978, pp. 46, 47, 49, 50. See also Patricia A. Renwick and Edward E. Lawler, "What You Really Want from Your Job," *Psychology Today*, May 1978, pp. 53–58, 60, 62, 65, 118.

13. James W. Walker and Harriet Lazer, *The End of Mandatory Retirement*, New York: John Wiley & Sons, Inc., 1979.

14. *The Changing Nature of Work, Trends Analysis Report 17*, Washington: American Council of Life Insurance, 1978. See also "The Great Male Cop-Out from the Work Ethic," *Business Week*, November 14, 1977, pp. 156, 161, 164, 166.

15. William B. Werther, Jr., "Government Control vs. Corporate Ingenuity," *Labor Law Journal*, June 1975, pp. 36–37.

16. George S. McIssac, "What's Coming in Labor Relations," *Harvard Business Review*, September–October 1977, pp. 22–23, 26, 30, 34, 35, 190.

17. Gus Tyler, "Labor in the 1980s—A New Challenge," *The AFL-CIO American Federationist*, November 1979, pp. 3–7.

18. Lawrence A. Wrangler, "The Intensification of the Personnel Role," *Personnel Journal*, February 1979, pp. 111–119.

19. D. Quinn Mills, "Human Resources in the 1980s," *Harvard Business Review*, July–August 1979, pp. 158–159. See also "The New Personnel Professional," op. cit., p. 49.

20. William B. Werther, Jr., "Flexible Compensation Evaluated," *California Management Review*, Fall 1976, pp. 40–46.

21. Joann S. Lublin, "Firms and Job Seekers Discover More Benefits of Part-Time Positions," *Wall Street Journal*, Western ed., October 4, 1978, pp. 1, 27. See also William B. Werther, Jr., "Beyond Job Enrichment to Employment Enrichment," *Personnel Journal*, August 1975, pp. 438–442; and William B. Werther, Jr., "Part-Timers: Overlooked and Undervalued," *Business Horizons*, February 1975, pp. 13–29.

Appendix

How to Find a Job
Glossary

How to Find a Job

You will probably face the challenge of finding a job several times during your career. If you have ever looked for a job, you already know that it can be both a frustrating and a rewarding experience. This appendix offers some suggestions on how to make your next job search more successful. It also answers many other questions you may have about finding a job. Even after you have found the job you want, this appendix will be useful if you ever decide to change jobs.

WHEN TO START PREPARING FOR A JOB

Even if you do not need a job immediately, there are two things you can do right now that will help you in the future. First, start a job folder. A *job folder* is merely a folder or large envelope in which you place employment-related information. It should contain the names of your past employers, their addresses and phone numbers, the names of your immediate supervisors, your job titles, dates of employment, and starting and ending salaries or wages. You may also want to add information about awards, scholarships, athletic or civic activities, and positions in campus organizations. Many employers will request this information when you apply for a job. And unless you keep a job folder, you may not be able to remember all this information years into the future.

Another action you can take is to get a detailed job application form. (The employment office of most large organizations will be glad to give you one for free.) Study it. What information does it seek? (An example of a typical application form appears in Figure 7-7, Chapter 7.) The answers to many of its questions will be found in your job folder. Also, notice the questions it asks about your involvement in civic, social, and professional associations. Most employers do not want just an employee; they want someone who will be active and outgoing. You may well strengthen your chances for a good job by joining such organizations, which are usually located on campus or in your community.

When should you start preparing for a job? Right now!

UNDERSTAND YOURSELF

One important part of finding a job is understanding oneself. What are your likes and dislikes? What do you seek from a job? Do you want just money, or do you want a job with opportunities for growth and advancement? In Chapter 8, Figure 8-8 lists other questions worthy of some reflection.

In understanding yourself, you eventually come to the question: What do I have to offer an employer? If you have relevant job experience, you can offer the skills you have developed from your experience. But what if most of the jobs you have held were low-level positions that gave you little relevant experience for the job you now want? Then you must be prepared to "sell yourself." You can point to your education, your initiative, your positive attitude toward work, and your desire to work for the particular employer. It is important to remember that most employers hire recent university graduates for their future potential. Anything you have done that shows initiative, leadership, or motivation helps the employer recognize your potential. If you paid some or all of your own university expenses, that shows initiative. If you have held offices in social or professional groups on campus, that shows both initiative and leadership ability. If you have earned high marks, that shows motivation.

It is important to uncover your strengths. It is your strengths that differentiate you from others and make you attractive to an employer. Once you have identified your strengths, it becomes easier for you to decide what your employment objectives are.

Many of the questions you face about yourself, about employment opportunities, and about your future goals are difficult to answer. Even when you find some answers, time has a funny way of changing them. In dealing with employment-related questions, there are no right answers; there are only right answers for *now*.

Do not ask yourself: What do I want to do for the rest of my life? There is no final answer to that question. Instead, ask yourself what you want to do during the next few years. After a few years, you may change so much that you decide to change your job or even your career. Besides, any decision you make about your future can always be changed.

SOURCES OF HELP

In trying to understand yourself, do not overlook outside sources of help. Although no one has the right answers for you, friends, family, and professionals can provide valuable information and advice.

Many campuses have counselling services that are free to students and alumni. Although the available services vary widely, many counselling centres offer vocational interest tests. These tests are usually in a forced-choice format that requires you to answer many questions about your likes and dislikes. Then your answers are compared with norms that have been developed by testing people who do different jobs. These tests will not provide any magic solutions to understanding yourself. But they may indicate areas of interest to you.

Besides tests, counselling centres may offer you sessions with trained counsellors. These people can help without telling you what you should or should not do. The big advantage of trained counsellors is that they are less likely to show their biases. Parents, relatives, and friends can also help you, of course, but compared to a trained professional, they may be less objective and may tend to project their interests rather than let you discover your own goals.

If you want information about career fields and job opportunities, many colleges and universities, and most Canada Employment Centres, offer career information. Again, the service is usually free. Although it may have a different name on your campus, the career services division of a university often maintains data about different careers and their future potential. Its records also can give you an idea of starting salaries.

YOUR RÉSUMÉ

Once you are ready to look for a job actively, you will need a résumé. A *résumé* is a brief summary of your personal and job-related background. It gives a prospective employer key information needed to help evaluate your suitability for employment. A sample résumé appears in Figure A-1.

The résumé usually begins with your name, address, and telephone number. This information is put at the top of the résumé for quick reference by the employer. It is often followed by your employment objective, which tells the employer what type of job you are seeking.

The remaining information on the résumé is usually placed in descending order of importance. That is, you should follow the employment objectives with whatever you believe to be your most appealing strength. If you are a recent university graduate, the most appealing information is probably your education. Once you have gained career-related experience, it usually appears before educational background. Next, the résumé lists honours and memberships. The résumé ends with personal data that may be of interest to the employer. References are normally omitted from the résumé, although you may wish to indicate that they will be furnished upon request.

The appearance of the résumé is important. It should be neat and eye-catching and all words should be spelled correctly. Brief phrases may be used instead of complete sentences to save space. Unless you have extensive experience, the résumé should be kept to one side of an 8½-by-11-inch sheet. The paper should be white or a light color that is easily photocopied. Résumés printed by a professional printer look better than photocopied ones. Armed with a professional-looking résumé, you are ready to look for a job.

SOURCES OF JOB OPENINGS

Where can you learn about job openings? There is no one best source. Most successful job hunters seek job openings through a variety of means.

CAREER SERVICES. If you plan to seek a job upon graduation from university, a good place to start is your university's career services division or a Canada Employment Centre. They are a good source of jobs because employers are looking there for trainees and others with limited job experience. At smaller colleges and universities, many employers that work with the career services division are from the local area. At large universities,

Figure A-1
A SAMPLE RÉSUMÉ

LESLIE S. APPLICANT

2451 Robie Street   Telephone
Halifax, Nova Scotia   (902) 429-9780
B3H 3C3

Employment Objective

Seeking an entry-level position in a personnel or industrial
relations department effective June 1.

Educational Background

B.Com. degree from Saint Mary's University with a major in
Personnel Management. Graduation expected in early May.
Personnel management-related courses include:

Personnel Management	Wage and Salary Administration
Training and Development	Collective Bargaining
Organizational Behaviour	Introduction to Psychology

Work Experience

Summer 1982	Payroll clerk in a summer internship program with Brookman Electronics Company
Summer 1981	Construction labourer with E. & J. Landscapers
Summer 1980	Assistant cook with Tarrow's Cafe

Honours and Memberships

AIESEC, International Association for Students of Economics
and Commerce
Vice President, Saint Mary's Commerce Society
Scholarship recipient, Atlantic Personnel Management Association

Personal Data

Birthdate: April 11, 1961	Height: 5'6"
Marital Status: Unmarried	Weight: 120 lbs.
Hobbies: Sailing, golf,skiing	Health: Excellent

References

References will be furnished upon request.

the employers usually are a blend of local and national firms and government agencies. Since many of these employers only visit your campus annually, you may want to contact your college's career services division about nine months before graduation. (Even after graduation, alumni are often welcome to use these services.) The division's counsellors can inform you of their procedures and the organizations that will be visiting your campus.

CANADA EMPLOYMENT CENTRES (CECs). These offices exist to match applicants with prospective employers. Each office maintains a listing of job openings with a brief description of the qualifications. Since this service is paid for through taxes, there is no charge to you. In the past, many jobs listed with the unemployment office have been for blue-collar workers. However, many universities now have CECs on campus. These offices are specifically tailored to the needs of the graduating student and can be a valuable source of information and assistance.

PRIVATE PLACEMENT AGENCIES. Some employers rely on private placement agencies to help them recruit. In some provinces these agencies are not allowed to charge the applicant a fee for their services; instead they charge the employer 10% or more of the first year's salary. These agencies may have knowledge of job openings that cannot be found in other ways. Usually a placement specialist at the agency will review your résumé and interview you to determine which openings are appropriate. Then the placement specialist will refer you to the employer who also will screen your résumé and conduct an interview.

PERSONAL CONTACTS. An excellent source of information about job openings may be your personal contacts. Family, friends, and faculty members may know of job openings that are not being publicized. The more people you talk with about job openings, the greater your chances of discovering the right job. Besides, if someone suggests you should inquire about a particular opening, you may have an advantage in getting an interview.

WANT ADS. Advertisements in newspapers and professional journals are another source of job openings. The major advantage of these advertisements is that they usually identify the employer and give a brief description of the job's requirements. If you are seeking a job in another city, you may want to write the leading newspaper in that area and get a mail subscription. Want ads are best used about one month before you plan to graduate, since most jobs advertised this way are ones the employer wants to fill promptly.

DIRECT APPLICATIONS TO EMPLOYERS. Another approach is to go to local employers and apply directly. Most organizations are equipped to handle "walk-in" applicants. Usually, you will be requested to complete an application form, like the one in Figure 7-7. Bring your job folder along since you will probably need to provide dates, names, and addresses of previous employers. Be sure to complete the application fully and neatly. If you can take the application with you, plan to type in your answers.

HOW TO GET AN INTERVIEW
After you learn where the job openings are, the next step is to get an interview. It is the interviewing process that usually decides who will be hired. There are two ways to get an interview: by an oral request and by mail.

BY ORAL REQUEST. When you seek a job through your university's career services division, through Canada Employment Centres, or by direct application to an employer, you can often get an interview by asking for one. As discussed more fully in Chapter 8, the first interview is usually little more than a courtesy that allows the employer to make a quick screening of your suitability. Although brief, this interview is important. If you plan to ask for an interview, be sure to have a résumé you can give the interviewer and be sure to be dressed the way you want to be remembered.

BY MAIL. When you hear of a job opening through a personal contact or advertisement, you may wish to request an interview by sending a covering letter and a résumé. The letter serves to stimulate the reader's interest and focus attention on the résumé you have included.

As Figure A-2 illustrates, the letter has three main parts. The first paragraph tells why you are writing and expresses your interest in the employer. The second paragraph highlights one or two of your most valuable characteristics in relation to the job. You want this paragraph to sell you to the reader; it often contains a reference to your résumé. The final paragraph asks the reader to take some action, such as arranging an interview.

The letter should consider the perspective of the reader. The best covering letters minimize the use of the personal pronoun "I." Instead, write the letter in the second person, as the example in Figure A-2 is written. Of course, the letter should be neatly typed and an original (not a photocopied form letter with the company's name typed on it). Use normal margins and limit the letter to one page.

THE JOB INTERVIEW

Perhaps the most important aspect of the entire job-hunting process is the interview. Although you may have to complete an application or take a pre-employment test, the hiring decision is usually made as a result of the interview. Chapter 8 discusses employment interviews in depth, and you may wish to review it before going to an interview.

Your success in the interview depends on your preparation, your answers to the interviewer's questions, and the subtle impressions you make during the interview.

PREPARATION FOR THE INTERVIEW. Never go to an interview without being prepared. As a minimum, you should know a bit about the company. Look up recent articles in the *Financial Post, Canadian Business*, or other business periodicals. If you can find one, read the company's annual report, which may be available from the career services division of your college or in your university's library. The purpose of this preparation is to demonstrate your sincere interest in the employer. For example, you do not want to waste the interviewer's time asking questions whose answers are available publicly, such as how many employees the company has or what its annual sales are. Nor should you use this information to overwhelm the interviewer with facts and figures.

Figure A-2
A SAMPLE COVERING LETTER FOR A PERSONNEL TRAINEE POSITION

```
                              Your Address
                              City, Province
                              Postal Code
                              Date

Recruiter's Name
Department
Company Name
Company Address
City, Province
Postal Code

Dear Mr. (or Ms.) Recruiter:

    Your recent advertisement for a Personnel Trainee sounds most
appealing.  Consideration of the size, location, and favourable
reputation of your company persuaded me to write you about the
possibility of employment with your firm.
    Your advertisement indicates that you are seeking someone with
a degree in business administration, preferably with a major in
personnel management.  As the enclosed résumé indicates, my
educational background meets your requirements and my degree will
be awarded in early May.  In view of the courses to my credit in
personnel management, wage and salary administration, collective
bargaining, and training, your opening and my background seem well
matched.  Though my experience in the personnel field is limited
to a summer internship as a payroll clerk, that job exposed me to
a variety of situations and gave me some insight into a career in
the personnel field.
    After you have had an opportunity to review my résumé, would
you please contact me to arrange for an interview?  Any additional
information you could provide about the trainee position would also
be much appreciated.

                              Sincerely,

                              L. S. Applicant

Enclosure:   Résumé
```

Another important part of your preparation is to be ready with questions about the company. These questions should focus on the nature of the job. It is acceptable to ask about training, job duties, responsibilities, job locations, and other work-related issues. Although you will be curious about pay and benefits, those questions are irrelevant until you are offered a job. To ask them before you get the offer shows that you are more interested in pay and benefits than in what is expected of you. The questions in Figure 8-8 are ones you should be prepared to discuss before you go to the interview.

YOUR RESPONSES IN THE INTERVIEW. Some people approach the interview by trying to determine what answers the interviewers want to hear. This approach is foolish for two reasons. First, interviewers are usually skilled professionals. They can sense when someone is not being candid with them. Second, even if an applicant fools the interviewer, he or she may end up with a job that is unsatisfactory. Candour is the best approach to responding to the interviewer's questions. Even when the answer you have to give is less than favourable, the interviewer may give greater weight to your candour than to the negative information.

SUBTLE IMPRESSIONS IN THE INTERVIEW. The interviewer's job is to form an opinion of you. This opinion is shaped by your preparation and your responses to the questions. But the impression you leave is also shaped by many subtle factors.

Your appearance is one of the first things the interviewer notices. The appropriate dress is a conservative suit—for both men and women. The suit should fit well, be well pressed, and not be flashy in design or colour. Well-groomed hair and clean hands are a must. Aftershave or perfume should not be overwhelming.

You should meet the interviewer on time. Offer a firm (not finger-crushing) handshake and a smile. Do not smoke during the interview. Do not glare at the interviewer, but do make eye contact. When the interview is over, shake hands and thank the interviewer for his or her time.

REJECTIONS

Unless you are an exceptional candidate with hard-to-find skills, you can expect rejections. They happen to everyone. They should not be taken personally. A rejection does not mean you are unworthy. It merely means at this time what you have to offer and what the employer needs do not match.

If the rejection occurs at the end of the interview, do not become hostile. Instead, ask the interviewer for suggestions about where else you might apply for employment. Often, interviewers may be able to give you good leads. If the interviewer seems genuinely concerned, you might ask if he or she has any suggestions that would improve your interviewing skills. Sometimes the interviewer may be able to give you good tips on how to conduct yourself in future interviews.

THE OFFER AND ACCEPTANCE

When you receive an offer, you should acknowledge it immediately. If it is for the job you want, your acknowledgement of the offer should express your acceptance. When the offer comes by mail, it is best to accept by calling the person who made the offer and expressing your appreciation. Then the acceptance should be followed with a formal letter.

But what if you do not want to accept the job immediately? You may want to wait until you hear from other employers before you accept an offer.

Under these circumstances, you should contact the employer and acknowledge the offer. When acknowledging it, tell the employer the date upon which you will be able to give your decision. If you are the right person for the job, an employer is usually willing to wait a week or two before demanding a final decision. However, with each job offer you will have to judge how long the employer is likely to wait. During interviews, the personnel department or line managers often indicate how anxious they are to fill the position.

A FINAL NOTE ON CAREER PLANNING

Finding a job is not the end; it is the beginning of a career. Once you have taken a new job, it is time to update your job folder. It also is time to begin planning your career with the new employer. A review of Chapter 10 will indicate the major career planning actions you might want to consider.

Glossary

Absentees. Employees who were scheduled to be at work but are not present.

Accident and sickness policies. Policies that pay the insured a specific amount during short periods when the employee is unable to work because of an accident or sickness.

Accreditation/certification. The process by which the standards and credentials for members of a profession are established. Accreditation may be based on, among other things, written or oral tests, letters of recommendation from established professional members, or experience.

Active listening. Requires the listener to stop talking, to remove distractions, be patient, and to empathize with the talker.

Adverse selection. This occurs when a disproportionately high percentage of those who are likely to file claims against their insurance are granted insurance coverage.

Advisory authority. (See *Staff authority*.)

Affirmative-action programs. Detailed plans developed by employers to undo the the result of past employment discrimination or to ensure equal employment opportunity in the future.

Agency shop. A provision in a collective-bargaining agreement which requires that all employees in the bargaining unit who do not join the union pay, as a condition of employment, a fixed amount monthly, usually the equivalent of union dues, to help defray the union's expenses in acting as bargaining agent. Under some arrangements, the payments are allocated to the union's welfare fund or to a recognized charity.

American Federation of Labor and Congress of Industrial Organizations (AFL-CIO). An American federation of many national unions in the U.S. and Canada. It exists to provide a unified focal point for the labour movement, assist national unions, and influence government policies that affect members and working people.

American Society for Personnel Administration (ASPA). The major association of professional personnel specialists and administrators in the U.S.

Applied research. A study of practical problems, the solution of which will lead to improved performance.

Aptitude Requirements (APT). One of the job attributes used in the *Canadian Classification and Dictionary of Occupations* to define a job. The aptitude factors measured are intelligence, verbal ability, numerical ability, spatial ability, form perception ability, clerical perception ability, eye-hand-foot coordination, and colour discrimination.

Arbitration. The resolution of a dispute by a neutral third party.

Arbitration board. A panel consisting of a neutral chairman and a member representing each of the parties to an arbitration. When the members of the board are unable to agree, the chairman's decision normally governs.

Arbitration clause. A provision in a collective agreement stipulating that disputes arising during the term of the contract be settled by arbitration. All jurisdictions in Canada except Saskatchewan have legislated for the insertion of an arbitration clause in all collective agreements.

Assessment centres. A standardized form of employee appraisal that relies on multiple types of evaluation and multiple raters.

Attitude surveys. Systematic methods of determining what employees think about their organization through the use of a broad survey of employee attitudes, usually done through a questionnaire. Attitude survey feedback results when the information collected is reported back to the participants who initially provided the information. This process then is usually followed by action planning to identify and resolve specific areas of employee concern.

Attrition. The loss of employees due to their leaving the organization.

Audit report. A comprehensive description of personnel activities, which includes both commendation for effective practices and recommendations for improving practices that are ineffective.

Audit team. Those people who are responsible for evaluating the performance of the personnel department.

Authorization cards. Forms that prospective union members sign to indicate their wish to have an election that determines whether the workers want to be represented by a labour organization in their dealings with management.

Autonomous work groups. Any of a variety of arrangements that allow employees to decide democratically how they will meet their group's work objectives.

Autonomy. Independence; in a job context, having control over one's work.

Bargaining book. A compilation of the negotiation team's plans for collective bargaining with labour or management.

Barriers to change. Factors that interfere with employee acceptance and implementation of change.

Barriers to communication. Factors that interfere with the receiver's understanding of a communication.

Behaviour modification. A psychological theory that behaviour depends on its consequences.

Behavioural modelling. Relies on the imitation or emulation of a desired behaviour. A repetition of behaviour modelling helps develop appropriate responses in specified situations.

Behaviourally anchored rating scales (BARS). Evaluation tools that rate employees along a rating scale by means of specific behaviour examples on the scale.

Benefit plan. One of various types of schemes established by employers to provide some degree of financial protection for employees against accident, illness, old age, and death.

Bereavement pay. Pay to a worker, usually for a limited period, for time lost because of the death and funeral of a member of the immediate family.

Blind ads. Want ads that do not identify the employer.

Body language. A form of nonverbal communication that communicates by body movements during face-to-face communication.

Bona fide occupational qualification (BFOQ). A justified business reason for discriminating against a member of a protected class.

Boulwarism. A negotiation strategy developed and used by the General Electric Company in the U.S. The strategy caused the company to make its "best" offer to the union at the beginning of negotiations. Then the company remained firm in not increasing its offer unless the union could find where management had erred in its calculations used to arrive at the "best" offer. This strategy has been ruled an unfair labour practice by U.S. courts.

Brainstorming. A process by which participants provide their ideas on a stated problem during a freewheeling group session.

"Buddy system." The "buddy-system" of orientation exists when an experienced employee is asked to show a new worker around the job site, conduct introductions, and answer the newcomer's questions.

Burnout. A condition of mental, emotional, and sometimes physical exhaustion that results in substantial and prolonged stress.

Business agent. Generally, a full-time, paid employee or official of a local union whose duties include day-to-day dealing with employers and workers, adjustment of grievances, enforcement of agreements, and similar activities.

Business unionism. The practice of unions that seek to improve the wages, hours, and working conditions of their members in a businesslike manner. (See *Social unionism*.)

Buy-back. A method of convincing an employee who attempts to resign to stay in the employ of the organization; normally, it involves an offer of an increased wage or salary.

Cafeteria benefit programs. Programs that allow employees to select the mix of fringe benefits and services that answer their individual needs.

Canada Employment and Immigration Commission (CEIC). A federal agency responsible for administering employment and immigration programs.

Canada Employment Centres (CECs). Centres administered by the Canada Employment and Immigration Commission (CEIC) that match jobseekers with employers who have job openings, and provide counselling and testing services.

Canada Manpower Training Program. A federal program that supports institutional (classroom) and industrial (on-the-job) training.

Canada Occupational Forecasting Program (COFOR). One of the publications of Canada Employment and Immigration providing long-term forecasts on the demand for various types of labour in Canada.

Canada Pension Plan (CPP). A mandatory, contributory, and portable pension plan applicable to all self-employed persons and employees in Canada, except those working for the federal government. It pays retirement pensions, disability pensions, pensions for surviving spouses, lump-sum death benefits, and benefits to children of disabled contributors.

Canadian Classification and Dictionary of Occupations (CCDO). A publication of Canada Employment and Immigration in 1971, periodically updated, providing detailed job definitions for all jobs in government and industry.

Canadian Human Rights Act. A federal law, enacted in 1977, prohibiting discrimination on the basis of race, national or ethnic origin, colour, religion, age, sex, marital status, conviction for an offence for which a pardon was issued, and physical handicap. It applies to all federal government agencies and Crown corporations and to businesses and industries under federal jurisdiction.

Canadian Human Rights Commission (CHRC). A federal body, consisting of a Chief Commissioner, a Deputy Chief Commissioner, and from three to six other members; all members are appointed by the Governor in Council. The commission supervises the implementation and adjudication of the Canadian Human Rights Act.

Canadian Labour Congress. A central labour congress formed in 1956 by the merger of the Trades and Labour Congress of Canada and the Canadian Congress of Labour.

Career. All the jobs that are held during one's working life.

Career counselling. A process that assists employees to find appropriate career goals and paths.

Career development. Those personal improvements one undertakes to achieve a personal career plan.

Career goals. The future positions one strives to reach as part of a career. The goals serve as benchmarks along one's career path.

Career path. The sequential pattern of jobs that forms one's career.

Career planning. The process by which one selects career goals and paths to those goals.

Career plateau. This occurs when an employee is in a position that he or she does well enough not to be demoted or fired, but not so well that the person is likely to be promoted.

Change agents. People who have the role of stimulating and coordinating changes in a group.

Change objective of the personnel department. The change objective of the personnel department is to manage change in ways that increase its benefits and reduce its costs.

Check-off. A procedure whereby the employer, by agreement with the union, deducts union membership dues and assessments from the pay of all employees in the bargaining unit and turns these monies over to the union.

Closed shop. A form of union security that requires the employer to hire only union members and retain only union members.

Codetermination. A form of industrial democracy, first popularized in West Germany, giving workers the right to have their representatives vote on management decisions.

Cognitive dissonance. Cognitive dissonance results from a gap between what one expects and what one experiences.

Cognitive models of motivation. These models depend on the thinking or feeling (that is, cognition) within each individual.

Coinsurance clause. A provision in an insurance policy that requires the insured and the insurer to share the costs of a claim on some basis.

Collective agreement. A legal document negotiated between the union and employer. It states the terms and conditions of employment.

Collective bargaining. The procedure by which the representatives of employers and unions negotiate the terms and conditions of employment. The term also applies beyond the negotiating process to encompass the actual interpretation and administration of the agreement, including the day-to-day activities of the employer and union.

Collective liability. In the Workmen's Compensation Act, the collective responsibility of all employers to pay compensation to workers for any work-related injury. The industries covered by the act are classified according to how hazardous they are, and employers in each group are collectively liable for payment of compensation to workers employed in that group.

Communication. The transfer of information and understanding from one person to another.

Communication overload. A condition that exists when employees receive more communication inputs than they can process or than they need.

Communication process. The method by which a sender reaches a receiver; it requires that an idea be developed, encoded, transmitted, received, decoded, and used.

Communication system. Provides formal and informal methods to move information throughout an organization so that appropriate decisions are made.

Comparable work. (See *Equal pay for work of equal value*.)

Comparable worth. U.S. terminology for *Equal pay for work of equal value*.

Compensation. Whatever employees receive in exchange for their work.

Concentration in employment. A condition that exists when a department or employer has a higher proportion of members of a protected class than is found in the employer's labour market. (See *Underutilization*.)

Conciliation. The process whereby a third party, usually a government official or a person appointed by the government, attempts to bring together the parties in an industrial dispute for reconciling their differences. The conciliator has no power to enforce a settlement.

Conciliation board. A board, usually legally required and consisting of a chairperson and a member representing each of the parties to the dispute, formed to effect a settlement in a negotiation dispute.

Conservative syndrome. A tendency to be guided by tradition, to accept the decision-making functions of elites, and to put a strong emphasis on the maintenance of order and predictability in society.

Constructs. Substitutes for actual performance; for example, a score of a test is a construct for actual learning.

Consumer Price Index (CPI). A monthly index prepared by Statistics Canada, to measure the percentage change through time in the cost of purchasing a fixed basket of consumer goods and services representing the purchases by families and individuals living in urban centres with populations of 30,000 or over.

Content theories of motivation. Describe the needs or desires within us that initiate behaviour.

Contract labour. People who are hired (and often trained) by an independent agency that supplies companies with needed human resources for a fee.

Contributory benefit plans. Fringe benefits that require the employee to contribute to the cost of the benefit. (See *Noncontributory benefit plans*.)

Cooperative counselling. A mutual counsellor-employee relationship that establishes a cooperative exchange of ideas to help solve an employee's problems. (See *Directive counselling* and *Nondirective counselling*.)

Corrective discipline. Action that follows a rule infraction and seeks to discourage further infractions so that future actions are in compliance with standards. (See *Preventive discipline*.)

Cost-of-living adjustment (COLA). An increase or decrease in wages or salaries in accordance with changes in the cost of living as measured by a designated index, such as the Consumer Price Index.

Council of Canadian Personnel Associations (CCPA). A Canadian federation of provincial personnel associations.

Counselling. Discussion of a problem with an employee, with the general objective of helping the employee cope with it better.

Counselling functions. The activities performed by counselling, which include advice, reassurance, communication, release of emotional tension, clarified thinking, and reorientation.

Craft union. A labour organization which limits membership to workers having a particular craft or skill or working at closely related trades.

Critical incident method. An employee evaluation method requiring the rater to record statements that describe extremely good or bad behaviour related to performance.

Decision-making authority. (See *Line authority*.)

Deductible clause. A provision in an insurance policy that requires the insured to pay a specified amount of a claim before the insurance company is obligated to pay. Usually the insured must pay the first $50 or $100.

Delegation. The process of getting others to share a manager's work; it requires the manager to assign duties, grant authority, and create a sense of responsibility.

Delphi technique. The soliciting of predictions about specified future developments from a panel of experts. Their collective estimates are then reported back to the panel so that members may adjust their opinions. This process is repeated until general agreement on the future trends emerges.

Demographics. The study of population characteristics.

Demotions. Demotions occur when an employee is moved from one job to another that is lower in pay, responsibility, and organizational level.

Dental insurance plan. A group benefit plan whereby the employer pays in whole or in part the individual premium for dental insurance coverage of its employees.

Development. A process of preparing an employee for future job responsibilities. (Compare with *Training*.)

Differential validity. The applicability of tests or other selection criteria to different subgroups (such as women or minorities).

Directive counselling. The process of listening to an employee's emotional problems, deciding with the employee what should be done, and then telling and motivating the employee to do it. (See *Nondirective counselling* and *Cooperative counselling*.)

Discipline. Management action to encourage compliance with the organization's standards.

Discrimination. The systematic exclusion of particular persons from consideration for a job, or the payment of different wages to such persons, because of their age, sex, race, or some other characteristic not relevant to job ability or performance.

Dismissal. The ultimate disciplinary action; it separates the employee from the employer for a cause.

Downward communication. Information that begins at some point in the organization and feeds down the organization hierarchy to inform or influence others in the organization.

Dual responsibility for personnel management. Since both line and staff managers are responsible for employees, production, and quality of work life, a dual responsibility for personnel management exists.

Due process. It means that established rules and procedures for disciplinary action are followed and that employees have an opportunity to respond to the charges made against them.

Early retirement. When a worker retires from an employer before the "normal" retirement age.

Empirical validity. Validity achieved through studies that relate test scores to a job-related criterion, usually performance.

Employee assistance programs (EAPs). Comprehensive company programs that seek to help employees overcome their personal and work-related problems.

Employee handbook. A handbook explaining key benefits, policies, and general information about the employer.

Employment freeze. Occurs when the organization curtails future hiring.

Employment function. That aspect of personnel which is responsible for recruiting, selecting, and hiring new workers. It is usually found in the employment section of large personnel departments.

Employment involvement (EI). Consists of a variety of systematic methods that enable employees to participate in the decisions that affect them in relation to the organization.

Employment references. Evaluations of an employee's past work performance, provided by past employers.

Employment tests. Devices that assess the probable match between applicants and job requirements.

Environmental conditions (EC). One of the job attributes described in the *Canadian Classification and Dictionary of Occupations*, consisting of the significant physical surroundings of a worker, such as noise, mechanical hazards, and fumes and dust.

Equal employment opportunity. The principle whereby employment is based on the qualifications of the applicant rather than upon sex, race, or other factors not related to ability or performance.

Equal pay for equal work. The principle or policy of equal rates of pay for all employees in an establishment performing the same kind and amount of work, regardless of sex, race, or other characteristics of individual workers not related to ability or performance.

Equal pay for work of equal value. The principle of equal pay for men and women in jobs with comparable content; criteria used: skill, effort, responsibility, and working conditions; part of the Human Rights Act.

Equifinality. The attribute of paths that lead to a common objective.

Equity theory. Equity theory suggests that people are motivated to close the gap between their efforts and the perceived amount and appropriateness of the rewards they receive.

Ergonomics. The study of biotechnical relationships between the physical attributes of workers and the physical demands of the job with the object of reducing physical and mental strain in order to increase productivity and quality of work life.

Error of central tendency. An error in rating employees that consists in evaluating employees as neither good nor poor performers even when some employees perform exceptionally well or poorly.

Esteem needs. The needs people have for recognition from others and for a personal sense of self-worth.

Evaluation interviews. Performance review sessions that give employees feedback about their past performance or future potential.

Existence-Relatedness-Growth (ERG) Theory. Alderfer's Existence-Relatedness-Growth Theory suggests that lower-order needs can be grouped under the heading of Existence; Relatedness needs encompass interpersonal relationships and include acceptance, belonging, and security that come from approval of those in the organization. Growth needs include challenging an individual's capabilities that cause personal growth on the job.

Exit interviews. Conversations with departing employees to learn their opinion of the employer, managers, policies, and other aspects of employment with the company. These interviews also seek to learn why the employee is leaving.

Expectancy. The strength of a person's belief that an act will lead to a particular outcome.

Expectancy theory. Expectancy theory states that motivation is the result of the outcome one seeks and one's estimate that action will lead to the desired outcome.

Experiential learning. Learning by experiencing in the training environment the kinds of problems one faces on the job.

Exposure. Becoming known by those who decide on promotions, transfers, and other career opportunities.

Extrapolation. Extending past rates of change into the future.

Facilitator. Someone who assists quality circles and the quality circle leader to identify and solve workplace problems.

Factor comparison method. A form of job evaluation that allocates a part of each job's wage to the key factors of the job. The result is a relative evaluation of the organization's jobs.

Family Allowances. A scheme introduced in 1944 by which all Canadian children under sixteen years of age are to be given monthly payments for their sustenance and education.

Feedback. Information that helps evaluate the success or failure of an action or system.

Field experiment. Research that allows the researchers to study employees under realistic conditions to learn how experimental and control subjects react to new programs or other changes.

Field review method. A method of preparing an employee performance evaluation, whereby skilled representatives of the personnel department go into the field and gather information about employee performance.

Flextime. A scheduling innovation that abolishes rigid starting and ending times for each day's work. Instead, employees are allowed to begin and end the workday at their discretion, usually within a range of hours.

Flexyear. An employee scheduling concept that allows employees to be off of the job part of the year. Employees usually work a normal work year in less than the twelve months.

Forced-choice method. A method of employee performance evaluation that requires the rater to choose the most descriptive statement in each of several pairs of statements about the employee being rated.

Ford Occupational Imbalance Listing (FOIL). A quarterly publication by CEIC that projects the short-term labour imbalances based on supply-and-demand information.

Forecasts. Forecasts predict the organization's future needs.

Functional authority. Authority that allows staff experts to make decisions and take actions normally reserved for line managers.

Funded retirement plans. A retirement plan in which the employer has set aside sufficient monies to meet the future payout requirements of the retirement plan.

General Educational Development (GED). One of the job attributes used in the *Canadian Classification and Dictionary of Occupations* to define a job; it reflects the approximate direction of schooling and/or qualification needed for effective performance on the job in question.

General Industrial Training Program. A federal program supported by CEIC that reimburses employers for the direct cost of industrial training and a portion of the trainee wages.

Good-faith bargaining. The requirement that two parties meet and confer at reasonable times with the sincere intention of reaching agreement on new contract terms.

Grapevine communication. An informal communications system that arises spontaneously from the social interaction of people in the organization.

Grievance. Any complaint or expressed dissatisfaction by an employee or by a union concerning the job, pay, or any other aspect of the employment relationship.

Grievance procedure. Usually, a formal plan set up in the collective agreement to resolve grievances, involving discussions at progressively higher levels of authority in the company and the union, culminating, if necessary, in arbitration.

Guaranteed annual wage plans. Agreements wherein an employer assures employees that they will receive a minimum annual income regardless of layoffs or a lack of work. The guaranteed amount is usually a fraction of the employee's normal full-time earnings.

Halo effect. A bias that occurs when an evaluation allows some information to disproportionately affect the final evaluation.

Handicapped workers. Workers whose earning capacity is impaired by age, physical or mental deficiency, or injury.

Harassment. Harassment occurs when another member of an organization treats an employee in a disparate manner because of that person's sex, race, religion, age, or other protective classification.

Health insurance plans. Health and medical insurance provided by provincial governments with assistance from the federal government. In April 1972, the scope of the Medical Care Act of 1966 was extended to all of Canada. Since that date, the cost of medical care has been paid for by taxes.

Hierarchy of needs. Since all needs cannot be expressed at once, they have some priority in the way in which they find expression. The ordering or priority of these needs forms a hierarchy beginning with physical and security needs and continuing with social, esteem, and self-fulfillment needs.

Higher-order needs. Higher-order needs include the need of social acceptance, esteem, and self-fulfillment.

Hiring hall. An office, usually run by the union, or jointly by employers and union, for referring workers to jobs or for the actual hiring operation. Common in construction and related trades.

Hot-stove rule. The principle that disciplinary action should have the same characteristics as the penalty a person receives from touching a hot stove—that is, the discipline should be with warning, immediate, consistent, and impersonal.

House organ. Any regularly published organizational magazine, newspaper, or bulletin directed to employees.

Human resource audits. An extensive survey of each employee's skills and abilities.

Human resource forecasts. Predictions of the organization's future demand for employees.

Human resource planning. Organizational planning based on systematic forecasts of an organization's future supply and demand of employees.

Human resources. The people who are ready, willing, and able to contribute to organizational goals.

Human rights legislation. Federal and provincial laws against discrimination. (See *Canadian Human Rights Act.*)

Imminent danger. An unsafe or unhealthy work condition that is likely to lead to death or serious injury if it is allowed to continue.

Incentive systems. Incentive systems link compensation and performance by paying employees for actual results, not seniority or hours worked.

Indexation. A method of estimating future employment needs by matching employment growth with some index, such as sales growth.

Industrial democracy. The policy of giving employees a larger voice in work-related decisions that affect them.

Industrial relations. A broad term which includes relations between unions and management, between management and the government, between unions and the government, and between employers and employees—the latter often being referred to as *personnel relations.*

Industrial union. A union that represents all or most of the production, maintenance, and related workers, both skilled and unskilled, in an industry or company. It may also include office, sales, and technical employees of the same companies.

In-house complaint procedures. Organizationally-developed methods for employees to register their complaints about various aspects of the organization.

Initiation fee. A payment to the union required of a worker when he or she joins, usually as set forth in the union's constitution.

Injunction. A court order restraining one or more persons, corporations, or unions from performing some act that the court believes would result in irreparable injury to property or other rights.

Insurable employment. Jobs covered by unemployment insurance.

Interest Factors (INT). One of the job attributes used in the *Canadian Classification and Dictionary of Occupations* (CCDO) to define a job. Five pairs of interest factors are provided in the CCDO; positive concern for one factor of a pair usually implies rejection of the other factor (e.g., routine vs. creative work).

International union. A union that charters locals in the United States and Canada.

Job analysis. Systematic study of a job to discover its specifications, its mental, physical, and skill requirements, its relation to other jobs in the plant, etc., usually for wage-setting or job-simplification purposes.

Job analysis schedules. Checklists or questionnaires that seek to collect information about jobs in a uniform manner. (Also called *Job Analysis Questionnaire.*)

Job banks. Job banks are maintained in employment offices. They are used to match job applicants with openings.

Job classification. The arrangement of tasks in an establishment or industry into a limited series of jobs or occupations, rated in terms of skill, responsibility, experience, training, and similar considerations, usually for wage-setting purposes.

Job code. A job code uses numbers, letters, or both to provide a quick summary of the job and its content.

Job cycle. The time it takes a worker to complete every task in his or her job before repeating the cycle.

Job description. A recognized list of functions and tasks included in a particular occupation or job.

Job enlargement. Adding more tasks to a job in order to increase the job cycle.

Job enrichment. Adding more responsibilities, autonomy, and control to a job.

Job evaluation. The process of assessing job content and ranking jobs according to a consistent set of job characteristics and worker traits, such as skill, responsibility, experience, etc. Commonly used for setting relative rates of pay.

Job families. Groups of different jobs that require similar skills.

Job grading. A form of job evaluation that assigns jobs to predetermined job classifications according to their relative worth to the organizaton. This technique also is called the job classification method.

Jobholder reports. Reports to employees about a firm's economic performance.

Job instruction training. Training received directly on the job and used to train workers in how to do their job.

Job performance standards. The work performance expected from an employee on a particular job.

Job posting. Involves informing employees about unfilled job openings and the qualifications for those jobs.

Job progression ladder. A particular career path where some jobs have prerequisites.

Job ranking. One form of job evaluation whereby jobs are ranked subjectively according to their overall worth to the organization.

Job rotation. A process of moving employees from one job to another in order to allow employees more variety in their jobs and to learn new skills.

Job satisfaction. The favourableness or unfavourableness with which employees view their work.

Job sharing. A plan whereby available work is spread among all of the workers in the group in order to prevent, or reduce the extent of, a layoff when production requirements result in a substantial decline in available work.

Job specifications. A written statement that explains what a job demands of employees who do it and the human skills and factors that are required.

Joint study committees. Committees which include representatives of management and the unions who meet away from the bargaining table to study some topic of mutual interest in hopes of finding a solution that is mutually satisfactory.

Jurisdiction, union. The authority of a union to represent certain groups of workers within specific occupations, industries, or geographic areas.

Key jobs. Jobs that are common in the organization and its labour market.

Key subordinates. Those employees who are crucial to a manager's success in a particular job.

Laboratory training. A form of group training primarily used to enhance interpersonal skills.

Labour agreement. A legal document, also called a labour contract, that is negotiated between the union and employer. It states the terms and conditions of employment.

Labour market. The area in which the employer recruits.

Labour market analysis. The study of the employer's labour market to evaluate the present or future availability of workers.

Labour relations board. A board set up in the federal and all provincial jurisdictions to administer labour relations legislation. Its powers and duties generally include the determination of appropriate bargaining units, the certification and the decertification of trade unions, decisions as to unfair labour practices, and failure to bargain in good faith.

Labour standards. Standards concerning employment and working conditions found acceptable by labour and management through collective bargaining and by the legislator through labour laws and legislation.

Labour standards legislation. Legislation designed primarily to provide protection to unorganized workers but which increasingly affects the operation of negotiated collective agreements. The legislation sets the minimum standards permissible in the areas of statutory school-leaving age, minimum age for employment, minimum wages, equal pay for equal work, hours of work, weekly rest-day, annual vacations, general holidays, termination of employment, maternity protection, and severance pay.

Labour union. Any organization in which workers participate as members and that exists for the purpose of dealing with employers concerning grievances, wages, hours, and conditions of employment.

Law of effect. The principle that people learn to repeat behaviours that have favourable consequences and to avoid behaviours that have unfavourable consequences.

Layoff. A temporary or indefinite dismissal of one or more employees because of lack of work.

Learning curve. A visual representation of the rate at which one learns given material through time.

Learning curve for change. A charted representation of the period of adjustment and adaptation to change required by an organization.

Learning principles. Guidelines to the ways in which people learn most effectively.

Leave of absence. A grant to an employee of time off from his or her job, generally without loss of job or seniority.

Legally required benefits. Employee benefits programs to which employers must contribute, or insurance that they must purchase for employees, by law.

Leniency bias. A tendency to rate employees higher than their performance justifies.

Leveraging. Resigning in order to further one's career with another employer.

Liability, joint. Responsibility on the part of both union and employer for unfair labour practices.

Life insurance plan. Group term insurance coverage for employees, paid for in whole or in part by the employer.

Life plan. A person's hopes, dreams, personal ambitions, and career goals.

Line authority. Authority allowing managers to direct others and to make decisions about the organization's operations.

Listening. A receiver's positive effort to receive an understanding of a message transmitted by sound.

Local. The basic unit of union organization, formed in a particular plant or locality. Members participate directly in the affairs of their local, including the election of officers, financial and other business matters, and relations between their organization and employers, and pay dues to the local.

Lockout. A temporary withholding of work or denial of employment to a group of workers by an employer during a labour dispute in order to compel a settlement at or close to the employer's terms.

Long-term disability plan. A benefit plan that provides the employee with an income, usually a percentage of normal take-home pay, in the case of long-term illness or injury.

Maintenance factors. Those elements of the work setting that lead to employee dissatisfaction when they are not provided adequately. These factors also are called dissatisfiers or hygiene factors.

"Make-whole" remedies. Measures taken when an individual is mistreated in violation of employment laws, whereby the wrongdoer is usually required to make up losses to the employee that were suffered because of the wrongdoing.

Management by objectives (MBO). Requires an employee and superior to jointly establish performance goals for the future. Employees are subsequently evaluated on how well they have obtained these agreed-upon objectives.

Management inventories. Management inventories summarize the skills and abilities of management personnel. (See *Skills inventories*, which are used for nonmanagement employees.)

Management rights. As used in union-management relationships, this term encompasses those aspects of the employer's operations that do not require discussion with or concurrence of the union, or rights reserved to management that are not subject to collective bargaining. These rights may be expressly noted as such in a collective agreement. Such prerogatives generally include matters of hiring, production, scheduling, price-fixing, the maintenance of order and efficiency, and the processes of manufacturing and sales.

Maternity benefit. Medical benefits, and partial compensation for loss of income for maternity, as provided under health and disability insurance systems or under private benefit plans.

Maternity leave. The period of time off work generally granted persons who are pregnant. Many jurisdictions have legislation setting minimum standards for maternity leave.

Maturity curves. A statistical device used to calculate compensation for workers based on their seniority and performance. Normally, such compensation plans are limited to professional and technical workers.

Maximum hours. The number of hours which can be worked at straight-time rates under federal and provincial laws.

Mediation. The process whereby disputing parties seek to reconcile their differences through a third party who actively seeks to assist by making suggestions, providing background information, and noting avenues open to the parties for settlement.

Mediator. A person who undertakes mediation of a dispute.

Medical and health benefits plans. Public and private insurance plans to protect the individual from the costs resulting from illness.

Medical and health benefits provisions. Provisions made by an employer, contractually or otherwise, to pay entirely or in part the cost to the employee of public or private medical and health benefits.

Mentor. Someone who offers informal career guidance and support on a regular basis.

Merit-based promotion. When an employee is promoted because of superior performance in the present job.

Merit raises. Pay increases given to individual workers according to an evaluation of their performance.

Metropolitan Order Processing System (MOPS). A computerized system that automatically conveys information about job vacancies to all Canada Employment Centres within a large metropolitan area.

Minimum wage. The rate of pay established by statute or minimum wage order as the lowest wage that may be paid for any category of work or workers. All provinces in Canada have legislation establishing minimum wages for most classes of workers. In 1935, the federal government passed the Minimum Wages Act, which applies to all governmental agencies.

Modified union shop. A union security provision that specifies that only new employees are required to join the union. It may or may not stipulate that present union members maintain such membership.

Motivation. A person's drive to take action because that person wants to do so.

Motivational factors. Those elements of the work environment that motivate people to perform and be satisfied.

National Job Bank (NJB). A national system for conveying information about vacancies in any region of the country to all other regions; it is administered by Canada Employment and Immigration and operates through Canada Employment Centres.

National union. A union that charters locals in Canada only.

Needs assessment. A diagnosis that presents problems and future challenges that can be met through training or development.

Net benefit. A surplus of benefits after all costs are included.

No-lockout clause. Statutory provision prohibiting lockouts during the term of a collective agreement.

Nominal group techniques (NGT). A group method of drawing out ideas from people on a specified topic. It requires participants to list their ideas and then share those ideas in round-robin fashion with the group and a facilitator. Once all ideas of the group are vented, duplicate ideas are eliminated and clarification follows. Following clarification, members of the group vote on what they believe to be the best or most important items they uncovered through the NGT process.

Noncontributory benefit plans. Fringe benefits that are paid entirely by the employer. (see *Contributory benefit plans.*)

Nondirective (or client-centred) counselling. The process of skilfully listening to and encouraging an employee to explain bothersome problems, understand them, and determine appropriate solutions. (See *Directive counselling* and *Cooperative counselling.*)

Nonverbal communication. Actions that communicate, as opposed to words.

Objectives. Benchmarks against which actions are evaluated.

Obsolescence. A condition that results when an employee no longer possesses the knowledge or abilities to perform successfully.

Open communication. A condition that exists when people feel free to communicate all relevant messages.

Open-door policy. A policy of encouraging employees to come to their manager or even to higher management with any matter that concerns them.

Open system. (See *System.*)

Organization character. The product of all the organization's features, such as its people, objectives, technology, size, age, unions, policies, successes, and failures.

Organizational climate. The favourableness or unfavourableness of the environment for people in the organizaton.

Organizational development (OD). An intervention strategy that uses group processes to focus on the whole organization in order to bring about planned change.

Organizational development process. A complex and difficult process that consists of seven steps. These steps begin with initial diagnosis, data collection, data feedback and confrontation, action planning and problem solving, team building, and conclude with inter-group development and evaluation and follow-up.

Organizing committee. A group of workers who guide the efforts needed to organize their fellow workers into a labour organization.

Orientation programs. Programs that familiarize primarily new employees with their roles, the organization, its policies, and other employees.

Outplacement. The action of an organization in assisting its present employees to find jobs with other employers.

Overtime. Hours worked in excess of the standard workweek or work day established either by law, by the collective agreement, or by company policy.

Pareto analysis. A means of collating data about the types or causes of production problems by arranging the data in descending order of frequency.

Participation rates. The percentage of working age men and women who are in the work force.

Participative counselling. This type of counselling seeks to find a balance between directive and nondirective counselling techniques with the counsellor and the counsellee participating in the discussion and solution of the problem. (See *Cooperative counselling.*)

Part IV of the Canada Labour Code. A section dealing with safety of employees and incorporating many of the provisions of the Canadian Safety Code of 1968.

Part-time layoffs. When an employer lays off workers without pay for a part of each week, such as each Friday.

Paternalism. The attitude of an organization whose management assumes that it alone is the best judge of employee needs and that it need not seek and act upon employee inputs about their needs.

Patterns and practices. When discrimination is found to exist against a large number of individuals who are in a protected class, a *pattern and practice* of discrimination exists.

Pension plan. Any plan whose primary purpose is to provide specific and determinable benefits to employees over a period of years following retirement. The term private pension plan is often used to distinguish voluntary plans from the social insurance system. If the employee shares in the cost, the plan is *contributory.*

Pension plan, registered. An employee's superannuation or pension fund or plan registered for purposes of the Income Tax Act.

Performance appraisal. The process by which organizations evaluate employee job performance.

Performance measures. The ratings used to evaluate employee performance.

Performance standards. The benchmarks against which performance is measured.

Personal barriers. Communication interferences that arise from human emotions, values, and limitations.

Personal failure. Nonachievement of one's most important goals in life. Research studies indicate that contradictory life demands, disconfirmation of one's expectancies and beliefs about the environment, a sense of external control, and feelings of loneliness are associated with a person's feelings of personal failure.

Personal leave days. Normal work days that an employee is entitled to be off. (In some firms personal leave days are used instead of sick days.)

Personnel audit. A systematic review of the personnel activities used in an organization.

Personnel management. The function primarily concerned with utilization and development of the human resources in a particular company or organization. It involves the planning of human resource needs, staffing, training, and compensation.

Peter Principle. The Peter Principle states that in a hierarchy, people tend to rise to their level of incompetence.

Physical Activities (PA). In the *Canadian Classification and Dictionary of Occupations*, the physical requirements of the job and the physical capacities or traits a worker must have to meet those requirements (e.g., seeing, lifting).

Picketing. Patrolling by union members at or near an employer's place of business in order to publicize the existence of a labour dispute or a union's desire to represent the employees, to attempt to persuade workers to join the work stoppage, to discourage customers from patronizing a business, etc.

Piecework. A type of incentive system that compensates workers for each unit of output.

Placement. The assignment of the employee to a new or a different job.

Point system. A form of job evaluation that assesses the relative importance of the job's key factors in order to arrive at the relative worth of jobs.

Portability clauses. Allow accumulated pension rights to be transferred to another employer when an employee changes employers.

Portable pensions. Pension plans with a feature allowing employees to move from one employer to another without losing their accrued pension credits.

Position analysis questionnaire (PAQ). A standardized, preprinted form that collects specific information about jobs.

Precedent. A new standard that arises from the past practices of either the company or the union.

Preferential quota system. This situation exists when a proportion of the job openings, promotions, or other employment opportunities are reserved for members of a protected class who have been previously discriminated against.

Prevailing wage rate. The wage rates most commonly paid for a given job in a geographical area. The prevailing wage rate is determined by a wage and salary survey.

Preventive discipline. Action taken prior to any infraction, to encourage employees to follow the standards and rules so that infractions are prevented. (See *Corrective discipline.*)

Price index. A statistical device used to show relative price changes over time. Prevailing prices in a selected base year are assigned a value of 100; in subsequent years, the prices of the components of the overall index are weighted by their relative importance in the base year in order to determine the current price level, which is then divided by the base year price to yield the index.

Private placement agencies. For-profit organizations that help job seekers find employment.

Proactive management. A type of management wherein decision makers anticipate problems and take affirmative steps to minimize those problems rather than waiting until after a problem occurs before taking action.

Probationary period. The initial period of employment during which a worker is on trial and may be discharged with or without cause.

Problem-solving interviews. Interviews that rely on questions limited to hypothetical situations or problems. The applicant is evaluated on how well the problems are solved.

Production bonuses. A type of incentive system that provides employees with additional compensation when they surpass stated production goals.

Productivity. The ratio of a firm's output (goods and services) divided by its input (people, capital, materials, energy).

Professional associations. Groups of workers who voluntarily join together to further their profession and their professional development. When these associations undertake to negotiate for their members, they are also labour organizations.

Profit sharing. A system whereby an employer pays compensation or benefits to employees in addition to their regular wages based upon the profits of the company. This is usually done on an annual basis.

Progressive discipline. A type of discipline whereby there are stronger penalties for repeated offences.

Promotion. When an employee is moved from one job to another that is higher in pay, responsibility, and/or organizational level.

Protected groups. Classes of people who are protected from employment discrimination under one or more laws.

Provincial federation. An organization formed by a labour congress at the provincial level that consists of the congress affiliates in the province. It functions similarly to the congress in the appropriate provincial area except that it does not charter local unions. Funds are obtained through a per capita tax on affiliates.

Psychic costs. The stresses, strains, and anxieties that affect a person's inner self during periods of change.

Pygmalion effect. The Pygmalion effect occurs when people live up to the highest expectations others hold of them.

Qualified handicapped. Those handicapped individuals who can perform jobs with reasonable employer accommodation.

Quality circles. A small group of employees with a common leader who meet together regularly to identify and solve work-related problems.

Quality of work life (QWL). A generic term emphasizing the humanization of work. The elements relevant to a worker's quality of work life involve the task, the physical work environment, the social environment within the workplace, the administrative system of the enterprise, and the relationship between life on and off the job.

Quality of work life efforts. Systematic attempts by an organization to give workers a greater opportunity to affect their jobs and their contributions to the organization's overall effectiveness.

Quebec Pension Plan (QPP). A mandatory, contributory, and portable pension plan applicable to all self-employed persons and employees in the province of Quebec except those working for the federal government. This plan is identical to the Canada Pension Plan in most of its provisions.

Quitting. Voluntary resignation from employment, initiated by the employee.

Raiding. The efforts of a union to bring into its organization individuals who are already members of another union.

Rand formula. A union security plan developed by Judge Rand, in an arbitration decision handed down in 1946, that requires the employer to deduct union dues from the pay of all employees, union and non-union, and remit the amounts to the union.

Rank and file, the. Union members, collectively, who have no special status as either officers or shop stewards in the plant.

Rap sessions. Meetings between managers and groups of employees to discuss complaints, suggestions, opinions, or questions.

Rate range. A pay range for each job class.

Ratification. Formal approval of a newly negotiated agreement by vote of the union members affected.

Rating scale. A scale that requires the rater to provide a subjective evaluation of an individual's performance along a scale from low to high.

Rational validity. A characteristic of tests that include reasonable samples of the skills needed to perform successfully or that are based on an obvious relationship between performance and other characteristics assumed to be necessary for successful job performance.

Reactive management. A type of management wherein decision makers respond to problems rather than anticipate them.

Realistic Job Preview (RJP). Allows the employee to understand a job and the job setting where the hiring decision is made. It involves showing the candidate the type of work, equipment, and working conditions involved in the job before the hiring decision is finalized.

Recall. The procedure followed by an employer for the return of individuals who have been laid off.

Recency effect. A rater bias that occurs when the rater allows recent employee performance to sway unduly the overall evaluation of the employee's performance.

Recognition clause. A mandatory clause in Canadian collective labour agreements which provides that the trade union is recognized as the exclusive agent of the employees in the bargaining unit.

Recruitment. The process of finding and attracting capable applicants to apply for employment.

Recruitment channels. Different sources of prospective applicants for a job.

Red-circle rate. A rate of pay higher than the contractual, or formerly established, rate for a job. The special rate is usually attached to the incumbent worker, not to the job as such.

Refreezing. Requires integrating what has been learned into actual practice.

Registered pension plan. (See *Pension plan, registered.*)

Regulations. Legally enforceable rules developed by governmental agencies to ensure compliance with laws that the agency administers.

Reinforcement schedules. The different ways that behaviour reinforcement can be given, in terms of frequency, type of stimulus, etc.

Relation to Data, People and Things (DPT). One of the job attributes used in the *Canadian Classification and Dictionary of Occupations* to define a job. DPT code numbers indicate the functional relationships of the worker in relation to data (e.g., analyzing, synthesizing), people (e.g., negotiating, supervising), and things (e.g., handling, tending).

Reliability. A quality of a selection device (usually a test) such that it yields consistent results each time an individual takes it.

Relocation program. A company-sponsored fringe benefit that assists employees who must move in connection with their job.

Repetition. Facilitates learning through repeated review of the material to be learned.

Replacement charts. Visual representations of who will replace whom in the organization when a job opening occurs. (See *Replacement summary.*)

Replacement summary. A list of likely replacements and their relative strengths and weaknesses for each job. (See *Replacement charts.*)

Resistance to change. Employee opposition to change.

Résumé. A brief listing of an applicant's work experience, education, personal data, and other information relevant to employment qualifications.

Reverse discrimination. This situation occurs when an employer seeks to hire or promote a member of a protected class over an equally (or better) qualified candidate who is not a member of such a protected class.

Reward-performance model. This model combines the strengths of other motivational approaches. It argues that behaviour which is properly reinforced enhances an individual's self-image and, therefore, the individual's self-expectations. These self-expectations lead to greater effort, which is met with rewards and continues to reinforce that behaviour.

Role ambiguity. Uncertainty of what is expected of one in a given job.

Role playing. A training technique that requires trainees to assume different identities in order to learn how others feel under different circumstances.

Sandwich model. The human relations principle that corrective comments should be sandwiched between two positive comments in order to make corrective comments more acceptable.

Scanlon Plan. An incentive plan developed by Joseph Scanlon, which has as its general objective the reduction of labour costs through increased efficiency and the sharing of resultant savings among workers.

Search firms. Private for-profit organizations that exist to help employers locate hard-to-find applicants.

Selection interview. A step in the selection process where the applicant and the employer's representative have a face-to-face opportunity to explore their mutual interests in the employment relationship.

Selection process. A series of specific steps used by an employer to decide which recruits should be hired.

Selection ratio. The ratio of the number of applicants hired to the total number of applicants.

Self-actualization. (See *Self-fulfilment needs.*)

Self-fulfilment needs. The needs people have that make them feel they are becoming all they are capable of becoming. This need is also called self-actualization.

Semantic barriers. Limitations that arise from the words with which we communicate.

Seniority. A certain type of employee status relative to other employees, used for determining order of promotion, layoffs, vacation, etc. *Straight seniority* is seniority acquired solely through length of service. *Qualified seniority* depends on other factors besides length of service, such as ability.

Seniority-based promotion. When the most senior employee is promoted into a new position.

Settlement. The agreement reached between labour and management.

Severance pay. Payment to a worker upon permanent separation from the company, usually for causes beyond the worker's control.

Shelf-sitters. This is a slang term for upwardly immobile managers who block promotion channels.

Shift differentials. A premium rate paid to workers on other than the regular day shift. Payment may be a fixed cents-per-hour above or a percentage over the regular day-shift rate.

Shop steward. A local union's representative in a plant or department usually elected by union members to carry out union duties, adjust grievances, collect dues, and solicit new members. Usually a fellow employee.

Shorter workweeks. Employee scheduling variations that allow full-time employees to complete their week's work in less than the traditional five days. One variation is forty hours' work in four days.

Sick leave. Time off work allowed to an employee because of illness, accident, or some other incapacity. A paid sick leave plan provides for full or partial pay for such absence.

Skills inventories. Summaries of each employee's skills and abilities. (Skills inventories usually refer to nonmanagement workers. See *Management inventories*.)

Social insurance. Insurance devised by governments to give wage earners and their dependents a minimum of income during periods when, through conditions largely beyond control, the workers' earnings are impaired or cut off.

Socialization. The process by which people adapt to an organization.

Social unionism. A characteristic of unions that seek to further their members' interests by influencing the social, economic, and legal policies of governments at all levels—city, district, province, and nation. (See *Business unionism*.)

Socio-technical systems. Interventions into the work situation that restructure the work, work groups, and the relationship between workers and the technology they use to do their jobs.

Specialization. Specialization occurs when a very limited number of tasks is grouped into one job.

Specific Vocational Preparation (SVP). In the *Canadian Classification and Dictionary of Occupations*, the additional special training (apart from general education) needed by a job holder to perform the job effectively. SVP ratings are shown in terms of a range; for example, 8 means: over 4 years up to and including 10 years.

Sponsor. A person in an organization who can create career development opportunities for others.

Staff authority. Authority to advise, but not to direct, others.

Staffing table. A list of anticipated employment openings for each type of job.

Statistics Canada. A federal agency responsible for providing a broad range of statistical information.

Steering committee. Part of a quality circle or other employee involvement effort. It usually includes the top manager of the work site (such as a plant manager) and his or her direct staff.

Steward. A union official elected by workers (or appointed by local union leaders) to help covered employees to present their problems to management.

Stock options. A fringe benefit that gives the holder the right to purchase the company's stock at a predetermined price.

Strategic plan. An identification of a firm's long-range objectives and its proposals for achieving those objectives.

Stress. A condition of strain that affects one's emotions, thought processes, and physical conditions.

Stress interviews. Job interviews that rely on a series of harsh, rapid-fire questions intended to upset the applicant and learn how the applicant handles stress.

Stressors. Conditions that tend to cause stress.

Stress-performance model. This model shows the relationship between stress and job performance.

Stress threshold. The level of stressors that one can tolerate before feelings of stress occur.

Strictness bias. A tendency to rate employees lower than their performance justifies.

Strike. A temporary stoppage of work by a group of employees to express a grievance, enforce a demand for changes in the conditions of employment, obtain recognition, or resolve a dispute with management.

Strike benefits. Union payments made to members who are on strike.

Structured interviews. Interviews wherein a predetermined checklist of questions usually asked of all applicants is used.

Suggestion programs. Specific procedures designed to encourage employees to recommend work improvements.

Suitable employment. For the purposes of unemployment compensation laws, employment in a position to which a person is suited by training, education, or experience. Those receiving compensation are not required to accept any available job, but only a suitable one in this sense.

Supplementary unemployment benefits (SUB). Private plans providing compensation for wage loss to laid-off workers, usually in addition to benefits provided under government unemployment insurance programs. SUB plans are employer-financed.

Suspension. A form of disciplinary action that consists in removing a worker from his or her job for a stipulated time with the consequent loss of pay.

System. Two or more parts (or subsystems) working together as an organized whole with identifiable boundaries. An *open system* is one that is affected by the environment.

Task identity. The feeling of responsibility and pride that results from doing an entire piece of work rather than only a small part of it.

Task significance. Means knowing that the work one does is important to others in the organization or outsiders.

Time studies. Measurements of how long a job takes to be performed.

Training. Teaching employees how to perform their present jobs. (Compare with *Development.*)

Transfer. When an employee is moved from one job to another that is relatively equal in pay, responsibility, and organizational level.

Transference. Applicability of training to actual job situations, as evaluated by how readily the trainee can transfer the learning to his or her job.

Tripartite board. A board whose membership is composed of three elements: one or more members selected by management, an equal number of members selected by the union, and one or more neutral members, whose selection may be achieved by agreement of the partisan members or by other means.

Turnover. The rate of loss of employees by the organization. It represents those employees who depart the organization for a variety of reasons.

Two-way communication. The exchange of messages between a sender and a receiver such that a regular flow of communication is maintained.

Type A persons. Persons who are aggressive and competitive, set high standards, and put themselves under constant time pressure.

Type B persons. Persons who accept situations and work within them rather than fighting them competitively or putting themselves under constant time pressure.

Underemployment. Employment which does not fully utilize a worker's potential, whether in terms of skill or time or both.

Underutilization. The condition that exists when a department or entire employer has a smaller proportion of members of a protected class than are found in the employer's labour market. (See *Concentration.*)

Unemployment benefits. Payments to those who have lost their jobs, are willing and able to accept new employment, and are actively looking for work.

Unemployment insurance. A program started in 1940 to help alleviate the monetary problems of workers in Canada during the transition from one job to another. The Unemployment Insurance Act of 1971 has made some significant changes and additions to the program.

Unfair labour practices. Those employer or union practices which are classed as "unfair" by labour relations acts.

Unfreezing. Refers to casting aside old ideas or practices so that new ones can be learned.

Union-management agreement. (See *Collective agreement.*)

Union organizers. Persons who assist employees in forming a local union.

Union rights. Those freedoms of action that individual union members or organizations claim as theirs by constitutional right, statute, or practices recognized over a period of time. These may include the right of assembly, the freedom to form a union, the freedom to strike, etc.

Union security. A provision in a collective agreement designed to protect the status of the union by establishing a union shop, a closed shop, an agency shop, or a maintenance-of-membership arrangement.

Union shop. A union security provision in which the employer may hire anyone he wants, but all workers must join the union within a specified period.

Unstructured interview. An interview using few if any planned questions, to enable the interview to pursue, in depth, the applicant's responses.

Upward communication. Communication that begins at some point in the organization and proceeds up the organization hierarchy to inform or influence others in the organization.

Valence. The strength of a person's preference for one outcome in relation to others.

Validity. An attribute of a selection device (usually a test) that exists when it is related significantly to job performance or some other relevant criterion.

Variable entrance requirement. The number of weeks an applicant for unemployment insurance needs to work before he or she becomes eligible for payments. The requirement varies with the unemployment rate in the economic region.

Variety. An attribute of jobs wherein the worker has the opportunity to use different skills and abilities.

Vertical mosaic. Canadian society, with reference to its multiracial, multiethnic, and multicultural nature.

Vertical staff meetings. When managers meet with two or more levels of subordinates to learn of their concern.

Vestibule training. Training that occurs off the job on equipment or methods that are highly similar to those used on the job. This technique is used to minimize the disruption to operations caused by training activities.

Vesting. A provision in employer-provided retirement plans that gives workers rights to a pension after a specified number of years of service. Once a pension has been vested, the employee is entitled to a pension payout even if he or she quits before retirement.

Wage and salary surveys. Studies made of wages and salaries paid by other organizations within the employer's labour market.

Wage compression. A narrowing of the difference between the top and lowest jobs in an organization or industry. This compression usually results from giving larger pay increases to the lower-paid jobs than to the higher-paid ones.

Walk-ins. Job seekers who arrive at the personnel department in search of a job without any prior referrals and not in response to a specific ad or request.

Want ads. Advertisements in a periodical that solicit applicants for a job; these ads describe the job and its benefits, identify the employer, and tell those who are interested how to apply.

Weighted checklist. Requires the rater to select statements or words to describe an employee's performance or characteristics. After those selections are made, different responses are given different values or weights in order that a quantified total score can be determined.

Welfare secretary. A forerunner of modern personnel specialists, who existed to help workers meet their personal needs and to minimize any tendency of workers to join unions.

Wildcat strikes. Spontaneous work stoppages that take place in violation of a labour contract and are officially against the wishes of union leaders.

Work flow. The sequence of jobs in an organization needed to produce the firm's goods or services.

Work measurement techniques. Methods for evaluating what a job's performance standards should be.

Workers' compensation. Compensation payable by employers collectively for injuries sustained by workers in the course of their employment. Each province has a workers' compensation act.

Work practices. The set ways of performing work in an organization.

Work sampling. The use of a variety of observations on a particular job to measure the length of time devoted to certain aspects of the job.

Work sharing. A plan whereby work available during slack periods is spread among all of the workers in the group by reducing each worker's daily or weekly hours in order to prevent or reduce a layoff.

Work simplification. The elimination of unnecessary tasks in a job, or the reduction of the number of tasks by combining them.

Work stoppage. Cessation of normal business operations due to a strike or lockout.

Write-ins. People who send in their written inquiry, often seeking a job application.

Name Index

Subject Index